The
Turbulent Crown

The Story of the
Tudor Queens

ROLAND HUI

The Turbulent Crown:
The Story of the Tudor Queens

Copyright © 2016 Roland Hui
& MadeGlobal Publishing

ISBN-13: 978-84-945937-9-6

M
MadeGlobal Publishing

For more information on MadeGlobal Publishing, visit our website: www.madeglobal.com

Cover: *Henry VIII and his Successors Edward VI, Mary I, and Elizabeth* I (detail), The Rijksmuseum, Amsterdam. Colour Tint and additional detail by Dmitry Yakhovsky. Copyright ©2016 MadeGlobal Publishing

Figure 1 The Tudor Rose with royal portraits and heraldic emblems
The Rijksmuseum, Amsterdam

Contents

THE RED QUEEN: KATHERYN HOWARD

THE GOSPELLER: KATHARINE PARR

THE UNCROWNED QUEEN: LADY JANE GREY

THE LAST OF HER RELIGION: MARY I

THE MAIDEN QUEEN: ELIZABETH I

List of Illustrations

PART 1
THE WHITE ROSE:
ELIZABETH OF YORK

One of the most gracious and best loved princesses in the world.
(Description of Elizabeth of York at her funeral)

Figure 2   Medal celebrating the marriage of
Henry VII and Elizabeth of York
The Los Angeles County Museum of Art

Chapter 1
Beginnings: The Cousins' War

ON CHRISTMAS morning of 1483, a young Welshman knelt before the high altar of the Cathedral of Rennes in Brittany. In the presence of the assembled company, he took a solemn oath. By all that was holy, he swore to take Elizabeth, daughter of the late King of England, as his wife.

The touching scene had the makings of a great romance - the devoted knight pledging his love to his lady across the sea. But to those witnessing the young man's pledge, the intended marriage was hardly a love match. The couple, they knew, had never laid eyes on each other, and the aspiring bridegroom was no catch for a royal Princess. Though Earl of Richmond by title, the twenty-six-year-old Henry Tudor was a wandering fugitive. He had spent nearly half his life on the run as a traitor with a price on his head. By promising to wed Elizabeth, he hoped to return home and even be ruler of England. But there was more to the bargain; Richmond must first depose England's present King, Richard III, and take his throne.

Long before that Richard, the events leading to the proposed marriage between Henry Tudor and Princess Elizabeth of the House of York began with another bearing the same name and title - King Richard II. As a boy, he had come to the throne displaying a knack for kingship – and for ruthlessness. When the peasants rose in revolt against his government in 1381, the fourteen-year-old Richard boldly rode out and pacified the rebels himself. But that he failed to keep any of the promises he made to them was indicative of the rest of his reign. Surrounding himself with ineffective counsel and sycophants, Richard became increasingly at odds with the nobility. His greatest mistake was banishing his cousin Henry of Bolingbroke to France, and later confiscating his inheritance from his father, the King's uncle, John of Gaunt, Duke of Lancaster. It was an insult too great for Bolingbroke to bear. In 1399, he invaded England, and in a bloodless coup, deposed Richard as a tyrant. No kingdom could afford two rulers, and by the next year, Richard was dead. Whatever was the manner of his death, it haunted his cousin – now King Henry IV - for his rest of his days, and it cast a long shadow over the new dynasty he founded.

Henry's probable hand in Richard's death seemed to have been forgotten in the next reign when England was swept up in the euphoria of his son's conquest of France. Unfortunately, Henry V had little time to savour his triumph as the newly appointed heir of the French King, Charles VI, or to know the pleasures of marriage to his daughter Catherine. Less than a year after the birth of his namesake in 1421, the victor of Agincourt was dead; not from fighting gloriously in another battle, but from that scourge familiar to all campaigning soldiers – dysentery.

Despite Henry V's achievements, many dreaded the days to come. 'Cursed be the land where the Prince is a child', the people murmured. No good would come from having a minor as King; Richard II was proof of that. The catastrophes appeared early on in Henry VI's reign. By the age of seven, his title of King of France was challenged by his Gallic subjects, who had never accepted England as their overlord. In May 1429, forces under the command of the visionary peasant girl, Joan of Arc, liberated Orléans from the English. Two months later, Henry's maternal uncle, the Dauphin, the son and heir of Charles VI, was crowned as the nation's rightful King. Emboldened, the French pushed on. In time, nothing would be left of England's possessions in France except the little port of Calais.

If the English hoped Henry VI would someday recover those losses, or even rival his father in new conquests, they were deeply disappointed. Henry had little ability for government. He was timid and easily dominated by competing factions all too willing to exploit his weaknesses. It was Henry's misfortune to be his father's only son. Had he an older brother groomed to be King instead, Henry would probably have been earmarked for the Church, often the path for a younger son. Were it not his duty to rule, a peaceful life in the cloisters would have been preferable to the pious Henry.

With the King 'more given to God and to devout prayer than to handling worldly and temporal things', the government was controlled by ambitious men at court like Edmund Beaufort, Duke of Somerset, and the King's French wife, Margaret of Anjou. Where Henry VI was meek and mild, Margaret was fiery and fearsome. 'She spareth no pain', it was said, 'to sue her things to an intent and conclusion to her power'.

Richard, Duke of York, the greatest nobleman at court and a cousin to Henry, resented Margaret and Somerset's hold over the King. He was no friend to Somerset or the Queen. Margaret's hatred for York was only matched by her fear of him. Margaret knew that as long as she remained without child, many were looking to York as the next King of England. Some were even whispering that he should wear the crown, not Henry of Lancaster.

The speculation was not entirely treasonous. Prior to Henry IV's seizing of the Crown, York's maternal grandfather, Roger Mortimer might have been King if Richard II were childless, but he died before Richard in 1398. Still, Mortimer's family had a stronger right to the throne. While the Lancastrian line drew from King Edward III's fourth son, John of Gaunt, the House of York sprang from Lionel, Duke of Clarence, the *third* son. Not only that, York also came from a fifth son of the old King. The question was whether Richard of York was ambitious enough to press his claim.

Henry VI's already weak government underwent a further setback in 1453, when the King suffered a mental breakdown. For more than a year, Henry sat staring into space, saying nothing and acknowledging no one. Not even the longed for birth of his son could bring him out of his stupor. When the newly christened Edward was brought for his blessing, Henry 'only looked on the Prince and cast his eyes down, without anymore sign of recognition'. With the King incapacitated, York, to the annoyance of Somerset and the Queen, was appointed Protector of England 'for the duration of the King's illness, until such time as Prince Edward should come of age'.

The new Protector, by all accounts, 'governed England most excellently'. But his rule ended when the King finally recovered his wits around Christmas 1454. He remembered nothing of the past eighteen months, and this time when Prince Edward was presented to him, Henry reacted as any proud father would. 'He held up his hands and thanked God thereof' for giving him a son. A reluctant York surrendered his powers back to the King, or as he saw it, back to the grasping Margaret and her crony Somerset.

Months of peace ended soon after Easter. Somerset had taken a vow never to let York eclipse him again. He whispered in the King's ear rumours of his cousin's ambitions to the throne, which the Queen of course confirmed. Their son Edward's claim, she lamented, would never be safe as long as the Duke was alive. Henry, ever putty in his wife's hands, grudgingly prepared for war.

On 22 May, the two armies clashed in the narrow streets of St Albans in Hertfordshire. While York engaged the royalist army directly, his kinsman Richard Neville, Earl of Warwick, a man of 'stout stomach and invincible courage', led the attack from behind. When the fighting was over, many Lancastrians lay dead, including Somerset. The King managed to find safety in a tanner's house until he was discovered. To his relief, York and Warwick dropped their weapons and knelt at his feet. They had only meant to remove him from the wicked influence of Somerset, they said reassuringly, and in the same breath, professed their undying allegiance to the Crown.

Henry 'was greatly cheered' by their declaration, though Margaret was anything but. The price of their loyalty, she knew, was York's re-assumed control of the government. With Somerset dead, all Margaret could do was wait to settle the score herself. She played her part well. When a day of reconciliation was organised in March 1458, Margaret walked through the streets of London arm-in-arm with the man she hated most, as if they were the greatest of friends. York was just as duplicitous. He treated the Queen with the utmost courtesy in public, but behind her back, he was mustering and arming his followers for the inevitable showdown.

In the following year, there was no more pretence. Margaret openly demanded York's head. In October, she marched towards Ludlow determined to take him down. At Ludford Bridge, the Yorkists were roundly defeated, forcing them into exile. Warwick took refuge in Calais with York's oldest son, Edward, Earl of March, while the Duke fled to Ireland. A joyful Margaret had them all attainted as traitors in Parliament.

Her victory was short-lived. The Queen was hated by the people for her misrule, and they welcomed Warwick and the Earl of March back from France in June 1460. The whole of London cheered on the returning exiles as they passed through the city on their way north to confront the Lancastrians headquartered at Coventry. This time, it was Margaret who was forced to run. The King, left behind, was taken and brought back to London in Warwick's keeping.

It was expected that York, who had returned from Ireland in the autumn, would take back the reins of government as the King's chief minister. But to everyone's astonishment - including that of his own supporters - he had other plans. On 10 October, the Duke made his way to the Palace of Westminster, and before the dumbfounded assembly, laid claim to the English throne by virtue of his ancestry from Edward III's older son. Even Warwick was shocked. York had never harboured such ambitions, and he was always faithful to his anointed King. But there was no denying that it was Richard of York, not Henry of Lancaster, who provided the country with a sound and stable government, and Warwick found himself coming over to the Duke's side. Eventually, so did Parliament. However, it was stipulated that York and his heirs would only inherit the Crown *after* Henry VI's death. The compromise was agreed to by both sides. To confirm the settlement,

> 'all the lords, spiritual and temporal, swore allegiance to Richard Duke of York, and the Duke of York swore allegiance to the King and the lords, saying that for his part he would abide by all the conventions and compacts agreed.'

For the sake of peace, Henry was willing to disinherit his son, but there was no such reaction from the Queen. When the news reached her in Scotland where she had taken refuge, she could not believe her ears. In a fury, she swore she would sooner see York's head on a spike than wearing her son's Crown. Supported by an army of twenty thousand men, Margaret attacked her enemies at Wakefield, near the city of York, on 30 December. Warwick's father, the Earl of Salisbury, was slain, as was the Duke of York. Margaret's revenge was the sweeter when she had his head severed from his corpse and mounted above the city gates. As a further humiliation, she adorned it with a paper crown mocking his kingly pretensions.

York's death did not go unavenged. In February 1461, at Mortimer's Cross in Herefordshire, his nineteen-year-old son, Edward, Earl of March, defeated the Lancastrian forces and made his way to London. Earlier, its citizens had refused aid to Queen Margaret and had shut their gates to her. She had no choice but to retreat north, taking the King whom she had rescued, and their son with her. The city was Edward's for the taking, and the people hailed him as their liberator from the Queen and her marauding northern troops. Without hesitation, they offered the throne to him. It was only after a decisive victory fought at Towton at the end of March that he allow himself to be crowned that summer as King Edward IV. In a reversal of fortune, Henry VI was pronounced a usurper as his grandfather had 'taken [the Crown] from King Richard II… whom he caused to be wretchedly murdered'. His deposition was thus retribution long overdue; for 'men say that ill-gotten goods cannot last'.

≡

For the next three years, Edward IV was continually harassed by Margaret of Anjou. But her uprisings were unsuccessful, and she was sent back to lick her wounds each time. After her last failed attempt, Edward was free to indulge in the pleasures of courtly life. Young and inexperienced in statecraft, he willingly left the business of government to the Earl of Warwick. As the Governor of Abbeville joked to his master Louis XI of France, there were actually *two* kings in England – the renowned Warwick, and one other whose name escaped him.

In the political arena, England's new ruler might have been a lightweight, but in person, he was every inch a king. Edward IV was tall (6 feet and 3 inches in height), powerfully built, and 'of comely visage'. A French observer said he 'had never beheld a more handsome person'. Like the 'sun in splendour', that was his personal emblem, Edward shone brightly and drew people to him. He was every bit aware of the attraction he held over others, and he revelled in their attention. A natural show-off, Edward 'seized any opportunity that the occasion offered of revealing his fine stature more protractedly and more evidently to on-lookers'. The beauty of his person was matched by his affable manner. Edward's gregarious nature won over all those he came across. Having the common touch, he effortlessly mingled with all classes, 'even the least notable'. Should Edward sense that one of his subjects was too shy to approach him, he would make the first move, putting the person at ease with a ready smile and 'a kindly hand upon his shoulder'.

Besides his great charm, Edward's other asset was his skill in warfare. In an era when a ruler was also expected to be a soldier and to lead his men into great battles, he fulfilled the part superbly. Strong and athletic unlike his bookish predecessor, Edward knew what it was like to wield a sword and fight to the death. In other words, he had all the qualities of a king that his uninspiring cousin lacked. When Henry was finally seized in Lancashire in 1465, few regretted his capture.

≡

As King, Edward IV's prospective marriage became an affair of State. Warwick, whose power was second only to his, was delegated

Figure 3   Edward IV by Bernard Lens III
The Yale Center For British Art, New Haven

to finding him a suitable bride. Despite being Europe's most eligible bachelor, Edward was still single three years into his reign. Discussions with Burgundy, Scotland, and Castile had come to nothing for one reason or another, and in 1464, Warwick was sent to France to open negotiations for Bona of Savoy, the sister-in-law of King Louis. By the beginning of autumn, the match was almost finalized, with only the papers to be signed. Or so it seemed. The Earl received astonishing news from his friends in England – the King had been secretly married since spring.

Warwick was infuriated. As a further insult, Edward had chosen a lady of inconsequence called Elizabeth Woodville. While it was true that her father held the title of Lord Rivers, and that her mother came from a prominent family in Luxembourg, Elizabeth was no match for a foreign princess. She was even five years older than Edward, and to boot, a widow with two sons. Furthermore, Elizabeth had prominent Lancastrian ties. Her mother had been formerly married to the Duke of Bedford, Henry V's brother, and both Elizabeth's father and her late husband, Sir John Grey, had fought against the Yorkists.

Despite the rumblings at court, Edward stuck by his wife. He defended 'her beauty of person and charm of manner', and as for offending Warwick, Edward answered that he would not suffer 'to be ruled by *his* eye than by mine own as though I were a ward that were bound to marry by the appointment of a guardian'. If he had surrendered that privilege, Edward said stiffly, he 'would not be a king'. His continued commitment to Elizabeth was evident when he had her crowned at Westminster Abbey in May 1465.

With Elizabeth Woodville as Queen, the court was overrun by her family. Elizabeth had five brothers and seven sisters – all ambitious and all expecting their share of her good fortune. She obligingly provided for them. Her sisters were all married off to great peers of the realm, and her brother Anthony, Earl Rivers, was appointed Governor of the Isle of Wight. Another sibling was made a bishop, and three others received preferment in the King's army and in his household. Elizabeth's father and her sons were not forgotten. Lord Rivers was made high constable and treasurer, while Thomas and Richard Grey were both handsomely endowed by their new stepfather. While her supporters took the view that Elizabeth was merely doing right by her family, her enemies censured her and the rest of her kin for greed. The Woodvilles, they grumbled, dominated the King, and made themselves rich and powerful at the expense of the older nobility. It seemed that they would stop at nothing. The Queen went so far as to arrange a marriage between her brother John, a young man of twenty, to the wealthy Dowager Duchess of Norfolk; a lady well into her sixties.

The Woodvilles' future seemed assured when Elizabeth found herself pregnant not long after her coronation. Because this was her first child as Queen, hopes were high that it would be a son. Elizabeth had already produced two boys by her prior marriage, and chances were good she could fulfil the expectation again. Her Italian doctor Dominic de Serigo was so confident that she would indeed have another son that he advised the King to prepare a most elaborate christening in honour of the forthcoming Prince.

On 11 February 1466, the Queen's labour pains started. Outside her chamber, de Serigo paced anxiously waiting for the result. He had stationed himself near the door to be the first to give King Edward the good news. Hours later, he heard a great cry - the child was born. De Serigo knocked excitedly on the door, asking what sex the baby was. A mocking reply came from one of the Queen's ladies. 'Whatsoever the Queen's Grace hath here within,' she said, 'sure it is that a fool stands there without!'

Insulted, de Serigo went away in a huff, missing his chance to congratulate the King, and as he hoped, to collect a reward.

Chapter 2
The King's Daughter

IT WAS a girl, but she was strong and healthy; a good sign that her future brothers would be as well. Despite her sex, the King and Queen took the child into their hearts and prepared for her christening. To calm the still resentful Warwick, he was asked to be the infant's godfather, and his brother, the Archbishop of York, was given the honour of baptising the child, naming her Elizabeth.

Regrettably, the christening did nothing to heal the rift between the King and Warwick. Tensions continued when they disagreed over whether to align England with the French or with the Burgundians. Edward, who favoured the latter, had the last word. He sealed the alliance by marrying his sister Margaret to Charles, Duke of Burgundy, in June 1468. In what appeared to be a concession to Warwick, Edward later offered up his daughter to the Earl's nephew, George Neville, son of his brother Lord Montagu. The Princess was only in her fourth year and her fiancé no more than nine, but both children conducted themselves with the utmost solemnity as they betrothed themselves in the presence of their elders.

This union between the families failed to appease Warwick. In fact, the Earl suspected an attempt on Edward IV's part to isolate him further. As he saw it, in matching the Princess Elizabeth with George Neville, the King was hoping to ally himself to the boy's father, Lord Montagu instead. With each passing day, Edward was asserting his independence from his mentor, and Warwick knew that soon he would be redundant. His pride would never allow that, and he was prepared to rebel.

To strike at the King, Warwick looked to Edward's brother.

George, Duke of Clarence had his sibling's looks and charm, but the similarities ended there. The young nobleman was arrogant, untrustworthy, and predisposed to violent jealousy. It took little to win Clarence over. The Duke was envious of Edward's royal title, and he sorely resented his brother's promotion of the Woodvilles. By advancing 'strangers of his wife's blood', the King was holding them in higher esteem than his own family, he complained. Knowing how ambitious Clarence was, Warwick reminded him how already, many were looking to him as Edward's heir. His niece Elizabeth was just a child, and a female at that. Few would accept her as Queen if her father were dead. There were even some, Warwick told Clarence, who were prepared to see him as King now. His brother Edward was 'unworthy of the regal sceptre [and] mete to be expelled by all means possible'. Itching for a crown, Clarence pledged himself to Warwick, and to cement their allegiance, took the Earl's daughter Isabel as his wife.

In July 1469, Warwick and his new son-in-law rose in revolt. Despite his valiant efforts to suppress their uprising, Edward IV was taken prisoner. The Earl now had two kings under lock and key - Henry VI in the Tower of London and Edward IV at Middleham Castle - earning him the nickname 'the Kingmaker'. But Edward did not remain a captive for long. The Lancastrians were on the rise again, and Warwick needed his cousin's authority in restoring order. He had little choice but to set him free. Edward was willing to forgive and forget, or so he said.

The opportunity for revenge came in March of 1470. After defeating those who had declared for Henry VI in Lincolnshire, Edward turned his forces against Warwick and the turncoat Clarence. Caught unprepared, they rode like the devil to Dartmouth to take ship to France. Warwick and Clarence were not the only refugees at the court of Louis XI; Queen Margaret was there seeking her kinsman's help in recovering her fortunes. Warwick's break with Edward was a godsend for the Lancastrian cause, but Margaret, still angry and distrustful of him, refused an alliance. Only after Louis convinced her to set aside her pride for the sake of her ambition, would she agree to settle her differences with Warwick. Putting the past behind them, she consented to have her son Prince Edward marry Warwick's other daughter Anne. In return, Warwick promised to wage war in England until the kingdom was in her hands again. Afterwards, he and Clarence were to be appointed as 'Protectors of the Commonwealth' until young Edward came of age. To seal the bargain, both parties swore on a relic of the True Cross 'in most devout and religious manner' to uphold each other.

With the support of Margaret and Louis, Warwick launched his invasion in September. Ill-equipped and deserted by his supporters who flocked to the Kingmaker, King Edward, taking his other brother Richard, Duke of Gloucester, his brother-in-law Anthony Woodville, and his friend William Lord Hastings with him, fled to the court of his sister Margaret in Burgundy. Penniless, with no money to pay the boatmen at their landing, Edward offered up the rich cloak off his back; the only thing of value he had with him.

≡

With her husband gone to do battle with Warwick, Queen Elizabeth had removed herself to the safety of the Tower of London. Before its reputation as a place of torture, execution, and murder, the great citadel on the banks of the River Thames also served as a royal palace. During his reign, King Henry III had done much to reinforce and enlarge the Tower. His programme of works included a range of private quarters facing the river front. Spacious and comfortable, they took up three floors, and Henry, who had a taste for luxury, had the apartment walls whitewashed and decorated with painted flowers and ornamental masonry work.

In these lodgings, in fact not far from where Henry VI was still imprisoned, Elizabeth Woodville waited anxiously, hoping for good news. The last year had been fraught with sorrow. Warwick and the treacherous Clarence had taken her husband prisoner, as well as her father Lord Rivers and her brother John. Fortunately, Edward was later released, but both Woodvilles were executed. Elizabeth had come from a close-knit family, and their deaths undoubtedly were deeply felt. Other than to have her husband back with her again, it could be well imagined that Elizabeth's great wish was revenge against the two men who had brought her so much grief.

The Queen put aside her sorrow as best she could. She had her daughters – Elizabeth and her two younger sisters: Mary, born a year after her, and Cecily, still a toddler – whom she had brought with her to the Tower to consider. There was also the baby in her womb to think about. Elizabeth was with child again, and she was set to deliver in a few short weeks. After a succession of girls, she might at last be blessed with a son. Not that the Queen was displeased with her daughters. On the contrary, all three were fine-looking children making her most proud. Her eldest, the Princess Elizabeth was already developing into a young beauty taking after both her parents. She would soon be the most attractive and sought after bride in Europe - not only for her loveliness, but for her status as well. Unless the child her mother was carrying was a boy, she remained her father's successor. Probably none of that concerned the four-year-old Elizabeth herself. Despite her father's absence, life went on as it had before at her mother's new court at the Tower. Elizabeth played with her little sisters, continued with her lessons, and at worship, prayed for the King's safe return. The routine was interrupted on 1 October. Word reached London that King Edward had fled the country. And there was more calamity – the victorious Warwick and Clarence were marching towards the city to restore Henry VI. The Queen was terrified. With her husband in exile, his family was left to fend for themselves. At her arrival, Elizabeth had taken the precaution of having the Tower stocked up and well fortified - but was that enough? She might have remembered how during the great Peasants' Revolt, Joan of Kent, the mother of Richard II, had taken refuge behind its thick walls but to no avail. The rebels stormed into the fortress, ransacked her apartments, and massacred her friends. Luckily, the Queen Mother was able to escape onto a boat outside. Should the Tower be breached again, would Elizabeth and her daughters be as fortunate?

On the moonlit waters of the Thames, a silent barge set sail from Tower Wharf. The Queen was on board with her children huddled beside her. Their journey was a short one - up the River to Westminster. There, Elizabeth and the Princesses crossed the yard in darkness with their servants in tow. They went past the great palace and continued towards the Abbey. For centuries, the grounds within its sacred precincts had provided refuge for those seeking protection, and they would do so again. The arrival of the royal party caused a commotion. Never before had such eminent persons sought asylum in the Abbey.

From her borrowed quarters within the church, Elizabeth Woodville received the shocking news of how Warwick and his Lancastrian army had entered London unopposed. True to his promise to Margaret of Anjou, the Earl released Henry VI from the Tower. The befuddled ex-monarch was cleaned up and furnished with a new velvet gown to give him some semblance of his former majesty. He was then paraded to St Paul's Cathedral where he offered thanksgiving for delivery. Along the route, the people – ever capricious – welcomed their restored King. Though they were once glad to be rid of Henry for keeping 'mischievous people' and 'false lords' about him, it was now Edward IV whom they denounced. He had promised England 'prosperity and peace, but it came not'. From the Abbey, Elizabeth and her daughters might have watched as Henry VI was taken in procession to the palace next door. With him, were the proud Kingmaker and the hated Clarence riding triumphantly beside their puppet sovereign.

Again, there could not be two Kings of England. Edward of York was formally deposed, his goods confiscated, and his laws overturned by Parliament. Warwick was appointed Lord Protector with Clarence as his right hand. The Duke was also made second in line to the throne if Henry VI's son Prince Edward failed to have issue. Of course, there was no mention of Edward IV's daughters in the succession; they were the offspring of a traitor and usurper. That same dishonour was extended to the former King's child born in sanctuary on 2 November. It was a boy named Edward. His christening was a low-key affair. The baby was baptised, not as his sisters were with all ceremony befitting their rank, but quietly 'without pomp' as if he was a poor man's son.

Even with the birth of a Yorkist prince, Edward IV's supporters remained pessimistic. As the new year of 1471 began, their ranks were still in disarray, and the King himself was still in exile. Day by day, the country was flooded with Lancastrians returning from abroad to reclaim their titles and properties. Among the expatriates was Henry VI's half-brother Jasper, Earl of Pembroke, the son of Henry V's widow Catherine of Valois by her second marriage to a Welshman named Owen Tudor. In February, Pembroke arrived at court bringing with him his thirteen-year-old nephew, Henry, Earl of Richmond, the child of his late brother Edmund and Lady Margaret Beaufort, a descendant of John of Gaunt. As Gaunt's great-great-grandson, many considered the boy to be one of the most distinguished representatives of the House of Lancaster. Henry VI felt so too. A story was told of how the saintly King had gazed on his young kinsman and prophesied that one day - 'this is he unto whom both we and our adversaries must yield and give over the dominion'.

In the middle of March, the Yorkists finally had reason to rejoice when Edward returned from Burgundy. From Ravenspur, he marched towards York but found its gates closed to him. The citizens, who had gone over to the enemy, only allowed Edward to enter when he declared that he had come back to England, not as its King but merely as Duke of York, being his late father's heir. Edward even went so far as to assert his allegiance to the House of Lancaster. As they entered the city gate, he and his men shouted out lustily, 'For King Harry! For King Harry!' By the time they got to Nottingham, however, there were no more such displays. Edward immediately proclaimed himself the lawful King of England.

True to form, his brother Clarence abandoned Warwick and offered himself to Edward again. Naturally, Clarence's intentions were entirely self-serving. Warwick had failed to make him King, and he was allowed little share of power. If he made peace with his brother, Clarence reckoned, he might be better used. Overlooking any designs his fickle brother might have had, Edward happily forgave him.

On 11 April, the Londoners, who had re-embraced Henry VI back in October, were in 'trembling fear' at the coming of Edward. They put up no resistance, and threw open the city gates. After a rapturous welcome, Edward gave his thanks at St Paul's Cathedral. Having done his duty to God, he then hurried to Westminster to meet his wife and his children – particularly his newborn son.

With his family safe, Edward swore they would never have to endure the 'great trouble' of the past months ever again. He would crush Warwick and the Lancastrians once and for all. On Easter morning, between 4 and 5 o'clock, the two armies met near the village of Barnet. The sun had still not yet risen and the battlefield was shrouded in a heavy fog. Unable to see, the Lancastrians unwittingly shifted their lines. It was a fatal mistake. At about 8 o'clock when the fog began to lift, thousands of Warwick's men were lying dead on the field, many having killed each other in confusion. In that mêlée was the Kingmaker himself.

Although Warwick was vanquished, Edward's victory would not be complete until Queen Margaret was taken. News of Warwick's defeat had stunned her at her landing at Weymouth, but she was resolved to do battle, hoping to rendezvous with Jasper Tudor's forces. She only got as far as Tewkesbury where her army was laid to waste. Afterwards, the Queen was found hiding 'in a poor religious place'. Margaret was a shadow of her former self. All the fight in her was gone – her troops were defeated and her husband's cause lost forever. Even more devastating was the death of her son. The Prince had been slain in combat, or as some reported, taken alive and butchered before King Edward. Whatever the manner, the child upon whom all her hopes were pinned was no more. 'Almost dead for sorrow', Margaret surrendered without a struggle.

21 May 1471 was a day of celebration. Whatever their loyalties – to Lancaster or York - all men were glad that the turmoil, later remembered as 'The War of the Roses', had finally ended. In their thousands, Londoners came out to observe the triumphal entry of the King. Waiting too was Edward's proud family – his Queen with the baby Prince in her arms, and her daughters beside her. The festivities would have certainly impressed the Princesses. Mary and Cecily had never seen such celebration before, and though their elder sister Elizabeth had witnessed the revels in honour of their aunt Margaret of York, when she left England for Burgundy in 1468, her recollections were probably vague with her being so young at the time.

Elizabeth and her sisters watched as the procession came into view. At the head were the King's troops bearing his standards of the sun in splendour and the Yorkist emblem of the white rose. The people cheered at the sight of them, but then suddenly they howled and hissed. Sitting alone in a carriage was Margaret of Anjou. Exhausted and unkempt, she rode through the city as a trophy of war. Then came the beaming King and his retinue. There seemed to be no end as far as the eye could see. As a demonstration of his might, Edward rode into the city in the company of 'all the noblemen of the land with many other able men… to the number of thirty thousand horsemen'. Edward savoured his triumph. His victory was complete; except for one loose end. The morning after, Henry VI was found dead at the Tower. It was announced that the old King, unable to bear the defeat at Tewkesbury and the death of his only son, departed this life simply out 'of pure displeasure and melancholy'.

The decade between the triumph of the white rose and the closing of her father's reign were idyllic years for Elizabeth of York. As brutal and callous as the murder - it was almost certainly that - of Henry VI was, it did restore order to the country. No longer would men - even brothers and cousins - raise arms against each other for one king over another. With his authority firmly established, Edward IV could devote himself to peaceful endeavours. He promoted trade with his European neighbours, and he encouraged new enterprises such as William Caxton's innovative printing presses. He also rebuilt St George's Chapel at Windsor with the intent of establishing a monumental tomb for him and his descendants. The Queen was just as busy. She gave her support to Queens' College, Cambridge, which she had re-founded earlier in 1465 (it was originally established by her rival Margaret), and to various charitable and religious organisations.

As the kingdom prospered, so did the House of York. In 1473, another son, Richard, was born to the King and Queen. The royal nursery continued to expand when three more daughters – Anne, Katharine, and Bridget followed. There was another girl and a boy – Margaret and George – but unfortunately, both died in infancy. To their seven surviving offspring, the King and Queen were affectionate parents who took much pleasure in their children. At Canterbury Cathedral, the proud Edward had his sons and daughters displayed with him and the Queen in a great stained glass window depicting the entire family at worship.

Growing up at their father's court, Elizabeth and her siblings lacked for nothing. The King had a taste for luxury and the best life had to offer. Edward tasted the finest foods, drank the best wines, and wore the latest fashions. One Christmas was particularly memorable when the King celebrated by appearing in 'a variety of most costly dresses of a form never seen before, which he thought displayed his person to considerable advantage'. Such magnificence was modelled on the splendour Edward experienced first hand in the Netherlands as a guest of his brother-in-law the Duke of Burgundy. On his restoration, Edward set about emulating his opulent court. He well succeeded, according to the Governor of Holland, the Lord of Grauthuse who visited England in 1472. He described the King's apartments at Windsor Castle as being richly hung with tapestries made from cloth of gold. Grauthuse's own lodgings were just as grand. The Governor was allotted 'three chambers of pleasance' decorated with white silk and linen cloth. The floors were even covered with carpets; a luxury at the time. At night, the pampered Grauthuse slept on a fine bed with sheets edged in gold and ermine, and with pillows provided by the Queen herself. For his relaxation, he bathed in the next room in a portable tub covered with a curtain of white cloth.

Throughout his stay, Grauthuse was treated with great honour. He was invited to the Queen's apartments where he joined Elizabeth Woodville and her attendants at their amusements. Later, the Governor had the pleasure of watching the King dance with his daughter Elizabeth. He was also invited to ride and to hunt with Edward, and to view his gardens. When they returned to the castle, Grauthuse was the Queen's special guest at 'a great banquet in her own chamber'. When supper was completed, the Princess danced before him again.

=

Elizabeth's appearance before the Governor of Holland gave her a sense of her importance. Although she was relegated in the succession by the birth of her two brothers, she was still a valuable asset to her father. By marrying her abroad, Edward could forge an alliance with another European power to the benefit of his kingdom. She would not wear her father's Crown, but for Elizabeth, a great future lay ahead of her nonetheless. She could be Queen Consort to a foreign king, or she could be a great duchess like her aunt Margaret of York, presiding over a glittering court as well.

In 1475, her parents' ambitions for her were realised when Elizabeth was affianced to the Dauphin Charles, son and heir of Louis XI. Her father had never forgiven the wily Louis for encouraging the unholy alliance between Margaret of Anjou and the Kingmaker. To settle the score, he imagined himself another Henry V and prepared to invade France. It was easier said than done, and in the end, Edward had to be satisfied by being bought off by Louis. By the terms of the Treaty of Picquigny, he was awarded an annual pension of 50,000 crowns, along with the hand of the Dauphin for his daughter. So although Edward would not recover England's lost territories himself, at least his future grandson would rule over them as King of France one day.

After her engagement, Elizabeth's betrothal to Warwick's nephew, made five years ago, was no more. She would now be styled as 'Madame La Dauphine' in anticipation of her future nuptials. However, for now, the Princess would remain in England until she was deemed old enough to be a bride. In preparation for becoming Queen of France one day, Elizabeth was most likely given lessons in the customs and history of her future country. She might already have been speaking some French. Her father was fluent in it having been born in Rouen and spending the first three years of his life there. The Queen could probably converse in French as well, as her mother Jacquetta hailed from Luxembourg and had lived in France as the wife of the Duke of Bedford.

The details of Elizabeth's schooling are unknown, but they may have been similar - though probably less rigorous - to those of her brother Edward. If so, like the Prince, Elizabeth rose at dawn at a 'convenient time' in preparation for the day ahead. After she had washed and dressed, her early hours were set aside for devotions. She attended Mass, and on feast days heard a sermon preached before her and her family. Afterwards, as she ate breakfast, Elizabeth was read 'noble stories' to move her mind to 'virtue, honour, cunning, wisdom, and deeds of worship'. When she finished eating, she spent about two hours in the schoolroom, and then occupied herself in practising the skills required of a girl of her privileged position. She was taught to ride, to hunt, and to manage a household. There was, of course, that time-honoured female pastime of needlework that the Princess was expected to devote hours to. It was perhaps dancing that was Elizabeth's strength. She was apparently most graceful when asked to perform before the Governor of Holland.

As happy as the royal family was, there were underlying tensions. The Woodvilles still held sway over the court, and their influence was begrudged by Elizabeth's paternal uncles. It was probably obvious to the Princess how strained her mother's relationship with the Duke of Clarence was, and how the Queen had few kind words for Richard of Gloucester as well. The Queen knew how Richard disliked her family, and she was ever vigilant of him. Gloucester seldom came to court, and he was happiest in the North as the King's lieutenant, living with his wife Anne Neville (daughter of the Kingmaker and widow of Edward of Lancaster) and their little son Edward. Richard and Anne had known each other since they were children, and their marriage may have had the advantage of being a love match. Gloucester's absences, coupled with his natural reserve, made him almost a stranger to his niece. What Elizabeth did know of her uncle was that her father held him in the highest esteem. Edward IV always spoke glowingly of his brother - of his courage, of his diligence, and most of all, his loyalty.

The King could not say the same of Clarence. The two had reconciled, but Edward never really trusted him again, and with good reason. In 1476, the Duke's wife Isabel passed away, and Clarence was looking to make a new marriage. He found one in Mary of Burgundy, stepdaughter of his sister the Duchess. Margaret of York, who had always loved Clarence the best, gave her approval. However, the King, whose opinion mattered, forbade the match. Mary of Burgundy was too great a prize for his ambitious brother. She was a wealthy heiress, and by her descent from Edward III, had English royal blood in her. Should Clarence have her as his wife, he would be powerful – and dangerous.

Clarence, still itching for a crown, would not be thwarted. He would be King one way or the other. To bolster his position, he revived a whispering campaign that Edward was not their father's son, but the result of adultery by their mother, Cecily. Clarence had already circulated such rumours years earlier when he was in league with Warwick. The charge, as it was then, was almost certainly untrue, but Clarence had no qualms about vilifying his own still living mother again for a kingdom. His sister-in-law was not immune either. Clarence spoke openly of how 'she was not the legitimate wife of the King'. Edward, he said, 'ought to have married a virgin wife', but instead, took 'a widow in violation of established custom'.

Clarence's recklessness knew no bounds. In April 1477, he suddenly arrested a woman formerly in the service of his late wife. Ankarette Twynyho was accused of poisoning her mistress, perhaps in connivance with the Woodvilles. Despite her protests of innocence, Mistress Twynyho was sent to the gallows. Clarence even went after the King. Edward, he said wildly, had resorted to sorcery against him. To protect himself, Clarence hexed his brother with the help of an astrologer who dabbled in the black arts.

At this latest revelation, Clarence was taken into custody and clapped in the Tower. At Clarence's trial before Parliament in January 1478, Edward himself appeared in person to accuse his brother of high treason. Clarence denied everything and even offered 'to defend his cause with his own hand' in a trial by combat. He was not taken up on it. On 8 February, the Duke was condemned by an Act of Attainder, and sentenced to death.

If Edward hesitated in what he must do, the Queen erased his doubts. She reminded him of the danger if Clarence remained alive. The Duke had already questioned Edward's parentage, and in traducing his marriage, cast doubt on the birthright of their children, particularly the heir to the throne. She also reminded him of an old prophecy. It was foretold that 'after King Edward, should reign someone the first letter of whose name should be G'. Afraid that George of Clarence was the usurper spoken of, the Queen was adamant that he must die. Edward agreed. On 18 February, the Duke was drowned in his cell.

———

A month before her uncle was put to death, Elizabeth of York attended the first great wedding in her family – that of the little Prince, Richard, Duke of York. Elizabeth watched as her four-year-old brother pledged his troth in a childish voice to Anne Mowbray, Duchess of Norfolk. Despite her lofty title, Anne was only two years older than the bridegroom. Her youth aside, the King and Queen considered the wealthy Anne too great a prize to pass up. Observing the ceremony, Elizabeth may have been reminded of her betrothal, at the same age as her brother, to young George Neville eight years ago.

The nuptials were made the happier by the presence of Prince Edward, whom Elizabeth seldom saw. Since he was three, Edward divided his time between the King's court and his own household at Ludlow Castle in Shropshire, where he was sent to establish himself as Prince of Wales. It was only on great feast days and special occasions like this that he was with the rest of his family. Those who saw him at court praised young Edward for his dignity and intelligence, and for the good looks he shared with all his siblings. An observer noted that in his face, the Prince had 'such charm that however much they might gaze, he never wearied the eyes of beholders'.

Elizabeth must have cherished such family gatherings. Soon they would be rare and even impossible. In a few short years, as she was told, she must sail to France to wed the Dauphin. Two of her sisters had duties to fulfil as well. When they were old enough, Cecily would marry the Scottish King's brother, while Mary would travel to faraway Denmark to be its queen.

Mary of York never made her journey. In May 1482, she sadly succumbed to illness at the age of fourteen. Of all her siblings, Elizabeth was probably the one most affected by Mary's death. The two were close in age, and unlike their other sisters, were bonded by shared memories of their time in sanctuary together. After mourning for her sister, there was more difficult news for Elizabeth and her family. In December, Louis XI, whom some said had taken perverse pleasure in telling King Edward of Clarence's treason, dealt him another blow. He defaulted on his yearly tribute, and to Elizabeth's shame, refused her for his daughter-in-law. The Dauphin, Louis reconsidered, was better-off marrying elsewhere.

Furious at his treachery, Edward vowed revenge. Parliament voted him money to prepare for battle, but privately, its members doubted whether he could wage war as he used to. In the last decade, with his realm 'in quiet and prosperous estate', the King had turned from a vigorous soldier to an indolent playboy. He seldom took exercise anymore, and he developed a great fondness for food and drink, becoming 'somewhat corpulent and burly'. Dominic Mancini, an Italian humanist and an observer of English affairs, was more blunt. He described Edward as being 'very fat' in his final years. When the King was not at the table gorging away or gambling at cards and dice, he was pleasuring himself with one of his many mistresses. Whether Edward could personally lead an army to war again was never put to the test. In March 1483, while on a fishing trip, Edward caught a chill from which he never recovered. He died on 9 April.

When the news spread throughout the city, the people hung their heads in sorrow – for their King who had ruled England well, and for themselves in what lay ahead. They recalled the turbulent days of Richard II and Henry VI, and lamented as those before them did – 'cursed be the land where the Prince is a child'.

Chapter 3
The King's Sister

FOLLOWING TRADITION, the royal family did not attend Edward IV's funeral at Windsor. Elizabeth Woodville and her children watched the obsequies in private, lamenting the loss of a beloved husband and father. Her grief was cut short at the reading of the royal will. According to the late King's wishes, the Queen – or rather Queen Dowager as his wife must now call herself - was denied any role in the new government. The Duke of Gloucester would govern in her son's name as Lord Protector. The notion filled Elizabeth and her kin with dread. Richard had never been a friend to them, and he had taken Clarence's death badly; blaming it on the Woodvilles' thirst for his blood.

To frustrate Gloucester's Protectorate, it was essential for the Queen and her party to have the new King in their power. Young Edward was still away at Ludlow, but thankfully under the guardianship of his Woodville uncle, Earl Rivers. The Queen wrote to her brother telling him to have his nephew brought to the capital with all haste, that he may be put into her care. Once the boy was formally crowned, Gloucester's authority would be set aside, and Edward would rule in his own name; under a Council dominated by his Woodville relations of course.

The plan was perfect, but on 30 April, on his way to London with the young King, Rivers was arrested at Stony Stratford by Gloucester and his confederate the Duke of Buckingham. Like Richard, Henry Stafford had no love for the Woodvilles since he had been forced into marriage with one of the Queen's sisters at the age of twelve. Even in his youth, Buckingham was conscious of his rank and dignity, and he resented his Woodville wife 'on account of her humble origins'.

After Rivers was taken away, Gloucester paid his nephew 'every mark of respect... in the way of uncovering his head, bending the knee', but the boy remained perturbed. Where was Rivers, he demanded? And why were his attendants being replaced by strangers? All that was being done, the Duke assured him, was for his own safety. Rivers was a traitor, as were others in his company, including Edward's half-brother Richard Grey and his chamberlain Sir Thomas Vaughan. Powerless, Edward put himself into Gloucester's hands.

≡

Just before midnight, the Queen was abruptly awoken at Westminster Palace. There was a messenger, she was told, who had ridden post-haste from Stony Stratford with urgent news. Her son, the King, was on his way to the city, but not in the company of his uncle Rivers, but of his *other* uncle, the Duke of Gloucester. The Queen was stunned. In a carefully orchestrated move, Richard had her brother Rivers, her son Grey, and the King in his custody. Having seized Edward, Richard had effectively taken control of the government.

Elizabeth Woodville's response was to fight, but when she sent for help, no one would take up arms on behalf of the unpopular Woodvilles. In fact, many on whose support she counted on 'even said openly that it was more just and profitable that the youthful sovereign should be with his paternal uncle than with his maternal uncles and uterine brothers'. Abandoned, the Queen Dowager quickly gathered up the little Duke of York and his five sisters. Accompanied by her other son, Thomas Grey, Lord Dorset, they fled to the nearby Abbey. At the door of the church, a desperate Elizabeth demanded asylum again.

In the small hours of the morning, even before the sun rose, there was another great knock on the Abbey door. The monks inside, thinking that the Queen's enemies had come to violate the privilege of sanctuary, were filled with fear. Thankfully, it was not Gloucester's men, but the Lord Chancellor, Archbishop Rotherham. One of the few friends left to the Queen, Rotherham had come to deliver the Great Seal of England (with which government business was transacted) to her. Brought into her presence, he saw mayhem all around. Throughout the night, servants had carried in the possessions of the fugitive royals. Everywhere, 'chests, coffers, packs, fardels [and] trusses' lay scattered in the Abbot's quarters, which were again offered up for the Queen's use. To hasten their work, the men had the walls broken down to bring in the rest of her property.

She was a pathetic sight. With her clothes dishevelled and her hair loose about her shoulders, Elizabeth Woodville 'sat alone, a-low on the rushes, all desolate and dismayed'. She would not let her daughters come to her, nor would she go to them. All was lost, she wailed over and over. Nothing the Archbishop said could comfort her. After handing the Queen the Great Seal, Rotherham left Elizabeth with his solemn promise that should any harm come to King Edward, he would see to it that her other son Richard assumed the Crown in his place. It was a bitter consolation.

≡

The Queen's fears appeared to be unjustified. The Duke of Gloucester continued to treat the young King with kindness and deference, and on 4 May, brought him to London where the boy was honourably received and homage paid to him. After a short stay at the Bishop of London's, Edward was transferred to the Tower. But there was nothing usual about that. The royal apartments would be more suitable to his rank, and he would be following the tradition of taking up residence there before his coronation. Meanwhile, everything else was going as it should. Laws were enforced in the name of King Edward V, coins were issued for the new reign, and preparations for the ceremony at Westminster Abbey - rescheduled for 22 June - were under way.

That the Queen and her other children would attend the coronation seemed unlikely. It had been well over a month since they had gone into hiding and they had yet to emerge. Elizabeth Woodville had good reason to remain in sanctuary. In early June, she had involved herself in a failed conspiracy to remove the Protector. The details are obscure, but it involved her husband's old friend Lord Hastings. Ironically, it was Hastings who had warned Gloucester about the Woodvilles' attempt to seize the King after the death of Edward IV. Hastings had never liked the Queen and her kindred, but what he disliked even more was being denied a place in Gloucester's inner circle. Courting Richard's favour had done him little good, he discovered, as it was Buckingham who reaped the rewards as the Duke's confidante. In his jealousy, Hastings went over to the Woodvilles. Aware of his duplicity, Gloucester had Hastings arrested at a meeting of the King's Councillors at the Tower on 13 June. He was then quickly beheaded on the Green outside.

By the urgency of his actions, Richard was clearly on the offensive. Lord Hastings had been dispatched without trial, and he had even taken the precaution of summoning his loyal retainers from the North to London. They were to come armed and prepared to do battle, he ordered, as the Queen and 'her bloody adherents… doth intend to murder and utterly destroy us and our cousin the Duke of Buckingham and the royal blood of this realm'. It was probably Richard's intention not only to remove the Queen from power, but also her son the King. Edward V was, after all, half a

Woodville. He would not forget the imprisonment of his uncle Rivers and his stepbrother Richard Grey, or the dishonour of his mother and his siblings in sanctuary. Inevitably, the Woodvilles would be restored to power, and with that, Gloucester's turn to have his head fall on Tower Green. Thus, for Richard to survive, his nephew must be deposed. Gloucester was also an ambitious man. He had governed in the North like a king, and had won the admiration of all men as an able administrator and as a dispenser of justice. With his experience, perhaps Gloucester felt justified in taking the Crown. In doing so, he would preserve England from the uncertainties of a child ruler.

It was not enough for Gloucester to have possession of the King. He needed the nine-year-old Richard of York as well. If free, the boy would undoubtedly be a focus of opposition to him in the future. Young Richard was still with his family in Westminster Abbey, which by now resembled a citadel under siege. Even on the day Rotherham visited the Queen, the Archbishop had noticed how the church was surrounded by the Duke of Gloucester's servants, watching that no man should go into the sanctuary, nor none pass unsearched. On 16 June, the already tense situation was heightened by the arrival of a 'great plenty of harnessed men'. Despite brandishing 'swords and staves', they had come in peace, they said. All they wanted was the Duke of York. He was being held against his will by his mother, and he was needed as a companion for his brother.

Expecting the Queen's unwillingness to surrender the Prince, the Archbishop of Canterbury was appointed to head a delegation to meet with her. Inside, he appealed to the Queen, but she would not cooperate. She feared the Prince would come to harm if she let him go. Undeterred, the old clergyman continued to press Elizabeth Woodville, promising her Richard's safety. Her worries were unfounded, the Archbishop said, not to mention unreasonable. If she would not leave the gloomy confines of sanctuary, she could at least let the little boy go and stay with the King. What danger could there possibly be in that, the Archbishop asked? Elizabeth had no answer, and she grudgingly gave in. She knew that outside the Abbey walls, armed men stood waiting. The inviolability of sanctuary meant nothing to them. If she refused to give up the Prince, they would storm the Abbey and take him - perhaps even the Princesses as well - by force. Relying on the Archbishop's promise, Elizabeth let Richard go. After a tearful send-off, she and her daughters watched as the boy was taken to meet with his uncle, Gloucester. They never saw him again.

≡

In seizing the throne, Gloucester may have been inspired by what his late brother George had made much noise about - the validity of Edward IV's marriage to Elizabeth Woodville. Clarence had thought it flawed merely because the Queen, as he put it, was a lowborn adventuress, but Gloucester had something far more substantial up his sleeve. He claimed to have recently learnt that before his marriage, Edward IV was discretely betrothed to a woman, now deceased, named Eleanor Butler. The King was a shameless womaniser, and when the lovelier Elizabeth Woodville came on the scene, Lady Eleanor was jilted and nothing more was said of her. The truth would never have been known had not the good Bishop Stillington, who pre-contracted Eleanor Butler to the King, come forward after all these years. The startling revelation, if true, was tailor-made for Gloucester's purposes. If the King were indeed pre-contracted before his marriage, his union with the Queen, by Church law, was bigamous, and thus invalid. His children, therefore, were all bastards and incapable of inheriting the Crown.

On 22 June, there was confusion all about London. The citizens had come out in droves to watch the celebrations in honour of Edward V's coronation - but there were none. Instead, the city was full of 'armed men, in fearful and unheard-of numbers, from the North, Wales, and all other parts' loyal to the Duke of Gloucester and the Duke of Buckingham. At St Paul's Cross, the people were told that Edward V was not their rightful Sovereign. His line was tainted as his late father was illegitimately conceived. No details were given, but the implication was that the family matriarch, Cecily Neville, had cuckolded her husband the Duke of York. In addition, the young King was further stigmatised by the unlawful marriage of his parents; Edward IV having been previously contracted to Lady Eleanor Butler. Because Richard of Gloucester was the undoubted son of the Duke of York, having his 'father's own figure…[and] the very print of his visage', and was the next in line after his brother's now bastardised children, he 'was to come to the throne as the legitimate successor'.

The announcement was met with scepticism at first, but by 26 June, whether through fear of sharing the fate of Lord Hastings (and of Rivers, Grey, and Vaughan executed at Pontefract Castle in the North three days earlier) or from a genuine conviction that Gloucester 'was legally entitled to the Crown, and could bear its responsibilities', the lords of the realm petitioned the Duke to assume the throne. Richard humbly accepted.

Chapter 4
The King's Niece

ON 5 July, the postponed coronation went ahead. Wearing royal purple, Richard of Gloucester set forth to Westminster Palace from the Tower of London where he had spent the night according to custom. The early doubts about his accession were all forgotten as the people hailed him with shouts of 'King Richard! King Richard'! along the way. At his arrival, Gloucester rode past the Abbey where the Queen Dowager and her daughters still immured themselves. Did Elizabeth Woodville look incredulously at the sight before her, or did she shut herself away, refusing to witness the takeover of her son's throne?

The next day, Richard and his wife Anne were crowned King and Queen by the Archbishop of Canterbury. He was said to have done his part 'unwillingly'; feeling shame for breaking his promise to the Queen Dowager to protect the rights of her two sons. Elizabeth, who stayed well away from the ceremony, found solace in the reports about them smuggled to her in sanctuary. Both Edward and Richard were unharmed, and they were even seen in public playing together in the garden of the Tower. However, these sightings would become increasing infrequent as the summer wore on. Soon, it was said that the boys were being

> 'withdrawn into the inner apartments of the Tower proper, and day by day began to be seen more rarely behind the bars and windows, till at length they ceased to appear altogether.'

Even more ominous was the statement of Edward V's physician who claimed that the deposed King, having a foreboding of doom, was preparing himself for death.

As she could do nothing for the 'Princes in the Tower', the Queen did her best to protect the rest of her children. She turned to conspiracy again in late July. Since his coronation, Richard III had relaxed the guard about Westminster Abbey, and Elizabeth saw her chance to act. Her sons were beyond her reach, but 'if any fatal mishap should befall the said male children of the late King in the Tower, the kingdom might still, in consequence of the safety of his daughters, some day fall again into the hands of the rightful heirs.'

Before her brother-in-law could get his hands on the girls, the Queen intended to sneak them out of sanctuary. The plan was to disguise the Princesses and have them taken abroad to safety. But before the arrangements could be made, the authorities caught wind of the plot. The Abbey grounds were refortified 'so that not one of the persons there shut up could go forth, and no one could enter'.

Not one to give up easily, the Queen involved herself in another scheme; incredibly enough, with the Duke of Buckingham. Next to Richard III, no man was more loathsome to her. But Elizabeth was desperate, and Henry Stafford was her only hope. Buckingham had become disillusioned with Richard and was turning to treason. His motive is unclear, though one source attributed it to the supposed murder of the Princes that autumn. Allegedly, the King, fearing for the security of his throne, had both his nephews smothered to death in the Tower. If that were true, Buckingham, appalled at the slaughter of innocent children, might have regretted siding with Richard.

Whatever his reason for abandoning his friend, the Duke switched his allegiance to Henry Tudor, still living as an exile in Brittany, and invited him to depose Richard. Henry would then be crowned England's King and he would have the Princess Elizabeth as his wife, or else her sister Cecily, if 'the other should die before he enjoyed the same'. This was not the first time Elizabeth of York was spoken of as a bride for Henry Tudor. Her late father King Edward had once hatched a plot to lure 'the only imp now left of King Henry VI's blood' into his clutches. If the Earl of Richmond would return to England and make peace with the House of York, he would be well favoured and have Elizabeth for his bride. Suspecting a trap, Henry stayed put.

As Henry Tudor was being offered the English throne, Elizabeth Woodville's participation in the conspiracy probably meant that she had no reason to believe her sons were still alive. Perhaps Buckingham had communicated his suspicions – or the fact – to her. According to one account, when told that her sons were dead or probably so, the Queen 'fell into a swoon and lay lifeless a good while; after coming to herself, she cried out loud… condemning herself for a madwoman for that, being deceived by false promises, she had delivered her younger son out of sanctuary to be murdered by his enemy.'

Elizabeth Woodville lent her full support to Buckingham and to Lady Margaret Beaufort, Richmond's formidable mother, who had masterminded the revolt. With the help of the Queen's Yorkist friends, Richmond set sail in early October. But the rebellion was a glorious failure. Henry Tudor's ships were driven back to the Breton coast by fierce gales, while in England, Buckingham's forces were overwhelmed by the King's. Richmond remained safe abroad, but the Duke was not so lucky; he was captured and beheaded.

≡

After the failed rebellion, Richard III took extra precautions to reinforce his authority. In January 1484, he introduced a blatant piece of propaganda entitled *Titulus Regius* to justify his taking of the throne. It invalidated the 'ungracious pretended marriage' of Edward IV and Elizabeth Woodville, making their children 'unable to inherit or to claim anything by inheritance by the law and custom of England'. *Titulus Regius* was especially denunciatory towards the Woodvilles. The Queen Dowager, with the help of her mother the Duchess of Bedford, was accused of bringing about her marriage through 'sorcery and witchcraft', and the rule of her grasping family was blamed for the 'discords, inward battles, [and] effusion of Christian men's blood' during the last reign.

Having declared his brother's children illegitimate in Parliament, Richard looked to the upbringing of his own son, the eleven-year-old Edward of Middleham as the next King of England. But in April, tragedy struck when the boy died unexpectedly. Richard and his wife Anne were devastated at their loss, both 'in a state bordering on madness'. But any hope the Queen would conceive again was unlikely. Within a year of her son's death, Anne herself grew ill, and by March 1485, she was on her deathbed.

The Queen's demise fuelled speculation that her husband had romantic designs on his eldest niece, Elizabeth. Just a year before, the Queen Dowager had made the extraordinary move of surrendering all five of her daughters into Richard's protective custody. Her decision remains controversial. Centuries later, it still seems inconceivable that

Richard the th King of Englād
and France, Lord of Ireland

Figure 4   Richard III by Wenceslaus Hollar
The Rijksmuseum, Amsterdam

Elizabeth would commit them to their uncle's care. Even if he did not kill the Princes in the Tower, he had stripped them of their birthright and their freedom. Did Elizabeth Woodville receive some word from Richard himself that he was blameless of the Princes' deaths, or that they were even still alive? Most likely, Elizabeth had gotten no such assurances. She was simply a pragmatist. She and her girls had been in sanctuary for close to a year, and they could not remain there indefinitely, living in continual fear and uncertainty. Rather than have Richard demand their release by force as he might eventually, Elizabeth made her peace with him under terms guaranteeing their safety.

Richard accepted her conditions. To lessen their mother's worries, he made a public oath on 1 March 1484, affirming that in leaving sanctuary, the Princesses Elizabeth, Cecily, Anne, Katharine, and Bridget would be in

> 'the surety of their lives, and also not suffer any hurt
> by any manner persons, nor any of them imprisoned
> within the Tower of London or any place.'

As well, Richard promised to provide for them and to find them suitable husbands. Each girl would receive 'in marriage lands and tenements to the yearly value of 200 marks for terms of their lives'. The King also pledged to be a fair and loving guardian to his nieces, swearing that 'if any surmise or evil report be made to me of them', he would give it no credence until the entire matter was brought forth and all sides heard. For the surrender of her daughters, 'Dame Elizabeth Grey', as Richard called his sister-in-law, was rewarded. She was given an annuity of 700 marks for her maintenance, on the condition that she live quietly and give Richard no further trouble.

Despite their reservations about their uncle, the return to court must have been agreeable to the Princesses after so many months shut away. The King treated them kindly, as did Queen Anne before she died. By December, it was noticed that Richard was playing particular attention to his attractive niece, Elizabeth. Richard's court was never known for its excesses, but during the Christmas festivities of 1484, he appeared uncharacteristically jovial and high-spirited, ordering rounds of entertainments. 'Far too much attention was given to dancing and gaiety' that holy season, according to his detractors. Furthermore, they rebuked the King for overstepping the bounds of propriety. Not only were his gifts of costly dresses to the

Queen excessively extravagant, but he also presented Elizabeth with similar clothing.

When Anne died the following spring, rumours flew far and wide that Richard, now a widower and in desperate need of an heir, was intent on marrying Elizabeth. His generosity that Christmas implied he was infatuated with her, as none of his other nieces were so well favoured. Richard's true intentions remain a mystery. If he had indeed fallen for Elizabeth, it would have been no great surprise. The girl was comely, and at nineteen, young and capable of bearing children. Though considered illegitimate, thanks to his own doing, Elizabeth's status would apparently not affect that of their offspring if Richard took her as his wife.

What Elizabeth thought of the King's overtures – if that was what they were - is another puzzle. Throughout her life, she left no clues about her feelings towards her uncle. *The Song of the Lady Bessy*, a poem written at the beginning of the 16th century about Elizabeth of York, naturally had the Princess repulsed by Richard's advances. However, the notion that Elizabeth was enamoured of her uncle - and even encouraged his attentions - was put forth in the early 17th century. The antiquarian George Buck claimed to have found a most revealing letter by the Princess in the collection of the Earl of Arundel. Written to the King's supporter, the Duke of Norfolk, Elizabeth asked his help in furthering her marriage to Richard - 'her only joy and maker in this world'. Like an impatient and smitten adolescent, the writer was anxious for the wedding to take place, and was annoyed how the ailing Queen Anne 'would never die'. If Elizabeth had written the letter, it remained a well-kept secret in the Howard family, and apparently no outsider knew of it except Buck. But its authenticity cannot be verified - the letter has since disappeared - and with it any real evidence that Elizabeth was keen on marrying Richard III.

Even supposing uncle and niece were in love; they faced stiff opposition from the King's own supporters. His two closest friends, Richard Ratcliffe and William Catesby, told him, in no uncertain terms, that the marriage would be ruinous. The late Queen was still held in great affection by the people, they said, and already there was talk that Richard had done away with Anne to gratify his 'incestuous passion' for Elizabeth. Also, such a union between close relations was contrary to Church law. To back them up, doctors of divinity were ushered into the King's presence to confirm the fact. That they were summoned suggests the seriousness of Richard's intentions, whether or not his niece herself was willing. If he had never considered marriage with Elizabeth, he could simply have said so, and there would have been no need for the King to have been lectured to. Whatever his objectives, Richard was forced into the awkward position of having to deny the rumours in public. Shortly before Easter of 1485, in the presence of the Lord Mayor and the citizens, the King denied he had any interest in his niece. That said, he had her sent away to Sheriff Hutton in Yorkshire.

Gossip regarding the King's love for Elizabeth of York was disturbing to Henry Tudor. Without marriage to her, he risked losing the support of the Yorkists wanting to overthrow Richard III. Just as troubling were the actions of late of the Queen Dowager. For releasing her daughters into Richard's care, she was seen as double-dealing and untrustworthy. Now she was even writing to her son Dorset, who had fled to Richmond's side, urging him to abandon his new Lancastrian friends. He must make his peace with the King, she begged Grey. But just as Richmond was resigning himself to her betrayal, news came from across the Channel that Richard had publicly repudiated her daughter Elizabeth. Henry Tudor's hopes were on the rise again. It was still possible that he might have the young woman to whom he had pledged himself at the Cathedral of Rennes.

Since January, the King was warned of an impending invasion by Henry Tudor. He showed no alarm, but instead, affected an air of bravado and cheer as he had that Christmas. He even boasted that no tidings were more welcome to him. A final confrontation with his enemies, Richard declared, would 'put an end to all his doubts and troubles'. When Richmond and his army finally landed at Milford Haven on 7 August 1485, Richard was well prepared. His army, comprising some ten thousand men at arms, outnumbered that of his enemy two to one. He also had the great lords, John Howard, Duke of Norfolk, and Henry Percy, Earl of Northumberland by his side, whereas the rebels only boasted one significant nobleman - the Earl of Oxford - in their ranks.

But could Richard trust his friends? On the evening of 21 August, a taunting note, written by an anonymous hand, was left for the Duke of Norfolk at Bosworth Field where the battle was to be fought. It read:

'Jack of Norfolk, be not too bold, For Dickon thy master is bought and sold.'

If Richard ignored the warning, when the battle was under way the next day, he knew he was indeed betrayed. When the Earl of Oxford attacked Norfolk's forces, the Earl of Northumberland did nothing to prevent their onslaught. Lord Stanley did likewise, holding back his men. As husband to Margaret Beaufort, he chose his stepson over his King. Fearing further disloyalty, Richard took a small band of his most trusted men with him to make a decisive attack against Richmond himself. Catching sight of his hated rival, Richard charged ahead. But before he could get close enough for the kill, he was cut down and slaughtered. His crown, which had fallen from his helmet, was later retrieved. As shouts of 'King Henry! King Henry!' filled the air, it was set on Richmond's head.

Chapter 5
The King's Wife

HENRY TUDOR and Elizabeth of York did not meet immediately after Bosworth was won. When the conquering Richmond rode in triumph towards London, his chief desire was to reunite with his mother again. The two had always been close even though they had spent so little time together. As a boy, Richmond was raised in Wales by his uncle, Jasper Tudor, and as a young man, was forced into exile by the Yorkists. Only during the short-lived restoration of Henry VI, did the Earl see Margaret Beaufort again before he had to go back in hiding. A deeply devout woman, the Countess believed she had been inspired by God to wed Henry's father, Edmund Tudor, and in that same confidence, she knew her son was marked for greatness. When she greeted Henry at Leicester as King of England, Margaret's ambitions for her 'dear heart' and her 'dearest and only desired joy in the world', as she called her son, were fulfilled.

After the happy reunion, the new King set foot in London on 3 September. It was there that Henry finally set eyes upon the young lady he had sworn to marry. At the death of her uncle and the proclamation of the new King, Elizabeth was conveyed from Sheriff Hutton to Westminster Palace, where she was returned to the care of her mother. There is no account of Elizabeth and Henry's first meeting, but protocol would have had her doing him obeisance when she was brought into his presence. Though she was the daughter, sister, and niece to three kings, and as some might say, the rightful heir to the Crown herself, the greater honour now belonged to the young man before her. On his part, courtesy would have Henry raise Elizabeth to her feet instead of keeping her on her knees. Standing face-to-face, both were undoubtedly pleased with what each saw. To Henry, his Yorkist bride-to-be was as beautiful as he had been told, and Elizabeth herself could not have been disappointed. We are familiar with the image of Henry VII in his later years - the drawn face with the hooked nose, suspicious eyes, tight lips, and thin greying hair - but at twenty-eight, before he was beset by age and the cares of State, Henry was described as tall, 'slender but strong', and quite handsome - 'particularly when his expression was happy in conversation'.

Elizabeth's meeting with her intended husband was brief and formal. Henry Tudor was cautious and reserved, his nature no doubt shaped by his years of exile. For his survival, he had to learn to watch his back and to rely on no one. Perhaps in time, when they had married and come to know each other better, Elizabeth may have thought, he would come to trust her - and even love her. For the present, she had to be content that she and Henry Tudor, by all appearances at least, were compatible. After all, theirs was not a love match, but one made 'for the profit of the commonwealth'.

That politics came before love was obvious when Henry planned his coronation. He decided on 30 October for the momentous day, but he set no date for his wedding. His subjects, especially the Yorkists who had defected to him, had expected Henry to fulfil his promise to marry Elizabeth of York, and to have her jointly crowned with him. But Henry was unmoved. He was determined to be made King of England *alone*, and he would not allow it to be thought that his right was by virtue of his wife. To make that clear, he was crowned a bachelor in Westminster Abbey, and a week later it was declared in Parliament that his rule was achieved by conquest alone – 'the sure judgment of God… giving him the victory in the field over his enemy'. There was no reference to Elizabeth.

Elizabeth and her supporters were disheartened as winter approached and there was still no word as to her marriage. Had the King renounced his oath, they wondered? Was she of no use to him now? Was he looking elsewhere for a wife? Despite the precariousness of her situation, Elizabeth was not without hope. Just as he declared himself King of England by his own right in Parliament, Henry also repealed many of the laws made by Richard III – including *Titulus Regius*. Since she was no longer deemed illegitimate, perhaps Henry would still marry her as promised.

It took Parliament to push the King along. On 10 December, the Commons petitioned Henry VII 'to espouse the Lady Elizabeth… [by] which marriage they hope God would bless with a progeny of the race of kings to the great satisfaction of the whole realm'. After the Lords endorsed the request, Henry submitted to their wishes. He had most likely intended to all along. In keeping with his policy of asserting himself as King without Elizabeth of York, he probably left it to Parliament to ask him to marry, as he knew they would. Giovanni de Giglis, a collector of papal taxes in England, wrote to the Vatican that at least four days before the petition was formally presented, Henry had already made up his mind to wed the Princess. That he did on 18 January 1486. Because the couple were related by blood, a dispensation from the Vatican was required for legality's sake. But rather than wait till it was granted by the Pope in Rome (which it was later in March), a special license for the nuptials to proceed was issued two days before the ceremony.

Within months of the marriage, a happy Elizabeth announced herself with child. As her pregnancy progressed, the King and his mother carefully orchestrated her lying-in. Sometime in the late summer, the heavily pregnant Queen was carefully moved to Winchester. It was not in response to her condition - that is to shield her from any possible infection in the capital - but to further the King's dynastic pretensions.

In staking his claim to the throne, Henry VII did not base his descent only from Edward III, but further back, to Cadwallader, the last King of the Britons. As a boy living in Wales with his uncle, Jasper Tudor, Henry had probably been enthralled by the stories and legends of the region. Cadwallader was popular. Brave and just, he was regarded as a hero - even as a saint - by the Welsh. His exploits were even more captivating to the young Henry who was told that he was a descendant of the great King himself. Not only that, but it was said in ancient times that Cadwallader's 'stock and progeny should reign and have dominion in this land again'. Henry might well have believed he was the fulfilment of that prophecy. Not only did he associate himself with Cadwallader, whose dragon he bore on his standard, but also with the legendary Arthur Pendragon, another great hero of the Welsh. Believing the Tudors to be descendants of him too, Henry would have his heir – and of course it would be a son – be his namesake. He would also have him born in Winchester - a city with associations to Arthur and the ancient kings of Britain.

In darkness, propped up in her great bed, Elizabeth of York felt as if time had come to a standstill. Three weeks had passed since she had taken leave of the court, but it seemed a lifetime ago; an eternity since she had seen the sky above her or breathed the open air. The ordinances for a royal childbirth, as laid down by her mother-in-law, dictated that Elizabeth be shut away - cocooned - to await the birth of her baby. Except for one window that 'she may have light when it please her', the rest were draped over with heavy tapestries. Even the walls and the ceiling of the Queen's bedchamber were covered by 'rich cloth of arras'. Their decoration must be minimal and nondescript. Under no circumstances, Lady Margaret ordered, should they contain images. In childbed, the mother was in a fragile state of mind and prone to fantasies. Pictures might upset her, causing harm to the child.

Despite the stifling atmosphere of her confinement, measures were taken to ensure Elizabeth's comfort. Rushes normally used to cover the floors were deemed unsanitary, and were replaced by luxurious carpets imported from the Near East. On Elizabeth's 'Bed of State' were fine sheets embroidered with golden thread and bordered with ermine. The bed itself was suitably grand, denoting her status as Queen and as mother of the King's heir. Across the room was a cupboard, also adorned with hangings, inside of which the Queen's sumptuous gold and silver plate was displayed. Although Elizabeth had retired from the rest of the court, she was not to be deprived of the tokens of her rank.

Nor did she lack company. To watch over Elizabeth and to carry out the delivery, the best midwives were in attendance, as were her ladies-in-waiting. The royal physicians were not present, nor were any other gentlemen of her household. After they had prayed God 'to send her the good hour', there were disbarred from her presence. All functions normally handled by them were now the responsibility of the Queen's women. During the confinement, they were

> 'made all manner of officers as butlers, stewards, etc.; the officers they represented being commanded to bring them all needful things unto the great chamber door, and the women officers to receive it there of them.'

For weeks, these ladies shared their mistress's exile away from the masculine world. They attended to Elizabeth's every need - conversing with her, comforting her, praying with her, and waiting with her for the impending childbirth. The monotony was relieved by small amusements - games of cards and chess, music played on the virginals or the lute by one of Elizabeth's more accomplished ladies, and snatches of gossip from the court beyond the bedroom door.

On 20 September, her time came. Elizabeth entrusted herself to her midwives and to God. Neither failed her, the infant - the reconciliator between Lancaster and York, and the future ruler of a new Camelot - was safely delivered to the joy of his parents. It was a boy as Henry VII had no doubt it would be.

The birth of Arthur, Prince of Wales, rather than advancing concord between the families of Henry VII and Elizabeth of York, encouraged new rebellion. In Burgundy, the Dowager Duchess Margaret, the Queen's aunt, had never come to terms with the demise of her royal House in England. She continued to uphold her family's right to rule, and she had deeply mourned the death of her brother King Richard. Even though her niece Elizabeth had become Queen of England, she was a Tudor now – and that was no comfort to the passionately Yorkist Margaret.

The Dowager Duchess' court became a refuge for Yorkist exiles who after Bosworth, fled to Burgundy rather than acknowledge a Lancastrian as their overlord. Among the exiles were Margaret's nephew, the Earl of Lincoln, whom Richard III had named as his heir if he remained childless, and Viscount Lovell, a long-time friend of the late King. With the Duchess' help, the two malcontents planned to invade England for Edward, Earl of Warwick – or so they claimed.

At Henry VII's accession, Warwick – the son of George of Clarence - who had lived with his cousin Elizabeth at Sheriff Hutton, was placed into custody. As the nephew of Edward IV and Richard III, the fifteen-year-old was considered too dangerous to be on the loose by the new King. Warwick's disappearance from the public eye led to rumours that he had escaped from prison. It seemed to be true when Warwick suddenly appeared in Ireland in January 1487. Accompanied by a priest named Richard Symonds who claimed he had helped the youth out of the Tower of London, Warwick laid claim to Henry VII's throne.

When the news reached London, the King was 'sorely vexed and angered' – not only by the challenge to his authority, but also by the fraudulence of the whole affair. The *real* Warwick, Henry knew, was still safely locked away. The young man who was rallying Irish sympathizers and discontented Yorkists to him was an impostor. In response, Henry brought out the actual Earl of Warwick in public to dissuade rebellion.

Having the real Warwick shown to the people had no effect. Even if Margaret of Burgundy and her friends believed the boy in Ireland to be a fake, they were still set on dethroning Henry Tudor. On 16 June, Margaret's forces, led by Lincoln and Lovell, and joined by the Irish, met the royal army near the village of Stoke. The rebels proved no match for Henry VII's troops, and four thousand of them, including

Lincoln and Lovell, lay dead by the time they surrendered. Symonds and Warwick were taken alive. Upon questioning, it was discovered that the captured 'Earl' was actually one Lambert Simnel. Symonds, who 'delighted in fraud and crafty behaviour', had first coached the lad to assume the role of the missing Richard, Duke of York. But perhaps thinking that Warwick would be a better sell, and that Simnel was 'of the same age and stature' of the real Earl, he had his pupil switch parts.

When all was made known, the King was surprisingly lenient. The priest, who had masterminded the deception, was merely imprisoned. His protégé, whom Henry spared because his young age, was put into service at court, working as a scullion in the royal kitchens. Later, having proved his ability to avoid trouble, he was promoted to King's Falconer.

What Elizabeth of York thought of the Simnel affair is unrecorded. The Queen was at least aware that the true Warwick was kept close in England, and that Margaret of Burgundy was championing an impostor. As Henry Tudor's wife, Elizabeth would probably have viewed her estranged aunt's actions as repugnant. Had she been made aware that Lambert Simnel was originally meant to be passed off as her lost brother Prince Richard, Elizabeth might have been more appalled.

The reaction of her mother the Queen Dowager is hard to gauge. At the height of the Simnel threat, it was reported that Elizabeth Woodville 'should lose and forfeit all her lands and possessions'. Her property was put into the hands of her eldest daughter, and the former Queen was placed in a nunnery. Henry VII's justification, as it was also reported, was that Elizabeth had betrayed him when she surrendered her daughters to Richard III in 1484. If this were all true, why did her actions three years ago suddenly matter now? Since Henry VII won the Crown, he had born no resentment towards his mother-in-law. He treated her well, restoring Elizabeth to her former dignity as Queen Dowager, and at the christening of her grandson Arthur, she was even given the honour of being his sponsor. Elizabeth's disgrace, if it was that, has been credited to her alleged sympathies for the Yorkist uprising for Lambert Simnel. But it is difficult to imagine why Elizabeth would have flirted with treason in the first place. She had no reason to back a conspiracy – one against her own daughter, and by extension her grandson – and least of all for the son of her old enemy Clarence. After the tumultuous days of Richard III, Elizabeth had finally found a measure of peace. Henry VII was good to her, and she was honoured as mother of the present Queen and as grandmother of England's future King. Why would she jeopardize all that?

If it was not treason that removed Elizabeth Woodville from court as it was said, perhaps it was simply her own desire to retire from public life. The loss of her property was perhaps no punishment at all, but done with the Queen Dowager's full consent; a transferring of her dower lands to her beloved daughter. In return for her generosity, Elizabeth Woodville received a pension and other cash gifts from the King. After her lands were put in her daughter's care, she may have intentionally moved to the nunnery at Bermondsey. It was not unusual for privileged widows, even queens, to seek retirement within a religious community. In doing so, Elizabeth was following the example of her predecessors such as Eleanor of Aquitaine and Isabella of France. Far from living a cloistered life of austerity, Elizabeth was allotted luxurious quarters at Bermondsey, and on occasion, she even visited court.

That is not to say her presence was always welcome. She was seemingly absent from her daughter's coronation, which would take place in November 1487. The reason was unlikely due to illness – the Queen Dowager seemed to have enjoyed good health until her death in 1492 – but most likely because she was asked not to appear, by request of the King. Though he was giving his wife a coronation at last, Henry VII was still reluctant to admit that she had a better claim to the throne than he did. By allowing Elizabeth Woodville no place in the ceremony, he would be calling attention to that fact her daughter was Queen, not by her descent from Edward IV and his spouse, but by her marriage. To underline the Queen's commitment to her new family, her redoubtable mother-in-law Margaret Beaufort would stand in for the Queen Dowager, as she was already doing at stately functions.

Elizabeth could only have been disappointed by the decision to exclude her mother. But had she raised any objection, it was the King who invariably had the last word. Convention and religion compelled her to obey her husband in all things, and Elizabeth by her gentle character, was not one inclined to disagreement. Throughout her life, she appeared to have been content, rather than resigned, in deferring to her husband. After his death, Henry VII was reputed to be chilly and distant towards Elizabeth, but that was almost certainly untrue. Though the King did come across as aloof to his subjects, he appeared to have a warm and loving relationship with his wife. Inventories taken in the reign of Henry VIII list items belonging to his parents as being decorated with their combined initials *H* and *E*. Despite his miserly reputation, Henry was generous to Elizabeth, giving her gifts including furs and jewels. He also paid many of her debts. On one occasion, Henry gave his wife £2,000 to satisfy her creditors. Evidence of their affection can be found in their private communications. In the margins of a prayer book, Henry wrote to his wife - 'Madam, I pray you remember me, your loving master, Henry R'. In reply, Elizabeth scribbled underneath – 'I pray you forget not me. Pray to God that I may have part of your prayers, Elizabeth the Queen'.

At Elizabeth's coronation in 1487, Henry was determined to do her honour, sparing no expense. To bring her to London, he organized a great water pageant. On 23 November, Elizabeth, with her mother-in-law and her ladies, rode in a sumptuously decorated barge taking her from the riverside palace at Greenwich to the capital. Surrounding the Queen were the Lord Mayor and the city officials in dozens of water craft 'freshly furnished with banners and streamers of silk richly beseen'. Completing the flotilla, were boatloads of musicians playing trumpets and horns in joyful celebration. At Elizabeth's arrival at the Tower, the King openly demonstrated his affection for her. He greeted his wife 'in such manner and form as was to all the estates, being present, a very goodly sight, and right joyous and comfortable to behold'. So much for the myth that Henry VII was an unfeeling husband.

Following tradition, Elizabeth spent the night in the Tower. While the King occupied himself dubbing new Knights of the Bath for the coronation, Elizabeth prepared for her special day, rehearsing the rituals she would undergo on the coming Sunday. Later, left alone to rest in the royal apartments, Elizabeth might have reflected on the Tower's gloomy past. It had always been a melancholy place for her family. It was here within its confines that she, her mother, and her sisters had once sought safety, where her uncle Clarence had been slain, and where her brothers were last seen alive, playing in the garden beneath her windows.

Whatever sadness she might have felt, by dawn, Elizabeth turned her attention to the day ahead. After she dined, Elizabeth stepped into an open litter for the journey to Westminster. As she rode through London, the city streets were packed with thousands of citizens wanting to see her as she passed. They were not disappointed. Elizabeth was striking. Following the custom of a queen going to her coronation, she was dressed all in white - white damask and white cloth of gold. Around her shoulders was a mantle of ermine to ward off the November chill. As protocol also demanded that she 'be bareheaded' and 'bare visaged till she come to Westminster that all men may see her', Elizabeth wore a jewelled circlet on her 'fair yellow hair' which was worn loose down to her shoulders.

The next day – 25 November - Elizabeth, clad in purple, set out to her coronation. Beneath her feet was the customary ray cloth stretching from Westminster Hall into the Abbey. Tradition also had it that after the King or Queen had passed, the onlookers were free to cut it up for souvenirs. For centuries, the custom was observed largely without incident, but this time, as Elizabeth walked by and turned into the church, the eager crowd suddenly rushed forwards to rip up the cloth. In the mad dash, several people were hurt - even trampled to death. In the commotion, Elizabeth's train of ladies 'was broken and distroubled'.

Order was quickly restored, and the ceremony proceeded as if nothing had happened. The Queen may not even have been told what had occurred. With her sister Cecily bearing her train, she was conducted down the aisle of the Abbey to a chair set before the pulpit. From there, Elizabeth was taken before the high altar. She knelt and prostrated herself on cushions as the Archbishop of Canterbury prayed over her. After Elizabeth was anointed with holy oil, her coronation ring and her crown were blessed. The ring was then slipped onto her finger, and the crown solemnly set on her head.

During the coronation and the Mass that followed, the King was nowhere to be seen. As Elizabeth was the star of the show, Henry had secreted himself in a viewing box above the pulpit, joined by his mother. The King and Lady Margaret also saw fit to absent themselves from the banquet that followed at Westminster Hall; again watching from a place of concealment.

Single-handedly, Elizabeth held court over the revellers. She sat at a long table on the dais where she was joined by the Archbishop, her sister Cecily, and the Duchess of Bedford. Even with this honour given to them, all three had to sit at the far ends of the table so as not distract attention from the Queen. For the feast, a long list of dishes was offered including venison, rabbit, deer, crane, capon, egret, quail, swan, peacock, chicken, plover, partridge, eel, perch, carp, sturgeon, and 'pike in Latymer sauce'. For dessert, there were selections of custards, tarts, wafers, marzipan, 'castles of jelly', and imaginatively prepared fruits. Throughout the meal, the Queen of course was served first, followed by the Archbishop, and then the guests according to precedence. Nearing the end of the meal, Elizabeth, following custom, offered gifts to her well-wishers. As she did so, the herald repeated several times around the hall in a loud voice:

> 'From the most high, most mighty, most excellent Princess, the most noble Queen of England and of France, and Lady of Ireland – largesse!'

When the banquet ended, Elizabeth was given the traditional drink of hippocras by the Lord Mayor. She drank, and gave the golden cup back to him as reward. The Queen then 'departed with God's blessing, and to the rejoicing of many a true Englishman's heart'.

The Queen's fecundity was proven again – and several times over – in the years following. In November 1489, Elizabeth gave birth to her second child, a daughter named Margaret in honour of the King's mother. The Princess was followed by a brother named Henry in June 1491, and then by a sister Elizabeth, born a year later. Sadly, the Queen's namesake died at the age of three. There was consolation when Elizabeth was pregnant again, producing another daughter, Mary, in March 1496. To the especial joy of the King, Elizabeth even managed another son, a boy named Edmund, born three years afterwards. But sadly, like the baby Elizabeth, Edmund did not live long.

Although her energies were chiefly directed to the care of her surviving children, the Queen was still attentive to the family she grew up with. As the oldest of Elizabeth's surviving sisters, Cecily of York was given a prominent role at her coronation, and was asked to grace many an occasion at court. The Queen's other siblings were well favoured too. Her sister Anne was in frequent attendance on her too, and at the baptism of Prince Arthur, she had the privilege of bearing his chrisom cloth. In 1495, Elizabeth helped to arrange Anne's marriage to Thomas Howard, son of the Earl of Surrey. The union was a great boon to the Howards. Ten years ago, the family was in disgrace when the Duke of Norfolk fought on the losing side at Bosworth. Fortunately, his son Surrey, Fortunately, his son Surrey, by his unwavering loyalty to the new dynasty, was able to revive the Howards' fortunes. His efforts were well rewarded by being brought into the royal family.

The Queen's other sister, Katharine of York, was provided with a good marriage as well. She was wedded to William Courtney, son of the Earl of Devon. Elizabeth continued to look out for her sister's welfare. Later, when Katharine's husband was imprisoned for alleged treason, it was the Queen who came to her aid, providing financial support to the Courtney children. She also took care of her youngest sister Bridget. Having chosen a religious life, her needs were modest. Still, Elizabeth saw to it that Bridget's maintenance was regularly paid to her convent at Dartford.

=

Having failed to best Henry Tudor, Margaret of Burgundy's hatred for him only grew stronger. After Lambert Simnel was exposed, the Duchess was 'incontinently devising, practising, and imagining some great and even more difficult enterprise by which she might vex and perturb' the King of England. She found means in a mysterious young man who showed up at her doorstep in November 1492. He spoke English and he had a noble demeanour about him. He also bore a striking resemblance to the late Edward IV - and with good reason as he told the Duchess – he was none other than her nephew, the lost Richard, Duke of York!

The stranger had quite a story to tell. After he and his brother Edward V were imprisoned, he escaped when one of the murderers didn't have the heart to kill him. The youth recalled that he was smuggled out of the Tower and allowed to live in obscurity until the opportunity came for him to reclaim his birthright. Since leaving England, he had already been received by the French King, Charles VIII, and now, he had come to be reunited with his aunt the Duchess.

It is unknown whether Margaret deluded herself into believing his fantastic tale, or she was merely using the young man to get back at Henry VII. Either way, the Duchess gave him a showy welcome at her court. Besides publicly recognizing him as her nephew, she raised support for his cause. She praised his many 'virtues and qualities with which he was endowed above the moon' to any Yorkist sympathizer willing to listen. She commended him to her Hapsburg son-in-law, the Holy Roman Emperor Maximilian I, and to the 'Catholic Kings' of Spain - Ferdinand of Aragon and Isabella of Castile. Writing to the Spanish Queen, Margaret told her how after speaking with the newly arrived youth, she was positive 'this man is the one whom they once though dead'; the 'sole survivor of our family through so many calamities and crises'.

Isabella sensibly ignored the Duchess, but in Scotland, King James IV was among those taken in, or pretended to be, in his grudge against his English neighbour Henry VII. James welcomed 'York' to his kingdom, and endorsed the young man's title of 'King Richard IV'. He even offered him his kinswoman Lady Gordon as his 'Queen'. James was also willing to provide troops. In September 1496, 'the White Rose, Prince of England', as his supporters called him, invaded England by way of Northumberland. The attempt was a fiasco.

When the Duchess' protégé took up arms again in 1497, he had the support of the Cornishmen, who, discontented by heavy taxation, rose in revolt. In July, news of thousands of rebels marching towards London threw the citizens into panic, including the Queen. During the crisis, Elizabeth was in the capital with the six-year-old Prince Henry. As the rebel army neared, mother and son sought safety in the Tower. But the Cornishmen got no farther than Blackheath, four miles outside the city limits. There, they were thoroughly crushed by Henry VII's army.

Although some two thousand Cornishmen lost their lives in battle, and hundreds more in the retaliatory executions that followed, they continued to resist. In September, the insurgents pledged themselves to 'King Richard', and marched towards Taunton. It was another disaster for them. By October, the revolt was suppressed, its leaders put to death, and the challenger to Henry VII's throne taken prisoner.

As with Lambert Simnel, Henry VII was again unexpectedly merciful. In return, the captured 'Duke of York' made a public confession. He was not the missing Prince Richard, he admitted, but a Fleming named Perkin Warbeck. Because of his looks and his ability to speak English, he was persuaded by Yorkist exiles to assume the role of Edward IV's younger son. Convinced he was a harmless dupe like Simnel, Henry pardoned him. After a spell in the Tower, Warbeck was even allowed to attend court under supervision. His presence must have been disconcerting to the Queen. Elizabeth disliked bloodshed, and she was glad Warbeck was spared, but his impersonation of her brother Richard - assumed to be long dead - must have upset her. Elizabeth did not have to endure Warbeck's presence for long. In 1498, fed up with being under constant surveillance, he tried to escape. Henry could not afford to be so forgiving again. He had Warbeck put back in the Tower.

Within a few short years of winning the Crown, Henry Tudor had established himself as a key player on the international stage. Through his ability to maintain his throne and to provide good government to his people, England's prestige was restored before the crowned heads of Europe. Maximilian I sought Henry VII's friendship, as did Ferdinand and Isabella - the unifiers of Spain and not long afterwards, the rulers of the mysterious new lands across the ocean. In 1489, the ties between England and Spain were cemented by the betrothal of Arthur Tudor and Katherine, the youngest of the Spanish Princesses.

At the time, Arthur was still a child of two, and his future bride barely a year older. Not until the two children were of marriageable age – in their teens that is – would Katherine be allowed to leave Spain. Until then, the relationship of the young couple was fostered by being the 15th century equivalent of 'pen pals'. There was an obstacle in that neither knew the other's native tongue. In England, no one spoke Spanish, and in Spain, English was an utterly foreign language.

Elizabeth proposed a solution. In July 1498, she suggested to Queen Isabella that her daughter ought to begin learning French, which Arthur was already fluent in. The idea was well received, and the Princess was put in the company of her French-speaking sister-in-law Margaret of Austria, the daughter of Emperor Maximilian, who had recently wed Katherine's brother Prince John. Katherine's time with Margaret paid off. Within two years she was speaking French very well, Isabella wrote in a letter to Elizabeth.

But since it was Latin, not French, which Katherine had started learning as a child, that was the language used in her initial correspondence with Prince Arthur, another student of the ancient tongue. Under the direction of their tutors, the couple wrote - or rather copied - 'sweet letters' to each other. Their sentiments, composed in extravagantly romantic terms, were of their constant mutual affection, and how regrettable it was that they could not meet sooner. "The procrastination about your coming', ran a typical communication from Arthur, was 'vexatious to me', as he told Katherine adoringly.

In 1501, the wait was over, or so it seemed at first. In May, Katherine bid farewell to her family at Granada. But because of bad weather, it was not until the middle of August that Katherine could set sail; only to be cast back to Spain by high winds and rough seas. The voyage had to be delayed until 27 September when it was finally thought safe to try another crossing. Conditions were favourable at first, but when the Spaniards neared the English Channel, a tempest rose causing 'thunderstorms every four or five hours'. The longer route to Southampton was abandoned, and the battered Spanish fleet anchored at Plymouth, the first port in sight. An exhausted but grateful Katherine headed straight to the local church in thanksgiving.

Not only was Arthur Tudor anxious to see his fiancée as he had always written to Katherine, but his parents too. Elizabeth of York was glad that after so many delays, the Princess from Spain had finally reached England. In a month's time, she and Arthur would be wed, and within a year - God willing - she would a mother. But the Queen's happiness had come at a price. Before his daughter could come to England, King Ferdinand had demanded the death of the hapless Earl of Warwick. The young man, though he was a prisoner, was a continuing threat to the security of England, he believed. Until he was properly dealt with, Ferdinand declared, he would not allow his precious daughter to leave Spain. Henry VII complied. To secure the alliance, Warwick and Perkin Warbeck were put to death in 1499.

Having made sacrifice of Warwick, Henry VII was even more curious to see the young woman for whose sake blood had been spilt. But Katherine's journey to London, done in stately procession, was slow, and heavy rains added further delay. Since her landing on 2 October, Katherine had only managed to cross into Hampshire in the month afterwards. The King could no longer contain his impatience. Instead of waiting to receive Katherine at his recently completed riverside palace of Richmond as planned, he would see her immediately. On the 4 November, Henry sent a message out to Arthur to rendezvous with him at Easthampstead. Together, they would ride to Dogmersfield to welcome the girl.

The Spaniards were caught unaware by the arrival of father and son. Meeting the royal party outside of town, Katherine's staff tried to reason with the King. Not only was their mistress unprepared to receive visitors, it was most improper. Spanish etiquette demanded that a bride be in seclusion until the day of her wedding. Henry brushed their objections aside. It was very well that the Princess followed the customs of her country, he replied, but she was now in *his*, and thus subject to *his* wishes.

Henry rode on ahead. He would inspect the Princess himself first, and then return to fetch the Prince. Perhaps Henry remained sceptical of Katherine's looks. During the marriage negotiations, portraits of her and of Arthur were undoubtedly exchanged. The girl looked pleasing enough, but painters could be notorious flatterers. Henry had to be certain with his own eyes that she was indeed the young beauty he was expecting. There must be no surprises and no embarrassments at the young couple's first meeting.

At her lodgings, Katherine had already retired for the day. It was only three o'clock in the afternoon, but she was exhausted having arrived just a few hours before. She was awakened from her sleep by a commotion outside – the King was here. Though told Katherine was resting, Henry announced he would see her nonetheless. She was quickly roused out of bed by her indignant ladies no doubt muttering curses against the uncouth English. Wearing a simple shift, with her long hair falling down her back, Katherine greeted the King with a deep curtsy. The meeting was brief. Just pleasantries to each other, before Henry, satisfied with what he saw, left to bring back the Prince.

By the time they arrived, Katherine made herself more presentable. Brought before the King again, she was formally presented to her fiancé. Despite professing their love to each other for years, Katherine and Arthur's face-to-face meeting at last must have been awkward nonetheless. But as he shyly gazed upon Katherine, Arthur must have been impressed as his father was. Following English ideals of beauty, Katherine of Aragon was fair skinned and golden haired. Her looks, it was said, were inherited from her English Plantagenet ancestors. Katherine, like the Tudors, was a descendant of John of Gaunt. She was also small in stature, which probably pleased Arthur; he was not tall himself. Katherine also had a becoming plumpness to her, he noticed, a sign of good health, and the ability to bear many children. The attraction was likely to have been mutual. Katherine would have appreciated Arthur's good looks. He was not unlike his father with his slender figure, auburn hair, long pale face, and aquiline features. However, he did not have Henry's rough manner to Katherine's relief. Arthur was gentle and unassuming taking after his mother, whom Katherine heard was a most sweet lady.

After speeches of welcome and of the concord between the two countries were made in both English and Spanish (and then immediately translated into Latin for mutual understanding), Henry and his son left to take supper - no doubt to compare notes on Katherine, as she probably did on Arthur with her Spanish attendants. When they returned, the couple had little time to converse and know each other better. Instead, minstrels were summoned into the Princess's chamber. Arthur and Katherine did not appear to have danced together, probably because neither knew the styles of the other's country. Instead, Arthur partnered Lady Guildford, one of the English ladies drafted into Katherine's service, dancing most 'pleasantly and honourably' together before the assembly.

≡

The Queen was not to meet Princess Katherine until her formal entry into London set for 11 November. Until then, she had to be content with what her husband and her son could tell her about the meeting at Dogmersfield. She was happy that Arthur had taken a liking to Katherine, and that her daughter-in-law was everything she imagined. According to the King, she was a pretty and dignified girl, and by all appearances – humble, virtuous, and intelligent. In short, Henry and Elizabeth could not have chosen a better wife for their son.

The citizens were as eager to see their future Queen. In preparation, the streets on which she was to ride through were cleaned and strewn with gravel, and the buildings hung with rich tapestries and colourful banners. To honour her marriage to the Prince, a series of living tableaux were set up from London Bridge to Saint Paul's Cathedral, with themes taken from classical mythology, the Scriptures, and from history. As carpenters, painters, and craftsmen worked on the elaborate stage sets, children and youths rehearsed their roles in the spectacle.

Due to poor weather on 12 November, the city welcomed the new Princess of Wales the next day instead. When Katherine set out from Lambeth, it seemed as if all of London had come out to welcome her. The people cheered at the sight of Katherine, noting her foreign attire and her unusual customs with fascination. Instead of being carried about in a litter like Queen Elizabeth had been at her coronation, Katherine, wearing a 'strange diversity of apparel', rode on a mule as she did in Spain. By her side, was her soon-to-be brother-in-law, the ten-year-old Henry, Duke of York, acting as her escort and guide through the city.

Coming to London Bridge, Katherine and her entourage stopped before the first tableau along the route. At the bottom of a two-storey stage made 'of carved work, painted and gilded in most costly manner', Katherine was received, appropriately enough, by a young girl dressed up as Saint Katherine of Alexandria. She gave welcome to her Spanish counterpart, expressing her affection for the Princess whom she would 'aid, assist, and comfort'. As Katherine knew no English, it was left to Prince Henry to translate (in the French or Latin they both knew) what was being said.

Katherine was then directed to St Ursula seated above. Ursula, believed to have been a British princess, made fitting reference to Katherine's own English roots. The genealogy of Prince Arthur was also pointed out. Not only was he related to Katherine, he was also of ancient royalty – a kinsman to Ursula herself and to the legendary King Arthur. The Prince, the Saint continued, would 'succeed the first Arthur in dignity', and he would shine bright on earth like the star Arcturus.

Astronomical allusions were continued in subsequent tableaux. Coming before the personification of *Policy*, it was told to Katherine that Hesperus, the evening star – that 'bright star of Spain', her alter ego - had guided her to him and to his companions *Noblesse* and *Virtue*. After listening to speeches proclaiming their qualities, and of their intention to lead her on to *Honour*, Katherine moved onto to Cornhill to the 'Pageant of the Moon'.

At a cleverly devised staging of the moon and the planets in orbit, Katherine met her ancestor King Alfonso in the company of Raphael the 'angel of marriage', the prophet Job, and the philosopher Boethius. Known for his interest in astronomy, Alfonso gave his descendant a discourse on the movement of the heavenly bodies. As the sun, 'the significator of kings', was in conjunction with the stars Hesperus and Arcturus, Alfonso said, a happy future was in store for Arthur and Katherine.

From Cornhill, Katherine went on to Cheapside. As a follow-up to the preceding tableau, a large scale 'Pageant of the Sun' had been erected. In the centre of a great revolving wheel, representing the heavens with the signs of the zodiac, was seated a prince – a representation of the Sun itself - in golden robes. At his feet were four additional spinning wheels symbolizing the evening firmaments. Positioned before them were children posing as living constellations, wearing costumes 'full of stars as… named in books of astronomy'. The whole contraption was powered by three strong youths dressed as knights, who climbed on a treadmill mechanism moving the wheels of the tableau. As Katherine and her retinue marvelled over the ingenuity of the display, the princely Sun welcomed her to 'Britain, the land of Arthur', telling the Princess to 'go ye forth to the joyful semblance now of the marriage between your spouse and you'.

The joy of their union was reiterated at the 'Temple of God', a pageant showing the court of Heaven itself. There, the Lord, in all His glory surrounded by blazing candles and carolling angels, exalted

Katherine and her future children. 'Blessed be the fruit of your body,' He said, 'your sustenance and fruits shall increase and multiply.'

Katherine's final stop, before she was to go on to St Paul's, was before *Honour*, the culmination of all the presentations she had come across. Robed in purple outside the churchyard of the Cathedral, *Honour* presented two empty seats to Katherine. The Princess of Spain, being endowed with noblesse and virtue herself, he said, shall with Arthur, mount these thrones 'to reign here with us in prosperity forever'.

=

Katherine may have found Henry VII intimidating, but the Queen, whom she finally got to meet the following day, was anything but. Elizabeth of York's reputation for goodness was universally known, and her mother Isabella who had corresponded with the English Queen, had assured Katherine that Elizabeth would prove a most loving second mother to her. From the Bishop's palace at St Paul's where she had spent the night, Katherine was taken to nearby Baynard's Castle on the banks of the Thames to be introduced to the Queen. The two ladies hit it off immediately. The afternoon to evening was spent in 'pleasure and goodly communication, dancing and disports', before Elizabeth finally bade Katherine a good night.

They did not see each other again until after the wedding. From a raised viewing box facing the high altar, the King and Queen, accompanied by the omnipresent Lady Margaret, watched in private as Katherine entered the Cathedral by the west door on Sunday, 14 November. The church was teeming with onlookers. For their benefit, Henry VII, who never underestimated the value of good showmanship, had a raised platform – 'a place like a mount' - built in the centre of the nave. Upon it, in the sight of God and all present, Arthur and Katherine would be joined as one.

As Katherine climbed the 'long bridge made of timber' to the stage, all eyes were on her. Her Spanish clothes, the like never seen before in England, elicited much attention. The white wedding dress consisted of a large gown with broad sleeves having many pleats. More unusual was Katherine's skirt. It was wide and bell-shaped, made by unseen hoops underneath. Her voluminous clothes had the effect of making the petite Katherine stand out. They also gave her an air of mystery. Following the example of Spanish brides, she wore a mantilla or long white veil, bordered with jewels which covered a 'great part of her visage and also a large quantity of her body'.

Katherine joined Arthur - also wearing white - in the middle of the platform. There, before the Archbishop of Canterbury, they were made husband and wife. 'The union between the two royal families and the two kingdoms is now so complete', Henry VII wrote jubilantly to Ferdinand and Isabella, 'that it is impossible to make any distinctions between the interests of England and Spain'.

A month after the nuptials, the newlyweds were packed off to Ludlow Castle. There, Arthur would re-assume his responsibilities as Prince of Wales, this time with Katherine at his side. Just before Christmas, Elizabeth and the rest of her family watched as the Prince and his bride left for their new life together in the Welsh Marches. As much as she missed them, Elizabeth was content knowing they were happy together. Arthur, as he wrote to his new in-laws in Spain, had 'never felt so much joy in his life'. He found Katherine so perfect, he said, that 'no woman in the world could be more agreeable to him'. By her son's exuberance, Elizabeth had no doubt that his marriage was immediately consummated. With joyful anticipation, she looked forward to the grandchildren to come.

From Ludlow, tidings about the Prince and Princess of Wales arrived regularly at court. His family heard how the pair were adjusting to life in the wilds of the Welsh border, how they played host to the locals come to offer their congratulations, and how Katherine had made a new friend in the Queen's cousin Margaret - the wife of the Prince's Chamberlain Sir Richard Pole, and the sister of the unfortunate Earl of Warwick. But not all the news was good. In the spring, an occurrence of plague was reported in the Marches. The King and Queen were grateful that Arthur and Katherine were secluded within the fortress-like confines of Ludlow Castle, away from town where disease would be most rampant.

On the night of 4 April 1502, a courier from Ludlow arrived in a sweat at Greenwich. He had ridden in haste with a message for the King. But the hour was late and he was intercepted by the Council instead. At his news, Henry VII's advisers hung their heads and crossed themselves. It would do no good to trouble the King now, they decided. Let him sleep, and let him know what he must tomorrow.

When morning came, a friar who was the King's confessor asked to see him. Solemnly, he bowed and approached Henry. 'If we receive good things at the hands of God,' he said sadly, 'why may we not endure evil things?' The King braced himself. He recognized the quotation from the *Book of Job* – Job who remained steadfast in his faith even in the face of great suffering. As gently as he could put it, his confessor announced that Arthur Prince of Wales was dead.

Stunned at first, Henry then gave way to an outpouring of grief. All he heard was that his son was dead, not the rest that the Princess, his daughter-in-law, who had also taken ill, was safe and out of danger. His thoughts were only on Arthur – his first-born son, the successor to his throne, and England's safeguard against the dynastic wars of old. In that moment, perhaps Henry found himself feeling empathy for his enemy Richard III. Both had lost their sons. Now he knew the pain his predecessor had felt.

Composing himself, Henry sent for the Queen and broke the painful news to her. Husband and wife then wept together. Henry had intended to console his wife, but it was Elizabeth who had to ease his sorrow instead. Arthur may be gone, she said through her tears, but they were still blessed with 'a fair Prince' and 'two fair Princesses'. Even though his dynasty now hung on the life of one male heir - their son Henry - Elizabeth also reminded her husband that he too was an only child, and 'God by His grace had ever preserved him, and brought him where he was'.

Elizabeth then left Henry to let him mourn in private. No sooner had she returned to her own apartments when she fell into anguished weeping again. She was so distraught that the King was sent for. Finding more comfort in grieving together than alone, Henry took Elizabeth in his arms, mingling their tears.

≡

At the age of thirty-six, Elizabeth still believed herself 'young enough' to have more children. Her last pregnancy was only three years ago, and Elizabeth was confident she could produce another son to safeguard the realm. Sure enough, the Queen became pregnant, and in January, her *accouchement* was prepared at Richmond Palace. However, during a stopover in London, Elizabeth's time came sooner than expected. Instead of journeying on to Richmond, the King and Queen settled in the Tower to await the childbirth. The Queen's chamber was hastily prepared following the Lady Margaret's directives as usual. The windows were covered with tapestries, carpets were laid on the floor, and an altar was set up near Elizabeth's bed that she might pray for a safe delivery. Again, her male servants were dismissed and replaced by her ladies.

On 2 February, the hoped for prince turned out to be a princess. Not only that, the infant was weak and its survival was in doubt. Nonetheless, she was baptised in the Tower chapel two days later and given the name of Katharine, after the Queen's sister. There were also concerns about the mother. Elizabeth had become feverish after giving birth. When told, the King put on a brave face. William Parron, his trusted astrologer, Henry reassured everyone, had predicted that his wife would live to the ripe old age of eighty.

The horoscope proved wrong. A week after the baby's christening, it was clear the Queen was dying. A priest was summoned, and she was given the last rites. By morning, she was dead. It was 11 February 1503; Elizabeth of York lived just long enough to see her thirty-seventh birthday.

PART 2
THE UNHAPPY QUEEN:
KATHERINE OF ARAGON

She preferred moderate and steady fortune to great alternations of rough and smooth. But if she had to choose, she would elect the saddest, rather than the most flattering fortune, because in the former, consolation can be found, whilst in the latter, often even sound judgement disappears.
(Juan Luis Vives on Katherine of Aragon, 1524)

Figure 5   Katherine of Aragon by an Unknown Artist
Hampton Court Palace, Photo © 2016 MadeGlobal

Chapter 6
The Greatest Trouble and Anguish in the World

THE WHOLE of England mourned the passing of 'Elizabeth the Good' - 'one of the most gracious and best loved princesses in the world'. Her death had hit the King hard. In less than a year, not only did Henry Tudor lose his son and heir, Prince Arthur, he also lost his beloved wife. His newborn daughter Katharine, who might have been a consolation to him, was sickly and unlikely to survive, his doctors said. Overwhelmed, Henry shut himself in 'a solitary place to pass his sorrow'.

The death of Prince Arthur had put the seventeen-year-old Katherine of Aragon in a precarious situation. Not only was she a widow, but she was also a foreigner living a country whose language she barely understood. Given a choice, Katherine would simply have gone home, but her wishes counted for nothing against the dictates of her parents. Ferdinand and Isabella decided that their daughter should take Arthur's brother Henry, Duke of York, as her new husband, thus preserving the alliance between Spain and England.

But such a union was considered incestuous by the Church. It was forbidden for a man to take his brother's wife according to the *Book of Leviticus*. However, due to the nature of Arthur and Katherine's relationship, a dispensation could be obtained from Pope Julius II to allow the marriage to proceed. Following Arthur's death, his widow vehemently swore she was still a virgin. Throughout their brief life together, she and her husband had never known each other carnally, Katherine declared. So said her Spanish duenna Doña Elvira Manuel too. As the Princess's chaperone in England, and the person closest to her, Doña Elvira's opinion carried considerable weight. Katherine, she confirmed, had confided in her about her virginity, and she, as her duenna, had drawn the same conclusion by her proximity to the young couple.

Katherine and Doña Elvira's assurances were good enough for Ferdinand and Isabella. Assuming they were to Henry VII as well, would he go for the marriage, they wondered? To feel him out, their envoy to the English court, the Duke of Estrada, was told to say nothing of it at first, but instead, demand the return of the 100,000 crowns paid out to England as the first instalment of Katherine's dowry, along with the surrender of her person. Worried she might be held hostage as a bargaining chip, Ferdinand and Isabella notified Estrada that 'without any delay', it was 'very important for us to have the Princess in our power'.

Henry VII, wanting to keep the goodwill of Spain, was eager to keep Katherine in his family. But seemingly in a more intimate way. In the spring of 1503, rumours reached Spain that the widower-King was to marry Katherine himself! Ferdinand and Isabella were aghast. It was not because Henry was so much older than Katherine - such marriages were not unusual - it was its very nature. For a father to take his son's wife was unheard of - 'an evil thing, one never before seen', the Spanish Queen exclaimed. Not only that, there were the consequences to consider. Even if a papal dispensation were issued, permitting father-in-law and daughter-in-law to wed, any son they had would only be King *after* Prince Henry and his children. Moreover, Katherine would only be Queen in the years left to her ageing husband.

How serious was Henry VII? After the death of Elizabeth of York, he did put himself in the marriage market. In fact, he had considered taking King Ferdinand's niece, the widowed Queen of Naples. If not from want of companionship, it was to strengthen his dynasty following Arthur's untimely death. But if the old King was indeed considering Katherine, he faced opposition. Her parents were dead set against the match, and it might have been difficult to get the Church's approval. Later, when it became clear that Henry had either changed his mind, or that he was the victim of slander, Ferdinand and Isabella breathed a sigh of relief.

By summer, the haggling over Katherine's marriage to the Duke of York was over. Their betrothal was announced on 23 June. But the wedding was not to occur immediately as the proper dispensation allowing 'brother and sister' to wed had yet to be obtained from the Vatican. As well, under the terms agreed to by both parties, the nuptials would not take place until the twelve-year-old Henry was at least fourteen; the customary age of consent.

In February 1504, Henry, who had been given his own establishment, came to live at court following his investiture as Prince of Wales. By assuming his late brother's title, Henry's life was forever changed. No longer was he second in importance to the realm and to his father – he was now the centre of attention. It was noticed that the King, who used to lavish all his affection on his eldest, now took an active interest in the young Henry, putting him under his wing. Of the new bond between father and son, the Duke of Estrada wrote to Ferdinand and Isabella - 'it is quite wonderful how much the King likes the Prince of Wales. He had good reason to do so, for the Prince deserves all love'.

But for the teenage Henry, being the apple of his father's eye had its drawbacks. In his apprenticeship as England's future King, he was mostly cooped up with his tutors all day. Even when he was not at his lessons, he lived in virtual seclusion. Access to the Prince was near impossible. To reach him, one had to go through the King's apartments. He was, it was reported to Ferdinand and Isabella, 'locked away as a woman'. Thus, many of Henry's outdoor activities were probably curtailed, especially the martial pastimes he was so fond of. Excessive swordplay was discouraged, as was the dangerous sport of jousting on horseback. Henry, it can be supposed, was made to sit on the sidelines, watching others like the Duke of Buckingham, the Marquis of Dorset, and his closest friend Charles Brandon win glory for themselves at the tiltyard. For one as energetic and athletic as Prince Henry, he suffocated under his father's watchful eye. Nonetheless, the King was well-meaning. After losing his eldest son, Henry VII was determined to let no harm be visited upon his second.

While young Henry continued his appenticeship in running a kingdom, there were great turns of events internationally. In October 1504, Queen Isabella passed away. As a result, the kingdoms of Aragon and Castile, united since 1479, were split. Isabella's realm of Castile would be passed on, not to King Ferdinand, but to their daughter Joanna and her Burgundian husband, the Archduke Philip, son of Emperor Maximilian. The loss of Castile did not please Ferdinand, neither did his daughter's new-found loyalties. Since she married, Joanna's interests were solely pro-Hapsburg. Not for nothing was Archduke Philip called 'the Handsome'. Her passion for him, it was said, bordered on the obsessive.

With Ferdinand's position undermined, Henry VII thought him a liability. An alliance with the Hapsburgs, he now believed, would be far more advantageous than one with a weakened Spain. With that in mind, Henry made grandiose new plans. As a widower, he could marry Archduke Philip's sister Margaret of Austria, while his children, including Prince Henry, could be matched to the rest of the Imperial family. But what to do with Katherine of Aragon?

On 27 June 1505, on the eve of his fourteenth birthday and on the verge of manhood, the Prince of Wales appeared before a select panel presided over by the Bishop of Winchester. On the instruction of his father, he declared that since his betrothal to Princess Katherine was made in his minority and against his wishes, he now utterly renounced it. The Bishop pronounced him a free man. However, no public announcement of the fact was made. The proceedings were done behind closed doors, allowing Henry VII to keep his options open. Should it be convenient for the Prince to marry Katherine after all, his declaration would remain undisclosed. But if a Hapsburg bride was preferable, his rejection of his Spanish fiancée was on record.

Needless to say, the ploy was kept secret from Katherine. She continued to believe that soon enough, with Henry being fourteen, she would be his wife. It had never occurred to her how much her mother's death had altered the situation. But as the weeks and months passed, Katherine sensed something was wrong. Despite the King's reassurances, still no wedding date was set. Just as frustrating was that she was allowed little if any contact with her intended husband. Only when she was invited to court did she see young Henry at all, and that depended on whether the King allowed him to appear in public or not. One time, as Katherine was to complain to King Ferdinand, both she and the Prince were under the same roof together at Richmond Palace, but after four months, their paths had yet to cross.

In the rare moments when Katherine did catch sight of Henry or was allowed to converse with him, albeit briefly, she would have noticed how he had changed since their first meeting in 1501. The ten-year-old boy she had known him as was developing into a comely young man - taller and stronger than his brother was at that age, and different in personality. While Arthur was gentle and retiring, Henry was boisterous and extroverted. He loved attention and eagerly sought the spotlight. Even at her wedding, it was obvious to Katherine that her brother-in-law was the star of the family. While dancing with his sister Margaret at the festivities, Henry, encumbered by his heavy cloak, 'suddenly threw off his robe and danced in his jacket… in so goodly and pleasant a manner'. His parents and all their courtiers roared with delight.

When she was not at court, Katherine lived at Durham House in the Strand. An episcopal palace belonging to the Bishops of Durham, it was built along the Thames, nestled between other fine mansions of the well-to-do. On the east side of the property was a fine garden for Katherine to take leisure in, and the windows of the house facing south gave her a spectacular view of the river bending towards Westminster. But to Katherine, her establishment was not the haven it ought to have been. Durham House was infused with discord. Stuck in a foreign land with their wages often in arrears, Katherine's Spanish attendants often bickered among themselves. The tension was so thick that Katherine was compelled to ask her father-in-law to intervene. Henry refused to step in. As her quarrelsome servants were no subjects of his, Katherine must refer the matter to Spain, he said.

Katherine's inability to be mistress of her own household was largely attributed to her dependence - though she was nearing the age of twenty - on her duenna. For the past four years, Doña Elvira had stayed faithfully by Katherine's side, sharing her troubles. In gratitude, Katherine looked to her as a second mother, allowing the older woman much influence over her affairs. She could not see that her loving duenna was all too human. Loyal and attentive as she was, Doña Elvira was also self-serving and manipulative.

The Spanish duenna could be blamed for much of the friction in Katherine's household. She permitted no challenge to her authority, and those who gave opposition faced her wrath. Even men of God were not immune to her displeasure. When Father Alessandro Geraldini, Katherine's tutor and chaplain, expressed doubts about her virginity - Doña Elvira had always been insistent that Katherine's marriage to Prince Arthur was never consummated - the duenna went on the offensive. She poisoned Katherine against her priest and slandered him to her parents. By his lies, the duenna wrote to Spain, Geraldini was unfit to serve the Princess, and he was also risking her marriage to Prince Henry. Ferdinand and Isabella (then still alive) agreed. Before long, the priest was sent packing back to Spain.

Doña Elvira also clashed with Doctor Roderigo Gonzalva de Puebla, the principal Spanish emissary to England. Her dislike of him was probably due to more than just disagreements over Katherine. De Puebla, while a Catholic, was a *converso* or Spanish Jew by origin. Doña Elvira, like many Spaniards, had wholeheartedly approved of the expulsion of some 170,000 Jews from the Iberian

Peninsula in 1492. The conversion of de Puebla's ancestors mattered not a jot to Doña Elvira – or to Katherine it seemed. Regrettably, she loathed the good doctor as much as her duenna, perhaps for the same reason. Katherine was, after all, the daughter of Ferdinand and Isabella, the great *Catholic Kings* who had forced the choice of Christian baptism or exile upon the Jews. They had also introduced the infamous Inquisition to Spain to enforce Catholic orthodoxy.

Suspicious of de Puebla and devoted to her father, to Katherine, one could do no right, and one no wrong. So it was when it came to the problem of her upkeep. Who should pay for it – Spain or England? The cash-strapped Ferdinand and the miserly Henry both shouldered the responsibility on the other. As Ferdinand saw it, it was the duty of the King of England to provide his daughter-in-law with her dower, that is, a third of her late husband's revenues. In response, Henry countered that he owed the young woman nothing, since only half of the 200,000 crowns of her dowry had been paid out her wedding. Only when Ferdinand made good on the remainder, the English King declared, would Katherine receive her full dower rights.

In playing hardball with Spain, Henry VII had the clear advantage; he had Katherine in his power. Though he treated Katherine as a mere pawn in his dealings with her father, Henry VII did show her kindness from time to time. One day, back in December 1501, before her departure for Ludlow, Henry noticed Katherine's sadness; some of her attendants were returning to Spain. To cheer her up, he took Katherine on a personal tour of his great library, showing her 'many goodly pleasant books of works full of delightful, sage, merry, and also right cunning, both in English and Latin'. Henry then allowed his daughter-in-law to choose and keep as many jewels as she wanted from his collection. After Katherine had been widowed, the King was seen to express concern for her. He provided the Princess with some funds to maintain herself and her household, and, on one occasion, took the bereaved Katherine to Windsor with him for a two-week hunting trip.

But when Ferdinand stalled on the dowry, Henry retaliated by treating Katherine like an unwelcome guest. His vow, made in happier times that he would 'never permit her to want anything that he can procure for her', was forgotten. Katherine found herself burdened with debts and unable to maintain her household. Rather than blame her father or her father-in-law, Katherine held Doctor de Puebla responsible. In December 1505, she wrote a furious denunciation of the ambassador. De Puebla had 'transacted a thousand falsities' against him, she scribbled crossly to Ferdinand, and now he was doing the same to her. 'Each day my troubles increase', she complained, 'and all this on account of the Doctor de Puebla'. Rather than securing money for her from King Henry as he was commanded to do, the envoy was always making excuses. If only Ferdinand would dismiss him, Katherine begged him, all would be well. De Puebla had given her so much 'pain and annoyance' that she had even fallen ill. For the past two months, she was sick with fever, she lamented, and she was sure it would be the death of her.

Katherine did not hold back her grievances, but she was less than forthcoming when it came to another matter - one involving intrigue against her father. In between her accusations, Katherine briefly mentioned that Doña Elvira would be leaving her service. Her poor duenna had developed an eye infection and would have to travel to Flanders for treatment. But Ferdinand need not be concerned, Katherine wrote. She intended to ask King Henry for an 'old English lady' as a replacement until Doña Elvira came back. Katherine had spared her father worry, but it was not out of daughterly concern. Truth be told, she was wracked with guilt for what she had unwittingly done. Doña Elvira was not unwell, nor was she ever returning to England. Back in August, she had conspired against King Ferdinand, and Katherine, to her shame, was her dupe.

Katherine's duenna, so kind and caring by all appearances, was not above using her mistress to suit her purposes. Doña Elvira's brother, the ambassador Don Juan Manuel was a fervid Castilian and no friend to Ferdinand of Aragon. With the break-up of Spain on Queen Isabella's death, Don Juan was determined that Castile should not remain in the hands of Ferdinand acting as Regent. Instead, he thought it should be handed over to Ferdinand's daughter Joanna and her husband, Philip. Perhaps Henry VII, who was now at loggerheads with Ferdinand and extending friendship to Philip, would prove useful, Don Juan considered. If only the two could meet, they could form an alliance against the Kingdom of Aragon. Who better to make that happen than his sister's young charge, the Princess Dowager?

Doña Elvira was agreeable, but was Katherine? Knowing she was loyal to her father, Doña Elvira resorted to deception. Playing on the Princess's yearning to see her sister again, her duenna suggested that she write to Philip and Joanna in Flanders. Why not arrange a family reunion, her duenna asked? She had not seen her sister for almost ten years, and she could finally get to meet her dashing brother-in-law, the Archduke. And of course, Doña Elvira added, they must include Henry VII as well. Perhaps her sister and her brother-in-law could get the King to be kinder to her, Doña Elvira suggested sweetly.

Katherine was delighted with the idea. She sent a messenger to Flanders asking Philip and Joanna to invite the English King over for a meeting. Philip needed little convincing. To the fledgeling monarch in his struggle against King Ferdinand, Henry VII had already proved himself an invaluable benefactor. In April 1505, he had loaned Philip a staggering £108,000, and he promised more to come. Writing back to his sister-in-law, an excited Philip 'desired with his whole heart' that she set up the get-together.

The interview might well have taken place as the Manuels planned - except for De Puebla's timely intervention. He had gotten wind of their scheme, and 'with tears running down his cheeks', told Katherine that her duenna and her brother were up to no good. They were using her, the ambassador explained, and if she allowed the King and the Archduke to meet, she would be the instrument of her father's ruin. As much as she hated him, de Puebla's desperation convinced Katherine he was telling the truth. She immediately wrote to Henry VII asking him to ignore her previous request for the meeting, and begged him to 'value the interests of her father the King of Spain, beyond those of any other King in Christendom'.

Katherine never told Ferdinand what had happened. She had sworn to de Puebla that she would keep the matter secret, and she took her promise to mean from her father as well. Still, Ferdinand learnt of the plot from the doctor himself. However, he never allowed Katherine to know that he had been fully informed about it, or of her part in the affair. He took de Puebla's word that his daughter, with her 'excellent heart', had been taken advantage of by the devious Manuels, and that 'she loves her father more than herself'.

Until Doña Elvira left her service, Katherine had to maintain all appearances of friendship with her, as she had promised de Puebla. That meant even lying to her duenna that she still wanted Henry VII and Philip to meet. However, the strain proved too great for Katherine. She could not find herself forgiving Doña Elvira, and at the end of November, there was a terrible blow-up. Katherine's pent up rage made Doña Elvira's dismissal a 'horrible hour'.

Not long after Doña Elvira packed her bags, Katherine was angry with de Puebla again. Without a duenna, Katherine had asked

King Henry for permission to live at court, and 'thinking to make of the rogue a true man', as she told her father, she had left the arrangements to the envoy. But after Katherine was brought to live at Richmond Palace, she discovered many of her servants had been let go, and all her household goods had been confiscated. In other words, she was reduced to being a poor pensioner at court. To Katherine, the contemptible little doctor was at fault. But in Spain, King Ferdinand knew otherwise – it was a deliberate move on Henry VII's part to force him to surrender the rest of his daughter's dowry. Unable to pay up and unable to help Katherine, he wrote to de Puebla, ordering his ambassador to see to it that the Princess 'yield and assent to the will and pleasure of the King of England, my brother'.

Caught in a tug-of-war between her father and her father-in-law, Katherine was miserable. Even the gaiety and excitement of court life failed to lift her spirits. Katherine's only comfort was in the half dozen or so Spanish ladies still with her. However, their continuing attendance on her was also a cause for shame. They had all come to England hoping for advantageous marriages, yet no one would have them. Good matches required good dowries. It was Katherine's duty to provide for her ladies, but being almost penniless, she could give them nothing.

Desperate for money, Katherine considered pawning her valuables - her rich plate and her jewels - to Henry VII himself for cash. When the offer was made, he was most indignant. To Katherine's face, he told her sharply that he would appear a miser to the world if he accepted her plate. As for her jewels, though 'valued at a great sum', he would not touch those either, not even at half their price. He had enough ornaments of his own, Henry said scornfully. What he truly wanted was the money, which King Ferdinand had *still* not sent him.

≡

From her exile in Flanders, Doña Elvira gloated. Despite Doctor de Puebla's efforts to prevent their meeting, the new King and Queen of Castile were guests of Henry VII in January 1506. By a twist of fate, Philip and Joanna, on their way to Spain to lay claim to their kingdom, were blown off course. Their ship ended up in English waters, landing at Weymouth on the 13 January. Like it or not, the couple was there to stay. The weather had to be waited out, repairs made, and Henry VII thanked in person for all the money (totalling £138,000) he had given Philip towards his struggle against King Ferdinand.

On 31 January, Philip was welcomed to England by his 'father', as he called Henry VII. While his wife remained behind at the port of Melcombe Regis, Philip was shown the splendours of Windsor Castle. He hunted in the great park and was entertained by his host in a style worthy of his Burgundian court. The series of pleasures were combined with rounds of negotiations. A commercial treaty was signed, as was a pact of mutual aid in war or defence of the other's territories - particularly Philip's claim to Castile. The alliance was backed up by a series of proposed marriages. The old King agreed to wed Philip's sister, Margaret of Austria, and when they came of age, Prince Henry would marry his daughter, Eleanor, while Princess Mary would be matched to his son Charles of Ghent – a young man who would one day inherit great dominions from his father and two grandfathers, the King of Spain and the Holy Roman Emperor.

None of this was made known to Katherine when she met Philip for the first time at a ball on 1 February. After being introduced to her brother-in-law, Katherine danced before him. While her partner, a Spanish lady, was described as being clothed in 'Spanish array', Katherine had chosen to wear English costume. In doing so, she was emphasising, in public, her commitment to her new country as Princess of Wales.

This was not lost on Philip. Katherine's unshakable resolve that she would be Prince Henry's wife, and her steadfast loyalty to his enemy Ferdinand, made for an uncomfortable evening. Throughout the festivities, Philip ignored his sister-in-law. He had not forgotten how she had foiled the Manuels' scheme to bring him and Henry VII closer. When Katherine asked him to dance, Philip rebuffed her. He was born a sailor, the Archduke said roughly, *not* a dancer. A dejected Katherine was later seen sitting forlornly by herself, until Princess Mary noticing her discomfort, went to keep her company.

Nine days later, the Queen of Castile finally arrived at Windsor. Eager to meet this paragon of beauty he had heard so much about, Henry VII, instead of waiting for Joanna in his lodgings, rushed down to the foot of the stairs outside to greet her. With him was Katherine. After ten years, the two sisters were finally together again. But their reunion, which gave Katherine 'great pleasure', was all too brief - a 'few hours' before Joanna made a 'sudden and hasty departure' the next day.

As Katherine would later write to Joanna, she was much distressed by her leave-taking, as was King Henry. Had he been able to, the King would have 'by every possible means, have prevented your journey'. But based on the advice of his Council, and other 'mysterious causes' of which Katherine herself was ignorant, he would not 'interfere between husband and wife'. It had been obvious to Katherine that Philip wanted Joanna kept out of sight. Perhaps she had never been sick at all at Melcombe Regis as it was given out. Joanna's late arrival at court was merely a ploy to keep her away from her sister. Katherine knew from Doña Elvira's plot that Philip was no friend to her father, and by his coldness at Windsor, nor was he hers. With her brother-in-law so against her, and with her sister under his thumb, Katherine's hopes that they could help her had been in vain.

After the King and Queen of Castile resumed their voyage to Spain, Katherine's position became even more desperate. In April, she had to beg Henry VII and his Council for money with tears in her eyes, she wrote to Ferdinand. Her father-in-law was unsympathetic as usual – even cruel. He had told her with great harshness how he was not obliged to give her a penny, and that he provided her with food on her table only because he was loath to see her starve. She had no one to blame, the King went on, but Ferdinand for defaulting on her dowry. When she assured him that her father would soon pay up, Henry just scoffed.

Ignored and insulted, Katherine pleaded with Ferdinand to fulfil his obligations, for she was in 'the greatest trouble and anguish in the world'. 'All but naked', she had been forced to sell her bracelets to buy a decent new gown. 'For the love of our Lord', she wrote desperately, Ferdinand must 'consider how I am your daughter', and put things right. Katherine also asked him for a new confessor. Since Father Geraldini's recall to Spain, she had received her absolutions from Doña Elvira's chaplain. But when she left in disgrace, she took him with her. Since then, Katherine had no priest who understood Spanish. Presumably, Henry VII had provided her with an English chaplain who spoke Latin at least, but Katherine preferred to make her confessions in her native tongue.

As with Katherine's financial welfare, Ferdinand was delinquent when it came to her spiritual one as well. A year later, when he finally got around to seeking a suitable priest for her, Katherine told him not to bother. She already had one with her, she wrote to her father in April 1507. Tired of waiting, it seemed that Katherine took the initiative and contacted the Franciscan Observant Friars in Spain herself asking for one of their number to be sent to England. In time, Ferdinand would regret not having acted sooner.

≡

Eighteen months passed before Katherine was in touch with her sister Joanna again. Since then, tragedy had occurred. In September 1506, the Archduke Philip died unexpectedly. Joanna, who loved him with an all-consuming intensity, was distraught. Katherine heard how her sister kept a constant vigil before her husband's coffin, and she would not allow it to be buried. In her letter to Joanna, dated a year after the Archduke's death, Katherine, knowing how upset her sister still was, made no mention of Philip by name. Nonetheless, she had a proposition for the Queen-Archduchess – would she like to marry again?

She had heard, Katherine told Joanna, that the French had captured the city of Tilmote belonging to her son Charles. What better solution 'to the increase of your state, the tranquillity and welfare of your subjects, and those of the said Prince, my nephew', Katherine asked, than for Joanna to take a powerful new husband? And who better than Henry VII? The King of England had a 'great affection' for her, and 'is much feared and esteemed… by all Christendom'. Being 'so possessed of immense treasures and having at his command, powerful bodies of wonderful troops', he could help Charles against the French. To sweeten the deal, Katherine promised that as King Henry's wife, Joanna would be 'the most noble and most powerful Queen in the world.'

Katherine's efforts at matchmaking were the result of her new role as her father's ambassador in England. To her satisfaction, de Puebla was being recalled to Spain, and until his departure was finalised, Katherine was accredited as co-representative to the English court. One of her first duties was to work with de Puebla to get her sister to accept Henry VII. With the King and the Prince of Wales wedded to Joanna and herself respectively, England would be completely tied to Spain. The plan was Ferdinand's, but even Henry VII himself was for it. He had need of a wife, and he had been captivated by the beautiful Queen-Archduchess. Though he had signed a treaty of marriage with her late husband, Philip, promising to wed his sister Margaret, Henry knew who was the greater prize. And as for her sister Katherine, she would be a fit wife for his son, after all, the King reconsidered.

Despite Henry VII's desire for Joanna, the marriage would never take place. From Spain, it was said that the Queen-Archduchess, increasingly unhinged by Philip's death, was in no state to take another husband. Henry, ever suspicious of Ferdinand, questioned the extent of her madness, accusing him of keeping Joanna a prisoner to assume control of Castile for himself. 'Sane or insane', de Puebla heard say, the English King still wanted her as long as she could bear him children. Perhaps, the ambassador suggested, a good marriage would serve as a cure. Joanna 'would soon recover her reason when wedded to such a husband'.

But she was beyond help. Joanna sank further into lunacy, spending the rest of her life in confinement. Deemed incapable of ruling, Castile was put under the governance of her father, and then of her son Charles. When Joanna died at last in 1555, few remembered her as the enchanting creature she once was, but as a raving old woman, 'Joanna the Mad'.

=

The arrival of her new confessor, Fray Diego Fernandez, in the spring of 1507, lifted Katherine's spirits. She was immediately taken by his great learning, sophistication, and charisma. He was also good looking. Katherine came to value him greatly, not only as her spiritual director, but as her confidante as well. Fray Diego spoke to her in her own language, was full of good advice, and was ever attentive to her well-being. With his wit and charm, he also brought much-needed mirth into her life. She could not have asked for a better chaplain and friend, Katherine declared.

Her opinion of the young friar was not universal. Others found Fray Diego more of a worldly courtier than a humble monk. Instead of being meek and mild, he was hot-headed and petulant. Instead of denying his flesh, he gratified it. His way with the ladies was notorious, it was said. And rather than ministering to the Princess, he was intent on dominating her as her duenna had done. It was gossiped at court that Fray Diego abused his position as confessor by making 'a sin of all acts of whatever kind they be if they displease him'. Katherine, being 'so full of goodness', obeyed him without question. If she ever went against his authority, his critics said, all Fray Diego had to do was to rebuke her for offending God, and a repentant Katherine would submit to his wishes.

The new Spanish envoy, Don Gutier Gomez de Fuensalida, was most displeased. While it was true that Katherine needed a strong guiding hand, de Fuensalida wrote in a communiqué to Spain, Fray Diego was 'unworthy of having such a charge, caus[ing] the Princess to commit many errors'. Even King Henry did not like him, the envoy said, and had 'very strong words' with Katherine about the young man. Fray Diego's hold over Katherine was so complete, de Fuensalida told King Ferdinand, that once when she was invited to go riding with her friend Princess Mary – an outing that would have given Katherine much pleasure – the priest would not let her go. Katherine was recently ill, Fray Diego said, and she must rest. If she disobeyed him, it was 'upon pain of mortal sin'. After being kept waiting for two hours, a fed-up Mary rode off alone.

And there was more, the ambassador complained, Fray Diego was meddling in Katherine's finances. Against the wishes of her father, she was selling her plate piece by piece each day at the priest's bidding. In a fortnight, she managed to unload gold worth 200 ducats, with much of the money going towards gifts for Fray Diego.

De Fuensalida's loathing of her confessor - the two came close to blows once - did not endear the envoy to Katherine. In filling Doctor de Puebla's shoes, when the old man finally retired in 1508, his replacement found himself subjected to the same scorn as his predecessor – thanks to Fray Diego. The friar 'put me so much out of favour with the Princess', de Fuensalida fumed, 'that if I had committed some treason she could not have treated me worse'.

However, Fray Diego could not be blamed for everything. The ambassador was not so different in fact from the young priest he so despised. He too was insensitive and arrogant in his own way. Henry VII, for one, found de Fuensalida so rude and demanding that he and his Council did not even wish to see or hear from the envoy anymore. Ironically, even Katherine was forced to admit that her former ambassador – the hateful de Puebla – at least knew how to handle the King of England.

With de Fuensalida shut out by the English, Katherine ran out of hope. After seven fruitless years in England, she was ready to admit defeat. She was in deepest despair, Katherine told her father in March 1509. She was ill served by her ambassador, her confessor – her 'greatest comfort' - was threatening to leave, and she was nowhere near being married to Prince Henry. All she wanted to do now was to go home to Spain. There, she would 'spend the remainder of her years in serving God which would be the best thing that could happen'.

For once, Ferdinand listened to his daughter. In April 1509, he appointed a new ambassador to settle the marriage. The residual of the dowry, he announced, would be paid up at last. As an added incentive to Henry VII, Katherine's dower rights would even be surrendered to him. But should the English refuse the offer, Katherine must be allowed to return to Spain. 'Her long-suffering', Ferdinand said with belated compassion, 'would be at an end'.

But if Katherine hoped to retire to a quiet private life, perhaps even to a religious one, she was fooling herself. Once Ferdinand took possession of his daughter again, it was his intention to seek out 'another very acceptable marriage for her'.

While Katherine was begging to be brought home, her release by another manner was at hand. Henry VII had fallen sick. The old King would not 'allow himself to be seen', and when foreign emissaries came calling, it was left to the Prince of Wales to receive them. By 29 March 1509, three weeks after Katherine had written so desperately to Ferdinand, it was reported that Henry was 'very ill and utterly without hope of recovery'.

Chapter 7
Well and Prosperous

IN THE last months of Henry VII's life, Katherine, when she was not overcome by despair, was in 'no doubt her wedding would soon be celebrated if the old King of England were to die'. When he finally expired on 21 April, nothing could prevent her marriage – or so Katherine believed. The days following the King's death were tense. Would his son, Henry VIII as he was now called, honour the old pact with Spain?

Since he had become Prince of Wales, his father had kept Henry by his side, teaching him the art of statecraft. There was speculation that Henry would mimic the late King in policy, choosing friendship with Burgundy over Spain, as Henry VII once did. If so, would he jilt Katherine and take a Hapsburg bride instead? Or would the handsome seventeen–year–old Henry, the greatest catch in Europe, look elsewhere? To a lady in France perhaps?

To Katherine's relief, Henry considered none of them. Sometime between his proclamation as King of England on 24 April and his father's funeral two weeks later, he announced that he would indeed marry Katherine. In Spain, an elated Ferdinand began collecting the remaining 100,000 crowns of the dowry; 50,000 to be sent upfront and the rest in forty days. As Ferdinand told his daughter, he had delayed payment as Henry VII proved 'neither his nor her friend', but he would gladly forward the money now 'in order to show the new King how much he loved him, and how much more highly he valued his friendship than that of his father'.

The marriage Katherine had fought for so tenaciously became a reality on 11 June. This time, there were no cheering crowds and a grand ceremony at St Paul's. Just a handful of witnesses gathered at Greenwich Palace on a quiet summer's day. In the Queen's Closet, Katherine's oratory within the royal apartments, the young couple solemnly pledged to 'fulfil the treaty of marriage concluded by the late King of England and the parents of the Princess of Wales, the King and Queen of Spain'.

The wedding was a private affair, but not the joint coronation that followed. Ten days after they were married, Henry and Katherine set out for the capital. The newlyweds went from Greenwich to Southwark by land, crossing over to the city at London Bridge. From there, they were taken to the Tower of London for the traditional layover. After a two-day rest, the couple was seen in public again. The royal entourage, winding its way from London to Westminster, was large in number and splendid to behold. Those in attendance on Henry and Katherine – the lords spiritual and the lords temporal - were all in 'cloth of tissue, cloth of gold, cloth of silver, embroidery or of goldsmiths' work'.

Of course, the King outshone them all. He wore a gown of crimson velvet furred with ermine under a golden coat set with innumerable pearls and precious stones. Around his neck was a rich collar set with rubies. Not only were his clothes magnificent, so was Henry himself. 'The gifts of grace and of nature that God had endowed him with' were evident to all who looked upon him. Those in the crowd old enough to remember the tall and strapping Edward IV swore Henry VIII was his spitting image. Like his grandfather, Henry was handsome, athletic, over six feet in height, and had limbs 'of a gigantic size'. He was like Apollo and Hercules in one.

Not all the attention was upon Henry. Katherine, who followed behind him, was a striking figure of her own. She was dressed in white from head to toe. Even her palfreys and the litter she sat in were covered with white cloth. Like Elizabeth of York at her coronation, Katherine too wore her hair unbound. 'Of a very great length, beautiful and goodly to behold', it shone golden bright under the summer sun as she turned her head this way and that, acknowledging the people's cheers.

The citizens' affection for their new King and Queen was witnessed by the old matriarch Lady Margaret Beaufort. Her joy in her grandson's accession was not without sadness of course. She had never thought to outlive her adored son the late King, but as a woman of great piety, Margaret accepted his death with resignation. She also came to terms with the severity of her own illness of late. She was in fact slowly dying, but she would not allow her condition to have the better of her. For the coronation, Margaret had ordered rich clothes of silk, satin, damask, and velvet to be made for herself and her attendants. She chose to remain inconspicuous, and she watched the procession in private from a house in Cheapside in the company of her granddaughter Princess Mary. When she died on 29 June, just five days after the crowning, Margaret had the satisfaction of seeing the dynasty she helped create being carried on into the next generation.

Figure 6   Henry VIII by Sylvester van Parijs
The Rijksmuseum, Amsterdam

Sunday 24 June, the Feast of St John, was Katherine of Aragon's moment of glory. Inside Westminster Abbey, after she and Henry were both anointed with holy oil, they received their crowns together as King and Queen of England. When those assembled were asked if they would take Henry VIII as their sovereign lord, they shouted, 'Yea, yea!' as one.

The accession of Henry VIII heralded an unprecedented optimism throughout England. William Blount, Lord Mountjoy, spoke for his countrymen when he described the exhilaration to his friend the esteemed Dutch scholar Desiderius Erasmus:

> 'If you could see how everyone here rejoices in having so great a prince, how his life is all their desire, you would not contain yourself for sheer joy. Extortion is put down, liberality scatters riches with a bountiful hand, yet our King does not set his heart on gold or jewels, but on virtue, glory, and immortality!'

It was out with the old and in with the new. To get his reign off to a fresh start, Henry VIII cleaned house. On the same day he was proclaimed King in April, he had Richard Empson and Edmund Dudley, his father's detested henchmen, arrested. As scapegoats for their late master's repressive policies, the two men were accused of corruption - 'not to the little rejoicing' of many people. They were later beheaded.

Katherine shared in the new euphoria too. No longer were her letters to Spain filled with anger and tears, but with joy and hope. In July, a month after her wedding, she told her father that she and the King were 'well and prosperous', and 'lov[ing] one another so much'. It was as if their time together was spent in 'continual feasting', she wrote blissfully.

The Queen's declaration was not one-sided. Henry VIII too wrote to Ferdinand about his great love for his wife. He was not play-acting the dutiful son-in-law for appearance's sake. To Henry, Katherine had all the qualities of a worthy wife. At twenty-three, she was still a lovely young woman, and she was virtuous, devout, and intelligent to boot. Most importantly, there was every reason to believe that she would bear many children, just like her mother Isabella and her sister Joanna. Henry was proud to have Katherine for his wife, and he wanted the world to know. At the jousts following their coronation, Henry had both his and Katherine's personal devices - the Tudor rose and the pomegranate of Spain – prominently displayed together. Also, their initials *H* and *K*, rendered in brilliant gold, were joined in love knots for all to see.

Katherine was equally in love with her new husband. Whether it was Eleanor of Austria or the other ladies the Emperor or the French King had thrown his way, Henry had turned them all down and had chosen her instead. Besides the attractions of his good looks and his boisterous love of fun, Katherine was also drawn to his inner qualities. Aware of the great position he was born into, Henry always had 'a certain royal demeanour' about him, and as Doctor de Puebla had noted, he was 'prudent as is to be expected from a son of Henry VII'.

The new King was also pious and learned like Katherine herself. He heard Mass three times a day, and sometimes five when he was not out hunting. In the evenings, he even liked to join his wife in her apartments for Compline and Vespers. Henry also shared Katherine's intellectual interests, thanks to the excellent education provided by his late father. Even as a boy, Henry had a 'dignity of mind combined with a remarkable curiosity' – a high compliment coming from the great Erasmus himself who visited England and met young Henry in 1499. Even as King, he continued in his thirst for knowledge. As he told Lord Mountjoy after his accession, without scholars in the world, 'we should scarcely live at all'. Mountjoy, an avid proponent of learning himself, passed Henry's comment on to Erasmus. 'What more splendid remark could a prince make?' he asked of him.

=

As if the royal couple could not be happier, Katherine discovered she was pregnant at the end of October. When Ferdinand was told the good news, he offered his daughter some fatherly advice. As this was her first child, she must watch her health and not exert herself. Even writing 'with her own hand' must be avoided, he cautioned. Better that she dictate all her correspondence from now on.

All seemed to be going well until 31 January 1510. Ferdinand's prayer that God give his daughter 'a good delivery', and Katherine's own petitions to St Peter the Martyr were in vain. That morning, she went into premature labour and delivered a little girl, born dead.

The death of her first baby was a blow to Katherine. As her father had told her, though she needed no reminding, her pregnancy 'was a great blessing, since she, her husband, and the English people have wished it so much'. Had the baby lived, even though it was female,

Katherine could have at least proved she was capable of bearing a healthy child. But as she mourned, all was not lost, her doctors and midwives told her. There was already another infant in her womb waiting to be born!

Relieved that all was not lost, Katherine prepared herself for the ordeal again. Meanwhile, nothing was said of the stillbirth. Only the King, Fray Diego, who stayed on as the Queen's confessor, her doctor, and two of her women who were present in the inner sanctum of the royal bedchamber, knew the truth. Since Katherine still appeared full bellied, it was announced at court that her delivery, her '*first*', was expected in March. But when the time came, no child was to be had, and the swelling in her belly gradually vanished.

Katherine did not fear her husband's anger as much as her father's. Henry was undeniably upset, but he was at least able to console himself that there would be better luck next time. But with King Ferdinand, Katherine dreaded his reaction. It was not until 27 May, and after repeated demands from Spain as to what was going on, that Katherine offered up her version of events. She began with a lie. '*Some days before*', Katherine answered, she had miscarried a daughter. She had not written her father sooner, she apologised, because a stillbirth was considered a 'misfortune in England'. Knowing he would be disappointed, even furious, Katherine begged Ferdinand not to blame her as it was the will of God.

At the same time Katherine sent her letter off to Spain, Fray Diego wrote to the King telling him the truth. He did not do so to undermine his mistress in any way, but to do what he thought best. Ferdinand had to know, and better that it came from *his* pen than from Luiz Caroz's, the new Spanish ambassador to England. Fray Diego was predictably at odds with Caroz as he had been with de Puebla and de Fuensalida.

Fray Diego told Ferdinand about the undisclosed stillbirth in January, not May, as Katherine reported, and of her false pregnancy in the spring, which from shame, she had said nothing of to her father. But there was good news after all, Fray Diego told the King, Katherine had recently confided in him that she believed herself to be with child again. So far, she did not tell her husband or anyone else, as she wanted to be certain first. Nonetheless, he and her doctors were sure she was pregnant. Katherine was 'very large', and he expected Ferdinand to have 'a hundred grandsons' in time. Until then, all was well, Fray Diego assured Ferdinand. Katherine was in good health

– still the 'most beautiful creature in the world' - and the King her husband adored her as he always did.

The priest was right to be optimistic. On New Year's Day 1511, Katherine gave birth to a son 'to the great gladness of the realm'. In celebration, London was ablaze with bonfires in honour of the new Prince and his proud parents the King and Queen. Heaven was not forgotten. 'General processions to laud God' were formed, and the King himself offered up his thanks. Before the Queen was 'churched', meaning when she was put into seclusion for thirty to forty days to be ritually 'purified' before returning to everyday life, Henry set out to the Shrine of Our Lady of Walsingham in Norfolk in gratitude for his new son.

When Henry returned to Richmond in February, he ordered two days of tournaments to be held at Westminster. The celebrations were not only in recognition of Prince Henry, as the child was christened, but of his mother Queen Katherine also. Pavilions along the tiltyard were affixed with 'a great *K* of goldsmith's work', and the Queen's pomegranate was everywhere, as was the scallop shell of St James, the patron saint of Spain. In tribute to his wife, an armoured Henry, in the guise of *Coeur Loyal (Sir Loyal Heart)* – wearing a skirt of cloth of gold decorated with *H*'s and *K*'s, and his horse covered with the same and with hearts – jousted before his lady love to the delight of the crowd.

But while the court was celebrating at Westminster, the nursemaids watching over the infant at Richmond were despairing. Young Henry was strong and healthy at his birth, but he was growing weaker by the day. The doctors could do nothing; neither could the priests praying for the boy's life. On 22 February, he was dead. The Queen 'like a natural woman made much lamentation', while the King, taking 'this dolorous chance wondrously wise... made no great mourning' – at least not in public.

To divert himself from his grief, Henry threw himself into recreations. 'Greatly delight[ing] in feats of chivalry', the King's love for jousting was already demonstrated at the celebrations for the late Prince. He would be a regular at the lists until an injury in 1536 put an end to his participation. A keen outdoorsman, Henry also enjoyed riding, hunting, hawking, and picnicking with his wife. For added fun, the King and his companions once disguised themselves as Robin Hood and his outlaws. They broke into the Queen's apartments where

Katherine and her ladies, first astonished, and then amused, accepted their invitation to an open-air feast.

Indoors, Henry found 'other innocent and honest pastimes' to occupy himself with. Like his father, Henry was an enthusiastic gambler, enjoying dice and cards even when he lost great sums to his friends. He also shared Henry VII's love of tennis, which was played inside in a specially built court. The Venetian ambassador said 'it was the prettiest thing in the world to see him play, [with] his fair skin glowing through a shirt of the finest texture'. There seemed to be nothing the multi-talented Henry could not do. One season, when the court was at Windsor, he was a whirlwind of activity, 'exercising himself daily in shooting, singing, dancing, wrestling, casting of the bar, playing at the recorders, flute, virginals, and in setting of songs'. Popular sixteenth-century English compositions such as *Pastime With Good Company* and *Green Groweth the Holly* are attributed to him, and the prolific Henry even 'set two goodly Masses...which were sung oftentimes in his chapel'.

But the mock battles Henry VIII fought on the tilting field were no match for the excitement and glory of actual engagement. Since the start of his reign, Henry had been itching for war. The peace and quiet of his father's reign did not suit his temperament. Instead, Henry looked to his celebrated forebears - the warriors Edward III and Henry V, hoping to win another Crécy or Agincourt for himself. His desire to follow in their footsteps was evident at the visit of the French ambassador, the Abbot of Fécamp, in August 1509. His Council, as Henry knew, had previously written to Louis XII, promising good relations with France. But when the Abbot came to offer his master's thanks, Henry was spoiling for a fight. He disavowed the Council's offer of friendship, and he shouted at his advisers in the ambassador's presence. 'Who wrote this letter?' he demanded to know, 'I ask peace of the King of France who daren't look at me, let alone make war!' Henry then stormed out of the room leaving the Council and the Abbot flabbergasted.

With Henry eager to win himself renown in France, his father-in-law Ferdinand, who hated Louis as much as he did, rubbed his hands with glee. While there was an interlude of peace between the two old monarchs when Ferdinand took Louis XII's niece Germaine de Foix as his second wife in 1505, it was fleeting. In a few short years, Ferdinand and Louis were at each other's throats again. This time, however, the King of Spain had an ace up his sleeve. Since his

accession, Henry VIII had been ever ready to 'obey all his behests'.
Now, Ferdinand expected him to keep that promise.

In 1511, when Ferdinand, the Holy Roman Emperor, and the
Pope joined forces in a 'Holy League' against France, Henry VIII
jumped on board. But things got off to a bad start. When the
English forces landed in Fuenterrabia in Spain in June 1512, they
found themselves stranded. The 'ordinance and carriages' they had
been promised were nowhere in sight, much less Ferdinand and his
Spanish army. Helpless, they had to seek aid from the nearby King of
Navarre, John III, who provided the English with victuals and with
tents for shelter.

Ferdinand offered up excuses and made new promises, but still,
his army never showed up. Each day, the English waited in vain
for the Duke of Alva and his troops to meet up with them for a
combined attack on the French at Guienne. But Alva had other plans.
Under Ferdinand's instructions, the Duke directed his men towards
Navarre. King John, who had been so generous to the English, was
driven out of his country, and his throne seized by Spain. Angered by
Ferdinand's duplicity, the English army was in no mood to remain
in this 'wretched country, to be defrauded, and mocked of by the
King of Aragon'. Besides being homesick, many were ill; even dying.
Eighteen hundred men had already perished of the flux by eating
food that 'was much part garlic', and by 'drink[ing] hot wines in the
hot weather'. In November, ignoring Henry VIII's orders to stick it
out until spring, the Englishmen sailed home.

Because of Ferdinand's double-dealing, Henry left for France in
June 1513 to continue the war in person. His homecoming afterwards
would be most joyful, he expected. He would return as King of France,
not only in title as he was already styled by virtue of his ancestors' old
conquests, but by his actual possession of the country. He would also
come back as a father, perhaps of a son, as the Queen had announced
herself to be pregnant again.

With Henry away at war, Katherine was appointed Regent with
the authority to rule England in her husband's absence. By such an
honour, Henry clearly recognized his wife's ability to govern. A female
ruler may have been a novelty to the English, but not so to Katherine
herself. Her mother Isabella and her sister Joanna were Queens in
their own right, and her former sister-in-law Margaret of Austria -
that 'most redoubtable lady' as she was called - was overseeing the
Netherlands for her nephew Charles.

While Katherine busied herself tending to government and to making pennants and badges for the King's army, Henry won himself a victory. On 16 August 1513, he took the 'small but very strong town' of Thérouanne at the Battle of the Spurs. It was so named because the French were forced to retreat, frantically digging their spurs into their horses as they fled. The prisoners of war included one of the flowers of the French nobility, the Duke of Longueville. It was Henry's intention to have him shipped over to England to live at court as his trophy. But as Katherine told Thomas Wolsey, the King's almoner who was with him in France, there was no suitable place for the Duke in her household. Better, Katherine thought, that Longueville should be placed in honourable confinement in the Tower. There, she would not have to keep her eye on him, especially with 'the Scots being so busy as they are now'.

On the home front, Katherine - as Regent - was facing the prospect of war herself. With Henry VIII distracted by the French, his brother-in-law James IV of Scotland, who had married Margaret Tudor in 1503, was planning an invasion across the border. 'Unmindful of ties of blood', James saw a greater advantage to himself in a new alliance with France. Katherine was up to the challenge of facing down the Scots. War ran in her blood as the daughter of Ferdinand and Isabella, the conquerors of Granada. Aware of the legacy she was born into, the Queen-Regent gave a rousing speech to her troops telling them that 'the Lord smiled upon those who stood in defence of their own, and they should remember that English courage excelled that of all other nations'.

The Englishmen's valour was proven at Flodden on 9 September. An army of about a thousand soldiers, led by the Earl of Surrey, crushed the Scots who outnumbered them ten to one, as Henry VIII later wrote to the Duke of Milan. 'No Englishmen of note have perished', Henry added proudly. Among the dead, brought down by his own arrogance, was the King of Scotland.

Henry's pride was matched by his wife's - and more so. Was it not *she* who roused her subjects against the invading Scots? And was it not under *her* authority that the English laid waste to them? When announcing her victory to Henry a week after the battle at Flodden, she sent along the dead James' coat - 'for your banner', she said. She had also thought of sending his battered corpse, but her subjects, being squeamish, did not think well of the idea. Katherine was not afraid to blow her own horn – and loudly even – according to the reports of Italian envoys. They mention how the Queen was openly competitive with her husband. Katherine bragged to Henry VIII that she had 'shown no less prowess than he in fighting the Scots', and whereas he was sending her a duke, she was going to send him *a king*. Katherine's boasting may have been exaggerated in the foreign communiqués. More in keeping with her character, she credited her victory to God, as she told her husband, and was setting out to Walsingham to pray for his safe return. But Katherine had more to her prayers than just Henry's homecoming. Since her husband had gone, her belly was growing larger as the months passed.

But while God had granted her victory at Flodden, He withheld the blessing of motherhood. The son Katherine gave birth to that October died soon afterwards.

≡

On 13 August 1514, all eyes were on the Princess Mary as she was escorted into a large chamber hung with cloth of gold at the Palace of Greenwich. There, the ravishing Mary Tudor - 'a 'paradise' she was called - made her curtsies to her brother the King and to her sister-in-law who was noticeably with child again. After the formalities, Mary took her place beside the Duke of Longueville before the Archbishop of Canterbury. She had come to him as a bride. However, the groom was not her brother's esteemed hostage - he was only a proxy - but his master the King of France. Even so, Mary took Longueville's hand, and the two were married.

Despite Louis' absence, a vital part of the ceremonial was not neglected. That evening, Mary Tudor was taken to her bedchamber where Longueville and a group of witnesses waited. As she laid herself down in full view of all, the Duke

> 'in his doublet, with a pair of red hose, but with one leg naked from the middle of the thigh downwards, went into bed, and touched the Princess with his naked leg. The marriage was then declared consummated.'

To conclude the ceremony, 'the King of England made great rejoicing', as did the visiting French dignitaries. There was no mention, however, of the bride doing the same.

As Mary Tudor wrote to her new husband, she was King Louis' to 'use and command', but being Queen of France held no joy for her, and she dreaded the impending journey set for October. Mary was close to Katherine, and she might confided in her of her distaste for the 'feeble, old, and pocky' Louis, a man more than thirty years older than herself. More than that, she was already in love. She had settled her heart on the handsome Charles Brandon. Although he was her brother's closest friend, and Henry had rewarded him with the title of Viscount Lisle and then of Duke of Suffolk, he was still considered an unworthy suitor against the King of France. Unable to have Brandon, Mary looked to a bleak future ahead of her.

As much as Katherine might have pitied her sister-in-law, she would be preoccupied with sorrows of her own. In November, she was 'delivered of a stillborn male child of eight months to the very great grief of the whole court'. The miscarriage had been compounded by her relations of late with the King. Since his return from France, Henry was incessant in reminding his wife of Ferdinand's treachery at Fuenterrabia. As he could not admonish his father-in-law to his face, Katherine got the brunt of his anger instead. All her excuses on her father's behalf were in vain, and in the end, even she had to admit that Ferdinand had acted in bad faith. Katherine continued to revere her father, but for the sake of her marriage, her interests, she decided, must now be entirely English.

Katherine's shift alarmed the Spanish ambassador. Caroz, already 'a bull at whom everyone throws darts' as the representative of the despised Ferdinand, was now even snubbed by his compatriot the Queen. The fault was not Katherine's. She was merely a misguided woman, Caroz believed. Instead, he blamed his old nemesis, Fray Diego. The troublemaking monk, Caroz complained, had advised Katherine 'to forget Spain and everything Spanish, in order to gain the love of the King of England and of the English'.

Caroz was elated when Katherine's reliance on Fray Diego came to an end at last. Unable to keep his hands off the ladies at court, the randy friar was finally sent back home to the Queen's dismay. Fray Diego's expulsion surely left a void in Katherine's life. As her priest and as her friend, she had always looked to him for comfort and counsel. He had steadfastly stood by her in her difficult years under Henry VII, and he continued to do so after she was Queen. Though many found him to be overbearing and belligerent, Fray Diego was unfailingly loyal to Katherine, and his advice was not always bad. His suggestion that the Queen should be of better service to her husband and his people was well given.

In the wake of Fray Diego's departure, there was some good news for Katherine - Mary Tudor was coming home. Her stint as Queen of

France had lasted less than three months. On New Year's Day 1515, she had suddenly found herself a widow. The old King, it was said, died happy; worn out by his young wife in bed. Secluded in mourning for forty days, to ensure she was not pregnant, Mary was at leisure to consider her options. The more she pondered, the more she was convinced that she would be forced into another miserable marriage. Before she had left England, Mary had made her brother promise that should Louis die, her next match could be of her own choosing. But would Henry keep his word? As fate would have it, Charles Brandon came to France to take her home. She was in a frenzy, and she begged him to marry her without delay lest Henry should change his mind. Moved by her tears and in love with her, Brandon gave in. The two married in secret.

The couple were in great trouble. Neither of them – Mary as the King's favourite sister and Suffolk as his closest friend - could expect Henry to accept what they had done behind his back. Brandon's action might even be construed as treasonous, costing him his head. But with Thomas Wolsey, the King's former almoner, now Archbishop of York, acting as an intermediary between the angry King and the errant lovers, the crisis blew over. In May, the Brandons - husband and wife - were allowed back in England, and back into Henry's good graces.

The return of her sister-in-law was even more joyous to Katherine when she and Mary, now Duchess of Suffolk (or 'the French Queen' as Mary was still referred to as), both found themselves pregnant in the summer of 1515. Katherine had even more to look forward to. Relations between England and Spain had improved with the two countries in alliance again.

It was Katherine who began her confinement first. But while the Queen was in seclusion, Ferdinand of Aragon breathed his last on 23 January 1516. Twelve years earlier, when her mother Isabella died, Katherine had been deeply affected by her death. With the Queen in the condition she was in, it was decided to withhold the sad news from her until after the delivery.

Unaware of her father's passing, Katherine's concerns were for the child in her womb. She was now thirty, and her chances for motherhood were diminishing as time passed. She must *not* fail again, she must have thought. Thankfully, the signs were promising. Her pregnancy was going well, and she could feel her child move inside her. Unlike its siblings, this one was determined to live.

On 18 February 1516, at 4 o'clock in the morning, God granted the Queen's prayers - though in part. It was not a boy as she had hoped, but a 'fair princess'.

In the weeks following her christening, the infant - named Mary - was still thriving, and there was every expectation that she would survive into adulthood. To her father, Mary was a sign of more children to come. Both he and the Queen were still young, Henry said optimistically, and 'if it was a daughter this time, by the grace of God, the sons will follow'.

Until Katherine conceived again, Mary was her father's successor. Unlike France for example, which followed the Salic Law disbarring a woman from the throne in her own right, England allowed the rule of a Queen Regnant, although such an event had yet to occur. The closest the country came to having a female monarch was the twelfth-century Empress Maud (or Matilda), the daughter of Henry I. After the untimely death of her brother William, her father had forced his barons to accept her as Queen. Maud might have worn the crown if not for her countrymen's prejudice against a female ruler, and the opposition of her cousin Stephen. The 'Lady of the English', as Maud was called, had to be content to see her son Henry, the first Plantagenet King and the second of that name, take the throne instead of herself after Stephen.

To Henry VIII and his subjects, the likelihood that Mary would succeed to the Crown was unlikely, but Katherine was open to the possibility. Unlike the English who had never lived under a woman with the title and authority of a reigning sovereign, Katherine herself only had to look to her own country and family. As a girl, she had watched her mother Isabella wielding absolute power as Queen of Castile, ruling as a joint monarch with her father Ferdinand of Aragon. Together, they were inseparable; so much that their motto was *As much as the one is worth so much is the other — Isabella as Ferdinand*. Not only was Isabella an able administrator, but she was also a warrior to be reckoned with. Not even her pregnancy with Katherine stopped the Queen of Castile from donning armour like an Amazon of legend to rally her troops against the Moors. When Granada fell to the *Catholic Kings* in 1492 and Christian rule over Spain was firmly established, Isabella gained further prestige as the patroness of Christopher Columbus's voyages to the New World.

As Mary might be the Queen of England one day, Katherine took a great interest in her education. She was influenced by the example set by her mother. While Isabella insisted that her daughters be taught traditional feminine skills such as 'spinning, sewing, and needlepoint', at the same time, she wanted them schooled in the Humanist tradition of the Renaissance like their brother Prince John. Isabella imported the best minds from Italy to educate her children. The poet Antonio Geraldini and his brother Alessandro (later Katherine's confessor) were appointed as tutors to the Queen's daughters, as was Peter Martyr of Anghiers, who proudly called himself the 'literary foster father of almost all the Princes and of all the Princesses of Spain'. Under their direction, Katherine and her sisters had embarked on a curriculum of classical literature and the works of the Church Fathers. These were of course written in Latin - the international language of Christendom - which Isabella insisted all her children become proficient in. As Queen, she had always regretted her own ignorance of Latin, and in later life, Isabella made a dedicated effort to master it herself.

During Mary's youth, Katherine personally directed her studies. But to ensure that her daughter received a most thorough education, she sought the expertise of her countryman, the esteemed scholar Juan Luis Vives. In April 1523, he presented to the Queen his treatise *The Instruction of a Christian Woman*. It was written with Mary in mind, encouraging her to emulate her mother – 'a model of an exemplary life'. The Princess, as Vives wrote to Katherine, 'will read these recommendations and will reproduce them as she models herself on the example of your goodness and wisdom'.

Essentially a guidebook on how to lead a 'virtuous and holy' life, Vives offered young women advice on everything from deportment – they must be discreet; attire – they must dress modestly; cosmetics - they must wear none; to married life - they must be obedient. Vives' views were entirely conventional, except in the notion that women should be educated. Though by nature, the fairer sex was 'a weak creature and of uncertain judgment and is easily deceived', females were nonetheless capable of attaining knowledge, Vives believed. Given proper instruction, girls such as Mary could imitate celebrated ladies of antiquity and the Bible – not to mention Queen Katherine herself and her three sisters – all renowned for their learning.

To be as 'well accomplished' as her mother and her aunts, Mary was to follow a plan of study drawn up by Vives entitled *De Ratione Studii Puerilis*. As Princess (and perhaps her country's future Queen),

Mary should familiarize herself with works about good government by Plato and Erasmus. She should also read *Utopia* by Thomas More, the respected English lawyer, historian, and Humanist, and friend to both her parents. It was also recommended that Mary study the Classics, the Bible, and theology to further 'right living'. As for languages, besides French, and some Spanish she learnt from her mother, Mary must pay particular attention to her Latin and her Greek.

Inherently bright, Mary, with her mother's encouragement developed a formidable intellect. She continued under Katherine's tutelage until the age of nine, when she was given her own establishment. Though Mary was never officially styled *Princess of Wales* as her father's heiress (the title was normally reserved for the wife of a Prince of Wales; there was no precedent for a woman having the title in her own right), she was nonetheless sent off to the Welsh border. There, she would hold court at Ludlow like her mother and Prince Arthur had done.

Katherine and Mary were close, and letters were often passed between them. One, written in reply to Mary's, had Katherine expressing gladness that her daughter was continuing her lessons in Latin with her new schoolmaster Richard Fetherston. She delighted in Mary's progress and asked for samples of her school work. 'It shall be a great comfort', Katherine wrote proudly, 'to see you keep your Latin and fair writing and all'.

Chapter 8
To Submit and Have Patience

TIME HAD not been kind to Katherine. By the time she reached thirty, the 'most beautiful creature in the world', as Fray Diego once called her, had become a dumpy, middle-aged matron. Though the Queen did retain her 'very beautiful complexion', the Venetian ambassador who saw her in June 1515, was unimpressed and thought her 'rather ugly than otherwise'. No doubt, Katherine's fading looks were even more apparent when she appeared next to her younger husband, a man of 'great personal beauty'.

Katherine's decline affected her marriage. With his wife losing her attractions, the King became less attentive towards her. But then Henry had always had a wandering eye. In 1510, he had been attracted to one of the Queen's women, Lady Anne Hastings. The flirtation – it seemed to have only gone as far as that – ended when the lady who was already married, was carried off to a nunnery by her outraged brother, the Duke of Buckingham. Lady Anne was soon forgotten, but Henry remained restless. He began an affair with Elizabeth Blount, another young woman in the Queen's service, who 'in singing, dancing, and in all goodly pastimes, exceeded all other'. In June 1519, she presented the King with their son. The birth of Henry Fitzroy, as the boy was named, was upsetting to Katherine. Elizabeth Blount had succeeded where she as Henry's wife could not. A year earlier, Katherine had found herself pregnant again, but when she went into labour in November, the child was a girl - and she was born dead. Katherine would never conceive again.

The Queen found solace in religion. She appeared less frequently in public, preoccupying herself with prayer and with good works. Her routine involved her rising at midnight and again at 5am to attend devotions. Katherine was most ascetic in her worship. She knelt on the bare stone floor, refusing the comfort of a cushion, and beneath her robes was the coarse habit of her cherished Order of St Francis. As well, she was assiduous in fasting on Fridays, Saturdays and holy days, taking only bread and water. To foster an atmosphere of piety in her chambers, the Queen read the lives of the saints to her ladies daily. Katherine's company seemed to have been strictly female. The days when the King diligently heard evening services with her were a thing of the past.

As the royal couple's lives became increasingly separate, Katherine's opinions and her advice mattered less and less to Henry. Once, he had trusted the Queen implicitly, and had even made her Regent, but since his falling-out with King Ferdinand, Henry's reliance on her had diminished. He turned instead to Thomas Wolsey. From his humble beginnings as a butcher's son, Wolsey, through hard work, intelligence, and personal magnetism had risen steadily in his chosen profession of the Church. He started out as chaplain to Henry VII, and under his successor, his career took off. After serving Henry VIII as his almoner, Wolsey became Bishop of Lincoln, and then Archbishop of York. In 1515, at the age of forty, he was at his peak as a Cardinal of the Church and as Lord Chancellor of England.

While Henry played, Wolsey worked, handling the tedium of government on his master's behalf. It was a relationship that suited them both, and the tireless Wolsey became invaluable to the King. Those whom Henry loved, he rewarded, and Wolsey became rich and powerful. To demonstrate his might, he chose Hampton Court in Surrey as his seat. After acquiring its lease in 1514, Wolsey began expanding the medieval manor house into a magnificent Renaissance palace. By the middle of the 1520s, it surpassed anything Henry VIII himself owned. As the poet John Skelton put it, 'the King's court should have the excellence, but Hampton court hath the pre-eminence'. To be closer to Westminster, the seat of government, Wolsey also took over York Place, near Durham House where Katherine had lived, and transformed it into another dazzling showplace.

Wolsey was as powerful as he was ostentatious. In May 1519, he flexed his muscles by banishing the King's 'minions' – Henry VIII's band of rowdy favourites. Their high jinks and their loose 'French manners', Wolsey felt, had brought dishonour to their master's dignity, and he ejected them from court. Such clout made him unpopular. The Cardinal's lowly origins, his standing with the King, and his own arrogance, made him enemies. He was especially resented by the nobility, and the Duke of Buckingham for one was known to hate Wolsey intensely.

Katherine was wary of the Cardinal too. She was always protective of her closeness to her husband, and Henry's new intimacy with Wolsey disturbed her. She was particularly bothered by the Cardinal's bias towards the French. Although it was Wolsey who organized Henry's war against Louis XII in 1513, he later encouraged a *rapprochement* with France. In the fall of 1518, the Cardinal negotiated peace with Louis XII's successor Francis I. To Katherine's vexation, her daughter Mary was included in the package. She was to be betrothed to Francis's son and heir, the Dauphin.

The ceremony was held at Greenwich on 5 October. The bridegroom, named Francis after his father, was not present - he was only seven months old. However, his age and his absence were of no matter. In the presence of witnesses, the four-year-old Mary, like her aunt the French Queen had been, was 'married' to a proxy instead. A representative of the French King stood in for the Dauphin, and with Wolsey's help, slipped a diamond ring on the Princess's tiny finger. Owing to her tender age, she was thankfully spared the ordeal of the ensuing consummation ritual her aunt had to go through.

To reinforce the 'Universal Peace', as it was called, it was planned for Henry VIII and Francis I to meet. From the beginning, their relationship was marked by rivalry. In 1515, when ambassadors from Venice came to court, Henry grilled them about the new King of France. Was he as tall as himself? Henry enquired good-naturedly. And was he as stout? Francis was about the same height, but not as well-built, they answered. "What sort of legs has he?" Henry then asked. "Spare", the envoys said. At that, Henry opened his doublet, showing off his muscular thigh. "Look here!" he said proudly, "And I also have a good calf to *my* leg!"

In truth, Henry and Francis were cut from the same cloth. Years later, the Admiral of France would remark how

> 'they be like, not only in wisdom and affection,
> delighting both in hunting, in hawking, in building, in
> apparel, in stones, in jewels, and of like affection one
> to another.'

Their so-called 'affection' was a merry-go-round of friendship and hostility, but the Admiral was not far from the mark. Both Henry and Francis were men of sophistication, each presiding over brilliant courts. But in splendour, Francis had the advantage. While England was an island kingdom on the periphery of Europe, and thus a cultural backwater in many ways, France, by its proximity to Italy, absorbed the ideas and ideals of the Renaissance. An enthusiastic patron of painters and sculptors, Francis would welcome Leonardo da Vinci, Andrea del Sarto, and Benvenuto Cellini among others to his court. Francis also had a passion for architecture. He embarked on ambitious building projects, rebuilding the Louvre and transforming the medieval hunting lodge at Fontainebleau into a sumptuous palace. His grandest undertaking was the construction of the Renaissance styled Château de Chambord in the Loire Valley. It was to arouse Henry VIII's envy, later inspiring him to build an equally magnificent monument to himself in Surrey called Nonsuch (as 'none such' was ever seen before).

The much-anticipated meeting of the two Kings was to take place in June 1520 near the French town of Ardres, close to Calais. But before Henry and Katherine crossed the Channel, they received a most exalted visitor. In May, the Queen's nephew Charles - ruler of the Netherlands, Spain, and Germany, and the newly elected Holy Roman Emperor - landed at Dover. He had come to seek England's help against his troublesome Spanish subjects - and to ensure that his uncle's meeting with Francis would not leave himself in the cold.

The young man Henry met on the evening of 26 May was not exactly the image of the most powerful man in Europe. His great titles aside, Charles, at twenty, was still wet behind the ears in his uncle's opinion. Albeit, Henry himself was King at only seventeen, but he had at least looked like one. In contrast, Charles seemed rather insipid with his grave and introverted demeanour, and to boot, he was awkward looking with his gaping mouth and ponderous chin. What Henry did not know was that beneath this solemn and unprepossessing exterior was a young man determined to take his place in the political arena.

Charles might not have impressed Henry, but his visit to England meant the world to Katherine. When she met him the next day at Canterbury, 'she embraced her nephew tenderly, not without tears'. Charles stayed for three days fêted by his uncle and aunt. But it was not all pleasure; on his last day in England, he and the King 'sat in Council until late in the evening'. No great settlements were reached, but it can be assumed that Charles at least received Henry's word that his visit with the French King would not be detrimental to him.

It took seventy-seven ships to transport Henry VIII and his court across the Channel. Some five thousand people accompanied him, from the highest in the land – the Queen, the Dukes of Buckingham and Suffolk, and Cardinal Wolsey, to the lowest - cooks, kitchen boys, stable hands, maids, laundresses, and such. The size of Henry's retinue was meant to impress the French, as were the rich furnishings, tapestries, plate, jewels, and clothes he brought along.

In France, Henry and Katherine settled into a newly built palace outside the Castle of Guisnes. It was meant to be a temporary structure – only its foundations were brick, the rest was wood and canvas - but nonetheless no expense had been spared to make it grand and luxurious. The exterior was decorated with heraldic emblems, Tudor roses, and festoons. To let in light, windows, measuring around eight feet high, were installed made of the finest glass. Up above, statues graced the rooftops. The interior was just as impressive. To entertain guests, a large banqueting chamber was set up, and connecting to it, two grand halls both measuring 750 feet in length. Outside, a special fountain was erected. Instead of water, it gushed out wine in endless quantities. The French were suitably impressed. The palace was 'so well designed', that the great da Vinci himself could not have done better, it was said.

Henry and Francis met on 7 June. They embraced each other 'very lovingly' on horseback, and then again when they dismounted. For the next two weeks, there were continual entertainments, feasts, and exchanges of gifts. While Henry and Francis took on challengers on the tiltyard, Katherine kept company with the ladies. Her sister-in-law, Mary, the former Queen of France sat with her, as did the current one, Claude, daughter of Louis XII. Katherine took a liking to Queen Claude. She was an amiable young woman - soft-spoken and devout like Katherine herself. Such was her nature, and perhaps she was also self-conscious of being rather plain, heavy set, and crook-backed. Francis was not entirely faithful to his wife, but he always treated her with the utmost respect as the mother of his children. At the time she met Katherine, Claude already had two fine sons, and she was pregnant once again. If Katherine felt envious, one could hardly blame her.

As the meeting came to a close, a special Mass was conducted by Wolsey on 23 June in celebration of the alliance between England and France. To seal their bond, Henry and Francis vowed to erect a chapel together on the spot dedicated to 'Our Lady of Friendship', along with a 'very handsome palace, promising to visit each other there once every year'.

═══

The great summit, remembered as 'The Field of the Cloth of Gold', achieved nothing. For all their promises made to each other,

Henry VIII and Francis I were no closer than before. No joint palace was ever built, nor did the Virgin ever receive her chapel. There was to be no marriage between Princess Mary and the Dauphin either. At their betrothal in 1518, Henry VIII had sworn before his court that if he failed to keep his bargain in giving away his daughter, Wolsey was to 'excommunicate him, and pass sentence of interdict on his kingdom'. Despite his solemn oath, and the threat of ecclesial punishment (which Wolsey obligingly withheld), Mary was released from her commitment to France in the summer of 1521. Katherine could not have been happier, especially when her daughter's new fiancé – and the kingdom's new ally – was her nephew, Charles V.

In May 1522, the Emperor arrived in England again, this time to discuss a joint invasion of France. At Greenwich, Charles greeted the Queen on his knees as before, and asked for her blessing following 'the fashion of Spain between the aunt and the nephew'. At Katherine's side was her six-year-old daughter - his cousin and bride-to-be, in whom Charles took 'great joy'. He stayed for six weeks, and for the rest of her life, Mary preserved the special memory of his visit.

As Charles' future bride, her daughter would be destined for greatness, Katherine thought proudly. Mary would be the most honoured woman in Christendom – Empress, Queen Consort, Archduchess, Duchess, and Countess of the various territories ruled by her husband covering the expanse of Europe and parts of the New World. Mary would also be Queen Regnant of her own country, as her father had confirmed at her former betrothal to the Dauphin in 1518. It was declared that if he died without a son, Mary would succeed him. Katherine had no doubt of the fact. Now in her mid-thirties, the Queen knew she was unlikely to conceive again, leaving Mary as Henry's only legitimate heir. As for his son, Henry Fitzroy, the boy being a bastard would be no threat to Mary.

Recognizing the Princess as her father's heiress would also dispel any unrest about the succession, Katherine believed. Without a Prince of Wales, Henry VIII's Yorkist cousins were often regarded as possible successors. The most dangerous of them were Edmund and Richard de la Pole, sons of Edward IV's sister Elizabeth. Henry VII had been so worried that his wife's kin would overthrow his new dynasty that he had Edmund imprisoned in the Tower in 1506. He was considered a threat even in the next reign. In 1513, when Henry VIII left to fight the French, he made certain his kingdom was secure by having de la

Pole executed before his departure. His brother Richard, called the 'White Rose', fled to France with a price on his head.

Then there was Edward Stafford, third Duke of Buckingham, whose father had supported, and then betrayed, Richard III. As descendants of Edward III, the Staffords boasted royal blood in their veins. Edward, despite his father's ignominious end, never forgot that. He was proud, in fact too proud, and he did not care who he antagonized. Stafford had quarrelled with the King over Henry's attempted seduction of his sister, and he was not afraid to provoke Wolsey, thumbing his nose at the Cardinal's humble origins.

Buckingham's arrogance, his closeness to the throne, and his popularity with the people, were a deadly combination. It was commonly imagined that 'were the King to die without heirs male, he might easily obtain the Crown'. Afraid of the possibility, Henry had Buckingham arrested in April 1521. The Duke was accused of conspiring the King's death, and even though his guilt was questionable, he was condemned to death nonetheless.

$$=$$

The alliance between England and the Holy Roman Empire was as brittle as the Anglo-French 'Universal Peace' made in 1520. The invasion of France was hampered by squabbling, mutual distrust, and self-serving interests on both sides. In February 1525, when Charles V's army defeated and captured Francis I at Pavia in northern Italy, the victory was attributed to the Emperor alone. Still, Henry and Katherine offered him their congratulations. Without its King, France was now up for grabs, and there was more reason to rejoice when it was learnt that among the dead, fighting with the French, was Richard de la Pole. In celebration of his troublesome kinsman's end, Henry ordered bonfires to be lit and free wine to be distributed in the streets.

The crushing of the 'White Rose' was England's only gain at Pavia. None of the terms Charles exacted from the captive Francis were to Henry VIII's benefit. The Emperor, now at the height of his power, began to see his English alliance as a burden. To sever his ties, Charles provoked a rift that June. He made unreasonable demands for military assistance and money, and he requested that the nine-year-old Mary be delivered to him immediately, as his wife-to-be. When Henry failed to respond as Charles knew he would, he renounced his betrothal to the Princess. Taking a page from the crafty Henry VII, the Emperor claimed that since his uncle had failed to deliver Mary to him, much less her dowry, he was free to look elsewhere. In March 1526, Charles wed his other cousin Isabella of Portugal instead.

The Emperor's hostility perplexed Katherine. He had always held her in high regard as his mother's sister, but in the past two years, he had ignored her many letters to him. In November 1526, with no end to his silence, Katherine wrote again. 'I cannot imagine what may be the cause of Your Highness having been so angry, and having so forgotten me', she told him. But if Charles was upset, as Katherine believed him to be, so was she: 'And yet I am sure I deserve not this treatment', she went on, giving her nephew a piece of her mind, 'for such are my affection and readiness for Your Highness' service that I deserved a better reward'.

≡

Charles' jilting of Mary was a great disappointment to Katherine. She had imagined a glittering future for her as the Empress, but it was not to be. Katherine was left with the consolation that Mary was still heiress to the English throne. But that reassurance, so important to her, came under threat on 18 June 1525. That Sunday, Henry Fitzroy, the King's natural son, was led in procession into his father's presence. The six-year-old boy knelt before the King, and was created Earl of Nottingham, and then Duke of Richmond and Somerset.

Katherine was furious. The honoured title of Richmond had belonged to the King's grandmother Lady Margaret and his father Henry VII. By his ennoblement, Fitzroy - a bastard - was now 'the highest grade in the kingdom', even 'next in rank to His Majesty'. To the Queen, it was an insult to her daughter the Princess, the King's *legitimate* child.

Afraid that Mary might be displaced by her half-brother, Katherine did not keep silent. She was extremely vocal about Fitzroy's advancement, and her rage was egged on by three of her most trusted Spanish women. His wife's open resentment was an embarrassment and irritation to Henry VIII. He struck back by banishing her ladies from court. When the dust settled, the Queen 'was obliged to submit and have patience'.

For Katherine, 'patience' meant having to endure her husband's infidelities as well. She reconciled herself to the miserable truth that men, even loving husbands, could be unfaithful. Her father Ferdinand, she recalled, was not blameless. At least, Katherine told herself, Henry's liaison with Fitzroy's mother had been brief. Hopefully, it would be the same with his new sweetheart Mary Boleyn. It was rumoured at court, that the son, named Henry, she gave birth to in March 1526 was not the child of her husband, William Carey, but of the King. Katherine paid no attention to such gossip, especially when Henry never acknowledged the boy as his.

Just as the Queen expected, Mary Boleyn was soon out of sight and out of mind. Henry's affairs, Katherine knew, were short-lived, and in the end, it was she – his wife of many years – whom he truly loved. With that reassurance, she had nothing to fear from the King's latest diversion – Mary Boleyn's sister, Mistress Anne. Once Henry had his fill and became bored with her too, she would go the way of the others, Katherine believed.

Figure 7   Charles V by a follower of Jan Cornelisz Vermeyan
The Rijksmuseum, Amsterdam

Chapter 9
The King's Great Matter

DURING HENRY VIII's short-lived friendship with the Emperor, Charles' ambassadors were entertained at the English court at Shrovetide in 1522. On 2 March, there was a joust in which the King himself took part, and two days later, on Shrove Tuesday, the Imperial envoys were treated to a sumptuous banquet at York Place by the Cardinal. After supper, a revel was staged before his assembled guests. In the great hall lined with torches and hung with tapestries, a castle - the Château Vert - was erected. Within its walls of timber, paper, and 'green tinfoil', a group of young 'ladies of honour' were held captive. They were dressed in gowns of white satin, and on their headdresses, written in gold, were their names: *Beauty*, *Honour*, *Perseverance*, *Kindness*, *Constancy*, *Bounty*, and *Mercy*.

Suddenly, a band of gentlemen disguised as *Amorous*, *Nobleness*, *Youth*, *Attendance*, *Loyalty*, *Pleasure*, *Gentleness*, and *Liberty* came into the hall led by *Ardent Desire*, clothed in 'crimson satin with burning flames of gold'. They stormed the Château Vert, and demanded the surrender of the maidens from their captors – young male choristers 'attired like women of the Indies'. While five of the 'ladies' - *Danger*, *Jealousy*, *Unkindness*, *Malebouche*, and *Strangeness* - gave in, *Scorn* and *Disdain* would not yield.

On cue, a great shot of ordnance was fired from outside the palace. At the signal, *Amorous* and his knights attacked the castle pelting the defenders with fruits. *Scorn* and *Disdain* defended themselves valiantly with 'rose water and comfits', but in the end were vanquished. *Beauty* and her attendants were released from captivity, and in celebration, they took their liberators by the hand, 'and danced together very pleasantly'. Afterwards, the participants removed their disguises and revealed their identities. The King, as everyone already guessed, had the role of *Amorous*, while *Beauty*, as expected, was his sister the ravishing French Queen. Among the supporting players were Mary Boleyn as *Kindness*, and as *Perseverance*, her sister Anne.

≡

Whether Anne Boleyn made her courtly debut as a fifteen-year-old teenager or as a young woman of twenty-one is a mystery.

Traditionally, her birth date has been given as 1507, but 1501 has been suggested as more likely. While her sister Mary was supposedly prettier, it was Anne who had the brains.

Anne's intelligence as a child did not go unnoticed by her father Sir Thomas Boleyn, a man of ability himself. Boleyn began his career at court as a Squire of the Body to Henry VII, and in the next reign, he distinguished himself as a competitor in tournaments, and as a linguist. Fluent in French and Latin, Boleyn went on to serve Henry VIII as ambassador to the Netherlands and France. By 1522, he was a member of the Council, Controller of the royal household, and Treasurer. Later, as his family reached greater heights thanks to his daughter Anne, Thomas Boleyn reaped the benefits as Viscount Rochford, Earl of Wiltshire, and Earl of Ormond, and then as Lord Privy Seal. Boleyn had done well in his marriage too. His wife was the aristocrat Elizabeth Howard, daughter of the Earl of Surrey. After he had defeated the Scots at Flodden, the Earl was rewarded with the dukedom of Norfolk, which Henry VIII gave back to his family. Through her Howard blood, Anne Boleyn, like Queen Katherine, was distantly related to the King, as were all his future wives, interestingly enough.

Ambitious for the precocious Anne as he was for himself, Boleyn placed her at the Flemish court of Queen Katherine's former sister-in-law Margaret of Austria. That Anne the younger daughter, not Mary, the elder, was given such a privilege in 1513, suggests that Thomas Boleyn recognized some quality in Anne lacking in her sister. Given Anne's later career in comparison to Mary's, he was correct in his assessment. The Archduchess took to Anne immediately. 'I find her so bright and pleasant for her young age', Margaret wrote Boleyn, 'that I am more beholden to you for sending her to me than you are to me'.

Whatever her actual age, Anne impressed the archduchess with her maturity. Margaret was a kind and generous guardian, and Anne aimed to please her. She worked especially hard at her French. It was Margaret's main tongue, and the subject her father particularly wanted her to excel at. Anne did Thomas Boleyn proud. After a year in the Netherlands as a maid of honour, she was speaking French well; so well that it landed her place at the court of Louis XII where she joined the household of his new Queen, Mary Tudor. Even after Mary sailed home with her second husband Charles Brandon, Anne stayed behind, improving her French even more, and gaining extra polish at the court of Francis I. She was transferred to the service of Queen Claude and became acquainted with the King's sister, the fascinating Margaret of Angoulême – a patroness of learning, and an author and poetess in her own right. Years later, Anne would speak of Margaret with affection, expressing a hope to see her again. Not only did Margaret's talents impress Anne, but also her particular brand of religion. Margaret was critical of the abuses in the Church, and though she was not a Lutheran, she was interested in religious reform. Within her circle were like-minded scholars and churchmen. Their ideas were to have an impact on Anne's beliefs in the future.

By the time she set foot in England again around the end of 1521 to serve Queen Katherine, Anne Boleyn had been transformed. She had left home as an English girl, but returned as a French woman. She spoke French with ease, and she even 'thought' French. Her time in the Netherlands and France had given Anne an air of sophistication none of her English counterparts could even hope to possess. No lady at Henry VIII's court was as elegant, witty, or as fashionable as she was. 'By her manners', a poet later wrote, 'no one would ever have taken her to be an English lady, but a native born French woman'.

Despite her Continental flair, her looks were less remarkable. Anne Boleyn was not beautiful in the conventional sense. Her hair was not golden, nor was her skin pale like that of the universally praised Mary Tudor. Anne's long tresses were dark, as was her complexion. Some thought her mouth too wide, and her neck too long. Nonetheless, there was something striking about Mistress Anne; the way she held herself, and the way she attracted people to her. Even her critics had to admit that there was something mesmerizing about Anne Boleyn - especially her eyes. They were 'black and beautiful',

> 'which she well knew how to use, holding them sometimes still, and at others, making them send a message, carrying the secret witness of the heart. And to tell the truth, such was their power that many a man rendered his allegiance.'

Of these many admirers was Henry Percy, the heir of the Earl of Northumberland, and a member of Wolsey's household. Like many young men of the aristocracy, Percy was placed in the Cardinal's care for his education. But Henry Percy had more on his mind than his lessons. Often, he would 'resort for his pastime unto the Queen's Chamber, and there would fall in dalliance among the Queen's maidens'. Of all the ladies-in-waiting, it was Anne Boleyn who won his heart, and within a short time, the young lovers pledged themselves to each other.

Had Percy and Anne been allowed to love and marry as they wanted to, the course of history would have been profoundly different. But Cardinal Wolsey stepped in. He summoned Percy before him and berated the youth for entangling himself with that 'foolish girl yonder in the court'. His attachment to Mistress Boleyn, Wolsey stormed, had offended both his father the Earl and the King. Anne, unbeknownst to her, the Cardinal went on, had already been promised to another, and there were similar plans for Percy. Crushed by the Cardinal, a weeping Percy gave in. He stopped seeing Anne, and would later wed another as ordered. Anne herself had no use for tears. Made of sterner stuff than the pliable Percy, she 'was greatly offended, saying that if it lay ever in her power, she would work the Cardinal as much displeasure'. No one took Anne seriously, and she was packed off to her family's home at Hever Castle in Kent to cool off.

Anne was eventually allowed back at court. A spell in the country had not diminished her charms, and a new host of admirers was at her door. Leading the pack was the poet and courtier, Sir Thomas Wyatt. Although he had a wife already – not that it mattered, especially when his marriage was an unhappy one – Wyatt indulged in the pastime of 'courtly love' with Anne. As it was played out, Anne was the aloof unattainable mistress whom Wyatt and his rivals pursued with gifts, songs, and verses. However, his pursuit of Anne – that elusive hind as he imagined her to be in a poem he wrote – was futile. She had spurned him and was bestowing her favours on others. As Wyatt wrote:

> 'The vain travail hath wearied me so sore, I am of them
> that farthest cometh behind.'

Ignored by Anne, Wyatt withdrew from the chase. His chief competition was none other than Henry VIII himself. As the poet explained:

> 'And graven with diamonds in letters plain There is
> written her fair neck round about: *Noli me tangere*,
> for Caesar's I am, And wild for to hold, though I
> seem tame.'

In other words, Anne Boleyn was off limits. 'Touch me not, for I am the King's', she declared. Wyatt's poem is undated, so when exactly did Henry VIII enter the picture? According to George Cavendish,

Wolsey's gentleman usher, to whom we owe the details of Anne's affair with Percy, it was shortly after the couple's forced separation that the King revealed his 'secret affection' for the lady. Cavendish provided no dates either, but it could have been as early as the summer's end of 1525. Around that time, Anne's sister Mary found herself pregnant. Whoever the father really was – Mary's husband or the King himself - Henry would have presumably ceased sexual relations with Mary, and probably even cut all emotional ties with her then as well. He had done so with Elizabeth Blount after she gave birth to young Fitzroy.

Just how honourable were the King's intentions towards Anne? Was he simply after a new paramour, or was he searching for a new queen? As he did not begin divorce proceedings against Katherine until Mary 1527, it can be assumed that in the beginning, Anne was just another mistress in the making. If that was the case, Anne was not as easily won over as Mistress Blount or her own sister. She was indeed 'wild for to hold' as Thomas Wyatt described her. Henry, who hated to write, found himself putting pen to paper to possess Anne.

Seventeen love letters from Henry VIII's hand survive, but unfortunately none from Anne's. In reading the King's correspondence, Henry unabashedly wore his heart on his sleeve. Anne, however, was not so forthcoming. When she replied (as gleaned from the King's letters), she was often ambiguous and cool, and sometimes she did not even reply at all. Was she simply uninterested or was she acting the tease? Was she playing Henry for a fool – payback for ruining her relationship with Percy, or was she indeed interested in him, but disdainful of being just a mistress? We can only guess.

The King's letters are undated, but one that seemed to have been composed early on in their relationship had him lamenting Anne's absence. Evidently, she had purposely withdrawn herself to Hever Castle, leaving 'I and my heart', as Henry described it, in great pain. His suffering was increased when Anne later made it clear in one of her replies that she had no intention of returning to court. She had 'entirely changed [her] opinion', leaving Henry - 'her entire servant' - as he called himself, most confused.

But in January 1527, Anne hinted at her intentions. She sent Henry a jewel – 'a handsome diamond and ship in which the lonely damsel is tossed about'. 'The fine interpretation' which she had sent with it is lost along with all her letters, but it can be inferred that Anne intended to finally surrender herself into the safe harbour of Henry's affection. In one of his previous letters, Henry had asked

Anne 'to give yourself body and heart to me'. Apparently, she would now. Like an infatuated schoolboy who had received his first kiss, the King signed himself 'Henry Rex seeks A.B. no other'. As further proof of his love – he enclosed Anne's initials within a heart.

But Anne's body, to which Henry also laid claim to, would not be his in the fullest sense until some years afterwards. It was probably after Anne's surrender that Henry made up his mind to divorce the Queen and to remarry. Perhaps the idea had occurred to him even before he met Anne. After losing her baby in 1518, Katherine was incapable of bearing any more children. Was it then that Henry began wondering if his marriage was cursed? The time frame is uncertain, but not Henry's grounds for a separation. Fancying himself a theologian, he sought an answer from Scripture, and sure enough, he found it in the Book of Leviticus. There, it was clearly stated that should a man took his brother's wife, he would be childless by her. That Katherine always claimed her marriage to Arthur was unconsummated, and that the prohibition in Leviticus was contradicted by the Book of Deuteronomy (which encouraged a man to wed his dead brother's wife), were ignored by Henry. The King's myopic view also allowed him to overlook his daughter Mary. Being without sons was synonymous to being childless.

If his marriage was cursed, as Henry truly believed it to be, then he must marry again, and with Anne Boleyn. Though she was not royal, she was of good lineage by her Howard blood. She was also young enough to bear him sons, and furthermore, she and Henry were in love. Determined as he was to have Anne, Henry would not bed her – not yet - not until she was legally his wife. Their sons must not be born out of wedlock like Henry Fitzroy. To achieve that end, they must proceed cautiously and in secret. Katherine and her supporters must not be allowed to mount an opposition. On 17 May 1527, Wolsey at Henry's command, summoned his master to appear before an ecclesial court. The King, it seemed, was living in sin with the Queen. There were grave doubts, the Cardinal declared, that Katherine was indeed the virgin she had always claimed to have been, and that the Pope truly had the authority to issue a dispensation for their marriage in 1504.

After the groundwork for the 'Great Matter', (as the divorce, or rather the annulment, was called) was laid, the Queen was kept in the dark. Already, she was seeing less and less of the King. She and Henry no longer slept together, and both were living in their own establishments within the palace. Unless one of them specifically called on the other, they only saw each other on public occasions. Despite her isolation, word still leaked out to Katherine of the manoeuvrings behind her back. But 'full of apprehension', and that she was being watched by the Cardinal's spies, she dared not confide her fears to Don Inigo de Mendoza, the new Spanish ambassador directly, but only through an intermediary. Alerted, de Mendoza was able to find out that the King himself was 'bent on this divorce', and Wolsey was merely his henchman. Even so, the Queen chose to believe otherwise. It was the Cardinal who was behind all her troubles, putting ideas into his master's head.

Having faith in her husband's love for her, perhaps Katherine thought Henry had come to warn her against the Cardinal when he paid her a visit on 22 June. She could not have been more wrong. The King sat Katherine down and bluntly told her how 'his conscience was much troubled'. For years, they had been living in sin together as man and wife. That they had no sons together was proof enough, and his doubts were supported by the many theologians he had already consulted in private. Therefore, they must separate, Henry stammered, and his 'sister-in-law' - as he believed Katherine only to be - was free to retire anywhere she pleased.

In shock and disbelief, Katherine burst into violent sobs. When she was finally able to speak, she professed her love for the King, and she vehemently swore that her marriage with Prince Arthur had never been consummated. Henry made no answer. At a loss for words at her incessant weeping, he left Katherine to her tears, only telling her to 'keep secrecy upon what he had told her'.

She did no such thing. Katherine's first response to was to get word to her nephew the Emperor. Though her relationship with Charles had been frosty of late, surely he would come to her aid in such a vital matter. But Katherine suspected she was still being watched. Unable to speak freely with de Mendoza still, she had to resort to deception. It was hinted that one of her servants, by the name of Felipez, had a sick mother whom he wanted to visit in Spain. To throw off suspicion, Katherine pretended to refuse to let him go, and she asked Henry to deny him permission as well. But the King, 'knowing great collusion and dissimulation between them', granted Felipez a passport, as Katherine suspected he would. Once the Spaniard was on his way, Henry intended to have him detained at his stopover in Calais. But Felipez, one step ahead, went straight to the Emperor instead.

Charles V was stunned 'to hear of a case so scandalous', and he immediately pledged his help to his aunt. He also wrote to Pope Clement VII, asking him to revoke Wolsey's authority as Papal Legate to try the case in England as the King wanted. The Emperor knew there would be little opposition from the Vatican as Clement was virtually his prisoner.

In May 1527, an Imperial army fighting in Italy had gone on a rampage laying waste to Rome. Houses were destroyed and looted, and citizens indiscriminately butchered. Even priests and nuns were tortured and killed 'that they might declare what money or jewels they had concealed'. The great church of St Peter was not left untouched. It was desecrated, stripped of its riches, and its floor littered with corpses. By the time the atrocities were over, the city was a smouldering ruin, and some eight thousand people were dead. 'Rome will not recover from this blow for five hundred years to come', it was said.

During the mayhem, even the Pope himself had been in danger for his life. Clement VII managed to save himself by fleeing to the protection of the fortress-like Castel Sant' Angelo. The Emperor later disavowed the bloodthirsty actions of his army, but even he could not deny that having the Pope in his power was not without its advantages. Clement would not dare offend him by divorcing his aunt.

Meanwhile, Henry VIII did not foresee any difficulty in getting the Pope on his side either. After all, Henry had always been a faithful son of the Church. When Martin Luther criticized its excesses in 1517, Henry leapt to its defence. He penned *The Defence of the Seven Sacraments*, a work upholding Catholic beliefs, as well as the authority of the Pontiff as the Vicar of Christ on Earth. In gratitude, Pope Leo X gave Henry the title *Defender of the Faith* in 1521. Now as he saw it, the Vatican still owed him one.

It was left to Wolsey to smooth the way to the divorce. The Cardinal, who had left for France in July for extended peace talks with the restored Francis I, was given the impression that Henry was interested in marrying not Anne Boleyn, but the French King's sister-in-law Renée. Such an alliance would be a natural conclusion to negotiations made earlier with the French in the spring. While Henry wed Madame Renée, his daughter Mary would be offered as a bride to Francis's younger son, Henry, Duke of Orléans.

But Wolsey's hard work in settling peace with the French was not matched by his efforts in handling the divorce. Once he discovered that Anne Boleyn was to be Queen of England, not Renée of France, he was in a quandary. Wolsey had never cared for Queen Katherine, but to bring her down for Anne's sake would only endanger his position. The young woman was highly intelligent, aggressive, and wilful – and most of all, growing more powerful each day. Wolsey might have recalled how livid Anne was when he parted her from Henry Percy, and how she had sworn revenge on him. He was only acting as the King's messenger, but if she hated him still nonetheless, he had much to worry about indeed.

Arriving back in England in September, Wolsey asked to see the King, inquiring as to where and when he might be received in private. His messenger found Henry VIII with his lady love by his side. Before the King could respond to the Cardinal's request, Anne cut him short. "Where else is the Cardinal to come?" she asked haughtily, "Tell him that he may come *here* where the King is". The messenger, taken aback by Anne's audacity in answering for the King, looked to Henry. He only nodded sheepishly in agreement. As the Cardinal came forth, he knelt before the King in greeting. Had he looked up, he would have seen Anne beaming in triumph.

As Henry VIII ploughed on with his divorce, life at court went on as usual. The King and Queen, were by all appearances, still a loving couple appearing together on ceremonial occasions. Katherine even went out of her way, it was said, to hold 'Mistress Anne in more estimation for the King's sake', showing her no 'spark or kind of grudge or displeasure'.

But to those who knew better, the Queen was 'dissimul[ating] the same'. By now, she was well aware that Anne Boleyn was intent on supplanting her, but in her pride, Katherine would not give her the satisfaction of seeing her jealous. Nonetheless, it was a façade not easy to keep up. Once, as it was told, she asked Anne to play cards with her – a scheme to keep her occupied and away from Henry VIII – Katherine could not resist a jab at her rival. After Anne won the round by drawing up a king, Katherine congratulated her. "My Lady Anne, you have good hap to stop at a king. But you are *not* like others, you will have *all or nothing*"

The new year of 1528 held out no great hopes for Katherine of Aragon. Anne Boleyn's star was still in the ascendant and rising higher, and England's relations with Charles V were only getting worse. On 22 January, Henry VIII and Francis I, united by the Treaty of Amiens made in August 1527, jointly declared war on the Emperor. The aggressions amounted to nothing, but with Charles as her husband's enemy, Katherine's reliance on him to help save her marriage was made more difficult. News had also reached England the month before that Clement VII was out of Imperial clutches, seeking safety in the town of Orvieto. Katherine had deplored the actions of the Emperor's mutinous army in Rome, but even she knew how her cause was set back with the Pope no longer her nephew's prisoner.

Conversely, the Holy Father's liberation was welcome news to Henry VIII. Clement, he expected, could now rule on his divorce without Imperial interference. When the English envoy William Knight met with Clement in Orvieto, the Pope appeared amenable to the King's wishes. Henry was given a dispensation to wed Anne Boleyn - the sister of his former mistress - with impunity. However, Clement, still a refugee, remained fearful of the Emperor. To satisfy Charles, he had the dispensation worded in such a way that before Henry could have Anne, he must be legally separated from his Queen, and such a judgement could only be given in Rome. When the technicality was discovered, Henry was furious.

In February, another embassy was sent to Italy, this time, headed by the more capable Stephen Gardiner, a secretary of Wolsey's trained in civil and canon law, and by Doctor Edward Fox, the King's almoner, and a brilliant theologian. The pair met the Pope in March at his court-in-exile. The episcopal palace he occupied was in a sorry state, 'ruinous and decayed'. The roofs were caving in, letting in damp and pestilence, and its interior was devoid of any luxury. The walls were bare and crumbling, and the meagre furnishings in the papal bedchamber were not worth '20 nobles, bed and all', Gardiner and Fox reported to Wolsey. As pathetic was Clement himself. A timid and indecisive man, he was driven to further distraction by the hardships - both mental and physical. 'It were better to be in captivity in Rome,' Clement sighed, 'than here at liberty'.

Though free from harassment from the Emperor's troops, Clement was still not yet able to fully oblige the English. After three weeks of talks with Gardiner and Fox, he agreed to a compromise.

The faults in the dispensation allowing the King to wed Anne Boleyn would be corrected, and a 'general commission' given to Wolsey to hear the case in England. As well, Cardinal Lorenzo Campeggio, as his representative, would sit beside him in judgement. However, the Pope withheld the more effective 'decretal commission' that Wolsey had asked for. Such a document would establish that Henry and Katherine's marriage was *indeed* faulty (not *perhaps*), and Wolsey would merely have to prove this in court. He dare not, Clement said, extend the Cardinal's powers for fear of the Emperor. However, he did promise that with the general commission Wolsey was given, the Church would abide by whatever decision was reached by an English court.

As Gardiner and Fox were finishing their business in Italy, back in England, it was decided that 'for her own better education, and for the consolation of the King and Queen, the Princess should reside near the King's person'. Mary's household at Ludlow, where she had been living for two years, was closed up, and she was back home by April 1528. Beset by troubles, having her daughter with her again was a comfort to Katherine. It was so for Mary too, especially when she fell ill of smallpox in May. Being with her mother at Greenwich, the Queen could nurse her personally.

Mary recovered from the pox, but another form of disease was to ravage England that summer. The 'sweating sickness', or 'the sweat' as it was commonly called, was deadly. When it last appeared in July 1517, 'it killed some within three hours, some within two hours; some merry at dinner and dead at supper'. When it finally ran its course months later, thousands were dead.

The spring of 1528 was excessively warm and wet, allowing the sweat to be carried quickly and easily from one place to another. Even as far away as Italy, Gardiner and Fox were fearful of the contagion. At the English court, some of the Queen's ladies had been stricken, along with an attendant of Anne Boleyn. There was reason to believe that the girl's mistress might have caught the epidemic as well, and Anne was quickly packed off to Hever Castle to be quarantined.

At the same time, Henry VIII, who had a great fear of infection, took off to the country to the fresh air of Waltham Abbey and his estates at Hunsdon, 'keep[ing] himself ever with a small company'. While he fortified himself with remedies, he wrote to Anne. He hoped that she was spared the sweat, and he reminded her that her brother

George Boleyn, who had fallen sick, had fully recovered, and that few women were affected by the illness. Or so he believed. About a week later, Henry wrote again, but in despair – for 'there came suddenly to me in the night the most unpleasant news that I could have received' – Anne had caught the plague.

Swearing to his beloved how he 'would willingly bear half of your illness in order to have you cured', Henry sent one of his best doctors to Hever. By his care, Anne was able to pull through, as did her father, who was also bedridden. Anne's brother-in-law William Carey was not so lucky. He succumbed to the sweat on 23 June, leaving Mary Boleyn a widow.

After her recovery, Anne Boleyn returned to court. To rectify the awkward situation of having his mistress in his wife's household, the King removed her from Katherine's service. She would no longer have to wait on the Queen, but have her own establishment; one obtained by 'my lord Cardinal's means', as Henry had him do. It is not certain which residence it was, but it may have been Durham House where Queen Katherine once lived. Showered with fine clothes and rich jewels by her royal lover, Anne kept estate 'more like a queen than a simple maid'.

With Anne back at the King's side, Wolsey was to do more than help her find a new house, he was prepared to make her Queen. The Cardinal had bowed to the inevitable. Henry would have Anne no matter what, and though he continued to disapprove of 'the night crow' as he called her behind her back, he thought it best to woo Anne's favour, than to bear her hostility. More than that, his very survival depended on it. 'The pride and ambition of the Cardinal' was resented by many nobles, and they were looking to Anne to see Wolsey brought down. Thomas Howard, Anne's maternal uncle, who had succeeded to the dukedom of Norfolk at the death of his father in 1524, was one of the Cardinal's enemies, as was her father Thomas Boleyn. Even Charles Brandon, whom Wolsey had helped restore to royal favour after his marriage to the French Queen, was no friend to the Cardinal.

Wolsey made efforts to ingratiate himself with Anne. When she had a craving for the delicious carp and shrimps from his ponds, he immediately sent her some, and when her mother Lady Boleyn asked for some fish, Wolsey graciously 'bestow[ed] a morsel of tunny upon her'. The Cardinal's benevolence and his commitment to her cause, won Anne over. She set aside her former hatred for Wolsey, writing to him in thanks for the 'great pains and troubles that you have taken for me, both day and night'. She was 'most bound' to him, Anne declared, and before she sealed the letter, she had the King add a postscript in his own hand expressing his good wishes to the Cardinal.

But behind their new-found friendship, there was still mutual distrust. Both Anne and Wolsey were strong personalities; each one trying to assert herself or himself over the other. Inevitably, they openly clashed. In the summer of 1528, there was debate as to who should be the new Abbess of Wilton. Wolsey supported one Isabel Jordan, but Anne, looking out for her family, had Eleanor Carey, the sister of her late brother-in-law William, in mind. Neither Wolsey nor Anne would give in. After some digging, the Cardinal discovered that Eleanor Carey, far from being unsullied, 'had two children by two sundry priests', and was currently the mistress of another man. Anne, who did some investigating of her own, unearthed an old scandal about Isabel Jordan. It was left to the King to arbitrate, and in the end, he decided against both ladies. 'I would not for all the gold in the world', Henry wrote to Anne, 'clog your conscience or mine' in appointing Dame Eleanor (or the equally unsuitable Dame Isabel) as Abbess.

Anne and Wolsey also disagreed over the so-called 'heretical' books being read in England. While the Cardinal was orthodox in his religion, Anne's beliefs were of a more radical sort. Though she was accused of being 'more Lutheran than Luther himself', Anne was not a Protestant. She remained a committed Catholic to her death, believing in the Eucharist, in confession and pilgrimages, and in good deeds as a means to Heaven. However, where she differed from traditionalists was in her passionate devotion to Reform. Anne was rather an 'evangelical'. She sought a better enrichment of her faith by actively debating, studying, and promoting the Word of God. At her table, Anne encouraged talk of religion, and her guests, which often included the King himself, would give 'themselves wholly in their dinners and suppers to the discussing of some doubt or other in Scripture'. When she was not arguing religion, Anne read up on it voraciously. The Humanists at the court of Margaret of Angoulême had advocated making the Bible available to the common people in their own language, rather than it being exclusive to the few who could read it in Latin. Anne took to this idea wholeheartedly, and she was to own a copy of the Bible in French, translated by Jacques Lefèvre d'Étaples, one of the scholars patronized by Margaret of Angoulême, and also one in English by William Tyndale. Her love for devotional works, particularly ones in French, was described by a visitor to the English court, Louis de Brun. In 1530, he complimented Anne on her studiousness and piety:

> 'I am not surprised that you are never to be found... without some French book in your hand which is useful and essential for teaching and discovering the true and narrow path of all virtue...I have you seen you this last Lent and the one before... reading the salutary epistles of Saint Paul, wherein are contained the whole teaching and manner of a good life.'

Anne's interest in inspirational literature was shared by her brother George. Lord Rochford was just as passionate an evangelical as his sister, and he actively sought out new books - even controversial ones - for them to study together. One that caught his attention was *A Supplication For The Beggars* by a London lawyer named Simon Fish. In it, Fish attacked the 'ravenous wolves' – the corrupt 'bishops, abbots, priors' and their sort who were seizing the riches of England from the people and from the King himself. Not only did the clergy already own 'the third part of all your realm', Fish told the King, but they were continually extorting money from his subjects by Church levies and crooked fees for their services. Furthermore, Fish wrote, the Church was most presumptuous in setting itself above the rule of kings.

Rochford advised his sister to show *A Supplication For The Beggars* to Henry VIII. They might have already supposed how Wolsey would react. As a churchman, he would be offended by Fish's attacks, and by his endeavours to distribute illegal English Bibles. Wolsey also nursed a personal grudge against Fish, as the lawyer was known to be critical of him. Ignoring what Wolsey might think, Anne brought the book to the King, imploring him to read it for himself. Henry was so taken by it that he went over the work for days. He even met with Fish, 'embrac[ing] him with loving countenance', and discussed the book with its author at length.

To the Cardinal's annoyance, Anne introduced another controversial work. William Tyndale, the translator of the Bible into English - not to mention a friend of Simon Fish - had written *The Obedience of A Christian Man* in 1528. It argued for the authority of secular rulers over the clergy, including the Pope himself. Anne had meant to show the book to the King, but it had found its way into the hands of Richard Sampson, the Dean of the King's Chapel. *The Obedience of A Christian Man* was banned in England, and the disapproving Sampson was looking to find out who had brought such a contentious work to court. But before he could report the matter to the King, Anne, swearing that 'it shall be the dearest book that ever Dean or Cardinal took away', went straight to her lover and commended the book to him. To Henry, Tyndale's book, like Fish's, was a revelation. He declared *The Obedience* was 'for me and all kings to read'.

Henry VIII's approval of the books encouraged Anne to be bolder yet. In a letter to the Cardinal written in August, she asked him to 'remember the parson of Honey Lane for my sake'. The cleric was Thomas Forman who was jailed by the Cardinal and the Bishop of London for possessing illegal publications. But Forman's plight had attracted Anne's attention, and she took him under her protection. Wolsey dared not refuse her request and he let Forman go.

In September 1528, Anne and the King were filled with excitement. Cardinal Campeggio, 'the Legate which we most desire', had arrived in Paris. Within a week, he would be in Calais, Henry told Anne, and then England at last. Campeggio's appointment as Legate had been made months ago, but there had been a delay in getting him to England. Elderly and afflicted with gout, it took him what seemed forever to reach Paris from Rome. The journey onwards to Calais, and then to Dover, also took longer than expected, and it was not until 7 October that Campeggio, exhausted and in pain, set foot in London at last.

As he could not 'ride nor walk, and could not sit without discomfort', Campeggio's audience with the King was delayed as well. When he did come to court at last on 24 October, Campeggio, following the Pope's instructions, was to dissuade Henry VIII from seeking a divorce. But after a few meetings with the King, Campeggio knew it was hopeless. 'I believe that an angel descending from Heaven would be unable to persuade him otherwise', the Cardinal moaned.

With the King determined to have his way, Campeggio tried another tactic. A trial could be avoided, he told Henry and Wolsey, if the Queen could be persuaded to step aside. Would she be willing to enter into religion, he asked? Katherine was renowned for her piety, and she might indeed welcome the idea of being a nun. It would be a solution to all their problems. Henry would get his divorce and Katherine a holy life. Charles V, abiding by his aunt's wishes, would make no more trouble on her behalf.

The three of them - Campeggio, Henry, and Wolsey - saw no reason why the Queen would refuse. The Legate was optimistic when he wrote to Rome:

> 'as she is nearly 50, and would lose nothing whatever, and as so much good would ensue, I cannot see why it should be impossible to induce her to take this course, which would be less scandalous and more secure.'

After Katherine was divorced, the King promised to treat her with great honour as his sister-in-law - the Princess Dowager as she once was. In fact, she would not be 'compelled to assume the monastic habit, or bound by any other vows than that of chastity'. She would live a life of comfortable retirement as a private gentlewoman much like the King's grandmother Elizabeth Woodville had in her final years. As a further inducement for Katherine, Princess Mary would be allowed to keep her place in the succession. Everything now hinged on Katherine.

She absolutely refused. What other answer could she give? Since she was a child in Spain, her destiny was to be Queen of England. Even after Prince Arthur died, Katherine had never given up hope of marriage to Henry, and in her resolve, endured years of humiliation. As for Campeggio's suggestion that she take the veil, Katherine was offended. While she was certainly a religious woman, she had no calling to such a vocation, she said. God had intended her to live by the sacrament of marriage, and she would not break the vows she made before Him and her husband at Greenwich nineteen years ago. She would go to her grave as King Henry's wife and Queen, Katherine declared.

Further entreaties proved useless. Her resolution 'does not much please me', Campeggio grumbled. At an impasse, he did agree to hear the Queen's confession. Upon the damnation of her soul, she swore that she had only shared a bed with Prince Arthur for no more than seven nights, and each time he had left her a virgin - 'intact and pure like when she had left her mother's womb'. Her declaration made no impression on the Cardinal. As if he were deaf to what she had said, he again proposed the nunnery, and again, Katherine refused. Her cause was just, she exclaimed, and she

> 'intended to live and die in the estate of matrimony, into which God had called her, and that she should always be of that opinion, and would not change it… that neither the whole kingdom on the one hand, nor any great punishment on the other, although she might be torn limb from limb, should compel her to alter this opinion; and that if after death she should return to life, rather than change it, she would prefer to die over again.'

To help her case, the Queen gave Campeggio permission to disclose her confession to the Pope. But that was not all. In her possession, Katherine revealed, was a copy of a papal brief her late mother had obtained from Rome. While on her deathbed, Queen Isabella had been troubled by the dispensation she had received allowing her daughter to wed Prince Henry. In describing Katherine's previous marriage to Arthur Tudor, Pope Julius had used certain terminology implying that it had indeed been consummated. Isabella, who had always believed the contrary, was greatly displeased. To placate the dying Queen of Spain, the Vatican issued a papal brief changing the wording to *perhaps* – the marriage had only *perhaps* been consummated.

When Katherine publicly presented the brief, accusations of forgery were made against her. She stood her ground. While hers was indeed a copy, the Queen stated, the original did exist and was in the Imperial archives with the Emperor. Katherine was reluctant to send for it as she feared it would be surreptitiously destroyed once it reached England. Nonetheless, she was ordered to 'use all possible means and diligence to recover the brief, wherever it be'. But Charles V, under his aunt's secret instructions, refused to hand it over to the Wolsey's court, saying that 'he should then consent to [its] jurisdiction; which he will not'. However, Charles did allow a notarised copy to be made and sent to England.

On 31 May 1529, Wolsey and Campeggio formally opened the trial. It was not until 21 June, that both the King and the Queen appeared before them at Blackfriars. There, the Parliament Chamber was set up with 'tables, benches, and bars, like a consistory, a place judicial'. The two Cardinals presided upon a dais. To one side of them was the King sitting under a cloth of estate, and to the other, the

Queen, 'some distance beneath' him. In the midst were the nobles, the bishops, and the experts in canon law for each side. Henry's team was represented by Doctor Richard Sampson, while John Fisher, the Bishop of Rochester, supported Katherine.

When all was in readiness, the crier called for silence. The Pope's commission setting out the cause of the hearing was read out, and both parties were summoned. Henry was first. 'King Henry of England, come into the court!' 'Here my lords,' he answered. After Henry opened with a short speech stating how his conscience had troubled him 'from the very beginning' regarding his marriage, Katherine was called. 'Katherine Queen of England, come into the court!' 'Here my lords', she answered in her 'broken English'. Even after so many years away from her native Spain, Katherine never lost her accent.

Henry's declaration about his long-held doubts touched a nerve in Katherine. She confronted him saying, 'It was not the time to say this after so long silence'. That was only because of the 'great love he had and has for her', Henry retorted. He assured the court that nothing would please him more than to have his marriage found to be in good standing. However, Henry protested, the Queen's continual request to have the case revoked to Rome was unreasonable. Equally irrational was his wife's insistence that she would not get a fair trial in England. The country was 'perfectly secure for her', the King said, and he had given her the best legal counsel possible.

To this, Katherine made no reply, but rose from her chair. Unable to make straight for the King because of the packed court, she 'took pain' to reach him on the other side. Everyone watched as Katherine, her face impassive, made a circuit around the chamber. When she came before Henry at last, she stopped and fell to her knees. She addressed him directly:

> 'Sir, I beseech you for all the loves that hath been between us, and for the love of God, let me have justice and right. Take of me some pity and compassion, for I am a poor woman, and a stranger born out of your dominion. I have here no assured friend, and much less indifferent counsel. I flee to *you* as the head of justice within this realm.'

Henry shifted uncomfortably in his chair as Katherine went on. 'Wherein have I offended you, or what occasion of displeasure?', she asked piteously. For close to twenty years, she had always been a 'true and humble wife', conforming herself to him entirely. She took interest in all things he did, and those whom he loved, she did too - even if they were her enemies. As for their many children, their deaths were the will of God, and not any fault of her own, Katherine reminded Henry.

Touching her virginity, in a firm voice, Katherine swore that 'when ye had me at the first… I was a true maid without touch or man'. She even challenged Henry to deny it on his conscience. Katherine had a last request to make of him. She begged to be spared this court – one so prejudiced against her - until she received advice from her friends in Spain. 'And if ye will not extend to me so much indifferent favour,' she said finally, 'your pleasure then be fulfilled, and *to God* I commit my cause!'

The Queen rose to her feet. Instead of returning to her place, she swept out of the court. When told she must return, Katherine looked straight ahead. "On, on", she said, not stopping, "it maketh no matter, for it is no indifferent court for me, therefore I will *not* tarry".

Katherine made good on her vow not to appear before the tribunal again. Wolsey and Campeggio had no choice but to declare her contumacious, and the hearing continued. Absenting herself from the proceedings, the Queen was spared the indignity of reliving her first wedding night in public. Depositions, taken over the summer from those present at the nuptials twenty-eight years ago, were introduced in open court. Most were damaging to Katherine's case. The Marquis of Dorset, for example, remembered Prince Arthur's 'good and sanguine complexion' during his honeymoon; a sure sign he had sex with his wife. Others, less certain, expressed the view that Arthur and Katherine most probably consummated their marriage, being old enough. Sir Anthony Willoughby certainly thought so after what Arthur allegedly told him. He recalled how on the morning after, the Prince had poked his head out of the bedchamber and asked for a drink. "I have been this night", the young bridegroom boasted, "in the *midst* of Spain". Marriage, Arthur said, was thirsty work!

Still, the Queen was not without her defenders. One of the few to testify on her behalf was the Bishop of Ely. He affirmed how Katherine had told him in person that 'on the testimony of her conscience', Prince Arthur never knew her carnally. Unfortunately, up against so colourful a statement like Willoughby's, the Bishop's sober recollection made less of an impact on the court.

After weeks of listening to witnesses and of hearing arguments from lawyers representing both the King and the Queen, Cardinal Campeggio made an unexpected move. Under orders from the Pope to delay and to make no judgement, he suspended all proceedings on 23 July. It was the custom in Rome, the Cardinal declared, to close all courts in midsummer. The trial would resume in the autumn.

Wolsey knew it was a ruse. But he could not stop Campeggio, and for that he was ruined. In October, the Cardinal was charged with *praemunire* – that is his loyalty was to the authority of Rome *before* that of his own sovereign lord the King. Wolsey was deprived of his office of Lord Chancellor, along with his many other powers and responsibilities. His great London residence York Place was seized (the Cardinal had already given Hampton Court away to Henry VIII as a gift in 1528), and he was exiled in disgrace to his archdiocese of York, which he was allowed to retain.

Later when Wolsey tried to raise himself up again, his enemies, including Anne Boleyn and the Duke of Norfolk, were ready to pounce. The Cardinal was arrested, and by Henry Percy of all people. He was accused of trying to regain his authority by treasonable means, and he was ordered to the Tower of London to await trial. Wolsey already knew what the result would be. He had failed his master in obtaining the divorce, and for that, Lady Anne, who had once vowed to work him 'much displeasure', would see his head on the block.

Wolsey managed to cheat Anne Boleyn of her revenge. On his way to London, the mortally ill Cardinal stopped over at the Abbey of Leicester. Telling the abbot he had come to 'leave my bones among you', Wolsey expired shortly after on 29 November 1530.

Throughout the divorce proceedings, the very sight of Katherine of Aragon was enough to stir a crowd into a frenzy. The people shouted out encouragement and 'wished her victory over her enemies'. Ladies in particular were the Queen's most fervent supporters. 'If the matter was to be decided by women', the French ambassador remarked, 'he (the King) would lose the battle'. It was they who cheered the loudest for Katherine, 'telling her to care for nothing, and other such words'. They were especially offended that Henry VIII would put away such an exemplary Queen, wife, and mother so he could gratify his lust for a younger woman. The people's love for Katherine was matched by their hatred for Anne Boleyn. To them, she was but plain 'Nan Bullen', 'a poor knight's daughter', and a 'naughty paikie' (a prostitute). Whenever Anne and the King rode out in public, she was often subjected to much 'hooting and hissing'.

Her fiercest critic was Elizabeth Barton, a young nun claiming to receive messages from the heavenly angels and the Mother of God Herself. By her reputation as a 'good, simple, and saintly woman', Barton was revered as 'the Holy Maid of Kent'. Great crowds gathered to hear her revelations, and her celebrity even won her prominent friends at court. Sir Thomas More, who replaced Wolsey as Lord Chancellor, and who was sympathetic to the Queen, 'gave much faith' to her prophesies, as did Bishop Fisher and the Marchioness of Exeter – two other supporters of Katherine.

In the beginning, the Nun of Kent's utterings were fairly innocuous – exhortations to the people to amend their lives and to shun heresy, but as Henry VIII's divorce became more contentious, so did her pronouncements. Dame Elizabeth was heard to say how the King must put away the Lady Anne - lest 'the vengeance of God should plague him'. Astonishingly, she was not punished for it. The young woman was too popular to proceed against, and the King even agreed to meet with her one time. Intending to buy her silence, he offered to make her an abbess. The offer was refused, and the Nun returned to her convent to stir up more trouble.

The many attacks on Anne Boleyn only served to make her bolder. During Christmas of 1530, Anne and her servants were seen wearing her new motto *Ainsi sera, groigne qui groigne! (Let those who would grumble do so!)* embroidered on their clothes at court. But behind Anne's defiance, there was also anxiety – worry that time and opportunity were passing her by. After years of waiting, she had yet to achieve the Crown. Katherine was still Queen, and she was still the King's mistress. Overwrought, Anne did not hold back even when speaking to Henry. Once, she railed at him saying, "I have been waiting long, and might in the meantime have contracted some advantageous marriage. But alas! Farewell to my time and youth spent to no purpose at all!"

Frustrated as she was, Anne was still determined to be Queen no matter what it took. She was becoming 'fiercer than a lioness', her enemies said. All Spaniards, Anne declared wildly to one of the Queen's ladies, should be 'at the bottom of the sea!' When told she must not say such things, Anne laughed. She cared nothing for Katherine, she cried, and would 'rather see her hanged than confess she is my mistress!'

In August 1529, a possible solution to his dilemma reached the ears of the King. Stephen Gardiner and Edward Fox told Henry VIII about a clever priest they had recently met; his name was Thomas Cranmer. Cranmer had offered a suggestion to the King's marital woes. What His Majesty ought to be doing, he proposed, was to solicit the opinions of the universities of Europe about the legality of his marriage, rather than to leave it up to the ecclesiastical courts. Their verdict, he believed, would 'compel any judge soon to come to a definite sentence'. When Gardiner and Fox reported this novel idea to the King, he was excited. 'I perceive that the man hath the sow by the right ear!' Henry exclaimed, and he summoned Cranmer to court.

After meeting Thomas Cranmer, an impressed Henry employed him right away. He was to help gather opinions from the universities and to 'write [his] mind therein' on the divorce, particularly on how the pope 'had no such authority, as whereby he might dispense with the Word of God and the Scripture'. As for his upkeep, the King made it the responsibility of the Boleyns. It was at Durham House that Cranmer, himself inclined to Reform, became acquainted with the religiously sympathetic Anne. In time, he would declare himself 'most bound unto her', even when that friendship proved deadly to him.

As Henry and Anne gained a new ally in Thomas Cranmer, in the autumn of 1529, the Queen found her own in Eustace Chapuys. Sophisticated, witty, and diligent, the new Imperial ambassador was to be Katherine's most zealous supporter. So dedicated was he to her cause that he would go beyond his duty, dabbling in intrigue and treason for Katherine's sake, often forgetting he was putting her in danger. Still, the ambassador always had the Queen's interests at heart, and winning her lasting gratitude as her 'especial friend'.

Chapuys detested Anne Boleyn. To the envoy, she was the absolute antithesis of the good-hearted and noble Katherine. 'The Lady', as he called her, was cruel and immoral; an adventuress greedy for a crown. But even Chapuys had to admit that Anne's hold over the King was remarkable. In November 1530, the envoy had a private audience with Henry VIII. They conversed pleasantly for a while, but then the King's mood suddenly changed. He began speaking of the divorce in angry tones, and he heaped abuse on the Emperor, complaining how Charles was meddling in his affairs. The ambassador was bewildered at first, but then from the corner of his eye, he noticed 'the Lady' spying on him and the King from a window. Henry had seen her too, and not wanting Anne to think he was soft in his dealings with the Emperor, put on a show of belligerence to impress her. Once the two were out of Anne's sight and hearing, the King was back to his affable self.

The Christmas of 1530 was observed with the usual solemnities culminating with revels on Twelfth Night. 'According to the old custom', the King and Queen sat in the great hall and presided over 'divers interludes, rich masques, and disports'. Afterwards, there was the traditional 'great banquet' to mark the end of another Christmas.

The festivities were as grand and full of cheer as any in years past, but Katherine could find no joy in them that season. She was under tremendous stress as it was, and relations between her and her husband were increasingly tense. They often quarrelled, and their latest row occurred only recently on Christmas Eve. Unable to contain herself, Katherine confronted Henry, complaining how he was ignoring her for his mistress and inviting great dishonour on himself. Henry protested. There was nothing indecent or scandalous in his relationship with Anne Boleyn, he shot back. He was in her company only to learn more about her character as he was *resolved to make her his wife*. – not words Katherine wanted to hear.

Adding to her troubles were the momentous events of late. On the advice of Thomas Cromwell - a crafty lawyer whose 'vigilance and diligence… ability and promptitude both in evil and good' had brought him to royal attention - the King bullied the English clergy into submission. The Church of Rome, it was obvious, would never grant him his divorce, but the Church of England, directly under his power, would. Before the year was out, the whole of the English clergy was charged with *praemunire*, as Wolsey had been. Remembering his fate, the churchmen put up no resistance and collectively pled guilty. To ensure the King's goodwill, they even agreed to surrender £100,000 towards his coffers. But that was not enough. Henry also demanded that the clergy's allegiance to Rome be completely severed. The pope had no authority in his realm, and it was he, Henry VIII, who must be recognised as 'Supreme Head of the Church and Clergy in England'. Browbeaten already, the clergy gave in. On 11 February 1531, they assented to his title after the King agreed to the addition of the proviso 'as far as the law of Christ allows'. But as far as Henry was concerned, there was no distinction between divine law and his right to rule absolutely even in matters spiritual. Thus, the 'law of Christ', far from restricting his powers, would allow him great leeway.

While Katherine grieved, her rival rejoiced. Anne made such good cheer over the latest change of events that it seemed 'as if she had actually gained Paradise'. Soon she would be Queen, if she was not one already. Since Wolsey fell, the King had installed her at York Place, or Whitehall as it was now called, where Anne, dazzling in the innumerable jewels Henry had given her, held court as if she were already first lady of the land.

Meanwhile, Katherine had to be tolerated still - but for how much longer? From the day the divorce proceedings began, she had insisted she would never abandon the King. More recently, she reasserted her position. 'I would not leave him', Katherine declared, 'not for my daughter nor anyone else in this world'. True to her word, she presided at court with the King while they were at Windsor Castle together that summer.

At last, Henry decided that if Katherine would not leave him, he must part from her. On 14 July 1531, after twenty-two years of marriage, he left his wife for good. He wanted no scenes. Accompanied by Anne Boleyn, Henry slipped quietly out of Windsor Castle.

PART 3
THE BLACK QUEEN: ANNE BOLEYN

Then she said, Master Kingston, shall I die without justice?
And I said, the poorest subject the King hath, hath justice.
And therewith she laughed.
(Report of Sir William Kingston on Anne Boleyn's imprisonment,
May 1536)

Figure 8   Anne Boleyn by an Unknown Artist
Hampton Court Palace, Photo © 2016 MadeGlobal

Chapter 10
The Most Happy

WHEN HENRY VIII and Anne Boleyn returned to Windsor, there was no more trace of Katherine of Aragon. She had been commanded to leave the castle and to take up residence elsewhere, even away from her daughter Mary. Heartbroken, Katherine submitted herself to the King's will, saying she would even go to the Tower if he so ordered.

Anne would have been happy to see Katherine in a prison, but the King would not have it so. Taken to The More, a great house in Hertfordshire, Katherine was still acknowledged as Queen and was treated as such. She was given a staff of two hundred, and she was even allowed to hold court. When she dined in state, Katherine was served by fifty waiters and butlers, while thirty maids of honour hovered about her. At public appearances such as these, Katherine was always aware of the need to uphold her dignity. Allowing no one to pity her as the King's discarded wife, she affected an air of cheerfulness - always smiling as if she had not a care in the world. Nonetheless, it was no secret how miserable she was.

Another step closer to being Queen, Anne, in joyful anticipation of her triumph, spent the summer preparing her 'royal estate'. She appointed a priest to be her almoner and assembled 'several other officers about her person'. Those sympathetic to Katherine would have no place at court. But not everyone was intimidated by Anne. Sir Henry Guildford, the Comptroller of the Royal Household and an old friend of the King, was unwavering in his loyalty to Katherine. Anne gave him a warning. When she was Queen, she threatened, she would deprive him of his office. Guildford stood his ground. He would save her the trouble, he retorted, for he would quit first!

Anne's expectation to be married in 'three or four months at the latest' was premature. Cardinal Campeggio had closed the proceedings at Blackfriars and the case had never been resumed. It was revoked to the Vatican, and in December, the King was summoned to Rome to plead in person. Henry was furious. He placed great blame on the Queen and her friends, for 'it was neither reasonable nor honourable that [he] should on that account abandon his kingdom, and that neither she, nor those who guided these affairs in Rome, took the right course to come to a feasible and loving end of this business.'

In her defence, Katherine argued that the pope 'was the only true sovereign and vicar of God, who had power to judge of spiritual matters, of which marriage was one'. As for Henry's new title of 'Supreme Head of the Church,' she was dismissive.

'She considered the King as her sovereign, and would therefore serve and obey him. He was also sovereign in his realm, as far as regards temporal jurisdiction; but as to the spiritual, it was not pleasing to God either that the King should so intend, or that she should consent.'

But the Pope's authority, which the Queen continued to uphold, suffered another blow in 1532. In March, the Commons, spearheaded by Thomas Cromwell, submitted to Parliament a list of grievances against the clergy entitled *The Supplication Against the Ordinaries*. Among the complaints were the ecclesiastical fees to which the Church believed itself entitled. Obligatory payments to the clergy had long been resented by English laymen who still remembered the injustice done to poor Richard Hunne.

In 1514, Hunne, a merchant-tailor of 'honest reputation', was imprisoned by the Bishop of London and his chancellor, Doctor William Horsey. The charge? Hunne had refused to surrender his dead child's rich shroud to a curate who claimed it as a mortuary fee. For his defiance, Hunne was accused of heresy. But before he was brought to trial, he was found hanged in his cell. The Bishop, who attributed the crime to the sin of suicide, had Hunne's body burnt in public 'to the abomination of the people'. There was further outrage when an inquest by the civic authorities confirmed suspicions of murder. Horsey, whom many believed was the killer, was set free. The scandal created much anti-clerical sentiment, which had not dissipated by the time the Reformation Parliament met in 1532.

Along with the fees charged by the English clergy, Parliament addressed those paid to the Vatican with a bill entitled *The Act of Conditional Restraint of Annates*. It had long been a requirement that when a new bishop was consecrated, his first year's income was sent to Rome. But with the Act, should the King allow to it be enforced, the pope would only receive a mere fraction, just five percent, of what he was owed. The *Restraint of Annates* was clearly meant to put pressure on Clement VII.

Two months later, an even bolder strategy was put in place to obtain the divorce. On 11 May, the King summoned the Speaker of the House to him, along with a delegation of Lords and Commons. In addressing them, Henry aired his displeasure about how the clergy of England was 'but half our subjects', and scarcely that. They 'make an oath to the Pope, clean contrary to the oath that they make to us', he said, 'so that they seem to be *his* subjects, and not ours'. Henry would not tolerate loyalty to two masters, and he charged the Lords and Commons to obtain the Church's entire obedience to the Crown. It took only four days for the clergy to buckle.

Encouraged by the Church's surrender, Henry and Anne now looked to the backing of France. Francis I had not always been a friend to England, but now he was supportive of Henry's impending marriage. To the French King, Katherine was expendable by virtue of her ties to the Emperor. Francis had not forgotten how her nephew had kept him and his sons prisoners after the defeat at Pavia, and how Charles had forced him as a widower (Queen Claude had died in 1524) to marry his sister Eleanor. A meeting between the two Kings was planned with Henry and Anne sailing across the Channel in October. There was however, a problem. Which great lady would receive Mistress Boleyn in France? Francis's Hapsburg Queen was out of the question. Anne herself had hoped that the King's sister, Margaret of Angoulême, whom she remembered from her days in France, would do her the honour, but she was unavailable. When the high-ranking Duchess of Vendôme was proposed, the idea was quickly squashed. The Duchess had a reputation for being notoriously promiscuous. In the end, it was decided that in the absence of a suitable French hostess, Anne would meet Francis only in private.

In preparation, she was awarded a great title. On 1 September, at Windsor Castle, Anne, 'completely covered with the most costly jewels', was led before the King and his nobles. Observing the expressions of those standing by, she held her head high savouring her triumph. The Duke of Suffolk, for one, was no friend to her. Charles Brandon resented the influence of the Boleyns at court, and he regarded Anne as an arrogant parvenu, as did his wife, Mary. As a long-time friend of Katherine of Aragon, the French Queen did not approve of her former lady-in-waiting usurping her sister-in-law's place. Earlier, when she found herself having to surrender precedence to Anne, Mary indignantly withdrew from court. Needless to say, when she was asked to accompany Henry and Anne to France, Mary refused.

At Suffolk's side was the Duke of Norfolk, another one of Anne's critics. There was no love lost between uncle and niece. While it was certainly advantageous to the Howards to have one of their own raised so high, Norfolk personally found Anne insufferable. Outspoken and abrasive, she did not spare him her razor tongue, and as for her religious opinions, they were too radical for his tastes. But Norfolk, like Brandon and the other nobles who disliked Anne just as much, wisely kept his silence. He watched as Anne knelt before the King, and from his hands received her mantle and coronet as Marquis of Pembroke. It was a most unconventional creation as the rank of Marquis was traditionally held by a man. But then again, there was little that was conventional when it came to his niece, Norfolk sighed.

Although the title of Queen still eluded her, the Lady Marchioness of Pembroke as Anne was more commonly referred to, was nonetheless determined to go to France looking like one. She spent vast sums on new dresses, and she packed chests full of the rich ornaments the King had given to her during their courtship. But even her own jewels were deemed insufficient; Anne had to have Katherine's as well. As they were still in her rival's possession, she got the King to send a messenger for them. But when asked to hand over her jewels, Katherine put her foot down. It was against her conscience, she exclaimed, to give them to a woman who was 'a scandal to the whole of Christendom, and a cause of infamy to the King'. Only when Henry sent an *order*, not a request, did Katherine obey.

With great hopes for their future together, Henry and Anne left for Dover on 7 October. There had been much murmuring at their departure. Those who watched them leave from Greenwich spoke uneasily of the many strange signs of late. 'A dead fish of marvellous size' was washed ashore in the North, and a great comet, first seen three weeks ago, was still blazing across the heavens. And just a day after the couple left, great tides appeared in the Thames. For nine hours, the flood waters rose so high they even lapped the walls of the chapel at Greenwich, 'a thing never hitherto seen or heard of'.

Along with these weird omens, the King's intentions were much mused on by the people. Some said he had it in mind to wed a French princess, but others insisted that he would take the Lady Anne instead.

Though Henry and Anne had indeed considered marrying in France, the idea was later abandoned. It was just as well as Anne had set her sights on a glittering wedding in England. She would be married, she insisted, in Westminster Abbey, the 'usual place appointed for the marriage and coronation of queens'; no other place would do.

They set sail from Dover on 11 October. When they landed at Calais, Henry went ahead to Boulogne to fetch Francis while Anne stayed behind at the Palace of The Exchequer. As the two Kings renewed their friendship in rounds of feasts and entertainments, calling each other 'brother' as they did at the Field of the Cloth of Gold, Anne prepared for her meeting with the French King. After Francis's arrival, she and her women, all disguised and wearing 'gowns of strange fashion', made their entrance following supper. The ladies selected partners from the men present, and together they danced. During the revelry, Henry removed their masks, and as expected, Francis found himself dancing with the King of England's sweetheart. Did Francis remember Anne from her days of service to his late wife Claude? Perhaps. Even if not, he was captivated by for her exquisite manners and by her excellent command of the French language - so unique in an Englishwoman. Before the evening ended, the two spent some time in conversation. Anne, no doubt, reminisced about her happy years in France, and mindful of why she had now returned, invoked Francis's help towards her marriage.

≡

Coming home in November, Anne was confident that her wedding and coronation would take place soon enough. Francis had promised to put pressure on the Pope and to come to England's aid should the Emperor prove aggressive. The support of France was a turning point in Anne's relationship with the King. Sometime, at the end of 1532, she and Henry at last made love together in the fullest sense. By January, Anne suspected she was pregnant. The happy event drove the couple to a momentous decision. They could no longer wait for the divorce to be finalised. For their child – the heir to the English Crown - to be born legitimate, they *must* wed immediately.

Instead of a great public ceremony at Westminster like Anne had hoped for, it was performed at Whitehall on 25 January 1533 'very early before day'. Only a handful of witnesses were present. It was later reported that none of them even knew why there were summoned that dawn until they came before the happy couple. After Henry and Anne had been declared man and wife, all were sworn to secrecy.

Even Thomas Cranmer, busy working towards the divorce, had not been told of it. He did not learn about the nuptials until two weeks afterwards. That the news was kept even from him was odd, considering the great plans Henry VIII had in store for Cranmer. In August 1532, William Warham, the aged Archbishop of Canterbury had died. Warham's efforts in the Great Matter had always been half-hearted, and his death opened the way for a successor who would truly commit himself to obtaining the King's divorce. That autumn, Cranmer, who was on embassy to the Emperor, was summoned home to take Warham's place. Despite Cranmer's known support for Henry and Anne, the Pope, afraid the King would make good on his promise to cut off English church revenues to Rome, gave his assent. The papal bulls confirming the appointment were dispatched, and in March 1533, Thomas Cranmer was consecrated Archbishop of Canterbury.

With a primate of his making ready to pronounce on the divorce, at last, the King had Anne publicly acknowledged as Queen of England on Easter Saturday. Dressed in gold and loaded with jewels (many confiscated from her rival), Anne was conducted to Mass with sixty young ladies to wait upon her. At the service, she was prayed for as Queen, in place of Katherine. 'All the world is astonished at it for it looks like a dream', Chapuys wrote depressingly to the Emperor, 'and even those who take her part know not whether to laugh or to cry'.

Still, Mistress Boleyn's sudden elevation could not have been a total surprise. Two months before in February, Anne, unable to keep a secret, informed the court in her own inimitable way that she was sleeping with the King. Bursting into a hall full of courtiers, she sought out an old admirer, probably Sir Thomas Wyatt. Teasingly, Anne told him how she recently had a sudden 'fierce desire to eat apples'. The King, she said, took her craving as *a sign she was with child!* As everyone gasped in astonishment. Anne took off laughing, leaving them speechless. Even Henry himself had dropped hints. At a banquet given in Anne's apartments that same month, the King, while chatting with her step-grandmother the Dowager Duchess of Norfolk, drew the old lady's attention to a sideboard piled high with gold plate; a gift from himself. It all belonged to Anne, he told the Duchess, asking whether she had ever seen such a 'great dowry' before?

To give Anne's new title legitimacy, on Good Friday, the day before Anne was publicly proclaimed Queen, Cranmer, as the new primate of England, asked permission from the King to reopen the inquiry into his first marriage, 'as much bruit exists among the common people on the subject'. Consent was granted of course. Neither the King nor Katherine were present in court that May at Dunstable. From nearby Ampthill, her current place of banishment, Katherine, as she had done at Blackfriars, refused to recognise the tribunal's authority. Her absence only made Cranmer's work easier for him. It took the new Archbishop only a week to reach his decision. On 23 May, Henry VIII's marriage of twenty-four years to 'the Lady Katherine' was finally declared 'void and of no effect'.

Even before Cranmer's verdict was delivered, preparations for Anne Boleyn's coronation were well under way. At the beginning of May, the City of London was ordered to make ready for the great day. Given such short notice to 'solemnize and celebrate the coronation of his most dear and beloved wife Queen Anne at Westminster the Whitsunday next ensuing', the City had to scramble. The streets and buildings on the processional route were cleaned and decorated, and artisans were put to work erecting pageants in honour of the new Queen.

The drapers and tailors had their hands full too. Imported silks, satins, velvets, brocades, damasks, and the much-prized cloths of gold and silver had to be acquisitioned to be made into clothes, trappings, and hangings. The many officials assigned to organise the coronation were no less busy themselves. Great quantities of food had to be obtained to feed all the 'lords, knights and squires… which came to London', not to mention their armies of servants. As well, lodgings in the already crowded city had to be found for all of them. There was also the coordinating of the river pageant, the city procession, the ceremony in the Abbey, and the closing banquet to consider. The preparations went around the clock, and it was not until the evening of 28 May, that the exhausted Londoners rested at last.

As if Heaven itself was blessing the King's new marriage, 29 May was glorious with 'no finer or more serene weather'. The sky was bright and clear, and a brilliant sun was rising above the turrets of the palace as Anne could see from her windows at Greenwich that morning. As excited as she was to set out to the city, she had to wait until the middle of the afternoon when the Lord Mayor and his party arrived to escort her to London.

At 3 o'clock, Anne, dressed in cloth of gold, stepped onto the pier where she was greeted by a 'goodly sight'. There, floating on the river before her, were fifty barges including one belonging to the Mayor, and the others to the various city companies. Each vessel was adorned with arms and escutcheons identifying the guild it belonged to, and with streamers and metallic cloths that shimmered in the sun. As impressive as these barges were, Anne's was even grander, for it had belonged to Katherine of Aragon. Stripped of her badges, it was now adorned with the Boleyn arms combined with those of the King.

As Anne and her entourage sailed leisurely towards the capital, boats along the way – about two hundred of them by one count - joined in the procession in a carefully choreographed parade. The Thames was so congested, an observer wrote, that it appeared as if the entire stretch of water from Greenwich to the Tower of London was occupied. Leading the fleet was a barge made in the shape of a Welsh dragon, the emblem of the King's father. To the delight of the spectators watching from the riverbanks, it spurted fire from its nostrils. Nearby were costumed 'monsters and wild men', shouting and dancing as they cast flames into the water. Lest their 'hideous noise' was too much for Anne, musicians serenaded her with instruments. Their 'sweet harmony' was only interrupted by the loud salvoes fired by ships moored along the Thames, and by the 'marvellous shot' of ordnance that greeted Anne when she finally landed at the water steps of the Tower.

On the wharf, Anne was greeted by Sir William Kingston, the Constable of the Tower. He led Anne through the crowd towards the drawbridge leading into the great citadel. There, standing beneath the Byward Tower entrance was the King himself. In sight of all, Henry VIII embraced his wife, and with a 'joyful countenance' laid his hands on her swollen belly, signifying the fruitfulness of his new marriage. Turning around, he then thanked the citizens with 'many goodly words' for welcoming their new mistress to London. The couple then walked inside to the royal apartments where they spent the next two days in seclusion in preparation for Anne's day of glory.

Anne emerged in public again on Whitsunday Eve. She was seen leaving the Tower in a 'costly and rich' open litter of white cloth of gold pulled by two white palfreys. Even Anne herself was in white from head to toe. Sitting in her litter, she would have been almost inconspicuous, if not for the contrast of her olive skin and her long dark hair flowing down her back.

The procession, extending some half-mile in length, made its way from the Tower towards Westminster. As Anne travelled the length of the city, the Barons of the Cinque Ports bore a canopy above her, shielding her from the heat of the sun. Ahead of them rode the justices, knights, nobles, and members of the clergy, including Archbishop Cranmer, who was to perform the sacred ritual of crowning the next day.

They all stopped at Fenchurch Street where a band of children, 'apparelled as merchants', saluted their new Queen with verses both in English and in French. The latter, no doubt, was in tribute to Anne's Francophilia and to the French ambassador and his party who accompanied her, demonstrating their master's support for the marriage.

After the children had finished their orations, the Queen moved on to Gracechurch Street. There, towering above her was a tableau, designed by the artist Hans Holbein, representing Mount Parnassus of Greek legend. Enthroned on the summit was Apollo with a fountain before him running with Rhenish wine. Around the sun god were the Muses playing on musical instruments. At their feet were placards with verses inscribed in golden letters praising Anne.

Further along the route, by Leaden Hall, was another pageant in the shape of a castle. Beneath it was a grassy mound with a wooden stump. As Anne watched, a child, joined by others portraying St Anne and members of her family, welcomed her. As everyone listened, the Queen was compared to her namesake. As St Anne counted Christ, the Apostle James, and John the Baptist as her descendants, so would her earthly counterpart produce 'such issue and descent' herself to 'the sure felicity and hope' of England.

When the child had finished, the audience's attention was diverted to the stump in the midst of the pageant. To the amazement of the onlookers, 'a multitude of white and red roses curiously wrought' suddenly sprang to life from it. Then, from behind a painted cloud above the castle, a white falcon (probably a mechanical contraption) swooped down. As it perched itself on the rose covered stump, an angel descended and set an Imperial diadem on its head, creating a tableau of Anne's personal device of the crowned white falcon. A ballad was then sung praising this bird 'of power regal' that had alighted on the Tudor rose (that is Henry VIII) to 'build her nest' to bring forth England's much-desired Prince.

Anne continued to the next set of presentations, nodding and waving to the crowd as she went. But her smiles became increasingly strained. Despite the festive appearance of the city with its 'goodly show' of banners and free-flowing fountains of wine, there was a conspicuous lack of enthusiasm from the citizens. They had come out in droves to see Anne Boleyn, but few offered up the customary salutation of 'God save the Queen!' Many also kept their caps on when she passed, prompting Anne's fool to joke aloud how they must all have 'scurvy heads, and dare not uncover'.

As her litter went by, the people glared silently at 'Nan Bullen', muttering of her behaviour. They whispered disapprovingly about how she had dethroned good Queen Katherine, and how she sat in her place looking haughty. To add further insult, the usurper was 'big with child', which she took no pains to hide. There were even sniggers of laughter. The passage through the city was decorated with Henry and Anne's initials entwined in love knots. To the annoyance of the city officials who were ordered to see to the people's good behaviour, the citizens mockingly read the *HA*'s as 'ha ha ha's!'

Hostile foreign observers were delighted by the English's disdain for Anne, and they compiled tales of her shortcomings – many highly imaginative - to send home. Anne, ran one, was a lady of low-born manners. When she was presented with a gift of cash by the city officials, unlike the noble Katherine who generously distributed the money among her attendants immediately, the greedy new Queen kept the purse to herself. Anne was also quite the sight, went another story. As if the *HA*'s were not amusing enough, ears belonging to a mule walking near her litter, when viewed from a certain angle seemed to belong to Anne herself! Also, her crown did not fit her properly, some said, and she was wearing a high ruff only to cover an unflattering goitre on her neck, others whispered. Such tales were certainly untrue, but Anne's enemies made the most of them. It was even reported that if one looked closely enough, one could see that her dress was decorated with a malevolent design of tongues pierced with nails - 'to show the treatment which those who spoke against her might expect'!

The response of the commons and the tales of the scandalmongers mattered little to Anne on this day. She, who had once adopted the motto *groigne qui groigne*, remained defiant in the face of her enemies. After all, was she not *The Most Happy* as her new device proclaimed? Even the nobles, many of whom had looked down on her, bowed the knee to her today. It gave Anne great satisfaction to see the Duke of Suffolk act as her High Constable, even if his wife Mary was a no-show. Steadfastly devoted to her sister-in-law Katherine still, the French Queen refused to acknowledge her brother's new wife. But her presence counted for little. Mary had exiled herself from court for some years, and she was in fact now dying from a wasting disease. Besides the ailing French Queen, there were two other notable absentees among the senior ladies of the realm. Neither the King's daughter, nor Anne's aunt, the high-ranking Duchess of Norfolk, took their places at the coronation either. Both ladies were unequivocal in their loyalty to Katherine, and they too refused to pay tribute to the new Queen.

At the Palace of Westminster, Anne stepped out from her litter in the middle of the great hall. On the dais beneath a royal cloth of estate, she and her ladies took refreshment. She drank a toast to the assembly and then retired to her chamber. Later in the evening, Anne went privately by barge to Whitehall to be with the King. Their reunion was only spoiled by Anne's caustic remark about the insolence of the Londoners. She liked the city well enough, she told Henry, but she heard few tongues and saw many covered heads.

By the following day, 1 June, the hostility of her subjects was forgotten by Anne. Robed in purple, she stood in the great hall again, ready to proceed to the Abbey for her moment of triumph. Her long train was carried by her step-grandmother, the old Dowager Duchess of Norfolk, who stood in for the Queen's disapproving aunt. Followed by her ladies clad in scarlet, Anne came before the high altar. After 'divers ceremonies used before her', she received a sceptre of gold and a rod of ivory. Cranmer then stepped forward with the crown. With great solemnity, he set it upon Anne's head as the choir burst out in a joyful *Te Deum*.

≡

Not long after her coronation, Anne remarked to the Venetian ambassador how God Himself had inspired the King to take her for his wife. It appeared foolish to contradict her. Heaven had exalted Anne Boleyn, making her Queen of England and blessing her with a child in her womb. Surely it would be a son, a Prince of Wales who would bring a 'golden world' to the English, as foretold in the verses celebrating her coronation. In raising Anne, God had scattered her enemies as well. Wolsey was dead, and Katherine, though still very much alive, was shut away in the country.

Anne's euphoria extended into the summer months. 'Pastime in the Queen's chamber', her Vice-Chamberlain said, 'was never more'. At her court, there were days and nights of music making, dancing, gambling, and other amusements. Gone were Katherine's dowdy old matrons. Anne surrounded herself with companions young and high-spirited as herself. Chief among them was her brother George, recently returned from embassy in France. Lord Rochford, besides being a devoted evangelical like his sister, was known for his wit and for his way with the ladies. Matching Rochford in his sexual prowess was the rakish Francis Weston. Although he was a married man, Weston was flirting with Anne's pretty cousin Madge Shelton, using the Queen's quarters as their trysting place. So popular was Mistress Shelton, that Sir Henry Norris, a favourite of the King, sought her out in the royal apartments too. Even Henry VIII took pleasure in the new gaiety. He seemed revitalized, observed the courtier Sir John Russell, and was never 'merrier of a great while than he is now'.

No one could threaten Henry and Anne's bliss – not even the Pope. In July, outraged by the King's secret marriage, Clement VII ordered Henry on pain of excommunication to abandon Anne. He was also charged to take back Katherine by the end of September. Should he refuse, the Pope warned, he would be denied the Sacraments of the Church, and would face an armed holy crusade against him. But Clement's threats of war rang hollow without any French or Imperial troops to back them. Neither Francis I, nor Charles V lifted a finger against schismatic England. The French King remained steadfast as Henry's ally, and the Emperor, who still valued diplomatic ties with his uncle, however strained they were, ignored the pope.

Helpless as she was, Katherine of Aragon remained defiant. Her resolve was unshakable – *she* was Henry's Queen. For her to say otherwise would stain her conscience, for which she would rather die a thousand deaths, Katherine said. In July, when she was officially notified of the new marriage, and that she must refer to herself as Princess Dowager again, Katherine refused. She would *never* accept that title, she exclaimed, and she would answer to no one who called her that. True to her word, each time a document came referring to her as Princess Dowager, Katherine scratched out each instance of the offensive title with her pen.

Anne gave little thought to Katherine's resistance. She was too preoccupied with the impending birth of her child to worry about an embattled old woman living in the past, fighting a lost cause. For her lying-in, Anne demanded nothing but the finest furnishings for herself, such as 'one of the richest and most important beds' owned by the King. It was so sumptuous that it was accepted as a ransom for a French Duke. At Anne's insistence, it was brought out of storage in July and set up for her at Greenwich. Shortly afterwards, the Imperial envoy Chapuys remarked that Anne was lucky to have asked for it beforehand, as recently, she and the King had quarrelled. With Anne bloated and irritable in her pregnancy, Henry had been on the prowl looking for distraction among the pretty young things at court. Nothing escaped Anne's attention, and she gave Henry a piece of her mind, using words 'at which he was displeased'. Forgetting her condition, Henry shot back, warning Anne that 'she would do better to shut her eyes, and endure as well as more worthy persons' - a reference to Katherine, who had put up with his flings. It was in his power, Henry warned, to 'lower her as much as he had raised her'. Chapuys was delighted by their quarrel, but even he had to admit that it was just a lovers' spat. After two or three days of avoiding her entirely, Henry had Anne in his arms again.

As her time approached, the ornate French bed was not enough for Anne; she must also have the beautiful christening cloth used by the former Queen. When Katherine was asked to give it up, she refused of course. She would never obey such a 'horrible and abominable' request, she answered. She had willingly surrendered her jewels as they belonged to the Crown, but the chrisom was hers entirely. She had personally brought it from Spain, and in it she had held Mary and those pathetic babies she had lost. So vehemently did Katherine protest that the matter was quietly dropped.

In the last week of August, Anne began her confinement. Having lost the battle over the christening cloth, Anne was determined to prevail over Katherine where it mattered most. Confident that God would bless her with a boy, Anne went into labour on 7 September. In the afternoon, the child was born. It was, however, not a *Henry* or an *Edward* as expected – it was a girl.

Chapter 11
She is My Death, and I am Hers

BEFORE THE birth of their child, the royal couple had been so certain of a son that letters had been prepared in the Queen's name announcing the 'deliverance and bringing forth of a prince'. But with the infant being a girl, the gender of the child had to be changed to 'princes' (the 16th century spelling of 'princess') before the letters were sent out.

Disappointed as she was in the sex of her child, there is no evidence that Anne bore any resentment towards her daughter. The birth was without complications, and the infant was a healthy beautiful little girl. Naturally, Anne expected sons to follow. But it was harder for Henry VIII - reminded of his previous ill luck with Katherine of Aragon - to come around. After all he had done to beget a prince, why did God frustrate him still? For the time being, he reconciled himself to the outcome and put a good face on it. After the delivery, he sent out letters informing his subjects that 'they ought to thank God for giving them a lawful heir'.

Three days after the birth, the honours due to the new successor to the throne went ahead as planned, though on a reduced scale without the usual 'rejoicings and solemn jousts' afterwards. The Church of the Observant Friars, which had not hosted the baptism of a royal infant since the birth of Princess Mary seventeen years before, was prepared for the ceremony. Its walls were hung with tapestries, and in the middle of the church, beneath a canopy fringed with gold, a silver font was placed. Close at hand was a 'pan over fire' to keep the baby warm as she was undressed, and to heat the holy water. Later, when a discontented friar learned that the 'little bastard' was christened with hot water, he unkindly remarked that 'it was *not* hot enough'.

Swaddled tightly, lest she catch a chill, the child was brought into the church by the Dowager Duchess of Norfolk and the Marchioness of Dorset acting as sponsors. At the font, the baby girl was christened by the Bishop of London, with Cranmer standing by as her godfather. Right up to the morning of the ceremony, there was talk of naming her Mary; an obvious slight against the King's elder daughter. It was not enough to strip her of her birthright, but her very identity as well.

Fortunately for Mary, the idea was abandoned. After her little sister was christened and confirmed, the herald cried out aloud, "God of His infinite goodness, send prosperous life and long, to the high and mighty Princess of England, *Elizabeth*"!

$$=$$

Elizabeth had not taken her name, and Mary saw to it that she was not to take her title either. Just as she would not acknowledge Anne Boleyn as Queen, Mary refused to call her daughter 'Princess'. But as she did recognise the King's natural son the Duke of Richmond as her brother, she said, she would do likewise with Elizabeth, calling her 'sister'. Like her mother Katherine who still referred to herself as Queen of England, Mary considered herself as the only legitimate Princess in the realm. When a letter in the King's name was sent to her as 'the Lady Mary - the King's daughter', she wrote back in protest. Believing Anne Boleyn to be behind the slight, Mary expressed astonishment to her father that she had not been addressed properly. Obviously, he had not known about the message, Mary wrote, as she was, after all, his 'lawful daughter, born in true matrimony'. If she believed otherwise, Mary added, she would offend her Maker.

But with a father who considered himself on intimate terms with the Almighty, Mary's argument of obeying God's will, especially when it was contrary to the King's, held no sway. Bit by bit, her cherished dignity was stripped away. As Mary no longer had claim to her royal title, her servants had to exchange their liveries. They were deprived of their golden coats embroidered with Mary's escutcheon as Princess, and were given new ones blazoned with the King's arms alone. Chapuys could only hope that Henry would 'do no worse to her'.

But in December, Mary was made to give up her household. At the King's command, she was to share one with Elizabeth at Hatfield House in Hertfordshire. Already, Mary's establishment had been being severely reduced. By the time she was forced to join her sister's, she had only two ladies-in-waiting in her service. Not much later she was down to one attendant, a mere 'chambermaid'.

The greater snub came when Mary learnt she was to be treated like her baby sister's subordinate. At Hatfield, Princess Elizabeth was given the best accommodations befitting her rank, while Mary was allotted 'the worst room in the house'. There were other humiliations. No longer was she allowed the privilege of taking her meals alone, but she had to eat in the common hall with the servants. When they travelled together, the distinction between Mary as bastard and Elizabeth as

Princess was made clear as well. Elizabeth, of course, was provided with a more sumptuous carriage, and when the two sisters journeyed by water, the younger was given the place of honour. One time, however, Mary managed to outwit her custodian Lady Shelton, Anne Boleyn's aunt. On a trip including the two sisters, Mary set out earlier by herself. Arriving at the waterside before Elizabeth, she claimed the better seat on the barge. Fortunately for Mary, Lady Shelton thought it best not to make a fuss about it and said nothing. But it was not always so easy. On another occasion, when Mary outright refused to accompany her sister somewhere, Lady Shelton had the defiant teenager manhandled into her litter.

There was even a close watch set over Mary. Under orders, Lady Shelton made certain no one addressed her as 'My Lady Princess', and offenders were duly reported. Mary's old friend, Lady Hussey, who afterwards insisted she only called Mary 'Princess' out of habit, found herself in the Tower. Close tabs were also kept on whom Mary kept in contact. Her friends had to correspond with her in secret, as did the trusted Chapuys. As her mother's friend, the envoy made it his responsibility to look out for Mary as well, but it was not easy, as he was never allowed to visit her in person. As they could not meet, Mary at least arranged for the ambassador to see her for a fleeting moment. On a trip to Greenwich, she sent a message to Chapuys telling him when and where her barge would pass. Disguised along the riverbank, the ambassador was able to get a glimpse of the Princess as she sailed by.

In the face of Mary's continual obstinacy and defiance, Anne Boleyn stormed and threatened. How dare she be so insolent, Anne exclaimed, and how dare she disobey her father the King? For her impudence, Anne told Lady Shelton that Mary must be 'slapped like the cursed bastard she was'. Even though Lady Shelton was the Queen's aunt, she did have pity on her charge. When Anne's brother Lord Rochford and the Duke of Norfolk berated her for being too lenient, Lady Shelton retorted that the Princess ought to be treated with respect and honour even if she were a poor man's daughter for 'her kindness, her modesty, and her virtues'. Empathetic as she was, even Lady Shelton could be exasperated by Mary's behaviour. One time, she was heard to say how the girl ought to be kicked out for defying her father.

Anne's hatred for Mary would become so obsessive that in her wilder moments, she even considered putting her to death. If the King should ever leave the country and appoint her Regent as he once did Katherine, Anne swore she would have Mary killed. She would not care, she boasted, if she herself 'were to be burnt or flayed alive in consequence'. 'She is my death, and I am hers!' In the battle of wills against her stepdaughter, she was determined to win. But if it were Mary who was triumphant, Anne swore to see to it that she at least would not have the last laugh over her.

As much as Anne ranted and raved, Mary, for the time being was still able to retain a good measure of her father's love. No matter how much he came to loathe her mother Katherine, Henry VIII still treated his daughter with affection. The French ambassador's praises of the Princess were enough to bring tears to his eyes, and when she took ill, the King immediately sent his best doctor to her.

But as much as he loved her, Henry was upset by her defiance. Until she was ready to conform herself to his will by acknowledging Anne Boleyn as Queen and herself a bastard, Henry would not see her. Nonetheless, Mary tried to reach her father. On his visit to Hatfield to check up on Elizabeth, the King had given orders that his elder daughter was not to come near him. Undaunted, Mary went up to the terrace above the house and waited. When the King was leaving, he saw her there kneeling silently in supplication. Henry still would not speak with Mary, but before he rode away, he did touch his cap in salute to her. The little gesture meant the world to Mary.

Unlike Henry VIII's, the people's love for the Princess was unconditional. Mary, like her mother, had always been popular – and she became even more so with the hateful changes of late. To most of the English people, Mary represented all that was proper and good. *She* was the true Princess of England, and *her* religion, with England in obedience to Rome, not schismatically adrift, was that of the faithful. For what Mary stood for, she naturally became a focus of opposition to all that was detestable as a consequence of the King's new marriage. Mary was not without influential friends. Among the conservatives at court who remained devoted to her and her mother were Nicholas Carew, a favourite of the King, the Marquis and Marchioness of Exeter, and the family of Mary's former governess, Lady Margaret Pole. They were all valuable allies should the succession be challenged. Mary, *not* Elizabeth, they believed, could still be Queen. Under Church law, the King's eldest daughter was arguably still legitimate as she had been conceived in 'good faith' – that is, at the time of Mary's birth, her father and mother truly believed themselves to be legally married. If this technicality was upheld, should the King die unexpectedly, Mary being the elder - and universally loved – would displace her sister as heiress of England. Chapuys for one, had no doubt Mary would do so if events should work in her favour, and he was determined to do all he could to help her.

In November 1533, Elizabeth Barton, the Holy Maid of Kent, was arrested for treason. For years, Henry VIII had tolerated the outspoken nun. When she prophesied doom against his new marriage, he stayed his hand, and when she warned him of offending God to his face, he let her go. But her mystic revelations went too far when she foretold how the King would be deposed and assigned a special place in Hell. Elizabeth and her supporters were quickly rounded up. The nun was so dangerous that the Council, in consultation with the judges, nobles, and prelates of the realm, sat continuously from morning to night for three days straight to decide what to do with her. After much deliberation, Elizabeth Barton was accused of 'damnable abuses and wicked deeds' for inciting rebellion.

Strenuous efforts were made to uncover the nun's supporters at court. When the Marchioness of Exeter was interrogated, the terrified lady quickly abandoned her friend and begged pardon. It was her 'fragility and brittleness', the Marchioness confessed, that led her to be hoodwinked by 'that most unworthy, subtle, and deceiving woman'. The Council also went after Sir Thomas More, who was said to be sympathetic to the nun. More had resigned his office of Lord Chancellor in protest the day after the Submission of the Clergy in 1532, but he was not allowed to retire in peace. He was questioned about his dealings with Elizabeth Barton, but More, being the shrewd lawyer he was, showed the Council a copy of a letter he had written to the lady advising her to stick to prayer and not to meddle in affairs of State.

Unable to pin anything on More, the authorities then approached the former Queen. Was it not true that Elizabeth Barton curried favour with her, they asked Katherine? And hadn't the nun pestered her for an audience? But no case could be made. Wisely, Katherine had always refused to meet or to correspond with the controversial young woman. Getting nothing from More and the Queen, the Council moved on to Bishop Fisher – this time with success. Unlike his two friends, Fisher had openly supported the nun. Accused of 'weeping for joy' at her pronouncements, the old man was arrested and was 'in great danger for his life'.

Shortly after Christmas, the Holy Maid of Kent and her closest associates were attainted as traitors by Parliament and condemned to die. In April 1534, they were taken from the Tower to the scaffold at Tyburn where criminals were usually dispatched. Looking over the people, many of whom had trusted in her utterings, Elizabeth Barton confessed her guilt, saying she was but a 'poor wench without learning' used by others to be 'profitable unto them'. She denounced her visions and expressed regret that her friends were to die with her. One by one, the nun and her accomplices were hanged. Afterwards, their heads were severed and displayed on the city gates and London Bridge – a dire warning of the King's terrible justice.

≡

In the spring of 1534, Anne Boleyn had every reason to be confident. The threats of the Emperor and of the Pope had proved empty, the Nun of Kent had been exposed as a charlatan, and the King had not abandoned her in spite of the birth of a daughter. In fact, Henry seemed to be even more loving. He would rather beg from door to door, he was heard to say, than to forsake her. Secure in Henry's affections, Anne had another reason to be happy - she was pregnant again.

During that carefree season, Anne even relented in her hatred for Mary. During a visit to Hatfield to visit Elizabeth, Anne asked her stepdaughter to see her. Normally, whenever the new Queen came by, Mary shut herself in her rooms. She did so again. A message was brought to her that if she were friendly, Anne would gladly reciprocate by speaking to her father on her behalf. When the messenger returned with Mary's reply, Anne could not believe her ears. She knew of no other Queen than her mother Katherine, the Princess replied boldly. However, if *Mistress Anne*, as Mary referred to her stepmother, would be so kind as to intercede with her father, she would be most grateful. Infuriated, Anne vowed to crush Mary's 'proud Spanish blood' and 'to reduce her pomp and pride'.

Angry as she was, Anne was still willing to meet Mary halfway. On a subsequent visit to Hatfield, both ladies found themselves in the awkward situation of attending Mass together. After the service was over, Mary was the first to leave. One of Anne's women, who was apparently not very bright, told the Queen excitedly how the

Lady Mary had bowed to her when she left. Gratified by Mary's gesture, Anne immediately sent kind words. Anne apologised for missing her curtsy, and wished 'an entrance of friendly correspondence' with Mary. Hearing this, the Princess had to suppress her laughter. Tell the *Lady Anne*, she said to the messenger, there was a misunderstanding. Her genuflection was solely meant for the Blessed Sacrament on the altar - to 'her Maker and mine'. Mary added that the messenger should refrain from saying the communication was 'from the Queen'; 'Her Majesty (that is her mother Katherine) being so far from this place'. Made a fool of, Anne stormed out of Hatfield in a rage.

Amazingly enough, Anne later made one last attempt to reach out to Mary. Anne wrote asking that their differences be set aside. If Mary came to court, she would find Anne 'another mother to her'. Additionally, she promised that Mary would not be obliged to bear her train as protocol demanded. Careful not to antagonise her stepmother too greatly this time, Mary simply ignored her invitation. When no reply came, Anne finally gave up. In a letter to Lady Shelton, that was left lying open on purpose so that Mary was sure to read it, Anne vented her exasperation. After all she tried to do for her, the girl was nothing but an ingrate. Her attempts to befriend Mary were out of charity, the Queen wrote, and out of regard for 'the word of God, to do good to one's enemy'. But since Mary had rebuffed her time and time again, she and the King no longer cared what Mary did. Anne finished off saying she hoped to have a son soon - then will Mary know the consequences for her 'rudeness and unnatural obstinacy'.

In provoking Anne, Mary had invited her father's wrath too. Henry had become so furious with his daughter that he was heard to be considering her execution on charges of treason. Terrified her father might proceed against her, Mary warned the Emperor. Still forbidden to receive Chapuys, she arranged to have her doctor visit her instead. In the presence of Lady Shelton, Mary engaged him in practising her Latin. It was rusty, she said, and 'she could hardly speak two words right'. As Lady Shelton, knowing no Latin, stood by, Mary told the doctor how her father might have her killed. He must notify her cousin Charles right away. Hiding his astonishment, the doctor nodded with understanding. Lest they arouse Lady Shelton's suspicion, he feigned confusion, telling Mary aloud in English that her Latin was indeed bad, and that he barely understood a word she said. Afterwards, he quickly communicated what Mary told him to the ambassador.

Despite Mary's fears, Chapuys sensed that Henry VIII was only speaking out of anger and frustration. Even he would not execute his own flesh and blood. Nevertheless, he addressed his concerns to the King. Tactfully, Chapuys avoided any mention that it was Henry himself who meant Mary harm, only her enemies. Should not the Princess - or rather 'the Lady Mary' as Chapuys had to call her in the King's presence - live with her mother for her own safety? She was in constant danger from opportunists who might do away with her 'perceiving his (the King's) displeasure against her'. Henry dismissed the ambassador of his worries. Mary was in perfect health, well provided for, and in no peril from anyone, he insisted. Besides, she was also *his* daughter to do with as *he* pleased, and Chapuys had no business to interfere in a family matter.

After his interview with the King, the ambassador warned Mary to show no resistance. Her father could only be provoked so far. It would be smart, Chapuys suggested, for Mary to at least pretend to be cooperative and submissive, making statement 'to the world that she was very much pleased to act according to her father's wishes'. Unless Mary treaded softly, Chapuys cautioned, Henry's threat that his daughter would find herself on the block would not be an idle one.

=

In March 1534, the pope finally declared in favour of Katherine of Aragon. But it was too little and too late. Henry VIII was too firmly tied to Anne Boleyn, emotionally and legally, that no decree from the Vatican could make him go back to his former wife. In the same month, the Act of Succession was passed. It confirmed the King's second marriage as 'undoubtful, true, sincere, and perfect hereafter', and it settled the Crown on his children by Anne. Unless the couple had a son, Elizabeth was to inherit. Provision was made that, in the event of the Henry VIII's premature death, Anne would be appointed Regent if his heir did not yet reach adulthood. There was no mention of Mary at all in the succession.

In November, an oath was drawn up to enforce the Act. Throughout the kingdom, the King's subjects were made to swear upon 'God, all saints, and the holy Evangelists', 'to bear faith, truth, and obedience alonely to the King's Majesty, and to his heirs of his body of his most dear and entirely beloved lawful wife Queen Anne'. Refusal to do so was treason, regardless of one's 'estate, dignity, or condition'. It was also a crime to have taken the oath, and then slander the King's marriage 'by writing, print, deed, or act'. The penalty was forfeiture of property - and death. To criticise the King or Queen verbally was equally criminal. Though the offender would not be executed under the law, he or she was liable to imprisonment and the loss of goods. To ensure the accused could not escape justice by taking refuge in a church, the right to sanctuary was denied. A person seeking such protection could be forcibly dragged out and tried for subversion.

The laws did not deter everyone. A woman in Suffolk named Margaret Chancellor cursed Anne Boleyn as a 'goggle-eyed whore'. 'God save Queen Katherine', she cried out, 'for *she* was [the] righteous Queen'. Mistress Amadas, 'the mad and distract' wife of the former Master of the Jewel House, also vilified Anne as a harlot. Like the Nun of Kent, she went into ecstatic trances. For twenty years, she had channelled messages from Heaven, Mistress Amadas claimed, and had recorded them carefully on a 'painted and written' scroll. In her reveries, Anne shall be burnt alive in six months, and Henry VIII – a monster cursed 'with God's own mouth' - shall lose his kingdom to the invading Scots. Afterwards, 'there shall be no more kings in England', she prophesied.

Before the summer of 1534 was out, the ornate silver cradle made for Anne's new child was quietly put away. There was to be no baby. The Queen had possibly miscarried or was the victim of a false pregnancy.

Frustrated again, the King indulged in another affair. Her name has not come down to us, but perhaps it was the same lady who had aroused Anne's jealousy before Elizabeth's birth. Whoever she was, she was reported to be a great beauty, and an ardent supporter of Katherine and Mary. In a message to the Princess, the King's new paramour told her 'to take good cheer, that her tribulations will come to an end much sooner than she expected'. All Mary had to do was to be patient.

The lady made no secret of her hostility towards Anne, and soon the Queen was complaining about her to the King. But as she had his protection, she could not be dislodged from court. Undaunted, Anne enlisted the help of her sister-in-law, Jane Parker. Lady Rochford was to engage Henry's mistress in a public row, which would lead to her dismissal from the palace. But the plan backfired when it was Jane who was banished instead.

There was further disappointment. In November 1534, Philippe Chabot de Brion, the Admiral of France, arrived as Francis I's emissary. Chabot, who had been friendly to Anne during her meeting with the French King two years ago, was now strangely cold. He avoided the Queen as much as he could, and he took scant pleasure in the company of her ladies. Instead, Chabot was often found chatting with Chapuys. A series of entertainments including dances and tennis matches, arranged especially for Chabot, were met with indifference. Even special visits to the Tower of London and other prominent landmarks in the city left the Frenchman unimpressed. The Admiral was heard to complain that he was not allowed to meet 'the most singular and valuable gem in all this kingdom, namely the Princess'. And by that, he meant Mary - *not* Elizabeth.

Chabot's mission, to Henry and Anne's astonishment, was not to seek Elizabeth's hand in marriage to Francis I's son, the Dauphin, as expected, but Mary's. Should his hosts refuse, he said, his master would look elsewhere. Henry was incredulous at the proposal, and he even thought it was a joke. It was only when Chabot showed him Francis's written instructions that Henry realised the envoy was entirely serious.

Seeing that the French were implacable, Henry reluctantly agreed to the Dauphin and Mary being betrothed once again. There was, however, the condition that the young couple renounce all claims to the English Crown. Francis, who had his sights set on Mary inheriting instead of Elizabeth, refused, as Henry knew he would. A counter offer was then made. Instead of a marriage involving Mary and the Dauphin, would Francis consent to have the Princess Elizabeth for his youngest son Charles, Duke of Angoulême, instead? The French agreed to take it into consideration.

Anne had been 'exceedingly annoyed' at Chabot's proposal. Such a match meant that France took Mary as Henry VIII's rightful heir, not Elizabeth. The betrayal was painful for Anne coming from the country she had always loved, and from its King whom she had counted on for support. Anne could barely hide her dismay, and she acted erratically. At a banquet, she suddenly burst into laughter. Chabot, who was sitting next to Anne, asked indignantly if she was laughing at him? She meant no disrespect, Anne replied, composing herself. She had found it amusing that her husband, in seeking out one of the admiral's countrymen in the crowded hall, had stopped to speak to an attractive lady (his mistress?) and plain forgot what he had set out to do!

Figure 9   Francis I, King of France by Titian
The Rijksmuseum, Amsterdam

The Queen's odd behaviour continued into the New Year. At a ball, Anne took the new ambassador, Palamedes Gontier, aside, and in a hushed voice, told him of the great danger she was in. His master King Francis must commit to the marriage between Elizabeth and the Duke of Angoulême, she said anxiously. Having still no son yet, her only safety was through an alliance with France. Glancing nervously about, Anne then told Gontier that she was lost if Francis continued to drag his heels. She was living in great fear, and could not see him again or even write, for she was being watched.

Before Gontier could say a word, Anne turned and vanished.

Chapter 12
Pride and Vainglory

BY THE end of February 1535, Henry's mistress was no longer seen at court. Perhaps Anne had succeeded in getting rid of her at last, or the King had simply tired of the lady. But even with her departure, Anne was still uneasy. It had been almost a year since her last pregnancy, or what she had thought was one, and she was troubled she might never conceive again. Anne confided her worries to her brother George with whom she had always been close. What if, they whispered, it was the King who was to blame? But to suggest that it was Henry VIII who was responsible was dangerous. With his immense ego, he was extremely touchy about his virility. Chapuys had greatly offended him once when he dared to tell Henry to his face that he might not be capable of a son by Anne. The King rounded on the ambassador and shouted, 'Am I not a man like others?! Am I not a man like others?! Am I not a man like others?'! Given the King's poor history as a father, Lord Rochford sniggered that it was almost a miracle that he had even managed to sire Elizabeth. It was a bad joke; one that would cost George Boleyn dearly later on.

Even though she still lacked the protection of an heir, Anne's position as Queen of England was strengthened by the enforcement of the laws upholding her marriage. In the spring and summer of 1535, London reeked with the stench of rotting corpses. It began with the execution of four monks. For choosing the Pope over the King, they were brought to the gallows at Tyburn. The monks did not walk in sad procession, but were instead, dragged on horse-drawn hurdles through the dust and mire. Normally, the condemned were assaulted with muck and insults on their way to die, but, this time, there was great sorrow and pity. As the monks went past, many crossed themselves or muttered a prayer for them.

On reaching Tyburn, the monks were untied and forced on their feet in the presence of the Duke of Norfolk, the young Duke of Richmond, and the Queen's father and brother, acting as the King's representatives. The monks were then marched up the scaffold stairs and hanged. But before the noose could fully do its work, they were quickly cut down. Not yet dead, the monks were then eviscerated. Their bowels were thrown into a fire before the awed crowd, and their corpses chopped into quarters. The monks' remains, like those of the Elizabeth Barton and her friends, were then distributed within and without the city.

In June, the Bishop of Rochester followed. His execution could only have been a relief to him. Old and weary, imprisonment had taken a further toll on Fisher. Placed in a draughty cell, the sixty-six-year-old had nearly frozen to death for lack of warm clothing. The King might have been content to let him die in bed, except for the Vatican's interference. The new pope, Paul III – no friend to Henry VIII - was intent on making Fisher a cardinal. Vowing that the cardinal's hat sent from Rome would sit on Fisher's headless shoulders, the King had the Bishop tried and condemned for refusing to take the Oath of Succession. Formerly a tall and impressive man, Fisher was stooped with infirmity when he emerged from the Tower on 22 June 1535. He was so weak he had to be carried to Tower Hill in a chair. After his head had been stricken off, it was spiked on the city gate. But instead of arousing fear in the people, it inspired awe. The hoary head would not rot, it was said, but instead 'looked fresher and fresher' as if the old Bishop were still living. Finally, to discourage such superstition, the authorities had it removed and tossed into the Thames.

The execution of the saintly John Fisher reverberated throughout Europe. Just as shocking was that of Thomas More on 6 July. The Council had not been able to link him to the Nun of Kent, but his refusal to swear the Oath of Supremacy was his undoing. Though More was willing to acknowledge Anne Boleyn as Queen as Parliament had decreed, he would go no further. He denied its power to renounce the authority of Rome. 'Looking first upon God, and next upon the King', More laid his head on the block defending his priorities.

The deaths of such eminent men were so atrocious that Chapuys begged his master to apply a remedy before it was too late. The Emperor, he wrote desperately, must take up arms and liberate this country from heresy and chaos. Thousands of Englishmen, Chapuys assured Charles, would join the Imperial forces and dethrone the tyrant Henry and his wicked 'concubine', giving the Crown to Princess Mary.

By encouraging rebellion, Chapuys was clearly overstepping his office as ambassador. Not only that, he was placing Katherine of Aragon in a precarious position. To ensure the success of the insurrection, Chapuys envisioned the popular Queen as its figurehead. Surely, as the daughter of Ferdinand and Isabella the conquerors of Moorish Spain, and as Regent overseeing the victory of Flodden Field, Katherine would prove a formidable leader. Even Henry VIII himself was heard to say that if his former wife ever took the field against him, she would be a fearsome opponent. However, Chapuys did not consider the alternatives if Katherine failed. She could justifiably be executed for inciting treason against her sovereign.

What did Katherine herself think? When she was approached in private, she refused to give ear to what Chapuys was proposing. It was not the fear of a failed enterprise that held Katherine back. Far from it. She simply would not condone conspiracy. She still believed herself to be the King's lawful wife, and as such, was bound to him in obedience and loyalty, in so far as her conscience allowed. Her struggle with Henry VIII was in the law court, not on the battlefield. Her scruples would not allow her to go beyond that. To Katherine, rebellion was a sin, and she would not plunge her adopted country into war. As she told Chapuys; 'she would rather suffer death than be the cause of such misery'.

Henry and Anne witnessed none of the horrors at Tyburn. That summer, the royal couple set out on progress from Greenwich. It was almost a second honeymoon allowing the pair to leave their cares behind. From Windsor, the itinerant court headed towards the West Country. The area was predominately Reformist in religion with few tongues to criticize events of late. The royal party travelled as far north as Tewkesbury, and then went down towards Bristol. An outbreak of plague, however, prevented a layover. The citizens had to be content with Anne's personal promise to them that they would be honoured with a visit in the near future. On the way south to Portsmouth, the King and Queen stopped for a few days at Wolf Hall in Wiltshire, home of Sir John Seymour and his family. Sir John had served both the King and his father, and two of his children were currently at court. His son Edward was an Esquire of the Body, and his daughter Jane served as a maid of honour in the Queen's household.

The royal couple, described as being 'very merry' throughout the progress, had even more reason to be happy when they returned in October - Anne was pregnant again. She was elated. No more would she have to worry as in the months past. In the coming summer, when her son was born - and it was sure to be a son this time, she would finally prove to the world that she was fit to be England's Queen. Katherine, that wretched old woman, would be forgotten at last.

≡

Katherine of Aragon's spirits were raised when she was allowed a visit from her friend Chapuys at the beginning of January 1536. The meeting would be bittersweet. The old Queen was slowly dying, though no one was certain of that just yet. She had not been well in the past months, and her low morale contributed to her decline. When Chapuys arrived at Kimbolton Castle in Huntingdonshire, where Katherine had been removed to in 1534, he found her oldest friend, Maria de Salinas, now the widowed Lady Willoughby, at her side. Maria, learning of Katherine's illness, had hastened to her beloved mistress. Nothing or no one could have stopped her; neither the journey through wind and snow nor Katherine's custodian Sir Edmund Bedingfield. Lying to her gaoler that she had permission to see the Queen, and that she was in great pain having fallen off her horse on the way, Maria was let into the castle. Taken to the Queen's chambers, she remained there for good. Bedingfield, a kindly man, let her stay.

The presence of her old friend and the ambassador brought much solace to Katherine, and she seemed to improve significantly. She was able to sit up in bed and converse. Over the past few weeks, Katherine had often been so tired that she could not even comb and dress her hair as she liked to do. When it came time for him to leave, Chapuys was confident that Katherine would get better, and that he might even get to see her again. But within days of his departure, Katherine had suffered a relapse. By the early morning of 7 January, it was clear the end was approaching. Calmly, Katherine waited for the coming of dawn, the time at which her confessor could celebrate Mass before her. She turned her thoughts to God – and to the King; Henry, who had welcomed her to England when he was just a boy, who had rescued her from her misery, who had jousted for her as Sir Loyal Heart, and who had once loved her and had children with her. That was the Henry Katherine chose to remember; the one before the coming of *that woman*.

In a final letter to him, Katherine asked Henry to have a care for her servants and their daughter the Princess. Mindful of the great Seat of Judgement she would soon come before, Katherine begged him to consider the state of *his* soul as well, 'which you ought to prefer before all considerations of the world or flesh…for which yet you have cast me into many calamities, and yourself into many troubles'. Whether God would forgive him or not, Katherine herself did. 'I make this vow', she wrote at the end of her letter, 'that mine eyes desire you above all things'.

After Mass was said, Katherine received the last rites. She slipped into a peaceful sleep, and in the afternoon she died, clutching the hand of the faithful Lady Willoughby.

'God be praised that we are free from all suspicion of war!' Such was the reaction of Henry VIII at the news from Kimbolton. Anne was equally overjoyed. At last, she was the undisputed Queen of England. To celebrate the death of the woman he had once loved but come to hate, an exuberant Henry dressed himself in bright yellow from tip to toe, as did Anne, and the two called for a round of festivities. During the celebrations, Henry called for the baby Elizabeth and carried her in his arms showing her off like a proud doting father.

Still in mourning for Katherine, Chapuys was disgusted by the callous disrespect shown for the late Queen. He had hoped the King would at least console his eldest daughter in person, or allow a sympathetic official to do so, but he did nothing of the sort. Instead, Mary received the sad tidings 'unceremoniously' from Lady Shelton, who had ceased to show her any more sympathy. After Mary's initial grief, she had composed herself by nightfall and was determined to find out what had occurred during her mother's final hours. Pleading illness, she asked her father to allow the doctors who had attended Katherine to treat her as well. Henry refused. Mary was not sick, he said, but merely overwrought by her mother's death.

Unable to see the doctors, Mary learnt what had happened at Kimbolton from Chapuys instead. As he wrote to Mary, the Queen was already suffering from 'despondency and grief'; all it took was a little poison to do the rest. Katherine's own doctor had thought so too, the envoy said. It was not for nothing that in the last months of her life, Katherine, in fear of being poisoned, had insisted that her meals be prepared in her own chambers. Chapuys believed her autopsy invited suspicion from the start. It had been performed in haste by the household chandler who had little experience in such matters. Why were the doctors not involved as well, he questioned? And where were her confessor and her officers to act as witnesses? The findings were just as mysterious. Katherine's organs were sound, but her heart was 'completely black'. Water could not wash away its 'hideous aspect', and when it was dissected, 'something black and round' was discovered within. By the King's instructions, Chapuys told Mary, the examination was to have been done in private, and nothing said. But horrified by what he found, the chandler had told the Queen's chaplain in secrecy 'as if his life depended on it'. However, the information was then been leaked to him, Chapuys said.

Despite the envoy's belief that a conspiracy of murder and cover-up had occurred at Kimbolton, Katherine probably just died of natural causes. At the age of fifty, she was old by the standards of her time, and the black core in her heart was probably a cancerous tumour contributing to her death. Nonetheless, her supporters suspected poison and pointed the finger at Henry VIII and Anne Boleyn.

Deprived of her mother's company for years, Mary was now denied her legacies as well. In her will, Katherine had left her daughter some furs and a golden cross she had brought over from Spain. But before Mary could lay claim to the bequests, the King had them seized. His daughter may have the gifts, Henry said, *if* she submitted to him. Mary refused. In place of the cherished reminders of her mother, she consoled herself with the Requiem Masses she ordered for Katherine's repose. Eventually, the cross was given to Mary; only after Thomas Cromwell had determined that it was of little worth.

In her last wishes, Katherine had asked to be laid to rest in a church of the Observant Friars of the Order of St Francis. Unbeknownst to her, the order was all but dissolved in England, and the Franciscans' property surrendered to the Crown. By the King's orders, Katherine was to be buried in Peterborough Abbey instead, and only as Princess Dowager, not Queen. Chapuys, upset over this final insult, boycotted the funeral.

≡

Despite her outward joy at the death of Katherine of Aragon, in private, Chapuys heard say, Anne Boleyn was in despair. As he communicated to the Princess Mary, there were rumours at court that even though she was pregnant again, the King was tiring of her. She lived in constant dread, knowing that unless she bore a son, Henry would get rid of her as he did her mother. Every day, Anne was 'visibly losing part of her pride and vainglory', Chapuys gloated.

With Anne's position still so insecure, the loyalty of her supporters was at a low ebb, the ambassador believed. Lady Shelton for one, could be made more amenable to Mary. If it were hinted that her niece the Queen would fall sooner or later, she would treat Mary with better respect. Chapuys even began bribing her. He sent Lady Shelton little gifts as Mary advised him to do, along with a promise that once Mary was restored to her father's good graces, the Princess would hold no grudges. To the contrary, her governess would find herself 'favoured and rewarded'. Concerned about her own future and won over by Chapuy's presents, Lady Shelton relaxed her guard over Mary.

With fewer restrictions, the Princess contemplated escape. Her late mother Katherine would never have considered such a move, having sworn that she would never leave her husband, but Mary was young with her future ahead of her. The prospect of having to spend more years in England 'in constant anguish, tribulation, danger, as well as annoyances of all sorts' had led her to a 'most ardent desire to escape'. But there were difficulties as Mary had recently been moved to another residence in Hertfordshire. Undeterred, she thought of drugging her attendants asleep to make her getaway. But after further consideration, Mary dropped the idea. Even if she managed to sneak away from her house, she wrote to Chapuys, there was still a forty-mile stretch to the coast at Gravesend. Many towns were situated along the way, and the residents would surely be alerted to her flight. An alternate plan was considered. Come next Christmas, Mary expected to be moved to another house closer to water. Perhaps then, other means could be found to spirit her away to the Emperor.

The wait was putting its toll on Mary. With each passing day, she was becoming more and more despondent, as she told Chapuys, and was 'daily preparing herself for death.' Mary believed that escape was not enough. More was required of the Emperor, and to this, the ambassador agreed. He wrote to his master that Mary's flight was an enterprise fraught with danger, and even if she did escape, it would achieve little in the long run. The Princess's concern, he said, was more for her people than herself. If Charles would only apply 'the remedy so often pointed out by her', it would 'be a most meritorious work in the eyes of God... saving innumerable souls now on the verge of perdition, and otherwise ensuring the peace and tranquillity of Christendom'.

What the 'sure and efficient remedy' mentioned by Mary specifically was, was vague in Chapuys' letter, but it was one to which he was agreed. As the envoy had constantly urged his master to make war on Henry VIII, perhaps Mary herself, in her desperation, had accepted such an enterprise as unavoidable and inevitable; the 'means to be employed for the general and total extirpation of the evil'.

If Mary was indeed dabbling in conspiracy whatever the manner, it was highly dangerous. Should it come to light how she thought it 'necessary to resort to force', the King her father would be justified in having her executed. Even Chapuys would face his wrath. The envoy, knowing the danger he too would be in for arranging Mary's escape and for the consequences to follow, advised the Emperor that once the Princess was safely out of England, he must be recalled as soon as possible. There would be no diplomatic immunity for him, as Chapuys wrote to Charles. 'Nothing would prevent him [the King] from wreaking his vengeance on me.'

Even into his forty-fifth year, Henry VIII continued to joust as he did in his youth. Though he had grown heavier with age and his eyesight was less keen, no one could tell the King that his prowess at the lists was anything less than it had always been. Confident of his abilities still, on a winter's day on 29 January 1536, Henry mounted his charger and prepared to meet his opponent. To the roar of the crowd, he rode furiously down the field with his lance held before him. There was a sudden clash of wood and steel, followed by a collective gasp. The King had been thrown off his horse, falling with a resounding crash. To the horror of the spectators, he did not get up but remained motionless on the tiltyard.

As frantic efforts were made to revive the King, news of the accident was sent to Queen Anne. She was not at the tournament. Perhaps the cold was thought too great for a pregnant woman, and she had remained indoors to rest. After two anxious hours, the King was finally conscious, to everyone's relief. He had 'fell so heavily' that it was a miracle he survived. With Henry VIII safe, all attention was diverted to his wife the Queen. Though only around four months pregnant, she had suddenly felt great pains in her stomach. The court prepared for the worst. Indeed, the Queen had miscarried, and the foetus was by all appearances a boy.

As she always did in times of misfortune, Anne put on a brave face. She admonished her women for their weeping, saying that soon, she would be pregnant once again. And next time, she assured them, she would have better luck now that Katherine of Aragon was gone. Her next child, born *after* her death, 'would not be doubtful' like this one.

But could Anne convince Henry? Denied a son time and time again, he had little pity for Anne as he hobbled into her bedroom on his injured leg. Gazing down at his wife, he muttered how it was evident, 'God did not wish to give him male children'. Brought to tears, Anne shifted the blame to the Duke of Norfolk. It was because her detested uncle had broken the news of the accident to her so abruptly that she had miscarried, she cried. Chapuys however, thought this nonsense. From what he had heard, the King's fall was 'told her in a way that she should not be alarmed or attach much importance to it'. In the end, it made no difference. The child was dead, and it was his wife whom Henry held responsible.

As the Queen made her recovery, the King spent the days in the company of her lady-in-waiting Jane Seymour. With her calm and sympathetic manner, Jane was so unlike his wife that Henry began to look to her as a refuge from his tempestuous marriage. The King's marked attention to Mistress Seymour did not go unnoticed by Princess Mary's supporters. They approached Jane advising her on how to maintain the fickle Henry's affection. Furthermore, according to Chapuys' sources, she was even coached to denigrate his marriage. In carefully scripted words, Jane would make it known to the King how it was an 'abomination', and was thus unlawful in the eyes of the world. Anne's enemies, who just happened to be standing by, would agree.

Nothing deterred Jane, not even the 'scratching and by-blows' from the jealous Queen. She was even bold enough to set the stakes higher. In a well-rehearsed episode, Jane presented her terms to the King. On receiving a purse of gold coins from him, she dramatically fell to her knees. She kissed the present and asked the courier to relay a message to the royal sender. 'Being a gentlewoman of good and honourable' upbringing, her honour was above reproach, she explained. The King should not compromise her reputation by offering her such gifts. If he must, be it so when *God might send her a good marriage*. The meaning was clear. It was the same tactic Anne Boleyn herself had used before. Jane would be Queen or nothing.

≡

Anne Boleyn had got on well with Thomas Cromwell, by now the King's secretary and his chief minister. He had helped pave Anne's way to the throne, and both were proponents of religious reform. But by April of 1536, their relationship had cooled. Queen and minister found themselves on opposing sides of policy. One cause of contention was the spoils of the Dissolution of the Monasteries and what to do with the confiscated wealth of the religious houses being shut down by Henry VIII as Head of the English Church. Anne, it was said, wanted the money to go towards educational and charitable purposes. Cromwell however, was intent on funnelling it into the royal coffers, making the King richer than he could ever have imagined.

Matters came to a head when the Queen's almoner, John Skip, gave a public sermon on 2 April. He recounted the story of the minister Haman who deceived the noble King Ahasuerus into persecuting the Jews. It was through Queen Esther's persuasion and wise counsel that Haman's plot was uncovered, and the minister brought down. Skip's denunciation was expressed in Biblical imagery, but the congregation did not miss the point. King Ahasuerus was Henry VIII, Esther - Anne, and Haman - Cromwell. The victimised Jews were the English Church pillaged by Master Secretary for greed's sake. By sanctioning such a provocative sermon, Anne made her displeasure known. As Cromwell had already confided to Chapuys, the Queen had promised that should he ever defy her, she would 'see his head off his shoulders'.

A further rift occurred that Easter involving the Emperor. With his aunt no longer in the picture, Charles V could put aside his family honour and make peace with England. Even Anne herself was open to the Emperor's overtures, having been snubbed by the French. Since January 1535, they had been less than enthusiastic about the marriage between Princess Elizabeth and the Duke of Angoulême. Their position had been made clear when Francis I finally rejected the proposal altogether. Humiliated, Anne had publicly denounced the French and looked to reconciliation with the Imperialists. There was one catch though - the Emperor still refused to recognise her as Henry's Queen.

During the rounds of negotiation with Chapuys, Henry VIII was just as stubborn as his nephew. He would not agree to a reinstatement of Mary as his successor, or to a re-acknowledgement of papal authority. And as for Anne, he would not abandon her. Things went from bad to worse when Henry lost his temper with Chapuys and then with Cromwell. He shouted at the envoy that he was not a child to be toyed with by the Emperor, and he demanded an apology for all wrongs, real and imagined. Cromwell, who avidly supported the alliance, tried to reason with the King. For his efforts, he was furiously berated by his royal master.

Cromwell was now in the precarious position of having offended both the King and the Queen. With Henry VIII, Cromwell was confident that their row was nothing; it would pass. But when it came to Anne, he remembered how his former master, Cardinal Wolsey, had been ruined for incurring her displeasure. Cromwell himself remembered how the Queen had already thrown down the gauntlet with her almoner's public attack on him. To ensure his survival, Cromwell had to assume the offensive. He considered the possibility of another royal divorce, and he canvassed the Bishop of London for his opinion. The cleric wisely abstained from offering one. He would only give his answer, he said, *after* knowing the King's feelings, and then *only* to Henry himself. 'Knowing his fickleness', the Bishop said, 'he would not put himself in danger'.

After consulting the Bishop, Cromwell dropped the idea of divorce. He would have to convince the King to discard Anne entirely. Despite her recent miscarriage and his new affection for Jane Seymour, there was no sign that Henry would take such a step. Even if he were somehow able to persuade the King to end his marriage, Anne would undoubtedly fight, and she was a formidable opponent. If the Queen must go, her removal must be swift and final.

It was to be Anne herself who would unwittingly provide Cromwell with his means. On 30 April, the court was rocked by a sensational quarrel between her and Henry Norris. The two were engaged in some teasing banter when the Queen asked Norris why he was delaying his marriage to her kinswoman Madge Shelton. He would wait awhile, he replied. Anne apparently took his meaning as a come-on. She shot back recklessly, "Then you look for dead man's shoes. If aught come to the King but good, you would look to have me"! Norris strongly denied harbouring such a thought, and 'then they fell out' in full earshot of the court.

After cooling her head, Anne realised the danger she and Norris were in. She had made suggestion of the King's death and had given the impression that she and Norris were intimate. Both were treasonable offences. Norris was quickly sent to her almoner to make a formal declaration that Anne was 'a good woman'. When news reached the King, he was livid. Did his wife really wish him ill? And could there truly be something between her and Norris? Later, as Henry fumed in silence by an open window, Anne came before him in supplication in the courtyard below. In her arms was baby Elizabeth. As they were both in full view of their courtiers, Henry concealed his rage. But, according to a witness, the tension was palpable; their 'faces and gestures... plainly showed that the King was angry'.

With the King suspicious of the Queen, Cromwell acted. He dared not touch Norris for the moment as the unpredictable Henry might still regard him favourably. Instead, Cromwell set his sights on Mark Smeaton, a musician of the court. When discrete inquiries were conducted within the Queen's household, a tale of a strange encounter between Anne and the handsome young man was brought to Cromwell's attention. Entering her Presence Chamber one day, the Queen had noticed Smeaton standing by a window. She asked the reason for his melancholy. "It was no matter", the musician sighed. Anne became offended. "You may not look to have me speak to you as I should a nobleman", she reproached him, "because you are an inferior person". Smeaton then made a shamefaced retreat. "No, no, Madam", he mumbled, "a look sufficeth me. And thus fare you well".

The exchange was odd, but seemingly innocent. Or was it? Cromwell invited the young man to his house for dinner. It was a great honour which Smeaton did not pass up. But when he arrived, he was seized and tortured. Broken and terrified, Smeaton admitted to sleeping with the Queen.

Chapter 13
Much Joy and Pleasure in Death

IN CELEBRATION of May Day, the royal couple attended the traditional tournaments at the Greenwich tiltyard. By all appearances, they had reconciled. The King, it was noticed, also bore no ill will towards Henry Norris, and he even lent him his horse. All was well until suddenly - with the jousts still going on - the King got up and left, taking Norris with him. Bewildered, Anne watched as they rode away.

On the way to London, Henry rounded on Norris accusing him of bedding his wife. Almost certainly, word had been brought to him of Mark Smeaton's confession, with Norris being implicated as well. He would show mercy, the King said, if his friend confessed. Norris denied the accusation. For that, he was packed off to the Tower to join Smeaton. Unaware of the net closing around her, a puzzled Anne presided over the rest of the day's festivities. It was to be her last function as Queen.

The next day, Anne received a summons to meet with the King's Council. Appearing before them, she was charged with high treason and arrested by her uncle, the Duke of Norfolk. She was told to make ready for the Tower and that she need not bring anything with her, not even her women. On the harrowing journey by water, Anne protested to Norfolk, Cromwell, and the lords who rode with her. Her pleas fell on deaf ears. Anne could expect no sympathy, especially from her uncle who had always disliked her. As Queen, she had been proud and haughty, insulting him like 'one would address a dog'. The tables were now turned, and Norfolk took pleasure in her calamity. As Anne went on defending herself, Norfolk shook his head disapprovingly, reprimanding his niece with a contemptuous 'tut, tut, tut'.

Landing at Tower Wharf in the late afternoon, Anne was led towards the great fortress by the Constable, William Kingston, who had welcomed her at her coronation not three years ago. Anne would have recalled how different her reception was then. On that day, endless rounds of ordnance saluted her. Now, there was but a singular cheerless boom sounding from the Tower - the official announcement of the arrival of a traitor. At the Court Gate, where Henry VIII had once greeted her with a kiss in full view of his subjects, Anne, overwhelmed, dropped to her knees. She was 'not guilty of her accusement', she cried, and she begged the lords to ask the King 'to be good unto her'. Saying nothing, they turned away, leaving her in the Constable's custody.

There was a small consolation for Anne in that she was not to be held in a dungeon as she expected, but in the royal apartments where she had stayed before her crowning. 'It is too good for me!' Anne exclaimed, and she fell into a great weeping. Kingston had expected tears, but not the bouts of uncontrollable manic laughter that immediately followed. Despair and then bravado were to be the pattern throughout Anne's confinement. It was as if, the Constable later wrote to Cromwell, 'one hour she is determined to die, and the next hour much contrary to that'.

Not only was Anne terrified, but she was also confused. Of what exactly was she charged? She was only aware that Henry Norris, Mark Smeaton, and an unnamed gentleman were imprisoned with her. "O Norris, has thou accused me"? she lamented. "Thou art in the Tower with me, and thou and I shall die together! And Mark, thou art here too"! When she asked Kingston, "Do you know wherefore I am here"? the Constable, following Cromwell's orders to keep Anne in the dark, said nothing. Whatever the allegations were, Anne was adamant about her innocence. "If any man accuse me", she said, "I can say but nay, and they can bring no witnesses".

Nor could they bring her to trial, Anne thought. Her arrest was just an elaborate scheme - perverse as it was - on the King's part to test her love for him, Anne laughed. It was all play-acting as in the masques in which they had performed. Again, Henry was *Amorous*, who would storm the Château Vert to free his captive love *Perseverance*. But in Anne's more lucid moments, the reality would have hit her that the Tower was no backdrop of courtly entertainment and that her husband the King had indeed deserted her. "Mr. Kingston", she asked soberly, "Shall I die without justice"? Kingston reassured her that "The poorest subject the King hath, hath justice". At that, Anne laughed.

—

Prisoner though she was, Anne Boleyn was still Queen, and she was treated accordingly. A generous sum of £25 was allotted for her maintenance, and she was allowed to send for her clothes and jewels - £100 worth – to adorn herself in the Tower. Four women - Kingston's wife, the Queen's aunt Lady Boleyn, a Mistress Cosyn, and a Mistress Stoner were assigned to her service. However, none of them were friendly. Lady Kingston, for one, was loyal to the Princess Mary and was a secret informant to the Imperial ambassador. The Queen complained how she was denied the company of her own trusted servants, and was instead, attended by ladies whom she had 'never loved'. They were good enough for the King, her gaoler protested, for he 'took them to be honest and good women'.

The only indulgence Anne requested in the Tower was the placing of the Holy Sacrament in her private oratory, before which she could 'pray for mercy'. She would not be doing so alone, she said, as 'the most part of England prays for me'. The Queen was certain the bishops she had appointed would do likewise, 'for they would all go to the King for me'.

But of the clergymen who owed their appointments and livings to Anne, only Cranmer made any attempt to plead on her behalf, and he did so with trepidation. Forbidden to come to court after Anne's arrest, Crammer, being 'cleaned amazed', set down his astonishment in a letter to his master. Next to the King himself, the Archbishop wrote, he 'was most bound unto her of all creatures living', and 'loved her not a little' for her great piety. It was his hope that the Queen would be found innocent. However, lest he appear too sympathetic to Anne, Cranmer conceded that the King 'would not have gone so far, except that she had surely been culpable... and if she be found culpable... then there was never creature in our time that so much slandered the Gospel'. The 'if' was as far as Cranmer could go in asserting the possibility of the Queen's innocence; any more would offend the King. But in a postscript to Henry VIII, Cranmer was no longer in doubt. He had just met with the Council who laid out Anne's crimes before him. In the face of the overwhelming evidence, he was 'exceeding sorry that such faults can be proved'. Whether he truly believed what he said, the Archbishop kept that to himself.

During Anne's confinement, the Kingstons moved into the royal apartments. Usually, a distinguished prisoner was placed with the Constable in his house. But since Anne, as Queen, was lodged in the palace, Kingston and his wife were obliged to live next to her 'at the door without'. The constable's easy access to the Queen was at Thomas Cromwell's bidding. Anne was to be spied on. Originally, the intention was to keep her incommunicado. None of the women assigned to the Queen, with the exception of Lady Kingston, were permitted to speak to her. But as the days wore on, Anne chattered incessantly. It was then decided to lift the ban on the rest of the ladies. It was Cromwell's hope that the women, now encouraged to converse with their prisoner, could goad her into making incriminating statements. Everything Anne said was to be noted by her ladies and then communicated to the Constable next-door.

Cut off from the outside world and surrounded by those who disliked her, Anne was under terrific strain. Her moods ran from one extreme to the other. At times, she could be 'very merry', and even indulge in light-hearted banter with her unfriendly gaolers. Referring to the accused men, Anne asked Lady Boleyn blithely, "Does anyone make their beds"? "Nay, I warrant you"! replied her no-nonsense aunt. Punning the word 'pallets' (for beds), Anne jested, "They might make *ballads*".

But equally, Anne could be sombre and even wild in her speech. "If I were to die", she told Kingston, "you shall see the greatest punishment within this seven years that ever come to England". In the same vein, Anne spoke of heavenly portents. The month had been uncomfortably hot and dry with no rainfall in sight. As if relief was contingent on her release, Anne vowed that 'there would be no rain' till she was delivered out of the Tower.

The Queen's strange utterings aside, her words were useful in building a case against her. Though Anne had said little or nothing about William Brereton, also charged with adultery with her, or about Lord Rochford, accused of incest with his own sister incredibly enough, she was more forthcoming about Sir Francis Weston. At court, the married Weston had been in hot pursuit of Madge Shelton like Henry Norris. Anne told her ladies how in the weeks before his arrest, not only had Weston been neglecting his wife, he had also stopped seeing Mistress Shelton. Why so, Anne had asked him - was there another woman? "It is yourself", he had answered. This was duly reported to Kingston.

As Anne languished in the Tower, Chapuys saw how the King played the cuckolded husband to great effect and with much enthusiasm. 'You never saw prince or other man who displayed his horns more or wore them so gladly', he wrote to Charles V. Henry was convinced – going so far as to boast even - that the Queen had bedded more than a hundred men. At a banquet at the Bishop of Carlisle's, he was in high spirits, displaying an 'extravagant joy' in the company of many ladies. Sitting next to the Bishop, Henry told him that the Queen's adultery was no surprise as he had long suspected her. He even admitted to having written 'a tragedy' on the subject.

But out of the public eye, the King dropped his façade. On the evening of his wife's arrest, Henry VIII broke down into tears when the Duke of Richmond came to bid his father good night. Embracing his son, Henry told him how he and his sister Mary ought to thank God for escaping Anne's clutches. Their stepmother, he said, 'was set on poisoning them both'.

≡

On 12 May, the trial of the four commoners took place at Westminster Hall, the setting of Anne Boleyn's coronation banquet. On the dais where the Queen once sat, were the judges and members of the King's Council - and, of all people, Thomas Boleyn. As a peer of the realm, he was obliged to appear as well. His only relief was that he would not be made to sit in judgement on his own children afterwards.

With the exception of Smeaton, who pleaded guilty to three incidents of bedding the Queen, the rest, Weston, Norris, and Brereton, maintained their innocence. There was talk that 'in case any do escape, it shall be young Weston'. His grief-stricken parents had offered the King money in exchange for his life, and Weston even had a friend in the French ambassador who intervened on his behalf. Neither approach was successful. Weston was found guilty with the others. For 'using fornication with Queen Anne… and also for conspiracy of the King's death'. All four were sentenced 'to be hanged, drawn, and quartered, their members cut off and burnt before them, their heads cut off'. As all the men were found guilty, it was a given that Anne herself would be too. Anticipating such an outcome, her household was broken up and her servants dismissed the following day.

Anne and George Boleyn were brought to trial on 15 May. The proceedings did not take place at Westminster, but within the precincts of the Tower. Inside the Great Hall, a 'great scaffold' was erected with benches and seats for the presiding lords and judges. At the far end was the Duke of Norfolk seated beneath a cloth of estate. In his hand was a long white staff signifying his office as High Steward of England. Before him was his son, Henry, Earl of Surrey, carrying his father's golden staff of Earl Marshal. Also present, was Anne's enemy, the Duke of Suffolk, and twenty-four other peers of the realm, all seated in order of rank. Even Henry Percy, now Earl of Northumberland, was there.

A hush fell on the packed chamber as the King's commission was read aloud. The Queen was then brought forward. She was conducted to the prisoner's bar, where she sat on a chair facing her accusers. The indictments were read out before some two thousand people who had crowded into the Great Hall to witness the sensational trial of a queen. They were not disappointed. The court heard salacious details of how 'led astray by devilish instigation, not having God before her eyes', Anne Boleyn 'most falsely and treacherously procured… by foul talks and kisses, touchings, gifts, and various unspeakable instigations and incitements' her various lovers. It escaped no one's attention how it was the Queen who was described as the aggressor through her 'most vile provocation and incitement day after day'. The charges became even more 'abominable and detestable'. Not only was Anne a great whore, but an incestuous one at that. 'Despising all the Almighty God's precepts', she had 'her tongue in the mouth' of her brother George who 'violated and carnally knew his own natural sister'.

Anne pleaded not guilty, and she 'made so wise and discreet answers to all things laid against her… with words so clearly as though she had never been faulty to the same'. Some of the charges were easy to refute. Anne was nowhere near the places where certain acts of adultery were said to have occurred. As to accusations that she had given 'great gifts' to the gentlemen squabbling for her attention, that was nonsense, Anne declared. Yes, she had given small tokens to Henry Norris and money to Francis Weston – but what of it? She was merely exercising her role as a generous mistress. Regarding Mark Smeaton, she hardly knew him, Anne testified. Other than the incident of the musician loitering about, she swore that he was only in her company one other time when he played on the virginals for her at Winchester, And as for the love she bore Lord Rochford, it was no more than that of a sister for her brother.

Unpopular as the Queen was, the absurd charges, along with her calm and dignified demeanour, won many over to her. Some even spoke 'variously about the King', censoring him for his treatment of his wife. The Queen's exemplary behaviour at her trial, in fact, was in marked contrast to the King's. While his wife was suffering in prison, the people said, Henry VIII was making a spectacle of himself. He caroused on the river in the company of musicians, and he was seen feasting with innumerable ladies late into the evening. The King's jaunts inflamed public opinion. It was no secret that he was visiting Jane Seymour, and soon, the two were lampooned in song, and a vulgar one at that, to the citizens' amusement.

The new sympathy for Anne was not shared by the jury. Knowing where their duty lay, the peers of the realm - including Northumberland - unanimously found her guilty. The Duke of Norfolk, despite his distaste for his niece, wept as he pronounced sentence. In offending 'the King's Grace in committing treason against his person', Anne was condemned to death. The lack of precedence in finding a queen guilty of treason presented a problem – what manner of punishment should be prescribed? As a female, Anne ought to suffer the usual penalty of being burnt alive, but because of her rank, she was no ordinary woman. Undecided, the court reserved the right to have her beheaded instead - if that be 'the King's pleasure'.

Retaining her composure, and perhaps expecting the result, Anne spoke. She told her judges she was sorry that guiltless men would have to die on her behalf, thus implying her innocence as well. Her only request was to have time to prepare herself for death. As the Queen was escorted back to her lodgings, there was a commotion. In the grip of an illness that would soon kill him, and perhaps overwhelmed by his part in the distasteful proceedings, Northumberland suddenly collapsed. After he had been tended to, the trial resumed with George Boleyn brought into court.

Like his sister, Rochford was prepared to put up a fight for his life. The principal charge against him was that he had had sex with Anne on at least two occasions. As proof, the prosecution claimed that George Boleyn had once spent an unusually long time with his sister behind closed doors. Just as incredible as the accusation itself was the fact that it was supposedly made by his own wife, Lady Rochford. Her role, if she was indeed involved, is mysterious. Did she willingly slander him, or was she forced to by the Crown? If she did testify, Jane Parker gained nothing. Burdened by her husband's debts, she later had to apply for support from Thomas Cromwell as 'a poor desolate widow without comfort'.

During the trial, Rochford

'never would confess anything but made himself as clear as though he had never offended... and made answer so prudently and wisely to all articles laid against him that marvel it was to hear'.

He defended himself so well that bets were placed - ten to one - that he would be acquitted. But Rochford foolhardily tipped the scales against himself. He was handed a paper by the court on which a 'delicate matter' was written; one that required a simple 'yes' or 'no'. Ignoring what he was told, Rochford read the charge out loud – did his sister, the Queen, ever make a statement that His Majesty the King was impotent?

George Boleyn's answer would have made no difference. His show of contempt, and his unwillingness to respond to the charge that he had once joked about Princess Elizabeth not being the King's, condemned him. Again, the Duke of Norfolk judged his kin. He commanded his nephew to be taken to Tyburn, and there suffer with the others found guilty.

The sentence was carried out two days later, not at Tyburn, but on Tower Hill. Fortunately for Rochford and the other four men, they were all spared any unnecessary butchery. The headmen's axe would be enough. On a hastily erected scaffold, 'of such a height that all present may see it', George Boleyn was the first to die. His final words were a warning to the crowd to take the example of him. He was a great promoter of the Gospel, he said, but had he been more diligent in practising what he preached, and had he avoided the vanities of this world, he would not have come to this. As to the specific crimes for which he was tried, Rochford made no comment. By not expressing remorse as he was expected to, he tacitly maintained his innocence. All he desired was the forgiveness of those whom he might have offended as he forgave them as well, and that 'God save the King'. Setting a good example for the others, George Boleyn knelt before the block and died bravely.

Henry Norris then took his place at the rail. Facing the throng, he was so nervous that he said 'almost nothing at all'. Francis Weston managed a short speech about making amends for his past 'abomination' - perhaps a reference to his raffish ways at court and for neglecting his wife - but nonetheless, he had 'thought little it had come to this'. Brereton too was resigned to his fate, and he admitted to deserving to die 'a thousand deaths'. However, he added, 'the cause whereof I judge not, but if ye judge, judge the best'.

The last to die was Mark Smeaton. Before laying his head on the block - now soaked with blood - he cried out, "Masters, I pray you all pray for me, for I have deserved the death"! It was left to the crowd to decipher his meaning. Was he sorry for his adultery with the Queen, or was he remorseful for falsely accusing her?

=

Before sending Anne Boleyn to her death, a nullification of her marriage was necessary. She would not die as Queen of England, but merely as 'the Lady Anne Boleyn'. To clear the way for any offspring Henry VIII might have with his future wife, Elizabeth must be disinherited as well. It was left to Cranmer who had once dared to speak up for Anne, to find the means of ending her marriage. He visited the Queen at the Tower on 16 May, and some justification was uncovered. Perhaps in hope of life, Anne corroborated the old rumour that in her youth, she did indeed betroth herself to Henry Percy (even though the Earl himself had vehemently denied it). Alternatively, Henry VIII's sexual relationship with Mary Boleyn, which Anne perhaps formally verified to Cranmer, may have been used instead to nullify his 'incestuous' union with her sister Anne. Whatever the cause, Cranmer thought it satisfactory, and he officially dissolved the royal union the following day. It was as if Henry VIII and Anne Boleyn had never been married. But still, she was to suffer death.

In the end, it was neither the flames nor the axe for Anne, but decapitation in 'the manner and custom of Paris' - that is with a sword. Anne, with her lifelong love of all things French, would have appreciated the gesture. But being a thing 'not before been seen' in the island kingdom, no Englishman had the skill to handle the requisite two-handed sword. It was thus necessary to send for the headsman of Calais, an expert with such a weapon. The King's graciousness, as his justice earlier, tickled Anne's black humour. "I heard say the executioner was very good", she joked. "I have a little neck". Again, she broke into peals of laughter. 'The lady has much joy and pleasure in death', Kingston noted with amazement in his report to Cromwell.

Anne's elation was in her certainty for what lay ahead. "I shall be in Heaven, for I have done many good deeds in my days", she assured her women. As well as the good Christian life Anne felt she had led to the best of her ability, she was also innocent of what she had been accused. By the injustice of her impending death, she was even more confident of her place in the next world. The Queen's last message to the King, thanking him for raising her from a gentlewoman to a marquis to a queen and then to the 'glory of martyrdom' can be dismissed as apocryphal, yet in her final days, perhaps such an exhilaration was indeed felt by Anne. Her conscience was clear, and what time was left to her was spent in prayer with her almoner. When she received Holy Communion on 18 May, she swore before Kingston and others present that she had never wronged her husband. The Constable would repeat this to the King, she was certain.

=

By tradition, executions normally took place in the morning with the Constable giving notice to his victims some hours before. But by daybreak no summons came. Eventually, the Queen was told that her death was to be postponed until after midday. "I hear I shall not die afore noon", she said anxiously, "I am very sorry therefore, for I thought to be dead by this time and past my pain".

It was not that Anne feared death; it was the waiting that unnerved her. The only comfort Kingston could offer was that when the time did come, Anne would feel nothing. The French executioner was exceptionally skilled and the blow would be 'subtle'. But the Constable's words of reassurance were dampened by further delay. The Frenchman had still not yet arrived, and Anne was to be given another day's reprieve. To fortify herself, Anne returned to her devotions.

It was a sleepless night, but not only for the Queen. Alexander Alesius, a Scottish reformer living in London, was awoken by a nightmare in the early hours of 19 May. He had a horrific vision of Anne Boleyn lying on the scaffold with her head off. Disturbed and unable to return to sleep, Alesius paid a visit to his friend Thomas Cranmer at dawn. At Lambeth Palace, he came upon the Archbishop, not abed either, but pacing nervously in his garden. The Scotsman inquired as to his restlessness. Cranmer answered, "Do not you know what is to happen today"? Alesius shook his head. "She who has been the Queen of England upon earth", the Archbishop said tearfully, "will today become a queen in Heaven". Having heard her last confession in the Tower, he paid tribute to her innocence.

Later that morning, the official witnesses to Anne's death - including Cromwell, Suffolk, Richmond, and the Lord Mayor - positioned themselves on a newly made scaffold. The headsman from Calais was also there, brandishing his double-handed sword. The platform had been built low so that only those closest could view the final ceremonial and hear the victim's last words. Nonetheless, Anne's execution was to be no private affair, but done with 'open gates', accessible to the common people. The 'reasonable number' Kingston expected had swelled to over a thousand Londoners, all drawn to an incredible and unprecedented event - the execution of the Queen of

England. There was worry about the mood of the crowd. People had 'spoken strangely' of Anne's condemnation. It was imperative that as soon as she was dead, any favourable account of her last moments must be suppressed. The rest of Europe must know her as 'a cursed and venomous whore' - as in the King's own words - who was justly punished for her crimes. To make sure the official spin made its way overseas via England's own ambassadors, all foreigners were ejected from the Tower.

The crowd waiting impatiently for the gory spectacle was not disappointed. At about 8 o'clock, the Queen came forward at last. For her final public appearance, Anne dressed carefully in a gown of grey damask edged with fur. A gabled hood, under which her long hair was tucked, framed her face. Determined to 'die boldly', Anne stepped onto the scaffold and addressed the crowd with a 'smiling countenance'. The officials drew in their breath. Would the Queen 'declare herself a good woman' in her last moments and make mockery of the King's justice?

To their relief, there were no surprises. Wanting to make a good end, and perhaps to protect her family from any royal reprisals, Anne made no accusation or criticism. But she admitted no guilt either. Following her brother's example, Anne merely submitted herself to the law and prayed for the King, asking the crowd to do likewise for her. Anne's only defence of her reputation was a reiteration of William Brereton's enigmatic plea. "If any person will meddle of my cause", she told the onlookers, "I require them to judge the best".

With nothing more to say, Anne removed her headdress, knelt upon the straw, and received the blindfold. The executioner advanced and raised his sword. With a single deft swing, it was done. Death was quick and painless as had been promised her.

Figure 10 The execution of Anne Boleyn by Jan Luyken, 1699
The Rijksmuseum, Amsterdam

PART 4
THE PEACEMAKER: JANE SEYMOUR

She would work in earnest to deserve the honourable name…
of pacificator, that is 'preserver and guardian of peace'.
(The Imperial ambassador in a letter to the Emperor, June 1536)

Figure 11   Jane Seymour by an Unknown Artist by kind
permission of the Chapter of Ripon Cathedral

Chapter 14
Bound to Obey and Serve

ANNE BOLEYN'S grave in the Tower of London bore no epitaph, but perhaps the most fitting tribute came from Thomas Cromwell. Shortly after her death, the secretary, in conversation with the Imperial ambassador, could not help but commend the late Queen, praising Anne 'beyond measure' for her 'sense, wit, and courage'. Coming from one who destroyed her, it was a great compliment indeed.

Freed from his marriage, the King seemed to be a new man. Later it would be said that it was as if he had 'come out of hell into heaven for the gentleness in this, and the cursedness and the unhappiness in the other'. But what to make of Mistress Seymour - the woman responsible for all this?

Surely, she must have been remarkable. But to the King's courtiers, she was anything but. What they did know of Jane Seymour was that she was originally a lady-in-waiting to Katherine of Aragon. She had served the Queen in her waning years, witnessing her many humiliations. As sympathetic as Jane was towards Katherine and her daughter Mary, her allegiances had to be set aside when she was transferred into the household of the King's new wife. It could only have been awkward for Jane. Shy and quiet, she could not make up or appreciate clever ballads and repartee like Anne Boleyn and the sophisticated gallants who surrounded her. Nor was Jane free and easy like the popular Madge Shelton. Unable to fit in and having no desire to, she affected an air of aloofness, one which many interpreted as arrogance on her part.

Eustace Chapuys too thought Jane 'proud and haughty' at first. He was also baffled by her looks – or lack thereof. What could the King possibly see in her? Being 'that nobody thinks that she has much beauty', the ambassador commented, Jane was hardly competition for her alluring mistress. Her complexion was dull, and her long nose, thin lips, and double chin did nothing for her. She was also about twenty-seven years old; hardly a young belle. Even Jane's virtue was suspect, snickered the ambassador, with her being a lady of the court. But that would pose no obstacle to the amorous Henry, Chapuys imagined. He had a great capacity for self-deception. If he wanted to believe

Jane was a virgin, he would convince himself of her purity. But should he then tire of her, the envoy added, Henry would conveniently find witnesses testifying to the looseness of her morals. With her dubious virginity, Mistress Seymour's motives were questionable as well. Her support for Princess Mary was perhaps insincere and entirely self-serving, Chapuys noted cynically. It remained to be seen whether Jane, once she was Queen, was as genuinely devoted to Mary's cause as she claimed to be.

≡

It was on 15 May - the day of Anne Boleyn's trial - that Jane Seymour received tidings of her condemnation. That morning, the King had promised his new sweetheart a verdict of guilty as if it was a foregone conclusion. True to his word, at 3 o'clock in the afternoon, Sir Francis Bryan brought Jane the welcome news. Did he address her on his knees? It would have been fitting. With Anne Boleyn sentenced to death, Jane was effectively England's new Queen. All she lacked was a wedding band.

Jane did not have to wait long. On the same day the executioner severed her rival's 'little neck', Archbishop Cranmer dutifully issued a licence allowing the King's new marriage. After 'mourning' as a widower for a brief eleven days, Henry married Jane on 30 May in Anne's former apartments at Whitehall. It was a quiet ceremony with little fanfare. Despite his new happiness, Henry felt no need to announce his third marriage to the world with a great public wedding. This was not meant as a slight to Jane. Henry's previous marriages had been performed in private, and his subsequent trips down the aisle after Jane were to be low-key affairs too.

Like Anne Boleyn before her, Jane Seymour's elevation was made known to the court at the royal procession to church. On Whitsunday, she was conducted to Mass at Greenwich adorned as Queen, followed by a great train of ladies as befitting her new rank. Later that day, Jane dined in state for everyone to see. Those present would have remembered how on the same day three years ago, it had been Anne Boleyn who sat as England's Queen in Westminster Hall; now Jane had that triumph. However, there were no immediate plans for a coronation. Rumour had it that the King would not crown his new wife until she was pregnant.

In place of a coronation, a great river pageant was organised in honour of Jane. On 7 June, the King and Queen travelled to Whitehall by water. The people had not seen anything like it since Anne Boleyn's coronation. This time, there were no sullen crowds, but joyful citizens who lined the banks of the river to cheer Henry VIII and his new bride. The Emperor Charles also gave his stamp of approval. Waiting along the way at Radcliff was a richly dressed Chapuys and his entourage stationed beneath a tent bearing the Hapsburg arms. As Henry and Jane sailed near, the ambassador sent a boatload of musicians towards their barge to serenade the happy pair. Before the procession passed out of sight, the Imperialists shot off forty rounds of ordnance in salute. Not to be outdone, the Londoners welcomed the royal couple with a hundred rounds of gunfire as they came in sight of the Tower. It was decorated with colourful banners; no more the gloomy place of execution as it was three weeks ago. With barely a thought given to the lives lost allowing their marriage to proceed, Henry and Jane glided past the fortress towards Whitehall.

The next day, Jane's triumph was all the sweeter as she stood in the gatehouse watching the King ride off to Westminster Palace. There, in the Parliament Chamber, the Lords and Commons began the process of revising the Act of Succession. With Anne Boleyn no more, her daughter Elizabeth was declared a bastard like her half-sister Mary. The Crown was instead settled on the offspring of Henry and Jane. But, as Chapuys noted, since the couple had yet to have children, it might *still* go to the Princess Mary - if she played her cards right.

=

The court hastened to pay its respects to the new Queen of England. The pallid wallflower was suddenly a blooming rose – 'as fair a queen as any in Christendom'. Jane Seymour was majestic, or so it was said. Decked out in her finery, she was a 'fair and goodly' sight to behold. The former Queen, everyone now agreed, had only looked 'the worse'. Jane surpassed Anne Boleyn not only in beauty and style, the courtiers said, but also in character. The King's new wife was no brazen hussy who laughed too loud and caused scenes. By all appearances, Queen Jane was gentle in nature and agreeable, looking to no other happiness than her husband's. She conducted herself meekly and with deference to his wishes, raising no objections or tantrums like his previous consorts. In other words, Jane was the perfect wife for Henry VIII. Her motto set out her duty as Queen. In contrast to Anne Boleyn's self-congratulatory motto of *The Most Happy*, Jane chose for herself the modest *Bound to Obey and Serve*.

Docile and submissive as she appeared to be, Jane did possess an intelligence and strength of character few gave her credit for. Though she had aligned herself with Katherine and Mary's supporters, Jane was no empty-headed tool to be used by them. It took calculation and nerve on her part to take on Anne Boleyn, and she did her part beyond anyone's expectations. That was more than can be said about Henry's previous mistress, that unnamed beauty who despite her assets failed to hold Henry's interest for long. Jane also had opinions of her own, and not all of them were in keeping with her husband's. Conjugal duty and fear of Henry's temper usually kept Jane in line, but when her conscience compelled her to take a stand, she was not shy to speak her mind. However, unlike the late Queen who had to have the last word each time, Jane knew when to hold her tongue.

Chapuys was impressed by Jane's conduct, and he echoed her subjects' admiration for her. His first audience with the new Queen was held within her apartments, a week after her marriage. Henry VIII was present, but preoccupied in chatting with her ladies, he let Jane receive the ambassador on her own. Chapuys offered her his congratulations. As the envoy spoke French, and Jane probably only English, their conversation was presumably made through an interpreter. During their exchange, it was Jane, the envoy proposed, who should bear Anne Boleyn's device of *The Most Happy*. As Henry's new wife, *she* would bring the title to fruition, he said. He also praised Jane as the peacemaker who would restore tranquillity and order to the realm and to the King's family. Even abroad, Chapuys told Jane, her benevolence towards the Princess Mary was recognised, and he hoped that she would continue in that vein. Jane uttered a few words of thanks and promised to do her best for her stepdaughter before becoming tongue-tied. Henry, who was hovering nearby, came to Jane's rescue. He apologised to Chapuys for his wife's nervousness. She had never received ambassadors before.

═══

There was none more excited at the great turn of events than Mary Tudor. Just three days after Anne Boleyn's arrest, she had noticed a change in the demeanour of her household officers. She was accorded more respect from them than before, as well as from Lady Shelton. Worried about her connection to the Boleyns, her guardian was eager to cut off ties to her disgraced niece. There was also an increase in Mary's staff. During a move to Hunsdon, many of her sister Elizabeth's attendants were transferred to her service instead. There was the possibility of even further expansion when many of Mary's former servants were found hanging about her gate. They had all heard of the Queen's downfall, and they were hoping to take up their old places again with the Princess.

Happy as she was to see these old familiar faces, Mary, on Chapuys' advice, declined to re-employ any of them without her father's approval. It was imperative that she regain his favour first, as the envoy was certain that Parliament would petition the King to restore her to her rights. If Mary played the obedient daughter, he would have no reason to refuse her anything, Chapuys believed. The ambassador also communicated to Mary his favourable impressions of the new Queen, especially how she promised to speak to the King on her behalf. With Jane as an ally, Mary was sure that her loving father would return to his senses now that he was freed from the influence of 'that woman', whom Mary charitably prayed God to pardon.

A week after Anne Boleyn's death, Mary wrote to Cromwell, commending herself to him. Master Secretary, as she heard from Chapuys, had always looked on her favourably. When her name was mentioned in conversation, Cromwell, the ambassador said, would touch his hat as a show of respect. Confident he would help her, Mary sent him a message. She 'would have been a suitor' sooner, but no one had dared speak for her while Queen Anne was alive. Now she was finally able to write to him freely. Would he, Mary asked, mediate between herself and the King?

Cromwell was receptive to restoring Mary. Although he had no taste for her commitment to the Pope, the Princess was valuable to his plan of re-establishing peace with the Emperor. After speaking with Henry VIII, Cromwell gave Mary permission to send a letter to her father. Writing lovingly and abjectly, she asked for his blessing. Without specifying her offences, she begged his forgiveness. Likewise, without reference to what she knew was required of her, Mary announced that she would 'most humbly and willingly stand content to follow, obey, and accomplish in all points'. There was nothing she wanted more than to return to court again, Mary also wrote, and to pay her respects to the new Queen.

Such words could not have been more pleasing to Jane. Mary and the King had been estranged for far too long, and it was time for them to be a family again. Though Henry had raged in frustration towards Mary, and had even threatened her life, Jane knew that he still loved her. It was unnatural that such a rift should befall a father and daughter. After all, Mary was so much his child. She inherited from Henry VIII his intelligence, his dignity, *and* his stubbornness.

For the benefit of his realm and his peace of mind, the King must bring Mary back to court.

But when Jane spoke up for Mary, she was rebuked. The King chided his wife for being a fool. Instead of being concerned about his unruly daughter, he said, she ought to be looking to her own future children. Undaunted, Jane continued to plead for Mary until Henry finally relented. He would receive Mary back into his affections, he promised, but *only* if she submitted to him entirely. She must admit she was a bastard.

Mary could not believe such a declaration was still needed. In the past, she had laid the blame entirely on Anne Boleyn - but now she was dead. Presently, it was her father himself who demanded her surrender. It was a chilling realisation for Mary. All the time, it was he too who wanted her browbeaten, and he was still intent on proceeding against her if she continued in her defiance. The word from court was that Henry was even actively consulting lawmakers on whether he could have her put to death for treason.

In desperation, Mary wrote to Cromwell again. She had done her utmost to appease her father. 'But if I be put to anymore', she told him, 'my said conscience will in no way suffer me to consent'. It was a useless appeal and Mary's fear of 'more business hereafter' was realised. In the middle of June, a delegation headed by the Duke of Norfolk went to Hunsdon to present the King's terms to her. A direct showdown was the last thing Mary wanted. Already, she was sick with grief and weakened by ailments largely attributed to anxiety. She suffered from headaches and a toothache, and she had barely slept for days.

Steeling herself before Norfolk and the delegates, Mary remained defiant. No, she would not accept her father as Head of the English Church; no, she would not accept the illegality of her parents' marriage; and no, she would not accept being a bastard. They turned to threats. Mary should not think she was immune from prosecution, the men warned, daughter or not, she was still the King's subject. One of the deputation, the Earl of Essex, went even further. With 'injurious language', he told Mary that she was so unnatural in her disobedience, that she was unfit to be the King's child. Were she his own, Essex swore, he would 'beat her to death' or bash her head against a wall until it was 'as soft as a boiled apple'.

Getting nowhere with the stubborn girl, the delegation left to report their failure to the King. Orders were left with Lady Shelton to see to it that the Princess spoke to and saw no one. But like she always managed to do, Mary smuggled out a message to Chapuys telling him what had just happened. The envoy counselled her to give in. She was clearly up against a wall, and she must surrender, or least seem to. Not only was she endangering herself, Chapuys warned, but also her friends. Several ladies at court sympathetic to her were being bullied into swearing to her illegitimacy. As well, her friend Lady Hussey had recently been arrested, accused of encouraging her into treason. The Marquis of Exeter and Francis Bryan were under suspicion too.

Mary must do whatever the King asked, Chapuys advised. For as long as she remained in England, the Emperor could do nothing to protect her. She must declare herself illegitimate. No one - not her friends, her cousin Charles, or the Pope - would begrudge her for wanting to preserve her life. And besides, any declaration she made under duress would not be legally binding. Her mother Katherine, if she were still alive, would have understood, as would her Maker. 'God looked more into the intentions', Chapuys consoled her, 'than in the deeds of men'. By saving herself, she might also serve His purpose in leading England back to Rome. Her chances were good, in fact, the ambassador believed. Since Elizabeth was to be dropped from the succession, and Jane Seymour was still without child, it was not impossible that Mary could indeed be Queen one day.

There was further pressure from Cromwell about the course Mary must take. Her message that she would obey her father in all things, save that which violated her conscience, earned a scathing response from Master Secretary. An exasperated Cromwell called Mary 'the most obstinate and obdurate woman that ever was', who ought to be made 'an example in punishment'. His anger was understandable. He had gone out on a limb for Mary, only to have her continue in her defiance. The King hated incompetence, and Cromwell began to fear for himself, so much that for days, he was 'considering himself a lost man and dead.' According to Chapuys, Cromwell's terror was very real. The King 'in a great passion' accused him of being in league with the Marquis of Exeter and his friends, and for that, they would *all* suffer for it. Even Queen Jane received the brunt of his anger. When she dared to intercede for Mary, she was 'rudely repulsed'.

Cromwell had gone too far to turn back, and he made one final attempt to force Mary into submission. He enclosed with a letter to her a 'book of articles' to which she must set her name. Should she refuse, he wrote, she should not even think about writing to him again. Pressured from all sides, Mary gave in. On 22 June, barely looking at the papers Cromwell prepared for her signature, Mary signed away her birthright and that which she held dear. She acknowledged the marriage between the King and her mother Katherine - not the Queen, but the Princess Dowager - 'was by God's law and Man's law, incestuous and unlawful'. Not only that, she recognised her father's title of 'Supreme Head in Earth, under Christ, of the Church of England'. As for the Pope, the Vicar of Christ, Mary with a stroke of her pen, refused his 'authority, power, and jurisdiction within this realm'.

With Mary's capitulation, her supporters, Chapuys, and Cromwell all breathed a collective sigh of relief. 'There was incredible joy throughout the court', and everyone looked to her return. Mary's own feelings however are an enigma. Did she regret what she had done? Chapuys had no doubt of it. Though she had saved herself, Mary, he wrote in his despatches, still retained 'some of her former sadness and sorrow'. Moreover, she had begged him to write to Rome in secret for absolution to clear her conscience.

But while Mary was imploring the Pope's forgiveness, she was writing to court as if the world was suddenly off her shoulders. In a letter to Cromwell, Mary rendered her gratitude:

> 'Good Mr. Secretary, how much I am bound to you, which have not only travailed, when I was almost drowned in folly, to recover me before I sank and was utterly past recovery, and so to present me to the face of grace and mercy but desisteth not since with your good and wholesome counsels, so to arm me from any relapse, that I cannot, unless I were too wilful and obstinate (whereof there is now no spark in me), fall again into any danger.'

Mary's other letters to Cromwell and the King speak of her new happiness and of the pleasure she took in rebuilding her household. She even had kind words about her sister Elizabeth. By her correspondence, she had no regrets. Or did she? Who was speaking from the heart? Mary who was ashamed of her past behaviour, or Mary who was haunted by guilt for betraying her ideals? Her true feelings are even harder to gauge when Mary by reputation was plain in her dealings and incapable of dissembling. Even when she became Queen, this view was still held. She is 'so good, so easy, without experience of life or of statecraft - a novice in everything' - was the opinion of the Imperialists who knew her best. But in truth, Mary was more complex. Essentially honest, she was nonetheless, able to deceive and to engage in intrigue when necessary. No 'novice' was capable of plotting an escape and dabbling in treason as Mary had done, and would find herself doing so again in the future.

Rehabilitated, at last, Princess Mary – or 'the Lady Mary' as she must now call herself - was paid a visit by her father and her new stepmother on 6 July at Hackney. According to Chapuys, the reunion went off splendidly. The King was 'kind and affectionate', and could not have been a better parent. He gave Mary a gift of a thousand crowns, promising her she would never lack for money again. Jane was equally generous. She presented her stepdaughter with a handsome diamond ring, and more importantly, she offered Mary her friendship. Starved of affection, Mary easily took to Jane, in time forging a genuine bond with her. At their departure, the next day, Jane and the King promised to have Mary at court soon.

To commemorate the new concord, Cromwell had a special ring made for the Princess. On it were minute portraits of her united family - Henry and Jane on one side, and Mary herself on the other. Inscribed on the band were verses celebrating, appropriately enough, the virtues of filial obedience. The gift was so exceptional, that before Cromwell was even able to put it into Mary's hands, the King took it and gave it to her himself.

=

Until Jane conceived a son, the succession was unsettled. The King had three children, all bastards. If he suddenly died, who would rule? Mary, the eldest, but female, or Richmond, the younger but male? Those betting on Henry Fitzroy, should the Queen prove barren, were let down when the young man died unexpectedly on 23 July 1536. According to malicious hearsay, the Duke had finally succumbed to a slow acting poison introduced by Anne Boleyn and her brother Rochford. As much as Anne was still reviled, in truth, Richmond had died from natural causes, perhaps from the same wasting illness that took away his aunt the French Queen in 1533. With the succession still so ambiguous, no announcement was made of Henry Fitzroy's demise for fear of raising public unrest. Instead, the King ordered his son's father-in-law Norfolk (Richmond had been married to the Duke's daughter Mary Howard) to convey the body without ceremony to Thetford Priory - away from the capital and prying eyes - for a discrete burial.

After the loss of young Richmond, Jane still showed no signs of pregnancy. At the age of forty-five, Henry VIII was feeling the weight of his years. He even wondered aloud to Chapuys whether he would ever be blessed with a son. Still, the King was hopeful and he remained committed to Jane. Fertile or not, she had proved to be a good wife. She was so widely adored that it was decided to have her crowned at the end of October. However, an outbreak of plague at Westminster meant a postponement until at least the following summer. All the same, cynics at court attributed the delay to Henry's insistence that the Queen fulfil her part of the bargain first in being a mother.

Until then, Jane occupied herself with managing her household. Hers was not to be like her predecessor's. Her court was to be free of any hint of light behaviour or scandal. People of questionable morals, such as Madge Shelton, were expelled and replaced by ladies of impeccable virtue. As always with a new Queen, there was a jostling for places in her establishment by the daughters of the elite. It was at court that alliances were forged, marriages contracted, fortunes made, and power obtained. Young women close to the Queen had her ear. A girl could reap great favours and rewards for her family and friends, or even influence policy if she were clever and her mistress pliable. But with the high demand for places, it was not easy to secure a position. When Lady Lisle, wife of the Governor of Calais, sought appointments for her two daughters, her efforts were only partly successful. Queen Jane allowed Lady Lisle to send over her two daughters, but only one would win the coveted spot. The position of lady-in-waiting was awarded to Anne Bassett. Her sister Katharine, considered less suitable, was packed off to her relatives instead.

The Queen's household was one of strict standards. Jane Seymour had definite opinions on how she wanted her servants to behave. They were to conduct themselves with decorum and modesty. That included what they wore as well. To Anne Bassett's dismay, all her fancy French clothes had to be put away. Jane thought them immodest, and Anne had to dress like the rest of her ladies in the more sedate English style. The days of Anne Boleyn's fashionable Francophile court were gone. Even Mistress Bassett's chic rounded French hoods were banished. Instead, she had to wear the cumbersome gabled headdresses favoured by the Queen. The French styles were far more flattering to Anne Bassett, but she had no say in the matter - 'the Queen's pleasure most be fulfilled'. Despite the demands she placed on her ladies, Jane was a generous mistress. She rewarded those who

Figure 12   Familia Regia (Henry VIII, Henry VII, Elizabeth of York,
and Jane Seymour) by George Vertu (after Hans Holbein)
The Yale Center For British Art, New Haven

served her well with gifts, including 'brooches of gold' and 'borders
enamelled with various colours' for their headdresses.

Besides the ladies recruited to serve her, Jane Seymour surrounded
herself with members of her family. Her brother Edward, who had
been in the King's service since an early age, was made Viscount
Beauchamp, and later Earl of Hertford. Edward's younger sibling, the
handsome and raffish Thomas, also basked in royal favour thanks to
Jane. He was appointed to the King's Privy Chamber and received a
knighthood. The Queen's sister, Elizabeth Seymour, also did well for
herself at court. She ventured out of the obscurity of Wolf Hall to be
married to Thomas Cromwell's son Gregory. Almost certainly, it was a
typical arranged marriage between two powerful families, rather than
a love match. However it came about, Elizabeth Seymour's father-in-
law would have viewed it in strictly practical terms. Cromwell had
already climbed high by his own merits, but even more could be had
if he became a kinsman of a future king.

Chapter 15
Most Precious Jewel

IN OCTOBER 1536, discontent that had been brewing in the North for some time took the form of open rebellion. Disturbances had broken out in Lincolnshire, beginning in the town of Louth. The call to arms gained momentum, receiving support from nearby Caistor, Horncastle, and the neighbouring communities. The ringleaders were a monk and a shoemaker, who together raised an army of over twenty-two thousand men. Added to this number were local officials forced to join in the insurrection. To refuse meant imprisonment or death. When the chaplain to the Bishop of Lincoln would not take part, he was killed as an example.

The Northerners, who still adhered to the old faith, abhorred the changes made by Henry VIII. His new Church had done away with the Pope, the worship of holy relics and images, and even four of the Seven Sacraments - what other blasphemies were next, the rebels asked? How many more monasteries were to be closed and stripped before the King had his fill of riches? The North was rife with rumour that if it stayed idle, 'God's service would be utterly destroyed and taken away; that no man should marry a wife, or be a partaker of the Sacraments… and that they should be brought into more bondage, and a more wicked way of life than the Saracens are under the Great Turk'. There were economic anxieties too - threats of forced subsidies, land enclosures, and increased taxation. Soon, people grumbled, a man would not even be able to 'eat a piece of roast meat but that he should for the same first pay to the King a certain sum of money'.

At first, the rebellion was short-lived. Receiving news of trouble in the North, the King threatened the malcontents with an army led by his brother-in-law Suffolk. After a tongue lashing from the Duke about their disloyalty to the Crown, the disheartened men of Lincolnshire returned in peace to their homes. Even so, to discourage any more disobedience, a few were made example of. For inciting treason, the principal agitators, including the monk and the shoemaker, paid with their lives. The rest escaped further north to stir up rebellion there. It was not difficult. The people of Yorkshire, unhappy with royal policy like their neighbours, needed little outside incitement. Some thirty thousand, supported by religiously conservative magnates such Thomas Dacre, Thomas Darcy, and John Hussey, banded together to carry on where their compatriots from Lincolnshire had failed.

Led by a charismatic lawyer named Robert Aske, a man of 'marvellous stomach and boldness', the insurgents carried the banner of the Crucifixion flanked by the Eucharistic chalice and the Host, and on their bosoms wore the badge of the Five Wounds of Christ. By adopting these symbols, their objective was a holy crusade - a 'Pilgrimage of Grace' as they called it. Their quarrel was not with the King himself - to whom they insisted they were still loyal - but with 'all villein blood and evil counsellors against the commonwealth'. The allusion to Thomas Cromwell by reference to his humble origins was obvious. Along with the dismissal of the hated minister overseeing the destruction of the religious houses, the rebels also demanded the expulsion of heretical bishops like Cranmer, a reunion with the Church of Rome, and the restoration of the Princess Mary as the King's legitimate heiress.

Some of the rebels' grievances might have been shared by Mary herself, but she wisely expressed no sympathy. As repugnant as the Royal Supremacy and its consequences were to Mary, she had made her peace with her father and she would no longer challenge his authority. Mary's good relations with the King brought her to court that October. More than an opportunity for Henry to see his daughter again, her visit was also meant to 'soften the temper of the people' as the crisis was brewing. Mary had always been popular, and it was pleasing to Henry's subjects to see her given the respect due to her. At banquets, Mary held precedence over all the ladies except Queen Jane, sitting just 'opposite her, a little lower down'. She also had the honour of presenting the napkin to her father and stepmother. For good measure, even the little Elizabeth was present, though seated at another table. This was due to her tender age, not neglect. Far from ignoring the little girl, the King was said to be 'very affectionate' towards his younger daughter, and 'loves her much'.

On 24 October, the distressing news came that Aske and his army had captured York. The Queen was troubled, becoming more and more convinced that God was favouring their cause. Was it not a sin for the King to covet Church property? And was it not wrong to displace holy men and women who aided the sick and the poor? Though Jane had vowed to 'obey and serve', her conscience would not let her keep silent any longer. Screwing up her courage,

Jane threw herself on her knees before Henry and begged him to restore the abbeys. The rebellion, she cried, was surely a sign of God's displeasure. Henry had tolerated Jane speaking up for Mary when the girl was disobedient, but this time, she had gone too far. Roughly, he told her to get up and not to meddle in affairs that were no business of hers. To make certain Jane understood, Henry reminded her of what happened to his former Queen.

Lacking enough troops to suppress Robert Aske's rebellion, it was necessary for the government to play for time. The Duke of Norfolk was dispatched to Doncaster to negotiate a truce. As a show of good will, Aske was even invited to court for Christmas. To meet with Aske, the King and his court left Whitehall for Greenwich on 22 December. The winter of 1536/1537 was bitterly cold, and the Thames had turned to ice preventing a journey by water. The trip had to be made on horseback and by carriage instead, but it allowed the people to witness the spectacle of the court on the move close-up.

Despite the chill, the people crammed themselves behind the barriers from Temple Bar to Southwark and beyond, hoping to catch a glimpse of the royal family. Those able to get a good look saw the Mayor of London leading the court towards London Bridge. Riding behind him were the King and Queen. At the sight of them, the people raised great cheers. Equal adulation was given to Mary as she went by. The procession headed to Fleet Street where a waiting group of friars censed the royal family. At St Paul's Cathedral, the choir sang anthems in their honour as they arrived, and the Bishop of London and his abbots greeted them with fragrant incense.

It looked to be a good Christmas, even for the rebels. At Greenwich, Henry VIII was the affable and forgiving monarch. He presented Robert Aske with 'apparel and great rewards', promising to right all wrongs done to his subjects in the North. As a further gesture of goodwill, he announced his intention to have the Queen crowned at York Minster. The rebel lawyer was just as accommodating. Won over by Henry's kindness and by his assurances, Aske ripped off his badge of the Five Wounds and vowed hereafter to take up only that of his sovereign lord the King.

But within weeks of Aske's return to the North with the royal pledge of clemency and compromise, revolt broke out again in February of 1537. Henry, who had never intended to keep his promises to the rebels, had his excuse to strike. He reacted with a vengeance. Norfolk hurried north again, this time not to bargain, but to make bloody punishment. The leaders - the Lords Hussey and Darcy - and their cohorts were tried and all sentenced to death. For many of them, simple decapitation was not enough. Traitors such as Lord Fitzgerald and his five uncles were drawn from the Tower to be 'hanged, beheaded, and quartered'. After the carnage, their heads were set on London Bridge and on the gates of the city. A special fate was reserved for Margaret Bulmer, wife of one of the chief rebels. Dragged to Smithfield, the 'very fair and beautiful' lady was burnt at the stake.

As a special warning to Lincolnshire, 'one of the most brute and beastly shires of the whole realm', Lord Hussey was specially brought there to be beheaded in full view of the people. Robert Aske also suffered. Though he was actually against the renewed violence, he was nonetheless taken to York where his pleas for a quick, merciful end were ignored. He was hung in chains on the wall of the castle tower till he slowly expired.

With the Pilgrimage of Grace put down, it was evident that God was on Henry VIII's side, even more so when Queen Jane was with child in May 1537. Determined not to lose what he was sure was a son, the King made certain that his pregnant wife was treated with the utmost care until the time of her delivery. Jane was pampered, but she was not difficult to please. Her only indulgence as her pregnancy progressed was a craving for delicacies. In the summer, she had an incessant appetite for quails. Nothing was too good for his expectant wife, and the King had them specially sent over from Calais by the bunch. Even Princess Mary made Jane a gift of them.

Because of the Queen's condition, the King's plan to visit the North to maintain the peace had to be postponed. 'Considering she was but a woman', Henry felt that Jane would fret over her his absence. Consequently, she might 'upon some sudden and displeasant rumours and bruits… take to her stomach such impressions as might engender no little danger or displeasure to the infant'. Her coronation at York - or even closer to home at Westminster - was also on hold. Perhaps the ordeal was thought too taxing for Jane, even though her predecessor Anne Boleyn had undergone the full rituals while pregnant.

Instead of a coronation, there was the celebratory singing of great *Te Deum* at St Paul's on 27 May in honour of the Queen's happy state. The elation extended well into the evening. Throughout the City, bonfires were lit, and free wine was given to all the citizens. They toasted the King and the Queen, and at the same time, prayed God to send England its long-awaited Prince.

In September, Jane took to her chamber at Hampton Court. But it was not until 11 October that her pains began. Alerted to the imminent birth, the clergy of St Paul's, joined by the Mayor, the city aldermen, and the guilds, formed a solemn procession beseeching God to grant the safe delivery of a prince. As surely as God was 'English', the child born in the morning hours of 12 October was indeed a boy. The country was in rapture. Not since the birth of the King's short-lived son in 1511 had there been such delirium. Church bells tolled continuously throughout the day, and the citizens danced and drank themselves into a happy stupor. At St Paul's, prayers for the Queen's delivery were replaced by those of thanksgiving. After so many years, it seemed almost a miracle.

Three days after his birth, the infant was carried into the royal chapel by the Marchioness of Exeter, recently restored to favour. At the font, he was baptised by Archbishop Cranmer acting as one of his godfathers; the others being the two dukes, Norfolk and Suffolk. At their side was Mary, serving as her brother's godmother. The baby's other sister had a role as well. Elizabeth had the privilege of bearing the chrisom. But being a child still herself, she had to be carried in the arms of the Queen's brother Edward Seymour. Elizabeth was probably too young to notice, but also present at the ceremony was that relic of the past, her grandfather Thomas Boleyn. Though he was no longer part of the King's circle, and his 'living of late [was] much decayed', Boleyn loyally took part in the christening.

After the boy was baptised and confirmed, the herald, Clarenceux King-of-Arms, presented 'the noble imp' to the assembly, calling out his name and titles - 'Edward, son and heir to the King of England, Duke of Cornwall and Earl of Chester'. As custom dictated, his parents were not present at the ceremony. But after all was done, Edward was taken back to the royal apartments where he received their blessing, along with that of God, the Virgin Mary, and England's patron saint, St George.

For Edward's safety and well-being, his father laid down strict rules for the care of his 'most precious jewel'. No one was allowed access to the Prince without the King's express permission. When such consent was granted, that person must at least be a knight in rank. Hygiene was rigorously enforced. Authorised visitors were not permitted to touch the baby in any way except to kiss his hand. Edward's linen was to be 'purely washed' each day, and his lodgings given a good scrub on a regular basis. The Prince's servants were expected to be clean and not resort to any 'infect[ious] or corrupt place'. They were to especially avoid London during the summer. Plague was most prevalent during the hot season. Any servant who had official business there had to be quarantined when he returned. Beggars were not to come into the vicinity of Hampton Court, but collect their alms elsewhere. Those who disobeyed were to be 'grievously punished'. After so many dead sons, Henry VIII refused to have another.

The Queen had survived the ordeal of childbirth, but sadly not its repercussions. Just days after the christening, puerperal fever set in. Again, prayers were offered and processions formed to intercede for her. Thomas Cromwell, looking to point fingers, placed the blame on Jane's staff. They had allowed their mistress to catch cold, he said, and they should have known better than to serve her the indulgent meals that her 'fantasy in sickness called for'.

After Jane suffered a 'lax' of her bowels, it was hoped that a discharge of her rich diet would be a curative. On the contrary, she worsened. The doctors could do no more for her, and her confessor was summoned. The court prepared for the inevitable. At 8 o'clock on the evening of 24 October, Norfolk scribbled a quick note to Cromwell requiring him to make haste to 'comfort our good master'. Jane was quickly slipping away, and Norfolk feared that by the time Cromwell received his letter, the Queen would already be dead. He was correct. She died shortly afterwards.

Henry VIII was beside himself with grief. Even when Jane was lingering between life and death, he was so agitated that he could not be at her side to offer comfort. Now with her gone, Henry could not bear to be at Hampton Court, not even with his newborn son. He immediately set out for Whitehall where he 'kept himself close and secret a great while'.

The arrangements for the funeral were put in the hands of Norfolk, as Earl Marshal, and of William Paulet, the Lord Treasurer. There had not been a proper funeral for a Queen of England since that of the King's mother in 1503, so the Office of Arms had to be consulted 'to show precedents'. Following the established procedures, after Jane's entrails were removed and buried separately, her embalmed corpse was laid in state in the Presence Chamber beginning on 26 October. For five days, Jane's women - in black mourning with white veils -

kept vigil around her hearse until it was removed to the royal chapel. There, Masses were said for the late Queen.

On 12 November, the coffin was transported in sombre procession to Windsor Castle. For its journey, the hearse was covered in black velvet. Upon it was an effigy of Jane 'richly apparelled like a queen, with a rich crown of gold on her head'. Surrounding the carriage were the greatest in the land, with Princess Mary acting as chief mourner. The common people who loved Jane Seymour too were also represented. Two hundred 'poor men' marched in the procession, each one wearing her royal badge.

When the hearse arrived at Windsor, the coffin was taken into St George's Chapel. Cranmer officiated at the service and saw Jane's body lowered into a great vault beneath the choir. Later, an inscription was placed over her grave:

'Here lies Jane, a phoenix By whose death, another phoenix was born How tragic that such a pair is rare indeed.'

As Queen, Jane Seymour had adopted the symbol of the phoenix. Just like the mythical bird, she had risen from destruction – that of another woman - only to die herself in bringing forth new life.

PART 5
THE KING'S WIFE AND SISTER:
ANNE OF CLEVES

That the pretended marriage between us is void and of no effect... ...
that Your Highness will take me for your sister,
for which I must humbly thank you..
(Anne of Cleves in a letter to Henry VIII, July 1540)

Figure 13   Anne of Cleves, attributed to Barthel de Bruyn
The Rosenbach Museum and Library, Philadelphia

Chapter 16
Of Excellent Beauty?

JANE SEYMOUR was barely cold in her grave when Thomas Cromwell began his search for the next Queen of England. No one doubted that Henry VIII would remarry. It was just a matter of *when*. But in his grief, Henry would not consider Cromwell's plea to take a new wife, and he remained in seclusion mourning his loss. 'Divine Providence', Henry wrote to the King of France, 'has mingled my joy with the bitterness of the death of her who brought me this happiness'. His bereavement went on for months, and Christmas at Greenwich that year was a gloomy one. It was not until the following February that Henry's mood lifted, and mirth and colour were brought back to court again.

With the King in better spirits, the Council pressed him to remarry. If not for his own pleasure and comfort, there was the state of the realm to consider. Prince Edward was healthy and thriving, and suckling in his cradle 'like a child of his puissance', but there was always the unthinkable possibility that he might not survive into adulthood. Henry only had to be reminded of the deaths of his brother Arthur and of his son Richmond.

Won over finally by the Council's petitions, Henry, out of 'tender zeal' for his subjects, agreed to play the eligible bachelor. The problem now was finding him a suitable mate. There was no one waiting in the wings to be Queen like there was when Katherine of Aragon and Anne Boleyn fell in their turns. There was talk that Henry's fancy had alighted on Jane Seymour's attendant Anne Bassett - perhaps due to her marked resemblance to the pretty Madge Shelton - but it was only a rumour.

Since Henry VIII showed no inclination towards any English lady, there was speculation that he would take a foreign wife instead. As early as mid-May 1536, when it was known throughout Europe 'that the King will put her (Anne Boleyn) and her accomplices to death', Charles V was considering a marriage pact between England and the Empire. He was certain Henry would not stay a widower for long, as he was 'of an amorous complexion and always desires to have a male heir'. The two young women Charles had in mind were his nieces, the Infanta of Portugal and the recently widowed Christina of Denmark, Duchess of Milan. Little was said about the Infanta's merits, but Christina was reported to be a 'goodly personage and of excellent beauty'. The Emperor's proposals, however, came to nothing when his uncle married Mistress Seymour instead. There was also Henry's reluctance to marry abroad as the Imperialists later learned. "Why so"? Chapuys asked Cromwell. The minister gave the extraordinary excuse that should the King marry a lady of 'great blood and high connections' who turned out be another Anne Boleyn, he would not find it easy to get rid of her!

But unable to find anyone at court to his liking, the King had to make himself amenable to a non-English wife. Lately, he had heard good things about certain ladies in France. Henry was particularly interested in Francis I's daughter Margaret, and his cousin Madame de Longueville (better known as Mary of Guise). Henry instructed his envoys to make discrete inquiries about their qualities, and whether either lady was already spoken for by his nephew James V of Scotland. After hearing from his ambassadors, the King was captivated by Mary of Guise. She was attractive and better yet, she was tall. Henry, being 'big in person', liked the idea of a 'big wife'. Mary, on the other hand, was not as interested in the King of England's portly physique. She set sail from France - past England - to Scotland to marry King James instead.

Undaunted by the rejection, Henry still aimed for a French bride. Audaciously, he suggested a beauty contest of eligible French princesses to be held in Calais, with himself as the judge *and* as the grand prize. Astonished, King Francis' ambassador asked Henry if he would instead, prefer to 'try them one after the other, and keep the one most agreeable'. Henry blushed full red and dropped the idea.

With a French consort out of the running, the possibility of Christina of Denmark was revisited. From what his envoys told him, Henry found her irresistible. She was young – only sixteen; tall - as Henry wanted his future wife to be; and best of all - she was lovely. John Hutton, the English representative in the Low Countries was enchanted by the girl. In her beauty and in her station, Christina had no rival in the region, Hutton said. 'She hath a singular good countenance, and when she chanceth to smile, there appeareth two pits in her cheeks, and one in her chin, the which becometh her right excellently well'. Christina had more than just good looks; she was fluent in three languages (French, Italian, and German), and she also enjoyed hunting, which Henry himself had a passion for. The King could not have chosen a better queen. But was the lady herself interested?

Christina, an obedient girl, was at the Emperor's command, she said. Encouraged by her response, one of the King's envoys, Sir Thomas Wriothesley, who met the Duchess in Brussels in February 1538, attempted to sell his master to her. He extolled 'his virtue, gentleness, wisdom, experience and goodness of person and all other gifts and qualities mete to be in a prince' to Christina. On and on he went until the teenager, so amused by Wriothesley's extravagant praise of the King, burst out in giggles like 'one who was tickled'.

Henry's celebrated court painter Hans Holbein, 'a man very excellent in making of physiognomies', was sent to Brussels to take Christina's likeness. The picture, described as 'very perfect', showed the young Duchess in full length, formally dressed in a widow's sombre black mourning. To liven up the portrait, Holbein took great care to emphasise her features, especially the delightful dimpled smile on her face. Henry was so smitten by the painting, according to Chapuys, that he had forgotten his foul mood of late, and called for musicians to play for him around the clock.

Meanwhile back in Brussels, Christina had misgivings regarding what she was getting herself into. Reviewing Henry VIII's marital history, she shuddered how 'her great-aunt was poisoned, that the second was innocently put to death, and the third lost for lack of keeping in her childbed'. The Duchess was especially mindful of Anne Boleyn's fate, and was said to have made a joke worthy of the witty Anne herself. 'If she had two heads', Christina allegedly commented, 'one of them would be at His Majesty's disposal'. Her reluctance to have Henry VIII, and the growing rift between England and the Empire, would throw all negotiations out the window.

In the summer of 1538, Charles V and Francis I entered an alliance, making England vulnerable. The fear of invasion by them and by papal forces led by the hostile Pope Paul III, who was determined to have the King of England excommunicated before the year was out, forced Cromwell to look to Protestant Germany for help. From his contacts there, he learnt that Cleves, a duchy situated in the lower Rhinc, might be what England needed. Its ruler, Duke John III had two daughters, Anne and Amelia, both ripe for the marriage bed.

Figure 14   Thomas Cromwell by Wenceslaus Hollar
Private collection

What better than for England to align itself with Cleves to counter any threats the Emperor and his friends might pose?

German representatives visiting the English court that summer were receptive to the proposal. Cromwell was intrigued by the Duke's elder daughter Anne, and he inquired of her from the King's envoys serving abroad. Hutton, for one, was unenthusiastic. He did not think Anne of Cleves had great value in the marriage market owing to the insignificance of her family. Also, he had heard 'no great praise' about her.

Despite Hutton's reservations, Cromwell believed Anne (or her sister at least) might still prove useful, and he pushed for her as Queen. When he had managed to convince the rest of the Council, Duke John had passed away and talks were conducted instead with his son, William, who had assumed headship of the family. As the new Duke of Cleves, the ambitious William was intent on aggrandizing his territories. Through his mother, Mary of Jülich and Berg, William claimed the province of Gelderland as his inheritance. Its inhabitants, wanting to throw off Imperial dominance, embraced William as their new ruler. Anticipating hostilities from the Emperor, William of Cleves welcomed the friendship of England.

In January 1539, Cromwell authorised the English ambassador in Germany, Christopher Mont, to begin formal negotiations. It would be a great match, or rather a great *double* match, Mont told the Germans. King Henry would wed one of the sisters, preferably Anne, and the unmarried Duke William would take the Lady Mary as his bride. Concerning the Princess, Mont had further instructions from Master Secretary. If the Germans should demand Mary's picture for William of Cleves' inspection, he was to refuse. Mary was the daughter of a king, and 'it was never seen that the pictures of persons of such degrees were sent abroad'. Besides, Cromwell added, the Vice-Chancellor Francis Burgart had already seen Mary in person on a diplomatic visit to England. He could vouch for her 'proportion, countenance, and beauty' to his master.

Protocol, on the other hand, did not prevent the English from obtaining a portrait of Anne of Cleves. She was, after all, only the daughter of a duke, not of a king. Day after day, Mont pressed Anne's brother for a picture, but each time he was put off. Until his painter Lucas Cranach recovered from his illness, Duke William explained, Mont would have to patient. While he waited, the envoy turned his attention to a list of questions Cromwell needed to be answered. What was the religious make up of the family? Were they still committed to the Pope? What were Anne's 'shape, stature, and complexion?' And would the King find her pleasing?

Mont could confirm that William of Cleves was not 'of the old Popish fashion'. He was inclined to Reform, though he did not consider himself a Lutheran. Plainly speaking, William took after Henry VIII in his religion. Just as gratifying was Mont's description of Anne. On paper, she was like a second Venus. 'Every man praiseth the beauty of the said lady', Mont gushed, 'as well for her face as for her person, above other ladies excellent'. She was even more beautiful than the Duchess of Milan, outshining Christina as 'the golden sun excelleth the silver moon'. Anne was a paragon of character as she was of looks. 'Everyman praiseth the good virtues and honesty, which plainly appeareth in the gravity of her countenance', according to Mont.

Henry VIII was enthralled by the glowing descriptions of Anne, and in no time, he was willing to consider marriage to her, or to her sister Amelia, as circumstances dictated. Since the King could not woo them in person, his representatives, Doctor Nicholas Wotton and Richard Beard would have to act as his eyes and ears.

Things got off to a rocky start. William of Cleves allowed the two emissaries to view his sisters, but the meeting was far from satisfactory. When presented to their English guests, both Anne and Amelia were heavily veiled and wrapped in voluminous gowns to preserve their modesty. Wotton and Beard were barely able to see their faces or their figures before their brother shuffled them off. William was overprotective. His sisters had been strictly brought up in the sheltered environment of their ducal court, under the careful supervision of their mother, the formidable Duchess Mary. They were not used to receiving visitors, and it would have been a breach of good manners to have them so closely scrutinised by the English strangers. The best he could do, William said, was to offer them portraits of Anne and Amelia. But when Henry Olisleger, the Duke's chancellor presented the paintings to them, Wotton and Beard were not pleased. They were not confident of the likenesses, they said, as they never got a good look at the sisters, smothered in their 'monstrous habit and apparel'. In that case, Olisleger answered with annoyance, perhaps the envoys would prefer to see them naked instead!

With the portraits judged unsatisfactory, it was decided that the trustworthy Hans Holbein should retake their images. Once again, the artist was packed off to the Continent with his paints and brushes, this time to the ducal court at Düren where Anne and Amelia were staying. Holbein's portrait of Amelia is lost, but the one of Anne still survives. As a bonus for the King, the artist also painted an exquisite miniature of her.

Along with Holbein's pictures, Wotton sent back a written description of Anne. Amelia was entirely ignored, apparently because she was not as seriously considered as her older sister. Anne, Wotton wrote, was raised by her mother, 'a very wise lady and one that very straightly looketh to her children'. Being strictly brought up, the King need not worry that Anne had any vices, Wotton continued. For example, unlike many of her countrymen, she did not indulge in drink. She was not 'inclined to the good cheer of this country', but instead, took after her strait-laced brother who 'doth so well abstain from it'.

As far as her education went, it was meagre, being neither academic nor courtly. Anne could read and write in her native tongue, but she was ignorant of any other. But she did have a sharp mind, and Wotton had no doubt that she could easily pick up English given the opportunity. Knowing Henry VIII's love of music, Wotton touched on Anne's talents in singing and in playing an instrument - alas, she had none. In Germany, it was 'a rebuke and an occasion of lightness' for a high-born lady to have any musical knowledge. To compensate, Anne was highly skilled in needlework instead.

Anne of Cleves' deficiencies did not deter the King. Jane Seymour was not musically talented or particularly educated either, but she proved to be a commendable wife. Apparently, what mattered in Anne were her looks, and those Henry saw when Holbein's finished portrait and miniature arrived in England on 1 September. He was pleased enough with them that the German representatives were summoned to court to finalise the marriage treaty.

There was one problem - a promise of marriage Anne had as a child with Francis, Marquis de Pont, the son of the Duke of Lorraine. Henry had been so keen on marrying Anne that even before Holbein took her likeness, he had instructed his envoys to investigate the matter with the aim of declaring Anne free of all impediments. Wotton, with the help of Doctor William Petre, searched through papers in the German archives about the betrothal, and he questioned the family about its legality. Duke William, eager for the alliance, was happy to oblige. An open declaration was made that Anne was not bound to any old contract made by her late father and the House of Lorraine. Therefore by law, she was 'free to marry as she pleases'.

On 4 October 1539, the papers were signed by both parties, but only for Henry and Anne; the plan of matching the Lady Mary with the Duke of Cleves was dropped. Under the terms of the agreement, Anne was to arrive in England by December, and after her wedding to the King, she was to receive a splendid coronation in February at Candlemas. William had little to offer as a dowry for his sister, but he could save face when he was assured by his future brother-in-law that he valued Cleves' friendship over its money. Now all that was left to do was to bring the bride-to-be over to England.

According to the officials in Cleves, it would be best to have Anne transported from Düsseldorf to Calais, and from there, across the Channel to her new country. They worried that a long sea voyage might damage Anne's delicate complexion and that she might catch cold. Worse, Anne might be kidnapped on the open seas by the Emperor's Dutch sailors if she did not have safe conduct. Charles V's possible interference was not lost on the English either. Since September, Henry VIII was considering a scheme to bring Anne over directly by sea, despite the objections of her brother. The plan involved smuggling her aboard an English ship moored near the harbour of Harderwijk, situated in the inlet of the Zuiderzee in the North Sea. Two English sea captains, Aborough and Crouch, were even sent ahead to study the possibility of the idea, and to produce charts of the area. To deceive the Emperor and his allies, it was given out that Anne would be travelling to England by land. The French ambassador in England, Charles de Marillac, however, was not fooled. He spied some of the King's ships being decorated and armed that October, and assumed correctly that they were being outfitted to spirit Anne away by water.

Before the swashbuckling escapade could be put into action, word was received by Henry's agents in Brussels, on 19 October, that Charles V, despite his resistance to his uncle's marriage with the House of Cleves, would not prevent it. Anne, the Emperor decreed, would be allowed to travel overland through his territories unmolested. Before Charles could change his mind, Henry wrote to his sister, Mary of Hungary, acting as Regent of the Low Countries, to confirm the safe conduct for Anne. Lest there be any confusion as to her brother's willingness to accommodate him, Henry forwarded her a copy of Charles' letter giving his 'satisfactory and conclusive' answer regarding Anne's journey.

≡

In early November, Anne of Cleves set out for Calais. At Düsseldorf, she bade farewell to her family, including her mother with whom since childhood, Anne was 'in a manner never far from her elbow'. There were no reports of a frightened, grief-stricken bride venturing into the great unknown. On the contrary, unlike Henry VIII's sister Mary who dreaded her arranged marriage in France, Anne was perfectly agreeable throughout the journey. Perhaps what she felt was relief and release at being away from her domineering mother and her stifling existence in Cleves, and joyful anticipation of a new life in a new country.

Meanwhile, Wotton wrote to Cromwell as to what to expect regarding her suite. Accommodations must be in readiness for at least eighty-eight people making up her personal household. A Mistress Lowe would be in charge of Anne's ladies-in-waiting, and a Mistress Gilman, an Englishwoman sent ahead by the King, would personally attend her. Several officials including Olisleger and Burgart would accompany their mistress as well, but they would return to Germany almost immediately afterwards. An additional staff of two hundred and sixty-three servants with two hundred and twenty-eight horses between them would go as far as Calais. However, they would only cross over to England if King Henry gave his permission.

Wotton also informed Cromwell of a German custom their master might want to observe after his wedding night. On the morning after, a great lord was obliged to make a present of money, a *morgengabe*, to his wife. He was also expected to provide gifts to the wedding party: jewellery for the ladies and clothing for the gentlemen. The value of such presents was always at the discretion of the groom, but Wotton saw fit to warn Cromwell that a great lady expected at least 1,000 francs.

It was not until early December that Anne of Cleves reached Antwerp. Outside the city gates, she was given a great welcome by the resident English merchants. Anne and her train were conducted into the city to their lodgings where they were 'honourably received', and an open house reception was given to all. It was a 'goodly sight'; not even the Emperor himself had received such a welcome in Antwerp, it was said.

Back in England, Henry VIII was impatient. The King had expected his wife-to-be to have trekked across the Low Countries, crossed the Channel, and settled in Canterbury by 25 November. But the day came and went, and Anne of Cleves was still nowhere to be seen. Owing to the large size of her train, the Germans were only able to travel in slow stages, at the most about five miles a day. It was not until 28 November that Henry was told Anne would be expected in England on 8 December. All he could do was grumble about the delay.

There was further interruption when Anne got to Calais a few days later than expected. The Governor, Lord Lisle, had ample time preparing for her coming, having been notified by Cromwell two months earlier. The Palace of the Exchequer was refurbished for Anne's stay and the nearby streets repaved to put everything in 'cleanly order'. The whole town was ready when Anne was finally spotted on the morning of 11 December. At Gravelines, outside Calais, Lord Lisle and his wife did obeisance to Anne of Cleves as their new Queen. They found Anne pleasant enough, and Lady Lisle wrote to her daughter Anne Bassett, still at court, that she would find her new mistress 'good and gentle to serve and please'.

Before entering Calais by the city gate, Anne was shown the King's great ships moored at the harbour - the Lyon and the Sweepstakes - by William Fitzwilliam, Lord Admiral and Earl of Southampton. The vessels were festooned with streamers and flags, and sailors perched on the masts waved down in greeting. As Anne went by, the ships fired such a mighty round of ordnance 'that all her retinue was astonished'. Inside the town, she was presented with purses of gold by the Lord Mayor and by the town merchants, and then she was brought to the Exchequer to hold court.

For 'lack of a prosperous wind', Anne was stuck in Calais for the time being. To relieve the boredom, her hosts entertained her with jousts and banquets. But after two weeks, even such diversions must have worn thin. With nothing to do but wait out the weather, Anne set herself to be a pleasing wife to her future husband. For starters, she learnt a card game called 'sent', in which, she was told, Henry VIII took much amusement. In no time, she gambled away 'as pleasantly and with as good a grace' as any seasoned player, according to Southampton her teacher. The Admiral found Anne most affable. Communication between the two could not have been easy with everything done through interpreters, but Anne was an astute pupil. Later that night, in a gesture of friendship and to learn more about the English, Anne asked him and his countrymen to join her for supper. With humbleness, Southampton demurred at first. But as it was the custom in Cleves, and as Anne was most insistent, he and the others accepted her invitation to dine at her table.

It was not until 27 December that the tempestuous weather died down and a fair wind prevailed, allowing safe passage across the Channel. Anne took ship at noon, and before early evening, she set foot at last on English soil at Deal. It was not an auspicious beginning. The gloomy skies above Calais had moved over to the English coast, and an impending snowstorm threatened to ruin Anne's reception. In fact, her hosts, the Duke of Suffolk and his new wife Katherine Willoughby, and the Bishop of Chichester, arrived late to welcome her because of the weather. Despite the bad conditions, the entire retinue – German and English - set out towards Dover that same night. Moving against wind and hail, it was not until 11 o'clock in the evening that they found relief in the warmth and shelter of the castle there.

The next day, the weather showed no signs of abating. Still, they all pressed on to Canterbury where Archbishop Cranmer was waiting to greet them. Outside the city, Anne was received by the Archbishop, the Mayor, and a crowd of citizens. As they welcomed her, a peal of guns was fired in salute. In a torch-lit procession, Anne was then taken to the former Abbey of St Augustine to retire for the night. Her rooms were comfortable and luxurious, having been specially prepared for her since early October when she was formally betrothed to the King. Henry's apartments next door were equally grand. Altogether, he had spent close to a lavish £650 on what was originally intended to be his honeymoon getaway. Anne was most impressed, and later that night was described as being 'very merry at supper'.

The snow did not let up the next day, but Anne was insistent that they set out regardless. According to Suffolk, she was 'so desirous to make haste to the King's Majesty, that Her Grace forced for no other'. Bowing to her wishes, they reached Rochester on New Year's Eve. There, Anne rested at the Abbey, formerly Bishop Fisher's episcopal palace, to prepare for what would be the last leg of her journey.

On the morning of New Year's Day 1540, a small band of travellers were seen galloping on the wintry roads towards Rochester. Those who caught sight of them would have noticed the urgency of the riders, and that one of their number was seen to be especially tall and powerfully built. Like the rest of his companions, he was heavily cloaked. Around noon, the horsemen dismounted at the Abbey. As they made their way inside, Anne's German staff was struck by the unusual deference shown by their English hosts to the large, heavyset gentleman heading the group. No doubt another nobleman, they gathered, sent to discuss the details of their mistress's meeting with King Henry, set for 3 January at some place the Englishman called Blackheath.

When the visitors were ushered into Anne's presence, they found her at a window watching a bull-baiting in the courtyard below. Without waiting for her to acknowledge them, the leader suddenly took hold of Anne and planted a big kiss on her cheek. Shocked, she said nothing. Even if she did, the man would not understand her. The stranger welcomed Anne in the King's name and presented her with a token from his master. Embarrassed, all Anne could do was to assume that the English had a peculiar way of greeting people, and she muttered her thanks in her native German. Not sure whether she ought to dismiss him or not, Anne turned her attention back to the bull-baiting outside, hoping the strange man would go away.

He did, only to return minutes later. Instead of his muddy travelling cloak, he was now wearing cloth of gold. Mortified, Anne fell to her knees.

When Henry VIII's returned to Greenwich the next day, his encounter with Anne of Cleves was all the news. Not since his courtship of Anne Boleyn was the King so romantic, his courtiers told one another. They spoke of how he rode for miles through the snow to 'nourish love' with his German fiancée, and how impressed she was by his ardour. The King was so taken with Anne of Cleves, they heard say, that he spent the evening supping with her and stayed till the next morning before finally taking his leave.

While the court was under the impression that all had gone well at Rochester, the King's intimates knew better – the meeting was a disaster. Instead of spending hours with Anne, as the story went, Henry had excused himself after some pleasantries and disappeared as quickly as he came. He had been so anxious to leave that he had neglected to present his sweetheart with a gift of furs he had brought especially for her.

Sir Anthony Browne, who had been with his master at the Abbey, was one of the first Henry VIII confided in. "I see nothing in this woman as men report of her", he fumed, "and I marvel that wise men would make such report as they have done"! The King then had words for the Earl of Southampton. He was especially hard on the Admiral as he had written so well of Anne from Calais. Did he still honestly think she was as beautiful as everyone said, Henry demanded to know. Her complexion was darker than he had been led to believe, the Earl stammered. "Alas, whom should men trust"? Henry retorted, "I promise you, I see no such thing in her as hath been showed me of her. I am ashamed that men have so praised her as they have done. I like her not"!

Cromwell, who had initiated the whole German alliance, was stunned. On the King's return from Rochester, Cromwell had hastened to his master, cheerfully inquiring as to his liking for the new Queen. He received a stinging reply. Anne was 'nothing as well as she was spoken of'. Had he known the truth, Henry bellowed, he would never have allowed her to enter his kingdom. Cromwell's blood ran cold. After all the good things reported of Anne, he had not expected such a violent reaction. "What remedy now"? Henry demanded. Cromwell had none.

What upset Henry VIII so much is still a mystery. By his account, he was tricked into marrying a gorgon. If there were any truth to what the King said, did Hans Holbein for one, make Anne of Cleves out to be more than she was? Apparently not. Though he would accuse many of deceiving him, Henry never blamed the great painter. Holbein was no flatterer when it came to his craft. His body of work in portraiture consistently proved that he was, as John Hutton called him, 'a master of that science'. In fact, when the picture of Anne was completed, Nicholas Wotton, who was with Holbein at Düren, positively stated that it was a most authentic likeness.

Was the fault, therefore, in the written and verbal descriptions of the lady? Anne's loveliness was certainly over exaggerated as in Christopher Mont's early assessment of her, but there was no indication that she was ugly like the King made her out to be. Virtually all his officials who met her, from the Lisles to the Suffolks, found her genuinely pleasing and suitable as Henry VIII's new Queen. Admittedly, none of them praised her for her reputed loveliness either. If not a great beauty, Anne was at least reasonably good-looking going by Holbein's two portraits. Her greater attraction was undoubtedly in her inner qualities - her gracious manner and her serene dignity so widely commented on by those who met her. Even the King himself, despite his criticism of Anne, admitted she had a 'queenly manner' about her.

Then was it Anne's lack of English or her unfashionable foreign costume that the King found detestable? Such considerations seem unlikely. Henry was clearly aware from the start that Anne spoke only German, and he had already seen portraits of her in the court dress of her country.

So what exactly had occurred at Rochester? In the few moments he had spent with Anne of Cleves, Henry VIII had been clearly disappointed, though he hid it well from those present. Beauty, as always, is in the eye of the beholder, and Henry, for reasons that will always remain elusive, saw nothing in Anne that pleased him. Perhaps he had expected too much. From the time he had agreed to marry her, until the moment he had stepped foot in Rochester Abbey, the King had been besotted with a woman of his imagination; a woman even more beautiful than the enchanting Christina of Denmark. But in the flesh, Anne of Cleves - a lady of just average looks - fell short of his fantasies. Sorely let down, Henry had found faults with Anne where there were none. In time, he would cast even worse slurs on her.

There was no hint of the New Year's Day fiasco at Anne's formal reception at Blackheath two days later. At the foot of Shooter's Hill, the entire court and a large crowd had assembled to greet the King's fourth wife. Anne appeared at noon and was taken to a tent where she changed into a gown of cloth of gold. Her rich clothes, and those of her German ladies, failed to impress the French Ambassador Charles de Marillac. They were 'heavy and tasteless', he sneered. What's more, the envoy was put off by their appearance. Anne's maids were inferior in looks to their mistress, and she was far from the beauty everyone was led to believe. He dismissed Anne as gangly, stern, and seemingly older than her twenty-four years.

The envoy's opinion aside, Anne made a good impression on her English subjects. They thought her regal and warm. When the King's courtiers presented themselves to her, she greeted each one of them with kisses, with 'a goodly manner and loving countenance'. She behaved impeccably with Henry VIII too. Unaware of his true feelings for her, Anne rode impatiently towards Greenwich where she was scheduled to meet him along the way. About a mile from the town, they came in sight of each other - Anne with excitement, Henry with dread. As she drew nearer, the King forced himself to play the lover. With his cap in hand, he bowed from his saddle to his beloved, and with 'princely behaviour, saluted, welcomed, and embraced her, to the great rejoicing of the beholders'. He then took his fiancée by the hand, and together they travelled towards Greenwich all smiles.

At the palace, out of earshot of the rest of his court, a frantic Henry VIII continued to harangue the author of his calamity. "How say you my lord"? he grumbled at Cromwell, "is it not as I told you? Say what they will, she is nothing fair"! Defending himself, the minister put the blame on the Earl of Southampton. Cromwell scolded him for misleading the King by his letters from Calais. But the Admiral stood firm. He was sorry their master disliked her, but his duty had been to escort Anne of Cleves across the Channel, not to judge her beauty.

There was little Cromwell could do but to reopen the question of Anne's pre-contract with Francis of Lorraine. That might at least buy the King a little time, perhaps even putting a halt to the wedding entirely. Summoned before the Council, Anne's ministers were 'much abashed'. Like everyone else, they had been under the impression that Henry VIII was most pleased with Anne and thought that the marriage was to take place the next day, on 4 January, as planned. Instead, the English were now stalling, saying that it had come to their attention that Anne was committed elsewhere. Olisleger and his colleagues were confused. During the negotiations, the King had considered the pre-contract so negligible that he would have married Anne regardless of it. But now, he was demanding guarantees that his fiancée was free from Francis of Lorraine. The Germans were given a day to present their case. But being given so short a time, all they could offer was reassurance that the agreement was mutually nullified by the Houses of Cleves and Lorraine. Therefore, there was absolutely no impediment to their mistress marrying Henry VIII. To this, the Germans pledged their word, and they even 'offered to be prisoners' of the English government until the matter was proven to the Council's satisfaction.

The King was not gratified by their response. "I am *not* well handled"! he complained to Cromwell. If Anne had not already come so far, Henry added, and so many preparations made, he would never take her for his wife. It was only his worry that her brother would join the Emperor against him that he dared not 'make a ruffle in the world' by sending Anne back home.

Since Anne's ministers were of no use in stopping the marriage, the lady herself was approached. Would she be willing to swear, the Council asked, that she was free to wed the King of England? They were grasping at straws. Anne herself would not have believed otherwise, and she assured the Council of the fact. If Anne was troubled by the King's attempt to examine her pre-contract, she gave no sign of it. She probably viewed the matter as a mere formality. All in all, she was oblivious to the his desperation to free himself from her. Already honoured as Queen, Anne was keeping 'a great court' with Henry VIII, and she was attending Mass - 'richly apparelled' - like Anne Boleyn and Jane Seymour were at their moments of triumph.

Finding no means to forestall the marriage, the reluctant groom had to 'put his neck in the yoke', as he described it. At 8 o'clock on the morning of 6 January, Henry VIII, wearing his best - a gown of cloth of gold with flowers in silver thread, and a coat of crimson satin embellished with diamonds - waited for his bride in a gallery at Greenwich. Already in a foul temper, he was further annoyed when Anne failed to appear on time. But the fault was not hers. The Earl of Essex who was supposed to take her to her husband arrived late. Before Anne appeared, Henry whispered to Cromwell. "My lord, if it were not to satisfy the world and my realm, I would not do that I must do this day for none earthly thing"!

At last, the bride appeared. For her happy day, Anne had chosen a dress of cloth of gold cut in the Flemish style. On her head was a crown set with precious stones, pearls, and sprays of rosemary. Her flaxen hair was worn long and loose as a still unmarried woman. Anne curtsied three times to the King. She then took his hand, and they walked into the Queen's Closet where Cranmer waited. Standing before the Archbishop, the couple made their vows and exchanged rings. On Anne's was the inscription *God Send Me Well To Keep*. After prayers had been offered, Cranmer joined Henry and Anne together as man and wife. The King cringed at the pronouncement.

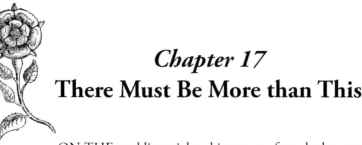

Chapter 17
There Must Be More than This

ON THE wedding night, things went from bad to worse. In attempting to know Anne in the flesh, Henry, as he would later claim, found her utterly repulsive. He was nauseated by her 'evil smells', and by what he considered her 'unsightly' belly and breasts. After some clumsy attempts at intercourse, he just gave up. He did not have the 'courage to proceed any further on other matters'.

Anne's performance in the bedroom was unrecorded. But far from discouraging his advances or distracting him with card games as imagined by modern dramatists, she would have made herself agreeable. That of course, meant having some knowledge of sex – what to do and what to expect. Contrary to the testimony of her ladies-in-waiting given months afterwards, Anne must surely have been aware that Henry's awkward gropes in the dark did not constitute married life in the fullest sense. This is suggested by Anne's own temperament. She was far from shy and ignorant. On her way to her new country, she had not been afraid to take initiatives. She had learnt card games to please the King, she had invited Englishmen to her table, and she had not let any bad weather prevent her from reaching her waiting spouse. Anne was determined to prove herself a good wife in every way. With that purpose in mind, she was undoubtedly certain of what was required of her beneath the bed sheets as well.

But when Henry failed to respond to her sexually, Anne became afraid. The success of the marriage depended upon her. If she failed, her family's honour would be tarnished, and her brother's alliance with England broken. As for herself, she was a stranger in a strange land. What would become of her if she disappointed the King? Her hope was that in time, he would find her pleasing. Until then, she must go on as if all were well. Perhaps she could confide her troubles to Master Cromwell and together seek a solution.

Meanwhile, Anne, as did Henry, acted as if nothing was wrong. On the morning after, both of them gave the impression that the wedding night had been consummated with great love between them. In writing to William of Cleves, his envoys described the match as an unqualified success. The day of the nuptials, they told the Duke, had been celebrated with 'costly suppers, comedies, dances, sundry plays and banquets'. The King was obviously pleased with Anne as he was 'very merry' the next morning. Instead of a mere gift of money as her *morgengabe*, he also presented her with jewels and dresses of great value. All things considered, the emissaries concluded, 'we think that His Royal Majesty is very well content with Her Noble Grace'.

In public, Henry and Anne could not seem happier. Five days after the wedding, the couple attended a tournament. Anne was said to be especially becoming. Gone were the dowdy German dresses and the cumbersome hats. Instead, Anne wore a fetching gown of English make, along with a stylish French hood. The rounded caps were making a comeback after the death of the fervently English Queen Jane, and even the friars who recorded the important events in the realm thought it noteworthy to mention how 'then began all the gentlewomen of England to wear French hoods with billiments of gold'. With her attention to fashion, was Anne trying to make herself more attractive to her husband? Her new dress sense was said to have 'set forth her beauty and good visage'. The people were certainly impressed. Anne of Cleves was fast becoming popular with her new subjects, so much that 'every creature rejoiced to behold her'.

As with every new Queen, places in Anne's household were eagerly sought. Katharine Bassett, who had been rejected by Jane Seymour in favour of her sister, was keen for a position and asked her mother for assistance. Lady Lisle, always wanting to ingratiate herself at court through her daughters, was more than willing to help. But despite her efforts, including bribing the King with home-made preserves and appealing to Olisleger and Mistress Lowe, Katharine was not given a place. The King was adamant that his wife's household was complete and that no more ladies would be admitted. Those lucky to have secured a place had already done so before Queen Anne's arrival. The Duke of Norfolk, for instance, had the foresight to place his niece, a girl named Katheryn Howard, in royal service back in December.

With her household put in good order, Anne may have expected to be crowned in February as promised. But the ceremony was postponed indefinitely, she was told, and no reason was given. It was not a good sign. Like Jane Seymour before her, Anne had to be content with a pageant on the Thames as the court moved from Greenwich to Whitehall on 4 February 1540.

A change of scenery did nothing to improve Anne's situation. Even though her husband was unfailingly polite and correct towards her as he always was, he would not be intimate with her when they slept. In private, he had told Sir Anthony Denny, who attended him in his Privy Chamber, how he could never 'be provoked and steered to know her carnally'. Anne's breasts sagged, and parts of her body were in 'such sort' that he suspected she was not the virgin everyone claimed she was, Henry confided. Anne heard none of these crude remarks thankfully, but nonetheless, frustrated by the King's continual aloofness towards her in the bedroom, she began to 'wax stubborn and wilful' with him. Henry's response was to pass her off to Cromwell.

If Anne did unburden her troubles to him, it did no good. The great Thomas Cromwell, who had spearheaded the English Reformation and made his master the wonder of Europe, was inept when it came to affairs of the heart. All he could do was to refer Anne to her Lord Chamberlain the Earl of Rutland, and to her Council. In turn, the only advice they could give their mistress was - as if *she* was the one at fault - to behave more pleasantly towards the King.

≡

Through no fault of her own, Anne was a failure as a wife, and she was beginning to outlive her usefulness as a political asset. For all his blustering, the Pope's holy crusade against heretical England never materialised, and the alliance between France and the Empire, so feared by Henry VIII, went cold. With no need of German help, Anne of Cleves was a liability.

During the summer, the court noticed the King's growing infatuation with one of the Queen's attendants, young Katheryn Howard. 'There is a talk of some diminution of love', de Marillac told the French King, 'and a new affection for another lady'. Just as Cromwell had promoted Anne to Henry VIII, so did the Duke of Norfolk with his pretty niece. Norfolk did not act alone; he had help from Stephen Gardiner, now Bishop of Winchester. A religious conservative who hated Cromwell as much as the Duke did, Gardiner obligingly offered the hospitality of his house to Henry and his new darling. The King gladly took up the invitation. He made no attempt to be discreet, and his trips on the river, both in broad daylight and by moonlight to rendezvous with Mistress Howard, aroused much attention.

Cromwell grew increasingly nervous. Would Katheryn Howard do to him what Anne Boleyn had done to Wolsey? A respite seemed to come his way in April, when Cromwell was created Earl of Essex and High Chamberlain in recognition of his services to the Crown. Surely, his ennoblement was a vote of confidence from the King, but even Cromwell knew that unless he could resolve Henry VIII's marital woes, he would 'smart for it'.

Taking advantage of the King's dislike of the Queen, Norfolk and his party began filling his ears with accusations about Anne's chief supporter. Far from being a faithful son of the Church, they whispered, Thomas Cromwell was a radical heretic. Not only was he aiming to upset the religion of England, but also the succession. The upstart planned to destroy the Prince, take the Lady Mary as his wife, and make himself dictator. The charges were rubbish, but where religious orthodoxy and the safeguard of his dynasty were concerned, Henry VIII would brook no opposition and take no chances. He ordered Cromwell's arrest.

The new Earl of Essex's fall was swift. On 23 June, as Cromwell was preparing to meet with the Council, he was ordered by Norfolk not to take his seat - traitors do not sit with gentlemen, he sneered. Before Cromwell knew what was happening, he was suddenly arrested. In anger and shock, he threw his bonnet to the ground, crying out that this was a fine reward for his loyalty to his King, and he challenged his colleagues to name him a traitor. And that they did, with Norfolk and Southampton ripping the insignias of the Order of the Garter from him. A humiliated Cromwell was then hustled into a barge heading straight for the Tower of London. At the same time, his worldly goods were inventoried and loaded into carts destined for the royal treasury.

In Parliament, indictments were put forth outlining the minister's various offences. Along with corruption and denial of the doctrine of the Real Presence in the Eucharist, Cromwell was also charged with contempt towards his betters who now bayed for his blood. 'That foul churl... so ambitious of others' blood', the Earl of Surrey gloated, 'now he is stricken with his own staff!' As if his crimes were not enough, Cromwell was also accused of maliciously concealing knowledge about the Queen. As charged, the minister had been well aware that she was legally pre-contracted elsewhere, but he had nevertheless encouraged the King into marriage with her.

Cromwell's skills as a solicitor enabling him to defend himself in open court were never put to use. On 29 June, he was condemned by an Act of Attainder. It denied him a trial and effectively sentenced him to death without a formal hearing. With no chance to plead his case in public, Cromwell appealed directly to the King instead. From his cell in the Tower, he wrote of how he had always done his utmost to serve Henry, despite whatever 'labours, pains, and travails' he had to endure. The King was 'more like a dear father to him... than a master', and had he the power, he would make him 'live ever young and prosperous'. But knowing he was unlikely to move the angry Henry, Cromwell ended his letter with a wretched plea – 'I ask mercy where I have offended... Most gracious Prince, I cry for mercy, mercy, mercy'. It fell on deaf ears.

Chapter 18
No More Spoken Of

CROMWELL'S FALL anticipated that of Anne of Cleves. Her final public appearance as England's Queen was at the traditional May Day festivities. She joined the King at the jousts held at Whitehall, and later in the day, the two dined together in state. On 23 June, Anne was unexpectedly told she was to be transferred to Richmond Palace the next day. Ostensibly, it was for her health. There were reported outbreaks of an epidemic in the city, but Anne was suspicious. The King, who 'was the most timid person in the world' when it came to diseases, did not hurry to her side for safety as expected. Instead, Henry headed in another direction. No doubt, Anne gathered, into the waiting arms of Katheryn Howard. She voiced her anxiety to her representative in England, Karl Harst. To her great shame, her husband's philandering was the stuff of common gossip, she lamented, and also, he had still not crowned her as promised. Was it his intention to do away with her then?

Anne was correct. Within a fortnight, Henry began the process to free himself of another wife. Reminiscent of his efforts to divorce Katherine of Aragon, on 6 July, an obedient Parliament petitioned the King for permission to investigate the validity of his latest marriage as it was fraught with 'doubts and ambiguities'. Henry graciously consented, seeing that their suit was 'so reasonable', and he empowered Convocation to render judgement. On the same day, Anne was notified of the proceedings. The delegation, led by the Duke of Suffolk and Bishop Gardiner, told her through an interpreter that 'she should be patient; everything would be for the sake of the realm'. If the clergy decided in her favour, the King would gladly accept it and come back to her. But if the ruling was against her marriage, she must comply, Suffolk explained. Perhaps the Duke suppressed a snigger as he spoke. These were the very words Henry VIII had used with Katherine of Aragon.

Two accounts - one from Anne's agent Harst, and the other from the King himself to his ambassador in France, Sir John Wallop - were in agreement about the Queen's initial reaction. Both mentioned how she was in shock, being 'much astonished therewith'. However, the reports diverge as to her subsequent behaviour. According to Henry VIII, after his wife was made fully aware of the 'reasonable grounds and causes' of the enquiry, 'she answered plainly and frankly that she was contented that the discussion of the matter should be committed to the clergy'. But Harst told another story. Instead of submitting gracefully, Anne declared that 'she would not know thereof but this, that His Majesty was given to [her] as husband, and therefore, she would consider him to be her espoused lord and husband, and that no one could divorce them but bitter death'. After Suffolk and the rest departed, Anne gave way to tears. 'She does weep and bitterly cry', Harst wrote to her brother the Duke, 'in such a manner as would move a stone heart to pity'.

In spite of the Queen's reaction - Harst's version of events being more credible - Convocation began its investigation. Gardiner and a committee of bishops authorised the gathering of statements from various witnesses. Thomas Audley, the Lord Chancellor, Cranmer, Norfolk, Suffolk, Southampton, and the Bishop of Durham all testified how the Duke of Cleves' envoys failed to offer legal proof that the Queen was entirely free of her pre-contract with Francis of Lorraine.

The King's personal aversion of the Queen was also presented as evidence. Sir Anthony Browne recalled how he had asked him at Rochester to go on ahead and announce his coming to the Queen. When Browne saw her in the flesh, he had been appalled by her appearance, and he had dared not tell his master at first. Henry had been similarly shocked on meeting Anne moments later, Browne continued; so much so, that he had immediately called for his Councillors, and for those of Anne's, for an all-night emergency session. His assertion of the King's unhappiness was backed up by Southampton and others, including Cromwell, who gave his statement from prison. All of them affirmed that Henry had 'sundry times lamented... his state in this pretensed marriage', and consequently never consummated his union with the Queen.

A medical opinion was even obtained from the royal physicians. They agreed that no intercourse had ever taken place. The King, by his own admission, had attempted the act at least three times on and after the honeymoon, but had to give up as the Queen's body was 'in such a sort disordered and indisposed to excite and provoke any lust in him'. However, just so no one was in doubt of his virility, the King also disclosed that he had two wet dreams (*duas pollutiones nocturnas in somno* – put more delicately in Latin) during his marriage. In other words, he was entirely capable of sex; just not with his wife.

No statement was taken from the Queen herself, but one was extracted from her ladies: the Countess of Rutland, Lady Rochford, and Lady Edgecombe. From them, came a curious account of Anne's side of the story - or so they claimed. As a married woman, they remembered, the Queen was shockingly ignorant as to what was supposed to occur in the bedroom. At midsummer, they had inquired of their mistress whether she was pregnant yet. She was not, Anne had replied, but it was not for lack of trying. At night, she said, the King 'comes to bed, he kisses me and taketh me by the hand and biddeth me - good night sweetheart. And in the morning he kisses me and biddeth me – farewell darling'. Wasn't that enough, she asked innocently? The astonished Countess of Rutland had answered 'there must be more than this' if Anne hoped for a child. Unaware that further effort was required from either her or the King, Anne had said simply that she was 'content with this'. When the Countess then asked if she had discussed the matter with her countrywoman and confidante Mistress Lowe, the Queen turned beet red and exclaimed, "Fie, fie, for shame! God forbid"!

The depositions of Browne and the Queen's ladies were a mishmash of truths, half-truths, and lies. Browne, who claimed that he had found Anne ugly, appeared to be just following his master's lead. That he was sent on ahead to the Queen's chamber at Rochester was suspect. Had he announced the arrival of the King's messengers, Anne would surely have prepared herself to greet her visitors as good manners dictated, instead of continuing to watch the bull-baiting outside. His story that Henry had summoned the Germans at Rochester for a conference that night was dodgy as well. Anne's representatives had no idea anything was wrong until days later when they had met with the King's Council at Greenwich shortly before the wedding.

The Countess of Rutland and her companions evidently gave a doctored deposition too, probably one prepared for them by the authorities. That the Queen was remarkably proficient in English to converse with her ladies raises a red flag. In reality, after only six months in England, Anne of Cleves still had trouble communicating in her new tongue. In fact, when she was later confronted by the King's delegation in July, an interpreter had to be present.

Additionally, it was improbable that Anne was so sexually ignorant. Even supposing for a moment that she was, it would have made far more sense for her to consult Mistress Lowe, whom she knew well and who spoke her own tongue, than to share intimacies with her newly acquainted English servants. Unbelievably, not only was the Queen forthcoming to them on this particular occasion, but according to her ladies, on 'divers and sundry times' as well.

=

On 9 July, Convocation ruled that Queen Anne was still pre-contracted to Francis of Lorraine. Her betrothal and the fact that the King had entered into matrimony with her unwillingly, failing to consummate it, rendered the marriage null and void in the eyes of the clergy. There were 'many other causes too… but they were not to be published to the world'. In other words, there was no need to broadcast the King's colourful remarks about Anne's alleged shortcomings in public.

The next day, both Houses of Parliament were informed of the findings. Anne too was notified. With the King employing all of his resources against her, she could hardly have expected another verdict. By Henry's own account as given to Wallop, Anne was 'somewhat troubled, perplexed, and aggrieved with the matter, yet giving place to the truth, preferring the same before all worldly affection… she did finally submit herself to the said sentence and decree of our clergy'.

This time, Henry's description was accurate enough. Before confronting another one of the King's delegations, Anne had braced herself. Though she could not hide her initial distress – she wept again before the deputation – Anne did manage to stay calm afterwards making no further outbursts about her titles and rights. What would be the point? She could appeal against the ruling, but who would help her? She was a foreigner with no friends in England, and she had no wish to incite Henry's displeasure. Anne made her decision. She would not assume the role of a resentful ex-wife. Katherine of Aragon did, and where had that got her? She must give in.

Anne sent off a letter to the King on 11 July. She had been notified of Convocation's judgement, she wrote, and had accepted it in good part. As the 'pretended matrimony' between them was found to be void, she would no longer call herself his wife. All she asked for was the continuance of his goodwill towards her. Instead of signing off as 'Anne the Queen', as she normally did, she signed as 'Anne, Daughter of Cleves'.

Anne was generous in her submission, and Henry responded in kind. 'For the honour of her house and parentage, and in respect of her true and comfortable behaviour', he would be pleased to adopt 'My Lady of Cleves', as she would henceforth be known, as his 'sister'. Anne would be permitted to remain in England with an income of £4,000 a year, and be given Richmond Palace and Bletchingley Place in Surrey as her own – 'That you may be near us', Henry lovingly proposed, 'and as you desire, able to repair to our court to see us, as we shall repair to you'.

Anne accepted the offer. She would stay in England, Queen or not. Of course, she could return to Cleves, but for what? To be shamed and ridiculed? *No.* Anne had become fond of England and of its people who had taken a great liking to her as their 'sweetest, most gracious, and kindest Queen'. Most importantly, the King was prepared to be considerate as a 'loving brother and friend'.

Having made her decision, Anne returned her wedding ring. She asked that it be broken into pieces 'as a thing which she knew of no force nor value'.

After the divorce - or the annulment as Henry preferred to call it – Anne retired from court. She nonetheless remained an object of scrutiny. The French ambassador reported that far from being sorrowful, Anne had blossomed. She was as 'joyous as ever', wearing new clothes and taking part in recreations every day, de Marillac wrote incredulously. He was puzzled by her behaviour. It was either 'marvellous prudence or stupid forgetfulness of that so closely touching her heart'.

Meanwhile, another was preparing to step into Anne's shoes. With everyone looking to a new Queen of England, Anne of Cleves was soon 'no more spoken of than if she were dead'.

Figure 15   Archbishop Thomas Cranmer by Hendrick Hondius
The Rijksmuseum, Amsterdam

PART 6
THE RED QUEEN: KATHERYN HOWARD

Whereas before she did nothing but dance and rejoice, and now when the musicians come they are told it is no more the time to dance.
(The French ambassador on Katheryn Howard's fall,
November 1541)

Figure 16   Katheryn Howard by Wenceslaus Hollar
Private collection

Chapter 19
Lambeth and Horsham

HAVING SETTLED his divorce, the King had no further use for Thomas Cromwell. On the morning of 28 July 1540, the disgraced minister was brought to the scaffold on Tower Hill. He was not to die as Earl of Essex, or as Lord Privy Seal or Baron Cromwell of Wimbledon, as he was also known, but as plain 'Thomas Cromwell, *shearman*'. As a commoner, he ought to have been 'hurdled… and then hanged and quartered', but the King was merciful. Instead, Cromwell would simply be decapitated. After a speech affirming that he died no heretic, but 'in the Catholic faith, not doubting in any sacrament of the Church', Cromwell laid himself down, 'and so patiently suffered the stroke of the axe' – or rather the *strokes*. It was not the quick death for which he had hoped. The headsman was either nervous or inexperienced. He botched the job terribly, prolonging Cromwell's agony.

On the day the dreadful sentence was carried out, Henry VIII celebrated by taking his fifth wife. The witnesses, no doubt, thought the couple a mismatched pair. In his fiftieth year, Henry VIII still stood head and shoulders above his courtiers like a Goliath. He looked even more so standing next to his new bride. All who saw Katheryn Howard commented on her diminutive stature. The new Queen was equally lacking in years as she was in height in comparison to her ageing giant of a husband. Between them was some thirty years difference.

Katheryn Howard owed much of her advancement to her uncle, the Duke of Norfolk. Her father, the Duke's younger brother Edmund, did little for his daughter except provide Katheryn with her proud Howard blood. His wife Jocasta Culpepper had died when Katheryn and her nine brothers and sisters were still children, and he had little involvement in their upbringing. He spent his life beleaguered by financial setbacks and career disappointments until he passed away in 1539. As an aristocrat, he could not be expected to 'dig and delve' to make his living as Edmund himself said, but instead had to depend on the Crown for employment. But being no warrior or diplomat like his brother Norfolk, Edmund was mostly regarded with royal indifference. He was often so short of money that he was reduced to begging and borrowing, and then had to hide from his creditors. Edmund fared no better in his personal life. He was a henpecked husband whose third wife had 'sore beaten' him when he urinated in bed after taking a remedy for kidney stones. His wife's scorn was shared by many who knew him. In a letter to Thomas Cromwell, the much put upon Edmund Howard mourned how 'smally friended' and 'beaten in the world' he was.

Early in their childhood, Katheryn Howard and the rest of her many siblings were farmed out among their relatives. The main reason was Edmund's inability to support his family, though he would have preferred to say he was merely following tradition. It was usual for aristocrats to send their offspring to other households for their education. Edmund's niece, Anne Boleyn had gone abroad to learn court etiquette and French, while her first love, Henry Percy, had resided with Cardinal Wolsey for his upbringing.

Katheryn in her turn was put under the supervision of her step-grandmother Agnes Tilney, Dowager Duchess of Norfolk, widow of the vanquisher of the Scots at Flodden Field. Wealthy and strong-willed unlike her feckless stepson Edmund, the Duchess would be able to provide for Katheryn and prepare her for the future. Having two great households, one at Horsham in Sussex and the other at Lambeth, the Duchess found herself saddled with a great many Howard dependants under her roof. Agnes Tilney was of an old-fashioned, practical frame of mind when it came to rearing her young charges. She was no advocate of higher learning or of any innovative ideas about education. Her only concern was to give them a basic schooling in reading and writing, music and dancing, and enough social polish to get them accepted at court or suitably married.

At her stepgrandmother's, Katheryn shared a dormitory with those of her sex. It was strictly off limits to the boys - or was supposed to be. The Duchess kept a tight grip on her household. When she retired for the evening, she saw to it that her 'maidens' had done the same. They were confined to their quarters, the door was locked, and the key brought to her for safe keeping.

Rowdy and resourceful, her adolescent wards did not find it difficult to have their fun right under the Duchess' nose. They got Mary Hall, a chambermaid of the old matriarch, to tiptoe into her room, steal the key, and unlock the door to the women's dormitory. There, it was passed off to a waiting Katheryn Howard who had assumed the role of ringleader. At a signal, the waiting young men sneaked in for the usual round of nightly entertainments. Lounging about, they all indulged in wine and strawberries until 2 or 3 o'clock in the morning. During the merrymaking, the youths were careful not to wake the Duchess. The old woman was a sound sleeper, but should she or any other uninvited guest approach unannounced, the young men knew to quickly hide in the little gallery next to the dormitory. As the hours passed, the conversation and laughter died down with couples stealing off to a corner or to bed to be more intimate. It was on such nights that Katheryn Howard - not older than 15 - began her schooling in lessons her grandmother never intended.

Katheryn's paramour at the secret soirées was Henry Manox, a music teacher employed by the Duchess. He was a married man, but that made no difference to him or to Katheryn. As Manox later recalled, their feelings were mutual. 'He fell in love with her, and she with him'. But from Katheryn's point-of-view, Manox took the relationship far more seriously that she ever did. Though considered one of the poorer Howards as the daughter of the family black sheep, Katheryn was still every bit conscious of her social position. Because of her tutor's inferior standing, not to mention that he already had a wife at home, her trysts with him never went beyond kisses and caresses. When Manox pressed her for more, Katheryn drew the line. "What token should I show you"? she asked disdainfully. "I will never be naught with you, and able to marry me you be not".

Not one to give up, Manox continued to pester Katheryn for more substantial proof of her affection for him. Worn down by his continual pleas, she finally relented. Under the cover of darkness one evening, the two met in her grandmother's private chapel. Unobserved, they laid themselves down on the flagstones.

Manox's passion for Katheryn Howard did not go unnoticed in the household. Mary Hall, ever observant, took it on herself to warn Manox. Taking him aside one day, she admonished him for getting himself in too deep. His affair with his pupil was bad enough, but he was also endangering himself. Katheryn was the granddaughter of a duke; a humble music teacher had no business consorting with his betters, she said. If he persisted, the Howards would surely kill him. The young man brushed off Mary's worries with a sneer. So what if his intentions were of a 'dishonourable nature'? Katheryn, in spite of her rank was easy and willing. More than that, the two were genuinely in love, Manox declared.

When all this got back to Katheryn, she was irate. She took great offence to Manox's bragging. "Fie upon him"! she cried out, "I care not for him"! Immediately, she and Mary Hall sought out Manox, and Katheryn upbraided him for his presumption. Chastised, he apologised 'that his passion for her so transported him beyond the bounds of reason, that he wist not what he did'. Katheryn, quick to anger, was quick to forgive. She took Manox at his word, and all was well between them again.

Mary Hall's fear of the Duchess discovering her granddaughter's extracurricular activities was not unfounded. Once when Katheryn and Manox were less careful than usual, she spotted them alone together. The old lady lashed out in fury and struck Katheryn with 'two or three blows'. However, the Duchess did not totally 'undo' them as Mistress Hall supposed she would. The misbehaving couple was let off with just a warning not to see each other alone again.

To Katheryn, it was just as well. She had grown bored with Manox. His lust for her and incessant demands for sex had become an annoyance. Setting her sights higher, Katheryn became enamoured with Francis Dereham, newly arrived at Lambeth around the end of 1536. Unlike Manox, Dereham was a gentleman, being a kinsman of the Duchess. Also, having been at court where he attended the Duke of Norfolk, he was far more urbane. Soon, Dereham was allowed into that inner sanctum of the ladies' dormitory - and into Katheryn's bed.

Inevitably, Manox caught wind of Dereham 'haunt[ing] her chamber nightly'. He did not fancy being replaced, and he looked for revenge. Manox wrote the Duchess an anonymous letter and left it in her pew in her private chapel. If she were to pretend to go to bed, as usual, he wrote, but then raid the girls' dormitory, she would 'see that which would displease her greatly'. But the plan went awry. After the Duchess had read the letter, instead of waiting until nightfall to catch the revellers red-handed, she reacted on the spot. She immediately 'stormed with her women', scolding them for their 'misrule'.

Katheryn set out to discover the cause of the uproar. Passing the chapel, she spied the letter the Duchess had left behind. She stole it and brought it to her lover's attention. Dereham was certain it had been penned by a jealous Manox. He confronted him, and the two had a furious row. Manox, realizing he had lost Katheryn's affection forever, left her to Dereham.

With Manox gone from the Duchess' house, Katheryn and Dereham continued their affair without interruption. But as she did before, Katheryn got careless. One day, she and Dereham were in each other's arms, with her friend Joan Bulmer acting as a lookout. Mistress Bulmer was apparently distracted as suddenly the Duchess appeared. Catching them in the act, she slapped Joan Bulmer, and 'gave also Dereham a blow'. Katheryn was hauled away, no doubt for another beating. No amount of punishment could dissuade the two lovers, and their passion for each other only deepened. To the irritation and titillation of Katheryn's roommates, there was much 'puffing and blowing' beneath her bed sheets whenever Dereham visited. Soon, the pair were even calling each other 'husband' and 'wife'. In using such endearments, Katheryn and Dereham were not simply engaging in sweet talk, but were considering themselves formally betrothed. Even if they lacked their families' consent and a formal wedding ceremony, they had committed themselves as far as Church law was concerned. Nonetheless, it seemed Katheryn never took this seriously. She was more concerned with other aspects of the relationship, such as the risk of an unwanted pregnancy. Each time she slept with Dereham, Katheryn was careful to know how to 'meddle with a man and yet conceive no child unless she would herself'.

At Lambeth, the 'betrothal' was an open secret. It was already common knowledge among their friends that 'Mister Dereham shall have Mistress Katheryn Howard'. The couple were openly affectionate, so much that as Katheryn later remembered, everyone joked that Dereham 'would never have kissed me enough'. "Why would I not"? Dereham would answer back. Who would prevent him from kissing his own wife? Despite her blatant affection for Dereham, Katheryn was nonetheless fearful that it 'should come to My Lady's ear'.

Her grandmother was not ignorant. She may not have known that Katheryn and Dereham were referring to themselves as a married couple, but she probably guessed that they were sexually involved. The Duchess knew that Dereham was a frequent visitor to the ladies' quarters and could be found sleeping 'upon one bed or another'. Other than sending her servant Edward Waldgrave to shoo him out, she seemed to have done nothing else to discourage the young buck. Against her better judgement, she had a soft spot for her kinsman, so much that she allowed Dereham to upset the strict discipline she imposed over her household. He went where he pleased and did what he pleased with impunity. All the Duchess could do was to resign herself to his romantic escapades. At times, she could even be strangely flippant about it all. If anyone was ever looking for Dereham, she would reply with a dash of humour – "In Katheryn Howard's chamber or in the gentlewomen's chamber, there shall you find him"!

In the final months of 1539, England was preparing for the arrival of the King's new wife from Germany. The Queen's household was being re-established, and the Duke of Norfolk was able to secure a place for his niece as one of Anne of Cleves' ladies-in-waiting. For Katheryn Howard, it was the chance of a lifetime. It was an opportunity to leave the humdrum of Lambeth and Horsham, and to get out from under her grandmother's thumb. To Katheryn, the King's court was the world itself, and she wanted everything it could offer - new clothes, new pleasures, new prospects, new friends, and perhaps even new suitors.

Looking to the future, Katheryn broke up with Francis Dereham. Their parting was bitter. If she should leave him, Dereham cried, he had no desire to remain in the Duchess' house. 'He might do as he list', Katheryn answered. All the world knew 'how glad and desirous I was to come to the court'. Still, Dereham found it hard to let go of Katheryn. After she was settled at the royal palace, he had a 'little woman in London with a crooked back', skilled in crafting flowers out of fabric, make her a French fennel to wear on her dress. Also, before he left to make his fortune in Ireland, Dereham entrusted Katheryn with his money; the great sum of £100. If he should not return, the money was hers, he said.

Chapter 20
Perfect Jewel of Womanhood

LIKE HER cousin Anne Boleyn before her, Katheryn Howard was said to have made quite a splash at her courtly début. According to her grandmother, 'the first time that ever His Grace saw her', he was smitten. By tradition, Katheryn was the most beautiful of Henry VIII's six wives. But the French ambassador, Monsieur de Marillac, was only partially impressed. He considered her looks average, but he did admit that Katheryn possessed a delightful expression, was exceedingly graceful, and had excellent taste in clothes - which of course were French.

If the King had indeed fallen in love with Katheryn at first sight, the couple were remarkably discreet. The court was always rife with gossip, but Henry VIII's attentions to Katheryn were not noticed until about the third week of June 1540 when 'it was whispered that the King intended to divorce his Queen… he was much taken with another young lady… whom he was seen crossing the Thames to visit'. Even then, Henry's interest in the Howard girl was dismissed as a mere fling. The people looked on it 'as a sign of adultery, not divorce'.

Katheryn's relatives saw the King's infatuation with their own as an opportunity. Through Katheryn, they could tip the balance of power at court in their favour, and at the same time rid themselves of their enemy Thomas Cromwell. Following the lead of Jane Seymour's supporters a few years before, the Duchess instructed her granddaughter on how to behave towards her royal admirer, and 'in what sort to entertain the King's Highness and how often'. Katheryn must not appear too easy, but play hard to get to whet his appetite. At the same time, she must not act the tease and the temptress like Anne Boleyn did. Instead, Katheryn must model herself after the humble and soft-spoken Queen Jane. For their part, Norfolk and the rest of the Howards commended Katheryn to the King at every chance, attesting to her 'pure and honest condition'. Henry agreed to her qualities, and 'being solicited by his Council to marry again… upon a notable appearance of honour, cleanness and maidenly behaviour… His Highness was finally contented to honour that lady with his marriage'. On 8 August, their wedding was publicly celebrated for the first time with the new Queen dining under a cloth of estate.

After 'sundry troubles of mind which have happened to him by marriages', barring his third with Jane Seymour of course, Henry VIII had at last obtained his 'perfect jewel of womanhood'. De Marillac could not help but notice how the King 'is so amorous of her that he cannot treat her well enough and caresses her more than he did the others... and he knows not how to make sufficient demonstrations of his attention for her'.

Henry's love was also expressed through gifts of land, fine gowns, and most notably by the treasure trove of ornaments - necklaces, pendants, beads, brooches, pomanders, and the like - that he showered on Katheryn. The fine craftsmanship and originality of Tudor jewellery were expressed in many of the pieces given to her. One 'fair brooch' was described as being:

> 'of gold enamelled with white, having a border of antique boys about the same, with a very fair square diamond held by a man whose coat and boots [were] enamelled with blue, and a king, crowned, with a sceptre in his hand at the one end thereof, and five persons more standing behind the same with scriptures over their heads, with the king's words under the said brooch.'

Another piece, just as unique was a:

> 'book of gold enamelled, wherein is a clock, upon every side of which book [are] three diamonds, a little man standing upon one of them, four turquoises, and three rubies, with a little chain of gold hanging at it, enamelled blue.'

Some of the jewels Henry gave to Katheryn were items once belonging to his beloved Jane. A 'Jesus of gold containing XXXII diamonds having three pearls hanging at the same' that the King presented to his fifth wife the following Christmas was probably the same brooch with the name of Christ (IHS) that Jane Seymour was known to have worn. Loaded with so many presents, Katheryn was grateful and gracious. For her motto, she honoured her husband by choosing the loving and deferential *No Other Will But His*.

By all appearances, Katheryn was elated to be Queen. She was adored by her husband, and she had all the riches and attention she could ever desire. But did Katheryn love the King as he did her – in the romantic sense? It is unlikely. The Henry she wed was far removed from the handsome, athletic youth her grandmother and her uncle once knew. Katheryn's Henry was fat and greying, often ill-tempered, and considerably older than she was. Perhaps in her own way, Katheryn was fond of him, but probably as a benevolent father figure rather than as a lover. Predictably, she would be drawn to company her own age; unfortunately, it was to the sort she had known at Lambeth and Horsham.

===

Spoiled by Henry VIII, Katheryn Howard expected to be indulged and obeyed in everything. If she felt slighted in any way, she reacted in the manner of a petty child. When the Lady Mary somehow failed to show her 'the same respect' as she did to her father's two previous wives, Katheryn retaliated. In December 1540, she removed two of Mary's favourite maids from her stepdaughter's household. It is hard to believe that Mary, who was always discreet, could somehow offend the Queen, especially when the two had even yet to meet. Perhaps the Princess was slow in sending her new stepmother her well wishes after the wedding.

Whatever was the cause of the rift, peace was eventually restored. Mary had been warned by her friends that she must find 'some means of conciliation' with the new Queen. Heeding their advice, she sent her a gift on New Year's Day. Touched by the gesture, Katheryn returned the kindness with a present of her own. A few months afterwards, in May, Mary even came to live at court with the Queen's approval. Despite the truce, some tension must have lingered. At twenty-five, Mary was in the awkward position of being older than her stepmother, and thus she had little taste for her frivolities. The Queen, on the other hand, was bored silly by Mary's bookish interests. Nevertheless, Katheryn and Mary managed to coexist peacefully under one roof. Later, the Queen even presented the Princess with a special gift of a 'pomander of gold, wherein is a clock, enamelled with divers colours'.

Katheryn got off on a better foot with Henry VIII's other daughter, the seven-year-old Elizabeth. The girl had barely known her two former stepmothers, and she easily took to her father's new wife. Katheryn became fond of her little cousin, and she gave her small trinkets, including a golden brooch set with a cameo, and a 'pair of beads of purple stones garnished with gold'. Enjoying Elizabeth's company, Katheryn had her boatmen bring her stepdaughter to her from Suffolk Place in the spring of 1541.

The warmth in Katheryn's relationship with Elizabeth was absent when it came to her other relative, the Duke of Norfolk. Although it was he who brought Katheryn to court, there was no love lost between uncle and niece. Later, Norfolk would play the victim placing the blame on the Queen, complaining of the 'malice' she bore towards him. The cause of their estrangement is unclear. The old soldier Duke and his giddy teenage niece had nothing in common except their blood ties. To Norfolk, Katheryn was merely a political asset; a Howard queen to promote Howard interests. Perhaps this was the root of their mutual antipathy. Katheryn might have resented being a tool, and Norfolk might have viewed his niece as an ingrate.

No other family at court was as fragmented as the Howards. In the past, Norfolk was at odds with his father-in-law the Duke of Buckingham, and with his other niece, Anne Boleyn. Relations within his immediate family were just as bad. Norfolk openly kept a mistress, and when his Duchess dared to complain, he had her beaten, so she said. As with many dysfunctional parents, their children took sides. Henry, Earl of Surrey, and Mary, Dowager Duchess of Richmond, defended their father, leaving their mother to bewail the unkindness of her 'so ungracious an eldest son, and so ungracious a daughter and so unnatural' towards her. In time, even brother and sister were to quarrel, leading to the ruin of the family.

Quarrelsome as they were, the Howards were united when it came to reaping the rewards of Katheryn's good fortune. The Queen, as she was expected to, did her duty in providing for her family. Her cousin, the Dowager Duchess of Richmond, held a senior position in the royal household, and two of Katheryn's sisters received preferment as well. Their brothers were not excluded, being appointed to the King's service. At Katheryn's urging, Henry VIII also made her uncle, William Howard, ambassador to France. A year before, an unfriendly Thomas Cromwell had blocked Lord William's appointment; he had been nervous about having too many Howards at court.

Similarly, Katheryn's friends from Lambeth and Horsham were not forgotten. Four of her old dorm mates - Margaret Morton, Katherine Tilney, Alice Restwold, and Joan Bulmer now served in the royal household. Mistress Bulmer, by her own initiative, was probably the first to be reunited with her former chum. When news reached her in York that the King had separated from Anne of Cleves on 10 July 1540, she saw a way to get out of her dreary existence and head for the pleasures of the capital. Just two days after the formal announcement was made in Parliament, Joan Bulmer sent Katheryn a note congratulating her. It had come to her attention, Joan wrote, that 'God in His high goodness' had revealed the illegality of the Queen's marriage, and will 'put you in the same honour that she was in'. Unfortunately, Joan continued, life had not been as kind to her herself. She was in 'the utmost misery of the world', and she begged Katheryn, in remembrance 'of the unfeigned love that my heart hath always borne towards you', to rescue her. Katheryn could not refuse her old friend, and she summoned Joan to London after her marriage to the King.

There was another familiar face at court – Francis Dereham. Katheryn had not seen him since his departure for Ireland shortly after she had left her grandmother's house. He reappeared in the winter of 1540 and was later received into the Queen's service as her private secretary. His advancement was not owed to Katheryn, but to her relatives. It was through the persuasion of her two aunts, the Countess of Bridgewater, and her uncle William Howard's wife, plus that of her grandmother, that Katheryn took him on. The young man had charmed the two matrons into speaking for him, and they in turn approached the old Duchess to have a word with the Queen. But did she, knowing of Katheryn and Dereham's past, do so out of her old fondness for him, or because - as the Queen's former lover - he was too dangerous a young man to deny?

In coming to court, Dereham hoped to rekindle his relationship with Katheryn. What he did not realise was that they were no longer in the cloistered world of Lambeth. The royal court was filled with other young gentlemen - more refined than he, and more exciting and more handsome - all hovering about the Queen. His main rival, Dereham discovered, was Thomas Culpepper, a cousin of Katheryn. As a member of the Privy Chamber, Culpepper was also a favourite of the King.

With so many competing for Katheryn's attention, Dereham set himself apart by putting on airs and bragging about his former relationship with her. Puffed up with pride, he often dined with her officials uninvited and would then remain seated when the others had finished and risen. When he was reprimanded by Master Johns, the Queen's gentleman usher, for his bad manners, Dereham just laughed. He sent a message back saying, 'Tell him I was of the Queen's Council before he knew her, and shall be when she hath forgotten him'. Johns failed to understand his meaning, but Katheryn did not. She met her ex-lover in private and ordered him to keep his mouth shut. As an incentive, she handed him £3, and later an additional £10 - at that time a good deal of money - to buy his silence.

≡

Anne of Cleves was determined not to be out of sight and out of mind. Despite her cheery demeanour as a divorcee, she had never really accepted her rejection by the King. Henry VIII had kept his word to be a 'good brother' to his ex-wife, and he had even visited Anne shortly after their separation, but the loss of her former dignity irked her. For instance, as Queen, Anne was by Henry's side when they dined, but now she was relegated to 'a little distance at a table joining the corner of the table where the King sat'. Tactfully, she made no fuss at such arrangements but instead made a great effort to show that all was well between her and Henry. Although the King had honoured her with his presence, Anne still felt neglected. Henry had once promised that she was always welcome at his court, but no invitation had ever come her way. As the year came to a close, and still no summons arrived, Anne took matters into her own hands.

On New Year's Day 1541, she broke the ice by sending her ex-husband a variety of gifts - silver plate and pieces of jewellery - all of great value according to the French ambassador. For good measure, Anne also offered him 'two fine and large horses caparisoned in mauve velvet'. Henry was touched by her generosity, and he asked her to Hampton Court. In her eagerness to go, Anne set out much sooner than expected. As she neared the palace, there was no official welcome for her. The only person to greet her was Lord William Howard, and that was only because he happened to meet her and her retinue on the road by chance. When Anne was brought to the royal apartments, the Queen was not there to welcome her either. Anne's early arrival had caught the palace off guard, forcing Katheryn to receive some impromptu instructions on how best to greet her. But Anne had already decided on what the protocol should be. Coming before her former lady-in-waiting, Anne abased herself as if 'she were the most insignificant damsel about court'. It was uncomfortable for Katheryn to see the woman she had once served humbling herself before her. She would have none of it. She raised Anne from her knees, and 'received her most kindly, showing her great favour and courtesy'.

The pairing of the Queen and the ex-Queen was made even more extraordinary when the King came on the scene. Henry may have been a poor husband to Anne, but he was a good 'brother'. He made a sweeping bow to her and greeted his 'sister' with a warm embrace. At the banquet following, there was nothing but mirth with the three of them 'looking as unconcerned as if there had been nothing between them'. When dinner had finished, Katheryn took her guest by the hand and the two ladies danced together into the night. The next day, there was more merriment. Before Anne left to go back to Richmond, Katheryn presented her with a ring and two lapdogs that Henry had given her.

On both evenings of Anne of Cleves' visit, Henry VIII had retired to bed early allowing the Queen to entertain his former wife instead. But of late, such episodes of fatigue were usually rare. Since his marriage, it had been noticed by all the court how rejuvenated the King was. It was as if Queen Katheryn's youth had been extended unto him as well. 'He has taken a new mode of living', de Marillac observed, 'to rise between 5 and 6 AM, hear Mass at 7, and then ride until dinner time, which is 10 AM'.

Still, exercise and diet could only do so much. At fifty, Henry VIII was an old man by the standards of his time, and his physique was not what it used to be. Like his grandfather, Edward IV, in his later years, Henry too had become 'very stout and marvellously excessive in drinking and eating'. A suit of armour made around this time showed the King having a chest measurement of fifty-seven inches.

At the beginning of March, before Lent, the precariousness of his health was made plain. At first, Henry was laid low by a fever. No one thought that much of it, and the French envoy even suggested the illness would do him good in helping him lose some weight. But complications followed when an ulcer on Henry's leg, which was normally kept open underneath bandages to help drain the harmful fluids, suddenly closed up. The royal physicians were in alarm. A similar occurrence about five years ago had almost killed the King. Luckily, after a few days, the sore reopened and the crisis was over.

During his convalescence, Henry VIII shut himself in his rooms. He would not see the Queen, nor would he admit his musicians with whom he always liked to surround himself with. Only his doctors and his servants tending to his most intimate needs were allowed near him. In Henry's absence, the court was so quiet that it resembled more the household of 'a private family than a king's train'. Those inside the Privy Chamber did not find him easy to serve. Irritable and sometimes still in pain, Henry was a most difficult patient. Often, he ranted about the ingratitude of his subjects - 'an unhappy people to govern' - and about his incompetent chief officials. He even grumbled about his regret in having the faithful and hard-working Thomas Cromwell put to death.

By 19 March, Henry was sufficiency recovered to take part in the public ceremonial of the royal progress from Westminster to Greenwich by water. As they had done for Henry's previous Queens, officials did honour to the royal couple by escorting them on the Thames. Passing by the Tower of London, Katheryn was reminded of Sir Thomas Wyatt, imprisoned for a misdemeanour. Taking advantage of her husband's improved humour, Katheryn asked his forgiveness for Wyatt. Unable to deny her, Henry graciously ordered his release. Encouraged, the Queen later spoke up for Sir John Wallop, the King's former representative to France, recently suspected of being a papal sympathiser. Again, Henry assented to his freedom, bolstering Katheryn's new reputation as the lady merciful.

As summer rolled by, Henry VIII was in much better health and spirits. It had been almost a year since he had wed Katheryn Howard, and their marriage was still a happy one. In the beginning, it was her beauty that drew the King to her, but in having Katheryn as his wife, Henry, to his great comfort, found her to be naturally kind and loving as well. She had no complications it seemed; all she wanted to do was to please him. Though Katheryn lacked her husband's intellectual prowess - she could never engage him in stimulating political or theological discussions like Anne Boleyn did - it was for the better. Henry was in no more mood for debate. Moreover, he considered a woman with opinions a nuisance.

The only thing lacking in the marriage were children. In April, the Queen was thought to be pregnant, but it was a false alarm. However, Henry imputed no blame to her. As much as he wanted a Duke of York, there were no reports of undue pressure on Katheryn to produce a son as there had been on his first three wives. She was still young, and as sure as God had blessed their happy union, He would in His good time exalt her with a son.

In his buoyant mood, the King planned a great summer progress to the North as far as York. There, a summit was to be held at which he and his nephew, King James V of Scotland, would meet. In travelling to York, the itinerant English court would be making its way into the regions that had rebelled during the Pilgrimage of Grace. The excursion would serve to impress upon the Northerners the authority of the Crown as embodied by the great Henry himself. A personal visit by their King would strengthen the people's affection for him and discourage any future discontent.

But before he had even set out, there was already trouble in the form of a small uprising in Yorkshire. It was put down, but Henry was determined to destroy any vestiges of treason before he travelled. For the safety of the realm, it was decided that a number of prisoners in the Tower awaiting execution should be put to death, including the old Countess of Salisbury, Margaret Pole.

The King had always been wary of threats posed by his own relatives, and the Yorkist branch of his family was troublesome. He had already dealt with Edmund and Richard de la Pole earlier in his reign, but that left the family of the Countess of Salisbury. Margaret, the niece of Edward IV and sister of the unfortunate Earl of Warwick, had been a great friend of Katherine of Aragon, and was governess to her daughter, Mary. Margaret detested the King's treatment of Katherine and Mary, but she was wise enough to know there was safety in silence. The rest of her family, conservative in politics and in religion, was not as prudent however.

Margaret's son, Reginald Pole, had already invited the King's displeasure by publicly denouncing his marriage to Anne Boleyn. Pole, made a cardinal in Rome in 1536, may have been safe living on the Continent, but his kin were within reach of a vengeful Henry VIII. In 1538, Reginald's brother Geoffrey was arrested and interrogated. Weak-willed and terrified, he provided the government with ample details of his family's discontent. Geoffrey's older brother, Baron Montague, and their cousin, Henry Courtney, Marquis of Exeter, were said to have muttered how they 'liked well the proceedings of Cardinal Pole', and how 'knaves ruled about the King'. Such talk was the venting of grievances rather than actual treason. Nonetheless, it was enough to land Montague, Exeter, and their two families in the Tower. Montague's son Henry, a mere child, was imprisoned too, along with Exeter's boy, young Edward Courtney. In January 1539, Montague and Lord Exeter were beheaded for conspiracy, as was Nicholas Carew, the former supporter of Queen Jane. Eventually set free, Geoffrey Pole was forever guilt-ridden for betraying them.

That left the old matriarch herself. Margaret Pole had been charged with promoting a marriage between her son Reginald and the Lady Mary. She was vigorously examined to no end, but the old lady proved tough. Her interrogators had to admit that they were up against 'one as men have not dealed with before'; the Countess being 'rather a strong and constant man than a woman'. Nonetheless, an Act of Attainder was passed against her. Like that used for Cromwell, it rendered her a dead woman in the eyes of the law. Owing to her advanced age, nearly seventy, and the fact that she was essentially harmless, Margaret was left unmolested in prison. But on the early morning of 27 May 1541, she was told to immediately prepare herself for death.

The bewildered old lady, not knowing the reason for why she must die, was led towards a 'corner of the Tower' to a wooden block placed on the lawn. The order for her execution was so sudden that there was no time to erect a scaffold beforehand, and only about 150 people were there to see her die. The executioner, perhaps the same clumsy headsman who dispatched Thomas Cromwell, botched his work. Several blows of the axe were needed before the Countess' head fell upon the Green.

With the kingdom thought secured, the court left London in June. The progress was to be a magnificent spectacle lasting four months on the road with hundreds on the move. Provisions were made for the King and Queen to travel in style and comfort. Brought with them were their richest tapestries, plate, jewels, and clothes to dazzle their subjects in the North. The enterprise had the appearance of 'an extraordinary triumph', according to the French ambassador, and he would not be surprised if it was concluded with Katheryn Howard being crowned in York.

As it was meant to, the progress boosted the King's popularity. Along the way to Lincolnshire, Henry VIII played, to the acclamation of his subjects, the benevolent Solomon dispensing justice to any man who 'found himself grieved for lack of'. All the old grievances against the Crown were forgotten. When news was received in Lincoln of the King's coming, the city officials, the clergy, and the common people all set out to welcome him at Temple Bruer. A clergyman greeted the royal couple in Latin, and presented them with a gift of deer. After they changed - Henry from green velvet to cloth of gold, and Katheryn from red velvet to cloth of silver - they advanced towards the city. Their entourage was an impressive one. Leading the procession were the heralds wearing their tabards emblazoned with the royal arms. Then came Lord Hastings bearing the Sword of State, followed by the King accompanied by six 'children of honour' dressed in cloth of gold and crimson velvet. Behind them were the Queen and her suite. Entering the city, they halted. The city recorder, along with the Mayor and his company, implored Christ's blessing upon the King. After a speech, this time in English (which Katheryn must have appreciated as she knew no Latin), the royal couple were received at Lincoln Cathedral.

From Lincoln, the King and his party moved towards Yorkshire. There, at Pontefract Castle, the citizens were put into two groups - those who had been faithful to the Crown during the Pilgrimage of Grace, and those who had fought against it. The former were 'graciously welcomed by the King and praised for their fidelity', while the latter, placed further off from the royal presence, were made to beg for mercy. On their knees, the ex-rebels confessed how 'for lack of grace and of sincere pure knowledge of the verity of God's word', they had 'grievously, heinously and wantonly' offended. They implored the King to remember his pardon given to them four years ago, and they pledged themselves to be ever loyal. Their promises were sweetened with purses of gold. With a 'benign answer', Henry graciously forgave them. He even allowed the men to attend his court-on-the-move. However, after two days, they were dismissed and told to go home. Though absolved of their offences, the King 'still distrust[ed] such assemblies, especially of the Northern men'. Henry felt the same about his nephew. To his infuriation, the Scottish King was a no-show in York.

Despite James V's boycott of their meeting, the progress had gone well. Henry had won and reinforced the goodwill of his subjects in the North, and he had shown off his new Queen to them. Though he did not honour Katheryn with a coronation as it was thought he might, the King was still most pleased with her for being the perfect wife.

When they returned to Hampton Court at the end of October, a content and grateful Henry ordered special prayers on All Hallows Day for 'the good life he led and trusted to lead' with his Queen.

Chapter 21
No More To Dance

THE KING'S hopes for a happy future with Katheryn Howard were dashed when Thomas Cranmer, who had remained behind in London while the rest of the court were on progress, quietly slipped him a letter. Before slinking away, he asked the King to read it in private. Lacking the courage to confront his master face-to-face, the Archbishop had set down on paper the sordid details of the Queen's past at Lambeth and Horsham.

Henry was incredulous. Far from being his flawless jewel, Katheryn was a lady with a reputation. She was no virgin on her wedding night, and this was widely known in the Duchess of Norfolk's household. Unpredictably, Henry stood up for his wife. He dismissed the accusations as slander and ordered a discrete investigation to be made so that no 'spark of scandal should arise against the Queen'. She would be exonerated from this malicious slur, of that he was certain.

The King was told that the smear on his wife's honour had been brought to light by a gentleman named John Lascelles. It had been his sister Mary Hall, a former servant of the Dowager Duchess, who made the accusation. It had all came about inadvertely. Queen Katheryn, being of a generous nature had provided places at court for many of her old friends. Surely, Lascelles thought, she could do as much for his sister. To his surprise, Mary had refused to have anything to do with Katheryn. She was 'very sorry for her… for she is light both in living and in conditions', she said.

On 5 November, brother and sister were secretly questioned by the Earl of Southampton. 'For the discharge of his duty' to the King, Lascelles would not retract what his sister had told him. When Mary Hall was examined in turn, she stuck to her story. Before the King had her, Mary testified, the Queen was intimate with Francis Dereham who had slept with her 'a hundred nights'. And there was another - Henry Manox. Katheryn and her music teacher had exchanged love tokens, and he knew of a private mark on her body. Katheryn was so promiscuous, Mistress Hall claimed, that one of her attendants at Lambeth named Alice Welkes refused to serve her any longer. Katheryn, she had said indignantly, 'knew not what matrimony was'.

While Southampton was taking Lascelles and his sister's depositions, Thomas Wriothesley tracked down the whereabouts of Manox. Under interrogation, he admitted that there had been more than just music lessons with his former pupil. Before Dereham had ousted him, he used to feel the 'secret parts' of Katheryn's body. However, their affair had gone nothing beyond that. 'Upon his damnation', Manox swore that she had only allowed him to fondle her most private part. The two had never engaged in actual intercourse.

To raise no alarm at court that the Queen was under investigation, Dereham was held on a charge of piracy in Ireland before he entered royal service. His confession was far more substantial than that of Manox. He had done what the musician could not – he had had full sex with Katheryn. In fact, he had 'known her carnally many times'. But that was all in the past - before Katheryn became the King's wife. Dereham refused to admit he had slept with her afterwards.

During the arrests, the Queen was ordered to keep to her apartments. She was given no explanation why. It was later said that Katheryn, aware that something terrible was afoot, broke free from her guard. She ran frantically down the gallery leading to the chapel where her husband was, begging to see him. But before the hysterical girl could get to him, she was dragged away kicking and screaming. The story is doubtful, part of a celebrated ghost story, where down the centuries, Katheryn's phantom re-enacts the pathetic scene of trying to reach the King. She never did see him again after All Hallows Day, and even if she had been able to, she would have unlikely moved him. Henry was shattered. With his 'heart pierced with pensiveness', he gave way to tears one day before the Council. It was an extraordinary scene. He had never done such a thing before, and it was perceived as 'strange in one of his courage'. On 6 November, the King quietly left Hampton Court, abandoning Katheryn to her fate.

The Queen's interrogation was set for the next day. The Council was sure that nothing she could say would help her cause. Based on 'what was done before the marriage', they said with cynicism, 'God knoweth what hath been done since then'. When she was confronted by Cranmer, the Queen rigorously denied everything that had occurred at Lambeth and Horsham. Undeterred, the Archbishop coaxed Katheryn further. It was useless for her to resist, he warned.

Mary Hall, Henry Manox, and Francis Dereham had all admitted everything. If she confessed, the King would be merciful.

Katheryn began weeping so terribly that even Cranmer felt sorry for her. 'It would have pitied any man's heart', he later wrote to the King. That Henry was still prepared to be kind to her, brought about another convulsion of grief. She was undeserving of his clemency, she cried. The King's mercy made her offences seem 'more heinous than they did before'. Katheryn calmed herself in the afternoon, but by 6 o'clock 'she fell into another pang'. This was the usual hour that the King's servant Master Hennage brought her tidings of her husband, she told Cranmer. Obviously, Hennage did not come by that day.

Between her outbursts of grief, Cranmer forced a statement from the Queen. Upon the Sacrament she received on 'All Hallows Day last past' and by all that was holy, Katheryn swore she had never been married, in any sense of the word, to Francis Dereham. Yes, there was talk in her grandmother's house of that, but as far as she was concerned, it was *just* talk. In fact, the only reason they had begun calling each other husband and wife, she explained, was out of amusement. Dereham had convinced her to do so to make the other young men around her jealous. Later, all their friends were in on the joke. It meant nothing, Katheryn insisted.

If so, why did she take him into her bed, Cranmer asked? Faced with Dereham's admission, Katheryn tried to make herself appear less guilty. She had never stolen her grandmother's key, she claimed, or asked anyone else to do so. It just so happened that the doors to her chamber were sometimes open at night or early in the morning, allowing Dereham and his friends to slip in. But it was never at her 'request nor consent', she said firmly. Regarding the various gifts that had passed between them, yes they did exchange presents, but not to the extent that Dereham claimed. Katheryn did not recall ever giving him rings or other jewellery, as he had stated, but she did remember providing him with a band and sleeves for a shirt, and a gift of £10 before the royal progress.

After making her statement to Cranmer, the Archbishop had Katheryn do the same for the King. Under his direction, she wrote:

> 'I, Your Grace's most sorrowful subject and most vile wretch in the world… do only make my most humble submission and confession of my faults… My sorrow I can by no writing express. Nevertheless, I trust Your most

benign nature will have some respect unto my youth, my ignorance, my frailness, my humble confession of my faults, and plain declaration of the same referring me wholly unto Your Grace's pity and mercy.

First, at the flattering and fair persuasions of Manox, being but a young girl, suffered him at sundry times to handle and touch the secret parts of my body which neither became me with honesty to permit, nor him to require. Also, Francis Dereham, by many persuasions procured me to his vicious purpose and obtained first to lie upon my bed with his doublet and hose, and after within the bed, and finally he lay with me naked, and used me in such sort as a man doth his wife many and sundry times... I was so desirous to be taken unto Your Grace's favour and so blinded with the desire of worldly glory that I could not, nor had grace, to consider how great a fault it was to conceal my former faults from Your Majesty...'

Despite her assertion of the 'whole truth being declared', Katheryn was not entirely straightforward. She swore that she had only slept with Dereham for about four months, and that the relationship had ended a year before Henry's marriage to Anne of Cleves in January 1540. But in fact, it had been longer than that, lasting from 1536, when Dereham had come to Lambeth, to the end of 1539, when Katheryn had received her place as one of Anne's ladies. She also downplayed her role in the affair. In referring to Dereham's 'vicious purpose', she was implying that her lover had forced himself on her.

These inconsistencies troubled Cranmer. At the beginning of their interview, Katheryn had presented herself as a willing participant in her relationships with both Dereham and Manox. But then 'she began to excuse and tamper those things which she had spoken... and set her hand... for she saith that Dereham used to her importune-force, and had not her free will and consent'.

Just as disturbing to the Archbishop was the Queen's mention of a strange conversation she had had with Dereham. She had recalled how her secretary had once asked whether she 'should be married to Master Culpepper' as he heard say. "What should you trouble me therewith"? Katheryn retorted. "For you know I will not have you. And if you heard such report, you heard more than I do know." Though the

Queen denied any intimacy with Thomas Culpepper, there was talk in her inner circle of her fondness for him, an affection so strong that a jealous Dereham had wondered if she ought to be married to *him* instead of the King. These were strong words indeed, and Dereham was further questioned. To save himself, the young man confessed that yes, Culpepper had 'succeeded him in the Queen's affections'.

On 11 November, Thomas Culpepper was detained after a carefree hunting trip spent 'merry a hawking'. Like Dereham at first, he steadfastly denied any familiarity with the Queen. However, a search of his possessions uncovered a most interesting letter - it was from Katheryn. In it she had written:

> 'Master Culpepper, I heartily recommend me unto you, praying you to send me word how that you do. It was showed me that you was sick, the which thing troubled me very much till such time that I hear from you, praying you to send me word how that you do, for I never longed so much for thing as I do to see you and to speak with you, the which I trust shall be shortly now. The which doth comfortly me very much when I think of it, and when I think again that you shall depart from me again, it makes my heart to die to think what fortune I have that I cannot be always in your company... praying you then that you will come when my Lady Rochford is here, for then I shall be best at leisure to be at your commandment... and thus I take my leave of you, trusting to see you shortly again, and I would you was with me now that you might see what pain I take in writing to you.'

Signing off, she had declared herself as Culpepper's - for 'as long as life endures'.

Were it written by anyone else, the letter might be considered tender and moving, but it was by the hand of a married woman - no less a queen - to her secret lover. Far from being romantic, it was treasonable. The discovery of the letter was a devastating blow to Katheryn's hope for leniency, for it hinted of an affair *after* her marriage. A queen with a past was bad enough, but a queen who kept going at it was worse.

The authorities then went after Jane Parker - Lady Rochford - mentioned in the letter. Despite the scandal of her husband and his sister Queen Anne only five years ago, Lady Rochford had remained at court. After the Boleyns had fallen, she had gone on to serve the King's two subsequent wives. Except for providing evidence about the non-consummation of Anne of Cleves' marriage, the Viscountess had kept a low profile. That was until Katheryn Howard became Queen.

It had been noticed at court how she and Lady Rochford were unusually close. The Viscountess became so invaluable to Katheryn that she had her own sister Lady Baynton dismissed from her Privy Chamber in favour of her new-found friend. Perhaps Isabel Howard was unable or unwilling to keep secrets like Lady Rochford. Her reasons for helping the Queen remain mysterious. Was she simply following orders, or was she actively encouraging Katheryn's indiscretions? Whatever her motive, she evidently enjoyed her privileged position as confidante. She would never reveal her secrets, Lady Rochford assured the Queen, and would rather 'be torn with wild horses'. Or so she said. Summoned before the King's men, Lady Rochford's resolve crumbled. Desperate to disentangle herself from the Queen, she had quite a story to tell.

As she remembered it, Katheryn and Culpepper's liaison had been in full swing during the Northern progress. Their meetings had been conducted at night at the various residences where the court had rested. The Queen had arranged them on her own, 'seek[ing] the back doors and backstairs herself', and having her (Lady Rochford) act as a lookout. Later, when everyone slept, Culpepper had stealthily let himself in by a designated entryway and had rendezvoused with Katheryn.

What occurred at these meetings, the Viscountess swore she could not say for certain. Katheryn and Culpepper had always sequestered themselves. On one occasion, Lady Rochford claimed she had even fallen asleep and so had no idea what the two had been up to. Still, 'considering all things that she hath heard and seen between them', she was certain they had been engaging in a sexual relationship. For what other reason, Lady Rochford recalled, would the Queen incessantly ask about Culpepper after her arrest? She also recollected how Katheryn in the same breath had muttered how if '*that* matter came not out, she feared not'.

Confronted with Katheryn's letter and with Lady Rochford's testimony, Culpepper came clean about his backstairs meetings with the Queen. But it was Katheryn, he said - not he - who was to blame. From the start, it was she who had started the affair. Culpepper went on to tell how at Easter, on Maundy Thursday, the Queen had summoned him to her Privy Chamber. As he knelt before her, Katheryn drew herself closer. Secretly she handed him a rich velvet cap and whispered to him to hide it under his cloak. It had been more than a gift, Culpepper said, it had been an 'invitation' – one he could not find himself refusing. Since then, he and the Queen had met nightly during the summer progress with Lady Rochford acting as a go-between. Contrary to what she might have said about her lack of enthusiasm, the Viscountess had been actively encouraging him 'to much love the Queen'. And it was not difficult to do, Culpepper confessed. Katheryn was a notorious flirt. She knew what she wanted - and she went after it. At one of their meetings in the North, she had reprimanded him for bedding others. "If I had tarried still in the maiden's chamber," she said seductively, "I would have tried you."

Despite the danger, Culpepper continued, they went on seeing each other in private. At Pontefract, they had almost been discovered by one of the Queen's maids, and Katheryn had even feared that the King suspected something. He had tightened the security outside her room. But none of this had deterred them. On one particular evening, Lady Rochford and the Queen had been waiting at a back door for his arrival but they were frightened away by a sudden flash of light. It had been a watchman with his lantern. The man had noticed the door ajar, shut it, and continued on his rounds. When the coast was clear, Culpepper said that he had to pick the lock to make his way to the Queen.

Throughout the progress, they had been able to carry on in secret as only Lady Rochford knew about the meetings. They had trusted no one else. Katheryn had even warned him not to tell his confessor, for 'surely the King being Supreme Head of the Church should have knowledge of it'. Not even the confessional was safe, Katheryn had believed, when a priest - in loyalty to her husband - would break his sacred oath of silence and inform on them.

Culpepper's deposition was damning, but there was something he nonetheless wanted to make clear. Whatever his interrogators might think, he had never betrayed the King. He and Katheryn had never gone as far as to actually have sex. He was adamant about that - as was Katheryn. On further questioning, Katheryn too swore that despite the secretive nature of her meetings with Culpepper and their risqué banter, it had all been innocent. All she and Culpepper were guilty of was poor judgement. Even when they had been alone together, they had done nothing, she said, but talk away the long hours of the night. As for Lady Rochford's accusation that much more had occurred, Katheryn vehemently denied it. The woman was a liar. If anyone was guilty, she countered, it was the Viscountess. It was Jane Parker who had goaded her into loving Culpepper, which she, of course, refused to do.

The King was unconvinced. How could Katheryn and Culpepper, whom he treated with great favour, make a fool of him? The thought of his wife, 'that wicked woman', in Culpepper's arms was unbearable. Overwhelmed with disgust, Henry one day 'called for a sword to slay her he had loved so much', shouting that she 'had never such delight in her incontinence as she should have torture in her death'. For all his blustering, the King was a broken man. He was a cuckold, and all the world laughed at cuckolds.

≡

As more evidence was gathered against her, it was decided to have Katheryn moved. She would be sent under guard to Syon House, a former convent converted into a royal residence. Despite his raging at her infidelity, the King was still willing to be somewhat generous, showing 'more patience and mercy than anyone might think'. He ordered his wife to be housed 'as her life and conditions hath deserved'. At Syon, three chambers were assigned to her and her staff. She would be allowed six servants of her choosing on the condition that one was her sister Isabel. It was not meant as an intentional act of kindness. Isabel was married to Sir Edward Baynton, the Governor of Katheryn's household. He would continue in the same position, though now serving as the Queen's jailer as well.

Katheryn arrived at Syon House on 13 November. Though she was still received 'in the state of a queen', she no longer had its trappings. In fact, she no longer had the title either. Before her transfer, a proclamation was made that she had 'forfeited her honour and should be proceeded against by law', and as such, was demoted to being just plain *Katheryn Howard* again. No longer Queen, all her jewels were confiscated at Hampton Court to be carefully inventoried.

Several pieces were retrieved by the King himself in his regret for having given them to her in the first place.

Besides losing her jewels, Katheryn was obliged to dress more modestly at Syon. By the King's instructions, Katheryn's gowns and headdresses were not to be adorned with gemstones or with pearls. Her diminished status was also made known by the lack of a royal cloth of estate above her chair. 'Till the matter be further ordered', Katheryn was to remain in detention.

≡

After Mary Hall had been examined and let go, the authorities went after the Queen's ladies. Margaret Morton, a childhood friend of Katheryn's, knew nothing of the escapades at Lambeth and Horsham, or so she said, but she did confess that 'she had never mistrusted the Queen until at Hatfield'. There she had seen Katheryn by a window gazing lovingly at Culpepper below. Also, the Queen had at times locked her chamber door against her own women. Mistress Morton was certain that on at least one occasion, Culpepper had been inside with her doing God knows what.

Katherine Tylney, who had shared a bed with the Queen as a girl, had much to say about Dereham's visits to the ladies' dormitory. She also remembered how at court, the Queen would be up until 2 o'clock in the morning engaged in mysterious matters, leading her to wonder whether she was 'abed yet'. Her old friend also described how the Queen would routinely have her pass on coded messages to Lady Rochford. They were so odd and nonsensical that 'she knew not how to utter them', Katherine Tylney said.

These depositions were added to those of Joan Bulmer, Edward Waldgrave, and other servants of the Dowager Duchess; all of them testifying to the Queen's 'unlawful, carnal, voluptuous, and licentious life' with Manox and with Dereham.

≡

Dereham and Culpepper were put on trial on 1 December at London's Guildhall. On the same day, Katheryn's brothers rode most conspicuously about the city affecting an air of indifference. It was their way of disassociating themselves from their sister's crimes, de Marillac noted. The Duke of Norfolk behaved similarly. During the trial, he would guffaw loudly, expressing his contempt for the accused.

The proceedings lasted six hours. Both men pleaded not guilty to adultery with the Queen. Dereham, of course, tried to point out that he had been involved with Katheryn *before* her marriage, and that they had also been pre-contracted to each other. The issue of the pre-contract was a sensitive subject for the authorities who did not want Dereham to escape punishment, or the Queen for that matter, by admitting to the lesser crime of bigamy. During the interrogations of the various witnesses involved, the King's officials were instructed to suppress this piece of information. Dereham's defence did him no good. His judges did not recognise the validity of the pre-contract, much less its existence. Ironically, Katheryn, who could have vouched for it, had minimised its worth in an attempt to save herself. Concerning his actions at court, Dereham insisted upon oath that he had acted the clerk - not the lover - when he had re-entered Katheryn's life. The jury believed otherwise. In joining the Queen's service, there was presumption that Dereham meant to resume their earlier relationship.

Culpepper fared no better. His nocturnal meetings with the Queen implied adultery. Even if the two had not engaged in sexual intercourse as they both claimed, there had still been the desire to do so. During his interrogation, Culpepper confessed that he had '*intended* to do ill with her, and *likewise the Queen.*' Though adultery was never sufficiently proved, presumption of guilt and intention of deed were enough to condemn both young men.

Nine days later, the two were taken from the Tower to Tyburn through the crowds. Was Henry Manox one of the bystanders? It is tempting to think that he was drawn to the grisly scene about to take place, thankful to have escaped punishment for his own past with the Queen. Culpepper, despite the greater enormity of his crime in betraying the King's trust, only had his head struck off. The wretched Dereham, despite his pleas for a more merciful end like Culpepper's, being lowly born was subjected to the full barbarity of the King's justice.

Even before the arrest of her granddaughter, the Dowager Duchess of Norfolk had sensed that something was wrong. When Francis Dereham had been picked up for piracy, she had not been fooled, and she had taken the precaution of sending a servant to Hampton Court - under the pretence of buying wood - to learn what he could. Her worry was justified when her man came back saying not only was Dereham detained for questioning, so were Henry Manox and the Queen herself.

Certain the King's commissioners would come knocking at Lambeth next, the Duchess sprang into action. She remembered how before he disappeared for Ireland, Dereham had stored some of his possessions with her. Could they contain incriminating material against him and Katheryn? On the evening of 14 November, Agnes Tilney, with the help of a servant named William Ashby, broke into Dereham's things. By candlelight, she ransacked his chests, pulling out piles of his old papers. According to Ashby, his mistress then locked herself in her room to study them in private. Whether she was worried by what she read or merely taking precautions, around the same time the Duchess had one of her grandsons consult the law books. She wanted to know if she would be eligible for a general pardon if implicated in Katheryn's misdeeds.

Her worst fears were realised in December. Dereham and Culpepper had been found guilty and executed, and now the authorities ordered her arrest. She was not alone; her son Lord William, his wife, and the Duchess' two daughters, Anne Howard and the Countess of Bridgewater, all joined her in the Tower. Thanks to their station, the Howards were fortunate enough to be assigned to the royal apartments. By this time, the fortress was so crowded with prisoners held for questioning in the matter of the Queen, that Henry VIII allowed his private rooms to be used for additional lodgings.

The Howards, in spite of their predicament, remained stubborn. When they first came for her, the Duchess feigned illness and took to her bed. Only when she was promised that she would be well provided for in the Tower did she go quietly. Lord William was no less difficult. His bearing was so arrogant that Wriothesley, who brought him to prison, did not 'much like his fashion'. Meanwhile, his sister the Countess was just as troublesome; she being truly 'her mother's daughter', her jailers complained.

Locked up in the Tower, the Duchess maintained she was 'as innocent as the child newborn'. She admitted to opening Dereham's coffers, but she had had no idea that he had been taken into custody, she claimed. Later, she tweaked her story saying she had been looking for evidence to send to the King when she learnt of his arrest. Her servant Ashby did confirm that his mistress had given him some papers to forward to the authorities, but only after she had gone through everything beforehand. As for her ignorance of any 'abomination' between her granddaughter and Dereham, Ashby would not corroborate that. Long ago, the old man remembered, the Duchess had told him that she had a notion that Katheryn and Dereham were up to no good behind her back.

As the weeks went by, the Duchess began to unravel. Agitated, she contradicted her statements and could not verify her claims. The Earl of Southampton observed with satisfaction how 'for my Lady of Norfolk, such matter there groweth continually against her, whereby she hath so meshed and tangled herself that I think it will be hard for her to wind out again'. The King's Councillors agreed. 'Her denial makes for nothing', they said.

Under interrogation, Lord William was as 'stiff as his mother'. But he at least had the excuse of being unaware of the seriousness of his niece's affair with Dereham. He had to be warned about it by the Duchess when the government was closing in on the family. But what he was guilty of was knowledge of the midnight romps at Lambeth and Horsham. He had even made light of them, as had his sister Lady Bridgewater. Her offhand approach had been simply to give advice to Katheryn not to overdo it, for 'it would hurt her beauty'.

With the Howards being brought down, the authorities cast greedy eyes on their wealth. The Duchess' house was carefully searched and her possessions inventoried. In a desperate attempt to appease the King, she revealed the location of a stash of money she had squirreled away. No stone was left unturned. A thorough investigation was even made into Lord William's claim that his goods were lost at sea on their way from Calais. Altogether, the authorities were able to seize some 5,000 marks in money and £1,000 in plate from the family. The windfall was transported to Westminster for Henry VIII's inspection.

No one denounced the fallen Howards louder than their own kinsman, the Duke of Norfolk, who was apparently clueless about Katheryn's past. The nobleman, who had already seen one niece sacrificed to the King's anger, knew where his loyalties lay. He denounced the Queen to anyone who would listen, saying she even deserved to be burnt alive for her crimes. Norfolk was no less kind about his other relatives. In a grovelling letter to the King, he condemned his 'ungracious' stepmother, his 'unhappy' brother William, and his 'lewd' sister the Countess. His one great hope, Norfolk wrote, was that Henry would not 'conceive a displeasure in [his] heart' against himself.

===

With her world crashing down around her, Katheryn Howard seemed to be unfazed by it all. Gone were the tears and hysterics she'd displayed at Hampton Court. Locked up at Syon, the ex-Queen was 'making good cheer, fatter and handsomer than ever she was... more imperious and commanding, and more difficult to please than ever she was when living with the King her husband'. But beneath her jovial and haughty exterior, Katheryn had no illusions regarding what was in store for her. She knew Henry would have her killed, 'for she owns that she has deserved death'.

To avoid any more grief and embarrassment to the King, his wife was proceeded against by an Act of Attainder on 21 January 1542. She had already been deprived of her title of Queen, now it was to be her life itself. Though Thomas Cromwell and Margaret Pole were both condemned by such a measure, Katheryn was no 'mean and private person but an illustrious and public one', as the Lord Chancellor had to remind Parliament. Before its members could vote on what was effectively her death sentence, it was agreed that Katheryn should at least be allowed to have her say.

The committee sent to Syon House found Katheryn subdued and resigned 'that her end will be on the scaffold'. There were no more tearful denials or retractions, in fact, Katheryn made no defence at all. She turned down the opportunity to defend herself before the Lords and Commons. Without going into specifics, she simply 'openly confessed and acknowledged... the great crime of which she had been guilty'. Perhaps she was referring to the concealment of her past from the King, as she had never confessed to adultery with Culpepper. But in the end, it did not matter. She had betrayed her husband's trust all the same. Katheryn's quiet submission made Parliament's grim task the easier. Her death warrant was made law, and on 11 February, the royal assent was given.

The might of the King's justice was moderated by the mercy he was prepared to bestow on those involved in his wife's misconduct. The Dowager Duchess, whom many supposed would go the block, only had her wealth forfeited. She was also sentenced to perpetual imprisonment, as was the rest of her family. Not long after, they were all released, including the others charged with concealing one thing or another. Only Katheryn was to die, along with Lady Rochford, convicted as her procuress.

≡

On the afternoon of 10 February, Katheryn was told to make ready for the Tower. The detachment and arrogance she had affected in the past weeks suddenly crumbled, and she had to be dragged shrieking into the waiting barge. Shivering with fear, the journey was all the more terrible when she passed beneath London Bridge. As a reminder of what was to come were the heads of Dereham and Culpepper impaled above a turret. When she landed at Tower Wharf, Katheryn had sufficiently calmed herself as there were no further reports of struggle. Dressed in sombre black velvet, she was conducted to the rooms where that other Queen - whose fate Katheryn was to share - had spent her last days.

Her composure was short-lived. Katheryn became so distraught that it was decided to have her execution postponed for at least three or four days. Lady Rochford was another cause for delay. Shortly after her arrest, she had suffered a nervous breakdown. The King, however, thought she was faking. To ensure Jane Parker could not legally escape punishment under 'a fit of madness', he had his own doctors attend to her daily. By the evening of 12 February, she was believed fit to face the executioner with her mistress.

When told to prepare herself for the next day, Katheryn was strangely calm. She was determined to die with dignity. Lest her courage fail her when the time came, she had the block brought to her room so she might practise laying her head on it. She also had another request – could she have a death in private? Regrettably, the execution of a distinguished person was an affair of State, she was told, and could not be conducted in secrecy. The public must see that justice was done and take example of her punishment. However, Katheryn was given the privilege of dying within the Tower's walls. There, the expected gathering would be considerably smaller than the mob of thousands who descended on Tyburn to witness the ends of Dereham and Culpepper.

Inevitably, Katheryn Howard's tragedy became the stuff of legend. It was reported that just before she put her head on the block on the morning of 13 February, Katheryn boldly proclaimed that rather than dying as Queen, she would have preferred death as the wife of Thomas Culpepper. Even Lady Rochford was excused from her part in Katheryn's follies. Her 'shameful doom', as she purportedly confessed, was divine retribution for another great sin. 'She was guilty of *no* other crime', the Viscountess said, than bearing false witness against her husband and his sister Queen Anne.

But according to an eyewitness named Ottwell Johnson, who was present on Tower Green that day, no such extraordinary speeches were made. Standing on the scaffold, Katheryn, at first 'so weak that she could hardly speak', paid no tribute to her dead lover, and Lady Rochford, in a 'long discourse' of her past sins, admitted to no wrong done towards George and Anne Boleyn. Instead, being 'justly condemned' and accepting 'their worthy and just punishment', both ladies made 'the most godly and Christian end'.

For a queen who did little but make merry till there was 'no more the time to dance', as the French ambassador described her fall, Katheryn Howard did leave her legacy. On her condemnation, Parliament passed a new law. From now on, it was high treason for a woman with a past to marry the King without making known her former indiscretions.

PART 7
THE GOSPELLER: KATHARINE PARR

…I am taught to say of Saint Paul - 'Non me pudet evangelii'.
['The Gospels cause me no shame']
(Katharine Parr in a letter to Cambridge University, February 1546)

Figure 17   Katharine Parr by an Unknown Artist
Sudeley Castle

Chapter 22
As Truly God is God

EUSTACE CHAPUYS, who had witnessed first hand Henry VIII's succession of Queens, reported how badly the King took the escapades of Katheryn Howard. Henry, he said, 'had certainly shown greater sorrow and regret at her loss than at the faults, loss, or divorce of his preceding wives'. After so many 'ill conditioned' marriages, he seemed resigned to live out the rest of his days as a widower. It was, Chapuys continued,

> 'like the case of a woman who cried most bitterly at the loss of her tenth husband than at the death of all the others together... it was because she had never buried one of them before without being sure of the next, and as yet, this King has formed neither a plan nor a preference.'

To alleviate his gloom, Henry VIII had hosted a banquet just a fortnight before Katheryn Howard's execution. He entertained twenty-six guests at his table, with another thirty-five nearby. It was a flashback to his rejoicing at the Bishop of Carlisle's when Anne Boleyn fell. To show he was unfazed by yet another wife's misconduct, Henry openly flirted with the ladies. Elizabeth Brooke, the estranged wife of Thomas Wyatt, received much attention, as did a niece of Anthony Browne. Anne Basset, whom the King had taken a fancy to after the death of Jane Seymour, was on the receiving end as well. Of the three, courtiers placed their bets on Mistress Brooke. She was the loveliest - a 'pretty young creature' - and according to Chapuys, the boldest. She had 'wit enough to do as badly as the others if she were to try', he said comparing her to Anne Boleyn and Katheryn Howard. If Elizabeth Brooke did try to entice the King, he did not bite. A month later, he was welcoming a new round of young belles to court.

Still, no one emerged as a possible frontrunner for the post of Queen of England. Fewer women were interested in catching the royal eye, Chapuys believed. The envoy, ever cynical about the virtue of English women, was sure that with the passing of the recent Act concerning old bedroom secrets of potential queens, no one dared to accept the honour of being Henry VIII's sixth wife.

But there was one brave enough to take on the King *again* - Anne of Cleves. After the disaster of his latest marriage, Anne, along with her brother Duke William, hoped that Henry VIII would reconsider their divorce. Anne's handsome settlement and her carefree life as a private gentlewoman meant little to her against the shame of being an ex-queen, a discarded old maid, and an embarrassment to her family. Interestingly enough, Anne apparently never blamed her former husband himself for her debasement. She seemed never to have understood his personal dislike of her, and she probably still attributed their break-up to trifling legalities concerning her old pre-contract with Francis of Lorraine. With Henry single again, Anne was hopeful he would take her back.

Their reunion was not as far-fetched as it sounded. Even Katheryn Howard, when wedded to the King, had been strangely afraid that her husband would leave her for his former wife. She was not alone in her estimation. Within a month of her arrest, courtiers were already saying how 'God was working His own work to make the Lady Anne of Cleves Queen again'. Such talk, while not treasonous, was an irritant to Henry VIII. When a lady of the court wondered aloud, "What a man the King is! How many wives will he have"? she found herself in trouble. So did one Frances Lilgrave. For spreading tall tales that the former Queen Anne was left pregnant by the King, she was punished with a spell in the Tower.

Anne of Cleves' 'restoration' was also speculated abroad. In France, a pamphlet was widely circulated condemning Henry VIII's divorce from her, and at the Imperial court, Charles V was so concerned about his uncle reuniting with the German Protestant princes, that he expressly ordered Chapuys to frustrate any plans for Henry and Anne's remarriage. But the Emperor worried for nothing. The last thing Henry wanted was life with his German Queen again. When the Duke of Cleves' ambassadors went to the English court to feel the King out, they were explicitly told that he would *never* consider having Anne back in his bed.

=

In the summer of 1542, the uneasy alliance between France and the Empire finally collapsed. Francis I and Charles V were at each other's throats again, and both reached out to England in friendship. Freed from his alliance with William of Cleves and having no interest in reviving it by taking his sister back, Henry VIII patched up his differences with the Emperor.

Their renewed amity pitted Henry against his other nephew, the King of Scots. Henry had not forgotten how James had 'stolen' Mary of Guise from him, and how he had failed to show up in York. If that was not enough, his nephew offended him by continuing his friendship with France. With England and the Empire united against Francis I, James was pressured by his uncle to abandon the French King, and to make an alliance with him instead. James refused. A pact with England, he knew, would effectively make his country subject to its mightier neighbour.

Henry VIII retaliated with raids on the Scottish border. When that proved futile, the Duke of Norfolk, restored to favour, was sent north to teach James a lesson. Still, the Scots remained defiant. They struck back with attacks of their own on English soil, boasting to 'stay as long in England as the Duke of Norfolk did in Scotland'. Norfolk, whose father had beaten the Scots at Flodden, was just as fearsome. On 24 November, he soundly defeated King James' army at Solway Moss. Learning that his fifteen thousand strong army was in the dust, James took to his bed and never got up again. He left his kingdom to his sole surviving heir – a girl, only six days old, named Mary Stuart.

The death of James V and the accession of his daughter were welcome news to Henry VIII. The little Queen was put under the governorship of the Earl of Arran, a Scotsman known to be pro-English. On 1 July 1543, Arran put his signature to the Treaty of Greenwich whereby Mary, when she came of age, would marry Prince Edward. Henry was already King of Ireland by the consent of its Parliament in June 1541. With Mary of Scots as his future daughter-in-law, he would assume complete mastery over the British Isles.

=

Under the terms of the treaty, Mary Stuart would not be delivered to England as a bride until she was ten years old. But in the meantime, Henry VIII had another marriage to celebrate – his own. On 12 July 1543, at Hampton Court, in the presence of a select company with Bishop Gardiner presiding, the King took his sixth wife.

The contrasts were obvious yet again. There was always considerable disparity between each of Henry VIII's wives, as if the King was intentionally compensating for the one before. He was attracted to Anne Boleyn because she was young and attractive in comparison to the ageing and frumpy Katherine of Aragon. Afterwards, when Anne proved too tempestuous, Henry was drawn to Jane Seymour's meekness. Jane had been no beauty, and when the King was selecting his fourth wife, Anne of Cleves' supposed charms brought her to England. But when she failed to live up to her reputation, Henry turned to the vivacious Katheryn Howard. Now in what was to be his last marriage, the differences were again noticeable. Katharine Parr, Henry's new bride, was no flighty teenager but a mature woman of thirty-one.

Katharine Parr's family had served the Crown for two generations before her birth in 1512. Her grandfather, Sir William Parr of Kendal in Westmorland, fought for Edward IV at Tewkesbury, and his son Thomas, Katharine's father, was an Esquire of the Body to Henry VIII. While Thomas Parr had attended to the King's needs, his wife Maud Green had served in the household of Katherine of Aragon. With both her parents in royal service, Katharine may have frequented her future husband's court as a young girl.

In 1517, Thomas Parr died, leaving Katharine and her younger siblings, William and Anne, in the care of their mother. Lady Parr, left with sufficient means as a widow, never contemplated remarriage. She was content to continue in the Queen's service, and at the same time, she saw to it that her children, probably living in the family estates in Northamptonshire, received the best education she could give them. Katharine and her two siblings learned to read and write - not only in their native tongue, but also in 'French and other languages'. As well, they had lessons in music, dance, and all the other necessary graces. It was Maud's intention that, on leaving home, her children would go on to make successful lives for themselves. For William, that meant following in his late father's footsteps of service to the King. Affable and handsome, not to mention sophisticated and well-polished thanks to her, Maud was certain that William would go far.

Katharine and Anne, as convention dictated, would seek advantageous marriages for themselves. Afterwards, their lives would be entirely domestic. With husbands to tend to, children to care for, and a staff of servants to run, there would unfortunately, be little if any opportunity to put their special schooling to use. However, despite their lot as married women, it was Maud Parr's belief nonetheless, that her daughters should be well educated. From her time at court, she had observed Katherine of Aragon's efforts to make the Princess Mary a learned young woman, and she would have heard from the Queen how her friend Sir Thomas More was having his daughters follow a curriculum of Latin, Greek, theology, philosophy, and the sciences just like his son. Taking Queen Katherine and More as her role models, Maud saw to it that both her girls were given the same advantages as their brother William.

Lady Parr's schoolroom was not restricted to her own offspring. In fact, she welcomed the children of her relatives and the neighbouring gentry, providing them room and board. The Parr household then was not unlike Lambeth and Horsham where Katheryn Howard grew up. But unlike the harried Dowager Duchess of Norfolk, Maud Parr genuinely cared about the well-being and education of the pupils under her roof. In a short time, the Parr schoolroom gained a sterling reputation.

One of Maud's boarders was Henry Scrope, the grandson of her kinsman Lord Dacre. Dacre had recommended his stay to his father Lord Scrope of Bolton. Not only would the boy get a good education under Lady Parr, Dacre promised, but he would also acquaint himself with her daughter Katharine, earmarked as his future bride. At the end of 1523, Maud began formal negotiations with Lord Scrope for their children to marry. Acting as the intermediary, Dacre advised his son-in-law that young Henry was fortunate in landing himself 'so good a stock as Lady Parr's considering her wisdom… and of that of the Parrs of Kendal'. But as good as their reputation was, their money mattered more to Lord Scrope. He and Maud Parr haggled over the dowry - he thought it too low and she too high - until with both parties being 'so far apart', the marriage between their children was abandoned.

Seeking a better offer for Katharine, Lady Parr looked to the more reasonable Lord Borough of Gainsborough. This time, there were no disagreements over money and a deal was struck. Around the middle of 1529, Katharine journeyed to Lincolnshire to be the wife of Borough's son Edward. The marriage was short-lived. About the end of 1532, Katharine donned black as a widow. How affected she was by her young husband's passing is unrecorded, but surely she had been deeply saddened by the loss of her mother who had died shortly after her wedding. But unlike Maud Parr, Katharine did not have the inclination - or the luxury - to remain single. With her brother William responsible for his own growing family (he had wed the Earl of Essex's daughter in 1527), and herself only adequately provided for as Edward Borough's widow, it was necessary for her to remarry.

In 1533, Katharine repeated her wedding vows with John Neville, Lord Latimer, a respected nobleman in Yorkshire. That Latimer was wealthy and almost twice her age, suggests that Katharine's priorities were probably more towards security than romance. Whatever her reasons, Katharine proved a devoted wife, and was a loving stepmother to her husband's two children John and Margaret. She was particularly close to the latter. Years later, when Margaret Neville fell fatally ill, she paid tribute to her stepmother in her will. For the 'tender love and bountiful goodness' Katharine rendered unto her, Margaret wrote she could 'never be able to render Her Grace sufficient thanks'. She was also grateful for the 'godly education' Katharine provided her.

Affectionate and dutiful, Katharine Parr was a model spouse. It was the obligation of all wives, she believed, 'to love their husbands, to love their children, to be discreet, housewifely and good'. The advanced education she had received from Maud Parr might have led Katharine to form some opinions of her own, but all in all, as Lord Latimer's wife, she was of one mind with him. If she did ever find herself disagreeing with her husband, she suppressed her views. As Katharine later wrote:

> 'If they be women married, they learn of Saint Paul
> to be obedient to their husbands, and to keep silence
> in the congregation, and to learn of their husbands
> at home.'

Like the majority of Northerners, Lord Latimer was conservative in his religion. So much so, that his private chapel was reputed to be one of the grandest in the north. Latimer disliked the changes the kingdom had undergone since Henry VIII's Great Matter, but as a loyal subject, he would not be moved to treason, despite the grumblings of his neighbours.

His neutrality was compromised by the Pilgrimage of Grace in the Fall of 1536. When the Northerners rose in revolt, they counted on the great magnates of the region – John Neville included – to lead the rebellion. Those who would not join them, the rebels declared, would be made to. Just two weeks after the commons of Lincolnshire raised their standard at Louth on 1 October, Lord Latimer found them at his doorstep at Snape Castle. Fearing for the safety of his family, Latimer tried to pacify the rabble. He was sympathetic to their grievances, he explained, but he dare not raise arms against his sovereign lord the King. Yes, the attacks against the Church were a sin, but so was rebellion. His words were met with angry shouts. Protesting in vain, Latimer was hauled away by the rebels in front of his terrified family and forced to ride away with them to their camp. Katharine, John, and Margaret were left to fend for themselves.

To justify their actions, the rebels made Latimer their spokesman. Forced to take an oath promising himself to them, he reluctantly negotiated on their behalf with the King. But after Robert Aske was tricked into peace, Latimer took the opportunity to change sides. His treachery led to his house being ransacked by the insurgents in January 1537. 'I do not know what they will do with my body and goods, wife and children', Latimer wrote fearfully to the Lord Admiral Fitzwilliam. His family emerged unharmed, but the experience of having their home turned upside down by an angry mob was terrifying in itself. Certainly, it left a permanent impression on the Nevilles, one that was perhaps life-changing to Katharine in terms of her later religious faith.

When the Pilgrimage of Grace was finally put down, a grateful Katharine welcomed Lord Latimer home. Happily, he was spared the fate of Robert Aske and the others. However, for his part in the rebellion - unwilling as it was - John Neville never regained the King's trust. He even endured a short spell in the Tower. In March 1543, Latimer passed away in his London house with Katharine by his side. He was lucky to die in bed, but his reputation had been tarnished. In the eyes of his King, he remained a suspected rebel, and in those of his neighbours - a turncoat.

After burying John Neville, Katharine set out to make a new start for herself. She would remain in the capital, she decided, where she and her husband had lived in the final months of his life. A return to Yorkshire, be it as a widow, or as the wife of another Northern lord, was not for Katharine. Her destiny lay at court.

As Maud Parr had once served Katherine of Aragon, it is believed that Katharine sought and won a place with her daughter Mary around the end of 1542. It was while she was at court that Katharine found herself attracted to Sir Thomas Seymour. Brother to the late Queen Jane and uncle to the Prince of Wales, Seymour was not a man Katharine, or anyone else, could have overlooked. Handsome, dashing, and charismatic, and at the same time brash, proud, and reckless, he swaggered about the court like his royal brother-in-law had done in his prime. Always having an eye for the ladies, Seymour himself was drawn to Katharine. Though his critics would suspect that he was solely after the Widow Latimer's fortune, it would be unfair to say that Katharine's wealth was her only attraction. Though she was not a beauty like the King's late sister the French Queen or Christina of Denmark, Katharine was reasonably attractive. But if not for her looks exactly, she was much admired for her lively personality and her 'cheerful countenance'. She had a kind and agreeable nature, everyone agreed. These qualities in Katharine appealed to Seymour, and she was captivated by his charms. Soon, she was in love. After two marriages made to protect herself in the world, Katharine now felt free to follow her heart. By the early summer of 1543, she planned to be married again.

But Katharine's merits, so pleasing to Thomas Seymour, won her another admirer too, one she least expected – the King himself. Having been without a wife for over a year, Henry VIII was a lonely man. Katheryn Howard's betrayal hurt him still, and his periodic bouts of ill health, mostly brought on by the ulcer on his leg and his increasing obesity, depressed him further. Having a wife to look after him would be a great comfort to Henry, but no lady had been deemed suitable. But, as the King observed Lady Latimer about court – how animated and gracious she was, and how well bred and how well she was spoken of - he became interested in the comely widow. The attraction became romantic, and Henry's thoughts turned to marriage. He was convinced that Katharine Parr would make an ideal queen, wife, and stepmother. Besides her evident virtues, she was a mature woman, having been respectfully married and widowed. Lady Latimer - unlike the Howard girl - would have no bedroom scandals behind her.

When Henry made his feelings known to Katharine, she was astonished at his proposal, perhaps even a little horrified. Emotionally, she had already given herself entirely to Thomas Seymour, and it had never crossed her mind that the King of England would desire her. The attraction was not mutual. For all his power and majesty, Henry VIII was a temperamental, fat, semi-invalid with a pus filled leg and a chequered history as a husband. Perhaps Christina of Milan's old joke about needing two heads as Queen of England crossed Katharine's mind in consideration of what had happened to Katheryn Howard.

If Lady Latimer did refuse him at first, Henry remained persistent - as did God Himself. What finally convinced Katharine Parr into marriage with the King were not his professions of love, but rather the mysterious ways of the Almighty. Years afterwards, when she was widowed once again, Katharine confessed to her cast off lover Seymour how

> 'as truly God is God, my mind was fully bent the other time I was at liberty to marry you before any man I knew. But God withstood my will therein most vehemently for a time.'

It was while she was agonising over the King's offer that prayer had enlightened Katharine to accept him. It was not so much the Lord's intention that she surrender herself in marriage as a loyal subject to her lonesome King, Katharine believed, as it was for her to be His divine instrument behind the throne. As Queen, she would be a dutiful helpmate to Henry VIII in furthering the cause of religious reform in England. Some time before she had accepted his proposal, Katharine had abandoned the Catholicism of her youth and embraced the new faith, coming 'in a new garment before God', as she put it.

The seeds may have been sown as early as Katharine's marriage to Edward Borough. Her father-in-law Lord Thomas was an avid proponent of Reform. He was also an enthusiastic supporter of the Boleyn marriage, and when Anne became Queen, he was appointed her Lord Chamberlain. Often, Borough dined with Anne, talking religion with her, the King, and their like-minded guests. Anne Boleyn had held such 'roundtables' even before she was Queen, and it is probable that at the time of Katharine Parr's first marriage, Lord Borough being part of Anne's set, was already a regular. Perhaps the stimulating table talk at court was brought back to Gainsborough on his visits home. But that Katharine, bright as she was, took part is unlikely. While it was acceptable for the King's clever mistress to argue Scripture (especially when it was she who initiated such pastimes), for Lord Borough, it was probably inappropriate that his daughter-in-law, a girl barely eighteen, do likewise.

Still, Borough's interest in Reform may have made an impression on Katharine. Supposing it had, even though she went on to wed the very orthodox Lord Latimer, Katharine's conscience might have become troubled. Perhaps she found herself drawn to the new religious thinking. If so, it challenged Katharine and it even invigorated her - both intellectually and emotionally. Eventually, she found herself in a spiritual crisis. But rather than give in to what she still considered heresy, Katharine suppressed her yearnings and clung to the faith she had been taught. Years later, she confessed her regret in a work entitled *The Lamentation or Complaint of a Sinner*. 'Bewailing the ignorance of her blind life led in superstition', Katharine wrote how:

> 'I would not learn to know the Lord and his ways, but loved darkness better than light. Yea, darkness seemed to me light. I embraced ignorance, as perfect knowledge and knowledge seemed to me superfluous and vain. I regarded little God's word, but gave myself to vanities and shadows of the world. I forsook Him, in Whom is all truth, and followed the vain foolish imaginations of my heart. I would have covered my sins with the pretence of holiness. I called superstition godly meaning, and true holiness error. The Lord did speak many pleasant and sweet words unto me, and I would not hear. He called me diversely, but through forwardness I would not answer.'

Still a devout Catholic, Katharine continued to seek out 'such riffraff as the Bishop of Rome... to receive full remission of my sins'. But no matter how much she prayed, or how often she received the Sacrament, Katharine found no comfort or meaning in the religion of her youth anymore. Her relationship with Christ her Saviour, as she put it, was 'cold and dead'.

Katharine's reawakening as a fervent Protestant is undated, but perhaps it was during the Pilgrimage of Grace. As sympathetic as she might have been to the rebels at first, the subsequent kidnapping of Lord Latimer and the looting of their family home might well have turned Katharine against them and their cause. With her growing alienation from her faith, it was possible that she came to equate the violence of the Pilgrimage with the religion for which it was fighting for.

Regardless of how God had inspired Katharine to a new faith, she responded with zeal. In that spirit, she gave up Thomas Seymour and 'most willingly' accepted Henry VIII's proposal.

Chapter 23
Most Illustrious Queen

AS HENRY VIII's wife, one of the first priorities Katharine set for herself was to win the trust of his children, as she had done with Lord Latimer's. The royal offspring were a disparate bunch to say the least - Mary, a frustrated spinster of twenty-seven who still bore the scars of her painful adolescence; Elizabeth, a solemn girl of nine whose cool intelligence masked her insecurities as an unwanted child; and Edward, a precocious boy of five who surrounded by nursemaids and attendants, had yet to know the warmth of a real family.

With Mary, Katharine had already gotten a head start by being in her service. A month before she married the King, Katharine appeared to be already on intimate terms with her eldest stepdaughter and even with her younger one Elizabeth. The Earl of Hertford, Edward Seymour, had noted in June that Katharine and her sister Anne were seen in the company of the two Princesses. While Mary had wanted little to do with Katheryn Howard, she took an immediate liking to her successor. She and the new Queen became close; probably more like sisters than mother and daughter, being so near in age. To Mary, Katharine's friendship was most welcome, coming at a still difficult time in her life. Though she and her father had reconciled, Mary could never entirely forget the past. Henry VIII was undeniably affectionate towards her, making up for their years of estrangement, but nonetheless, his interests always come before Mary. "I love my daughter well", the King said unabashedly, "but *myself* and honour more". Still officially 'the Lady Mary', her illegitimacy shamed her, and the stigma was often an obstacle to her desire to be married. Nearing thirty, Mary still lived under her father's thumb, and time was passing her by. With no prospects, or hope of any, Mary resigned herself to life as the 'unhappiest lady in Christendom'.

Katharine was able to ease some of Mary's misery. Knowing her love of finery, the Queen made frequent presents to her. Not long after she married Henry VIII, Katharine gave her stepdaughter 'a pair of bracelets of gold set with diamonds and rubies, and in either of them one emerald'. Later in January 1544, Mary received a New Year's gift of 'a book of gold set with rubies' and a bracelet adorned with pearls.

Besides the jewels that Mary was so fond of, Katharine provided her with purses of cash; £20 on the day of Katharine's wedding, and another £20 the following September.

Katharine was far too sensible to cultivate her friendship with Mary with just money and trinkets. Well aware of her stepdaughter's intellectual abilities, the new Queen encouraged Mary to put her talents to good use. In 1545, Katharine sponsored a translation, from Latin to English, of Erasmus's *Paraphrases Upon the New Testament*. While sections were assigned to select scholars, Katharine was confident that Mary, with her grounding in Latin, was ideal for tackling the *Paraphrase* of St John. Mary began the undertaking with enthusiasm, working on it diligently until a bout of illness forced another to finish it on her behalf. Though modesty prevented her from setting her name to the work, Nicholas Udall, who acted as editor of the project and as one of the translators, paid tribute to the Princess for her 'pains and travail' in the book's preface. Queen Katharine was not forgotten. As 'chief patroness' of the *Paraphrases*, Udall acknowledged her role in 'sew[ing] abroad the word of God', and in 'plant[ing] true religion in all His realms and dominions'.

While she was more of a companion and confidante to Mary, Katharine assumed the role of a parent to the King's younger children. Elizabeth welcomed the Queen's presence in the family. She had got to know Katharine in the weeks before her marriage, and on the big day, Elizabeth, with her elder sister, was one of the special guests present at the nuptials. Perhaps it was at the Queen's insistence that they were invited; neither of the King's daughters attended his three previous weddings.

Before Katharine Parr's arrival, Elizabeth's only parental figures had been her appointed caretakers. She seldom saw her father, and as for his parade of wives, she was too young to remember Jane Seymour, and she had little time to know Anne of Cleves or Katheryn Howard either. Elizabeth's affections, therefore, had been directed towards her governesses – her 'Lady Mistresses' - as they were called. The first of them was Margaret Bryan, a woman of experience having looked after the King's elder daughter in her infancy. Lady Bryan became devoted to the little Elizabeth, telling Thomas Cromwell in August 1536, that the King 'shall have great comfort in Her Grace, for she is as toward a child and as gentle of conditions as ever I knew any in my life'. Sadly, Lady Bryan had to move on when she was promoted to Prince Edward's nursery in 1537. Filling her shoes was Katherine

Champernowne, better known by Elizabeth's affectionate nickname for her – 'Kat', and by her subsequent married surname of Ashley. Kind-hearted, loyal, and of some education, Kat Ashley proved to be a commendable choice.

Elizabeth's upbringing under her two governesses would have done Henry VIII proud. Thomas Wriothesley, who visited the Princess in 1539, could not contain his admiration for her. At only six, Elizabeth had the bearing and deportment of a forty-year-old, he observed, and she would prove an 'honour to womanhood and shall be seen to be her father's daughter'. Wriothesley's praise would have made Elizabeth glad. Throughout her long life, she maintained her awe and affection for Henry VIII, despite the fact he had set his hand to her mother's death warrant and made her herself a bastard.

Though Elizabeth continued to live in a separate establishment, sometimes sharing one with her brother the Prince, Katharine saw to it that the whole family was together whenever possible. The idea of individual households was alien to Katharine, and she wanted to recreate the close-knit family life she had known at her childhood home and with the Latimers as much as she could. By the end of summer 1543, Katharine had succeeded. Mary was lodged with her, and Elizabeth stayed at court for a time. Even Edward was brought to meet Katharine. The novelty of all the King's children gathered under one roof aroused the curiosity of the Emperor's sister. In December, Mary of Hungary, while inquiring about the royal family's health, asked whether 'the Queen's grace, my lord Prince, my lady Mary, and my lady Elizabeth… continued still in one household' with the King? To Elizabeth's regret, they had not. Although Mary had stayed on with the Queen, she and Prince Edward had returned to their own establishments. Elizabeth was not to see Katharine again until a year later.

While Elizabeth was away from court, the Queen nurtured their friendship through letters. Sometimes it was more than just messages, as in Elizabeth's New Year's gift sent to the Queen in 1544. She had undertaken an English translation of a devotional poem *The Mirror of the Sinful Soul*, written in French by Margaret of Angoulême, whom her mother Anne Boleyn had known during her stay in France. Not only did Elizabeth translate and transcribe the work, but she also made the cover herself. On a background of blue cloth, she embroidered a pattern of intricate knot-work in silver thread. In the corners, Elizabeth added pansies, and in the centre, the initials 'KP', which she knew from Katharine's letters to her were always added by the Queen to the end of her signature. The result was impressive, especially coming from an eleven-year-old. But Elizabeth was humble. She asked its recipient to 'rub out, polish and mend' any mistakes she might have made, and not to show the translation to anyone else until then, lest 'my faults be known of many'.

The Queen was also a keen correspondent with Prince Edward. Barely six years old, he was already seen to be cut from the same cloth as Mary and Elizabeth. Edward was an attractive child, sharing the pale skin, reddish-gold hair, and dignified bearing of his sisters. Like them, he was also very bright, and in time would be their equal intellectually. By his natural gifts and by his training, there was every expectation that the boy would fulfil the great destiny in store for him. As early as January 1539, when Edward was not even two years old, verses beneath a portrait of him by Hans Holbein (meant as a New Year's gift to the King) called upon the Prince of Wales to 'emulate thy father and be heir to his virtue'. If he did, the prodigious Edward would then 'outstript all, nor shall any surpass thee in ages to come'. It was a heavy burden on his shoulders, especially when Edward was still amusing himself with 'pretty toys', as Lady Bryan reported in the spring of 1540.

By the time his father married Katharine Parr, Edward was beginning to set aside his playthings. In 1544, he officially left the care of Lady Bryan and his nurses to take up his education with 'well-learned men who sought to bring him up in learning of tongues, of the Scripture, of philosophy, and all liberal sciences'. Aided by his tutors, Edward composed letters to his various family members, including his stepmother, in English, French, and Latin. While Katharine was fluent in French, and presumably in Italian too (a letter from Elizabeth to her in that language exists), she may have read Edward's Latin letters with some difficulty. Katharine may have had only a basic understanding of it as Maud Parr's programme 'of other languages' apparently put more of an emphasis on contemporary ones. Probably, it was as Queen that Katharine began studying Latin in earnest to which Edward lent his enthusiastic encouragement. In a letter to his stepmother dated June 1546, Edward praised Katharine's progress in her Latin lessons. Much of Edward's writings, whatever their language, were intended as schoolboy exercises, but they still had an air of intimacy to them. In one communication, Edward's feelings for his stepmother were touchingly expressed when he thanked

Katharine, whom he often addressed as 'most illustrious Queen and beloved mother', for her 'loving and tender letters, which do give me much comfort and encouragement'.

To Edward, Queen Katharine was also a kindred spirit in religion, as she was in learning. Under the influence of his Reform-minded tutors Richard Cox, John Cheke, and Roger Ascham, Edward was exposed to doctrines at which conservatives at court would have cringed. Not only were the Prince's schoolmasters instilling new beliefs in the Prince, but also a new sense of morality. Edward's Catholic sister became a target of his growing priggishness. In a letter to their stepmother written in May 1546, Edward tried to persuade Katharine, whom he obviously believed felt as he did, to protect Mary

'from all wiles and enchantments of the Evil One, and beseech her to attend no longer to foreign dances and merriments which do not become a Christian Princess.'

Katharine, who loved dancing and a good time as much as Mary did, tactfully said nothing to her.

After six months of marriage, Katharine Parr still showed no signs of pregnancy. Perhaps Henry VIII had come to believe that his chances of having another child - a son that is - were slim. After all, even Katheryn Howard who had been much younger than his current wife, had failed to conceive. In the back of his mind, Henry may have even considered that the fault was not entirely theirs, but his. He was now an old man, not likely to have many years left to him. After him, young Edward would succeed, but from the King's own experience, fortune was fickle. His father Henry VII had fathered three sons, but only *he* had survived into adulthood. Should Edward himself die before having an heir, England might be plunged into chaos again.

In February 1544, a new Act of Succession modified the one of 1536 that had settled the Crown on the children of Henry VIII and Jane Seymour. Edward was still first in line to the throne, of course, followed by any children the King might have with Katharine Parr. A significant change in the Act was that Mary was back in the picture, as was Elizabeth – though both were still considered illegitimate. As it was now laid out, should Edward die childless, the throne would go to Mary and her heirs if the King had no offspring by his current Queen. If Mary, in turn, had no children, Elizabeth and her descendants would rule. Henry was even far-sighted enough to plan beyond that. After his youngest daughter, the succession would be passed to the line of his sister Mary, the late French Queen. The offspring of his elder sister, Margaret, Queen of Scotland, were entirely ignored. Henry had detested her husband and her son, James IV and James V respectively, having made war on them both. As well, Margaret's descendants being Scottish were looked on as foreigners with no rights in England. The fact that her daughter Margaret Douglas was born on English soil in Northumberland counted for nothing.

=

Katharine Parr was as eager to form good relations with the King's foreign allies as she was with his children. Envoys coming to court found Henry VIII's latest Queen most congenial. While Jane Seymour had been shy and at a loss for words in the presence of the Imperial ambassador, Katharine conducted what was probably her first important audience with flying colours. The occasion was the arrival of the Spanish Duke of Najera on 17 February 1544. On behalf of the Emperor, he had come to follow up on negotiations for England's help against France. After Najera had met with the King, he was taken to see the Queen. Henry did not join the Duke; signifying his complete trust in his wife's ability to entertain him on her own.

In the Queen's apartments, Najera and his party were introduced to their royal hostess. Aiming to impress, she was magnificently arrayed in

> 'a robe of cloth of gold, and a petticoat of brocade with sleeves lined with crimson satin, and trimmed with three-piled velvet. Her train was more than two yards long. Suspended from her neck were two crosses, and a jewel of very rich diamonds, and in her headdress were many and beautiful ones. Her girdle was of gold, with very large pendants.'

In her company were the Lady Mary, the King's niece Margaret Douglas, and the Queen's brother William Parr, now Earl of Essex and a rising courtier thanks to his sister. Despite being 'slightly indisposed', Katharine greeted her guests with all graciousness. After kissing her hand, the Duke of Najera was led into a chamber filled with music and dancing (thankfully the opinionated Prince Edward was not present!). Katharine, refusing to give in to her fatigue, danced 'very gracefully' with her brother, while Mary and her cousin Margaret partnered the other gentlemen in the room. The entertainments lasted several hours. When the evening finally came to a close, Katharine gave out presents to the Spaniards before retiring.

≡

In the summer of 1544, the Queen was given the highest accolade. After continuing talks with the Emperor following the Duke of Najera's embassy, Henry VIII announced himself his nephew's ally against the French. But he would not be an armchair general, the King insisted, he would cross over to France to lead his armies himself as he did thirty years ago. In his absence, his wife would govern England as Regent. It was an honour the King had not bestowed on any of his Queens other than his first. Assured that his kingdom was left in safe hands, Henry sailed for France on 11 July, just a day short of his first wedding anniversary with Katharine.

As Queen-Regent, Katharine met regularly with the Council headed by the Earl of Hertford and by Archbishop Cranmer. Like Katherine of Aragon before her, she found herself dealing with a difficult Scotland in the King's absence. Even before Henry crossed the sea, trouble had been brewing across the border. James V's widow had repudiated the Treaty of Greenwich and was looking to renew the 'auld alliance' with her native France. Instead of marrying her baby daughter Mary Stuart to Prince Edward, Mary of Guise intended to match her with Francis I's new grandson. Henry VIII, furious at the Scots' treachery, dispatched Hertford and his troops north with orders to burn and destroy 'every pile, fortress, and village that was in their wake'.

With Henry now gone to France, the Scots remained defiant against his 'rough wooing' of their infant Queen. Katharine, always a keen letter writer, kept her husband well informed on the Scottish situation. In early August, Katharine could report that the Earl of Lennox, recently married to his niece Margaret Douglas, had gone north in the King's name to engage the insolent Scots. With Lennox serving 'a master whom God aids', she was confident, the Queen wrote, that he would bring them to heel.

Katharine kept Henry up to date on more mundane matters as well. Even as Regent exercising kingly powers, Katharine still felt obliged to seek her husband's approval on ordinary domestic concerns. Later in the month, she asked Henry for his advice about the ladies she kept about her. Some of them had fallen sick, Katharine wrote, and she wanted his permission to take on new ones. The Queen's letters were never purely business though. She habitually asked about Henry's health and expressed her affection for him in terms both loving and submissive, signing herself off as his 'humble, obedient, loving wife and servant'. Katharine's wifely concern even had her sending provisions such as venison across the sea to ensure Henry ate well on campaign.

In her letters, Katharine also described the progress of his children. This was made easier when Elizabeth and Edward were brought to Hampton Court to stay with her and Mary in their father's absence. Elizabeth was especially excited at the invitation since she had not seen the Queen since the summer of her marriage. Katharine was pleased to have all her royal stepchildren with her, and together they would present a unified front before the court until the King's 'happy return' as Elizabeth had put it. Her hopes for her father's victory in France were echoed in one of the prayers Katharine had written herself. When Elizabeth and her siblings accompanied their stepmother to the royal chapel, they listened to it being read:

> 'O Almighty King and Lord of Hosts… our cause now being just, and being enforced to enter into war and battle, we most humbly beseech Thee, O God of Hosts, so to turn the hearts of our enemies to the desire of peace that no Christian blood be spilt. Or else grant, O Lord, that with small effusion of blood and little damage of innocents, we may to Thy glory obtain victory, and that wars being soon ended, we may all, with one heart and mind, knit together in concord and amity, laud and praise Thee who livest and reignest world without end. Amen.'

The Queen's prayer for victory was answered with the surrender of Boulogne on 14 September. Henry savoured his triumph and was determined to keep the port town in English hands. But his plans for further conquests came to a standstill when startling news arrived. Behind his back, the Emperor had made peace with Francis I, leaving the English to carry on the war alone. With 'no little grief and displeasure' to himself, Henry packed up at the end of the month. Even though his conquest had been spoilt by Charles V's underhandedness, Henry received a hero's welcome on his return home.

The falling-out between uncle and nephew continued into the spring of 1545. That May, Katharine, who had always valued amity with the Imperialists, stepped in to do what she could to mend fences. On the eve of Eustace Chapuys' departure from England due to his declining health, Katharine made it a point to speak with the envoy before he left. She 'was very sorry' that he was going away, she told him, but the climate in the Low Countries would do him much good. Katharine then commended herself to his master the Emperor, trusting that Chapuys would continue to do his best in furthering 'the increase of the existing friendship' between England and the Empire. Admittedly, relations between Henry VIII and Charles V had soured of late, but Katharine reassured the ambassador of the King's 'sincere affection and goodwill', and begged him to relay these sentiments. By speaking to Charles in person, the Queen said, Chapuys would do more good than in writing any letter to him.

In meeting with Charles' trusted ambassador, especially during the crucial time of his final days in England, Katharine hoped to restore peace. Though her powers as Regent were terminated on the King's return, Katharine remained true to the motto she had chosen for herself as Queen – *To be useful in all I do* – and that included her taking on the role of mediator between powerful princes when necessary.

In making herself 'useful' as she had vowed, Katharine encouraged learning and piety in her court. She formed a circle of women who were as interested in education and the reformed religion as she was. Significantly, many of these ladies were the wives of important courtiers. Most prominent were: Joan Champernowne, sister of Princess Elizabeth's governess Kat Ashley, and married to Sir Anthony Denny, a favourite of the King; Anne Stanhope, wife of Lord Hertford; Jane Guilford, married to John Dudley, Viscount Lisle; and Katherine Willoughby, wife of the now ailing Duke of Suffolk. The Queen also included members of her family: her sister Anne Parr, now Lady Herbert; their cousin Maud, Lady Lane; and Margaret Neville, the Queen's stepdaughter, newly come to court.

In the Queen's chambers, 'every day in the afternoon, for the space of an hour', Katharine and her ladies discussed and debated Scripture, and they listened to sermons by 'learned and godly persons' committed to the new faith. They also prayed together; almost certainly in words of the Queen's own composition. In November 1545, Katharine published a devotional entitled *Prayers and Meditations*. The collection proved so popular - a Tudor best-seller - that it was a consistently in print during the following reigns of Katharine's three royal stepchildren. Despite the Queen's growing evangelicalism, the prayers she had written were middle of the road; nothing explicitly Catholic or overtly Protestant, enough to satisfy her religiously conventional husband.

The virtuous nature of the Queen's court was highly praised. A member of Katharine's household, Francis Goldsmith, saluted her for the atmosphere of godliness she fostered. 'Her rare goodness had made every day a Sunday', he congratulated his mistress, 'a thing hitherto unheard of especially in a royal palace'. Katharine's reputation even spread beyond the confines of the court. The universities, particularly Cambridge, were most anxious to have her as their patroness – and their intercessor.

In the same month that Katharine's *Prayers and Meditations* was released, Parliament voted that 'all colleges, chantries, and hospitals [be] committed to the King's order'. Despite Henry VIII's solemn promise that their wealth would only be put 'to the glory of God and to the common profit of the realm', Cambridge University, remembering the fate of the monasteries, was wary. If the King could not be moved to forego its endowments, its chancellors thought, perhaps the Queen could help. And so she did. Katharine, as she wrote back to the University in February 1546, had 'attempted my lord, the King for the establishment of your livelihood and possessions'. Her husband, she said

> 'being such a patron to good learning, doth tender you so much, that he would rather advance learning and erect new occasion thereof than confound your ancient and godly institutions.'

In other words, the King had agreed to pass up their wealth, and was even willing to establish new colleges - at *her* pleading. It was another feather in Katharine Parr's cap.

Chapter 24
The Lord Chancellor's Plot

THE QUEEN'S influence over the King troubled the conservatives at court. Bishop Gardiner, who had married Katharine to Henry VIII, became increasing concerned about her religious convictions. Queen Katharine was seen to worship as the King did, but did she believe as he did? Was she flirting with heresy, as her enemies believed? That would be something of which the King would never approve, not even in his wife.

In spite of his break with Rome, Henry VIII remained a staunch Catholic at heart. In 1539, the Act of the Six Articles was passed which affirmed tenets central to traditional Catholicism, especially the doctrine of Transubstantiation, which upheld the belief that consecrated bread and wine truly became the Body and Blood of Jesus Christ. Critics dubbed these measures 'the Whip with the Six Strings', as severe penalties were put in place 'that no man upon pain of death to speak against them'. At court, many of the 'laudable ceremonies' of the Church were performed daily, and the centuries-old rituals were still in place during the great religious observances. At Easter, for example, until it was finally prohibited in 1546, the King retained the ancient practice of 'creeping to the cross' on Good Friday, where he humbly made his way on his knees from the door of the royal chapel to the crucifix at the altar. As he so venerated the cross, so did he revere the Eucharist. On the adoration of the Host, Henry made a grand pronouncement on the sanctity of the Real Presence: "If I could throw myself down, not only to the ground", he declared, "but *under* the ground, I should not then think that I gave honour enough to the most Holy Sacrament".

Knowing her husband's views on religion, Katharine was careful in how far she expressed hers. While *Prayers and Meditations* was issued with the King's approval, another book she was privately working on would have been met with quite a different response had he been aware of it. Entitled *The Lamentation or Complaint of a Sinner*, it was critical of the old ceremonies and trappings of the Church. Katharine denounced her former acceptance of 'visible idols, and images made of men's hands, believing by them to have gotten

Heaven'. As for the Blessed Sacrament to which her husband was so devoted, Katharine made no mention of it in the *Lamentation*. Its omission was significant, hinting at her scepticism of the Mass.

Concerning salvation, it was not, as Katharine wrote, achieved through rituals but rather through a personal knowledge of Christ as Redeemer. In reading St Paul that 'we be justified by faith in Christ, and not by the deeds of the law', Katharine came to accept that 'good works' were not, as traditionally understood, a prerequisite for achieving God's mercy. It was actually through faith. 'For out of this faith spring all good works', Katharine came to believe, even if the King did not.

So for the meantime, the *Lamentation* remained a secret project of the Queen's, especially with the kingdom becoming so increasingly divided with Englishmen calling one another 'heretic' or 'papist'. At least the King did not discriminate the one from the other when it came to treason. In July 1540 at Smithfield, he had three Protestants burned and three Catholics hanged and quartered - all at the same time.

In such a climate of fear and uncertainty, Katharine was cautious not to make waves. The same could not be said of some of her ladies. They patronised religious radicals, brought banned books to court, and openly scorned the old faith. The most outspoken was the sharp-tongued Dowager Duchess of Suffolk. Having buried her husband, Charles Brandon, in August 1545, the widowed Katherine Willoughby came into her own as a woman of very definite opinions. Not only was she critical about traditional religion, but she also did not hold back when it came to those she held in contempt – chiefly the Bishop of Winchester, a man 'whom she loved worst'. One of the Duchess' chief amusements, Gardiner learnt, was to dress up her pet dog in a miniature priest's surplice and call it by *his* name. Believing the Queen's apartments to be a nest of heresy where the Mass was mocked and forbidden books read, Gardiner conspired to bring down Katharine Parr and her clique in the summer of 1546.

His plan involved a remarkable young woman named Anne Askew. Formerly known by her married name of Kyme, Mistress Askew became a passionate convert to the new faith during her unhappy marriage in Lincolnshire. After being kicked out of their home by her devoutly Catholic husband, Anne sought out a new existence for herself in London. Very soon, she became part of a network of Reformers, gaining fame for her 'gospelling'. Anne's notoriety led to run-ins with the law, and eventually she was brought before the Council where she was brought to Gardiner's attention. For denying the divine nature of the Eucharist- a mere 'piece of bread', Anne scoffed - she was sentenced to death as a heretic. Anne's condemnation did not mean a rush to the flames at Smithfield. To Gardiner, she was far more valuable kept alive for the meantime; for it was rumoured that Mistress Askew had high placed friends at court, including the Queen of England herself.

With the connivance of Thomas Wriothesley, now Lord Chancellor, and Sir Richard Rich of the Privy Council, Anne was taken from Newgate Prison and brought to the Tower of London. Wriothesley had been full of praise for Katharine at her wedding, calling her 'a most gracious lady', but by 1546, her religion had alienated him from her. With gusto, Wriothesley interrogated Anne hoping she would name Katharine as one of her group. To protect her friends, Anne said she knew no one. Wriothesley and Rich then inquired about the Queen's attendants - the Ladies Suffolk, Sussex, Hertford, Denny, and Fitzwilliam. Did she know them, they demanded, and were they her benefactresses? Anne refused to incriminate them.

To loosen her tongue, Anne was hauled to a dungeon and shown the rack. But to the Lieutenant of the Tower, Sir Anthony Knevet, the use of torture was highly irregular. The prisoner was already condemned as a traitor, and her status as a gentlewoman protected her from harm. Also, such methods could not be employed without the express command of the King or the Council. But browbeaten by Wriothesley and Rich, Knevet reluctantly put Anne to the rack. He was careful to minimise her pain. Hoping this was enough to frighten Anne into being cooperative, Knevet then released her. The Lieutenant's ruse did not go unnoticed by Wriothesley and he ordered the prisoner to be racked again. This time, Knevet refused. He immediately left the Tower to report the abuses being carried out to the King himself.

Left to operate the machinery alone, Wriothesley and Rich, 'throwing off their gowns', began racking Anne themselves. Throughout her agony, she made no outcry or any confession linking herself to the Queen, to the fury of her torturers. 'Nigh dead', Anne was at last untied and brought back to Newgate in secret. However, Mistress Askew was seen being returned on a chair as her 'bones and joints were almost plucked asunder'. News quickly spread about her ordeal in the Tower, and the people shook their heads at such a distasteful 'strange thing'. Even the King, hearing Knevet's report of 'so extreme handling of the woman', was appalled - but not enough to pardon her. On 16 July 1546, Anne Askew, her broken body still on a chair, was burned at Smithfield.

Anne Askew may not have been useful as Gardiner had hoped, but he was not done. Knowing the Queen's zeal for her religion, perhaps she would bring about her own destruction. The Bishop bided his time, and she indeed fell into the trap. Like Anne Boleyn, Katharine Parr had developed a fondness for religious discussion with the King. Henry, with his own keenness for debate, indulged her. But on one occasion, Katharine went too far. She began lecturing him, forgetting she was arguing theology with one who considered himself the Head of the Church. Henry boiled in silent rage.

Afterwards, when Katharine retired, Gardiner played up to the King, commiserating with him on his wife's presumption. In disputing with 'his learned judgement in matters of religion', the Queen was surely a misguided woman who needed to be shown the error of her ways, he said in mock sympathy. Already, the Bishop added, it was whispered about at court that the Queen held opinions dangerous to the 'policy and politic government of princes'. Might not a discreet inquiry be made to look into her activities, Gardiner asked? With a heavy sigh, Henry consented. Katharine, he agreed, was to be investigated along with certain of her ladies. They were to be taken to the Tower to be questioned, and a search was to be made for any heretical books in their possession.

If Katharine were found guilty of contravening the Six Articles, the outcome would be no mystery. Precedents for queens condemned of treason had already been twice established. But was Henry really so upset that he was willing to sacrifice another one of his wives? Or was he playing an elaborate game with Gardiner and Katharine – a bishop and a queen appropriately enough - as his pawns? Henry was not above such tricks. He would allow the one to go about an attack, only to put a shielding arm around the other as demonstrated in his managing of Cranmer's enemies. In January 1544, when the conservatives at court had hoped to bring down the Archbishop on charges of heresy, Henry had given them the green light to proceed. But just before his arrest, Cranmer had been personally tipped off by the King. The next day, when a gleeful Duke of Norfolk came to take him into custody, the Archbishop flashed a ring that their master had given him the night before. By this token, Cranmer had declared, he had their sovereign's favour and protection - thus thwarting his opponents.

Again, Henry VIII was set on manipulating the situation. His intention was twofold - to teach Katharine a lesson, and to warn Gardiner he had overstepped himself. Henry brought into play his physician Doctor Wendy. In vague terms, Wendy was told by the King how he was determined not to be 'troubled with such a doctress' - meaning the Queen. But at the same time, he spoke mysteriously of 'what trouble was in working against her by certain of her enemies'. About all of this, the doctor was sworn to secrecy.

Meanwhile, Katharine had caught wind of the charges against her. Her arrest warrant had been accidentally dropped - or so it seemed - and immediately shown to her by one of her attendants. Katharine's reaction was of absolute terror. Weeping and shaking with fear in her chamber, her cries reached the ears of the King. Doctor Wendy was sent to see what the matter was - as if Henry did not already know. The doctor, 'having remorse to the shedding of innocent blood', forgot his promise to the King and confessed what he knew to the woeful Katharine. Her only recourse, Wendy advised her, was 'to frame and conform herself unto the King's mind', otherwise, she and her friends would be utterly lost.

That evening, Katharine made her way to the King where she received a surprisingly warm welcome. To test her, Henry tried to draw her into their usual conversations touching religion. Katharine saw right through him. Excusing herself for her 'womanly weakness and natural imperfections', she begged his pardon. She had meant no impertinence, she told Henry. She had engaged him in discussion only to 'learn of her husband, and to be taught by him' - he being so 'excellent in gifts and ornaments of wisdom'. Convinced of her sincerity and satisfied that she knew her place at last, Henry embraced his wife saying, 'Then perfect friends we are now again, and ever at any time heretofore'.

With all well between them once more, Henry invited Katharine to spend time with him in the gardens of Whitehall the next day. When Wriothesley came to arrest the Queen as originally planned, he found to his amazement, Katharine with the King. From the corner of his eye, Henry spied his baffled Lord Chancellor. Limping up to Wriothesley on his walking stick, he took him aside and ordered him away shouting, "Arrant knave! Beast! And Fool"!

Katharine shuddered in relief. It was a close call.

As his reign drew to a close, Henry VIII's trust was put into men of the new religion such as Edward Seymour and Thomas Cranmer. Those like Stephen Gardiner, who tried to destroy the Queen, and his allies the Howards, were cold-shouldered. In December 1546, the Duke of Norfolk's son, the Earl of Surrey, was even arrested. The young man had made much noise about the right of himself and his father to be governors of the Prince should the King die. To further his plan, Surrey was even prepared to pimp his sister Mary into the royal bedchamber. Fortunately for Katharine Parr, the Dowager Duchess of Richmond wanted nothing to do with the scheme, especially one that had her sleeping with her former father-in-law, and she gave evidence against her brother. Surrey's presumption landed him and his father in the Tower. The Earl was beheaded on 19 January 1547, with the Duke scheduled to follow.

Satisfied that the succession would pass peacefully to his son Edward, Henry VIII, tired and sick, awaited death. Later, his subjects would say how their King, so unlucky in his many marriages, had the good fortune 'to die in the arms of so faithful a spouse'. But the truth was that the Queen was not at his side. In his last moments, he would only agree to see Cranmer. Grasping his faithful Archbishop by the hand, Henry, wheezing and beyond speech, gave up the ghost on the morning of 28 January 1547. Cranmer, clergyman that he was, assured those present that the King's final gesture had been made in recognition of his faith in Christ his Saviour.

Katharine, absent from the King's deathbed, was also out of sight at his funeral held on 16 February. Secluded in an elevated viewing box in St George's Chapel at Windsor, and wearing widow's weeds once again, she watched as another husband was brought to the grave. After Henry Tudor's soul had been commended to God, his massive coffin was lowered into a vault where his 'true and loving Queen Jane' had been laid to rest. In life, Henry had loved her the most, and so too in death.

Before the mourners departed for the funeral banquet, the herald announced the accession of the new King:

> 'Almighty God of His infinite goodness give good
> life and long to the most high and mighty Prince, our
> sovereign lord Edward VI, by the grace of God, King of
> England, France, and Ireland, Defender of the Faith,

and in earth, under God, of the Church of England and Ireland, Supreme Head and Sovereign, of the most noble order of the Garter. Vive le noble Roi Edward'!

Chapter 25
The Merry Widow

IF KATHARINE Parr expected a place in the new government, she was sorely disappointed. Her nine-year-old stepson and his kingdom were not put into the capable hands of the Queen Dowager, but under the authority of a regency Council, from which she was entirely excluded under the terms of the late King's will. To the end of his days, Henry VIII was wary of having his kingdom run by a woman.

At the head of Edward VI's regime was the boy's uncle, Edward Seymour. Contrary to Henry VIII's wishes that the Council govern collectively, its members had elected Hertford as Lord Protector. He was also ennobled as Duke of Somerset even before the old King was buried, and his brother - Katharine's old flame Thomas - was made Lord Admiral and Lord Seymour of Sudeley. Those in good standing with the Seymours were also rewarded. John Dudley was elevated to Earl of Warwick, and William Parr became Marquis of Northampton. The Queen's enemy, Thomas Wriothesley, having abandoned the disgraced Gardiner, was retained as a Councillor and created Earl of Southampton. As for the Bishop of Winchester himself, he was ejected from the Council. Later, he was even sent to the Tower for opposing the religious changes set forth by Cranmer.

Having denied his wife any say in government, Henry VIII did see to it that she lived comfortably as his widow. For her 'great love, obedience, chastity of life, and wisdom', he bequeathed to her '£3000 in plate, jewels, and stuff of household goods, and such apparel as it shall please her to take'. She was also granted £1,000 in money, along with several properties as part of her dower and jointure.

Back in private life once more, it was Katharine's intention not to spend it alone. As Queen, she was forced to banish Thomas Seymour from her mind, but she had never truly forgotten him. Now that Henry VIII was dead, and Seymour still a bachelor and wanting her as much she did him, it was plainly the will of Providence that she was now 'at liberty' to accept the proposal he made to her three years ago before the King had stepped in. Quoting a favourite expression of the

Duchess of Suffolk's, Katharine wrote to her former lover that with events coming full circle – 'God is a marvellous man!'

Katharine indulged her passion for Thomas Seymour with intensity. A stream of love letters went back and forth between the couple in the weeks following. In one message, Katharine even arranged for a secret rendezvous with her fiancé at her dower house in Chelsea. He must, she wrote to Seymour, 'take some pain to come early in the morning, that ye may be gone again by 7 o'clock'. Katharine, calling herself 'his portress', would wait for him 'at the gate to the fields'.

Despite their secret meetings, it was her intention to wed Thomas Seymour after two years had passed. That was ample time for her to observe a proper period of mourning, not to mention to show she was not carrying any child of the late King's body. Writing back to the Queen, her impatient lover demanded a mere two months wait instead. Powerless against her desire for Seymour, Katharine gave in. Sometime in the spring, Katharine, with only a few witnesses present – and all sworn to secrecy - took her fourth husband.

Her joy was mingled with worry. How was she to break the news to the young King? To her advantage, Katharine had remained on excellent terms with her stepson. After his father's death, Edward had written to Katharine commiserating with her on their 'common grief' and calling her his 'most dearest mother' and 'venerable Queen'. As well, her new husband's relationship with his nephew was just as warm. Jovial and extroverted, it was Thomas Seymour who was Edward's favourite uncle; not his stern and aloof brother the Lord Protector. Nonetheless, it would be difficult to broach the delicate subject of their marriage to Edward.

It would be better, the Queen and her husband decided, to keep him in the dark about the *fait accompli*. Instead, Seymour would confide to the King his desire to marry. The plan would then have Edward being the one to propose Katharine as a suitable bride for his uncle. In June, the Admiral dispatched his friend John Fowler to speak with the King. Fowler was to play dumb, asking Edward his opinion of which suitable lady his 'bachelor' uncle should take as his wife. Innocently, Edward suggested Anne of Cleves. He also named his sister Mary - his Protestant uncle could turn her from her papistry, the King said. With more coaxing from Fowler, and by Thomas Seymour himself, Edward finally came around. He offered up the Queen Dowager to his uncle with his blessing.

At the same time that the King was writing to his stepmother thanking her for accepting 'his' suggestion of marriage, he also noted in his diary that 'the Lord Protector was much offended' at what had happened. To Edward Seymour, his brother's union with the Queen was a deliberate attempt on Thomas' part to challenge his authority. Since Somerset had been created Protector, his younger sibling had grown jealous of him. Nothing it seemed would satisfy the Admiral unless he wielded power equal to his brother's. There were even rumours at court that before marrying Katharine Parr, Thomas Seymour had been hoping to net a bigger catch – the Lady Mary, or even the Lady Elizabeth.

Somerset reacted with pettiness. He began to snub his new sister-in-law, and when she requested the jewels she had left behind at court, he refused to hand them over. Such valuables, he said, were never her personal property, but those of the Crown. As Queen Dowager, not to mention the wife of another man, she had lost her right to them, even to the wedding ring King Henry had given her.

Katharine was livid, even more so when Somerset's wife entered the fray. She had never really liked the Duchess, thinking her undependable and two-faced. Anne Stanhope, her new sister-in-law thought, was the sort of woman whose habit it was 'to promise many comings to her friends and to perform none'. She became positively unbearable when Somerset was elevated to Lord Protector. The Duchess took on airs, becoming proud and disdainful, and she was especially rude to her former mistress. What was Katharine Parr now, Anne Stanhope sneered? She was no longer Queen, but the wife of her husband's *younger* brother. When she came to court, the Duchess made sure to put her in her place. As Queen Dowager, etiquette demanded that Katharine's train be carried by high-ranking ladies. When asked to perform her duty, the Duchess flatly refused, saying that as the Protector's wife, *she* outranked the ex-Queen. Further rows between the sisters-in-law had Katharine writing furiously to Thomas Seymour, venting her rage at 'that hell', as she called the Duchess. As for her equally insufferable husband, the Duke, Katharine added it was well that he was not standing close by; otherwise 'I should have bitten him!'

As the family feud raged on, Katharine looked to her royal stepdaughters for support. Regrettably, the Lady Mary would not take her side. Not only was she a good friend of Lady Somerset – her 'good Nan' as Mary affectionately called her – she was against her stepmother's remarriage. In late May, when Thomas Seymour had written to Mary asking for her endorsement of their match, she had been uncooperative. 'Considering whose wife Her Grace was of late', Mary replied indignantly, she refused to be 'a meddler any ways in this matter'. She was also upset that Katharine and her lover were already man and wife, pulling the wool over everyone's eyes. To Mary, the wedding, by its haste and secrecy, was an affront to the memory of her father.

Rebuffed by Mary, Katharine sought Elizabeth's approval. The teenager's love for her stepmother had always been constant, and she was not put off by the marriage like her sister was. Elizabeth gave her wholehearted approval to the match.

Not long after Katharine and Seymour made their marriage public, they offered Elizabeth a home with them. She accepted with delight. Boarding with her was her ten-year-old cousin, Lady Jane Grey, the eldest daughter of Henry VIII's niece, Frances Brandon, and her husband, Henry Grey, Marquis of Dorset.

Nothing is known of Elizabeth and Jane's relationship while they lived together at Chelsea. It would be reasonable to assume the two cousins struck up a friendship. They were only four years apart in age, both intellectually gifted, and both brought up in the new religion. However, they did not seem to have been close at all. No letters exist between them, and little of interest was said by either one about the other. On one occasion, Jane did express her admiration for Elizabeth as a model of Protestant virtue, but she had only brought up her cousin to reprove the Lady Mary for her Catholicism.

Chelsea was far from dull with Thomas Seymour around. Outgoing and full of life, the Admiral strode about the manor house filling it with his hearty laughter and thunderous voice. A servant of his recalled afterwards how employment with Thomas Seymour was 'ever Joyful'. His home was made more the happier when the Queen Dowager discovered she was pregnant in the spring of 1548. It was unexpected, considering she had been childless by her first three husbands. Elated, Katharine Parr joined Seymour in the high-spirited fun and games he loved so much. On one occasion when they were in the gardens at Hanworth with Elizabeth, she playfully held down her stepdaughter while the Admiral cut her gown 'in a hundred pieces'. In the mornings, if Katharine and Seymour awoke before the Princess, they would go to her bedroom and tickle her awake.

As her pregnancy progressed, Katharine withdrew herself from her husband's high jinks. It gave her time to think, and she became uneasy. Were the amusements, in which she took part, as innocent as they seemed, Katharine wondered? She was not blind to her husband's increasing attention to Elizabeth. Her stepdaughter, truth be told, was developing into an attractive young woman. Though she no longer accompanied Seymour to Elizabeth's bedchamber in the mornings, Katharine heard how he would still go by himself. 'In his nightgown, barelegged in his slippers', he would rouse the girl with a cheery 'good morrow' and a good slap on her behind. If he found her bed curtains closed to him, the Admiral would sweep them open, and 'make as though he would come at her'.

Her stepfather's familiarity - amusing though it was at first - became no laughing matter to Elizabeth. While it was probable that the Princess was drawn to the handsome and captivating Thomas Seymour, she was always careful in her conduct towards him. Nonetheless, things were getting out of hand, and she was beginning to be 'evil spoken of' by the servants. To discourage any more such talk, Elizabeth began waking up very early as to be dressed and at her studies before her guardian could come around and tease her.

Still, matters spiralled out of control. In a curious episode, Katharine had taken Kat Ashley aside, telling her that the Admiral had seen Elizabeth with 'her arms about a man's neck'. Incredulous, the governess confronted her charge. In tears, the girl vehemently denied the accusation, even going so far as to have her ladies swear to her good behaviour. Convinced of her innocence, Mistress Ashley had to conclude that the Queen made the whole story up as to warn Elizabeth. Despite Katharine's good intentions, she handled the situation badly. Being so anxious to protect her marriage, the Queen was willing to slander her stepdaughter before her governess rather than to impute blame on her own husband.

Katharine's fears were confirmed when one day – and the circumstances remain hazy – she unexpectedly came upon Elizabeth and Seymour alone together, he 'having her in his arms'. Astonished, Katharine lost all control of herself and tore into both of them. When she finally calmed down, she was insistent that Elizabeth leave Chelsea. Already, there was too much gossip in the house about her stepdaughter and her husband. Even if it was not true, Katharine reasoned, for her peace of mind and for the sake of her marriage, Elizabeth and Seymour could not remain under the same roof together. In May, the Princess was sent away to Cheshunt to stay with her friends Sir Anthony Denny and his wife.

Peace was eventually restored. At her leave-taking of the Queen, Elizabeth had 'said little' in her defence, but Katharine bore no grudges. Instead, she promised to have 'a good opinion' of her stepdaughter and to warn her if any lingering scandal should arise. In June, Elizabeth wrote to Katharine acknowledging her 'manifold kindness' to her, adding grateful thanks to God for 'providing such friends to me'. She also corresponded with the Admiral, expressing no ill feelings towards him either. At the end of July, Elizabeth wrote again to Katharine. She prayed for her safe delivery, and joked that the child kicking so vigorously in her stepmother's belly deserved a good beating for 'the trouble he had put you to'.

The boy Elizabeth imagined it to be turned out to be a girl, born on 30 August at Sudeley Castle in Gloucestershire. The Lord Protector, who for the time being put aside his differences with his brother, congratulated him - adding his regrets. It would have been more of a 'joy and comfort' had the infant been a son, the Duke wrote. However, Somerset was glad that Thomas and his wife had 'so pretty a daughter', and that Katharine had escaped 'all danger'.

Somerset spoke too soon. As with his sister Queen Jane, complications had set in. In the days following the birth, Katharine suffered, not only in body but mind as well. In her delirium, the events of late involving Elizabeth preyed on her mind. From her bed, she lashed out at Seymour, saying he had given her 'many shrewd taunts'. She even accused him of bringing about her present illness as if he had some sinister intention towards her. Even her attendants, Katharine murmured fearfully, 'care not for me, but stand laughing at my grief, and the more good I will to them, the less good they will to me'.

Katharine's frenzy eventually abated, and she was lucid enough to make her last requests. 'Sick of body, but of good mind', she prepared for death, making her husband the beneficiary of her worldly goods. She even forgot her suspicions about him, and lovingly wished her legacies 'to be a thousand times more in value than they were or been'.

Having made her peace with Thomas Seymour and with the world, Katharine Parr died in the early hours of 5 September 1548.

PART 8
THE UNCROWNED QUEEN:
LADY JANE GREY

'Jana non Regina' 'Jane the Queen'
(Correction in William Cecil, Lord Burghley's hand of a
document signed by Jane Grey as Queen of England)

Figure 18 Lady Jane Grey by Francesco Bartolozzi
The Yale Center For British Art, New Haven

Chapter 26
A Maiden Professing Godliness

THE CHIEF mourner at Katharine Parr's funeral was the
Lady Jane Grey. Dressed in black, Jane followed the Queen's coffin
as it was taken from her Privy Chamber, where she had been laid
out, to the chapel on the grounds of Sudeley Castle. The church was
hung with black cloth and decorated with Katharine's arms joined
with those of Henry VIII and Thomas Seymour. As if her first two
marriages held no significance, no references were made to Katharine's
life as Lady Borough or as Lady Latimer.

In keeping with the Queen Dowager's religion, the service was
conducted by the rites of the new faith. No Requiem Mass was
celebrated, the Psalms were sung in English, and the sermon - 'good
and godly' - was read by Katharine's almoner, Miles Coverdale, who
held the distinction of being the translator of the first authorised
English Bible. To further emphasise the Protestant nature of the
ceremony, Coverdale reminded the mourners that the offerings they
made were not 'to benefit the dead, but for the poor only', and that
the candles surrounding the deceased 'were for the honour of the
person, and for none other intent nor purpose'.

After Katharine Parr was laid to rest, Jane's parents, the Marquis
and Marchioness of Dorset, demanded their daughter back from her
guardian Thomas Seymour. It would not be seemly, they argued, for a
young lady to be living the household of a widower. Perhaps rumours
of the Admiral's conduct with the Lady Elizabeth had reached the
Dorsets' ears. However, Seymour wanted to keep Jane with him. As
third in line to the throne after Henry VIII's two daughters, she was a
valuable young lady indeed.

Appealing to the Henry and Frances Grey's ambition, which was
as great as his own, Seymour approached them with an offer. If they
would allow him to buy Jane's wardship for £2,000, in return, he
would arrange her marriage to her cousin the King. The scheme was
worthy of consideration by the Dorsets. Despite their daughter's place
in Henry VIII's will, her chances of succeeding were still remote.
Edward VI and his sisters, and any children they all might have,
would all have to die before Jane could ever become Queen. That

said, if she could not rule in her own right, at least she could wear the Crown as King Edward's wife. The Greys accepted the Admiral's deal.

Jane was allowed to stay with Seymour, but for propriety's sake, she was put under the care of his aged mother. While Jane returned to her lessons, her guardian worked on putting his scheme in motion. But the Admiral was his own worst enemy. In his attempts to ingratiate himself further into the King's favour, he openly challenged the authority of his brother the Protector. He and Somerset had already clashed over his marriage to Katharine Parr, and now, the Admiral was heard to say bitterly how 'it was never seen, that in the minority of a king, when there hath been two brethren, that the one brother should have all rule, and the other none'. Inevitably, Thomas Seymour's unbridled jealousy led him to conspiracy. In a madcap attempt to govern the King alone, he planned to kidnap his nephew. He got as far as the King's bedroom when Edward's pet dog, who always slept at his master's side, sounded the alarm. Seymour was arrested on the spot and taken to the Tower the next day.

Throughout his imprisonment, the Admiral was unrepentant, and he remained so when he went to the scaffold on 20 March 1549. Intrigue was on his mind to the very end. After he had been beheaded, unsent letters to the Ladies Mary and Elizabeth were found amongst his effects warning them against the Protector. Hearing of his execution, the only words Elizabeth had for Thomas Seymour were that 'this day died a man of much wit - *and little judgement*'.

≡

The fall of the Lord Admiral meant the end of the Dorsets' grandiose plans for their daughter Jane. Without Seymour to sway the King into marrying her, there was nothing left to do but to bring the girl home. That spring, Jane was sent back to Bradgate, a large estate near Charnwood Forest in Leicestershire. It had been the family seat since Jane's grandfather Thomas Grey, 2nd Marquis of Dorset, built himself a fine palatial home there in the 1520s. Lord Thomas and his son, Henry, the current Marquis, may be excused for their lavish tastes, they were, after all, descendants of a queen. Henry Grey's great-grandmother was Elizabeth Woodville, making him related – though not by blood - to the Tudors.

The pedigree of Grey's wife, Frances, was even more illustrious. She was the granddaughter of King Henry VII and the daughter of the beautiful Mary Tudor and her second husband, Charles Brandon. Despite the heavy fine the couple had incurred as punishment from

Henry VIII for their secret marriage in 1515, they had no regrets. The Suffolks' union had been a happy one, producing Frances herself and her siblings Henry and Eleanor.

The marriage, for which Charles Brandon had risked so much, ended when his wife passed away in the summer of 1533. But he did not grieve for long. On 7 September, the very day the Princess Elizabeth was born, the Duke found consolation in taking another wife - a clever, pretty young girl of fourteen named Katherine Willoughby. The marriage was regarded with some distaste. Not only was Katherine originally intended for Suffolk's son Henry (already sickly and soon to die), but also Brandon had remarried with indecent haste. Eustace Chapuys, ever the cynic, congratulated Suffolk on setting a new precedent for English widows everywhere. Now 'when they are reproached, as is usual, with marrying again immediately after the death of their husbands', the ambassador quipped, the ladies 'can point to *his* example'.

Earlier that same year, Suffolk had given away the hand of his teenage daughter Frances to his young ward Henry Grey, Marquis of Dorset. Frances' reputation has suffered much over the centuries. Based on accounts of her daughter Jane's life, and some later embellishments of it, the Marchioness has been presented as an abrasive and forceful woman who ruled her family with an iron hand, henpecking her husband and terrorising her daughters. Frances' temperament has also relied on a supposed likeness where she was depicted as a hefty woman with a bloated face and disdainful expression. Taking after her notorious uncle Henry VIII in looks, Frances must have behaved like him too. But in actuality, she was not the brute she was said to be, especially when the portrait, so instrumental in forming her character, was later re-identified as being of someone else entirely.

A fairer assessment of Frances Brandon is that she was a woman of good sense who knew how to stay out of trouble. During her years under Henry VIII, Frances avoided dangerous entanglements – both political and romantic. No scandal ever touched her, unlike her cousin Margaret Douglas. The amorous Margaret so enraged her royal uncle with her reckless love affairs that he had her imprisoned on two occasions.

Frances cultivated a friendship with her other cousin, the Lady Mary. Their bond began early on. At Frances' christening in July 1517, Mary, even though she was only a year older than her baby cousin, was made her godmother, along with Katherine of Aragon.

As the two cousins grew older, their affection for each other was often expressed through the exchanging of gifts. At New Year 1543, Frances sent Mary a smock and six handkerchiefs, and in the following January, another smock and a pair of decorated sleeves. In 1546, Mary was recorded as giving Frances 'a pair of beads of crystal trimmed with gold'.

The friendship between the two ladies did not appear to have been strained by Frances' marriage to Henry Grey, a young man with strong inclinations towards the new faith. His contemporaries described Dorset as

> 'a man of high nobility by birth, and of nature to his friends gentle and courteous, more easy in deed to be led than was thought expedient...upright and plain in his private dealing, no dissembler, nor well able to bear injuries, but yet forgiving and forgetting the same... he could patiently hear his faults told him, by those whom he had in credit for their wisdom of faithful meanings towards him.'

But Grey was not without his flaws. He was also overly ambitious and 'lacking in circumspection', his detractors said. The Imperial ambassador, Francis van der Delft, even went so far as to dismiss him as a 'senseless creature'. The Marquis' greatest weakness was in being easily manipulated. Even his friends at court had to admit that Grey was an easy target for ruthless men, lending himself to their intrigues.

Continental Reformers, on the other hand, thought highly of Henry Grey. He was held in the greatest esteem as their ally in religion and as their patron. John Ab Ulmis, a German student living in England who was the recipient of a pension from the 'exceeding liberality' of Dorset, described Grey in glowing terms:

> 'He is descended from the royal family with which he is very nearly connected, and is the most honourable of the King's Council. He has exerted himself up to the present day with the greatest zeal and labour courageously to propagate the Gospel of Christ. He is the thunderbolt and terror of the papists, that is, a fierce and terrible adversary... He is learned, and speaks Latin with elegance. He is the protector of all students, and the refuge of foreigners.'

Dorset as the larger-than-life foe of the English Catholics was an exaggeration, but the rest of Ulmer's assessment was essentially accurate. The Marquis possessed an evangelical fervour, and he was genuinely committed to upholding the Protestant faith. Included among his friends was the renowned Reformer Heinrich Bullinger. The two men had corresponded, and soon Grey was addressing the theologian in friendly and familiar terms as 'my very dear Bullinger'. In turn, the Swiss pastor dedicated the fifth volume of his *Decades* to the Marquis, hailing him as a 'vigorous maintainer of real godliness'.

By all indications, Frances did not share her husband's religious zeal. Though she and her sister Eleanor were said to have been friendly with the martyr Anne Askew, Frances' enthusiasm for the new faith seemed to have waned by the time her cousin Edward ascended the throne. The Protestant clerics who lauded Henry Grey, and later his daughter Jane, were entirely silent when it came to his wife. Throughout her life, Frances uttered no religious opinions and simply conformed to whatever the State religion was during the four reigns she lived under. The Marchioness' indifference can be inferred from a letter written by her daughter to Bullinger, dated July 1551. Like her father, Jane corresponded with him, and she thanked Bullinger for his treatise on *Christian Perfection* that he had recently sent to her and her father. She had derived much pleasure from it, Jane wrote effusively, likening it 'a most beautiful garden' from which the 'sweetest flowers' sprang. Her father, Jane added, was also reading the treatise with delight. However, there was no mention of her mother doing likewise.

Religion aside, the Greys were more alike in their pursuit of life's pleasures. Husband and wife were especially fond of courtly entertainments, especially the chase and games of chance. Though Dorset had forbidden his servants to gamble, 'he himself and his most honourable Lady with their friends, not only claim permission to play in their private apartment, but also for money', their straight-laced chaplain James Haddon complained. Before Christmas, Haddon took the opportunity to preach before the Dorsets on the vice of gambling. Henry and Frances grumbled, but they agreed to stop. But as the holy season came and went, the couple and their guests were at it again, playing 'games of hazard' behind closed doors.

Haddon may have disapproved of Henry and Frances' pastimes, but he could not criticise them as parents. The couple set very high standards in raising their three children Jane, Katherine, and Mary.

The ideals they were to attain were outlined in one of Dorset's letters to Bullinger. The Marquis thanked his friend for continually encouraging his eldest girl to 'a true faith in Christ, the study of the Scriptures, purity of manners, and innocence of life'. Only Jane was mentioned as she was in contact with Bullinger, but Dorset and his wife would have had the same expectations for their two younger daughters as well. However, when it came to their studies, Jane outshone both Katherine and Mary. Intellectually gifted from a very young age, Jane had an innate curiosity and a burning desire to learn. By the time she was fourteen in 1551, she was skilled in French, Latin, Italian, and Greek, and she was even beginning to learn Hebrew.

While Bullinger encouraged Jane with words of kindness, her parents took a less enlightened approach. According to Jane herself, life with Henry and Frances Grey could be misery. Her home life outside the little haven of her schoolroom, she said, was nothing but 'grief, trouble and fear'. According to Jane's tutor, Roger Ascham, who set down the distressed teenager's side of the story, her parents were impossible to please.

As he told it, Jane had taken him into her confidence one summer day at Bradgate in 1550. Ascham had come upon Jane reading indoors. She alone had stayed behind while the rest of her family had gone hunting. Ascham asked her why she was not enjoying the chase with everyone else. Jane answered, "I wist all their sport in the park is but a shadow to that pleasure that I find in Plato. Alas, good folk, they never felt what true pleasure meant". Being a respectful daughter, Jane thanked God for her 'so sharp and severe parents', but in the same breath she complained of their harshness:

> 'For when I am in presence of either father or mother, whether I speak, keep silence, sit, stand, or go, eat, drink, be merry or sad, be sewing, playing, dancing or doing anything else, I must do it as it were, in such weight, measure, and number, even so perfectly as God made the world, or else I am so sharply taunted, so cruelly threatened, yea, presently sometimes with pinches, nips and bobs, and other ways – which I will not name for the honour I bear them - so without measure misordered, that I think myself in hell...'

Her only solace, Jane said, was in her lessons with her other tutor, the kindly John Aylmer. Aylmer, like Ascham, was an advocate of a new approach to teaching. Rather than to instil knowledge through pressure and fear, a pupil should be encouraged to learn through gentleness and praise. It was a novel concept in that most educators - and parents - believed that children did better if threatened with a beating. Over a century ago, Dame Agnes Paston had instructed her son's tutor that if his young charge 'has not done well, and will not amend at all...truly *belash him* until he will amend'. In the Tudor period, the same opinion held sway. Ascham, in his treatise *The Schoolmaster*, argued however that the 'common use of teaching and beating' was detrimental as it drove children to despise learning.

Nonetheless, the Dorsets preferred Dame Agnes's old-fashioned methods. Being an excellent student, Jane was unlikely to have been disciplined for a lapse in her studies, but still, she was not spared the rod for what seemed to be other infractions. Physical punishment at the time was fairly common and was by no means unusual, but Jane's vocal resentment certainly was. Unless she or Ascham were exaggerating, Henry and Frances Grey were exceptionally strict. Was it because they had high expectations of Jane as their eldest child? Or was it because she was inclined to be too outspoken for her own good?

Her exchange with Ascham revealed Jane's tendency for being both candid and critical - two qualities which would not have gone over well with her parents. Perhaps it was Jane's forthrightness that made them so harsh towards her. An old letter from Henry Grey to Thomas Seymour hinted of an unruliness in Jane that her father felt needed correction. It was written shortly after the death of Katharine Parr when Dorset was asking for the return of his daughter. With the Queen Dowager no longer present as a role model, he was concerned that considering her 'tender years', Jane 'should for lack of a bridle, take too much heed and conceive such opinion of herself that all good behaviour as she hereto hath learned ... should either altogether be quenched in her, or at least much diminished'. It would be better, the Marquis went on, if Jane were returned to her mother's care 'by whom for the fear and duty she oweth her, she shall most easily be ruled and framed towards virtue', which he wished 'above all things to be plentiful in her'.

Under the Queen Dowager's tutelage, Jane had developed the virtuous qualities demanded of her, but according to her father, she was apparently still predisposed to be stubborn and defiant. Later episodes in Jane's life bear out the Marquis' opinion. As disagreeable as her strength of character was to the Greys, it was to be a quality in Jane that was to sustain her well in the face of the calamities ahead.

≡

Apart from her lessons, Jane Grey's only other comfort was her religion. A child of the English Reformation like her cousins Edward and Elizabeth, Jane took to the Protestant creed with a fervid intensity. She embraced it both inwardly and out. In December 1551, Aylmer had written to Bullinger asking him to counsel the Lady Jane 'as to what embellishment and adornment of person is becoming in young women professing godliness'. He had probably sought Bullinger's advice after the recent visit of Mary of Guise to the English court in October and November. Jane and her parents, with over a hundred other courtiers, had been commanded to accompany the Queen Dowager of Scotland from the Bishop's palace in London to Westminster for a great feast with the King. Jane, as the daughter of a great nobleman - her father Dorset having been recently made Duke of Suffolk – was dressed in all her finery. But it was her cousin Elizabeth who stood out from all the belles of the court. After the fallout of the Seymour scandal, the Princess had reinvented herself as a paragon of maidenly virtue. Eschewing all magnificence, 'her plainness of dress was especially noticed'. Aylmer was suitably impressed, and he hoped that Jane would follow Elizabeth's example and 'look down upon gold, jewels, and braidings of the hair'.

Indeed, Jane needed little encouragement from Aylmer. She well liked her cousin's 'maidenly apparel', and she sought to emulate her. She was put to the test when the Lady Mary sent her a gift. Mary had always been kind to Jane, and on this occasion, she presented her with a gown of 'tinsel cloth of gold and velvet, laid on with parchment lace of gold'. It was a lavish present, but Jane, true to her convictions, thought little of it. "What shall I do with it"? she sniffed; such finery smacked of popery. She would rather be like her *other* cousin Elizabeth, who dressed like a respectable Protestant lady. It was she, Jane thought, who 'followeth God's word', implying that Mary did not.

If Mary was astounded by Jane's reaction, she was positively appalled at what followed when her cousin paid her a visit. It so happened that Jane and one of Mary's women Lady Wharton passed by the household chapel. A devout Catholic, Lady Wharton reverently paused and genuflected towards the Tabernacle where the Sacrament was kept. Jane, knowing full well the significance of her gesture,

Figure 19   Edward VI by Unknown Artist
The Rijksmuseum, Amsterdam

baited her. "Why do you do so? Is the Lady Mary in the chapel"?
"No madam", Lady Wharton replied, surprised at the girl's seeming
ignorance. "I make my curtsy to Him that made us all". "Why, how
can He be there that made us all, and the baker make Him"? Jane
answered mockingly. Lady Wharton was left dumbfounded. When
told of Jane's impertinence, it was said that Mary 'did never love
her after'.

Chapter 27
More Suffering Than Any Illness

MARY TUDOR could dismiss her cousin Jane's objections to her faith, but she could not do so when it came to her brother the King. The two had formerly been close. Mary was Edward's godmother, and she had been a frequent visitor to his nursery. Because of the years between them, Mary was almost like a mother to him, and Edward returned her affection. In a letter to his sister from 1546, he wrote that although he did not correspond as often as he should, he was not 'ungrateful and forgetful' of her. 'For I love you quite as well if I had sent letters to you more frequently', Edward wrote tenderly, 'for in the same manner as I put on my best garments very seldom, yet these I like better than others. Even so I write to you very rarely, yet I love you most'. But as he grew older, that relationship became increasing distant. Edward was not only Mary's brother, but he was now also her King with the power of the State behind him - one that was increasingly hostile to her religion.

Inheriting his father's mantle of Supreme Head of the Church of England, it was his duty, as Edward saw it, to define and defend religious doctrine in his kingdom. His life's work was set out for him at his coronation when Cranmer hailed Edward as another Josiah, the young King of Judah who had purged God's Temple of idolatry. With the help of the like-minded Archbishop, Edward stripped the English Church of its Catholic remnants from his father's time. Gone were the trappings and trimmings, and the images revered by the faithful for centuries. They were now regarded as superstition, as were traditional practices like the telling of beads (rosaries) and Masses for the dead.

Even more revolutionary was the redefining of the Lord's Supper. As set out by Cranmer's revised Prayer Book of 1552, the service was now performed in English, not Latin, and on a plain 'communion table' instead of an altar. As a further innovation, the laity received the consecrated elements in *both* species. When they did, they were told they were no longer consuming the actual body and blood of the Son of God, but mere bread and wine, and only in 'faithful remembrance of Christ's death'.

To Mary, such changes were repugnant. She abhorred her father's break with Rome, but at least Henry VIII had maintained the essentials of the Catholic faith. But now with him dead, the religion of England was turned upside down by her brother and his heretical Archbishop. Protestantism may have been the rage at court, winning the hearts of men such as Henry Grey, but where Mary was concerned, it would never be tolerated in her house. Back in 1547, when Cranmer began tinkering with forms of worship in the realm, she showed her displeasure by flaunting her opposition. Wherever she was, Mary ordered her chaplains to say Mass in all its 'ancient manner'. She even made a point of receiving the Host at least four times a day. With the Emperor backing her, Mary even won a small victory for herself. She received permission from the Lord Protector to hold Catholic services in the privacy of her house, but with no more than twenty people present.

Despite this indulgence, by 1550, Mary found the religious situation more and more intolerable. With the recent passing of the Act of Uniformity establishing Protestantism as the State religion, Mary knew her permission to hear Mass would eventually be withdrawn. Already, the Council was harassing her for allowing her entire staff and even visitors to attend her chapel. Mary had not felt so oppressed since her estrangement from her father, and once again, she believed her only recourse was to leave the country and seek asylum with the Emperor.

At the beginning of July, Mary, with Imperial assistance, attempted escape. Charles V authorised his sister, Mary of Hungary, to dispatch a convoy of Flemish ships towards England's Essex coast to convey their cousin to safety. While the four larger vessels remained anchored at sea near Harwich, four smaller ones were sent to the port of Maldon in the early hours of Wednesday 2 July. Three of them acted as lookouts while the other - dressed up as a boat for transporting produce - was rowed ashore by Jehan Dubois, secretary to the new Imperial envoy, Monsieur Scheyfve. To put off suspicion, he disguised himself as a merchant come to sell his corn in town.

Dubois' contact was Sir Robert Rochester, the controller of Mary's household. The two met that morning and pretended to bargain for the corn. After being certain they were not being watched, Dubois was taken to a house where he and Rochester could talk freely. Though he boasted of giving up his hand 'to see My Lady out of the country and in safety', the controller was not enthusiastic about the scheme. In speaking with Dubois he gave out a list of reasons why the Princess should *not* go abroad – there was an increased watch along the roads, there might be spies in the household, and his mistress was not in any immediate danger, in his opinion.

Nevertheless, Rochester agreed to take Dubois to Mary's house at Woodham Walter later that night. Before Mary received the Imperial agent, Rochester again tried to dissuade him. He let Dubois in on a 'mighty secret'. The Princess's supporters had recently commissioned Edward VI's horoscope (though it was illegal to do so), and according to his chart, 'the King could not outlast the year'. If Mary took flight now, the controller warned, she would forfeit her right to the Crown. Dubois, who had met Mary once before, answered that she had personally told him how she wanted to escape no matter what. By her own reckoning, her chances of becoming Queen were near impossible. 'If my brother were to die,' Mary believed, 'I should be far better out of the kingdom, because as soon as he were dead, before the public knew of it, they (her enemies) would dispatch me too'.

When Dubois was finally able to meet with her again, Mary had not changed her mind, but there was a hitch. She was willing to go - but not yet. Contrary to Dubois' plan for them to sail away that very evening, Mary was still unprepared. She could not leave until the day after next, she insisted. If Dubois and his men could only wait until Friday, Mary begged, she could come to him after 4 o'clock in the morning. At that hour, the sentries retired from their posts, and she, on the pretext of visiting the seashore for recreation, could leave her house without suspicion. The change in plans did not please Dubois, but seeing how Mary would have it no other way, and that the tide at least would still be in their favour come Friday, he went along with it.

As detailed plans for her getaway were being made, a frightened Rochester suddenly appeared. Dubois and his corn boat, he sputtered, were under suspicion by the local folk. They believed the stranger was linked to the Flemish ships anchored out at sea. At the news, Mary panicked. She began wailing over and over, "What shall we do? What is to become of me"? Dubois implored her to come with him straight away, but Rochester vetoed the idea on account of the risk. Mary, having completely lost her nerve, agreed not to go. Fearing discovery, Dubois left Woodham Walter giving Mary his promise they would try again in ten or twelve days time. However, there was to be no second attempt. An increased surveillance over Mary – not to mention her continuing indecisiveness - ended any more talk of escape.

With the prospect of having to stay in England indefinitely, Mary was left with no alternative but to defend her faith. 'She would die sooner', she told the Emperor, 'than lose her devotion to Holy Mass'. Mary was forced to make her stand in December 1550 when she was roused to protest on behalf of her chaplains. The authorities were attempting to arrest them for saying Mass for the entire household, instead of just for Mary and a handful of her servants as they were permitted to do. Until now, such attacks were essentially the work of the King's advisers, but now Edward himself was getting involved. He was taking a more active role in government, and with his mind already framed towards purifying the English Church, he was determined to crush his sister's nonconformity. The Lord Protector spoke for Edward when he said that 'if the King and his sister, to whom the whole kingdom was attached as heiress to the Crown in the event of the King's death, were to differ in matters of religion, dissension would certainly spring up'.

Mary's only option was to appeal directly to Edward himself. But she knew she had more than just her brother to contend with; there was also the powerful John Dudley, Earl of Warwick. The son of Henry VII's despised minister Edmund Dudley, he had risen to favour under Henry VIII, and he was now at his ascendant having bested the Duke of Somerset. Although the people admired Edward Seymour and he earned their respect as 'the good Duke', his nephew and the rest of the Council disliked him intensely. Edward found his uncle cold and stern, while his colleagues viewed him as arrogant and autocratic. Despite Seymour's popularity with the masses, economic and religious unrest had led to the peasant uprisings of 1549 and Catholic opposition against the new Prayer Book. When Somerset finally lost the confidence of the King, Warwick forced him from office and assumed his powers.

Mary was apprehensive of the newly appointed Lord President of the Council as Warwick was titled. The Earl was no friend to the old religion, unlike Somerset who had grudgingly tolerated her faith. He was also dangerous by his lack of scruples. Warwick, by Mary's estimation, was the 'most unstable man in England'; a power-hungry opportunist who moved against the Protector solely out of 'envy and ambition'. With Warwick in control, Mary saw nothing but turmoil ahead for herself and the kingdom. 'You will see that no good will come of this move', she told the Imperial ambassador, 'but that it is a punishment from Heaven, and may be only the beginning of our misfortunes'.

By January 1551, a showdown between brother and sister over religion was imminent. When Mary refused to back down over her household Masses, Edward VI brought himself into the fray. Adding his say to the Council's admonitions to his sister, he rebuked her in a letter written on 28 January. Edward did not mince words. He berated Mary for her disobedience, and for her 'lack of knowledge' towards true religion. By her defiance, she 'wish[ed] to break our laws and set them aside deliberately…and moreover sustain and encourage others to commit a like offence'.

As to Mary's argument before that he was too immature to decide matters of faith, Edward turned the tables on her saying that the 'best ordered Church of the people of Israel was instituted and upheld by kings younger in years than we', and that it was Mary who was set in her ways. And to her claim that she was following religion as their father had left it, Edward reminded her that he 'possess[ed] the same authority' as Henry VIII, and he expected to be obeyed. The letter was written by a secretary, but Edward was so fired up that afterwards he added a postscript in his own hand. In a long diatribe, he ordered Mary to amend her errors as a 'reasonable person and loyal subject'. He ended with a warning – 'I will see my laws strictly obeyed, and those who break them shall be watched and denounced'.

Edward received a reply just a few days later. His letter, his sister said, had caused her 'more suffering than any illness even unto death'. As she always did in dealing with the Council, Mary reminded Edward of the promise Somerset had made to her cousin Charles allowing her to attend Mass. Now, Mary lamented, that guarantee was being withdrawn, and was even said to have been 'never given' in the first place. To clear up the matter, she begged the King to have his representative at the Imperial court verify from the Emperor himself that such a promise was truly made to him by Somerset. Finally, Edward was indeed 'gifted with understanding' beyond his young years, Mary told him, but still she beseeched him not to deny her her religion until he reached his majority. For the present, she asked to be allowed 'to live as in the past'. Rather than offend her Maker, she would rather lose everything, including her life itself. Despite the defiant tone of her letter, Mary was not entirely prepared to risk martyrdom. After writing to her brother, she dashed off a message to her Imperial contacts. The King himself was now threatening her, she wrote desperately, and she begged the Emperor's intercession if the situation worsened.

By the spring, there was such likelihood. The exchange of letters between Edward and Mary had got them nowhere, and the Princess was summoned to Court to explain herself in person. She could not refuse since she had already turned down the King's invitation to visit him at Christmas saying she was sick. What Edward and the Council really had in mind that December, Mary suspected, was to make her attend Protestant services while she was at court. 'I would not find myself in such a place for anything in the world', she said boldly. Also, she wanted to 'avoid entering into argument with the King', which Mary knew would be impossible.

Unable to plead illness again, Mary set out for court in the middle of March. Her resistance and the righteousness of her cause were blazoned on the journey to Whitehall. Mary proceeded as if she were on a great triumphal progress. Before her, rode fifty knights and gentlemen wearing her livery, with another eighty of her household following along. With her sizeable entourage, Mary was proclaiming herself as a great magnate to be reckoned with. Not only that, she was the hope of England's Catholics. Each of her attendants carried 'a pair of beads of black' – a rosary – as a mark of devotion to the old faith.

Mary had always been popular, and the people were heartened at the sight of her. During her journey, the road to the palace was congested with hundreds of well-wishers surrounding their beloved Princess. Her rapturous welcome annoyed the Council, and its members saw to it that she received no such greeting at court. When Mary finally arrived at Whitehall, no one met her except the palace controller. Her entourage was told to stay behind while Mary was ushered in to face her brother the King alone. Edward received her 'kindly enough', and she apologised for not coming earlier at Christmas, as she had been ill. Edward replied that when she was indisposed, God had 'sent *him* health' instead.

Behind closed doors, Edward and his Council got straight down to business. It was their intention that Mary abandon the Mass. The King had run out of patience with her, and 'grave troubles might arise', his advisers put forth, 'if she, sister to the King and heiress to the Crown, observed the old religion'.

In her defence, Mary returned to the Council's old promise to the Emperor, and for Edward to wait until he was of 'riper age and experience' before proceeding against her. In response, the Council again insisted that the pledge to Charles V 'had always been meant to be limited', and Edward, who had taken issue with her remark on his youth, stepped in saying that 'she also might still have something to learn, for no one was too old for that'. She could not change her ways, Mary answered, having lived as a Catholic all her life.

Mary was then charged with violating her father's will in disobeying the wishes of the Council. It was a futile accusation. She had read the document carefully, she countered, and under its terms, she was only subject to its approval in regards to her marriage. If the Councillors were so devoted to the late King's memory, Mary then asked, why had they not provided him with the Masses for his soul as he had requested? It was evident to her, she added, that Edward 'alone cared more for the good of the kingdom than all the members of the Council put together'. The Earl of Warwick who had remained quiet all the while was offended. He leapt from his seat and cried out, "How now My Lady? It seems Your Grace is trying to show us in a hateful light to the King, our master, without any cause whatsoever"! Unprepared for John Dudley's outburst, Mary backed down. She closed the matter saying that she did not come to make accusations, but the Council's haranguing had provoked her anger.

The interview proved futile. As neither her brother and his Council, nor she would give in, Mary brought it to an end declaring that 'in the last resort, there were only two things – soul and body'. The first she committed to her God, and the second to her King. Her life was in Edward's hands, Mary said, and she would rather he end it than to deny her the comforts of her religion. For a moment, Edward's posturing as the Supreme Head of the Church dropped. "I wished for no such sacrifice", he replied meekly. As angry as he was, he could never bring himself to harm his sister. With that hope in mind, Mary took her leave and went home.

If not her life, the King was still determined to have Mary's submission. It was only the Emperor's intervention that stayed his hand. Two days after the confrontation at court, Charles V delivered on his promise to help Mary. He threatened England with war should his cousin be denied her Mass. Edward, who was becoming more and more like his father, dared the Emperor to make good on his word. However, Cranmer and his fellow bishops, knowing how disastrous war could be for the realm, urged Edward to reconsider. 'Giving license to sin was sin', they said, but it was more prudent to 'suffer and wink at it for a time'.

The truce lasted until summer's end. In August, the government went on the attack against Mary again. A new strategy was devised in which the Princess's staff would do what the Council could not; they would persuade her to adopt the revised liturgy. Three of her household officers, including Robert Rochester, were summoned before the Council. To get their cooperation, they were told that *they* were the cause of Mary's obstinacy. If not for them, she would have converted to the new faith long ago. The accusation was rubbish and was clearly designed to put a scare into the three men. Calling their bluff, Rochester answered that Mary ever was her own mistress concerning her conscience. Nonetheless, the controller and his two colleagues were ordered to convince Mary to capitulate.

Knowing full well what her servants were commanded to do, Mary refused to see or to speak with them, forcing the authorities to deal with her directly again. A delegation, sent from the Council, presented the Princess with a letter from her brother. She knelt and kissed it for the honour she owed to the King, she said, *not* in deference to its contents. Even before she read the paper, Mary guessed correctly that was a rehash of the arguments used against her time and time again. With the King and his Council having nothing new to add, Mary answered as she did in March. But with Edward absent, this time, she did not hesitate in holding back her scorn. She snapped at Richard Rich, now Lord Chancellor, for being long-winded, she refused to hear the list of her offences, and she declared 'she would lay her head on a block and suffer death' rather than deny her conscience.

Again, Mary invoked the protection of her cousin Charles V. But even if they 'esteem[ed] little the Emperor', she told the delegates, they ought to still render her the respect due to a daughter of Henry VIII. It was her father, she reminded them, who had raised most of them to power - before then they were nothing. And if the Council insisted on removing her servants as it threatened to do, Mary went on, she would not abide replacements. She would rather 'go out of her gates, for they two should not dwell in one house'. Similarly, if the new communion service were forced on her household, she would 'not tarry' to hear it.

Before ending the interview, Mary left Rich and the others with these words:

'I am sickly, and yet I will not die willingly, but will do the best I can to preserve my life. But if I shall chance to die, I will protest openly that you of the Council be the cause of my death.'

For the next year, Mary maintained a low profile. The Council could not have been unaware that she continued to worship by the old rites, but it opted to turn a blind eye to her activities. There were more pressing issues at hand. In October, Somerset was arrested once again. Despite his reinstatement to the Council, Edward Seymour proved too dangerous an opponent to Warwick, now raised to Duke of Northumberland. He found himself in the Tower again on dubious charges of treason. This time, however, he did not leave his prison except to walk to Tower Hill where he was executed on 22 January 1552. Somerset's death was greatly mourned by the citizens. Up to the last minute they had expected a reprieve, but none came. When Seymour's head fell on the straw, the people rushed up in droves to dip their handkerchiefs in his blood as keepsakes of their 'good Duke'.

≡

Except for an attack of measles in April 1552, the King enjoyed good health. Though he was never the athlete his father had once been, Edward VI still found enjoyment in sports such as tennis, archery, hunting, and riding. He had even developed an interest in mock combat. The Imperial ambassador, who visited the court at Greenwich the year before, described how Edward 'was beginning to exercise himself in the use of arms and enjoys it heartily'. Scheyfve even had the opportunity to see the young King in action displaying his skills at a tournament. At the tiltyard, Edward and his companions of 'other young lords' ran at the ring with their lances while on horseback, but they, unfortunately, lost to the opposing team. The French ambassador, Antoine de Noailles, who was also present at the lists, nonetheless complimented Edward on how he had 'borne himself right well and shown great dexterity'. "It was a small beginning," Edward replied. Next time, 'he hoped to do his duty better'.

In spite of Edward's budding prowess in the martial arts, his vigour appeared to be slipping beginning in the fall of 1552. The King was often exhausted, looking gaunt and pale, causing Northumberland alarm. The Duke took the precaution of having the boy's horoscope drawn up by Girolamo Cardano, a visiting Italian physician who dabbled in astrology, and who had even spoken at length with the King about their mutual interest in astronomy. He had nothing to fear, Cardano assured Northumberland. According to his calculations, Edward would live at least 55 years; a reasonably good age for the time.

The forecast proved false. Throughout the winter and into the spring of 1553, Edward continued to worsen becoming more 'thin and wasted'. Anxious about the future, Northumberland considered the consequences if the King should die. The notion of Mary Tudor succeeding filled John Dudley with dread. As a Catholic, she would undo the newly established Protestant Church, and she would surely avenge the slights she had endured from her persecutors, including Northumberland himself.

Mary's unmarried state would also invite dissension. She would, of course, choose a Catholic husband, most likely a foreigner whom the people would find disagreeable. Even if she took an Englishman, it would encourage division within the court. The Lady Elizabeth, raised as a Protestant, was a better alternative as Queen, but like her sister, she too was unwed. She was also tainted by illegitimacy; a technicality Henry VIII ignored when he restored both his daughters to the succession.

Northumberland looked elsewhere. If neither of Henry VIII's children had offspring, the throne would then go to the family of his sister Mary, the French Queen, beginning with Lady Jane Grey (her mother Frances having been written out of the succession). With an eye to the future, Northumberland proposed an alliance with the Greys wherein Jane would marry his younger son Guilford.

The Duke and Duchess of Suffolk were most pleased with the arrangement and they expected Jane to be as well. But when the Greys told their daughter of their plans for her, they were met with a most unexpected response. Handsome though he was, she did not love Guilford, Jane answered, and she had no intention of being a wife. Henry and Frances were furious. How dare she? How could she be so ungrateful and so unnaturally disobedient? It was their duty as parents to provide a husband for Jane, and hers to accept. For the nobility, marriages were all about the strengthening of alliances and the achieving of power and wealth. The selection of one's spouse was not a privilege afforded to the ruling class. Jane's parents did not wed for love, nor did her grandmother Mary when she was sent off to

France. What right did Jane think she had to marry or not marry as she pleased, her parents demanded?

The Suffolks continued to threaten, but Jane would not give in. Tearfully, she said that even if she were inclined to have Guilford, it would be impossible. She reminded her parents how they had once spoken of betrothing her to Edward Seymour, son of the late Lord Protector. Was the intention itself not a binding contract, Jane asked? But Jane's legal niceties meant nothing to Henry and Frances Grey. Exasperated, they took to more shouting and even to blows. Unable to resist any further, Jane accepted Guilford Dudley.

On 21 May, the young pair were joined as one. Unlike Jane, Guilford had presumably obeyed his father without question. While the young man was not known to have shared Jane's intellectual or religious interests, he probably appreciated that his wife was an attractive young lady. However the newlyweds regarded each other, their nuptials were a joyous occasion for both their families. The Dudleys and the Greys were now united by marriage, as were their supporters. On the same day that Jane and Guilford were wed, the Suffolks married their daughter Katherine Grey to Lord Herbert, son of the Earl of Pembroke. Not to be outdone, Northumberland gave away his daughter Katharine Dudley to Henry Hastings, heir of the Earl of Huntingdon. Mary Grey, the Suffolks' youngest child, was not excluded from the matches made that Sunday. Too young to be wed, the eight-year-old Mary was at any rate formally betrothed to her kinsman, Arthur, Lord Grey. As if that was not enough, there were also plans to have Northumberland's brother Andrew take Margaret Clifford (the daughter of Frances Brandon's late sister Eleanor) as his wife.

At such an event with so many families joined, no expense was spared. The festivities - lasting two days - were 'celebrated with great magnificence and feasting', with many in attendance. There was one notable absentee - the King. Edward VI was too ill to grace the revels with his presence, but to signify his wholehearted approval, he supplied the new couples and their guests with rich clothing and jewels - some of them the property of the late Protector - from the royal storehouses.

≡

In the weeks following the weddings, Edward VI took a turn for the worse. Northumberland tried to allay the people's concerns by propping the ailing boy in front of an open window to wave at the crowds below. It did more harm than good. Everyone was shocked at the young man's emaciated appearance. The Imperial ambassador, making discrete inquiries, found out that the King had a 'suppurating tumour on the lung' and had not long to live.

Aware that he might die soon, Edward's only concern was to put his kingdom in order before he was called to his Maker. To do that, he set aside his father's will and replaced it with his own *Device for the Succession*. Unable to accept a female successor, and a Catholic one at that, Edward denied his sister Mary the Crown. Even Elizabeth - a Protestant - was deprived of her rights. Instead, the throne was to go to 'the Lady Frances' heirs male', or 'for lack of such issue to the Lady Jane's heirs male'.

But a male succession was near impossible, Edward realised. The Duchess of Suffolk had no son, and she had not had a child since her daughter Mary in 1545. The succession would then go to Frances' grandson by Jane instead. However, Jane was only newly married, and such a child had yet to appear. With no male successor in sight, the Device was worthless.

As his throne would almost certainly go to a woman, Edward re-worded his will. If the Lady Frances had no sons before he died, the Crown would go 'to the Lady Jane and her heirs male', and following them, to the sons or grandsons of Katherine or Mary Grey, but not to the two girls themselves. Once again, their mother the Duchess was barred from the succession as she had been by Henry VIII. Edward's reason for excluding his cousin (and her two younger daughters) was based on the hope that Jane, still young, would produce a male child, frustrating the claims of all his female relatives.

Once the document had been properly drawn up, it required the assent of the Council and the lords temporal and spiritual of the realm. Despite the arguably illegal Device - Edward was technically still a minor, and Henry VIII's will for the succession had been made into an Act of Parliament - the dying boy, stubborn as his father was, brooked no opposition. Even his godfather Cranmer could not change Edward's mind. Ordered by the King and cowed by Northumberland, the Council and as many lords as could be summoned, swore to uphold the Device. The Mayor and the city elders, and the justices of the realm were also called upon to subscribe to the new will. Though reluctant to do so, seeing that the Council had agreed to the King's wishes, they too signed. Only Sir James Hale, a judge from Kent, refused. Although he was a Protestant, his conscience would not allow him to disinherit the Lady Mary.

To prepare the people for Jane's accession, a campaign was begun to vilify the rightful heiresses Mary and Elizabeth. While preaching in London on 2 July, the Bishop of Bedford made the customary prayers for the King, but left out those for his sisters. The oversight was not lost on the congregation and there was much discontent. The week after, the Bishop of London, Nicholas Ridley did not mince words. From the pulpit at Paul's Cross, he loudly denounced the Princesses as bastards and thereby unfit to wear the Crown. The sermon was not well-received, and the audience was reported to be 'sore annoyed'.

Even if his decision was unpopular, the succession was settled to Edward's satisfaction. His conscience was clear. Lying in his great bed of State with his physicians hovering about but unable to do anything for him, the young King awaited the glories of Heaven. He was anxious for it to all end. Edward was in great pain, and he was a piteous sight to behold. Northumberland, in a desperate attempt to save him, engaged 'a woman who professes to understand medicine' to attend to him, but her dubious efforts only increased his suffering. Gasping and coughing, his body swollen and covered in scabs, and his hair and nails falling out, Edward prayed for release. When death finally came on the evening of 6 July, the boy muttered gratefully,

> "Lord God, deliver me out of this miserable and wretched life, and take me amongst Thy chosen... defend this realm from papistry, and maintain Thy true religion... for Thy Son Jesus Christ's sake. Amen".

Chapter 28
The Reluctant Queen

SOME WEEKS before the King's death, Jane Grey was given warning of the seriousness of his condition and was told to prepare herself. Since her marriage to Guilford Dudley, Jane and her husband had lived apart, an arrangement, which strangely enough, suited both families. If Monsieur Scheyfve can be believed, the couple did not even consummate their marriage 'because of their tender age'. Whether his information was correct is uncertain. Jane's ancestor, Lady Margaret Beaufort, was already a wife and mother by the age of fourteen, and Arthur Tudor and Katherine of Aragon had been allowed to spend their wedding night together as young people. Jane, at sixteen and Guilford, at about the same age, would have presumably been ceremoniously put to bed together at their nuptials in May. Whether their relationship was consummated or not, with the throne now at stake, Northumberland and his wife would have seen to it that they began cohabiting.

Jane would later recall that on a visit to the Dudleys in the early summer with her mother Frances, she was informed by her in-laws that

> 'if God should have willed to call the King to
> His mercy, of whose life there was no lingering hope,
> it would be needful for me to go immediately to the
> Tower, I being made His Majesty's heir of his realm.'

She was in utter disbelief at first, Jane remembered, but once the initial shock had worn off, she refused to take them seriously, attributing their remarks to 'mean little but boasting'. Taking 'little account' of the matter, Jane proposed that she and her mother should return home. The Duchess of Northumberland, a woman of short temper, flew into a rage. With King Edward gravely ill, she wanted the heiress to the throne in her keeping. Jane must not go, she insisted, her place was here with her husband. A furious row then ensued between the two Duchesses. Finally, to keep the peace, Jane agreed to remain behind.

It was during her stay at Durham House that she and Guilford began living together as a married couple. The new arrangement did not last long - no more than four or five days - as Jane began feeling unwell. Only then did the Duchess of Northumberland allow Jane to leave the city and to take the air at Chelsea, where she had once lived with Queen Katharine. The change did her little good for she appeared to worsen for a time.

It was from Chelsea that Jane was summoned to Syon House, which belonged to the Dudleys at that time. To get her to come with little resistance as possible, Northumberland dispatched his daughter, Mary Sidney, a girl of about Jane's age, to fetch her on 9 July. Following her father's instructions, Mary was to say little, except to tell her sister-in-law with 'extraordinary seriousness' that she must accompany her without delay. Jane had no inkling that Edward VI had died just three days earlier.

Throughout the river journey, Mary Sidney was evasive, only telling Jane that she was to 'receive that which had been ordered for [her] by the King'. When they arrived at Syon, the house appeared to be quiet and deserted, but then Northumberland, the Marquis of Northampton, and the Earls of Pembroke, Huntingdon, and Arundel entered the hall and welcomed her. They engaged Jane in small talk, but their manner was strange. At first, the men did her 'such reverence as was not at all suitable to my state', Jane later wrote. They then knelt at her feet, as did – incredibly - her mother and her mother-in-law who had also shown up.

In a daze, she followed Northumberland towards a dais. There, the Duke announced the death of Edward VI. "Whosoever should acknowledge the Lady Mary or the Lady Elizabeth, and receive them as the heirs of the Crown", he cried out, "shall be had for traitors"! Northumberland then turned towards his daughter-in-law. "His Majesty hath named Your Grace as the heir to the Crown of England". The whole assembly - including Jane's parents and her husband - knelt on cue, calling out "The King is dead. Long live the Queen"! Overwhelmed, Jane dropped to the floor.

In her recollection of what followed, Jane remembered how she 'lay as dead' on the ground weeping over the death of her cousin and her own 'insufficiency' to the throne. But no one, not even her parents or Guilford came forward to comfort her. Instead, they all stood by and waited until she had composed herself. When Jane finally stopped weeping, she began praying aloud. She cried out to God that since it was His will that she succeed to the Crown, to grant her the 'grace and spirit' to govern England 'to His glory and service'.

≡

Shortly after midday on 10 July, Jane was taken from Syon to Westminster in preparation for her triumphal entry. There, a 'great company of lords and nobles', were summoned to do her honour and escort her to the Tower. After Jane was suitably robed, she and her entourage rode in a flotilla of barges towards Tower Wharf, arriving there at about 3 o'clock in the afternoon. Followed by her ladies and by her mother who bore her train, Jane, with an attentive Guilford beside her, climbed the river steps to take possession of the Tower, and to live there until her coronation set for two weeks after.

On the short walk towards the Byward Tower drawbridge, Jane smiled to the people and conducted herself with the utmost dignity. But for all her efforts there was no mistaking that the affections of the people lay elsewhere. Like the crowning of Anne Boleyn twenty years earlier, there was much ill feeling. A Frenchman visiting England at Jane's accession described how 'the people neither made any great feasts, nor expressed great satisfaction, neither was one bonfire made'. Even the crowd present at the wharf was sparse. Where was the Lady Mary, the citizens asked each other? Why was *she* not Queen? And what of the Lady Elizabeth? Bewildered, no one saluted Jane as she passed. It was left to the heralds to shout, "Long live the Queen! God save her"!

Inside the Tower, Northumberland set Jane to work immediately. He lay before her letters patent of her accession to which she must put her signature. After she had done, they were affixed with the Great Seal and readied for distribution throughout the kingdom. In London, Jane's coming to the throne was proclaimed by the two principal heralds of the realm, the Kings-at-Arms. In the early evening, in four parts of London, they formally announced the death of King Edward, and his appointment of the Lady Jane Grey as 'Queen of England, France, and Ireland, Defender of the Faith, and of the Church of England, and Ireland the Supreme Head'. The Lady Mary and the Lady Elizabeth, the heralds declared, were removed from the succession as both their mothers' marriages with Henry VIII were 'clearly and lawfully undone by sentences of divorces according to the word of God and the ecclesiastical laws'. Furthermore, the two Princesses were a danger to the realm by their unmarried state. Should either one of them be matched with any 'stranger born out of this realm', the husband would 'bring this noble free realm into the tyranny and servitude of the Bishop of Rome' - an obvious reference to Mary Tudor. Thus in his wisdom, the late King had made the descendants of his father's sister – namely, Jane, Katherine, and Mary Grey, and their cousin Margaret Clifford – as his heirs.

Throughout the lengthy proclamation, the people kept silent, and they remained so when the heralds finished and cried, "God save Her Majesty Queen Jane"! But there was one young man, Gilbert Potter, who dared say aloud what everyone else would not. In outrage, he shouted how the Lady Mary had a better right to the throne, and thus, "God save *Queen Mary*"! But before he could rally others to his side, Potter was immediately seized. The next day, for speaking 'seditious and traitorous words', his ears were nailed to the pillory and 'cut off cruelly'.

═══

Days before the King's death, Mary had been told of the plot against her. Northumberland, her supporters said, knowing Edward VI was ill and had not long to live, was planning some 'conspiracy aimed at her destruction'. If she were to come to London as bidden, she would find herself in a prison. Mary took the warning to heart. She remembered how sick Edward had looked when she had seen him last in February, and she knew that in the event of his death, Northumberland would never countenance her - a Catholic - on the English throne. That it was her own brother who had displaced her, probably never occurred to Mary. Northumberland and his cronies, she believed, were behind it all.

Since it was too dangerous for her to remain at Hunsdon 'where it would be much easier to seize her', Mary made up her mind to take refuge in East Anglia. In that region, she had many supporters, and at Framlingham Castle in Suffolk (formerly owned by the Duke of Norfolk until his arrest by Henry VIII) she could summon her supporters. And should she fail, the eastern coast would provide her with means of escape to the Emperor.

Fearing she might be spied on in her own household, Mary left Hunsdon with only a handful of her most trusted attendants on 4 July. To raise no suspicion, she had used the ruse that some of her staff had fallen ill, and fearing the spread of infection, she would be changing residences. Once she set out, Mary and her party rode quickly. By late evening, Mary managed to reach Sawston Hall in Cambridgeshire, home of her supporter Sir John Huddleston. When daybreak came, she was on the move again, this time stopping at the house of the loyal Lady Burgh near Thetford. Mary had made preparations to spend the night there but then her goldsmith Robert Reyns suddenly showed up. Reyns had ridden post-haste from London with the news that the king was *apparently* dead.

Mary found herself with a problem. It had always been her intention that once Edward VI's death was announced, she would immediately proclaim herself his successor. Tradition dictated it and it served the practical purpose of calling support to her claim. However, she could not be certain whether what her goldsmith had heard in the city was truth or rumour. It might, in fact, be a trick of Northumberland's. If she declared herself Queen while her brother was still alive, she would be guilty of high treason. She must not act precipitously, Mary decided, but wait for more news. Meanwhile, for safety's sake, she must continue.

It was at Kenninghall (another former property of the Howards), in Norfolk, that Mary received confirmation of Edward's death. The message was brought to her by her physician, Thomas Hughes, a man she trusted implicitly. He corroborated what Reyns had heard, but that was not all. The succession had been overturned in favour of her cousin the Lady Jane Grey. The news was upsetting, but Mary and her supporters remained undaunted. She was still the rightful Queen of England, and they would fight to win the Crown from their enemies.

As popular as she was, Mary's chances of achieving that 'which was owed to her as much by hereditary right as by her father's will' appeared slim. Even the Emperor's agents in London had to agree. 'The Lady Mary's person will be in danger', they wrote to Charles V, 'and her promotion to the Crown so difficult as to be well nigh impossible in the absence of a large force to counterbalance that of her enemies'. Northumberland had a strong advantage over her. Besides controlling the capital and the Tower of London, the Duke had

> 'managed to contract alliances between his family and the foremost in the land... he has seized the treasury and money-reserves of the kingdom, has appointed his own men to the command of the fortresses, has raised a force of artillery, fitted out warships for service, and has men ready to go onboard as soon as he shall issue the order.'

It would even be a miracle if Mary evaded capture, Scheyfve wrote glumly. Already, Northumberland has sent his son Robert Dudley with over three hundred horsemen to catch her.

Giving no thought to the odds against her, Mary gathered hundreds of her supporters to her at Kenninghall. To 'eschew bloodshed and vengeance', she dictated a letter to the Council on 9 July demanding its surrender. She put forth her claim as the country's lawful sovereign, which 'hath been provided by Act of Parliament, and the testament and last will of our dearest father. No good true subject... can or would pretend to be ignorant thereof' of her right, she continued, and because of that, she was astonished at being kept in the dark about her brother's death:

> 'yet we consider your wisdoms and prudence to be such, that having eftsoons amongst you debated, pondered, and well weighted this present case with our estate, with your estate, the commonwealth, and all our honours, we shall and may conceive great hope and trust, with much assurance in your loyalty and service, and therefore for the time interpret and take things not to the worst, and that ye will, like noblemen, work the best.'

Surely, the Council had acted out of 'consideration politic', Mary wrote tactfully. But at the same time, she warned them, saying she was well informed of their treachery:

> 'We are not ignorant of your consultations, to undo the provisions made for our preferment, nor of the great bands and provisions forcible, wherewith ye be assembled and prepared - by whom, and to what end, God and you know, and nature cannot but fear some evil.'

However, if the Council was willing to submit to her as Queen, she, in turn, would be generous and forgiving.

Later that same day, Jane and her court were sitting down to dinner when a horseman showed up at the Tower gates. He had come from *Queen Mary*, he said, and wished to speak to the Council. Ushered into Jane's presence, the messenger Thomas Hungate, a gentleman 'bordering on old age yet second to none in his obedience and diligence' to Mary Tudor, read his mistress's letter aloud before the startled assembly. When he had finished, Jane's mother and the Duchess of Northumberland wailed in terror. The members of the Council, being no less 'astonished and troubled', broke into pandemonium. What were they to do, they cried? Should they oppose Mary? Would there be civil war? Already, the Earl of Bath, the Earl of Sussex, and other important gentlemen had declared for her.

It was left to Northumberland to restore order. Hungate was arrested and tossed into prison with the intention of having him hanged. The Duke then turned his attention to Mary. She was a traitor on the run, he assured everyone, and even her cousin the Emperor would not take up her cause. The Princess would be captured in no time and locked up within this very place, he promised.

Northumberland drew up letters to his supporters. Upon their allegiance, they were to 'repel and resist the feigned and untrue claim of the Lady Mary, bastard daughter of... Henry VIII of famous memory'. At the top of each one, the Duke had his daughter-in-law affix her signature – *Jane the Queen*. He also began preparations to engage Mary in battle. 'A great number of men of arms', along with carts loaded with 'all manner of ordnance [such] as great guns and small, bows, bills, spears, morris-pikes, harnesses, arrows, gunpowder, and victuals, money, tents' - were brought to the Tower to make ready to march on her. As an added precaution, the city gates were guarded around the clock against any invasion by Mary's forces.

Northumberland, with the rest of the Council, also fired back a response to Mary. The late King, they wrote to her, by 'letters patent signed with his own hand, and sealed with the Great Seal of England in presence of the most part of the nobles, councillors, judges, with divers other and sage personages' had made Lady Jane Grey Queen. Mary, they reminded her, was 'justly made illegitimate and inheritable to the Crown Imperial of this realm, and the rules, and dominions, and possessions of the same'. That Parliament had later restored Mary to the succession was ignored by the Council. The Princess was ordered to be 'quiet and obedient', and not 'vex and molest any of our Sovereign Lady Queen Jane's subjects from their true faith and allegiance due unto Her Grace'.

To frustrate Mary, it was essential she not receive any help from abroad. Diplomatic letters were drawn up, seeking Imperial recognition of Queen Jane. Sir Philip Hoby, the English ambassador, was instructed to notify the Emperor of King Edward's death, and of the universal acceptance of Lady Jane Grey as his successor. Just as important, Hoby was also to emphasise England's continuing desire to maintain its 'ancient amity' with the Empire.

Shortly after her installation at the Tower, the new Queen had been presented with her crown by the Marquis of Winchester. She had obeyed God and her King in accepting the throne, but she cared nothing for its trappings. Indignantly, Jane had asked the old nobleman why he had brought it to her - she had never made the request. Winchester, thinking Jane was merely being modest, answered that she need not be afraid to wear it. As Lord High Treasurer, he was responsible for supplying her regalia, and therefore needed to know whether it fitted properly. Jane gave in and allowed the crown to be set on her head. Encouraged, Winchester then presented her with 'parcels of money, jewels gold, stone, pearl, and other stuff' taken from the royal storehouses at Westminster and from the Tower's Jewel House.

If Jane thought little of the riches before her, Guilford Dudley was positively dazzled by it all. He might have pictured how nicely the jewels would go with the crown Winchester promised to have made especially for him. Being husband to the new Queen of England was a heady experience for the young man. He took pleasure in being addressed as 'Your Grace' and as 'Your Excellency', and he enjoyed the privilege of dining alone, apart from the lords and his own family members who had to eat together in the hall. He even had the services of Sir John Gates, the Captain of the Guard, who was given the honour of waiting on him. With everyone at his beck and call, Guilford flaunted his new authority. He even took part in government. When the Council met, he insisted on being present and sat at the head of the table.

Jane tolerated Guilford's regal airs, but her patience snapped when he asked her to surrender her powers to him. His wife may reign, but she should not rule, he insisted. It was unthinkable that Jane, as a woman, should exercise power. Better that she step aside and allow *him* to assume the burden of government. Jane, displaying a streak of pride inherent in her Tudor blood, refused. Under no circumstances, she exclaimed, would she surrender her authority to him, or grant him the title of 'King' without Parliament consenting. The best she could do, was to make him Duke of Clarence.

A dukedom was a poor substitute for a kingdom, and Guilford complained in tears to his mother. Naturally, the Duchess took his side. Guilford was her favourite son (he was christened with her family surname) and she had indulged him all his young life. She scolded Jane on her wifely obedience, but her daughter-in-law would not be intimidated and she held her ground. Again, she would *not* make him King, she exclaimed. In a huff, the Duchess ordered Guilford to stop conjugal relations with his unruly wife immediately. Better yet, his mother said spitefully, he should leave Jane's company all together and return to Syon House with her. The family squabble ended with Jane putting her foot down. Both mother and son were made to stay put.

Having to contend with her demanding husband and her difficult mother-in-law, and faced with the pressures of being Queen, Jane's health took a downturn. She started feeling weak, and her skin began to peel. This was not the first time this had happened to her, Jane thought. She had suffered the same symptoms during her stay at the Duchess of Northumberland's. In her sickness, Jane thought that her in-laws were trying to poison her. She might even have imagined that if she were dead, John Dudley would declare himself Lord Protector, putting Guilford in her place as King.

Most likely, Jane's illness was due to stress rather than to any machinations of the part of the Dudleys. In both instances - Jane's row with her mother-in-law before she became Queen, and then with her husband (and his mother again) in the Tower, Jane was put under great strain. There is no reason to believe that the Duchess and her husband were poisoning their daughter-in-law. They would have known that the people would never abide a Dudley as England's ruler if Jane were put out of the way. She was far more valuable alive.

On 12 July, with the royal forces ready to march on Mary Tudor, all that was left to do was to appoint a commander. The Council chose Henry Grey as the Queen 'could have no safer defence for Her Majesty than her most loving father'. The Duke gladly accepted. But when her father's lieutenancy of the army was proposed to Jane, she would not let him go. In tears, she begged the Council to reconsider. Moved, the lords nominated Northumberland instead. John Dudley was certainly better qualified than Suffolk, having so bravely suppressed rebel uprisings in the last reign. The Duke's reputation was so fearsome that none would dare

> 'lift up their weapon against him. Besides that, he was the best man of war in the realm, as well for the ordering of his camps and soldiers both in battle and in their tents, as also by experience, knowledge,

and wisdom, he could animate his army with witty persuasions, and also pacify and allay his enemies' pride with his stout courage, or else to dissuade them, if need, from their enterprise.'

On the morning of 13 July, Northumberland, taking his kinsman Lord Grey, and the Marquis of Northampton with him, set out to Norfolk to do battle against the rebels. Even with more than 'three thousand horsemen well equipped and about thirty pieces of cannon and ammunition wagons' behind him, and more to follow the next day, John Dudley's spirits were dampened from the start. As he rode out of the city, the Duke could not help but notice the sullen faces of the crowd seeing him off. "The people press to see us", he commented to Lord Grey, "but no one sayeth God speed us".

Chapter 29
Queen Jane or Queen Mary?

TO RAISE support against the Lady Mary, Bishop Ridley was again ordered by the Council to preach against her. But as before, the crowd was unreceptive. The Londoners' affection for the daughter of Henry VIII was shared by the rest of the country. United by their allegiance to Mary Tudor and by their hatred of Northumberland, 'large numbers, both gentlemen and ordinary folk', rallied to her banner at Framlingham Castle. In Norfolk, Mary was proclaimed Queen by the Earls of Bath and Sussex, and soon the counties of Oxfordshire and Buckinghamshire, and the city of Norwich followed suit. In response, the Council addressed letters to their supporters, signed by Queen Jane, calling on them to defend her throne. One ordered them to

> 'assemble, muster, and levy all the power that you can possible make, either of your servants, tenants, officers, or friends, as well as horsemen as footmen... to repair with all possible speed towards Buckinghamshire, for the repression and subduing of certain tumults and rebellions moved there against us and our Crown, by certain seditious men.'

The traitors would no doubt, the Council wrote optimistically, 'lack hearts to abide in their malicious purpose, or else receive such punishment and execution as they deserve'.

Despite the government's boasts and threats, the people continued to flock to Mary in droves. Her 'forces were wonderfully strengthened and augmented' both on land and at sea. Off the coast of Yarmouth, six great ships had been lying in wait to capture Mary should she try to escape to the Low Countries. However, an unexpected storm blew the ships back near the shore. As the captains waited out the weather, one Henry Jerningham fighting for Mary was emboldened to take a boat out to the anchored ships. Asked if they would come over to his side, the sailors who in their hearts were for the Princess, declared for her. If their captains refused to join them, they shouted, "We shall throw them to the bottom of the sea! Long live our Queen Mary"!

When news of the mutiny reached London, both jubilation and panic set in. Mary's supporters 'much rejoiced', and the tenants and servants of the lords upholding Jane were emboldened to defy their masters by refusing to take up arms against the Princess. With so many turning to Mary, the members of the Council were in great apprehension. Clearly, their countrymen were in support of King Edward's sister, not his cousin. Away from Suffolk's watchful eyes, many of his colleagues were considering abandoning his daughter. Suspecting certain Councillors of wavering in their loyalty, Henry Grey took the precaution of forbidding them all 'to go out of the court, even to their own houses'.

Even so, the Marquis of Winchester sneaked out in the early evening of 16 July. By 7 o'clock that evening, Jane and her father had been alerted to his disappearance. Alarmed, they immediately ordered the Tower gates to be shut, and the keys brought to Jane for safe keeping. Later that night, Winchester was discovered at his London house and brought back to the Tower by force. Emboldened by his attempt nonetheless, more were ready to defect. On 19 July, under the pretence of going to the French ambassador to seek help, the Earl of Arundel and a handful of his friends headed straight for Baynard's Castle instead. Out of Suffolk's reach, they proclaimed their allegiance to Mary Tudor.

Once the announcement was made known, the tidings swept through the city like wildfire, and the streets were swarmed with jubilant Londoners. Everywhere one looked there were

'such expressions of popular rejoicing, such a clamour and din and press of people in the streets... men ran hither and thither, bonnets flew into the air, shouts rose higher than the stars... and all the bells were set a-pealing.'

Nothing of the like had been seen before. Even 'men of authority and in years could not refrain from casting away their garments, leaping and dancing as though beside themselves'. Caps were thrown into the air, and money was tossed out of windows as if it were of no worth.

The proclamation of a new government was made by the royal herald who just days before had announced the accession of Lady Jane Grey. At the sound of trumpets, he declared Mary Tudor 'Queen of England, France, and Ireland, and all dominions'.

As London celebrated, Jane Grey was unaware that her nine days reign had ended. She was sitting at supper when her father suddenly appeared. Without any greeting, Suffolk tore down her cloth of estate. "You are no longer Queen", he announced, adding that she must be content with 'a private life' once again. When Jane asked when she could go home - back to Bradgate, back to her books - Suffolk gave no answer.

Hardly anyone in London slept that night. The celebrations for Mary Tudor ran well past the late hours with continuous festivity until the sun rose. The next day there was more revelry. The Lord Mayor hosted a banquet to which the Council was invited. Among the guests was Henry Grey. Even Archbishop Cranmer, who had avidly supported Jane, was present.

That same day, the Councillors made their formal submission to their 'true natural Sovereign Liege Lady and Queen'. A letter was drawn by up William Cecil, Northumberland's secretary, in which they swore, with God as their witness, of having 'remained Your Highness' true and humble subjects in our hearts ever since the death of our late sovereign lord and master, your highness' brother'. However, they could not proclaim her Queen, 'for there was 'no possibility to utter our determination herein, without great destruction and bloodshed, both of ourselves and others, till this time'. When the letter was presented to Mary afterwards by Arundel, she was willing to be merciful. To prove his new loyalty, the Earl promised to deliver up Northumberland to her himself.

As Arundel rode out to Cambridge to apprehend the Duke, things were going very badly for John Dudley. When news of Mary Tudor's victory reached his army, his men deserted him. Fearing they would be arrested along with their master, they tore off their liveries of service 'in order to not be known as his men'. Before long, the streets of Cambridge were littered with the Duke's badges. There was also a price on Dudley's head. A grant of £1,000 in land was promised to any nobleman who took him, with lesser amounts going to a knight, gentleman or yeoman.

Hoping to save himself, Northumberland proclaimed Mary Queen. He even made a great show of throwing up his cap and tossing coins to the people. But still fearing for his life, the Duke, with his son John, Earl of Warwick, planned to take flight. They were ready to ride away at dawn, when without warning, Arundel appeared at their door and arrested them both in the Queen's name. Knowing all was lost, Northumberland fell to his knees and begged the Earl to be 'good to him, for the love of God'.

On 25 July, Northumberland, with three of his sons, was taken back to the capital. Three thousand soldiers were needed to maintain order. The mood of the crowd was especially ugly, and the new Queen had to intervene. Mary issued a command that 'under pain of punishment, they should allow the prisoners to pass peaceably'. The order was ignored. Every step of the way, from Bishopsgate to the Tower, the Duke was pelted with muck and reviled as a 'great traitor'. He was even nearly killed. Gilbert Potter, who had had his ears cropped on Dudley's orders, came at him with a sword. Only the protection of his guards saved him from the young man's fury. Northumberland showed no reaction, but with a touch of his old hauteur asked his escort Arundel, "Ought this most impudent fellow be allowed to afflict me while no accusation has yet been laid against me"? Even when he saw the Tower looming before him, John Dudley did not react. But one of his sons, it was noticed, did not have his father's fortitude. At the threshold of their prison, he gave way to tears.

In the late afternoon of 3 August, Mary Tudor set out in procession from Wanstead to take possession of her kingdom. Those who stood along the processional route to London were astounded by the great number in her party. Mary had an escort of some ten thousand people with her – 'gentlemen, squires, knights and lords', and not to mention, the various peeresses, clergymen, judges, heralds, and foreign dignitaries come to pay her tribute. Most conspicuous was the forgiven Earl of Arundel, who was given the privilege of bearing the Sword of State before her.

Following the Queen were her ladies and the noblewomen of the realm. The Duchess of Norfolk, an old friend of Katherine of Aragon, was there, as was the Marchioness of Exeter, who had also stood by Mary and her mother in their darkest days. Despite their intimacy with the Queen, precedence still belonged to the Lady Elizabeth, who rode immediately behind her sister. At the King's death, she too had been summoned to court, but like Mary, she had been warned about Northumberland's takeover. As events played out, Elizabeth took no sides but waited for the outcome. When Mary was victorious, she hastened to her sister's side with congratulations.

In London, the citizens awaited Mary with anticipation. In preparation for her coming, placards inscribed '*Vox populi, vox Dei*' –

'the voice of the people is the voice of God' - were seen everywhere. No one doubted that Heaven had glorified Mary Tudor. In His goodness, God had delivered her from her enemies as He did Moses from Pharaoh. When Mary came into sight at last at Aldgate, the cheers were deafening. The Londoners could not refrain from crying out, "Jesus save Your Grace"! over and over.

At St Botolph's Church, the 'poor children' of Christ's Hospital presented a Latin oration in the Queen's honour. After they had finished, an observer noticed how Mary remained aloof, saying nothing in response. Perhaps she was deeply touched and at a loss for words. Or maybe off the cuff remarks were simply not her forte. However, Mary was seen to take great pleasure in the singers and musicians performing for her on the way to the Tower.

There, Mary was welcomed by resounding shots of ordnance 'the like had not been heard'. Inside the Tower, on the way to her lodgings, Mary was met by a dishevelled little group kneeling before her on the Green. Coming closer, she recognised their faces. There was Edward Courtney, son of the Marchioness of Exeter, who had been confined for close to fifteen years, following his father's execution, and beside him the old Duke of Norfolk, the Bishop of Durham, the Duchess of Somerset, and Bishop Gardiner – all of them prisoners under the previous reigns. The Queen embraced each one of them. "These are *my* prisoners"! she said effusively, granting all of them their freedom.

There was one, however, to whom Mary would not be so merciful. For usurping her Crown, it was the Queen's pleasure that the Lady Jane Grey be 'committed to ward'.

PART 9
THE LAST OF HER RELIGION: MARY I

God grant she be the last of her religion.
(Raphael Holinshed on Queen Mary and her
persecutions, *Chronicles*, 1577)

Figure 20   Medal of Mary I by Jacopo Nizolla da Trezzo
The Walters Art Museum, Baltimore

Chapter 30
Queen Regnant

DAYS BEFORE Mary Tudor's astounding victory, 'not a soul imagined the possibility of such a thing'. Even the Imperial ambassadors in England were gloomy about her chances. They wrote to Charles V, saying that the Princess will be defeated and end up as Northumberland's prisoner. But when the tide turned in her favour, the envoys were among the first to offer Mary their congratulations. Their master's advice to the new Queen was to begin her reign as a 'good Englishwoman' and to foster the goodwill of her people. It would do her good to appear merciful, the Emperor suggested. She should not give the impression of being too vengeful in punishing the rebels who stole her Crown.

Mary heeded Charles' counsel as she always did, but even she found it hard to forgive. Mary was soft-hearted by nature, but the treason of the Dudleys greatly offended her, and she turned a deaf ear to all pleas for mercy for them. Even when Northumberland's wife came to beg for the lives of her husband and sons, she ordered the woman to turn around and go home. As Mary would not receive the Duchess, she would not see the Lady Jane Grey either. Although they were lodged in the Tower together, there is no record of any meeting between the two. If Jane had indeed requested an audience, Mary turned her down. She did, however, receive a letter from her.

Writing to Mary, Jane explained her actions in assuming her Crown. She was contrite for accepting that 'which I was not worthy', but in her defence, 'no one can ever say either that I sought it… or that I was pleased with it'. Her only real crime, according to Jane, was to allow herself to be misled by dishonourable men who with 'shameful boldness tried to give to others that which was not theirs'. It was for her 'lack of prudence' in going along with them that Jane begged Mary's forgiveness.

Softened by the letter, Mary was prepared to be merciful. She even found herself becoming Jane's defender. Despite the protests of the Imperial ambassador, Simon Renard, and Bishop Gardiner, newly appointed as her Lord Chancellor, the Queen could not be convinced that Jane posed any threat to her. Her cousin, Mary believed, had been in no way privy to Northumberland's intrigues. In fact, she argued, the girl was not even tainted by the Dudley name. Jane's marriage to Northumberland's son was never legal, Mary insisted, as her parents had betrothed her to young Edward Seymour before.

Unconvinced, Renard and his fellow envoys put pressure on Mary to reconsider. 'Jane of Suffolk' must be brought to account, they insisted. She was too dangerous a rival to be kept alive, even at her 'tender age'. Citing Roman history, the ambassadors reminded Mary how Theodosius the Great, regretful though it was, did not flinch from killing the young son of the traitor Maximus. If left alive, the boy, however blameless of his father's crimes, would have been a focus of dissension. The Queen herself would do well to follow such precedence, advised the Imperialists. But Mary stood her ground. "My conscience would not permit me to put her to death", she declared, closing the subject.

She did agree however to bring Northumberland to justice. On 18 August, the Duke was taken to Westminster to stand trial for high treason. Accused alongside him were his son, Warwick, and the Marquis of Northampton. As he surveyed the court, the Duke knew he had little chance of acquittal. There was not one sympathetic face to be seen; all 'beheld him with a severe aspect'. Old Norfolk, who presided, had not forgotten his long imprisonment under the Protestant regime, and the judges were still sore at being bullied by the Duke into accepting Jane Grey as Queen.

Before the court, Northumberland affirmed his loyalty to the Queen's lawful Majesty - even though he had borne arms against her. As to the indictment of treason, he challenged the court on two points. One - whether a man acting under the authority of the Council and the warrant of the Great Seal could be judged guilty, and two – whether those who were just as culpable as he was supposed to be, should be permitted to act as jurymen. Northumberland's defence caused a stir of uneasiness from the peers sitting in judgement on him; many of them had supported Queen Jane as he had done. But John Dudley's bold move failed. After conferring among themselves, the judges declared his arguments to be groundless. The Duke, they ruled, had acted under the seal of a usurper, and so long as there was no record of attainder against the individual, any man might serve at the Duke's trial, even if he did originally uphold the Lady Jane.

Crestfallen, John Dudley confessed himself guilty, and he begged Norfolk to request the Queen's mercy for him. Following the Duke's condemnation, Northampton, and then Warwick, took their places at the prisoner's bar. They too were found guilty. The punishment of death was pronounced on all three prisoners.

≡

There was great excitement outside the Tower on the morning of 21 August – the day Northumberland was scheduled to be executed. Around the great castle, the Queen's guard was put on duty to maintain control of the crowd. Some ten thousand strong had gathered on Tower Hill to witness the death of the notorious Duke. All was in readiness with the scaffold strewn with sand and straw, and the headsman standing by, when suddenly the spectators were told to disperse. As they turned away in disappointment, they caught sight of the city officials making their way towards the Tower. It was learnt that just before he had been led out to die, the Duke had announced his desire to return to the Catholic faith. His wish was quickly conveyed to the Queen who immediately ordered a stay of execution.

Instead of being taken out to Tower Hill, Northumberland was led to the Tower chapel. It was arrayed in splendour as it was in the days of Henry VIII. Cranmer's plain Communion table was gone, and its place was the high altar of former days with its rich covering cloth and golden ornaments. Around the church were the restored images of God the Father, Christ upon the Cross, the Virgin Mary, and the saints of old. Sweet incense filled the air as Northumberland, his brother Sir Andrew Dudley, Sir Henry Gates, and Sir Thomas Palmer - all renouncing their error in faith - heard Mass. The ancient ceremonies were revived, complete with 'elevation over the head, the pax giving, blessing and crossing on the crown, breathing, turning about, and all the other rites and accidents of old time appertaining'. Before he knelt to receive the Blessed Sacrament, the Duke turned around. This was 'true religion', he exclaimed, and it was through the 'false and erroneous preaching of the new preachers' that he had been 'seduced these fifteen years'.

Northumberland's conversion bought him only a day's reprieve. The next morning, he, Gates and Palmer, who were to die with him, marched up the hill to the scaffold. Having had their bloodlust postponed for a day, the mob was in a hostile mood. A woman ran up to Northumberland and shook a handkerchief in his face. It was stained with the blood of Edward Seymour, Duke of Somerset. "Behold the blood of that worthy man which now revenges itself upon thee"! she screeched before she was dragged away.

Surveying the crowd before him from atop the scaffold, John Dudley was resolved to die a Catholic. Before he laid his head on the block, he warned all against the dangers of Protestantism. It had brought nothing but 'wars commotions, tumults, rebellion, pestilence, and famine' to the realm. This, he truly believed, the Duke affirmed, of 'mine own free will'. After he had been beheaded, he was taken back to the Tower for burial. It was noted with some irony that he was laid next to his old enemy the Duke of Somerset.

Northumberland's death went unmourned, except by his wife and children. The least sympathetic was his daughter-in-law, Jane Grey. She could not forgive him for the troubles she had endured, and least of all, for his return to the old religion. From her window in the Lieutenant's house, where she was kept prisoner, she had seen her father-in-law taken across the Green to the Tower chapel for his reconciliation. Northumberland had set a terrible example, Jane believed, one that many, in the hopes of gaining pardon, would be quick to follow. Already, the Duke's eldest son, Warwick, had declared himself a Catholic, as had Northampton. In return, both had had their death sentences commuted to indefinite imprisonment. Later, Parr was even given permission to exercise outdoors. When not strolling about the Tower garden, the grateful Marquis was seen attending Mass at the chapel.

Jane held her tongue about Warwick and Northampton, but she could not contain her contempt for her father-in-law. Just a week after his execution, in conversation about his hope for pardon in returning to Rome, Jane railed against him. All her resentments – her marriage, her queenship, and her imprisonment - were vented in a passionate outburst. "Pardon"? she cried disdainfully, "Woe worth him"! It was Northumberland's 'exceeding ambition' that had brought the Greys and the Dudleys to ruin. As for his reconciliation, Jane had nothing but scorn for such a cowardly act. Northumberland should not have converted to save himself, Jane went on, as what man 'would hope of life' being so 'wicked and full of dissimulation'? Even if he had been spared, there would be no redemption for him in the next life. "For whoso denied Him before men", Jane said piously, "he will not know Him in His Father's Kingdom".

On 27 September, the Tower's booming cannons welcomed Mary Tudor again. Landing at the water stairs, the Queen was taken to the royal apartments to prepare for her coronation. After a short stay, Mary set out for the city. Seated in a canopied 'chariot of tissue' drawn by six horses, she was robed in splendour wearing a gown of blue velvet bordered with ermine. Her reddish gold hair was bound in a net of tinsel attached to a golden circlet encrusted with gems of 'inestimable value'. The headdress was magnificent but ponderous. Throughout her journey, Mary was seen to 'bear up her head with her hands'.

As her mother had been more than fifty years before, Mary was greeted by various staged pageants. The best displays, however, were not those set up by Mary's countrymen, but by foreigners living in London. At Fenchurch, the Genoese erected a great triumphal arch, which 'exceeded all the rest in novelty and elegance of design'. It was supported by four large sculpted giants, and in the midst, a child, sitting in a chair, was lifted high while making an oration to the Queen. Upon another arch, made by the Easterling society of merchants, was an artificial mountain. At the peak was a fountain flowing with wine surrounded by children making speeches in praise of Mary. The Florentines were just as creative. On Gracechurch Street, they had set up their own arch built in three tiers, each inscribed with verses celebrating the new reign. Though considered 'not so beautiful as that of the Genoese', it received a great deal of attention nonetheless. At the very top was a mechanical angel. To the amazement of the crowd below, it lifted a trumpet to its lips and played as if by magic.

Approaching St Paul's Cathedral, Mary's attention was directed towards its high steeple. It was decorated with streamers and a great banner displaying the city's arms of the red cross and the sword. At the apex, was a Dutch acrobat performing daredevil acts. Standing with one foot on the weathervane, he skilfully balanced himself on it on his knees; a feat thought to be 'a matter impossible'.

The next morning, 1 October, Westminster Abbey received the first Queen Regnant of England. At 11 o'clock, Mary was escorted from the nearby palace to undergo the time-honoured rituals of her male predecessors. She was taken into the church where the 'Princes of the realm, each in his proper attire', and all the clergy in their vestments did obeisance to Mary as she was led down the aisle. Before the altar was a platform built high up so that all could witness her receiving of the crown. With Bishop Gardiner's help, Mary climbed the twenty steps leading to the first tier. There, she paused to catch her breath because her coronation robes - made from cloth of gold - were heavy. Mary then ascended the last ten steps and seated herself in the coronation chair.

Gardiner took Mary by the hand again, and he led her around the four corners of the upper stage. At each stop, he asked in a loud voice whether the people had just cause why Mary should not be their Queen. "Is this the true heir to this kingdom"? he cried. Four times, a loud, 'yea, yea!' rang out from each section of the Abbey. "Are you willing to receive her as your Queen and mistress"? Gardiner then asked. Again, the answer was a fervid yes, followed by shouts of "Queen Mary! Queen Mary"!

Her right to the Crown unchallenged, Mary climbed down from the platform to be anointed. After prayers were said over her as she lay before the altar, Mary was divested of her robes in the privacy of a curtained off 'apartment' by the side. Standing in her corset, she was led back before the people and anointed. The sacred oil used by Gardiner was specially sent over by the Bishop of Arras at Mary's request. The old supply used at the coronations of her father and brother would not do, she insisted, because of the 'ecclesiastical censures upon the country' in both their reigns.

Having been blessed, the Queen was wrapped in a surplice of white taffeta. Though she was a woman, Mary received the traditional accoutrements of martial kingship - spurs on her feet and a sword about her waist. In her hands were placed the sceptre and the orb. The moment came. Standing before the seated Mary, Gardiner crowned her three times, signifying her triple titles of Queen of England, France, and Ireland.

≡

There was every expectation that the new reign would bring 'true justice, continual quiet, piety, mercy, and mild government' to the realm. That Mary took her duties as Queen most seriously was evident even before she was crowned. During her stay at the Tower, she had summoned the members of the Council to her. In their presence, Mary had done something extraordinary. She had risen from her chair and knelt in abasement before her own subjects. Before the astonished Councillors could implore her to raise herself up, Mary spoke. She recalled her difficulties in attaining the Crown, and said that now she was Queen, she would, 'acquit herself of the task God had been pleased to lay on her to His greater glory and service, to the public good and all her subjects' benefit'.

Still on her knees, Mary reminded her Councillors of their responsibilities too. 'She had entrusted her affairs and her person' to them, she said, and 'wished to adjure them to do their duty as they were bound by their oaths'. She then made a special plea to Gardiner as her Lord Chancellor to administer justice fairly in her name. When Mary had finished, not a man had spoken. All were overwhelmed by her 'humble and lowly discourse, so unlike anything ever heard before in England, and by the Queen's great goodness and integrity'. There was not a dry eye in the room.

As she had promised, Mary set herself to work with diligence. Two pressing issues she tackled at the start of her reign were the reform of the coinage and the repayment of debts. Beginning in 1542, English money had been continually debased to fund Henry VIII's wars with France and Scotland. Gold coins had been alloyed with inferior metals, while silver ones, formerly regulated to be at a standard of 11 ounces per 12 in precious content, had been incrementally reduced to only 4 ounces by 1546. Inevitably, with money having been so devalued, the country had been hit by inflation. English merchants bitterly complained how 'the exchange on foreign coin was so low and unequal, that it was impossible to trade or carry on commercial transactions at all without heavy loss'.

The financial mess had been left to the Duke of Northumberland to deal with. In 1551, he had addressed the problem by minting coins with their original metal content, and by assigning new face values - lower ones of course - to old debased currency. Mary was determined to continue his reforms. Her coins, she declared by proclamation, would be made of 'the perfect fineness'. The old 'base money', unfortunately still in circulation, would retain the values given in the last reign. Mary's efforts were much lauded as inflated prices began decreasing by a more than a third.

Mary was also determined to pay off outstanding debts accumulated by Henry VIII and Edward VI. The announcement was greeted with surprise. Many had assumed Mary would neglect her commitments

> 'in punishment of the attempt to cut her off by
> force or arms from the succession, and to be revenged of
> those who undertook to deprive her of her good right,
> she might well have refused to pay the said debts.'

Mary had no such intentions. It was 'for her own honour and the honour of the realm' that she fulfil her obligations. Despite the royal treasury being nearly depleted, it was her wish that every 'old servitor, minister, officer' be given their due, along with any 'merchants, bankers, captains, pensioners, soldiers, and others' that the government owed money to. Mary was equally magnanimous when it came to a subsidy granted by Parliament to her late brother. One third was still owed to the Crown, but Mary remitted the amount back to the citizens. They rejoiced at her generosity, crying out, "Long live the Queen! Long may she prosper"!

Mary's financial policies were well received, but there would be contention when it came to the settling of religion in the realm. The Queen was firm that her heretical kingdom be returned to the papal fold. Anticipating resistance, Mary had no choice but to dissemble, as the Emperor had advised her to at the start of her reign. She promised to make no changes, and she would not 'compel or constrain other men's consciences'.

But after she was safely crowned, the Queen made her true intentions known. Mary began expressing her wish - more a subtle command - that the Catholic faith be re-embraced by the whole country. In truth, she could never compromise on so great a matter. The Church of England broken off from Rome had made her a bastard and persecuted her for the beliefs she had held dear since childhood. That Providence had raised her high as Queen, replacing the errant Edward VI and the Lady Jane Grey, was confirmation that *hers* was the true Church. It was now her divine mission to reunite England with Rome. To achieve her purpose, Mary summoned her expatriate cousin, Cardinal Reginald Pole, home to be the new Archbishop of Canterbury, in place of Cranmer, and she put legislation in motion to end the Great Schism.

A few weeks after her coronation, a submissive Parliament began to dismantle the Protestant church of Edward VI. The English Communion service was banned, and, in its place, the Mass was celebrated as in the days of old. Only unmarried clergymen were allowed to dispense the Sacrament. Those who had taken wives under the late King were removed from office. The altars and crucifixes were restored, as were the accoutrements of 'holy bread, holy water, palms, and ashes'. As these measures were carried out, the Queen's title of Supreme Head of the Church was put into debate as to whether it should be retained. The title was especially abhorrent to Mary.

Equally repugnant to the Queen was her illegitimacy. The divorce of Henry VIII and Katherine of Aragon was repudiated by Parliament, and Mary's status proclaimed once again as 'lawful, legitimate, and legal'.

With England being turned from heresy and her birthright restored by law, Mary turned her thoughts to marriage. Like many of her contemporaries, she subscribed to the idea that the 'great part of the labour of government could with difficulty be undertaken by a woman, and was not within [a] woman's province'. But in having a husband, she would be 'assisted, protected, and comforted in the discharge of those duties'. And of course, as her Lord Chancellor reminded Mary, it 'would mean much more if she could leave an heir to succeed her'. Gardiner and the rest of the Council expected their say in the Queen's choice of a husband, but as she had always done, Mary looked to the Emperor instead for guidance. He was more a parent than a cousin to her, Mary said unashamedly, and she even regarded him more highly than her own father.

Even before her coronation, the Queen had had private talks with Charles V asking him to play matchmaker. Her English advisers must know nothing of this, Mary had warned the Imperial envoys, for already she resented their influence over her affairs. Not only was the Council she inherited from her brother a factious bunch – self-serving and argumentative among themselves – many of its members, Mary knew, were disdainful of her abilities, looking down on her as if she were a novice when it came to politics.

Determined to allow the Council no say in her marriage, Mary resorted to subterfuge. After long experience of being in peril, Mary was an old hand when it came to employing deception. At all times, the Queen warned the Imperials agents, they must relay their messages to her verbally; written communications were too risky. Their meetings must also be in secret. There was a back passage the envoys could use to reach her apartments undetected. And when she formally received them at court, Mary cautioned, they must not bring up the question of her marriage even in the most general terms. She might unwittingly betray herself before her advisers, who to her annoyance, were constantly at her side 'whenever she gave a public audience'.

The Queen especially insisted that Gardiner be kept in the dark. The Lord Chancellor, she knew, was hoping to drive her into the arms of Edward Courtney, now Earl of Devon. Gardiner had got to know him when they were both prisoners in the Tower, and he had developed a fatherly interest in the young man. To Gardiner, Courtney was a most suitable King of England. He was born of the nobility, popular with the people, and a Catholic to boot. Also, Courtney was not without good looks, and at the age of just twenty-seven would prove a virile husband in fathering a Prince of Wales. The Lord Chancellor spoke up for his protégé at every opportunity, and he was not alone. The Earl's mother, the Marchioness of Exeter, and one of Mary's closest friends, did her part, as well as the Earl of Pembroke and the Queen's ladies. In marrying Courtney, they all told her, Mary would also make up for the various wrongs done to his family by Henry VIII.

Even Parliament thought Courtney was the perfect King, and the speaker made a long-winded speech urging the Queen to have him. Despite Devon's qualities, Mary felt no attraction to him, and having spent almost half of his life in prison, he had no experience of the world, she felt. And most of all, the Emperor did not think much of him either. Feeling bullied by the Lords and Commons, Mary lashed out and scolded Parliament. It must not 'use such language to the Kings of England', she said angrily, 'nor was it suitable or respectful that it should do so'. She would wed as her duty called, but she if were forced to take a husband she did not love, she would 'not live three months and would have no children'.

Unsympathetic to Mary's personal feelings, Gardiner continued to hold out for Courtney. To boost his young friend's chances, the Lord Chancellor thought it best to remove any competition. For instance, there was Reginald Pole to consider. Mary had known him since her youth, and both their mothers were the closest of friends. In fact, the two women even hoped their children might wed some day. Reginald had taken holy orders while in exile in Rome, but Gardiner thought that the Queen might nonetheless be misguided into marrying him from a sense of loyalty. To dismiss the possibility, Gardiner reminded Mary that the Cardinal could not by Church law give up his vows, and that the English clergy had agreed to make him Archbishop of Canterbury on his imminent return to England.

Gardiner's concern over Reginald Pole was unfounded. Mary had no intention of marrying him, for she had her heart set on another – the Emperor's son Philip. For Mary, there was no greater catch in all Europe. Philip was a widower, a Catholic, and a Spaniard; born and bred in the country of her beloved mother. The twenty-six-year-old

Prince of Spain was even considered of 'manly countenance'. Mary would insist such a concern never entered her mind, but privately, she was much taken by the portrait of Philip she had received in November. Her cousin, Mary of Hungary, eager for the match to take place, forwarded her much-cherished picture of her nephew, done by the great Titian, for Mary's inspection. It had been painted three years before, the Regent admitted, but it 'was still considered a very good likeness by everybody'. She was so sure Mary would be captivated by the Prince that she asked for the portrait to be returned once the nuptials were performed. "I am to have it again, as it is only a dead thing", the Regent insisted. Her cousin will be compensated by having 'the living model in her presence'.

Her attraction to Philip may have caught Mary herself by surprise. The Queen was naïve when it came to sexual matters. In all her life she had 'never felt that which is called love', she confessed. Back in her twenties, after her restoration at court, Mary did entertain the idea of marriage and children, but as a bastard daughter with a father making only half-hearted attempts to find her a husband, her hopes went unfulfilled. As a private person, Mary seemed destined for spinsterhood - she may even have come to prefer her life as such - but now as Queen, it was her obligation to marry and produce an heir to the throne. The prospect of marriage also offered Mary companionship - the chance to love and to be loved. Philip's younger age did not seem to present a problem to her. Mary's chief concern was to obtain a loving husband, one as devoted to God as she was. Together, they would return her kingdom to Rome, and have a son – a son who would continue the line of Henry VII and carry on the true faith in England.

If it were left solely up to her, Mary would accept Philip without question, but there was also the will of God to consider. As she always did, the Queen sought guidance through prayer. On the night of 29 October, in the presence of Renard, and Susan Clarencieux, her favourite attendant, Mary knelt before the Blessed Sacrament. As the three sang the *Veni Creator Spiritus* together, invoking the Lord's help, Mary waited for an answer - and it came. God, she told her companions ecstatically, had heard her prayer. It was His wish that she wed the Prince of Spain.

Chapter 31
I Fear Them Nothing At All

ON 13 November 1553, Lady Jane Grey was let out of the Tower, but it was to go to her trial in the city. Though promised leniency by the Queen, the charges of high treason against her, her husband Guilford, and his two brothers, Ambrose and Henry, had not been lifted, nor that against Archbishop Cranmer. All five were made to walk in sombre procession to the Guildhall.

The mile long journey could have been done by carriage, but instead, the entire route was made on foot. Perhaps it was meant to strike fear in the little band of prisoners and to degrade them before the multitudes. If so, the intention succeeded. Passing through the Bulwark Gate towards Tower Hill, the prisoners caught sight of the public scaffold where Northumberland and so many others had perished. Along the route, some four hundred guardsmen were posted to maintain order, allowing Jane, the Dudleys, and Cranmer to pass unmolested. Shouts of sympathy, mixed with heckling, were directed at the group, but the former Queen, for one, was oblivious to it all. She fixed her attention entirely on the open prayer book she carried in her hands.

At the Guildhall, the accused were charged with

> 'compassing to depose the Queen, and that on the 10 July, they took possession of the Tower of London, and then and there proclaimed the said Lady Jane to be the true and undoubted Queen of England, and that she, the said Jane, signed various writings 'Jane the Queen' against her allegiance.'

It was of no matter that it had been of Northumberland's making; each of them had played their part in upholding an unlawful government. Jane and the three Dudleys admitted their guilt before the court. Only Cranmer held out. The Archbishop maintained that he had been merely obeying the late King's wishes in supporting the Lady Jane. The prosecution was unmoved. It argued that Edward VI had flouted the law in contravening the Act of Succession, and that the Archbishop had actively denied Queen Mary her right. He had 'received, acknowledged and proclaimed [Jane] to be Queen', and he had even sent troops to Cambridge to aid Northumberland. Unable to deny the charges, Cranmer changed his plea.

For obstructing Mary's rightful authority, all five prisoners were sentenced to death. Cranmer and Northumberland's three sons were to be taken to Tyburn and there suffer the full horrors of the executioner's knife. Jane's punishment was no less terrible. She was to be burnt alive or decapitated 'as the Queen should please'.

In the aftermath of the trial, Renard was confident that Mary would finally put her rival to death. But still, even backed by law, the Queen would not consent. As she saw it, her cousin was no longer a threat to her. Jane had been condemned as a traitor and therefore unfit to be Queen ever again. Also, the possibility that her parents' union was illegal was being explored. Before his marriage to Frances Brandon, Henry Grey had been betrothed to the Earl of Arundel's sister. Under Church law, his marriage with Frances was therefore bigamous. The taint of illegitimacy would be shameful to Jane (and to her sisters) but it would at least preserve her life; a traitor and a bastard could not inherit the Crown. In the meantime, Jane must remain in the Tower, Mary decided. Perhaps in time when her throne was more secure, she could send her cousin home as she had wished.

On a snowy day on 2 January 1554, the Imperial emissaries arrived in London to begin talks regarding the Queen's marriage to Philip of Spain. The news of their coming was 'very much misliked' and 'heavily taken' by the people. Their passage from Tower Wharf to Westminster was observed by Londoners - both Catholic and Protestant - who 'nothing rejoicing, held down their heads sorrowfully'. The only pleasure they took was in seeing some rowdy boys pelt the envoys with snowballs. When news of her sullen and unruly people reached the Queen, she reprimanded the city officials, telling them to ensure the citizens behaved themselves with 'humbleness and rejoicing'.

No amount of scolding could make the English embrace the foreigners. Shortly after the official announcement of the Queen's engagement had been made on 14 January, rumours of rebellion began to circulate. At the heart of the conspiracy, it was said, was the Earl of Devon. Dejected by Mary's preference for Philip, Edward Courtney hoped to depose the Queen, marry the Lady Elizabeth, and assume the throne as King Consort of England.

While Courtney was more of an opportunist looking to take advantage of the unrest in the kingdom than an actual instigator of treason, others like Sir Thomas Wyatt the Younger, son and namesake of the great poet, were prepared to act. On 25 January, under his leadership, the people of Kent rose up in arms against the coming of the Prince of Spain. Though Wyatt was a Catholic, the thought of Spanish rule over England drove him into revolt. He was not alone. In the West, Sir Peter Carew was gathering forces against Mary Tudor, as was Sir James Crofts in Herefordshire. Meanwhile, the Duke of Suffolk, who had been pardoned by the Queen, but 'had not the hap to reform himself', lent his support. On his part, he was to bring troops from Leicestershire, joining the other three leaders in a combined attack on London.

The city might well have been caught unprepared, if the government had not got wind of the plot just days before. Under interrogation, a frightened and contrite Courtney confessed all to his old friend Gardiner. Expecting an invasion, London was immediately fortified and suspected traitors arrested. The Marquis of Northampton, formerly pardoned, was thrown back in prison, and Suffolk, who was at his house in Surrey, received a summons to come to London. But fearing 'he should be put again into the Tower', the Duke fled to Leicestershire with his brothers to raise war.

Meanwhile, Wyatt's ranks had swelled to some five thousand men, all sworn to resist the 'proud Spaniards'. On 27 January, the Duke of Norfolk, still a tough old warhorse to be reckoned with at the age of eighty, was given instructions to march to Kent to engage the rebels. Leading a considerable number of men-at-arms himself, the Duke confronted the insurgents at Rochester Bridge. When an offer of royal pardon was made to any man who would put down his weapon, there was much laughter and only one taker.

After a brief skirmish, Norfolk was sent packing back to London - minus eight pieces of artillery and hundreds of his soldiers who had deserted to the enemy. The Queen and her court were shocked at the sight of Norfolk and his ragtag army limping back to the capital with their 'coats turned, all ruined, without arrows and string, or sword'. They had obviously underestimated Wyatt and the attraction of his cause, and it became necessary for the government to buy time to defend the city. Word was sent to the rebels to know their demands. Their reply was most brazen. Not only must Mary abandon her marriage; she must also surrender the Tower – and herself into their hands.

As Wyatt and his army marched towards London, Mary went to the Guildhall to rally the city to her. In a gruff voice, she addressed her subjects asking for their 'allegiance and obedience' as their anointed Queen; rightly descended from Henry VIII and 'wedded to the realm and laws of the same'. It was true, she continued, that she knew nothing of the love a mother bore her child, having never been a parent herself. But as a sovereign devoted to her people, such affection was comparable. As for her marriage, which had caused so much contention, it was not for any personal pleasure, Mary assured her listeners, but merely for the provision of an heir. But on the 'word of a Queen', she promised that 'if it shall not probably appear to all the nobility and commons in the high court of Parliament that this marriage shall be for the high benefit and commodity of the whole realm', she would willingly break off her engagement to the Prince of Spain. "And now good subjects, pluck up your hearts", she cried, "and like true men stand fast against these rebels! And fear them not, for I assure you, I fear them nothing at all"! At this, the citizens broke into thunderous cheers; Mary had won them over.

Though the Queen had promised to marry by the consent of Parliament, she no intention of doing so. She had long determined to follow her own conscience in the matter. The Londoners, nevertheless, took her at her word, and made ready to defend the city against Wyatt. On 3 February, when news came that the rebels were preparing to cross over the Thames via London Bridge, the citizens on the south bank scrambled to demolish the drawbridge access and shut the gates. Meanwhile, the Mayor and the sheriffs called on all able-bodied men to do their part. Amidst the pandemonium, their families took cover – 'aged men were astonished, many women wept for fear, and children and maids ran into their homes shutting the doors'.

Finding London Bridge inaccessible to him, Wyatt had no choice but to seek another river crossing. While the Londoners were unreceptive to his cause, the people of Southwark welcomed the rebel leader with open arms. There, his ranks were increased when many of the men raised by Lord William Howard defected to him. Wyatt was so emboldened that on hearing a bounty of £100 was being put on his head, he defiantly wrote his name on his cap and dared any man to take him down.

With the rebels making camp across the river, the Queen's permission was sought to bombard them with cannon fire from the Tower 'to beat down the houses upon their heads'. Mary refused. She would not have innocent people killed, she said. But later that night, a boat carrying the Lieutenant of the Tower's men was attacked by the rebels, leaving one dead. Provoked, the Lieutenant ignored the Queen's order and pointed his guns over the Thames. The cannon blasts went from evening till morning, and they so terrified the inhabitants of the south bank that they begged Wyatt 'for the love of God', to leave. Not wanting anyone, least of all any children, to be hurt, he complied and headed towards Kingston to look for another way across the river. But there, the southern end of the bridge was found to be partially destroyed. Wyatt brought out two pieces of ordnance and fired at the troops guarding the other side. After driving them away, he had some of his men swim across the water and seize the boats left behind. Once the rebels were all transported to the opposite shore, they marched towards the city.

On 7 February, Wyatt entered London. To his dismay, he found no support. Still, he set up his cannons near St James' Park and engaged the Queen's men led by the Earl of Pembroke. During the fighting, Wyatt raced towards St James' Palace, only to find the gates shut to him. In the noise and confusion of battle, the courtiers within were certain Wyatt had forced his way inside, causing much 'running and crying of ladies and gentlewomen'. Outside the palace there was even more chaos. The shrieking of women and children was so great it was even heard from the rooftops of the Tower. Wyatt and his army, now in disarray, ran towards Temple Bar to Fleet Street, and then to Ludgate which he also found closed to him. He turned back to Temple Bar. After a short scuffle, Wyatt, knowing all was lost, dropped his sword and surrendered.

For rising against their lawful mistress, the rebels could expect no mercy. Mary was not cruel by nature, but their treason hardened her. She had pardoned men before, only to have them betray her trust afterwards. One of the worst offenders was the Duke of Suffolk. Despite being 'truly irritated' by Henry Grey for siding with Northumberland, Mary, against her better judgement, had released him from the Tower at his wife's pleading. The Duke had then promised to return to the old faith, for which Mary remitted the fine imposed on him and showed him some semblance of her old favour. But in return, the ungrateful Suffolk had betrayed her by joining forces with Wyatt. His rebellion was equally a fiasco. Unable to flee the country to Denmark as he intended, Grey disguised himself and hid in a forest. For days, he lived like a hounded fugitive, concealing himself in an old hollow tree. Either bribed or threatened, a servant eventually revealed his master's whereabouts.

Because of Suffolk, his daughter and his son-in-law had to die. Though Jane Grey and Guilford Dudley had no part in his treason, Mary, encouraged by Gardiner, came to believe that her Crown would never be safe until all threats had been removed. Although the Duke's intention had been only to get rid of the Spaniards, *not* to put his daughter on the throne again, Mary and her government believed otherwise. With reluctance, she signed the death warrants of the young couple.

But before the Lieutenant of the Tower, Sir John Bridges, could carry out his commission set for 9 February, an unexpected postponement was granted. The news in London was that it was to allow the captured Duke of Suffolk to be brought safely to the capital, but the real intention appeared to be a last ditch attempt on the Queen's part to save her cousin's immortal soul. Jane must die, of that Mary was convinced, but she need not as a heretic. If Jane would convert to the old faith, she would be ensured of Heaven, and Mary's conscience would not be so burdened in killing her.

The Queen sent John Feckenham, a Benedictine, to meet with Jane. The learned monk could surely turn her cousin from her opinions, having so eloquently preached the 'goodliest sermon that ever was heard of the Blessed Sacrament of the Body and Blood' back in November. Their meeting in the Tower started cordially enough with Feckenham offering Jane his condolences. "Madame, I lament your heavy case", he said sympathetically, "and yet I doubt not but that you bear out this sorrow of yours with a constant and patient mind". Jane was equally courteous, and thanked him for his concern. But, she assured him, neither he nor anyone else should feel sorry for her; her troubles were but a 'manifest declaration of God's favour'. Jane's confidence and peace of mind were not what Feckenham had expected. Her impending death did nothing to diminish her faith but only strengthened it the more. Feckenham came directly to the point - it was the wish of the Queen and her Council that she embrace true religion. Of course, Jane refused. But she did tell Feckenham that she would consent to debate with him on matters of faith.

Their disputation ran the gamut from the definition of good works to the number of Sacraments and to the very nature of the consecrated Host. Worthy actions, Jane declared, were commendable in imitation of their Saviour, but in themselves they did not have the power to save. Salvation could only be achieved 'through faith only in Christ's blood', she said adamantly. Regarding the number of the Sacraments, there were only two – baptism and Holy Communion - as her faith dictated, not seven according to Feckenham's. Jane did not shy away from the controversy of the nature of Sacrament of the Altar either. Was it not the 'very body and blood of Christ?', Feckenham asked her. "No", she said emphatically,

> "I do not so believe. I think that at the supper I neither receive flesh nor blood, but bread and wine which… puts me to remembrance how that for my sins, the body of Christ was broken, and His blood shed on the cross. And with that bread and wine, I receive the benefits to come".

"Did not Christ speak these words - take, eat, this is My body"? Feckenham interjected. Yes, He did, Jane answered, but it was metaphorical. Did not Christ also say "I am the vine, I am the door"? Even St Paul understood that his master 'called things that are not as though they were'.

Getting nowhere with such a staunch young lady, Feckenham admitted defeat. Taking his leave, he turned to Jane saying sadly how they should not see each other in the afterlife. Yes, Jane concurred. "Except God turn your heart", she said, "for I am assured unless you repent and turn to God, you are in an evil case. I pray God in the bowels of His mercy to send you His Holy Spirit". Still, even if they were never to meet in Heaven - as both agreed - they could at least see each other one last time, the monk said. In spite of herself, Jane had come to respect and even like the old man. If not his religion, she did admire his 'great gift of utterance'. Jane granted Feckenham his request to attend her on the scaffold when the time came.

Feckenham reported his failure to the Queen. She was sorry to see her cousin die as an unrepentant heretic, but what more could she do for her? She had prolonged Jane's life for as long as possible even against the advice of her Councillors and of the Emperor. She could no longer hesitate to do what she must, but still, Mary was hesitant to allow the execution to proceed.

It took Gardiner to stiffen her resolve. Preaching before the court on 11 February, he praised the Queen for being a merciful lady, but her gentleness, the Bishop lamented, had allowed much treason to flourish. If she must show mercy, let it be to the 'body of the commonwealth', he implored. The preservation of her kingdom could only be guaranteed by 'cutting off and consuming' its 'rotten and hurtful members'. Mary got the point. She ordered the death warrants of Lady Jane Grey and Guilford Dudley to be carried out without delay.

On the morning of 12 February, Jane could see the crowd gathering on the Green from her window. They had come to witness her execution, which was to take place on a scaffold alongside the White Tower. To the citizens who arrived from all directions of the city that day, this was but one of many they had passed along the way to the citadel. Throughout London, across the river at Southwark, and as far as Kent - innumerable scaffolds and gallows had been erected for the rebels who were to suffer over the week. There were so many condemned men in the capital alone that the city jails were filled to capacity, and parish churches had to be used as makeshift prisons. Wyatt's followers were to be hanged in their dozens and their bodies left dangling in chains as a warning to others. Less fortunate were those who must endure the axe and disembowelling knife; their heads and parts to adorn the city gates.

For Jane, her end was to be more merciful. There was to be no fire, no writhing in the flames in agony as prescribed at her judgement - just a quick death on the block. The same clemency was extended to Guilford, but he was not to die alongside his wife. As a commoner, he must mount the scaffold on Tower Hill as his father and grandfather had done. At 10 o'clock in the morning, Guilford took leave of his sorrowful brothers. He was led out of the Beauchamp Tower where he passed beneath Jane's window. If he did look up, she was nowhere to be seen. Brought to the hill before the crowds, Guilford was too overwrought to say much. He only managed a 'short declaration' before he submitted himself to his fate.

Before he died, Guilford had been given permission to visit with Jane. However, she declined. It was not out of unkindness, she said, but only because a last meeting would be too upsetting for them both. Anyway, Jane added, she and her husband would be together soon enough in the hereafter. In the meantime, although she would not see him in life, she would look on him in death. And so she waited. About half an hour later, the sound of rumbling wheels was heard. Guilford had returned - his body on a cart with his head wrapped in a cloth stained red. To Jane, it was 'a sight to her no less than death', but she maintained her composure at the terrible sight. Perhaps in a strange way, it even fortified her for her own ordeal ahead.

When Jane stepped outside, those who had come to witness the sad proceedings might have noticed that she was wearing the same black dress she had worn to her trial. Once again, a book of prayers was in her hands. As she had done then, Jane read and walked - entirely detached from the tragedy she was to play out. Stepping onto the scaffold, Jane was met by Feckenham, waiting to attend her to the end. She addressed the spectators. "I am come hither to die", Jane said, "and by a law I am condemned to the same. The fact in deed against the Queen's Highness was unlawful, and the consenting there unto me". However, she went on, it was never her intention or her desire to seize the Crown; for that she did wash her 'hands thereof in innocency before God'.

After praying with Feckenham, Jane was motioned towards the block. As she knelt, she uttered nervously to the executioner, "I pray you dispatch me quickly". Perhaps the bungled executions of Margaret Pole and Thomas Cromwell had been made known to her. Afraid that the executioner would strike before she was ready, Jane suddenly turned to him again and blurted out, "Will you take it off before I lay me down"?

Assured he would not, Jane tied a kerchief around her eyes and stretched out towards the block. Instead of a last prayer, she cried out in distress. "What shall I do? Where is it"? Blindfolded, she could not find the block. "Where is it? What shall I do"? Jane asked desperately, her hands still finding nothing. No one moved. All the participants - her ladies, the officials, even the headsman - were rendered speechless and immobile by the pathetic scene before them. Finally, a compassionate onlooker climbed up the scaffold to end her agony. Taking hold of her arms, he gently guided the girl forwards. With one blow the executioner did his work cleanly and quickly as Jane had begged him to.

Figure 21 The execution of Lady Jane Grey by Jan Luyken, 1698
The Rijksmuseum, Amsterdam

Chapter 32
The Marriage With Spain

THE WYATT Rebellion brought to the forefront a far more dangerous threat to Mary I than the Lady Jane Grey – the Lady Elizabeth. The people had not taken to Jane, a mere cousin of the Queen and one tied to the Dudleys, but Elizabeth was another matter altogether. She was half-sister to Mary, and until the Queen had a child, her heiress under the will of their late father Henry VIII.

By her place in the succession, Elizabeth was a natural focus of treason against Mary's authority, especially in her religion. Even with England preparing to embrace Rome again, Elizabeth still clung to her Protestant faith. When a requiem service, according to the ancient rites, was held at the Tower for Edward VI, the Princess failed to attend. She was also conspicuously absent from the royal pew at the Masses – up to 'six or seven every day' - celebrated at court throughout the summer. By her behaviour, Mary was convinced Elizabeth was setting herself up as the hope of the English Protestants.

Not wishing to provoke her sister, Elizabeth yielded, or at least pretended to. In early September, while the court was at Richmond, Elizabeth sought an audience with the Queen. Tearfully, she prostrated herself before Mary and begged her indulgence. Being brought up in another faith, she wept, she was ignorant of any other. Seeing how this displeased the Queen, Elizabeth asked to be granted instruction in the old religion. Mary, wholly convinced of Elizabeth's sincerity, was overjoyed. Raising her to her feet, she offered Elizabeth books and a priest to enlighten her.

Elizabeth was hardly an enthusiastic convert. At Mass, on the Feast of the Nativity of the Virgin Mary on 8 September, she made a nuisance of herself by loudly complaining of a stomach ache all the way to the chapel. Throughout the service, she wore a 'suffering air', moaned and groaned, and had the Queen's ladies rub her belly to relieve the pain. About a week later, Elizabeth did not even attend Mass at all to the vexation of the Queen. 'She has half-turned already', Mary complained, 'from the good road upon which she had begun to travel'. But by 21 September, Elizabeth was apparently back in her pew and making no more scenes as demonstrated by Mary's renewed affection for her. She gave Elizabeth a rosary carved from white coral and trimmed with gold, along with a brooch depicting the myth of the doomed lovers Pyramus and Thisbe. Perhaps there was significance in the Queen's choice of subject matter. According to legend, the young couple, defying their disapproving parents, fell in love only to meet an untimely and unhappy end. Was Mary discreetly warning Elizabeth of the dangers of challenging authority?

The Imperial ambassador did not share Mary's renewed confidence in her sister. Renard thought Elizabeth deceitful. The heretical young woman would engage in treason sooner or later, he thought. When the Queen allowed Elizabeth to leave court in December, Renard was delighted. Thinking herself unobserved, Elizabeth would surely conspire with her Protestant friends and incriminate herself, he believed. To lure Elizabeth into a false sense of security, Renard advised Mary to part on the best of terms with her sister. Elizabeth responded in kind, asking for 'copes, chasubles, and chalices' for her private chapel to demonstrate her continuing devotion to her new-found faith.

Elizabeth's return to Hatfield House was only temporary. Though she had lain low during Wyatt's uprising, Mary's government was convinced that Elizabeth was a co-conspirator, even though the captured rebels had refused to name her as an accessory. The Duke of Suffolk, executed shortly after his daughter Jane, had said nothing to implicate her either. Nevertheless, correspondence between Elizabeth and the Queen was found in the diplomatic pouch of the French ambassador. The Princess was known to be on friendly terms with Monsieur de Noailles, whose agenda was to undermine Imperial influence at the English court. Far worse, it was alleged that Elizabeth had corresponded with Wyatt, responding to his advice to remove herself from her house at Ashridge to the safety of her fortified castle at Donnington. To her enemies, Elizabeth's relocation was part of a plan to avoid capture as a hostage by the government, allowing her to give free aid to the rebels. Fortunately, Elizabeth had had the foresight to put nothing down in writing and replied verbally by messenger. She had neither endorsed the revolt nor had she denounced it. Instead, Elizabeth had merely told Wyatt that she would do what she saw fit. And so she waited – *video et taceo* - 'I see and I say nothing', as was to be her motto throughout her life.

Elizabeth's inactivity during the crisis failed to exonerate her in the eyes of the authorities. On 9 March 1554, the Council charged her with high treason and ordered her back to court. At the summons, Elizabeth pled illness, saying 'she much feared her weakness to be so great that she should not be able to travel and to endure the journey without peril of life'. Unconvinced, the Queen's Councillors sent the royal physicians to Ashridge to examine her. Contrary to their suspicions - and those of the Spanish ambassador, who believing the worst of the Princess, were convinced she was secretly pregnant! - Elizabeth was indeed unwell. She was bedridden with no strength left to her, and an inflammation had bloated her face and arms severely. It was indeed a 'sad sight to see', the doctors reported to the Council, but nonetheless, the Princess' symptoms would not prevent her from travelling to London, they concurred.

The sights and stenches of the city did nothing to improve Elizabeth's health. From her travelling sickbed, everywhere she looked were the rotting remains of Wyatt's supporters scattered throughout the capital. Beneath the gibbets, the citizens stood along the route to catch a glimpse of the Princess. Using her infirmity to her advantage, Elizabeth swept aside the curtains of her litter so that all might see her. Looking weak and pitiful, she played on the sympathies of the crowd. Renard, ever her enemy, thought her expression proud and disdainful as she was carried to Whitehall. At her coming, Elizabeth received word that the Queen would not see her, and she was told to make her way into the palace through a back gate in the garden. Once inside, Elizabeth found herself under house arrest.

While Elizabeth remained in isolation, the government worked on incriminating her through Wyatt. Under interrogation, Wyatt admitted sending a message to Elizabeth telling her to leave Ashridge for Donnington Castle. However, on further examination of witnesses, it could not be proved that Elizabeth had entered into any intrigue with him. Even at his trial, the rebel leader repeated his earlier confession. Yes, he had contacted Elizabeth, but no, she had never written back to him.

Wyatt's testimony did nothing for Elizabeth. On 16 March, she was told to prepare for the Tower of London. That evening she was given a taste of her coming ordeal. Many of her servants were dismissed and replaced by those chosen by the Queen, and the grounds below her chamber were guarded by soldiers keeping watch throughout the night. In the morning, the Marquis of Winchester and the Earl of Sussex came to take her into custody. Desperate, Elizabeth implored the lords for permission to see her sister. If she could only plead her case in person, perhaps her sister would change her mind. Winchester and Sussex refused. Queen Mary was implacable and would not receive her. Unable to move them, Elizabeth played for time. She begged the two noblemen for permission to write to the Queen before they set out.

As the lords waited, Elizabeth grabbed pen and paper to fight for her very life. In her fine Italic hand, she began her letter by reminding the Queen of their last meeting in December. At their parting, Elizabeth had asked her sister 'not to believe anyone who spread evil reports of her without doing her the honour to let her know, and give her a chance of proving the false and malicious nature of such slanders'. Mary had agreed, and now Elizabeth begged her to fulfil her vow, for the 'word of a king' was far greater than any man's oath. Surely, she would not condemn her sister 'without answer and due proof' as she had promised. Her arrest and committal to the Tower - 'a place more wonted for a false traitor than a true subject' - was the work of those in the Council set against her. It was such men, who in their brother's reign, had conspired to discredit Thomas Seymour. 'I have heard in my time', Elizabeth continued, 'of many men cast away for wont of coming to the presence of their Prince'. Seymour would not have died, she was certain, if he had been allowed to see his brother, the Lord Protector. But lest she offend the Queen by comparing her to Edward Seymour, who was but a Duke - and later a condemned traitor himself as well - Elizabeth tactfully added that 'these persons are not to be compared to your Majesty'.

Concerning Thomas Wyatt, he might have indeed written to her, but Elizabeth swore she had received nothing from him. And as for a letter found in the French ambassador's possession supposedly linking her to the rebel, she denied any knowledge of it. 'I pray God confound me eternally', Elizabeth assured Mary, 'if ever I sent him word, message, token or letter by any means. And to this truth I will stand to my death'.

Though Sussex had promised to deliver the letter personally to the Queen and await her answer, Elizabeth feared it might be tampered with afterwards. Having set down all she could to defend herself, there remained an empty three-quarters of the second page on which incriminating words could be added in imitation of her handwriting. Taking no chances, Elizabeth drew a series of diagonal lines across the blank space. Before sealing the letter, she signed her name, declaring herself 'your Highness' most faithful subject that hath been from the beginning and will to my end'.

As the Marquis of Winchester had expected, the appeal did Elizabeth no good. Far from winning the Queen's sympathy, it made her furious. An angry Mary scolded Sussex. How could he let himself be beguiled by her sister? Thanks to him, they had missed the outgoing tide and the departure would have to wait till morning. An evening voyage was out of the question as the Princess's supporters might be emboldened to attempt a rescue under the cover of darkness. Before dismissing the chastened Earl, Mary raged at how her authority was so little respected and obeyed. Would to God, she said, that Henry VIII was alive again - if only for a month. Her father would know how to deal with such ineptitude!

The next day, 17 March, there was to be no more delay. At 10 o'clock in the morning, Elizabeth and a handful of her servants were led towards the riverbank to a waiting barge. As she was hurried along, Elizabeth might have looked towards the Queen's apartments on the chance that Mary might be watching from her window. If she were, she could attempt a direct appeal. But it was a vain hope; there was no sight of Mary at all. Most likely, the Queen was busy preparing for the observance of Palm Sunday. The old ritual of the carrying of palms had been revived, and all citizens were ordered to keep to their churches so that the Princess 'might be conveyed without clamour or commiseration to her prison'.

Elizabeth went meekly to the Tower, but on her arrival, she loudly proclaimed her innocence to the benefit of the onlookers. "I come in no traitor", she cried, "but as true a woman to the Queen's Majesty as any is now living, and thereon will I take my death"! Elizabeth was brought in by the Byward Tower drawbridge and conducted to the royal lodgings. It was the same path Anne Boleyn had taken on her way to judgement and death. All her life, Elizabeth had identified herself with her father. Now it seemed she was more appropriately her mother's daughter. Certain she would share her fate, Elizabeth petitioned the Queen to provide her with an executioner proficient with a sword. She would die with grace as her mother did.

Happily, there was no need to send for a French swordsman. It was to Mary's credit that despite the animosity she bore her sister, she proceeded no more against Elizabeth than the law would allow. There was no tainted evidence to entrap her, not even an Act of Attainder to condemn her without trial. In fact, such legislation was so repugnant to the Queen that she had all previous criminal convictions acquired by such means overturned. That being said, the authorities were forced to deal with Elizabeth by fair means. Scared as she was, she rose to the challenge. Under interrogation, she would admit to nothing, and even when cornered, she managed to cover her tracks. Donnington Castle, which was the government's trump card in linking Elizabeth to the rebels, was badly played when Elizabeth was able to convince her interrogators that her intention to move there was entirely innocent. They dropped the subject, and even apologised for troubling her on 'so vain matters'. Except for the Lord Chancellor, who was bent on destroying her, no one was willing to push Elizabeth too far. With the Queen still unmarried and childless, she was still heiress to the throne. Should Elizabeth come to power, she would remember those who were unkind to her.

Elizabeth was also popular, more so than her sister. Not only did men speak well of the Princess, but apparently Heaven did too. At Aldersgate, hundreds had gathered at a wall to hear an angel - or perhaps the Holy Ghost itself – extol her. Whenever a bystander called out, "God save Queen Mary"! there was silence. But when one cried, "God save the Lady Elizabeth"! a voice from the wall answered with an approving, "So be it"! It was only later that the oracle was found to be a fraud. The messages were transmitted through a specially made 'whistle' (a pipe that is) by a young woman hiding nearby. Despite the deception, the people did not waver in their love for the Princess. They were glad when, on 11 April, Thomas Wyatt publicly exonerated her and the Earl of Devon before his execution. He declared that it was 'most true' that neither one of them were privy to his 'rising or commotion'.

Unable to accuse them of anything, Mary was forced to release Courtney and Elizabeth. The Earl was allowed to go into exile abroad while Elizabeth was discharged from the Tower on 19 May 1554, the anniversary of her mother's execution. But she was not completely in the clear. Until she confessed, she would remain a prisoner at the Palace of Woodstock.

≡

With Elizabeth out of sight, Mary awaited Philip's arrival. He was supposed to arrive in June, but there was still no sign of him as July approached. The weeks dragged on as if he would never come at all. In the house she had prepared for the Prince near Southampton, the servants grumbled at having nothing to do, and then had more cause to complain when they were dismissed having no master to wait on. Mary's longing for her fiancé was evident when the jovial Lord William Howard noticed the Queen's melancholy one day. Howard said he knew what would cheer her up – the Prince of Spain sitting in the empty chair next to her. Mary could not help but smile and blush. She even found herself laughing aloud.

In the meantime, until her fiancé arrived, Mary took pleasure in the betrothal gifts sent to her. The Emperor forwarded a large table-cut diamond, while Philip, not to be outdone, presented his future bride with an assortment of magnificent jewels. There were chests full of bracelets, rings, pins, pendants, and the like, all of the finest goldsmiths' work, and adorned with brilliant stones – rubies and sapphires from the East, and emeralds of the deepest green, unlike any ever seen before, from the New World. Three pieces were especially noteworthy - a diamond, 'longer and thicker' than the one the Emperor gave her, 'mounted as a rose in a superb gold setting;' a necklace set with eighteen diamonds; and a 'great diamond with a fine large pearl pendant from it' described as 'the most lovely pair of gems ever seen in the world'. Mary was particularly fond of the third piece, and she wore it constantly as a brooch - a symbol of her ties, both political and romantic, to the Hapsburgs.

Finally, after months of delay, Philip and his fleet of ships coming from A Coruña were seen off the English coast on 19 July. The English lords who met Philip on-board found their new King to be nothing like the fiend Wyatt and his supporters had made him out to be. On the contrary, Philip was affable, gracious, and courteous. He made every effort to win over his new subjects, even ordering his entourage to learn and adopt English customs. At a reception in his honour, the Prince, with an air of informality about him, mingled and chatted - through an interpreter of course - with his hosts. To their amusement, Philip even took a swig of English beer. The Emperor was most pleased by the reports of his son's conduct. Prior to his departure, Charles had been so worried that he would make a mess of things that he had the Prince's travelling companion, the experienced Duke of Alva, see to it that Philip behaved himself. 'For otherwise', the Emperor wrote, 'I tell you I would rather never have taken the matter in hand at all'.

Being 'so obedient a son', Philip was determined to do his duty. Life in dreary England, away from the glorious sunshine of Spain, and with a woman considerably older than himself was not what he would have preferred, but 'in a matter of such high import', he put himself entirely at the service of his father and his God. In marrying Mary, he would help return her realm to the true Church and, at the same time, extend Hapsburg interests abroad. With these purposes in mind, Philip set out to meet his cousin at Winchester. The gathering storm clouds did not deter him. Even when the skies opened up releasing a torrential downpour, Philip, soaked to the skin, pressed on. Trudging through the rain, and through mudslides and flooded roads, he and his entourage finally came in sight of the great vault of the city's cathedral in the early evening of 23 July. When a *Te Deum* was sung in celebration of his arrival, Philip offered up his thanks - his gratitude for a safe sea voyage, and for being out of the miserable English weather at last.

Mary, who had already arrived in Winchester, was so excited to see her fiancé that she insisted on meeting him that very night. After he had rested, Philip was taken to the Bishop's lodgings at 10 o'clock that night. To the English onlookers, the couple's first encounter could not have gone better. Mary greeted her sweetheart with the exuberance of a schoolgirl. Just before the Prince's coming, she had been nervously pacing the length of the gallery. At the very sight of him, she could not contain herself. She rushed up to Philip, and 'very lovingly… and most joyfully received him'. The two then sat and conversed, probably in Latin and some Spanish (Mary's understanding of the latter was said to be limited). Their conversation lasted no more than half an hour, as the Queen took into consideration Philip's long journey and the lateness of the hour. Before, he retired, she taught him to say 'good night' in English. The Prince had trouble remembering the words, and with his heavy Spanish accent, he ended up saying something like 'God ni hit' instead. Still, the English were delighted and impressed.

But the same could not be said of Philip. Behind closed doors, he regretted what he had gotten himself into. The Queen of England was so unlike his late wife, the young and pretty Maria of Portugal. Philip had, of course, been well aware of Mary's age beforehand, but she looked far older than what he had expected. Her portrait painters, he complained, had overly flattered her. 'She is not at all handsome', one of the Spanish courtiers agreed, 'being of short stature and rather thin than fat'. Her complexion was overly 'red and white', and the lightness of her eyebrows made it look like she had none at all. Furthermore, the clothes she wore - of the English style - were unflattering to her. The only kind thing that could be said about Mary was that she was a most devout lady; even 'a perfect saint'.

His private feelings aside, Philip's outward demeanour was impeccable. At his formal reception the next day, he was the charming and loving

Prince Mary had longed for. Again, he and the Queen were found sitting together, talking pleasantly 'and each of them merrily smiling on [each] other, to the great comfort and rejoicing of the beholders'.

While his companions snickered how it would 'take God Himself to drink of such a cup' like the Queen, Philip summoned the courage to do just that. On 25 July at Winchester Cathedral, he was made a married man. The sanctity of the occasion was impressed upon the witnesses by the bride's great piety. Throughout the ceremony, her attention was fixed, not on her handsome groom, but on the Holy Sacrament before them. Not only was she commendable in her devoutness to God, but also in the simplicity of her joy as a bride. Eschewing her usual love of display, Mary had asked for a 'plain hoop of gold without any stone in it' for her wedding band 'because maidens were so married in old times'.

Ignoring his wife's lack of 'fleshly sensuality' as best he could, King Philip, as he was now styled in England, did his duty where it mattered most. That autumn, an elated Mary announced her pregnancy. Her joy was made even greater when in November, Reginald Pole returned to England to be its new Archbishop of Canterbury. Since they had last laid eyes on each other some twenty years previously, both Queen and Cardinal had known much suffering. But at their reunion, neither of them dwelt on the past. Instead, Pole joyfully greeted his cousin, hailing her by her namesake the Mother of God. The analogy could not have been more obvious. The child in Mary's womb would be a son and another saviour, rescuing England from heresy as the Queen herself was intent on doing.

The groundwork for Mary's reconciliation was laid on 28 November. Both Mary and Philip attended a momentous session of Parliament where schismatic England was received back into the 'unity of Our Mother the Holy Church'. Presided over by Pole, the Lords and Commons knelt together in penitence to receive the Cardinal's absolution. But the return to Rome was not achieved without compromise. To get the owners of confiscated Church lands to acquiesce, it was agreed that they would not have to surrender their properties once the reunion was in effect. Both Mary and Pole had opposed such a concession, but in the end, the secularised lands had to be given up to obtain Parliament's submission. With her kingdom lifted from sin at last, Mary wept tears of joy. Now, there was only the impending birth of her child to complete her triumph.

Chapter 33
Bloody Mary

IN THE spring of 1555, the country held its breath, awaiting news of the Queen's delivery. There was no doubt that it would be a prince, as God, so favourable to Mary, could not do otherwise but provide England with a future king. Already, the peers and peeresses of the realm were gathering at Hampton Court for the birth and for the christening to follow. An unexpected invitee was the Lady Elizabeth. After ten months at Woodstock, she was finally permitted to see the Queen. After so long, there was no justification for keeping her in detention. If Elizabeth could not be put under house arrest, she ought to at least be at court where she could be closely monitored. The request was not made by Mary - she wanted nothing to do with her sister - but by her new husband. It was not so much as to keep her out of trouble, but that Philip was most intrigued by this remarkable young lady of whom he had already heard so much.

Mary's lingering distaste for her sister was emphasised by the welcome - or rather lack of one - Elizabeth received at Hampton Court. 'The doors were shut to her', and she was obliged to enter 'on the back side' and without fanfare. After settling into her apartments, Elizabeth waited for the Queen's summons. The days became a week, then two, and still there was no word. Mary, it appeared, would not see her after all. Instead, she sent Bishop Gardiner and a handful of Councillors to harass the Princess as before. If she would finally admit her treason, they told Elizabeth, Mary would forgive all and grant her favour. As expected, Elizabeth maintained her position. She had had no dealings with Wyatt, she answered, and she would stand by that truth even if she were imprisoned again for the remainder of her life.

At last, at 10 o'clock one evening, Elizabeth was summoned to the royal apartments. As much as she had longed for this meeting, Elizabeth feared the worst. She told her servants that 'she could not tell whether ever she would see them again or no'. In Mary's chamber, Elizabeth came face to face with the sister she had not seen for more than a year. Her attention was undoubtedly drawn to the Queen's swollen belly. So this was the child who was the hope of Catholic England, Elizabeth might have thought to herself, the one who would

Figure 22   Medal of Philip II by Jacopo Nizolla da Trezzo
The National Gallery of Art, Washington D.C.

displace her in the succession. Once the infant was born, what would
they do with her?

Mary offered Elizabeth no greeting but sat in stony silence, her
eyes ablaze. Taking the initiative, Elizabeth prostrated herself, telling
the Queen she would find her 'a true subject as any', despite any
contrary reports she might have heard. When Mary spoke at last, she
came directly to the point. "You will not confess your offence, but
stand stoutly to your truth", she said sharply. She then demanded
to know if her sister thought she had been wrongfully punished and
would say this to others. Prudently, Elizabeth made no criticism. She
had 'borne the burden, and must bear it', and she implored Mary to
'have a good opinion of her… as long as life lasteth'. The reunion
was as uncomfortable for Mary as it was for Elizabeth. Getting no

further with the young woman than Gardiner had, the Queen finally dismissed her sister with 'very few comfortable words'. What else she had to say - and not meant for Elizabeth's ears - Mary vented in Spanish under her breath.

The sisters' battle of wills had ended in stalemate, but the Queen was setting her sights on a greater victory - the birth of her heir. In the third week of April, Mary took to her chamber. She was so certain it would be a son that announcements 'to signify the happy deliverance of a prince' were prepared in advance. On 30 April, news reached the city that the Queen was delivered of a fine baby boy. London exploded with joy. Not since the birth of King Edward, almost twenty years before, had there been a prince in England. However, the merrymaking came to a stop when officials confirmed the news to be false. Bells ceased tolling, banqueting tables were put away, and the people went home.

Despite assurances that all was still going well, the whole kingdom continued to wait - and wait. By the calculations of the physicians and midwives, Mary's child should have been born within a few short weeks of her confinement, but still, the 'sumptuously and gorgeously trimmed' cradle lay empty. In response, the delivery date was pushed further ahead. The baby was not expected until sometime in June, it was now said. Disappointed, but still convinced she was carrying Philip's son, Mary left her confinement chamber around the third week of May. A Spaniard who saw her in public at this time remarked how the Queen walked with such vigour that an imminent birth seemed highly improbable. Was he right?

Mary soon took to her chamber again, but as before, she had no labour pains. Even the very signs that she was pregnant began to wane. Her belly shrank and her breasts stopped producing milk. Often, Mary was seen sitting on the floor in a daze with her knees drawn up to her chin; a position that ought to have been difficult and painful for a woman in her condition. Apparently, it was all a false pregnancy, brought on most likely by Mary's overwhelming desire to have a child. By the end of July, the pretence could no longer be maintained. To spare the Queen any more humiliation, there was no announcement. But as she packed up and moved to Oatlands Palace on 3 August, it was clear that there was no child to be had.

Denied motherhood, Mary was soon dealt another blow. News had come from Brussels that the Emperor, in consideration of his advancing years and his declining health, was abdicating his powers.

His possessions in Germany would go to his brother Ferdinand, King of Hungary and Bohemia, while Spain and the Low Countries would be passed onto Philip. With his aunt, Mary of Hungary, stepping down as Regent of the Netherlands, it was necessary for Philip to assume the rule of his new territories there immediately. With the tidings coming so shortly after her ordeal, Mary was shattered. She had come to love and depend on the King immensely. She was also confident that if Philip were allowed to remain with her, given time, she would make up for her phantom pregnancy.

But the new King of Spain was impatient to leave. His father's abdication could not have come at a better time. His year in England had been nothing but frustration. As King Consort, he was allowed no say in government, in accordance with his marriage contract, and his hopes of remedying the situation were met with fierce opposition by the English lords. Married life with Mary Tudor was another cause of tension. While he was always careful to treat his wife with kindness and affection, privately, Philip continued to find her unappealing. The Queen was nothing but a clinging, lovesick woman, and likely a barren one at that.

Having done his conjugal duties as best he could, Philip's new obligations beckoned him from across the sea. His men were as eager to leave as he was. Several of his courtiers had already returned home, and those who did not, were begging permission to do likewise. Since their arrival, the Spaniards had regretted ever stepping foot in England. Though they liked the beauty of the country well enough, and were most impressed by London - 'a capital of magnificent things, grand buildings, and noteworthy achievements of industry' - they found its inhabitants 'the worst in the world'. Englishmen were quarrelsome in nature, barbaric in custom, and heretical in opinion. They 'disobey God, disregard the saints, and think nothing of the Pope', a Spanish courtier wrote. They were also highly xenophobic, hating all foreigners 'worse than they hate the Devil'. They openly mocked the Spaniards when they saw them in the streets, and they grossly overcharged them at their taverns, inns, and shops. Few of his companions dared to travel at night, the courtier continued, lest thugs rob them. Even being about the city in the daytime was unsafe. The Englishmen were always looking to pick a fight. Already, a few Londoners - and unfortunately a bunch of his own countrymen - were hanged for public brawling, the Spaniard reported.

As for the womenfolk, they were no better in his opinion. Like Queen Mary, the ladies at her court were 'not at all handsome', had no dress sense, and were ungraceful. Their idea of dancing, the Spaniard laughed, consisted of clumsily 'strutting and trotting about'. Worse was their immodesty. When greeting someone, even of the opposite sex, they kissed on the mouth – a practice Continentals found vulgar. As well, when English ladies went walking or riding, or even when they were seated, they exposed their legs as their skirts were too short. 'Not a single Spanish gentleman is in love with them', the courtier added, which was really to their own benefit, as they would not be obliged to spend money on them.

Philip, no more in love with his wife than his countrymen were with her ladies, prepared to set sail on 29 August. The only comfort he could offer Mary was his promise that once his affairs were settled, he would come back to her immediately. Consoled, Mary escorted Philip as far as Greenwich, where she bade him Godspeed till his return. Watching him go from the top of the staircase overlooking the Thames, she managed to avoid 'any demonstration unbecoming her gravity'. But overcome with emotion, Mary retired to the privacy of her room facing the river. Unseen by anyone, she broke down and wept.

In the following months, a stream of letters crossed the sea from England to the Low Countries. Almost every evening before bed, Mary sat at her desk and wrote page after page to Philip. But the King was not as prolific a writer as she was. Even a week of silence from him seemed an eternity to the Queen. Once, after seven days of receiving not a word from Brussels, Mary 'very passionately' wept and unburdened herself to the sympathetic ambassador of Venice, Giovanni Michiel. He became one of the few at court who knew that underneath the calm and dignified exterior Mary always affected in public, was immense suffering. The Queen, as Michiel knew, when 'supposing herself invisible to any of her attendants', cried inconsolably over Philip's absence. Desperate to see him, she even suggested to her husband, in a letter written at the end of September, that her ships escort the Emperor to his place of retirement in Spain. At the same time, she would make her way to the English coast to await Philip's return. But as usual, the King was evasive about his intentions, forcing Mary to abandon her plans.

By December, Mary had begun to lose patience. For every letter she wrote to Philip, there was usually no reply. When he did write, it was a litany of excuses regarding why he must stay put – he had to oversee the transfer of the Low Countries to him, tour his new dominions, meet his subjects, and at the same time, take on countless administrative duties. Mary tried to be understanding, but she was increasingly annoyed by rumours of her husband's extracurricular activities. She heard how instead of tending to his responsibilities, Philip was having the time of his life in Brussels and Antwerp. His waking hours were spent in continual rounds of parties, banquets, and balls, all lasting well into the night – and in the company of fair ladies. It was even said that he was two-timing his wife. Philip's alleged liaisons wounded Mary deeply, leaving her more heartbroken than ever. With Philip continuing to ignore her, and the tales of his love affairs circulating far and wide, Mary moved from tears to rage. She even became a subject of gossip herself. As it was told, exasperated by Philip, the Queen ordered his portrait to be taken down from the Council chamber. Not only that, she then gave the picture a good kick out of the door.

=

In addition to her husband's absence, Mary Tudor was troubled by the religious discord in her realm. Her reconciliation with Rome almost a year before had so far failed to instil absolute orthodoxy in the land. In fact, her Protestant subjects were growing even bolder. Not even the revived anti-heresy laws, for which punishment was a fiery death, could deter them. In London and other predominantly Protestant regions in the kingdom, many willingly went to the flames rather than acknowledge the pope and the 'filthiness and idolatry [that] is the Church of Rome'.

The first to die was John Rogers, Vicar of St Sepulchre's, in February 1555. Not the sight of his sorrowful wife and eleven children, or the promise of a royal pardon, could make Rogers recant. Instead, he went boldly to the stake at Smithfield and 'washed his hand in the flame, as if it had been in cold water' until the fire consumed the rest of him. Thomas Cranmer, who was burned at Oxford the following year, died likewise. In fear and hope of life, he had denounced all his achievements as Archbishop of Canterbury at first, but, at the eleventh hour, he recovered his courage. Cranmer retracted his recantation and was dragged to the stake. As the flames rose around him, Cranmer plunged his hand into the fire. With it, he had signed away his faith, he said, and therefore, it had to suffer first. The deaths of Rogers and Cranmer, and later of Bishop Latimer who exhorted his companion at the stake, Bishop Ridley, that their sacrifice would 'light such a candle, in England as... never be put out', edified the Protestants who stood witness. By the end of Mary's reign, close to three hundred people - men and women, young and old - were put to the fire; their bravery recorded by John Foxe in his *Acts and Monuments* – popularly known as *The Book of Martyrs*.

Mary cannot be excused for her part in the persecutions. While Philip, and even Gardiner, had advocated a more moderate approach, the Queen was implacable. Though she had winked at treason committed against her person when she could, she could not pardon the great sin of rebellion against the Church. Those guilty of heresy must be punished lest they 'deceive the simple', and contaminate the whole of England with their false doctrines. In a memorandum to her officers, the Queen ordered that 'good sermons' be preached at the burnings, and that none were to die 'without some of the Council's presence'. Their attendance would impress on the public her personal stamp of approval. But the executions did nothing but strengthen her enemies' resolve and lower her popularity. Mary's marriage with Spain was still begrudged by many, and her false pregnancy had made her a laughing stock. The harvests of the past two years had been poor, and her government's inability to deal with the widespread suffering led to even more resentment against the Queen.

But Mary was not without her defenders. Those closest to her, such as her devoted attendant, Jane Dormer, saw their mistress as a living saint. Far from being the Nero of the Protestants, she was the embodiment of goodness, as Jane would later recall. The Queen's devotion to God was exemplary, as was her love for her subjects. At Easter, for instance, when monarchs traditionally washed the feet of the poor in imitation of Christ on Maundy Thursday, no one did so with more humility than Mary. She even visited the needy in disguise and would personally dispense money and justice to them. As for her persecutions, Jane leapt to her mistress's defence:

> 'she caused no new laws to be made but only recalled such as were used and of force in God's Church since the Christian religion was established in England. And when in any did concur the faults of heresy and treason, or felony, her will was that the law should proceed, heresy being directly offensive and immediately against God.'

As Jane Dormer and her fellow Catholics saw it, Mary was only doing her duty as her royal predecessors had. But her Protestant subjects disagreed. In persecuting them, the Queen was a zealous tyrant, rightly earning herself the opprobrium 'Bloody Mary'. That firebrand of a preacher, John Knox went even further. Mary Tudor, he thundered from his pulpit, was a 'cruel monster' who had betrayed her kingdom to Spain, and by her 'bloody tyranny', a second Jezebel. When Mary's reign finally did come to an end, the chronicler Raphael Holinshed breathed a sigh of relief. 'God grant she be the last of her religion', he wrote.

As the burnings continued, Philip announced his return to England. He had promised to do so before, but this time, he intended to keep his word - he needed England's help. Philip was at war with France and with Pope Paul IV who was in alliance with its King, Henry of Valois. To win, it was necessary for Philip to bring his wife into the fray. Would she, he asked Mary, support him - even against the papacy itself? Mary, torn between her allegiance to Rome and her love for her husband, chose Philip. As Spain's ally and as a dutiful wife, she would commit her resources to his disposal. As Mary justified it, France was England's ancient enemy, and though she had no personal quarrel with the Pope, he had never been a friend to her cousin Reginald Pole, and was in fact, investigating her Archbishop for heresy. Even though she knew her Council would be against antagonising the French, Mary, desperate to please her husband, gave Philip her solemn promise that she would do everything in her power to sway her government to war.

The King's homecoming on 18 March 1557 was soured by the presence of his travelling companion. With him was his cousin, the lovely Duchess of Lorraine, a lady rumoured to be his mistress. The Duchess was no stranger to Mary. Better known as Christina of Denmark, she could have been her stepmother. In the years since she had turned down Henry VIII's proposal, Christina had not lost her famous beauty, and her attendance on Philip made Mary uneasy. But overjoyed to see her husband again, the Queen swallowed her pride and showed nothing of her jealousy. She treated Christina with the utmost courtesy and even set her up at court.

Not only did Mary have to put up with Christina's unwelcome presence, but she also had to deal with her unruly Council. Its members were strongly opposed to meddling in King Philip's war.

As her advisers reminded Mary, a clause in the marriage contract prohibited her country's involvement in Imperial conflicts. It explicitly stated that England 'shall not directly or indirectly be entangled with the war that now is betwixt the victorious lord the Emperor… and Henry the French King'. Philip, the terms continued, was required to see that England and France remained at peace.

Determined to keep her promise to Philip, lest he leave her again and never come back, Mary fought with her advisers. She reminded them about England's obligations to Philip as its King, and of the risk of a France left unchecked. When persuasion failed, Mary took to threats, accusing her Councillors of disloyalty. A godsend came her way when Thomas Stafford, an old supporter of Thomas Wyatt, and, ironically, a nephew of Reginald Pole, took up arms against the government. On 23 April 1557, he and a ragtag band of followers seized a castle in Scarborough in Yorkshire. Stafford then publicly accused Mary of being an 'unrightful and most unworthy Queen' who had delivered the nation into Spanish hands. He absolved all Englishman of their allegiance to her and declared himself Protector and Governor of the realm. Apparently, Stafford was even bold enough to proclaim himself King. His 'rule' lasted only days when he and his men were swiftly put down. According to English intelligence, Stafford had received 'armour, money, munition, and ships' from France. True or not, the madcap rebel gave Mary the justification she needed for war.

With hostilities formally declared on 7 June, Philip got what he came for, and he announced he would be leaving on campaign before the month was out. Mary was crushed, but, at the same time, she was optimistic that Philip's absence would not be as prolonged as before. Since he depended on England's help against the French, Mary reasoned that she would have some clout in demanding his return if he stayed away too long. More importantly, during Philip's homecoming, he had re assumed the bedroom duties of a husband. It was Mary's hope that she would truly be pregnant this time around.

At the end of June, Philip prepared for Brussels. Unlike his last leave-taking when Mary had contented herself with watching him go from Greenwich, she now insisted on accompanying him as far as she was able. In what were to be the last days of happiness she would know, the Queen rode to Dover with Philip, wishing him success. She ensured him of her and her country's unwavering support, and of the happy times to come. When the couple parted at last on 6 July, there were no reports of Mary's anguish as before. As Philip sailed out across the Channel, she was certain she would see him soon enough. Perhaps, Mary even imagined herself welcoming him home with their son in her arms.

=

Alone once again, the Queen looked to the faithful Reginald Pole for comfort. Philip himself would have approved of the Archbishop's attendance upon her. When he had left England before in 1555, the King had especially sought out his wife's cousin and appointed him to head her government. Leaving his episcopal palace at Lambeth, Pole took rooms at court to be near the Queen, offering her advice and solace until Philip returned. With the King now gone again, Pole resumed his duties, with Mary 'delighting greatly in the sight and presence of him'.

The same could not be said of her sister. Elizabeth was allowed to retire to her house at Hatfield, and when she did come to court, Mary had to make an almost superhuman effort to conceal the 'hatred and anger' she bore her. According to the Venetian ambassador, the Queen

> 'endeavours when they are together in public to receive her with every sort of graciousness and honour, nor does she ever converse with her about any but agreeable subjects.'

But he was not fooled. Mary, Michiel knew, had never forgotten the humiliations she had suffered under Anne Boleyn. When Anne had fallen, Mary's loathing for her stepmother was transferred to her child. Elizabeth may have glorified in being the daughter of Henry VIII, and thus her sister's equal, but to Mary, she was nothing more than the 'illegitimate child of a criminal who was punished as a public strumpet'.

But that is not say there weren't moments of closeness. As a toddler, Elizabeth had been such a precocious little thing that even Mary had taken to her. She had found herself writing to their father commending Elizabeth as 'such a child toward' that the King 'shall have cause to rejoice in time coming'. But as Elizabeth had grown older, it was Mary's belief that the apple had not fallen far from the tree. She had said nothing of Elizabeth's part in the Thomas Seymour affair, but the fact that her younger sister had opened herself to such a scandal would not have endeared her to Mary, who possessed an unblemished reputation throughout her life. Likely, she did not see

Elizabeth as entirely blameless, and she probably imagined how the sins of the mother were now visited on the daughter.

As time went on, not only was Elizabeth lacking in morals, she was also a traitor and a heretic. Mary still believed her sister had been in league with Wyatt, and she was never sure about the sincerity of her devotion to the old faith. So intense was her dislike of Elizabeth at times that the Queen even harboured a fantasy that she was no sister of hers, being the daughter of Anne Boleyn's 'lover' Mark Smeaton. Mary swore Elizabeth resembled him.

That Elizabeth was well received by her husband Philip was further cause for bitterness. Mary could well have thought that her sister was out to charm Philip from the start. While Elizabeth had no romantic inclinations towards her brother-in-law, she was, however, interested in cultivating a friendship with him to ensure her survival. Her instinct paid off. Philip liked her well enough, admiring Elizabeth for her youth, good looks, and intelligence. He also recognised her political worth. Until his wife conceived, Elizabeth was heiress to the throne. But should she come to harm, many might turn to her cousin Mary Queen of Scots. While Mary Stuart's Catholic credentials were commendable, her ties to France were not. By birth, the young Queen of Scotland was already half-French, and now at fourteen, she was living at Henry II's court betrothed to his son, the Dauphin Francis. In time, she would be Queen of France as well, and possibly Queen of England too after Mary and Elizabeth Tudor. In considering the options, a Protestant Elizabeth as Queen was preferable to Philip, over a Catholic – but pro-French - Mary Stuart wearing the multiple crowns of Scotland, France, England, and Ireland.

With Elizabeth as an asset against the French, Philip appointed himself as her protector to his wife's chagrin. 'No one favoured her more than he does', according to Michiel. It was said that at Philip's insistence, the Queen was dissuaded from disinheriting Elizabeth by Act of Parliament. The King also intervened on her behalf when one Christopher Ashton and his friends had dabbled in treason the year before. The government was intent on implicating Elizabeth in their plot until Philip personally stepped in. He defended her once more when her name was linked to the traitor Thomas Stafford. So valuable was Elizabeth to Philip, that he was even willing to consider her as an addition to his family. It was Renard's advice to the King during his brief return to England that Elizabeth should wed his cousin Emmanuel Philibert, Duke of Savoy. Philibert was a man 'true to God and Your Majesty', Renard noted, and should Elizabeth become Queen, England would again be under Hapsburg influence. Philip agreed.

Mary, however, did not approve. Despite the considerable pressure Philip put on her by his letters to get Elizabeth's consent, she could not bring herself to encourage such a match. Her hatred for her sister proved stronger than her obedience to her husband. To Mary, the Savoy marriage was a personal affront. To see her illegitimate, heretical, and treacherous sister given such an honour was more than she could bear. But even if Mary had been keen on the idea, Elizabeth, who had already turned down a proposal from Prince Eric of Sweden, wanted nothing to do with the Duke. The Savoy matter was to drag on into the following year, and all a harried Mary could do was to write to Philip, asking him, 'in all humility to put off the business until your return'. She also begged him not to be cross with her, for 'that will be worse than death for me, for I have already begun to taste your anger all too often, to my great sorrow'.

As Christmas neared, Mary was certain her husband's irritation with her would soon be smoothed over. She had good news for Philip – she was pregnant. Mary may have known since autumn, when she thought herself experiencing symptoms, but she waited until she was certain before announcing it. The baby, she wrote exuberantly to Philip, was expected in March. By that time, the King would be done on campaign and be able to return to his wife and his child.

But the happy tidings were to be overshadowed by events in France. Philip had won a great victory at Saint-Quentin in August, but he was unable to prevent the devastating loss of Calais. On 7 January 1558, the town, the last of England's possessions on the Continent, was taken by the French. The defeat was deeply felt by all Englishmen, and it hit Mary extremely hard. Not since the disastrous reign of Henry VI had England allowed its territories to be conquered. The humiliation haunted her until her dying day. On her deathbed, Mary would lament how after she was dead and cut open, Calais would be found lying in her heart.

Despite the loss, Mary continued to style herself by her ancient title of Queen of France when she made her will in March. In preparation for the impending childbirth, the Queen, mindful 'of the great danger which by God's ordinance remain to all women in their travail of children', decided to set her affairs in order. Upon her death, her soul was to be commended to the company of Heaven, while her earthly goods were to be generously distributed. Her greatest possessions – the 'Imperial Crown of England, and the Crown of Ireland, and [her] title to France' with all their 'honours, castles, fortresses, manors, lands, tenements, prerogatives, and hereditaments' were to be left to her soon-to-be-born heir.

But when the will was made, it was already the end of March. Mary was still convinced she was pregnant, though no one else was, including Philip. To him, it was déjà-vu. For the next seven months, Mary stubbornly clung to her delusion until even she found it impossible to. On 28 October, weary and defeated, she added a postscript to her will ending all her hopes. Seeing that God had 'hitherto sent me no fruit nor heir to my body', she entrusted the Crown to 'my *next heir and successor* by the laws and statutes of this realm'. Hating her still, she would not do Elizabeth the courtesy of acknowledging her by name.

By this time, Mary was mortally ill as she admitted in her codicil. 'Sick and weak in body', the Queen sank into a decline at St James' Palace in November. Her cousin, Archbishop Pole, was dying too, along with their dream of an England permanently restored to the Catholic Church. From Hatfield, Elizabeth had expressed her willingness to maintain the Catholic faith as her successor, but as Mary might have suspected, she had no intention of doing so.

Abandoned by her husband and vilified by her people, Mary looked to be called 'out of this transitory life'. From her bed, she spoke of angelic children appearing before her, singing 'pleasing notes, giving her more than earthly comfort'. Having had so little happiness in her life, it was a dream Mary eagerly slipped into.

With her sister on her deathbed, Elizabeth and her supporters were discretely preparing for the change in regime. She had already received the support of the local gentry, and even the congratulations of Count de Feria, the new Spanish ambassador, who was anxious to maintain her friendship. Now there was only the waiting.

According to tradition, the suspense ended on 17 November 1558 beneath an oak tree at Hatfield. Elizabeth had stopped beneath it when she caught sight of a delegation of lords galloping across the fields from the direction of the capital. Her heart raced - at last, at last! Approaching the Princess, they dismounted,

Figure 23   Henry VIII and his Successors Edward VI, Mary I, and Elizabeth I by Hendrick Goltzius
The Rijksmuseum, Amsterdam

doffed their caps, and knelt. With one voice they cried out, "The Queen is dead! Long live the Queen"!

Prepared as she was for the news, Elizabeth was overwhelmed nonetheless. Falling to her knees, she exclaimed with both awe and joy, quoting from the Psalms, "This is the Lord's doing, and it is marvellous in our eyes"!

PART 10
THE MAIDEN QUEEN: ELIZABETH I

But sorrows, care, and cruel broils likewise
This sacred Queen Elizabeth exiled
Falsehood did fall before her gracious eyes
And persecution turned to mercy mild
Plenty and peace throughout her days are seen
And all the world admires this maiden Queen
(Verses from a picture celebrating the family of Henry VIII)

Figure 24   Elizabeth I by Nicholas Hilliard
The Rijksmuseum, Amsterdam

Chapter 34
The Husband This Woman May Take

THE TUDORS were great believers in astrology. Henry VII, concerned about the longevity of his new dynasty, had commissioned horoscopes of his family. In the next reign, Henry VIII, anxious for a son, also sought reassurance from those who read the heavens. Of his children, Edward VI readily acknowledged celestial phenomena as manifestations of the 'glory of God and His Power over the whole world', while Mary, in that same belief, heeded omens foretelling her brother's early demise. Elizabeth, no different from her predecessors, placed her trust in the stars as well. She left the date of her coronation to the mystic Doctor John Dee. Based on the Queen's nativity, Dee chose 15 January 1559 as the most auspicious day.

In preparation, Elizabeth arrived at the Tower of London a few days earlier. She 'was seen but by very few persons', but on 14 January, thousands came to pay her tribute. Happily, the 'foul weather' of late had abated, and there was only a light snowfall as the parade of knights, nobles, clergy, and the rest of the Queen's entourage emerged from the great fortress. Behind the wooden barricades, the citizens stood deep in slush to catch a glimpse of the new mistress of England. She did not appear until near the tail end of the procession, but she was well worth the wait. Seated in a litter covered in brocade, Elizabeth was dressed in white cloth of gold, and on her head was a jewelled crown. With her slender build, reddish hair, pale skin, and aquiline features, she was a striking and majestic figure.

Elizabeth's deportment was in marked contrast to her sister's. Unlike Queen Mary, who had ridden to Westminster looking uncomfortable holding up her head, Elizabeth was completely at ease. Perhaps remembering Mary's dilemma with her heavy crown, she may have chosen a less cumbersome one to wear. Unhampered, Elizabeth made good use of her hands – much admired for their whiteness and elongation - holding them up to express her joy and thanks to the people.

While Il Schifanoya, a Venetian observer, may have censured Elizabeth for 'exceed[ing] the bounds of gravity and decorum', her

subjects were delighted by her openness. Whenever they called out
to her, wishing her well and asking God's blessing on her, she would
answer in kind. Elizabeth did not hold back her 'loving behaviour'.
Any time a citizen offered her a gift or made a private supplication
of her, the Queen had her litter stopped to thank or speak to the
individual. She also gave her complete attention to the various
pageants she came upon. At Fenchurch, she paused to hear the speech
of a child welcoming her, and she did likewise at a triumphal arch
depicting 'The Uniting of the Two Houses of Lancaster and York'. It
was of particular interest to Elizabeth as it set forth her right to the
Crown. At the bottom of the tableau were her grandparents Henry VII
and Elizabeth of York; in the centre, Henry VIII and 'the right worthy
Lady Queen Anne'; and at the top was a child dressed up as Elizabeth
herself. Because the arch was set far back and the noise great, the
Queen made a special request 'to have the matter opened unto her'.
She wanted 'to hear all that should be said unto her', at the same time
making certain that her subjects understood the significance of the
display as well.

The next pageant, 'The Seat of Worthy Governance', was an
allegory as to how Elizabeth should rule. A representation of her
was flanked by the figures of *Pure Religion*, *Love of Subjects*, *Wisdom*,
and *Justice*. Vanquished before them were their enemies: *Superstition*,
Rebellion and Insolence, *Folly and Vainglory*, and *Adulation and
Bribery*. It was explained to all that Elizabeth would rule long and
prosperously, 'so long as she embraced Virtue and held Vice underfoot'.

But was what was meant by 'Pure Religion', and what by
'Superstition'? Even with the death of Queen Mary, England was still
a Catholic country by law. Would Elizabeth continue to abide by the
religion of the State, or would she dissent in following her conscience?
Her inclination and what direction her government would take was
demonstrated at a subsequent pageant staged by the Little Conduit. It
consisted of two sections. On one side was 'A Decayed Commonwealth'
with a ragged figure weeping below a withered tree, and on the other
'A Flourishing Commonwealth' where a comely youth stood beneath
a tree 'very fresh' surrounded by blooming flowers. As Elizabeth and
the people watched, old *Father Time* emerged from a cave in the
middle. With him was his daughter *Truth* with the English Bible in
her hands. When it was presented to the Queen, she 'kissed it and
with both her hands held up the same, and so laid it on her breast,
and gave thanks to the city therefore'. Elizabeth's reverence for the

Bible in English, and her exclamation that she would read it 'most diligently', ended any ambiguity about her faith.

Elizabeth's Protestantism was further emphasised at a pageant on Fleet Street. Sitting on a great throne, and crowned and sceptred like the Queen herself would soon be was the Biblical Deborah, 'the judge and restorer of the House of Israel'. She was hailed as a 'worthy precedent' to Elizabeth for her victory over King Jabin of Hazor and his oppressing Canaanites. With Elizabeth compared to Deborah, needless to say, Jabin stood for the Pope, and the Canaanites the Catholic clergy.

Still, England's new Deborah was required to undergo the centuries-old coronation rituals as her ancestors had done on 15 January. There had been some difficulty in finding a clergyman willing to perform the actual coronation. The Archbishop of Canterbury, Reginald Pole was dead, and the highest churchman after him, the Archbishop of York, Nicholas Heath, declined. His conscience, he insisted, would not permit him to omit the Elevation of the Host, as Elizabeth demanded he must, at the coronation Mass. The Bishop of Carlisle, Owen Oglethorpe, had already been reprimanded for doing so before the Queen at Christmas. As nothing could persuade Heath to change his mind, a reluctant Oglethorpe was ordered to take his place.

In Westminster Abbey, Elizabeth was led up to a 'lofty tribune' set between the high altar and the choir. After she had been presented to the people at the four corners of the stage, Elizabeth descended and made her offering at the altar. She then prostrated herself on cushions to be prayed over and was subsequently anointed. Later, she was heard to complain that the holy oil, which her sister had taken pains to obtain from Flanders, was putrid. Enthroned, she then received the symbols of her authority - the sword, the spectre, and the orb. A great hush came over the abbey as the Bishop of Carlisle solemnly set three crowns– gold for England, silver for France, and iron for Ireland – each in turn on the Queen's head

At the ensuing Mass, the Bishop read out the Epistle and the Gospel in Latin, and then 'in the vulgar tongue' as he was ordered to. But when it came to the most solemn part of the service, Oglethorpe was as stubborn as he was at Christmas. To the Queen's annoyance, he would not perform the ceremony 'without elevating the Host or consecrating it'. All Elizabeth could do was to temporarily remove herself into a transverse by the side of the altar; an act of protest like the one she had been forced to make when Oglethorpe had disobeyed her before.

The day after the coronation had been set aside for tournaments in the new Queen's honour. But as 'Her Majesty [was] feeling rather tired', the celebrations had to be postponed. Exhausted by days of ceremony, Elizabeth withdrew herself from the public eye, preparing herself for what would certainly be a contentious Parliament.

=

In his observation of English affairs, Schifanoya was hopeful 'God of His goodness and mercy' would inspire the next Parliament 'to do what may be according to His holy will'. Being a Catholic, the Venetian, of course meant England's continuing adherence to the old faith. But Count de Feria, who had met with Elizabeth already and had got a taste of what to expect from her, was not optimistic. 'The kingdom', he lamented, 'is entirely in the hands of young folks, heretics, and traitors', and leading the pack was a 'young lass' 'without prudence'. But even de Feria had to admit that Elizabeth was clever, with a definite air of confidence and authority about her. 'She is incomparably more feared than her sister', the envoy warned King Philip, 'and gives her orders and has her way as absolutely as her father did'.

While the common folk were certain of better days ahead as demonstrated by their outpourings of joy at the coronation, those in the inner circles of government were as gloomy as the Spanish ambassador. England, as inherited by the young and inexperienced Elizabeth, was weak in 'strength, men, money, riches'. Sir Thomas Smith, who had served under Edward VI, agreed. 'Here was nothing but fining, heading, hanging, quartering and burning; taxing, levying, and pulling down of bulwarks at home, and beggaring, and losing our strongholds abroad', he observed with pessimism. Adding to the kingdom's woes were the French. England was still at with France, and with 'the realm exhausted' and lacking in 'good captain and soldiers', it was in no position to continue aggressions. Already, the French King was like a colossus casting his mighty shadow over the country, 'having one foot in Calais, and the other in Scotland'. What would prevent Henry II from also laying claim to poor England in between?

Mindful of the many problems before her, Elizabeth's first order of business had been to appoint her Council. At Hatfield, on the day after she had been acknowledged Queen, Elizabeth had gathered her sister's Councillors to her, along with a company of fresh faces. The make-up of the new Council, she announced, would include some who had advised Queen Mary, along with some new appointees of her own. To those she had to exclude, Elizabeth apologised. She meant no disrespect to their persons or to their abilities, but 'a multitude doth rather make discord and confusion than good counsel'.

The new government retained thirteen of Mary's advisers. Among them were the Archbishop of York, 'a man of great wisdom and modest disposition' whom Elizabeth had forgiven for refusing to crown her, and four Earls - Arundel, Shrewsbury, Derby, and Pembroke. Keeping his seat, as well, was the septuagenarian Marquis of Winchester who had once taken Elizabeth prisoner. She bore him no grudge whatsoever. For over thirty years – through changes in monarchs and in religion – William Paulet had served the Tudors faithfully. When the old man was asked how he had been able to survive the 'change and ruins of so many chancellors and great personages', Winchester replied, "I am made of pliable willow, not of stubborn oak".

To offset the conservative flavour of her Council, seven new members were added – all Protestants. The most prominent of them were the Queen's step-uncle, the Marquis of Northampton; the Earl of Bedford; Sir Francis Knollys, husband of the Queen's Boleyn cousin, Katherine Carey; Sir Nicholas Bacon, the new Lord Keeper of the Great Seal; and his brother-in-law, Sir William Cecil, whom the Queen favoured above them all. Educated at Cambridge and then at Gray's Inn as a lawyer, Cecil began his courtly career working for the Duke of Somerset, and he was later advanced to Secretary of State. Upon Edward VI's death, he had reluctantly declared for Lady Jane Grey but fortunately avoided her fate. Pardoned by Queen Mary, Cecil kept his religious opinions to himself, conforming to her faith. At the same time, he maintained his friendship with the Lady Elizabeth and acted as surveyor of her properties. Now, in recognition of his political acumen and of his reputation as 'an exceeding wise man and as good as many', Elizabeth appointed Cecil (whom she nicknamed her *Spirit*) to be her principal secretary. The Queen's special regard for Sir William was evident when she singled him out in a speech to her new band of Councillors:

'This judgement I have of you, that you will not be corrupted by any manner of gift, and that you will be faithful to the State. And that without respect of my private will, you will give me that counsel which you think best.'

In the years to come, through all the ups and downs, Cecil well earned that trust.

≡

The burning question put before the Lords and Commons of the Queen's first Parliament was the settlement of religion in the land. Elizabeth herself had already set her course. She aimed to restore her nation's independence from Rome and to re-assume the title of Supreme Head of the Church in England, which her sister had found so repugnant. In relinquishing that authority, Mary had diminished the prestige of the English Crown, and Elizabeth had no intention of following her example. She would also break her promise to her sister to maintain the *status quo*. While a dying Mary had hoped that Elizabeth would uphold the old faith, it was entirely unreasonable that she would. The Catholic Church had never recognised the marriage of her parents, nor her own legitimacy. Furthermore, having been brought up in the new religion, Elizabeth had even less reason to love Rome, and her sister's persecutions had only strengthened her resolve. Even now, the Pope had the audacity to declare that she was not the rightful Queen of England, but rather her cousin Mary Stuart - a faithful daughter of the Church.

Elizabeth's hostile relationship with Rome ought to have made her a fervid Protestant – in the mould of her brother Edward or her cousin Jane Grey – but it was not in her nature to embrace one extreme or the other. Elizabeth was a religious woman, but a moderate. Her relationship with her God was a private and personal one, and in that spirit, she recognised and respected the right of her Catholic subjects to believe as they would as well - so long as they remained loyal to the State. As Elizabeth would later sum up her beliefs, 'there was one Jesus Christ and one faith, and all the rest they disputed about but trifles'. However, with England having been tossed and turned by upheavals in religion in the last three reigns, the country needed the stability of a unified national Church. As God had made her Queen, that institution would naturally be one in accordance with Elizabeth's beliefs. But unlike her sister Mary, who sought the very souls of her subjects, Elizabeth had no such desire. All she demanded for the sake of peace in her realm was outward conformity of her people to her Church. 'Not liking to make windows into men's hearts', she left their consciences to themselves.

Elizabeth's objective of a Protestant settlement was demonstrated by her contempt for the Catholic clergy at the opening of Parliament on 25 January. When Abbot Feckenham (the same who had tried to convert her cousin Jane Grey) and his monks welcomed her at Westminster with lighted torches in hand, Elizabeth reacted angrily. "Away with these torches", she exclaimed, "for we see very well"! Queen Mary's churchmen had more reason to worry when Doctor Richard Cox, known for his Protestantism, gave a sermon before Parliament. Cox's oration turned out to be a rant against the monks for their role in persecuting his co-religionists, and he called on the new Queen to reform the English Church. The Lord Keeper, Nicholas Bacon, spoke in the same vein when he beseeched Parliament to 'unite the realm into a uniform order of religion', saying that 'idolatry' and 'superstition' must be put to an end.

A bill, drafted by the mainly Protestant Commons, was introduced on 9 February to have Elizabeth re-assume her father and brother's title of Supreme Head. After some debate in the Lower House, it was submitted to the Lords, incorporating another measure about uniformity of worship in the English Church. It was rejected. While the clergy and the peers were willing to acknowledge the Queen as Head of the Church (with the unusual rider that the title was of *her* own choosing, not theirs, as to clear their consciences), they opposed any tampering of religious doctrine as it stood. Viscount Montagu, one of the dissenters, and a man of 'burning zeal to religion', argued that 'it were a great dishonour to England, if it so soon revolted from the Apostolic See, to which it had of late humbly reconciled itself'. Furthermore, the kingdom would be 'exposed to the fury of her neighbouring enemies' in calling itself a Protestant nation again, Montagu warned.

In a fix, Elizabeth sought to mollify the Upper House. By proclamation, she ordered that 'no man should speak irreverently of the Sacrament of the Altar'. At the same time, as a concession to the Protestants, she also permitted communicants at the Lord's Supper to drink from the chalice when receiving the Host. In the hope of bringing the Bishops over to her, it was arranged for a selection of them to debate with a group of Protestant clerics at the end of March.

Three questions were put to both sides: whether English could be used in the liturgy, whether each church could dictate its own form of worship, and whether Masses were effective in gaining favours for the living and the dead.

The deliberations got off to a bad start. The Catholic contingent complained they were at a disadvantage from the very beginning. They were not notified of the topics beforehand, and they were forced to assume the defensive as if they were on trial. Also, the moderator was the Lord Keeper, 'a man little versed in matters of divinity, and a bitter enemy of the Papists'. Infuriated, the Catholics, led by John White, Bishop of Winchester (Gardiner having died in 1555), and Thomas Watson, Bishop of Lincoln, demanded an end to the debates just after the second sitting. Bacon had no choice but to shut it down - 'the assembly was dissolved, the expectation frustrated, the purpose disappointed'. Nonetheless, the Lord Keeper had the last word when he had White and Watson arrested for contempt.

When Parliament reconvened after Easter, the Queen's government made another attempt at pushing the settlement forward. Prepared to be conciliatory to her Catholic subjects, Elizabeth agreed to the less offending title of 'Supreme *Governor of* the Church in England' rather than the loftier 'Head of' as used by Henry VIII and Edward VI. The move served a double purpose. It also appeased those Protestants who were adamant that no mere mortal - least of all a woman - could set him (or herself) above Christ. To Elizabeth, it was all semantics. 'Head' or 'Governor', her authority remained intact and unchanged.

Concerning the form of worship, it would be according to the explicitly Protestant Prayer Book of 1552, but with some traditional elements maintained. Inserted into the Communion service would be language implying a tacit acknowledgement of Christ's presence in the Sacrament. The Host would also retain its traditional form of a wafer, which the people would receive on their knees according to the old practice. However, the actual taking of the Eucharist in church would be voluntary. Furthermore, the clergy would keep their old vestments and the churches their ornaments, as laid out in the earlier Prayer Book of 1549. With the settlement made as acceptable as possible to both Catholics and Protestants, all the Queen's subjects were required to attend Anglican services on Sundays and holy days. Absentees would be fined.

Despite the continuing resistance of some bishops, Parliament passed the Bills of Supremacy and Uniformity on 29 April. It was a close call. The Queen and her government won by only three votes - but it was enough to re-establish an independent national Church and to bring to an end entirely its millennium-long ties to Rome.

≡

'Everything depends on the husband this woman may take,' wrote Count de Feria to Spain. His concern was shared by the Queen's own countrymen. At her first Parliament, besides the settlement of religion, the issue of her marriage was also addressed by the Lords and Commons. The consensus, as it was with Queen Mary, was that no woman could rule alone. Elizabeth must marry as well, though more wisely it was hoped. On 6 February, while the debate over religion was still in progress, a deputation was sent to the Queen at Whitehall 'to declare unto her [a] matter of great importance concerning the state of this Her Grace's realm'. The Speaker, on behalf of her loving subjects in Parliament, begged Elizabeth to consider marriage, 'whereby to all our comforts we might enjoy the royal issue of her body to reign over us'.

But the Queen was of a different mind. In reply, Elizabeth expressed her preference to remain unwed until 'it may please God to incline my heart to another kind of life… my meaning is not to do or determine anything wherewith the realm may or shall have just cause to be discontented'. In the meantime, Elizabeth announced, "This shall be for me sufficient; that a marble stone shall declare that a queen, having reigned such a time, lived and died a virgin".

No one took Elizabeth seriously. Even her sister, before she had settled on Philip of Spain, had insisted she preferred the single life she had always been accustomed to. Elizabeth was merely being coy, as well, her contemporaries thought, as she was expected to be. She was simply waiting for a proper husband to come her way. De Feria, for one, was convinced Elizabeth was interested in a foreign match - and with the Hapsburgs. The Duke of Savoy, whose name had been linked to Elizabeth's once before, was under consideration again, as was Archduke Ferdinand, a cousin of the King of Spain. But it was his belief, de Feria told his master, that the Queen 'will fix her eyes on Your Majesty'. Their relationship as in-laws should be no impediment to marriage. For one, his great aunts, Isabella of Aragon and her sister Maria, had both been wives of the King of Portugal. As well, the Pope would certainly grant him a dispensation to marry Elizabeth to safeguard the unity of Catholic Europe.

From experience, the title of King of England was not one Philip relished again, but he did recognise the benefits. Marriage to Elizabeth would prevent her from forming an alliance with France, and, as de Feria had reminded him, he might well succeed in fathering a King of England this time around; Elizabeth's 'age and temperament' being so much better than her late sister's. In acknowledgement of 'the enormous importance of such a match to Christianity, and the preservation of religion, which has been restored to England by the help of God', Philip offered up his hand in marriage to Elizabeth in February; coincidently, at the time Parliament was urging her to marry. Having inherited a kingdom on the verge of decline, he was certain his former sister-in-law would gratefully and immediately accept him as her husband and protector.

She did not. Elizabeth remembered how unhappy her sister's marriage had been, and how, far from protecting her kingdom's interests, Philip had dragged England into a disastrous war with France. Besides, there was the major stumbling block of their respective religions. Philip was left hanging until March when Elizabeth finally gave him her answer. She and his master could never marry, Elizabeth told de Feria with exaggerated regret, as 'she was a heretic'.

Philip took his rejection well. He had never been that keen to marry Elizabeth, and her decision allowed him to withdraw honourably. He also had better prospects elsewhere. He had recently made peace with France, and to seal their new friendship, Philip announced he would wed Elisabeth of Valois, daughter of Henry II. When she heard how quickly Philip found himself a new bride, Elizabeth, 'giving little sighs that bordered upon laughter', scolded him through his envoy saying he could not possibly have loved her that much seeing he 'had not the patience to wait four months'.

The Queen's rejection of a Spanish match raised the hopes of those looking for her to marry within the kingdom, not to mention those wanting the honour themselves. While his master was wooing Elizabeth, de Feria had kept a careful watch over the Earl of Arundel. As one of England's great peers, Henry Fitzalan fancied himself a worthy catch for the Queen, despite the fact that he was Catholic, more than her twice her age, and often laughed at behind his back for being 'silly and loutish'. To boost his chances of making a royal match, the Earl had his son-in-law, Lord Lumley, a favourite of the Queen, speak well of him to her. He also distributed 2,000 crowns worth of jewels to her ladies, expecting them to do likewise. But for all his efforts, Elizabeth was simply not interested in this 'flighty man of small ability'. Instead of marriage, she offered Arundel the post of Lord Steward, an office he had held under her sister.

Arundel was not the only Englishman vying for the Queen's hand. 'It is said by the vulgar', Schifanoya reported, 'that one Master Pickering will be her husband'. William Pickering, a courtier and diplomat, had known Elizabeth for years, and the two had always enjoyed each other's company. When Pickering returned from embassy abroad to congratulate her on her accession, Elizabeth sat with him for five hours in private, causing many tongues to wag. Good-looking and refined, Pickering's chances of becoming King Consort were deemed quite favourable, and in London bets were placed 'twenty-five to a hundred' on the possibility. But while Elizabeth was fond of Sir William, she never thought of him romantically.

The London bookmakers then turned to Prince Erik of Sweden. Erik had already made a bid – unsuccessfully - for Elizabeth's hand during the reign of her sister, but he was not one to be easily dissuaded. In October 1559, he tried again, this time sending his half-brother, Duke John of Finland, to England to woo the Queen on his behalf. Elizabeth had never shown interest in Erik, even though he was a Protestant and heir to the Swedish throne, but still, she was obliged to play hostess. She came to like Duke John even though he came across as being rather stuffy at first. But after getting used to the English and their strange customs, the Duke let go of 'his high looks', and was admired as a 'good fellow'.

But after months at court, Duke John overstayed his welcome. Becoming Queen of Sweden had never appealed to Elizabeth, and there was nothing to be gained by encouraging Erik any longer. In February 1560, she wrote to the Prince personally, regretting she could not 'gratify [His] Serene Highness with the same kind of affection' he had always shown her. Contrary to what his brother might have told him, Elizabeth continued, it was not because she had not seen him in person that she was turning him down, but simply because she did 'highly commend this single life'. Therefore, it was her hope that he would 'no longer spend time in waiting for us'. After receiving Elizabeth's final word on the subject, Erik gave up and recalled Duke John back to Sweden.

All those wanting to marry Elizabeth might have had better success if she were not already in love. In truth, no man could hope to compete with Robert Dudley. Lord Robert had the advantage over his all rivals by his long history with the Queen. By his own account, he had known her since they had been children together; Elizabeth had been seven, and he a year older. A friendship had quickly blossomed when the Princess, not one to easily share her feelings, had made Dudley her confidante, telling him things she would not to others. It was at that time, as he later recalled, that Elizabeth 'invariably declared that she would remain unmarried'.

It is unclear how often Elizabeth and Dudley met during the reigns of Henry VIII and Edward VI, but what was certain was that in 1554, they were in the Tower of London together. When Elizabeth had been brought in as a prisoner that March, Lord Robert had already been condemned. His sister-in-law Jane Grey, his brother Guilford, and his father Northumberland had all gone to the block, and he was expected to follow. As prisoners, Elizabeth and Dudley were not permitted contact, but it is possible that they did at least catch sight of each other now and then when they were allowed outdoors 'for want of air'. Fortunately, Dudley escaped the fate of his family. Pardoned by Queen Mary, he proved himself loyal, even going so far as to fight for King Philip against the French in 1557. When Mary died the year after, Dudley was not forgotten by Elizabeth. She appointed him her Master of Horse, and he had the privilege of riding close behind her litter at her coronation.

Elizabeth was bound to Robert Dudley not only by the tribulations they had shared but by mutual attraction as well. A striking woman herself, the Queen had an eye for good-looking men. Dudley certainly fit the bill, being tall and darkly handsome. He was called 'the gypsy', but as the nickname came from his enemy, the Earl of Sussex, it was not meant as a compliment to his looks, but as a slur on his character. While Dudley was undeniably ambitious with a streak of arrogance to him, his detractors believed far worse of him. He was not unlike his hated father the Duke, they said, accusing Robert Dudley of being just as self-seeking, unscrupulous, and ruthless in furthering himself at court. But ultimately it was Elizabeth's opinion that mattered, and she was deaf to criticism about her *Sweet Robin* - or her *Eyes,* as she also liked to call him.

Naturally, the intimacy of their relationship – Dudley was consistently at her side riding with her, dancing with her at balls, and dallying about her chambers – led to much talk about just how far Elizabeth's special friendship with Lord Robert went. The hearsay at court, according to de Feria, was that she was already in his bed.

Elizabeth herself might have laughed at such nonsense, but to those closest to her it was no joking matter. The situation was to get so out of hand that Kat Ashley, now Elizabeth's Mistress of the Robes, found it necessary to confront the Queen about her familiarity with Robert Dudley, begging her to 'put an end to these disreputable rumours'. In her defence, Elizabeth swore that nothing improper had ever passed between her and her Master of Horse. However, as sure as she was her father's daughter, Elizabeth, in a fit of rage, declared that should she choose to lead a life of ill repute, 'she did not know of anyone who could forbid her'.

While no one could indeed prevent her from indulging her passions, as Elizabeth exclaimed, there is no evidence that she took advantage of her freedom to do so. While certainly there was no end to the stories surrounding her alleged promiscuity – even decades into her reign, scandalous tales of Elizabeth bearing Dudley a houseful of children in secret were still circulated – there is no proof that the Queen slept with him, or with any other man for that matter, throughout her life. In the cramped confines of her palaces, even a queen had little privacy. If Elizabeth did enter into a sexual relationship with anyone, it could hardly have been kept secret, least of all by her ladies who were in almost constant attendance on her. When the Imperial ambassador set out to uncover the truth about the Queen's 'affair' with Dudley in the summer of 1559, her women admitted that while her behaviour towards Lord Robert was certainly intimate, she had 'never been forgetful of her honour'.

As Queen, Elizabeth had to make her relationship with Dudley appear respectable. But she was not entirely successful - he was a married man. In 1550, Dudley had taken as his wife, Amy Robsart, the daughter of a Norfolk gentleman farmer. It was probably a love match, as William Cecil later said of the pair - 'carnal marriages begin with happiness and end in strife'. But by the time of Elizabeth's accession, the young couple appeared to be living separate lives. Dudley preferred the excitement of court, while Amy stayed quietly in the country. Whether it was of her own choosing or not, we do not know. But to the gossipmongers, Lady Dudley's seclusion was forced on her by her husband who, in his pursuit of Elizabeth, considered her an encumbrance. If not for Amy Robsart, they believed, 'the Queen might take him for her husband'. This view was even shared by Cecil, who never liked Dudley. On 27 August 1560, he confided to Bishop de Quadra, the new Spanish ambassador, that he suspected Dudley of plotting to kill his wife, and that she was taking precautions against being poisoned.

In less than a fortnight, Amy Robsart was dead – just as Cecil believed she would be. On 8 September 1560, Amy was found at the bottom of a staircase in her house in Oxfordshire with her neck broken. From the very start, her death was viewed with suspicion. No one was present in the house when the tragedy occurred, and Amy had been acting strangely before she died. It was a Sunday, and she had insisted - with some agitation - that her staff attend the local fair leaving her all alone. Upon their return that evening, their mistress was lying in a heap, 'but yet without hurting of her hood that stood upon her head'. Had she fallen by accident, or had she taken her own life? Or had she been pushed?

Dudley was with the Queen at Windsor when he received the sorrowful news the next day. His reaction was shock. He immediately wrote to his kinsman Sir Thomas Blount asking him to set up an inquest into Amy's death. The 'most discreet and substantial men' were to act as jurors in the investigation, and his late wife's stepbrother was to observe the proceedings. Dudley was as anxious to exonerate himself from any suspicion as he was to uncover the truth. Already, as he admitted to Blount, he was well aware of 'what the malicious world would bruit' about the whole affair.

The investigators found no evidence of foul play, or of suicide, and they ruled the death as the result of an accidental fall. Despite Robert Dudley's unpopularity, the inquest's findings were largely accepted. Even Cecil, who had suspected him of wanting to do away his wife, was satisfied that Amy Robsart had died 'by a misfortune'. Before the inquiry was closed, Cecil even made a visit to Lord Robert offering him his condolences, for which the bereaved widower was most grateful. Whether Cecil did so out of genuine concern or to ingratiate himself with the exonerated Dudley is unclear. Whatever his intentions were, he had the satisfaction of knowing that the Queen, as a result of the scandal, could never marry Robert Dudley.

≡

At Elizabeth's first Parliament, even before her religious settlement was introduced before the Lords and Commons, her right to the throne was duly established by law. The Queen's entitlement was based on the Act of Succession of 1544, wherein Henry VIII had enabled his two daughters to succeed after their brother. That her father never formally legitimised her was remedied by Parliament who now declared Elizabeth (and the future heirs of her body) to be 'rightly lineally and lawfully descended and come of the blood royal'. The wording was satisfactory to the Queen, and she saw no need to repeal the previous Act, made in 1536, that had bastardised her. As Elizabeth saw it, her father had made amends by putting her back in the succession, and her title as England's 'Sovereign Liege, Lady and Queen' was confirmed by her subjects. In contrast, her sister who had been determined to right all old wrongs, was insistent that her parents' marriage be validated again after twenty years to the contrary, with her own legitimacy properly recognised. The gesture was as much for her mother, Katherine of Aragon – restored as Henry VIII's 'loving, godly, and lawful wife' - as it was for Mary herself. That would perhaps help explain Elizabeth's lack of interest in establishing her birthright beyond what she thought was necessary. Unlike Mary, who had known and loved her mother, Elizabeth barely remembered hers. Having virtually no emotional ties to Anne Boleyn, Elizabeth had no reason to pay tribute to her memory as Mary did to her own. When Anne's name was brought up in Parliament, it was not to restore her reputation, but only to confirm Elizabeth's right to any legacies belonging to her mother and her Boleyn and Howard relatives that she might be entitled to.

Elizabeth's reluctance to make much ado about her legitimacy was exploited by her enemies. Upon Mary Tudor's death, Henry II of France immediately proclaimed his daughter-in-law, Mary Stuart, Queen of England and Ireland. Her coat of arms, formerly signifying only her titles in Scotland and France, now incorporated those belonging to her English cousin. Even after King Henry died in a jousting accident in July 1559, Mary and her husband Francis II continued to style themselves as the rulers of Elizabeth's two kingdoms. Later, Mary would blame her overreaching father-in-law for the transgression, but Elizabeth never forgave her. In laying claim to her throne, whatever the circumstances, Mary had set the stage for their tumultuous relationship ahead.

But from Mary Stuart's point-of-view, Elizabeth was hardly one to point fingers. Her English predecessors had long interfered with the Scots' autonomy as a nation. In the 13th century, Edward I had attempted to reduce Scotland to a mere fiefdom of England's, and more recently, Henry VIII had made war on Scotland and had even wanted to kidnap Mary as a bride for Prince Edward. The Scots' hatred for the English was further intensified by the Protector Somerset,

Figure 25   Medal of Francis II and Mary Queen of Scots,
attributed to Guillaume Martin
Private collection

who was as aggressive as the late King was in his wars against Mary's
countrymen. Now with Elizabeth as Queen, it was inevitable that she
too would meddle in Scottish affairs.

While Mary was in France, her kingdom was governed by her
mother, Mary of Guise, acting as Regent. Her French Catholic rule
was resented by the Protestant Scottish nobles who banded together
as the Lords of the Congregation to overthrow her. However, they
lacked the necessary money and arms, for which they had to look
to England. William Cecil's eagerness to intervene was matched by
Elizabeth's unwillingness to interfere. Certainly, the defeat of the
French would mean their expulsion from Scotland, not to mention
the triumph of Protestantism there, as Cecil argued, but to Elizabeth,
the matter was not as clear-cut. War was costly and giving aid to the

Scots would provoke the French King. Also, the Queen was faced with a moral dilemma. As one appointed by God to her high station, she was loath to unseat another whom He had similarly raised. If she condoned rebellion, she would set a terrible precedent. She would tacitly be admitting that any ruler - including herself - could be removed by force of arms. She would then be playing into the hands of men such as John Knox, the spiritual leader of the Lords of the Congregation, whom she found 'most odious'. Knox's hatred for Catholics was matched by his disdain for female authority. The full force of his contempt was laid out in his book *The First Blast of the Trumpet Against the Regiment of Women* written in 1558:

> 'to promote a woman to bear rule, superiority, dominion or empire above any realm, nation, or city, is repugnant to nature, contumely to God, a thing most contrarious to His revealed will and approved ordinance, and finally it is the subversion of good order, of all equity and justice.'

That was not all. For women rulers who were particularly wicked, Knox openly advocated overthrowing them, and 'then after to execute against them the sentence of death'. Needless to say, Elizabeth found Knox's rantings both treasonous and revolting.

Opposed as she was to rebellion, Elizabeth found herself having to agree with Cecil. The opportunity to remove the French from Scotland once and for all was too great to pass up. Putting her personal feelings aside, Elizabeth dispatched English coin and English troops north. She came to regret her decision. On 7 May 1560, her army suffered defeat before the fortified town of Leith. The loss was even more humiliating when it was learnt that it was also at the hands of the 'Frenchmen's harlots'. During the siege, the ladies had fought valiantly alongside the French soldiers throwing down stones and fire 'with great violence' on the hapless English.

Dishonoured, Elizabeth eventually saved face, not by arms but by negotiation. In June, Master Secretary Cecil was sent to Scotland for talks with the French. Even before he arrived, the situation looked promising from the English's perspective. Mary of Guise was dying, marking an end to the French presence in Scotland. From her deathbed, the Queen Dowager made her peace with the Lords of the Congregation, and they, in turn, pledged to support her daughter as their sovereign.

After the Regent's death on 11 June, the disheartened French sat down with Cecil. By the Treaty of Edinburgh, made on 6 July, they promised to withdraw from Scotland leaving the reins of power to Mary Stuart's older stepbrother, James Stewart, Earl of Moray – an able statesman and a Protestant. The French also renounced Francis II and his wife's claims to the English Queen's titles. Elizabeth had hoped that Calais would be included in the deal, but in the end, she was disappointed. The return of the port-town, so important to England as its foothold on the continent and to its honour, was non-negotiable and would remain irrevocably lost, to Elizabeth's regret.

The establishment of a wholly Protestant Scotland was at risk just months after the signing of the treaty. After twelve years in France, its Catholic Queen was coming home. No one, least of all Mary Stuart herself, had envisioned her setting foot in her native country again. She might have lived out her entire life in France if not for the tragedy that winter. Having just grieved over her mother, Mary Stuart found herself in mourning again – this time for her husband. Young King Francis, never healthy, died on 5 December leaving his wife a widow three days short of her eighteenth birthday. The loss of her husband also meant the loss of her French Crown. Her mother-in-law, the formidable Catherine de' Medici saw to it that Mary and her grasping Guise relatives were excluded from any future power. Until the new King, her son the ten-year-old Charles IX, came of age, Catherine was Queen of France in all but name.

Having outlived her usefulness at the French court, Mary had little choice but to return to Scotland. From what she knew of her birthplace, it was a world away from France, being neither as 'pleasant nor plentiful'. The Scots - 'hard to be held in bridle' - were difficult to govern, and increasing numbers of them were turning to the religion of John Knox. Still, Mary was Scotland's Queen, and it was her duty to assume her inheritance, which her late mother had gone to great lengths to preserve.

Having made up her mind to journey home, Mary wrote to her English cousin asking for permission to travel through her realm on her way to Scotland. Elizabeth was wary of Mary's homecoming, but it was not in her power to prevent it. In response to the request, Elizabeth was prepared to grant Mary safe conduct, even to receive her with 'all kindness which could be expected from a queen, from a kinswoman, and from a neighbour'. There was one condition: Mary must ratify the Treaty of Edinburgh, renouncing her claim to the English throne during her cousin's lifetime.

Mary refused. She would not endorse the treaty, the Scottish Queen replied, until she had returned to Scotland to consider her best interests. Angered, Elizabeth denied her cousin passage through her kingdom. At a deadlock, Mary was nonetheless determined to take possession of her country. Instead of journeying north by land, she announced, she would take her chances on the open sea, hoping 'the wind would be so favourable that she need not come on the coast of England'. But if she were forced to, Mary told Elizabeth's envoy Nicholas Throckmorton,

> 'then the Queen, his mistress, would have her in her hands to do her will of her, and if she was so hard-hearted as to desire her end, she might then do her pleasure and make sacrifice of her.'

Mary set sail on 14 August 1561, reaching the port of Leith five days later. As fate would have it, had she delayed her journey a bit she would have received Elizabeth's message. Before Mary's departure, the English Queen had a change of heart. She had decided to allow Mary to come through England – but too late. Had the two met and settled their differences face to face, perhaps much future unhappiness might have been averted - including the doom Mary spoke so prophetically of.

Chapter 35
Both King and Queen

UNTIL ELIZABETH married and had an heir, England's security against Catholic Europe hung on the life of its maiden Queen. Happily, she was still young and blessed with good health. She always ate and drank in moderation, and she exercised regularly. Elizabeth especially enjoyed the outdoors. When she rode or hunted, she could get away from the routine of government and from constantly having to be on show at court. Even when she was preoccupied with affairs of State, the Queen still found time to be in the open air, taking leisurely walks in her gardens and parks. Bad weather was no deterrent to her small pleasures. When she could not go out, Elizabeth would stroll back and forth across the long galleries in her palaces to keep fit. Her trim and graceful figure made Elizabeth a superb dancer. She excelled at dancing, mastering even the demanding Italian style where she had to do great leaps in the air. Elizabeth took much satisfaction in hearing how the Queen of Scots 'danced not as high and disposedly as she did'.

Despite the care Elizabeth took of herself, she was not immortal. Should she die, England might be plunged into chaos by rival claimants to the throne, and in its weakened state be vulnerable to foreign enemies. To the Queen's subjects, the danger inherent in an unwed childless queen could be lessened somewhat if Elizabeth would only nominate her successor. But that she would not do, she declared. She remembered how in the last reign, she had been the focus of plots against her sister. Elizabeth had no desire to put herself in Mary's shoes, living in dread of the 'second person' after her. Though well-loved by her people, Elizabeth was not ignorant of the fickleness of human nature. She recalled how even before her sister was pronounced dead, scores had flocked to her at Hatfield as the new ruler. During the talks surrounding the Queen of Scots' passage through England, Mary's representative Lord Maitland had suggested his mistress's agreement to the Treaty of Edinburgh in exchange for her being appointed Elizabeth's heiress. Elizabeth was favourable to Mary's claim, but she would put nothing in writing. "I know the inconstancy of the English people", she told Maitland, "how they ever mislike the present government and have their eyes fixed on that person who is next to succeed. Men look to the rising sun, never the setting one". Naming her successor, Elizabeth shuddered, would 'require me in mine own life to set my winding sheet before mine eyes'.

With the succession left dangling, Elizabeth's kingdom came under peril – as many imagined it would - when she fell dangerously ill in October 1562. What was initially thought to be a mere chill developed into something far worse. When Doctor Burcot, a German émigré physician, was brought to Hampton Court to examine the Queen, he diagnosed smallpox. The disease was most deadly. Its victims counted themselves lucky if they were only scarred by the red spots, however severe, even on the face; those who were less fortunate wound up dead. Horrified, Elizabeth ordered Burcot out of her sight. As the days passed, she only got worse.

While all England prayed for Elizabeth's recovery, her government prepared for what seemed inevitable. With no heir, the succession was left to the Council. Elizabeth herself had always favoured the Queen of Scots, but she was deemed unacceptable by her Councillors. Under Henry VIII's will – still law by Act of Parliament – Mary's Scottish line had been excluded from the English Crown. That she was a Catholic and a foreigner, were also to her disadvantage. The more popular choice was the Queen's other cousin, Lady Katherine Grey, sister of the ill-fated Jane. Unlike Mary Stuart, Henry VIII had allowed her family to ascend the throne should his own children produce no heirs. Along with her good standing as a Protestant, Katherine was the mother of a son. Should she be Queen, she would have already secured the succession for the next generation.

But backing for Katherine Grey was not unanimous. She was currently in disgrace - a prisoner in the Tower - and her son illegitimate, according to the Queen at least. In 1560, Katherine had married her lover Edward Seymour, son of the late Lord Protector and the young man originally intended for her sister Jane. Knowing how touchy the Queen was about marriages involving those close to her throne, Katherine kept her nuptials a secret. But the news could no longer be contained when Katherine found herself with child. Elizabeth, who had never liked her cousin much to begin with, had her thrown in prison where her son was later born. An investigation was then launched into the validity of the marriage. As no witnesses to the wedding ceremony could be found, and Katherine had stupidly lost the documents proving she was Seymour's wife, their union was found to be invalid and their son a bastard.

One alternative to the discredited Lady Katherine was the Earl of Huntingdon. Besides his royal descent from Edward III, he was suitably Protestant too. Outside the Council, Huntingdon had the support of Thomas Howard, 4th Duke of Norfolk, and of his brother-in-law, Robert Dudley (the Earl was married to one of Dudley's sisters). To assure Huntingdon's accession should the Queen expire, Dudley assembled a 'large armed force under his control' to uphold his claim.

A civil war, not unlike that of Lancaster and York, might well have broken out if not for the efforts of Doctor Burcot. He was summoned back to Hampton Court where he found that Elizabeth had been 'unconscious and speechless' for two hours. He gave her medicine, and he had her brought near the heat of a fire to draw out the disease. His intervention proved timely and the crisis passed.

During her convalescence, Elizabeth summoned the Council to her bedside. Still very weak and apparently convinced she was not yet out of danger, the Queen made an astonishing request. She asked the men to make Robert Dudley Lord Protector in the event of her death. Along with his new powers, he was also to receive a peerage and an income of £20,000. Before anyone could protest, Elizabeth spoke again. She swore that although she had always loved Lord Robert, 'nothing improper had ever passed between them'. Consequently, nothing should prevent his appointment should she die. 'Everything she asked was promised', Bishop de Quadra wrote to King Philip, 'but will *not* be fulfilled'. The Council, and the whole of England, would never stomach being ruled by another Dudley.

Before long, Elizabeth made a complete recovery. Always vain about her looks, she was glad very little damage, if any, was done to her appearance. Lady Mary Sidney, Robert Dudley's sister, was not so fortunate. While caring for her sick mistress, she was afflicted by the pox. Lady Mary's face was so pitted with scars afterwards that she retired from court.

≡

Robert Dudley was never made Protector of the Realm, but after the Queen's recuperation, she did appoint him as an advisor in her government. Lord Robert's seat in the Council put him closer to the Queen again as she had had to distance herself from him after his wife's mysterious death. While it was true that he was cleared of all suspicion, Elizabeth knew that any marriage between them – if she ever indeed considered the possibility - would be impossible due to the lingering scandal. Unable to marry him herself, Elizabeth had other plans for Robert Dudley.

After Mary Stuart had been safely installed in Edinburgh, she had only one thought on her mind – marriage. Unlike Elizabeth, who was reluctant to wed, Mary was keen on taking another husband. As a Catholic Queen in a Protestant country, she had need of a good match to bolster her position. But even Mary, certainly the most beautiful Queen in Europe with her tall, slender figure (she was about six feet in height), porcelain skin, deep brown eyes, and alluring expression, had trouble finding herself a suitable mate. Of the possible candidates, Mary was most in favour of Don Carlos, son and heir of the King of Spain. However, the union was thwarted by Catherine de' Medici. With her daughter Elisabeth married to Philip II, she would not have Mary eclipse her own daughter's influence in Spain. Catherine also silenced any talk of marriage between her son Charles IX and his former sister-in-law. Mary's return to the French throne would restore her despised Guise relatives back to power. Of the other possibilities for Mary's hand, all were unsuitable for one reason or another. The Archduke Charles was considered too poor, while the Kings of Denmark and Sweden were too Protestant.

Then there was Elizabeth to consider. Still wanting recognition as her successor, it was necessary for Mary to take into account what her cousin had to say. Indeed, Elizabeth had made it clear that the Queen of Scots' marriage to a great Catholic prince would be viewed as an act of aggression against England. Despite her threats, Elizabeth had no desire to be hostile towards Mary if she hoped to match her with a husband suitable to herself. Her cousin, she suggested, should take an English husband, and who better than her own Robert Dudley? As reluctant as she was to lose him, Elizabeth was mindful of her policy. As Mary's husband, Dudley would see to it that Mary was no longer a danger to her, and at the same time, pro-English in her all her dealings. To sweeten the offer, Elizabeth dangled the prospect of being named heiress of England before Mary's eyes - *if* she accepted Lord Robert.

On 29 September 1564, the Scottish ambassador to England, Sir James Melville, witnessed the ennoblement of Robert Dudley. Since he was offered up as King Consort to Mary, he must have great titles. Brought before the Queen, her Master of Horse went 'upon his

knees before her with a great gravity'. The solemnity of the occasion
was lightened when the Queen, placing a mantle about his shoulders,
gave her favourite a little tickle on the neck, a gesture of affection
which did not go unnoticed by Melville. After his creation as Baron
of Denbigh, Dudley retired to change into new robes. When he came
before the Queen again, he was made Earl of Leicester.

During his stay in London, Elizabeth grew fond of Melville. He
was a sophisticate and a great flatterer. Knowing he would give a full
report of her to her cousin in Scotland, Elizabeth intended to dazzle
her ambassador. Whenever Melville saw her, the Queen was dressed
in a different gown. One day she would wear the English style, then
the next a French, and then an Italian gown. She also showed off her
command of languages. Besides conversing with Melville in French,
she also spoke to him in Italian, and then in Dutch (which the envoy
privately thought 'was not good').

Intrigued by Mary, Elizabeth sought to learn as much as she could
about her through Melville. Elizabeth's curiosity was not limited to
the political, but also to the personal. Who had the lovelier hair and
who was the fairest, she would ask? Mary or herself? Who was of
better stature? Who was the better dancer? And who was the better
musician? Elizabeth's vanity and her competitiveness were obvious
to Melville. With great tact, he replied that while Elizabeth was the
'fairest Queen in England', Mary was the 'fairest Queen in Scotland'.
However, the envoy had to admit *his* mistress was taller. Then she
was 'too high', Elizabeth sniffed, for she herself was 'neither too high
nor too low'. When it came to their musical abilities, Elizabeth was
determined to outshine her cousin. She arranged for Melville to
hear her play in private. After dinner, the ambassador was quietly
ushered into her chamber while the Queen practised on the virginals.
When she had finished, she feigned surprise in seeing him. She was
not accustomed to playing before company, she told the envoy with
assumed modesty, but only 'when she was solitary to shun melancholy'.
Obviously, Elizabeth was fishing for a compliment, and Melville, who
was genuinely impressed, obliged her by saying she surpassed Mary
of Scots in her skill.

But not all their talk was trivial. As Elizabeth discovered, Melville
was also a man of great insight. During their discussions, the subject of
her unmarried state was brought up. "Your Majesty thinks if you were
married, you would be but Queen of England", Melville observed,
"and now you are *both* King and Queen. I know your spirit cannot

Figure 26   Robert Dudley, Earl of Leicester by an Unknown Artist
The Yale Center For British Art, New Haven

endure a commander". Elizabeth could not have put it better herself.
Placing her trust in Melville to bring about an understanding with her
cousin, she hoped he could convince Mary Stuart to have Leicester.
"If the Queen would follow her counsel", Elizabeth promised, "she
would in process of time get all she had".

As tempting as the offer was, it still rankled Mary to have to
accept Robert Dudley - the offspring of a traitor, a heretic in religion,

a person touched by scandal, and not to mention, her cousin's cast-off lover – in return. Mary's disdain was matched by Leicester's own. Ambitious as he was, having to be away from England and away from Elizabeth was not worth being King of Scotland. Behind the Queen's back, he dropped hints that he was not interested in the idea.

While Mary stalled and Leicester resisted, Henry Stewart, Lord Darnley had ridden from England to the Scottish court in February 1565. At the first sight of him, Mary was besotted. He was young (nineteen years old), tall (like Mary herself was), good-looking, and charming. Not only that, his pedigree was commendable. His mother was Henry VIII's niece, Margaret Douglas, Countess of Lennox, making Darnley cousin to both Mary and Elizabeth. He was also a Catholic. Within weeks, Mary was head over heels in love with the 'properest and best proportioned long man that ever she had seen'. By the end of July, the two were married.

Elizabeth was irate at the frustration of her policy. All she could do before the ceremony took place was to order Darnley home on his allegiance as an English subject. He refused. His new life as King of Scotland suited him just fine, he answered back. With Darnley out of her reach, Elizabeth took her anger out on Leicester instead. That summer it was observed at court how the Queen started 'to display a certain coolness towards him', and how she was turning her attentions to Thomas Heneage, 'a young man of pleasant wit and bearing'. Heneage had always been on good terms with Dudley, but now their friendship was strained by the latter's jealousy. Their animosity became so great that in August, the Queen's new favourite was obliged to leave court, and Leicester was banished from her sight for three days.

The Earl began a flirtation of his own, seeking out the Queen's maternal cousin, Lettice Knollys, 'one of the best-looking ladies of the court'. Lettice, though married to Walter Devereux, Viscount Hereford (and later Earl of Essex), was not unreceptive to Leicester's advances. His intention to make Elizabeth jealous succeeded. At the beginning of September, he and the Queen had it out in a furious row, ending with the two of them not speaking for days again. While Lord Robert sulked in his rooms, Elizabeth wept in private and raged in public. Seeing the emotional distress their mistress was under, Cecil and the Earl of Sussex put aside their mutual dislike for Leicester and intervened, patching things up between the bickering pair. Very soon, the Queen and the Earl were in each other's arms again.

Elizabeth's renewed happiness with her favourite was so very different to the state of affairs between the Queen of Scots and Lord Darnley. Not long after their honeymoon, the 'handsome lusty youth' Mary had wed in defiance of her cousin and of her Protestant nobles, showed his true colours. Darnley was nothing but an arrogant, immature, and self-indulgent lout. When he was intoxicated, as often was the case, he was worse. He would be positively vicious and verbally abusive, driving his wife to despair. After six months of matrimony, Mary regretted ever laying eyes on Henry Stewart. For a drunkard, she had jeopardised her relationship with Elizabeth and with her Scottish nobles. Her stepbrother Moray even rebelled against her. Though the rising failed, it was made clear to Mary how very unpopular her marriage was. In her misery, she came to rely on the friendship of her Italian secretary David Rizzio. Darnley, already jealous of any man around Mary, was easy prey for certain Protestant lords who hated Rizzio for his influence with the Queen. It did not take much for them to persuade the gullible Darnley that the base-born foreigner was bedding his wife behind his back. They even insinuated that the child Mary was now carrying was Rizzio's.

Convinced he was being made a cuckold, the King and a band of intruders interrupted a small dinner party held in the Queen's supper chamber at Holyrood Palace on the night of 9 March 1566. Before a pregnant Mary and her guests, Rizzio was dragged away screaming and was stabbed over fifty times. Mary was certain she was next as one of the ruffians held a pistol to her stomach while Darnley restrained her. But it was Rizzio they wanted, and after his bleeding corpse was carried off, Mary was made her husband's prisoner.

Whatever her faults, cowardice was not one of them. Banishing her tears and thinking only of revenge, Mary sprang into action to free herself. Knowing how weak-willed Darnley was, she threw herself at his feet. She feigned remorse for her neglect of him, and she convinced Darnley that the Protestant lords were sure to turn against him. Terrified, Henry Stewart was putty in Mary's hands. Together, the royal couple sneaked out of Holyrood and rode desperately towards the safety of Dunbar Castle, some twenty-five miles away. During their escape, Mary's contempt for Darnley only intensified. For the sake of their child inside her, she had begged him to slow down, but he would not. Concerned only for himself, Darnley urged his horse onwards, shouting back to his wife that if the baby died, they would simply have another.

Fortunately, Mary did not miscarry. At the safety of Dunbar, the Scottish Queen gathered her supporters - some eight thousand of them - to her. In just a week, the tables were turned with the conspirators running for their lives. Regardless of her differences with the Queen of Scots, Elizabeth offered Mary her congratulations. Treason was hateful to her even if it was backed by Protestants against a Catholic queen. She also commiserated with her cousin over her ordeal at Holyrood, even saying that had she been Mary, she would have taken Darnley's dagger and plunged it into him herself!

In the latter part of June, Sir James Melville returned to England with news from Scotland. Elizabeth was enjoying herself at a ball at Greenwich when William Cecil whispered the envoy's message in her ear. The Queen froze. The musicians ceased their playing, and those dancing stopped in their tracks. 'All mirth was laid aside' as silence fell over the great hall and all eyes turned towards Elizabeth. She looked absolutely stricken. The Queen of Scots had just given birth to a 'fair son', Elizabeth moaned, 'while she was but a barren stock'.

≡

Elizabeth was made godmother to Prince James of Scotland, but she had yet to be a mother herself. It had been four years since her brush with death, and since then she had done nothing, her subjects complained, to secure a husband or the succession. When Parliament was summoned in the fall of 1566, its agenda was to force the Queen into marriage, or at least to have her designate an heir. At a previous session, Elizabeth had still been resistant to being wed, but she did admit that while a life of celibacy was 'best for a private woman', it was 'not meet for a prince'. It was hoped that the Queen meant what she said, but as matters turned out, it was the Queen of Scots, not the Queen of England, who became a wife and mother to the joy of her Catholic supporters, while Elizabeth was no closer to marriage than she was in 1559.

This time, Parliament intended to use money as their leverage. The Queen was in need of funds to maintain herself and her kingdom, and it was hoped that with her finances at a low, she would be more amenable to its demands. The members of the Lower House, in particular, were more outspoken than ever before. By her refusal to name a successor, they complained, the Queen 'doth both provoke the wrath of God and alienate the hearts of her people'. In fact, she would be the very 'parricide of her country', the Commons warned. 'England which now breathed with her breath, should together with her expire than survive her'. Since the Queen would not budge, Parliament, its members demanded, must take the initiative. The names of Katherine Grey and James of Scotland were introduced, and all that was required was for the Queen to say whom she preferred as her heir.

To Elizabeth, the language used against her by Parliament, and its assumption of her prerogative to name her successor were insulting. She was even angrier when she discovered how members of her own Council had betrayed her. Far from supporting their mistress against Parliament's onslaught, they approved of its measures to coerce her into marriage. Enraged, Elizabeth summoned the troublemakers before her. The Duke of Norfolk, sworn in as a Councillor at the same time as Leicester, was accused of being 'a traitor', and his cohort the Earl of Pembroke was belittled as 'a swaggering soldier'. The Queen did not spare her step-uncle, the Marquis of Northampton either. He of all men should know better than to give her advice, she told William Parr crossly, seeing how he was now on his second wife, being barely divorced from his first. When Leicester defended his colleagues, Elizabeth had words for him too. If all the world abandoned her, she stormed, she thought she could at least depend on him. By the day's end, all four men, and those that supported them, were banished from the royal presence.

Having slapped down her Councillors, Elizabeth still had Parliament to deal with. She was not prepared to be conciliatory, as she confided to the new ambassador from Spain, Don Diego de Guzman de Silva. The Commons, she learnt, were willing to grant her £250,000 in subsidies but only if she settled the succession to their satisfaction. She had no intention of doing so, Elizabeth told de Silva. Such tactics smacked of bullying, and she refused to be backed into a corner.

The first showdown was on 5 November when representatives from the Lords and Commons presented themselves at Whitehall. The Queen was in a testy mood. After complaining of 'unbridled persons' in Parliament, she demanded to know:

> 'Was I not born in the realm? Were my parents born in any foreign country? Is there any cause I should alienate myself from being careful over this country? Is not my kingdom here? Whom have I oppressed? Whom have I enriched to others' harm? What turmoil have I

made in this commonwealth that I should be suspected to have no regard to the same? How have I governed since my reign?'

Coming to the crux of the matter, Elizabeth swore 'upon the word of a prince', that the vow she had made to Parliament to marry had never been broken. It was simply a matter of the right time, and she even went so far as to hint how she already had a husband in mind, though she did not name him. 'I will marry as soon as I can conveniently', the Queen promised once again, 'if God take not him away with whom I mind to marry - or myself'. She would even have children, she assured the delegation, that being her only desire for matrimony.

But in naming her successor, Elizabeth was less generous. It was 'a strange thing that the foot should direct the head in so weighty a cause', she stated with indignation. The Queen reminded the delegates of her troubles when she was 'a second person' to Mary Tudor. 'There were occasions in me at that time', Elizabeth reminisced aloud, 'I stood in danger of my life; my sister was so incensed against me. I did differ from her in religion, and I was sought for divers ways'. As a result, for her to name a successor would only endanger herself, not to mention the person who was to inherit as well. As she must say nothing of the matter for the time being, so must Parliament.

When the audience drew to a close, Elizabeth reasserted her authority, leaving the delegates with these words:

> 'And though I be a woman, yet I have as good a courage answerable to my place as ever my father had. I am your anointed Queen. I will never be by violence constrained to do anything. I thank God I am indeed endued with such qualities that if I were turned out of the realm in my petticoat, I were able to live in any place in Christendom.'

The Queen's arguments defending her position – sound as they were from her point of view – were taken by Cecil as being too provocative. He dared not present her speech to the Commons in its original form, but opted to submit a watered down version of it to the Lower House. Parliament was mollified by the Queen's promise to marry, but there was still dissatisfaction at her handling of the succession. The silencing of any debate about who should succeed was viewed as an attack on the Parliamentary privilege of free speech.

When the Commons issued a formal complaint, Elizabeth stood firm; rabble-rousers were to be hauled before the Council for a reprimand.

Before things got out of hand, Parliament and the Queen were able to come to terms. Before they were dissolved on 2 January 1567, both Houses agreed to trust Elizabeth that she would wed and appoint an heir in due time. She would not, however, have it committed to writing. When the subsidy bill – of which the Queen generously remitted a third part - was passed and presented to her, her discerning eye noticed its preamble of her promise to 'declare the succession in such convenient time'. Seeing a distinction between a binding clause and what she considered her 'private answers to the realm', Elizabeth had the offending text removed. Again, her 'word as a prince' must suffice.

Chapter 36
The Daughter of Debate

ON THE early evening of 16 May 1568, fishermen bringing in the day's catch at the little port of Workington in Cumbria were alerted to a curious sight. Not far to the north, a fishing boat carrying a band of strangers was heading towards shore. As the score of passengers landed, one of them, in particular, stood out from the rest - a woman dressed in a tattered riding cloak. She was of remarkable height, and much deference was paid to her by her companions. Despite her exhaustion, her ragged clothes, and her roughly cropped hair, she was still noticeably lovely. While the weary travellers were taken to the village for rest and refreshment, word quickly spread – Mary Queen of Scots had come to England seeking asylum.

No one could have foreseen the events leading to her arrival. Two years earlier, Mary Stuart had been at the apogee of her rule. She had avenged the death of David Rizzio, sending his killers into exile, and she had 'happily brought to bed of her son James'. For the sake of peace, Mary even pardoned her half-brother Moray and extended an olive branch to the Protestant lords. Unfortunately, she had not been so forgiving towards her husband. Estranged from Darnley, Mary had found herself attracted to James Hepburn, Earl of Bothwell. His loyal service to her late mother had commended him to Mary, and he had qualities in him so missing in the feckless Darnley. Bothwell was courageous and forceful, and with his stocky build and ruggedly handsome looks, a fine specimen of manhood, unlike the 'beardless and lady-faced' rather epicene Henry Stewart. Desperately unhappy with Darnley and needing a take-charge hand in her life, Mary fell hopelessly in love with Bothwell. She gave herself so completely to him that nothing else mattered – not his self-serving ambition, not his coarseness, not his Protestantism, and not even his wife. Mary was so impassioned, her enemies said, that she would do *anything* to have him - even murder.

Early in the morning of 10 February 1567, Edinburgh was shaken by a thundering blast. The explosion had come from a house – or what was left of it – at Kirk o' Field at the edge of the city. It had been reduced to rubble by gunpowder placed in its cellar. Discovered in a garden nearby were the intended victims – the King of Scotland and his manservant. From what could be determined, both men had escaped the devastation only to be strangled afterwards.

It was common knowledge that the Queen despised Henry Stewart, but it was still expected that at least for honour's sake, she would bring his assassins to justice. Mary did no such thing. Instead, she heaped honours on Bothwell, who was whispered to have orchestrated the murder. When public opinion compelled the Queen to bring her favourite to trial, the process was a mockery of justice. On the day of the hearing, the city was packed with Bothwell's armed supporters. Since no one, not even Darnley's grief-stricken father, the Earl of Lennox, dared to come forth and accuse Bothwell in person, he was acquitted. To add insult to injury, after Bothwell was quickly divorced, Mary took him as her third husband, even marrying him by Protestant rites.

The whole country was outraged. Even those who had rallied to Mary's side after the slaughter of Rizzio, denounced her as a murderess and whore, and rose up in revolt. By the middle of June, Mary was in the hands of the Protestant lords, and her beloved Bothwell was a fugitive on the run. At Lochleven Castle, where she was imprisoned, the Queen was forced - not without threat of violence - to abdicate her Crown to her son James. Until the child reached his majority, his uncle Moray would act as Regent.

After ten months in captivity, Mary escaped in May 1568 and prepared to do battle with Moray. Despite her larger army, the Queen was defeated and forced to take flight. Wearing a borrowed cloak and with her hair cut short to evade detection, Mary and her small party fled south. Escape to France was an option, but Mary's former in-laws had made it clear how she could expect no help from them as she had 'behaved so ill and made herself so hateful to her subjects'. The alternative was England. Trusting in Elizabeth's old promises of friendship, Mary took her last look at Scotland at Dundrennan Abbey on the border, setting her hopes across the Solway Firth.

The Queen of Scots' presence in England put Elizabeth's government in a panic. Despite her reversals of fortune, Mary was still regarded by many English Catholics as their rightful Queen. It was William Cecil's great fear that they would flock to her in their thousands, offering their allegiance. He could only hope that with the Scottish Queen presently lodged - and under surveillance - at Carlisle Castle in Cumbria, he would have time to neutralise her before she proved too great a danger. Meanwhile, Mary, Cecil instructed her custodians, was to receive no visitors, be they 'English, Scottish, or French', without his approval.

Elizabeth however, did not share Cecil's concern. She was sympathetic at what had befallen her cousin. Already, Mary had written to her explaining her plight and asking for help:

> 'Being assured, hearing the cruelty of my enemies, and how they have treated me, you will, conformably to your kind disposition and the confidence I have in you, not only for the safety of my life, but also aid and assist me in my just quarrel, and I shall solicit other princes to do the same. I entreat you to send to fetch me as soon as you possibly can…'

Elizabeth was prepared to do just that. Disgusted as she was at Mary's behaviour with Bothwell, she was equally appalled at the conduct of the rebel lords. To Elizabeth, it was outrageous that the Queen of Scots should be stripped of her Crown by her subjects. As a fellow monarch and as her kinswoman, Elizabeth could not abandon Mary. She had it in mind to bring her cousin down to London, as she had asked, and to even provide her with fine accommodations, befitting her station and her nearness in blood.

Cecil disapproved of Elizabeth taking Mary under her protection. If she welcomed and helped her cousin, he advised, she would sully her own reputation. Mary, Cecil reminded her, was still under suspicion for Darnley's murder, and for her to receive her kinswoman with honour might be interpreted as approval of her actions. It was also unthinkable, in Cecil's opinion, to provide Mary with the English army she was asking for. As a Protestant queen, it would be unseemly, to say the least, for Elizabeth to wage war against the Lords of the Congregation on behalf of a Catholic ruler. Nor could she allow her cousin to seek help elsewhere. If Mary were to regain her throne with French or Spanish troops behind her, the danger she then posed to England would be immense.

Cecil's assessment was sound, and Elizabeth gave in. She would not meet with the Queen of Scots after all, nor would she allow her to leave her realm. Her cousin, it was decided, would remain in England for the while as a 'guest'. Mary would prove to be a most burdensome one. Her upkeep, with the English government bearing the expenses, included not only herself, but also her ever-expanding household made up of dozens of her old friends trickling down from Scotland to serve her. Though she was a queen without a kingdom, Mary was allowed to live like one. Maintaining her little court in exile did not come cheap, costing Elizabeth some £56 a week.

For Mary's own 'safety', as it was put to her, she was moved. In July, she and her household were brought fifty miles south to Bolton Castle in Yorkshire. It was here that Mary received news that Elizabeth might receive her and help restore her to her throne – *if* she submitted herself to an inquiry. As it was presented to Mary, far from being a trial investigating her complicity in Darnley's murder, it was an opportunity for her to present her grievances against the Protestant lords. Elizabeth would not act as a judge, but only as a mediator between both parties. Under these circumstances, and an understanding that she would regain her Crown afterwards, Mary agreed. Unbeknownst to her, the very opposite was promised to the Earl of Moray. His sister, he was told, would *never* be Queen again.

The 'conference', as it was called, met in York on 4 October. Mary herself did not appear but was represented by the loyal Lord Herries, who had crossed into England with her, and by her old friend from Scotland, John Leslie, Bishop of Ross. Acting as Elizabeth's eyes and ears was the Duke of Norfolk. As England's only Duke, Thomas Howard was the most powerful aristocrat in the land, and thus second only after the Queen herself. He was also her maternal cousin, his father being the unfortunate Earl of Surrey executed by Henry VIII in 1547. Owing to his rank (inherited on his grandfather's death in 1554) and his familial closeness to her, Norfolk was held in special regard by the Queen, and as such, was appointed chief commissioner of the hearing.

In December, Norfolk reported back to London the astonishing evidence Moray had presented against the Queen of Scots at the conference. In his possession was a series of love letters (called the 'Casket Letters' after the silver gilt box in which they were found) purportedly written by Mary to Bothwell. In perusing them, Norfolk had expressed shock at their contents. If the letters were genuine, as Moray claimed they were, his stepsister was another Clytemnestra consenting to her husband's murder in her lust for another man. Mary, of course, denounced them as forgeries, and Elizabeth seemed to have agreed. But despite her reservations about the authenticity of the letters, she could not bring herself to Mary's side. As much as she still looked on her cousin as God's anointed like herself, to allow

Mary freedom would only threaten the safety of England and its Protestant religion. Elizabeth had not forgotten how Mary had once claimed her throne. A possible solution to the dilemma was to restore the lady as a powerless figurehead. She would reign, but not rule. The idea, however, was rejected by Moray, who did not want her back in Scotland. It might have occurred to Elizabeth to simply deport Mary over his protests, but her safety could not be guaranteed. Instead of just locking Mary up as before, the Scots might have her condemned and executed for Darnley's murder.

Under these circumstances, the conference, which had been moved from York to Westminster at the Queen's instructions, was quietly closed on 11 January 1569. No verdict was given for or against either party. The Protestant lords were not charged with deposing their sovereign, and Moray was allowed to leave in peace for Scotland. Before his departure, he had an audience with Elizabeth, who assured him of her friendship. To back up her promise, she presented Moray and his government with £5,000 as a gesture of good will. No judgement was given against Mary either, but clearly she got the short end of the stick. While her base-born brother had gone back north richer and as the 'King' he had always wanted to be - she was forced to remain a prisoner still.

═══

With her reign entering its second decade, Elizabeth was still unmarried, despite her many promises to the contrary. But it was not for want of trying. After she had turned down Erik of Sweden, Elizabeth had expressed an interest in Charles IX of France in 1565. But owing to his young age - he was only fourteen – and the Queen's habitual unwillingness to fully commit herself, nothing had come of it to the disappointment of Catherine de' Medici. The wily Queen Mother, acting as Regent, had hoped to absorb England into France with Elizabeth as her daughter-in-law.

After young Charles was out of the picture, Elizabeth was wooed by the Habsburgs on behalf of Archduke Charles, the brother of Ferdinand of Austria with whom the Queen had once been linked. By the summer of 1567, both sides were interested enough for Elizabeth to send the Earl of Sussex as her representative to meet with Charles' older brother, Emperor Maximilian.

While Sussex found the entertainments in Vienna most agreeable, the negotiations were less so. There was 'much arguing' from both sides as to the terms of the marriage contract. What was mutually agreed was that should the nuptials occur, the Archduke would be largely responsible for his upkeep. In return, the English were prepared to recognise Charles as King Consort. Of course, there were conditions. Should his wife predecease him, the Archduke would not be allowed to claim the Crown for himself, but he was permitted to act as the legal guardian of any children he might have with Elizabeth.

But when it came to religion, both sides were at loggerheads. The Archduke was willing to marry a Protestant, but he was not prepared to abandon his faith in the process. If he came to England, he demanded the right to hear Catholic Mass in public at court. His request was rejected by Sussex. Surely then, the Emperor proposed, the Queen would at least let his brother worship as he would in private. If that were acceptable, Charles, Maximilian promised, would support the Protestant religion in England, and he would even accompany his wife to her Anglican services. The compromise was fair, but it was met with resistance back home in November. Leicester, who did not want to lose Elizabeth to anyone, and who was building himself up as a champion of English Protestantism, made no bones about his opposition He was even supported by some of his fellow Councillors. Cecil and Norfolk, however, disagreed, and they urged the Queen to accommodate the Archduke.

In December, Sussex had to tell the Emperor, that with regret, his Queen could not see her way to him. It would 'offend her conscience', she had written, to 'openly break the public laws of the realm, not without great peril, both of her dignity and safety'. Since the Archduke would never convert to her religion - or she to his - there could be no marriage. Sussex was upset by the decision and understandably so. Five months of negotiations had come to nothing, ruined by Leicester and his cronies, not to mention by the Queen herself. Even back in October, Sussex had already had an uneasy feeling that she might frustrate his attempts using religion as an excuse. If she would not allow Charles to hear Mass even in private, the Earl believed, 'she wanteth or meaneth never to proceed in the matter'.

After all talks had fallen apart, the Queen was still careful to keep the friendship of the Hapsburgs. As a show of amity, she admitted the Emperor into England's prestigious Order of the Knights of the Garter. Maximilian responded in kind. Before Sussex departed, the Emperor gave the Earl his assurance that the 'dearness of love and mutual kindness' between himself and Elizabeth would not be diminished in any way.

Having had three husbands already, Mary Queen of Scots was ready for a fourth. As she surmised, her hopes lay not in Elizabeth's promises - which had proved so empty – but on making a new match for herself. The bridegroom she had in mind was England's premier nobleman, the Duke of Norfolk.

Such a prestigious match was the idea of Mary's old supporter, Lord Maitland. By marrying Thomas Howard, his mistress would secure her freedom and the restoration of her Estate. The scheme would even meet with Elizabeth's approval, Maitland believed. She had never wanted Mary in England in the first place, and if her cousin were matched to a husband who was both an Englishman and a Protestant, as Norfolk was, she might be willing to send her back to Scotland as Queen.

Before the idea was even presented to Elizabeth, Maitland and his agents discretely canvassed the English and Scottish lords for their opinion. Many were in favour of it. Even Moray, who had been against his sister's return to power, appeared to have approved the plan. The marriage was also agreeable to Mary's Catholic supporters, but for different reasons. Though Norfolk was a Protestant, as a Howard he had ties to powerful aristocrats – particularly his brother-in-law, the Earl of Westmorland, and the Earl of Northumberland - adhering to the old faith. Once Mary was free, she could ride at the head of Catholic army to depose the usurper Elizabeth and restore true religion to the land.

But what did the couple themselves think? Mary had apparently never met Thomas Howard, but she had become acquainted with his sister when she was in the custody of her husband, Lord Scrope, at Carlisle and Bolton. The sympathetic Margaret Howard had almost certainly commended her brother to Mary, no doubt mentioning that Thomas was a bachelor once again after the recent death of his third wife. Single, good-looking, and not to mention the wealthiest man in England - Mary agreed to have him.

When the Duke in turn was approached, he was not unresponsive either. This was not the first time that his name had been associated with the Queen of Scots. During Mary's first widowhood, he had been one of the Englishman suggested as her suitor before Elizabeth confirmed Robert Dudley instead. At the York conference, Norfolk had again been spoken of as a husband for the ex-Queen by his colleagues who were toying with an idea similar to Maitland's. But at the time, the Duke had wanted nothing to do with her, or so he said. "I love to sleep upon a safe pillow", he said, in reference to Lord Darnley's violent demise. But now, with Mary offered up to him again, Norfolk reconsidered. His ambition was certainly a factor, and the lady had much to recommend her. Mary Stuart was still regarded as one of the most beautiful women in Europe, and despite her abdication, many, including Elizabeth herself, still recognised her as Queen of Scotland. Furthermore, with the recent death of Lady Katherine Grey, Mary was one step closer to the English throne.

With their marriage so mutually agreeable, Mary and Norfolk began a secret courtship through letters in the spring of 1569. The Scottish Queen wrote in affectionate terms, calling Thomas Howard 'my Norfolk' and declaring herself 'yours till death'. Like true lovers, the two also exchanged gifts. In preparation for their nuptials, Mary began proceedings to have her marriage to Bothwell – with whom she had once sworn to follow 'to the end of the world in her petticoat' – annulled.

All the while, Elizabeth was kept ignorant. No one dared broach the marriage with her - not the couple themselves, not Maitland, not Cecil or Sussex, who knew what was afoot, and not even Leicester, who was in on it too. They were all well aware how sensitive the Queen was on the subject of marriage, whether it be hers or of someone close to her throne. The tragedy of the late Lady Katherine Grey was still fresh in memory. Held prisoner, denied the company of her husband, and her two sons made bastards by the Queen, Katherine's life had been one of misery – the price of falling in love without royal permission. Her sibling Lady Mary Grey had fared no better either. For following in Katherine's footsteps with a secret marriage of her own, she too had been made to suffer the brunt of Elizabeth's displeasure. By her treatment of her Suffolk cousins, the Queen was expected to react in kind – and probably with greater severity - towards Mary and Norfolk.

Even with the conspiracy of silence around her, Elizabeth did eventually learn the truth from the ladies of her court 'who do quickly smell out love matters'. Elizabeth was incensed, but she held her rage and said nothing, wanting those involved to come clean themselves. If they did, she was willing to be forgiving. But when she cornered Norfolk that August, he gave her no indication that anything was amiss. Elizabeth then dropped a broad hint, asking the Duke pleasantly if he had 'news of a marriage'. Norfolk played dumb. Disappointed, Elizabeth offered him another chance. She invited her cousin to supper with her, but again he was not forthcoming. When their meal finished, Elizabeth gave Norfolk a meaningful look, advising him 'to take good heed of his pillow' (in reference to his former resolve to avoid the Queen of Scots). But seeing how he would not take her into his confidence in spite of all her efforts, Elizabeth gave up. She dismissed Norfolk knowing she could not trust him again.

With Norfolk too scared to confess, Leicester decided he had best tell the Queen himself before she found out that he too had knowledge of the affair. He knew he could rely on her affection for him to calm the storm clouds of her fury, but just in case, he took to his bed and announced himself gravely ill. When Elizabeth hastened to him in worry, Leicester 'with sighs and tears' played on her pity admitting his knowledge of the intrigues under her nose. Elizabeth could forgive him, and later the others in on the marriage, but not Norfolk. She summoned him to her once again, but this time, she played no more games. With 'sharp speeches and dangerous looks', she admonished her kinsman for involving himself with the Queen of Scots, and she forbade him to have anything more to do with her. Chastised, Norfolk gave her his word. He vowed that henceforth, his princely aspirations would go no further than his tennis court at Norwich, where he 'thought himself in a manner equal with some kings'.

Norfolk's promise was not reassuring. Having lost faith in her cousin, Elizabeth grew suspicious when he suddenly left for London on 15 September. Why his hasty departure, she thought? Why did he not seek her permission first? Was he still involved with the Queen of Scots? Afraid Norfolk was up to no good, Elizabeth ordered his return to court immediately. His reply seemed to confirm her doubts about him. He could not come, the Duke said, for he was unwell. Or was he? Instead of taking to his bed, Thomas Howard retreated to his estates in East Anglia. Convinced he was turning traitor, the Queen demanded his presence without fail. Once more, he ignored the summons pleading illness.

Again, if Norfolk had been more open with the Queen, he would have saved himself a great deal of grief. He had left court not because he intended treason, but because of his injured pride. After his dressing down by Elizabeth, Norfolk suddenly found himself a pariah. No one, not even his friends, dared to associate with him lest they bring down the Queen's wrath on themselves too. When Elizabeth's summons arrived, it meant only one thing to Norfolk –

his arrest. The very thought of the Tower – that place of 'too great a terror' where his father, his grandfather, and many of his relatives had been imprisoned or lost their lives - filled him with dread. Rather than surrender himself to what was surely imprisonment and death, he began to contemplate treason. Though shunned at court, Norfolk was not without friends elsewhere. In the North, his brother-in-law, the Earl of Westmorland and the Earl of Northumberland were ready to strike. All they needed was a sign from him.

After Norfolk had refused to submit a second time, an apprehensive Elizabeth cancelled her plans to travel to Hampton Court, and instead, removed herself to the better protection of Windsor Castle on 23 September. She put the country on alert and dispatched a contingent of guards to watch over the Scottish Queen in case there was an attempt to liberate her. For the next two weeks, Elizabeth was on tenterhooks preparing herself for what could be the first and greatest challenge to her authority. Thankfully, no threat materialised. Just as the North was ready to strike, Norfolk backed down. He begged the Earls not to proceed. It was just too risky an enterprise, he wrote, and he would surely lose his head for it. They abandoned their plans, but not without bitterness. The fiery Lady Westmorland spoke for them all when she lashed out at her brother for his spinelessness. "What a simple man the Duke is", she exclaimed, "to begin a matter and not go through with it"!

On 3 October, Norfolk, on his way to submitting himself to the Queen's mercy, was taken into custody. From the Tower, he was silent on his dealings with Westmorland and Northumberland. Nonetheless, the Council was sure something was brewing in the North. Reports were being received about how the Catholic Earls were amassing weapons in secret, and how they were training their tenants for battle. Sussex, already in York serving as President of the North, was asked to investigate.

It was Sussex's request for the Earls to appear before him that reactivated the rebellion. Suspecting it was a trap to lure them into prison like Norfolk, Westmorland and Northumberland took up arms. On 14 November, they and hundreds of their followers - with banners depicting the Five Wounds of Christ like the rebels of the Pilgrimage of Grace a generation ago - raided St Cuthbert's Cathedral in the city of Durham. The Protestant Communion table was smashed, and the Book of Common Prayer and the Bible in English defiled. Afterwards, priests in the company of the rebels, who had not said Holy Mass since the reign of Queen Mary or did so only in secret, celebrated the Eucharist in public according to the old rites. From Durham, the insurgents then marched south. At each stop, Mass was openly conducted, and to attract others to their cause, the Earls had a proclamation read out saying:

> 'That they had not taken arms with any other intent than that the religion of their forefathers might be restored, corrupt councillors removed from the Queen, the Duke and other faithful lords that were put from their rank and degree, restored to liberty and grace.'

Furthermore, 'they attempted nothing against the Queen, to whom they vowed themselves now and ever to be most dutiful and obedient subjects'. That the rebels intended to free Mary of Scotland, and to put her on Elizabeth's throne, was of course never mentioned.

The enthusiasm of the insurgents counted for little when few flocked to their side. The letters they sent out to the great Catholic magnates exhorting them to their cause went unanswered, but instead were forwarded to the Queen as proof of their loyalty to her. With so few numbers, and news of a great army marching north against them, the rebels lost heart and scattered. While Westmorland made his way to safety in the Netherlands, Northumberland was not so lucky. He was captured by the Scots and handed over to the English.

Norfolk was never implicated in the Earls' folly, and he was even well treated by the Queen. During his confinement, she saw to it that her cousin was comfortably lodged in the Tower of London as his rank dictated, and she did not press for a trial. When a bout of plague infected the Tower in the summer of 1570, she even had Norfolk released that August and put under house arrest instead. But despite his declarations of loyalty and his promises to distance himself from Mary Stuart, Elizabeth remained sceptical. When New Year came and Norfolk sent her a costly jewel to win back her favour, she declined the gift. She could not accept it, she said regretfully, until they were 'better friends' again.

Elizabeth's mistrust of Norfolk was well warranted as he had never given up hope of marrying Mary Stuart. Even during his incarceration, Thomas Howard had continued to correspond with her through smuggled letters. In them, Mary reaffirmed her devotion to the Duke. Once their marriage was a *fait accompli*, 'the Queen of England and country should like of it', Mary assured him.

Should Elizabeth not approve, there was also conspiracy at Mary's disposal. The time was opportune. Earlier in January 1570, the Regent Moray had been assassinated in Linlithgow. With her hated half-brother gone, Mary had high hopes of wearing the Scottish Crown once again, and, if Heaven allowed it, the English one as well. In February, Pope Pius V, in response to the collapse of the Northern rising, excommunicated her cousin. Henceforth, all English Catholics were absolved of their allegiance to 'the pretended Queen of England'. In other words, it would be no crime to depose or kill such a 'servant of all iniquity', as the Pope called Elizabeth.

The challenge was taken up by one Roberto Ridolfi. A banker by profession and a conspirator by nature, the eloquent and persuasive Florentine contacted Mary in January 1571, promising her everything her heart could desire. With her approval, he said, he would arrange for the Pope and the King of Spain to assist her with military aid and make her ruler of England with Norfolk at her side. Excited, Mary agreed, and she named the Bishop of Ross as her go-between. Norfolk, however, was more difficult to convince. As he had done before, to the dismay of the Northern Earls, he hemmed and hawed. But by the third week of March, when Ridolfi was leaving for the Continent, Norfolk made up his mind and gave his endorsement as well.

While Ridolfi was busy soliciting the help of the Spaniards and the Vatican, Norfolk arranged for a consignment of cash - 600 gold coins - to be conveyed to Mary's supporters in Scotland that summer. The money never left London. The Duke's baggage was opened up by a suspicious messenger and its contents duly reported to the authorities. Cecil, or rather Baron Burghley as he had been since February, was already suspicious of Norfolk when a packet of strange letters written in code was found on a servant of the Bishop of Ross at Dover. When deciphered, the Duke's name was mentioned. Evidently, he had forsaken his promise to his Queen, and in September, he was back in prison.

The Bishop of Ross was also arrested. John Leslie invoked his right to diplomatic immunity, but to no avail. For engaging in treason 'against the Prince to whom he is sent', Leslie had 'forfeited the privileges of an ambassador, and is liable to punishment'. His servant had already been put to the rack, and the Bishop himself was next if he remained uncooperative. Terrified, Leslie confessed all. With the unravelling of the plot, there was much finger pointing among the conspirators. The Queen of Scots denied all, as did Norfolk. Both of them blamed Ridolfi and their overzealous friends for encouraging treason in their name. For his part, Leslie excused himself as a mere servant acting on his mistress's behalf, and then, to save his skin, utterly deserted her. Mary, Leslie blurted out, was a notorious adulteress and murderess. Having done away with three husbands already, she intended to kill Norfolk once he had served his purpose. After listening to the Bishop's wild accusations, his flabbergasted interrogator could not help but exclaim, "Lord! What a people are these! What a queen! What an ambassador!"

On 16 January 1572, Thomas Howard stood trial at Westminster. Never one to accept responsibility for his actions, he pleaded not guilty. However, the evidence proving his ties to Mary Stuart and Roberto Ridolfi was overwhelmingly against him. The Duke was convicted of high treason, and like his father before him, was sentenced to go to the block. But would he? For months afterwards, the Queen delayed putting her cousin to death. It was not that she was unsure of his guilt – she was convinced of it - but still she hesitated. Norfolk was of her own blood, and he was second in rank only to herself. It took all of Burghley's persuasive powers to convince Elizabeth that the Duke must be brought to justice as an example to other traitors. But in February, when Elizabeth did finally affix her signature to his death warrant, she had it recalled at the last minute. She would do so again and again in the months to follow.

Elizabeth was just as reluctant to proceed against Mary – that 'daughter of debate that discord aye doth sow'. Her cousin, she still insisted, was a God anointed Queen - accountable to *His* judgement only, not an earthly one. But Elizabeth's regard for Mary's sacrosanct nature was not shared by her subjects. To them, the Queen of Scots was a criminal and must be dealt with as such. When Parliament met in the spring, its members howled for her blood along with Norfolk's. To avoid the unpleasantness of a public trial, the Lords and Commons hoped to have Mary condemned by an Act of Attainder. Elizabeth rejected the idea, but she was open to compromise, she said. She allowed a motion (later rejected) to have Mary legally stripped of her rights to the English Crown go to debate.

To preserve Mary's life, Elizabeth gave up Norfolk. Lest she be perceived as weak, and unworthy of her high station by both her subjects and her enemies, justice must be carried out. After many delays, the Queen allowed Norfolk's death warrant – the *fifth* – to go to the Lieutenant of the Tower without a retraction. Perhaps an end to the agony of waiting was a relief to Norfolk himself. On 2 June 1572, he mounted the scaffold on Tower Hill – the very spot where his father Surrey had perished. Before he submitted himself to the headsman, the Duke addressed the onlookers. "For men to suffer death in this place is no new thing", he said, "though since the beginning of our most gracious Queen's reign I am the first, and God grant I may be the last."

The crowd responded with a collective 'amen'.

Chapter 37
The Frog Prince

THE QUEEN'S vacillation over Norfolk that spring had driven Lord Burghley to set down his frustrations on paper. In a private memorandum to himself written in April 1572, he criticised Elizabeth for her various shortcomings: she did not better advance the Protestant religion; she appeared more favourable to Mary Stuart than to her son King James VI's government, and she was slow to promote men in her service. Topping the list of his grievances was Elizabeth's continuing 'coldness and forbearing' towards marriage. At almost forty, her chances of having children were diminishing with each passing year. As such, there would surely be 'doubtfulness in foreign princes to contract and establish amity otherwise than to serve their own turns', Burghley worried. Even if the Queen did finally agree to marry at this late stage in her life, she might end up like her sister - bereft of children and unloved by her husband.

Nonetheless, Elizabeth *must* marry, according to Burghley. Besides the provision of an heir, the foreign situation demanded she take a husband to protect her kingdom. King Philip was no friend to England and to the Protestant religion; not by his support of the Ridolfi Plot, and certainly not by his warlike posturing. His army - numbering thirty-five thousand strong – stationed in the Netherlands since 1567, was too close for comfort. In fact, his troops might actually have invaded England except that their commander, the Duke of Alva, had considered Ridolfi's plan harebrained. Added to the threat of Spain was the danger posed by fanatical Catholics both within and without the kingdom. Given free licence to kill Elizabeth with impunity, all it took was a pull of a trigger or the thrust of a dagger for a man to win the gratitude of the Pope.

The precariousness of her position was not lost on Elizabeth herself, and in June 1572, she welcomed an embassy from France. Her dealings with the House of Valois had not always been so cordial. In the past, both Henry II and Francis II had claimed her Crown on behalf of Mary Queen of Scots, and more recently, there was a suspicion that Charles IX had lent support to the Northern rebels. But of late, relations between the two ancient enemies had warmed. Like England, France had become distrustful of Spain ever since their alliance was severed by the death of the French King's sister, Elisabeth - King Philip's third wife - in 1568. Charles and his mother, Catherine de' Medici, were now just as eager to check the power of their former in-law, the 'proud Spaniard', as Elizabeth was. To counteract Philip's ambitions, particularly in the Netherlands, Charles' youngest brother, Francis, Duke of Alençon, was formally offered up to Elizabeth.

Burghley might have been sceptical as to how far the Queen would commit herself to marriage this time around. She had already rejected Erik of Sweden, Archduke Charles, Charles IX, and, two years earlier, the French King's younger brother Henry, Duke of Anjou. The Duke had proved too stiff-necked a Catholic for Elizabeth's taste, and he was rumoured to prefer the company of his male favourites. There was also concern about his age. At nineteen, Anjou was eighteen years younger than the Queen. At the height of the negotiations, Elizabeth had made light of the difference, but it was clearly a sensitive subject for her. When the outspoken Lady Cobham alluded to the 'great inequality' of age between her mistress and the Duke, Elizabeth angrily retorted, "There are but *ten* years between us"! Lady Cobham knew better than to correct the Queen's arithmetic.

The gap was even wider with Anjou's younger brother, Alençon, born in 1555. As expected, Elizabeth was cool to the idea of marrying a man who could well have been her son, and she dismissed the French ambassadors with her regrets. But within days, they were recalled to court. The triple threat of Philip of Spain, the Pope, and Mary Stuart was too great to ignore, and England needed a powerful friend in Europe. Elizabeth told the French she would consider Alençon if - and only if – he agreed to come in person that she might see him beforehand. Catherine de' Medici, who was already expressing affection for Elizabeth - 'I already love you as a mother does her daughter', she had written - was delighted. Intent on dominating Europe through her children, the Queen Mother ordered Alençon to make ready for England.

≡

As Elizabeth prepared for the coming of the Duke, she spent the summer on progress. It was one of her great pleasures to leave behind the cares of government when she could and tour her kingdom. These excursions were not just holidays for Elizabeth, but exercises in public relations. By allowing herself to be seen by her people, the Queen

Figure 27   Francis of Valois, Duke of Alençon by an
Unknown Artist
The National Gallery of Art, Washington D.C.

fostered their good will and their loyalty to her. This was particularly important as the vast majority of her subjects outside the capital had never laid eyes on her. They knew her only as a face on a coin or a name in a proclamation rather than as an actual person of flesh and blood.

Throughout her long reign, Elizabeth would never venture beyond the borders of her kingdom. Her itinerary was mostly confined to the southern region of her realm, and the farthest north she ever went was Staffordshire. Like her father's expedition to York in 1541, Elizabeth's travels were a veritable court-on-the-move. The logistics involved both the Queen's officials and her hosts. The former had to ensure that provisions of food were on hand and that lodgings were in readiness once Elizabeth and her retinue arrived at their destination. The Queen would, of course, stay in the best accommodations available with her most intimate ladies, and, if there were room, quarters would be allotted to her best-favoured courtiers. The rest would be put up in billeted houses and inns close by, or, if necessary, in great moveable tents.

Given notice of the Queen's coming ahead of time, the civic authorities made certain that everything was shipshape. As if it were a coronation, the city was cleaned up and decorated, particularly the areas through which Elizabeth would pass. Buildings were repaired and repainted, the royal arms prominently and loyally displayed, and the streets paved and covered over with rushes and sweet smelling herbs (Elizabeth was particularly sensitive to odours). To give her a proper greeting, scaffolds were erected for the presentation of speeches and entertainments. As these were being set up, costumed performers rehearsed orations, poems, pantomimes, and songs in honour of their special visitor. There was also the matter of a welcoming gift for the Queen. A purse of money was sufficient, but if the city fathers wanted to give something extra special - like a jewel or a piece of goldsmith's work for her table – a trip was made to London to acquire something appropriate.

While the people were delighted to have the Queen in their midst, the great lords or magnates along her route were sometimes less so. At each stop she made, Elizabeth expected to be lavishly entertained and housed - at the owner's expense of course. Keeping in mind how large her entourage was, the costs for even a short stay could be crippling to her host. Whenever Elizabeth visited Lord Burghley's country estate of Theobalds in Essex, his expenditure was about two to three thousand pounds. Burghley, a wealthy man, was always glad to receive the Queen, but not all the lords could afford to be so hospitable. When the impoverished Earl of Lincoln heard Elizabeth was planning to pay him a visit, he quickly closed up his house and disappeared.

For her progress that summer of 1572, Elizabeth spent three days at Theobalds, before gracing the homes of Lord Keeper Bacon and the Earl of Bedford. By 12 August, she was in Warwick as the guest of Ambrose Dudley and his wife Anne. As an old friend, she had the honour of sitting with the Queen in her carriage.

In spite of the bad weather, thousands showed up to greet the Queen. The town recorder, a visibly nervous Edward Aglionby, gave a speech of welcome comparing Elizabeth to Alexander the Great, Gaius Marius, Caesar Augustus, and to her forbears Henry VII and Henry VIII. This was followed by a lengthy discourse on the borough's history, from its origins in the time of the ancient Britons down to Queen Mary's benefaction of the town. If Elizabeth was bored, she never showed it. She gave Aglionby her complete attention until he had finished. After she graciously accepted a gift of £20, she called the 'little Recorder' to her and put him at ease. "It was told to me", she said smiling, "that you would be afraid to look upon me, or to speak boldly, but you were not so afraid of me as I was of you".

Elizabeth stayed with her hosts at Warwick Castle. She was entertained by dances put on by the townsfolk, by mock battles between Ambrose Dudley and the Earl of Oxford, and by fireworks in the evenings. As Kenilworth, Leicester's great estate, was nearby, Elizabeth spent a few days there with him in private, taking only a handful of her attendants with her while the rest of her court stayed behind at Warwick Castle.

Elizabeth's holiday was interrupted by shocking news from abroad. France, embroiled in a decade-long civil war between its Catholics and its Protestants (known as Huguenots), had imploded. Paris, it was reported, was soaked in blood; the blood of Huguenots massacred in their thousands. The Queen returned to London as quickly as possible to meet with her Council. From Francis Walsingham, her representative in France, it was learnt that the atrocities had been triggered by an attempt on the life of the Huguenot leader, the Admiral de Coligny. His enemies, the fervidly Catholic Guises – Mary Stuart's relatives - were behind the plot, as was Catherine de' Medici, who resented de Coligny's influence on her son the King. Fearing exposure when the Admiral survived the assassination, Catherine convinced Charles that the Huguenot leaders assembled in Paris to attend the wedding of his sister Margaret to the Protestant Prince Henry of Navarre – a union meant to pacify the warring factions - were planning to topple his government. Believing his mother's story, the King ordered their deaths.

What was meant to be the slaughter of a handful of Protestants on 24 August - St Bartholomew's Day - turned into a bloodbath. Once the killings started, hoards of zealous Catholics unleashed their hatred for their heretical neighbours. No man, woman, or child known to be or suspected of being a Huguenot was spared. Some three thousand corpses littered the city - and it did not stop there. The carnage spread beyond Paris, even as far as Bordeaux, despite the French government's desperate pleas for the violence to end.

Burghley called the massacre the greatest crime since the Crucifixion, and Walsingham, who was an eyewitness to the event and an ardent Protestant like Cecil, echoed his revulsion. Writing from Paris, he advised the Queen to abandon any alliance with the House of Valois, and to regard them 'as enemies than as friends'. But Elizabeth, though she was as shaken as the rest of the Protestant community, could not act so precipitously. She still needed a powerful ally against her enemies, even if it was Catholic France. When the French ambassador came to court to offer his government's side of the story, Elizabeth, after a show of shock and anger, had to accept his explanation that the 'late accident' was a regrettable event, which King Charles had not ordered and could not contain. As a sign of her continuing goodwill to France, Elizabeth agreed to act as godmother to Charles' newborn daughter in October.

After relations with England had been smoothed over, Catherine de' Medici turned from murder to matchmaking. In 1573, the Queen Mother offered up her son Alençon to Elizabeth once again. Needing the friendship of France and perhaps reconciling herself to the idea of marriage and children, at last, Elizabeth consented to his coming. But again, she imposed conditions. Not only must the Duke woo her in person, as she had insisted the year before, but he 'should hold it to be neither prejudice nor disgrace unto him, if he returned without speeding in his suit' as well. On behalf of her son, Catherine agreed.

But six years were to pass before Elizabeth laid eyes on the Duke - or 'Monsieur', as he was usually called. In May 1574, Charles IX died at the age of twenty-three of tuberculosis – though his enemies preferred to say of remorse over the St Bartholomew's Day Massacre - and was succeeded by his brother, the Queen's former suitor, Henry of Anjou. Now next in line to the French throne after the still childless Henry, Alençon imagined a great future for himself. Besides being King of England, the Duke, a half-hearted Roman Catholic, envisioned himself as the defender of the Dutch Protestants struggling against the oppressive yoke of Spain. His ambitions in the Netherlands kept him occupied for the next few years, and it was not until 1579 that he began his formal courtship of Elizabeth.

In January, Alençon despatched his agent Jean de Simier to England to play Cupid. 'A most choice courtier, exquisitely skilled in love toys, pleasant conceits, and court dalliances', the Frenchman easily charmed the English Queen. She took pleasure in his company and was amused by his mischievous ways. When de Simier crept into her bedroom one morning and stole her nightcap, she allowed him to send it to his master as a token of her affection.

The Duke reciprocated with an unending stream of love letters and gifts. With Elizabeth so receptive to his wooing, Alençon set out to England as promised. On 17 August, he arrived at Greenwich, but kept himself incognito as prearranged. When she set eyes on him at last, she did so with trepidation at first. She had been forewarned - particularly by those opposed to the match - that the Duke was not handsome. He was short, had a big nose, and was scarred by a childish bout of smallpox. But what Alençon lacked in beauty, he made up with abundant charisma and a unique brand of sex appeal. Elizabeth found Monsieur captivating, and in a short time, she was swept off her feet. The Queen always had nicknames for her favourites, and the Duke was christened her *Frog*, and his spokesman, de Simier, her *Monkey*.

Alençon's visit was meant to be a secret, but Elizabeth's behaviour easily betrayed his presence at court. During his short stay, she was in an exuberant mood, and she could not stop talking about the Duke. 'She danced much more than usual', and when she did, she would gaze lovingly towards a curtained alcove where a certain someone had concealed himself. With Elizabeth dropping so many hints, her courtiers were well aware of having the Duke among them. Nevertheless, they indulged the Queen in her charade and said nothing. When Alençon took his leave at the end of August, Elizabeth saw him off with tears. By her affection for him, everyone was convinced that when he returned, they would be man and wife.

To Elizabeth's subjects, the prospect of having a Catholic foreigner yet again as their King was anathema, especially one whose family was blamed for the St Bartholomew's Day Massacre. John Stubbs, 'a fervent professor of religion', spoke for his countrymen when he published a pamphlet in September entitled *The Discovery of a Gaping Gulf whereunto England is like to be swallowed by another French marriage if the Lord forbid not the bans by letting Her Majesty see the sin and punishment thereof.* Its wordy and bombastic title said it all. Elizabeth was greatly offended at Stubbs' presumption, and she ordered him punished. It was an unpopular move, but no one could shake her resolve - not her lawmakers who thought the author had committed no real crime, and not de Simier who thought it best to simply ignore such rabble-rousers. On 3 November, Stubbs was brought to the public scaffold to lose his right hand. Swearing perpetual 'duty and affection toward Her Majesty', he submitted himself to punishment. Immediately after the axe did its work, Stubbs, with his remaining hand, pulled off his hat and shouted, "God save the Queen"! before he collapsed from shock.

The widespread opposition to Monsieur the Duke did not deter Elizabeth. Determined to have him still, she pushed her Councillors for a unanimous recommendation for her to marry. Her request only created division. While Burghley, Sussex, and a few others supported the Queen, another faction, led by a very vocal Leicester, was wholly opposed. As no consensus could be reached, the Council, weary of the bickering amongst themselves, agreed as a whole to abide by whatever decision the Queen made.

When told, Elizabeth exploded. After years of begging and badgering her to take a husband, it was now her Council who had cold feet. She had expected them to press her into accepting the Duke, but they had utterly failed her. The decision as always was hers alone, and she did not know which way to turn. Deeply upset, Elizabeth tore into her Councillors heaping blame on them. Was there no better 'surety to her and her realm', she demanded, 'than to have her marry, and have a child of her own body to inherit, and so continue the line of Henry VIII?' How foolish she was, she went on, in 'committing this matter to them', for instead of 'a universal request made for her to proceed in this marriage', all she got was 'doubt in it'. For days afterwards, the Queen was observed to be in the foulest of moods.

Of her naysayers, Elizabeth was most angry with Leicester, and de Simier saw his chance to get him into even more trouble. During his stay at the English court, the Frenchman always kept his ears open for any news, information, or gossip to further his master's cause. It was a godsend when he heard that Robert Dudley had secretly taken another wife. Unbeknownst to the Queen, his relationship with Lettice Knollys, her vivacious cousin, had turned from a mere flirtation into a clandestine romance. When Lettice's husband, the Earl of Essex, died in service in Ireland in 1576, she and Leicester married in secret two years later.

All it took to undo Leicester were a few whispered words into the Queen's ear by her *Monkey*. Elizabeth was beside herself with rage. Not only had she trusted Lord Robert since they had been children together, but it was he who for years had dissuaded her from marriage, only to enter into that estate himself. Leicester's tears and his excuses that he had only meant to provide himself with a Dudley heir, availed him nothing. Elizabeth had him put under house arrest at Greenwich.

She would have transferred Leicester to the Tower afterwards if not for the great uproar on his behalf. To the Queen's subjects, it was outrageous for the Earl to be treated as such. He had committed no offence in marrying, and as a good Englishman and a committed Protestant, he had done his duty in speaking his mind against the Queen's union with a French Catholic. Even Sussex, no friend to Leicester, pleaded for him. He knew that if the Queen dealt too harshly with Dudley, the Alençon marriage would be jeopardised by universal hatred for the Duke. Eventually, Elizabeth relented and she released Leicester. But his betrayal still wounded her deeply, and it was some time before Lord Robert was back in her good graces. On the other hand, the Queen never forgave her cousin Lettice. The Countess of Leicester was told to keep herself away from court.

Ironically, Leicester found himself appointed to a committee finalising the Queen's marriage in April 1581. A contract was drawn up in which Alençon's obligations and rights were clearly defined. In short, like Philip of Spain before him, he would have the 'title and honour of a king', but would exercise no power. He was not to elevate any Frenchman into government, and as a Catholic, 'alter nothing in the religion now received in England'. He was also bound not to engage his new country in a foreign war. If he and Elizabeth had children, the Duke would be their guardian if the Queen predeceased him, but only until they came of age. As her husband, Alençon was also expected to provide Elizabeth with a dowry worth forty thousand crowns. In return, the Queen would bestow on him an annual pension during their marriage, and even afterwards should he outlive her. She would even grant him the extraordinary right – denied to her previous Catholic suitors – to hear Mass in private.

The terms were acceptable to the French. Once Henry III ratified the documents, they expected to see the couple wed in six weeks time. But just when it seemed that both sides were in perfect agreement, Elizabeth prevaricated. Because of the present circumstances, she said, the marriage must be delayed. Her people were still opposed to her accepting the Duke, and with him fighting the Spaniards with the Dutch, she would inevitably find herself 'engaged in her husband's war' (even though she herself was giving the Netherlanders aid discreetly). Once her people were more accepting of the idea of Monsieur as their King, and once his commitments in the Low Countries were over, she would have him without hesitation, Elizabeth promised.

Wanting to hasten the marriage, the French were certain that if Alençon made another appearance in England, matters would come to a happy conclusion. Sure enough, they seemed to be right. When the Duke returned on 31 October, there was a joyful reunion between him and the Queen. As before, Elizabeth appeared entirely infatuated with him, and she and Monsieur were seldom seen apart. Shortly after Accession Day - 17 November, when the Queen's coming to the throne was celebrated throughout the kingdom – Elizabeth made a startling announcement. "You may write this to the King", she told the French ambassador, "the Duke of Alençon *shall* be my husband". And as if the nuptials were being performed then and there, the Queen took a ring off her finger, slipped it on the Duke's, and gave him a loving kiss.

Reaction to the Queen's declaration was decidedly mixed. The Dutch, who looked to Elizabeth and Monsieur as their saviours from the Spaniards, were thrilled. In Antwerp, bells were rung and bonfires lit in anticipation of the joyful event. But closer to home, while some 'leaped for joy', 'some were astonished, and some were cast down with sorrow'. Even the Queen was a jumble of emotions. After pledging herself to Alençon, she began to have doubts. What those were she never revealed. Was it concern about her advancing age, the dangers of childbirth, or even sexual intimacy? Whatever it was, the more Elizabeth thought about what she had got herself into, the more fearful she became. Burghley and Sussex's reassurances did little to comfort her, and she paid increasing attention to Leicester and Walsingham's predictions of doom and gloom should she marry.

Even in her privy chamber, there was a chorus of disapproval. Instead of being happy for her, her ladies did nothing but wail and weep as if their mistress were going to her death as Alençon's wife.

After a 'night in doubtful care without sleep', Elizabeth summoned Alençon to her. No one was present at their meeting, but it was clear what was said. After a long talk, a dejected Monsieur returned to his room. He drew the Queen's ring off his finger and cursed 'the lightness of women, and the inconstancy of islanders'. It was all over.

Before ever coming to England, Alençon had promised Elizabeth he would bear no resentment should she reject him. If not his vow, English gold had Monsieur keeping his word. £60,000 was sufficient to redeem his injured pride and to finance his ambitions in the Netherlands. 'She would give a million… to have her *Frog* swimming in the Thames rather than in the stagnant waters of the Netherlands', Elizabeth was heard to say, but the Spanish ambassador, Bernardino de Mendoza, scoffed. The Queen, he reported to King Philip earlier, had danced for joy when she finally wiggled out of her engagement, and she had even supposedly told Lord Burghley that were she to be made an empress, she would still not marry the Duke. The envoy was correct that Elizabeth had come to regret pledging herself to Monsieur, but that she had never wanted him to begin with was an overstatement. It appeared that Elizabeth had genuinely hoped to marry, but 'for reasons which she would not indulge to a twin soul, if she had one, much less to a living creature', she could not commit herself in the end.

≡

While Alençon was keen to be protector of the Dutch Protestants, Elizabeth was ever reluctant to accept the role. She had no ambitions towards military glory, and she was no petty prince needing to prove herself on the international stage. Nonetheless, circumstances forced Elizabeth to intervene in the Netherlands.

Philip of Spain's relationship with his Dutch subjects had never been good. His encroachment of their traditional liberties earned their hatred, as did his policy to stamp out the Protestant faith in the Low Countries. Spanish rule become even more detestable when Philip dispatched his henchman, the Duke of Alva, to quell dissent and to strengthen his authority. Alva introduced unpopular taxes, and his so-called 'Council of Troubles' (or 'Council of Blood' as his enemies called it) brutally suppressed any opposition to his master and to the Catholic Church.

Alva had taken no part in the Ridolfi Plot, but the English remained wary of the Spanish presence just across the sea. When the Duke was recalled in 1573, Elizabeth saw an opportunity to reach a settlement with Philip. Though she did not approve of his actions towards the Dutch, as a sovereign herself Elizabeth recognised Philip's right to rule as he pleased. That said, she expected the Dutch – including those who were Protestant – to conduct themselves as obedient subjects. As her own English Catholics were obliged to live by her Protestant Settlement, so must the Dutch abide by the religion of their King.

Unfortunately, Elizabeth's efforts to mediate foundered. Philip was inflexible, as was William of Orange, leader of the resistance against Spain. In hopes of inducing England to his side, William had offered Elizabeth sovereignty of Holland, Zeeland, and Utrecht. She declined. To accept would be to condone rebellion, and she had no wish to be drawn into an open war with Spain. Snubbed by the Queen, the Dutch appealed to France instead for help. Elizabeth's reaction was totally unexpected. Having no desire to see the French occupy the Low Countries, she sent an envoy to Spain to warn Philip against William.

In a twist of diplomacy, Elizabeth was, however, willing to finance Alençon against the Spanish. Estranged from his brother the French King, the Duke posed no threat to England in himself, and even though she had made up her mind to remain single at the end of 1581, Elizabeth continued to dangle the prospect of marriage before him. From the Low Countries, Alençon addressed letters to her as 'my wife the Queen of England' as she had asked him to. But Elizabeth's frog prince was a better lover than he was a soldier. Puffed up with pride at his welcome by the Dutch, he failed to live up to their expectations of him. His campaigns were disasters, and Alençon eventually limped back to France in disgrace. Before he had a chance to redeem himself, he became ill and died in June 1584.

Upon the tragic news, the Queen donned mourning and took to calling herself 'a widow woman'. The French ambassador dismissed it as play acting, but he was too cynical. Elizabeth was genuinely affected by Alençon's death, and she wrote to Catherine de' Medici to express her condolences:

'Your sorrow cannot exceed mine, although you are his mother. You have several other children, but for myself I find no consolation, if it be not death, in which I hope we shall be reunited.'

Elizabeth's sentiments might have been exaggerated for the Queen Mother's sake, but that is not to say she was insincere.

Her bereavement was interrupted by another tragedy. Barely a month after Alençon's death, William of Orange was assassinated. In the ensuing turmoil, the States General again offered to make Elizabeth their sovereign lady, but again she turned them down. She was unwilling to provoke the King of Spain too far, but at the same time she could not sit on the fence. In December, Elizabeth received intelligence that Philip had allied himself with the Guises to establish a 'Catholic League' against their Protestant foes. Elizabeth was certain that after they had vanquished the Dutch and the Huguenots, the English would be next.

To defend against the threat, the Queen agreed to meet with delegates from Holland beginning in June 1585. By the Treaty of Nonsuch, she would provide the Dutch with military aid, but not without guarantees from them in return. After the Spaniards had been expelled, her treasury was to be reimbursed 'to the last farthing', and in the meantime, 'a town in each province' was to be handed over as collateral.

The number of troops Elizabeth was willing to lend had to be increased when in August Antwerp surrendered to Philip's new governor, his nephew, Alexander Farnese (later made Duke of Parma). The four thousand foot soldiers the Queen had originally committed were raised by another thousand, and an extra six hundred cavalrymen were added to the initial four hundred. Such a force required a leader of distinction, and Leicester offered to take on the role.

At fifty-two, Robert Dudley was no longer the athlete of his youth. He had become portly with age, requiring the Queen to watch over his diet, and various aches and pains had him frequenting the spas at Buxton. Nonetheless, an opportunity at military glory revitalised Leicester, and he prepared himself for battle. Elizabeth had mixed feelings about letting him go, but in the end, she wished him luck and success. However, by her express command, his wife the Countess was not to accompany him. Knowing how the Dutch would give Leicester a hero's welcome, Elizabeth had no desire to see her insufferable cousin Lettice received by them as well.

'The General of the Queen of England's Auxiliary Forces', as the Earl was known, received a rapturous welcome in the Netherlands that December. Triumphal processions, tournaments, and feasts were held in his honour, and in the evenings the skies above Holland were ablaze with fireworks. Leicester's reception by the Dutch got to his head, and he gladly accepted the lofty title of Governor General from them. After he was formally installed in January 1586, the United Provinces even struck coins in commemoration. Leicester was depicted like an emperor of antiquity. In his fists were the emblems of war – arrows and a great sword, and on his brow was a crown of laurel anticipating his glorious feats ahead.

But back home, Elizabeth was not pleased. How dare the Dutch make Leicester Governor, she stormed, and how dare he accept? She had not rejected sovereignty over the Netherlands only to have it handed over to Leicester. What also piqued Elizabeth was that Dudley had given her his word that he would not take on any great titles even if pressed by the Dutchmen. She dashed off a scathing letter to the Earl holding nothing back:

> 'How contemptuously we conceive ourself to have been used by you… we could never have imagined… that a man raised up by ourself, and extraordinarily favoured by us above any subject of this land, would have in so contemptible a sort broke our commandment in a cause that so greatly toucheth us.'

She included a warning to Leicester that it would be to his 'uttermost peril' should he disobey any further instructions. Dudley was cowed, but ultimately, it was the Queen who yielded. He was allowed to keep his precious title of Governor, but not without more harsh words from her.

Elizabeth had more reason to regret appointing Leicester in the months to follow. Quarrelsome, arrogant, and insensitive, the new Governor general alienated many of the Dutch he had been sent to relieve, raising 'great hatred against himself among the people'. He was also not the great warlord he thought himself to be, when he lost Grave, a strategically important town, to the Duke of Parma. Leicester unfairly blamed its governor Van Hemart, 'a young man unskilful in military matters', for its surrender, and in a move that made him even more unpopular, he had the innocent Van Hemart executed for colluding with the Spaniards.

Leicester did better at Zutphen in September when his army valiantly prevented the enemy from transporting provisions to the Spanish-held town. But the victory came at a personal cost to Dudley. His nephew, Philip Sidney, an ornament of the Queen's court as a rising statesman, intellectual, and soldier of ability, was killed. Leicester was devastated. The young man was, in his uncle's own words, his 'greatest comfort, next her Majesty'. Sidney's passing was universally mourned. When his remains were sent back to England, he was given a lavish hero's burial at St Paul's.

Disheartened by his nephew's death and by his own lack progress in the Netherlands, Leicester requested a leave of absence from his duties. Elizabeth, who had not seen him for almost a year, gladly consented.

Chapter 38
That Wicked Murderess

'THE QUEEN of Scots is and shall always be', William Cecil told Elizabeth in 1569, 'a dangerous person to your estate'. In the years following his warning, Burghley never wavered from his opinion of Mary Stuart. Even after the Northern Rebellion was crushed and the Ridolfi Plot unravelled, the Scottish Queen remained a focus of conspiracy.

Mary's remarkable talent for inspiring devotion had not been diminished by her being kept close or by the onset of age on her person. By the 1580s, the celebrated beauty who had dazzled the courts of France and Scotland was a middle-aged invalid. She had grown fat from want of exercise, and she was often ill. But to her supporters, unaware of her decline, the Queen of Scots was still the romantic figure of her youth. This view of Mary was especially appealing to a new generation of Catholics - idealistic young men attracted to her plight. Far from the murderess and adulteress she had been painted as, they regarded Mary as a virtuous princess much wronged by circumstances. Since the Pope had already deprived the 'tyrannical' English Queen of her Crown, Mary's new admirers took it as their duty to execute the sentence. Only by the death of Elizabeth could true religion be restored and the persecution of the faithful be lifted with Mary Stuart as Queen of England.

The discontent of these English Catholics was not unjustified. The government of Queen Elizabeth was becoming increasingly intolerant of the old faith, which it virtually equated with sedition. In their efforts to squash the Catholic religion, laws against recusancy had been tightened and expanded. Fines for non-attendance at Anglican services had been raised, and private celebrations of Mass, often ignored by sympathetic officials, were strictly forbidden. Parliament even made it an offence to convert anyone to the Catholic religion, or even to allow one's self to be turned.

To revive the faith in the kingdom, the seminary college in Douai, founded by an English clergyman named William Allen, trained and ordained his countrymen to be priests and then smuggled them back to England. There, these dedicated men went from town to town, house to house, to administer the sacraments and to give comfort to their fellow believers in secret. Hounded by the authorities, many found themselves having to hide in concealed 'priests' holes' in Catholic homes to evade detection. Those unfortunate enough to be discovered were arrested and questioned. Who and where were the other priests in England? Who were their protectors for whom they performed Mass? And what plots have they heard of involving the King of Spain, the Pope, or the Queen of Scots? Those who remained silent were subjected to the rack. But even torture could not dissuade these priests, as in the case of Edmund Campion. Arrested in 1581, the charismatic Jesuit would not betray his friends despite the excruciating pains he was subjected to. A proud Englishman still, he gladly declared his loyalty to Queen Elizabeth before he was hanged and quartered. For their suffering, Campion and his fellow priests were revered as martyrs.

Against this backdrop of suppression and fear, Mary Stuart's name was linked to a new conspiracy in 1583. That spring, Francis Throckmorton, a nephew of the late Sir Nicholas, Elizabeth's envoy to Scotland, had aroused suspicion by his furtive visits to the French embassy. Francis Walsingham, head of the Queen's secret service, put a tail on him. Throckmorton, it was discovered, was also in contact with de Mendoza, the Spanish ambassador, as well as Mary of Scots. In November, Throckmorton was arrested and put to torture. He would reveal nothing at first, but unable to endure the agony a second time, he cracked. He poured out a confession detailing a joint invasion of England by Mary's kinsman the Duke of Guise, and by Philip of Spain. The Queen of Scotland herself had fully approved of the plot by smuggling out letters behind the back of her custodian the Earl of Shrewsbury.

Thwarted though she was again, Mary did not give up. When another scheme was formed in the beginning of 1586, she was elated. Secret communications had reached Mary at Chartley Hall in Staffordshire recommending the services of a Catholic named Gilbert Gifford. He would be most helpful to her, she was told, in forwarding her messages to her supporters. Mary agreed to use him. She thought Gifford's idea of sending out and receiving messages by hiding them in the stoppers of the barrels of ale coming in and out of Chartley most ingenious. What she did not know was that Gifford was in the pay of Walsingham.

She was then put in touch with a wealthy Catholic gentleman named Anthony Babington. The young man, like Throckmorton before him, was devoted to her cause, and would do all he could to see Mary as Queen of England. De Mendoza, expelled from England for his plotting, gave Babington his support from France, where he was now serving as ambassador, and he promised him and his like-minded friends the help of King Philip. After they had done away with Elizabeth, a Spanish army would overthrow her government and install the Queen of Scots on her throne.

Unbeknownst to Mary and her supporters, Walsingham was keeping close tabs on their every move. The Queen of Scots was falling into his trap, but she still had yet to incriminate herself in writing. Knowing how reluctant Elizabeth was to proceed against Mary – she had refused to bring her to justice after the Throckmorton Plot had been uncovered – Walsingham needed irrefutable proof of her complicity. Overseeing Mary's correspondence, the spymaster was made aware that on 14 July she had received full details from Babington of his intentions to assassinate Queen Elizabeth. But would she go along with him?

The plot invigorated the prisoner at Chartley. In reading Babington's letter, Mary saw a lifeline. It could not fail, she thought, it *must* not. Diplomacy had failed to secure her freedom, thus conspiracy was the only means left to her. If that meant death to Elizabeth, so be it. Mary abhorred violence, but she was determined to be free no matter what it took. Her decision was no doubt made easier by her personal feelings for her kinswoman. Over the years, Mary had come to hate Elizabeth. She was double-dealing and deceitful, and she had dared to appoint herself her judge and jailer. Elizabeth had even stolen her son's affection from her. Not long before, Mary had opened talks with James and with her cousin to be allowed back in Scotland to rule jointly with him. She was utterly let down. James ultimately rejected his mother's proposal, and if that was not enough, he made an alliance with Elizabeth instead. Of the many sorrows in Mary's life, James' betrayal of her probably hurt her the most, leading Mary to the reckless course she would take. On 17 July, Mary agreed to Babington's proposal and placed her life in his hands.

Once the fatal reply had made its way to Walsingham, instead, the spymaster acted. Babington and his friends were rounded up and thrown in the Tower, and Mary herself was formally arrested. A search of her effects revealed the desperation of a woman kept close for eighteen years - letters to and from her English supporters, correspondence with France and with Spain, and dozens of ciphers used to encode her secret messages. Mary's communications, all painstakingly cracked by Walsingham's agents, implicated her in the plotting of her cousin's death.

Elizabeth was horrified. Whatever Mary might have thought of her, Elizabeth always believed she had done her utmost to preserve her cousin's life. Was it not she who had saved Mary when Parliament had been baying for her blood? And was it not she who had protected her again when she had been implicated in the Throckmorton Plot? While there were times that Elizabeth had felt so threatened by Mary that she had called her 'the worst woman in the world, whose head should have been cut off years ago', by and large, she had continued to uphold her kinswoman as a sovereign like herself. Their actions were answerable to no man, but to God alone.

But that argument was worn thin by Mary's inability to stay out of trouble. No longer could Elizabeth defend her cousin's privilege to heavenly judgement alone. She had to agree with her Councillors that Mary – that 'wicked murderess' as even Elizabeth now referred to her as - must face a more earthly tribunal for her crimes. In September, the Queen of Scots was moved to Fortheringhay Castle in Northamptonshire to stand trial.

Naturally, Mary protested. As 'a queen, the daughter of a king, a stranger, and the true kinswoman of the Queen of England', she denied the competency of an English court to try her. She was no subject of her cousin, and thus exempt from her laws, of which Mary added, she was entirely ignorant of as a foreigner. Not even a letter from Elizabeth herself commanding her to submit could move Mary. Only when she was told that she would be tried in her absence, did Mary agree to cooperate.

Beginning on 15 October, she faced her accusers. Mary put up a passionate defence denying all charges against her except her desire to obtain her freedom, which was her right. Sir Amyas Paulet, Mary's current jailer, who was present at the proceedings, dismissed her testimonies as nothing but 'long and artificial speeches'. A Puritan by religion, and a great enemy to papistry, Paulet was convinced of Mary's guilt, especially in light of the fact that Babington and his co-conspirators had already been condemned for high treason. Paulet took grim satisfaction in hearing how they were executed 'not without some note of cruelty'.

The judgement against the Queen of Scots was not rendered at Fortheringhay, but in the Star Chamber at Westminster. On 25 October, the commissioners found Mary guilty of 'tending to the hurt, death, and destruction of the royal person of our sovereign lady the Queen.' Now all that was required was Elizabeth's assent that her cousin be punished.

The Parliamentary delegation, which appeared before the Queen on 12 November, was sorely let down. While expressing gratitude for her preservation and the continual love of her people, Elizabeth was still unwilling to proceed against Mary. She was shocked, she told her audience, that the Scottish Queen – one of her own sex, rank, and blood – should fall 'into so great a crime', but still, she had been willing to forgive her. She had even gone so far, Elizabeth admitted, as to write to Mary in private - though in vain - telling her that if she confessed all, she would be pardoned. As Mary had been found guilty, the matter of her death was 'of greatest consequence', Elizabeth continued, and as such, she dare not act rashly. 'I hope you do not look for any present resolution,' she cautioned the assembly, 'for my manner is… to deliberate long upon that which is once to be resolved'. Beseeching God to guide her, the Queen dismissed the delegation giving them no indication of what she intended to do.

Clearly, Elizabeth was in a quandary. Once again, Parliament was after Mary's life, and even those closest to her were adamant that the lady must die. Leicester, for one, suggested doing away with Mary in secret using poison. But Elizabeth would not hear of it, and she sent a message to Parliament asking for a solution to spare her cousin's life. It had none. 'For the preservation of Christ's true religion, the quiet of the realm, [and the] safety of the Queen's person', Mary must go to the block, the Lords and Commons agreed.

On 24 November, another committee was sent to pressure the Queen. In her speech to the delegates, Elizabeth was tormented by indecision as before:

> 'What will my enemies not say, that for the safety of her own life, a maiden Queen could be content to spill the blood even of her own kinswoman? I may therefore well complain that any man should think me given to cruelty, whereof I am so guiltless and innocent. Nay, I am so far from it that for mine own life, I would *not* touch her.'

And again, she left Parliament in suspense:

> 'And now for your petition, I pray you for this present to content yourselves with an answer without answer. Your judgement I condemn not, neither do I mistake your reasons, but pray you to accept my thankfulness, excuse my doubtfulness, and take in good part my answer answerless.'

Shortly after midnight on 29 January 1587, a strange light illuminated the skies above Fortheringhay Castle. Such portents were always believed to signal doom to princes. Before the Battle of Hastings, a great comet had warned King Harold against the invading Normans, and in 1572, a new star, appearing and then disappearing, in the constellation of Cassiopeia had heralded the demise of Charles IX. To those who witnessed this latest phenomenon, Mary, Queen of Scots was now clearly marked for death.

Even if the heavens decreed Mary must die, it was still left to Elizabeth to do her part. In the weeks since she had met with the delegates from Parliament, she had remained 'answerless' to their petition for her cousin's execution. Besides her long-held regard for Mary's position, Elizabeth was fearful of the reaction from the rest of Europe. Would Scotland and France avenge their former Queen, and would Spain use the killing of a Catholic ruler as justification for war? Whatever the consequences, Elizabeth knew she and her realm would never be safe while the Queen of Scots was alive. When she was alone, Elizabeth was often heard to mutter to herself, 'Suffer or strike! Strike or be stricken!'

As it came down to either herself or Mary, Elizabeth, in what was almost certainly the most agonising decision she ever made, asked for the death warrant to be brought to her on 1 February. When William Davison, the clerk of the Council, placed the document before her, the Queen calmly set pen to paper, putting her name to it with her usual flourish. Having done so, she then told Davison to have the Great Seal affixed to the warrant immediately, and that the execution was not to take place in the courtyard of Fortheringhay, but 'secretly as might be' within the castle. That said, she wanted to hear nothing more of the matter till Mary's head was off.

But as she had done with the Duke of Norfolk, Elizabeth hesitated. After Davison had the warrant sealed as instructed, she stopped him and asked what the hurry was? She saw no reason for haste, she said, but nonetheless the execution *must* proceed – necessity demanded it. It was only the responsibility she dreaded. Perhaps what Leicester had once suggested had Elizabeth jotting a note to Mary's keeper Paulet. Would he, she asked the old man, personally get rid of the Scottish Queen for her?

Elizabeth was referring to the Bond of Association drawn up in 1584 and aimed at Mary Stuart. Its signatories – loyal Englishman throughout the land – had pledged to put to death anyone intending harm to the Queen. Since Paulet had loyally subscribed to the Bond, Elizabeth expected him to do his part – though in secret. Once Mary was killed, it could be given out that she had simply died of natural causes. As much as he hated the Queen of Scots, Paulet refused. He could not, he replied to Elizabeth, shed blood in a manner 'God and the law forbideth', and thus make 'so foul a shipwreck of my conscience or leave so great a blot to my posterity'.

Turned down by Paulet, the responsibility of killing Mary was laid on Elizabeth's shoulders once again – that is until the Council stepped in. Knowing the Queen would put off the deed, as she had done with Norfolk, the members, led by Burghley, agreed to dispatch the warrant to Fortheringhay without further discussion with her.

The Queen of Scots went to her death on the morning of 8 February 1587. Composed and dignified, and with a 'smiling countenance' on her face, she was determined to end her life not as a criminal, but as a martyr to the Catholic faith. Mary had a crucifix borne before her as she entered the Great Hall, and on disrobing on the scaffold, she was seen to be wearing a dress of dark red – the liturgical colour of martyrdom. She refused the ministrations of the Protestant Dean, and before she laid her head on the block, one of her women covered her eyes with a Corpus Christi cloth.

When the news reached London that Mary was no more, the city exploded with joy. Bells were rung and the citizens offered their grateful thanks to God. Unaware of what had happened, Elizabeth asked the meaning of the uproar. When told of Mary Stuart's death, she was aghast. 'Her countenance and her words failed her', and she gave way to profound grief. After weeping copious tears, she let loose her anger. She demanded that Davison be put in the Tower, and even Lord Burghley was banished from her presence. Desperate to extricate herself from the terrible deed, Elizabeth even considered having her Councillors tried for treason, demanding of her judges whether she

THE TURBULENT CROWN

had grounds to proceed. A frightened Cecil had to write in secret to one of his friends telling him to convince the justices not to side with the Queen.

To the courts of Europe, the official line given by her ambassadors was that Elizabeth had never meant for her cousin to die. She had only signed the death warrant to satisfy her people, but Davison and her Councillors had deceived her acting on their own initiative. As she had 'sworn to God with many oaths', she was innocent of Mary's execution. That, of course, was not entirely true, but Elizabeth's remorse was genuine. Years afterwards, when her own end was approaching, it was said that her grief was only matched by the sorrow she had felt for the Queen of Scots.

Chapter 39
The Enterprise of England

'THE THEATRE of the whole world is much wider than the kingdom of England,' Mary Stuart had warned her accusers. Indeed, the repercussions of her death were felt throughout Europe. In the streets of Paris, angry mobs denounced the killing of their former Queen, and in Edinburgh, a horrified King James spoke of retaliation by arms. The furore eventually subsided with the French and the Scots accepting Mary's execution as the 'miserable accident' Elizabeth claimed it to be, but the Spaniards were not convinced. Hearing of the tragedy at Fortheringhay, Bernardino de Mendoza wrote to King Philip urging him to take action:

> 'And as God had so willed that these accursed people, for His ends should fall onto *reprobrium sensum*, and against all reason commit such an act as this, it is evidently His design to deliver these two kingdoms into Your Majesty's hands.'

Philip needed no convincing. 'Deeply hurt' by the Scottish Queen's execution, he vowed to avenge her death. Philip's grand gesture, it must be said, was not so much for Mary as it was for himself. Sometime during a rift with her son, Mary had impulsively disinherited James. Unless he became a Catholic, she vowed, she would bestow her claim to the English throne on the King of Spain instead. Even though Mary had later regretted making such a bequest, Philip had it in writing, and he intended to take possession of the English Crown. After all, by lineage, he was a descendant of the royal House of Lancaster, and by religion, more suitable, in the eyes of the Catholic Church, to rule England than Elizabeth or that 'young heretic' James. In that resolve, Philip ordered his envoy in Rome to obtain the Pope's blessing.

Even before Philip had begun preparing his great 'Enterprise of England' in secret, Elizabeth was aware that her relations with Spain were deteriorating. Her protection of the Dutch Protestants, and the plundering of Philip's treasure ships and his strongholds overseas by her 'sea–dogs' like Francis Drake and John Hawkins, had not endeared her to her former brother-in-law. With the prospect of any peaceful settlement with Spain bleak, Elizabeth was determined not to leave her kingdom undefended. In the autumn of 1586, she ordered a new programme of shipbuilding.

As her navy expanded, Elizabeth also went on the offensive. To prevent, or at least delay, any attack on her kingdom, Drake, with an army under his command, was ordered to frustrate the Spaniards. In April 1587, he attacked the port of Cádiz, destroying provisions earmarked for the invasion of England. He then sailed up along the coast to Cape St Vincent, where he did similar damage to the cargo of incoming supply ships. By the time he returned to England in June, after pillaging a great Spanish merchant ship in the Azores, Drake had a king's ransom in treasure with him to present to his Queen.

While Drake's 'singeing of the King of Spain's beard' did much to hamper Philip's preparations for war, Francis Walsingham and like-minded Councillors pushed for similar action to be taken in the Netherlands. However, the Queen was hesitant. Her support of the Low Countries was 'a sieve that spends as it receives to little purpose'. From the beginning, war had been costly, and Elizabeth was loath to burden her subjects with another request for subsidies. Already, Parliament had voted enormous sums to her only to have the Duke of Parma and his army still at large and now besieging the port town of Sluis.

Again, the Dutch appealed for assistance. This time, with Philip readying for war, Elizabeth could not allow Parma to remain unrestrained. In June, the Queen saw Leicester off to battle again. His performance abroad had been a fiasco the first time around, but it was hoped that given a second chance, he might redeem himself. But having learned nothing from past experience, Leicester was his haughty and inept self all over again. As before, he treated the Dutch shabbily, and he even allowed Sluis to fall to Parma. Before the situation deteriorated even further, Dudley was relieved of his duties and ordered home in December.

By the movement of the stars and planets, sages and seers were convinced that 1588 would prove to be 'the climactical year of the world' – a time of great tribulation. Even a century earlier, the famed mathematician and astronomer Regiomontanus had observed ominous signs in the heavens. 'Empires will dwindle', he had predicted, 'and from everywhere will be great lamentation'. Elizabeth, who heeded such warnings – her coronation day, after all, was determined by a horoscope – could only pray that should nations fall, they would be those of her enemies, not her own.

But as grim as it all seemed, Elizabeth still held out hope that war with Spain might be prevented. The signs of a *rapprochement* were good. From the Low Countries, Parma had announced his willingness to talk peace. Believing him to be sincere, Elizabeth dispatched representatives to meet with the Spaniards near Ostend that spring. There, and later at Bourbourg, great courtesy was extended to the English with Parma's commissioners giving their guests the 'prerogative of dignity, both in going and sitting'. The Duke himself was equally gracious. During the summit, he expressed his regrets that the Pope had gone so far as to excommunicate the Queen of England. In fact, Parma said, Elizabeth had no greater admirer than himself.

It was all a smokescreen. Contrary to making peace with the English, Parma was actually under orders to delay. The negotiations being 'spun, as it were, and unspun upon the same thread', bought King Philip valuable time in building up his floating army of a hundred and thirty warships – his Armada – to invade England. On board, would be some nineteen thousand infantry with over fifteen hundred great ordnance at their disposal. But that was not all. As William Allen assured Philip, in addition to his own troops, there would be the thousands of English Catholics waiting to help the Spaniards once they landed in Kent. For too long they had suffered under Elizabeth – 'this woman hated of God and Man' - and they were prepared to lay down their lives for the restoration of their 'ancient glory and liberty'.

In later years, it would be said that Elizabeth was onto Philip from the start, and that her peace talks were as much a ruse as those of Parma's. Whether Elizabeth was indeed playing a game of her own or that she was close to being duped by Spain is unclear. Ultimately, what mattered was when the Armada was known to be coming, England was fully prepared to meet the challenge. In the previous two years, Elizabeth had succeeded in strengthening the English navy. The new ships she had built were not cumbersome vessels like those preferred by the Spaniards, but ones of innovation. The English crafts were lighter and smaller in design, allowing them to move about with greater agility, and, in battle, to outmanoeuvre the enemy.

The improvements were tested when the Armada, under the command of the Duke of Medina-Sidonia, was sighted off Cornwall on 19 July. It was an awesome sight, and not for nothing was the colossal fleet called 'the invincible' - 'sailing as it were with labour of the winds and groaning of the ocean'. At the Armada's approach, those manning the series of hilltop signal towers along the English coast were ready to act. From Cornwall to London, they lit beacons one by one until the last could be seen from the capital. Alerted to the coming of the Spaniards, Lord Howard of Effingham, a kinsman of the Queen and her Lord Admiral, gathered his ships at Plymouth, and with Drake set sail to take on the invaders.

The English fleet - numbering a little under two hundred vessels - engaged the Spaniards off Eddystone on 21 July. Neither side had the advantage. The Armada's densely packed crescent-shaped formation - 'castle-like in front like a half moon, the horns stretching forth about the breadth of seven miles' - proved a formidable barricade, and Howard and Drake were afraid to come too close to fire at the enemy. Medina-Sidonia also wanted to engage the English at better range, but their quick moving ships were too elusive. The battle was indecisive, as were the subsequent clashes off Portland and the Isle of Wight.

By 27 July, the Armada had managed to sail up the Channel and anchor off Gravelines as planned. There, it would rendezvous with Parma and his troops, and together land in England in the south-east. But ill planning and poor communications delayed the King's nephew. While Medina-Sidonia waited in open water, the English seized their opportunity. At midnight, they set fire to eight of their boats and launched them against the Armada. Terrified by the oncoming fire ships, the Spanish sailors cut anchor and the entire fleet scattered in confusion. With its formation broken, the English attacked, inflicting great damage on the unwieldy vessels. Those able to escape by sailing north with the wind found themselves pursued by the Lord Admiral.

At summer's end, only a remnant of the Armada was left. The rest – both ships and crew - were lost in battle or on the hellish journey around Scotland and along the western coast of Ireland to Spain. Crewmen who were not swept away by storms perished from disease or starvation along the way. In October, when a proper tally could be made of the damage, Philip was told that of the hundred and thirty vessels that had left Lisbon, only about a half returned, and only a third of his men lived to see their loved ones again. And, as if God had indeed laid His hand on Queen Elizabeth, none of her ships were lost, and only about a hundred Englishmen perished in battle.

Mortified as he was, Philip accepted his defeat as the will of God. The failure of the Great Enterprise was not for him to question, and all he could do was to order a thanksgiving to be made throughout Spain that the loss 'was no more grievous' than it had been.

At her palace of St James, Elizabeth received a steady flow of reports updating her on the progress of the invasion. By the beginning of August, she had been told of the great 'Protestant wind' dispersing Philip's crippled fleet into the North Sea. But Elizabeth did not allow herself the luxury of safety just yet. The Armada might regroup and then backtrack to rendezvous with Parma as planned. With danger still looming over England, the Queen had been advised to remain in the safety of the capital, but she would not listen. Instead, she announced her intention to rally her army in person.

Like 'an Amazonian empress' with a gleaming cuirass on her chest, a commander's baton in her hand, and riding a great white horse, the Queen was led into the camp at Tilbury on 8 August by Leicester acting as her Lieutenant and Captain-General. With a 'manly courage', she inspected her troops, walking amongst them 'sometimes with a martial pace, and sometimes like a woman', stopping before individuals to offer them personal words of encouragement. There had been resistance amongst her officers in letting their mistress appear in public and in such close proximity to her subjects. The Catholic threat at home had not been forgotten, and the likes of Francis Throckmorton or Anthony Babington could have concealed themselves among those at Tilbury. But Elizabeth was dismissive of such concerns. William Allen's dream of a great English Catholic uprising had proved to be just that - a dream - and she had no desire 'to live to distrust of [her] faithful and loving people', as she told her army assembled before her the next day. Mounted on her white steed once again, she addressed them:

> 'Let tyrants fear; I have so behaved myself that under God I have placed my chiefest strength and safeguard in the loyal hearts and goodwill of my subjects. Wherefore I am come among you at this time but for my recreation and pleasure, being resolved in the midst and heat of the battle, to live and die amongst you all; to lay down for my God and for my kingdom, and for my people, mine honour and my blood - even the dust!

I know I have the body but of a weak and feeble woman; but I have the heart and stomach of a king - and of a King of England too - and take foul scorn that Parma or any prince of Europe should dare to invade the borders of my realm. To the which rather than any dishonour shall grow by me, I myself will venter my royal blood; I myself will be your general, judge, and rewarder of your virtue in the field!'

After promising her soldiers 'a famous victory over these enemies of my God and of my kingdom', Elizabeth vowed to stay at Tilbury until all danger had passed, for it was believed that Parma might still attempt a crossing to England on his own. But by nightfall, the invasion was confirmed to be false, and Elizabeth returned to London. But it was not until November that she was entirely satisfied the Armada was vanquished. On 24 November, the Queen and her court proceeded to St Paul's in thanks and celebration.

Elizabeth's victory was bittersweet. One of those lost during the crisis was the Earl of Leicester – not in battle at sea, but in his bed. On his way to take the waters at Buxton, a weary Lord Robert had stopped at Rycote. He had penned a note to the Queen on 29 August, commending himself to his 'gracious lady', and wishing 'good health and long life' on her. Sadly, the same was denied the author. Less than a week after the letter had been sent, the Earl passed away on 4 September.

She had known him since she was a child, and if circumstances had allowed it, perhaps Elizabeth might have accepted Robert Dudley's many proposals of marriage. To his great disappointment, she never did, but Leicester still had the satisfaction of knowing that of all men, Elizabeth regarded *him* with the greatest affection. Over the years, they had had their shares of quarrels, but when Lord Robert was writing to the Queen from Rycote, their disagreements – most recently over his conduct in the Netherlands - were things of the past, and they were in harmony again as two bound by long friendship. Elizabeth took Leicester's death 'most heavily', and on his note, she scribbled 'his last letter' before locking it away.

Chapter 40
No So Old As They Think

ELIZABETH I had no shortage of favourites. She unabashedly enjoyed attention, and her male courtiers eagerly vied for her favours. None of them were ever able to eclipse Robert Dudley, but Christopher Hatton, for one, did very well for himself regardless. Good looking and elegant in manner, Hatton had caught the royal eye with his skilful dancing – a favourite pastime of Elizabeth's. With the Queen's fondness for him, Hatton reaped great rewards. In 1572, he was made Captain of her bodyguard, and he was later promoted to the Privy Council. By 1587, he was at the zenith of his career as Lord Chancellor of England. Throughout his life, Hatton remained steadfastly devoted to the Queen, going so far as never to marry for her sake.

Hatton's devotion was matched by Sir Walter Raleigh's in the later years of Elizabeth's reign. A man of many talents – courtier, soldier, sailor, writer, scientist, explorer, and founder of the Virginia colony which he named after the Queen - he was said to have introduced himself to Elizabeth by laying down his cloak over a puddle in her path. True or not, in 1584, after two years at court, the thirty-one-year-old Raleigh was awarded a knighthood, and subsequently made captain of the royal guard like Hatton had been. Elizabeth was generous to Raleigh, heaping monopolies (exclusive business licenses) and estates on him. Naturally, his preferment was resented by others competing for the Queen's favour, and Raleigh – not the most humble of men - made enemies. His chief rival was the Earl of Essex.

Unlike Hatton and Raleigh, who had had to make their own way in the world, Robert Devereux had been born to privilege. His father was the deceased first Earl of Essex, and his mother, the seductive Lettice Knollys. Robert was thus a cousin of the Queen, and stepson of the Earl of Leicester. Although Elizabeth had continued to detest Lettice for marrying Robert Dudley, her displeasure did not extend to her son. In 1577, the Queen had allowed the nine-year-old Earl to be presented at court. She had found the boy to be intellectually precocious – he was already speaking French and Latin with ease – and utterly courteous. When Elizabeth had offered to kiss him, Essex

Figure 28   Robert Devereux, 2nd Earl of Essex from the
Studio of Marcus Gheeraerts the Younger
The National Gallery of Art, Washington D.C.

with modesty 'humbly altogether refused', and when she had allowed him to wear his cap in her presence, he respectfully declined.

They did not meet again till seven years later. By then, the humble lad Elizabeth had met had grown into a tall, darkly handsome young man keen to make his mark on the world. His purpose was driven by necessity as much as his own expectations for himself. Despite his earldom, his late father had left his family in debt. Money was in short supply with Robert at the mercy of his creditors, and his taste for the good life put him in further arrears. For an impoverished young nobleman like Essex, the royal court with the prospect of rewards and favours was a magnet to his steel. It did not take long for the Queen to reacquaint herself with Robert Devereux. She had always had an eye for a pretty face, and that certain air of danger about Essex – like that which had attracted Elizabeth to Thomas Seymour, Leicester, and Raleigh – drew her to him. When she was not tied up by affairs of State, Elizabeth was most likely to be found in the Earl's company, playing cards with him well into the night until 'birds sing in the morning'.

By 1588, Essex's star was on the rise. He was already a military hero having fought with Leicester in the Netherlands, and his career at court was promising. Following in Dudley's footsteps, Essex was made Master of Horse, and he was subsequently admitted to the Order of the Garter. More importantly, he had firmly established himself as the Queen's favourite like his late stepfather had done. But the parallels between Leicester and Essex ended there. Robert Dudley always knew who was the sovereign and who the subject. When he and Elizabeth had fought, as they sometimes did, and he was reminded how she would 'have here but *one* mistress, and *no* master', Leicester had always backed down, and by doing so, had kept her love for over thirty years. Unfortunately, it was an example Essex himself was never able to follow.

Bought up in Lord Burghley's household and educated at Cambridge, Robert Devereux had emerged with 'a kind of urbanity, and innate courtesy' so admired by all. But where Cecil and his schoolmasters failed him was by their inability to rein in his less attractive qualities. For all his 'goodly person', Essex was also reckless, stubborn, and overly proud, heeding 'no counsel save his own'. He was quick to anger, and even Elizabeth was not immune to his sharp tongue. He was also demanding towards her, expecting one favour or another. Should she deny him, he would take it as a personal affront and withdraw from court in a huff. Incredibly, it was often the Queen who was the first to make amends, and having done so, would then receive the Earl back into favour as if nothing had ever come between them. Perhaps an ageing Elizabeth saw in Essex another Leicester, and with Robert Dudley now taken from her, she was unwilling to lose his stepson as well. She would have him close by her even if it meant having to swallow her pride in the process.

But card games with an old woman bored a young man like the Earl of Essex. Feeling stifled at court, he longed for another chance at military glory. When it was announced that Francis Drake was launching an expedition against the Spaniards in Portugal in April 1589, Essex jumped at the chance of joining in. Knowing Elizabeth's unwillingness to let him go, he had to sneak away from court. After she had found out her favourite was at sea, Elizabeth was furious. His 'sudden and undutiful departure' was most offensive, she wrote to Essex, and she ordered him home immediately on his 'uttermost peril'. He ignored her. He stayed on until June, when disheartened by his inability to capture Lisbon, he finally set sail for England. Overjoyed to see Essex safe, Elizabeth forgave him his defiance. She was even willing to overlook his marriage to Walsingham's daughter, Frances, widow of the hero Sir Philip Sidney, in the following year.

Essex hoped to make up for his failure in Portugal by another campaign in France in 1591. Two years earlier, Henry III had been assassinated, and his brother-in-law, the Protestant Henry of Navarre, had assumed the Crown. But the new French King found himself besieged by the powerful Guises backed by Spain, and by his own Catholic subjects unwilling to accept a heretic as their sovereign. To keep his Throne, Henry IV appealed to England for help. The risk of France overrun by Philip and the Guise's Catholic League, and of another Armada headed towards England, was enough to convince Elizabeth to support Henry in his struggles. The French King had spoken of Essex as a suitable commander of her forces, and as much as she wanted him to remain at court, she eventually let Essex go off to war after much pleading from the young man.

Elizabeth's reluctance to let Essex go that August was justified. Her army had succumbed to camp fever while in Dieppe, and the Earl himself fell ill and was unable to fight. His younger brother, Walter, who did see action, was cut down by a bullet, leaving Essex guilt-stricken by his death. His lack of progress in France led him to be temporarily recalled to England. But before he left, Essex took it on himself to confer knighthoods against the Queen's wishes, for which he received a stinging rebuke. Elizabeth's confidence in Essex was not restored on his brief return to France that autumn. Instead of the great victories he promised, he only managed to capture the little town of Gourney before he was summoned home again in December.

With his military aspirations on hold, Essex turned his attentions to making a name for himself as a statesman. By 1592, his father-in-law Walsingham was dead, as was the Lord Chancellor, Hatton. The septuagenarian Burghley was still active in the Council and in his duties as Lord Treasurer (an office he had held since 1572), but he was growing increasingly frail and had to be carried about in a sedan chair. 'Very old and white', plagued by gout, and almost completely deaf, Burghley, conscious of his own mortality, was grooming his son to take his place in government. At first sight, the twenty-nine-year-old Robert Cecil was unimpressive. 'Not much beholden to nature', he was puny in size (the Queen, in fact, nicknamed him *Pygmy*), and his back was crooked. But what he lacked in looks, the younger Cecil made up with his keen brain, industriousness, and ambition to emulate his father's greatness. Essex had grown up with Robert Cecil, but the two had never been friends - one handsome and athletic, the other frail and bookish. Reunited at court, Essex continued to look down on Cecil, dismissing him as an inconsequential little clerk.

Walter Raleigh, on the other hand, was regarded by Essex with open contempt. The two men were not that much different from each other; both were attractive, dashing, and adventurous. But they were also easily stirred by their emotions, and in their rivalry for the Queen's attention, tempers ran high, even to the point of drawing swords. On one occasion, Elizabeth had to step in, forbidding them to duel. But Essex had his revenge when Raleigh fell from favour that May. For months, there had been gossip surrounding the long absence of Bess Throckmorton, one of the Queen's maids of honour. The court was no place to hide secrets, and it eventually came out that Mistress Throckmorton - or rather *Lady Raleigh* as she was discovered to be – had given birth to Sir Walter's child while away. The Queen's reaction was swift. For marrying without her permission, the couple were committed to the Tower.

With Raleigh out of his way, Essex poured his energies into establishing himself in the Queen's government. His diligence was noted by a servant of his, who, observing the Earl's sudden maturation into a dedicated statesman, wrote:

> 'His Lordship is becoming a new man, clean forsaking all his former youthful tricks, carrying himself with honourable gravity, and singularly liked of both in Parliament and Council-table for his speeches and judgement.'

But Essex's conduct was not always exemplary. After he had been admitted into the Privy Council in 1593, he quarrelled with the Cecils over the appointment of the new Attorney General. The Earl was insistent that Francis Bacon, a protégé of his, should have the position, while his rivals were in favour of the far more experienced Edward Coke. When the Queen agreed that Coke was the better man, Essex reverted to his childish sulking.

Not to be made a fool of, in January 1594 Essex announced that he had uncovered a conspiracy against the Queen's life. Unbeknownst to everyone – even the Cecils – Doctor Lopez, Elizabeth's Portuguese-born Jewish physician, was in the pay of Spain and was intending to poison the Queen. However, the evidence was found to be questionable, and Elizabeth, in conjunction with Burghley and Robert Cecil, thought Lopez, 'a man of noted fidelity', innocent. But once he was in the Tower, the terrified doctor told Essex what he wanted to hear. His confession left Elizabeth with no choice but to order his execution. There was a three-month delay before Lopez was put to death. Perhaps Elizabeth had doubts about his guilt. A confession made under the threat of the torture was always doubtful, and Lopez's origins as a foreigner and as a Jew (even though Lopez was a convert to Christianity) had undoubtedly prejudiced the jury at his trial. Certainly, none of this concerned Essex. In detecting the alleged plot and 'saving' the Queen's life, he brought further prestige on himself and managed to outshine the Cecils.

Essex added another feather to his cap when he fought against the Spaniards in 1596. In April, Calais was besieged by King Philip's new Governor of the Netherlands, Archduke Albert of Austria. Though the town defended itself valiantly, it was no match for the ferocity of the Archduke's onslaught. His artillery was so powerful, it was said, that it was heard as far as Greenwich. When Calais finally surrendered, the outlook was bleak. The town was 'the shortest cut over into England', and it was now in Spanish hands. In response, Essex, Lord Howard, and a forgiven Raleigh were put in command of an Anglo-Dutch expedition 'to set upon the enemy in his own ports'. In June, a force of one hundred and fifty vessels set sail for Spain – its target Cádiz. After the English sank two of Philip's warships and captured two others, Essex, 'full of courage and youthful heat', took Cádiz by storm on 20 June. By the next day, the town was his.

But instead of congratulations from the Queen, she was full of reproaches. Why had he again dispensed knighthoods against her wishes, she demanded to know? And where was the great plunder of which she expected her share? Elizabeth's chilly reception caught Essex off-guard. He could not deny that he had made new knights, he stammered, but they were deserving of the honour for their bravery. And as for the Spanish loot, Essex could only guess that much of it was pilfered on its way home.

For what she perceived as the Earl's disobedience and negligence at Cádiz, the Queen was determined to teach him a lesson. His triumph was none at all, Elizabeth decreed, and she ordered all writings hailing Essex as a hero to be suppressed.

At the end of 1597, André de Hurault de Maisse arrived in England as Henry IV's ambassador. Observant and insightful, the Frenchman kept meticulous notes about his time in London and at the royal court. In the week before his audience with the Queen, de Maisse played tourist. The expanse of the Thames covered with innumerable ships was a sight to behold, he wrote, and he liked how well ordered the city was. Thanks to the various houses of charity and schools established by the government, hardly any beggars or idle youths were seen hanging about the streets. The envoy also had the opportunity to view the palaces of Greenwich and Whitehall, but he was not overly impressed. In his opinion, they were not as magnificent as what he was used to in France. He was, however, delighted by Westminster Abbey with its splendid monuments to the Queen's ancestors. Perhaps it was during his visit there that de Maisse first noticed how religion was practised in the realm. It was 'like that of Geneva', he observed, but strangely enough, incorporated elements of the old faith. English clergymen were 'habited in the Catholic manner', and some belief in the Real Presence was implied at Holy Communion.

On 8 December, de Maisse was summoned to court to meet Elizabeth I. She wore cloth of silver with an abundance of jewellery, he noticed, and on her head was a large red wig with 'two great curls of hair' about her ears. The lowness of her collar allowed de Maisse to see the old Queen's bosom, which he thought was 'rather wrinkled'. Her great age was reflected in her face as well. 'It is long and thin, and her teeth are very yellow and unequal', the envoy observed, and 'many of them are missing so that one cannot understand her easily when she speaks quickly'. Nevertheless, 'her figure is fair and tall and graceful in whatever she does'. In spite of her years, Elizabeth was still an active woman, de Maisse added, and she took great pleasure in dancing as she did in her younger days.

The Frenchman found Elizabeth very gracious, but she was not without her eccentricities. At their first interview, the Queen gave the impression of being impatient when de Maisse spoke, and she was unable to keep still. She would stand and sit, stand and sit, forcing the envoy to do likewise. When she was in her chair, Elizabeth was 'forever twisting and untwisting' the long sleeves of her dress, and opening and closing the front of her gown 'as if she was too hot'. She was also terribly vain. During the envoy's stay at court, she made certain he knew how proficient she was in languages, how skilled she was in music, and how talented she was at dancing. As expected, de Maisse responded with praises each time. There was no end to Elizabeth's desire for flattery. One time, with feigned modesty, she told the ambassador what a 'foolish and old [woman]' she was, and how 'after having seen so many wise men and great princes', she must have been a huge let down to him. Of course, the ambassador, 'not without an answer', assured her of the contrary.

Elizabeth never missed an opportunity to impress de Maisse. When he praised her on her extensive knowledge of foreign affairs, the Queen quoted from the poet Ovid on how kings had 'far reaching hands'. To demonstrate that it was even literal in her case, Elizabeth removed her glove and showed de Maisse her hand with its long elegant fingers. The Frenchman was amused. For a woman who liked to say how 'she was never beautiful', he noted, 'she speaks of her beauty as often as she can'.

For all her quirks, de Maisse found himself admiring the Queen. Initially, his only knowledge of Elizabeth was by her reputation, and not all of it was good. From what he had heard, she was a 'haughty woman', impossible to deal with, and grasping to the extreme. But after having met Elizabeth in person, his opinion of her changed. She was indeed a proud woman, but she was not arrogant, and though she was sometimes difficult, she was still greatly respected by those in her service. That she was 'very avaricious' was a misconception, de Maisse discovered. Although the Queen had an annual income of over 600,000 crowns, she had great expenses. She had to maintain her court, her soldiers in the Netherlands and Ireland, and her defences along the Scottish border. At the same time, she was allocating pensions to individuals, such as King James, to maintain their goodwill as part of her policy to safeguard her realm. While on the subject of her money, de Maisse wrote approvingly that Elizabeth's coinage, which she had taken great pains to reform at the beginning of her reign, 'is very good', and 'neither alters nor ever depreciates'.

By Elizabeth's good governance, 'the friendship that her people bore her' was extraordinary, de Maisse noticed - even 'unbelievable' as the Queen herself described it to him. When the ambassador followed up with a comment on how fortunate her subjects were to have such a great ruler, Elizabeth, suddenly feeling the weight of her years, answered that she was not long for the grave. But then, as if the notion were the most absurd thing in the world, she smiled and assured de Maisse, 'I think not to die so soon, Mister Ambassador, and am *not* so old as they think.'

Nicander Nucius, a Greek travelling in the suite of an Imperial embassy to England in 1545, set down his impressions and observations of the British Isles. Ireland, in particular, fascinated Nucius, having heard 'certain strange and marvellous tales' about the island. From what he was told, it was a place of mystery with 'perfumed springs' and 'milky water'. But beneath its natural beauty, there was terror. Ghosts and demons roamed freely about, and Hell itself could be found there. If one listened carefully, the horrific cries of the damned could even be heard. Nucius dismissed such stories as nonsense, but he did give credence to what he learnt of the country's inhabitants. While the Irish living within the English Pale had 'something of human polity', those outside its borders were simple-minded, half naked, warlike savages dwelling in bogs and forests. It was 'only by their human form', the Greek attaché wrote, 'whereby they may be distinguished to be men'.

The English, who had passed on such information to Nucius, truly believed what they told him. The opinion of William Thomas, a clerk of Edward VI's Council - and thus a man of education - was typical:

Figure 29 An allegory of the Tudor Succession (The Family of Henry VIII) by an Unknown Artist
The Yale Center for British Art, Paul Mellon Collection

'the wild Irish, as unreasonable beasts, lived without any knowledge of God or good manners, in common of their goods, cattle, women, children, and every other thing, in such wise that almost there was no father which knew his son, nor no daughter that knew her father, nor yet any justice executed for murder, robbery or any other like mischief.'

The much-maligned Irish had their own distaste for the English. Since the 12th century, their mightier neighbour had sought to impose rule over their country. Later, with the Reformation taking hold of England, that effort became spiritual as well as secular. But the Irish remained staunchly devoted to their religion as handed down by St Patrick, and the new faith made no converts of them. That Ireland stayed Catholic could be attributed to Elizabeth's policy. She had been cautious in forcing Protestantism on the people for fear of driving them into the hands of Catholic Spain. Nonetheless, Irish militants eager to shake off England's authority over them were looking to King Philip for support.

The latest of these rebels, Hugh O'Neill, Earl of Tyrone, made his stand beginning in 1595. For three years, O'Neill confounded the English, making war one moment and then suing for peace the other. When Elizabeth agreed to a truce in the summer of 1598, Tyrone betrayed her by inflicting a humiliating defeat on her forces at Blackwater Fort on 14 August. Buoyed by his success, the whole of Ireland was ready to follow Tyrone.

The news from Ireland was not the only blow to Elizabeth. Ten days before the 'glorious victory' of the Irish, the venerable Lord Burghley died at the age of seventy-eight. In his forty years of service to the Crown, Cecil had more than fulfilled the special trust Elizabeth had placed in him at the beginning of her reign. Near the end of Burghley's life, the Queen's great affection for him was demonstrated by her frequent visits to his bedside. With her own hands, she would feed soup to the ailing old man, comforting him, not as his mistress, but as his loving friend. When word came that Burghley had finally slipped away, Elizabeth mourned his passing deeply. For weeks, she barely went outdoors as she so liked to do, but kept to her rooms, finding solace in being alone, and in penning letters, probably about her loss of Cecil, to her closest friends.

But with the situation in Ireland growing desperate, Elizabeth had to set aside her grief. Tyrone had to be put down, and Robert Devereux was the man to do it. Since his return from Cádiz, Essex's relationship with the Queen had been rocky. He had taken great offence at her ingratitude, and the elevation of the 'little pygmy' Cecil to Secretary of State had made him even more resentful. But, as it always was between them, both Elizabeth and Essex did not stay angry for long. In the spring of 1597, the Queen renewed her confidence in her favourite when she allowed him to embark on another campaign against the Spaniards. However, she thought her trust was misplaced once again when Essex, instead of battling his foes at sea as he was ordered to do, sought riches for himself by chasing after treasures ships in the Azores.

A full blow up between Elizabeth and Essex was in the making, and that indeed happened as the Irish were rebelling. Before Tyrone had seized Blackwater Fort, the Council had met to appoint a new Lord Deputy to Ireland. The tension in the room was palpable, and tempers flared. The Queen was adamant that Lord Mountjoy should go, but Essex strongly protested. When he was finally vetoed, the Earl scornfully turned his back on Elizabeth. Incensed, she struck him on the head. Unable to restrain himself, Essex spun around and put his hand to his sword. He shouted that he would not endure such an insult - not even from Henry VIII himself! It is certain how the late King would have reacted, but as for Elizabeth, she did nothing. After sufficient time had passed for Essex to nurse his wounded pride at his estates, she had him brought back to court.

Appointed Lord Lieutenant, Essex was dispatched to Ireland in April 1599. As she saw him off, the Queen was confident he had turned over a new leaf, at last, putting his delinquencies behind him for good. She was also assured of victory, given the great army put at his disposal. Essex would command a force of sixteen thousand foot soldiers and thirteen hundred horsemen, and with additional reinforcements to come. No expense was spared either in providing Essex with the necessary ordnance against the rebels.

But once her new Lord Lieutenant was in the field, Elizabeth's former doubts about Essex resurfaced. As a strategist, he was inept. Instead of obeying orders about where and when to engage the enemy, the Earl stubbornly followed his own course. What victories he did have were mostly inconsequential. After months in Ireland, he achieved little, and his men were succumbing to disease. With his campaign in dire straits, Essex looked for a way out.

As Elizabeth grew older, the artifice required to maintain her image as Queen became more and more elaborate. Layers upon layers of powder and paint were used to conceal her years, though the result in truth emphasised her advanced age. With her face covered in white and her lips and cheeks made glowing red, Elizabeth looked more outlandish than rejuvenated. The garish effect was heightened by the elaborate hair-pieces she wore in gaudy yellows, oranges, and reds. Elizabeth's wardrobe was equally flamboyant. At sixty-six, the Queen, far from being outdated in her attire, dressed in the latest fashions. Her bodices were stylishly cut low to accentuate her bosom, and her skirts were correctly bell-shaped according to the style of the day. Around her neck, Elizabeth usually wore enormous ruffs of starched lace, and on her back were wired frames of fine lawn shaped as outsized hoops, lending her the appearance of a human butterfly.

This was the Elizabeth of public adulation – the goddess Diana, as Walter Raleigh hailed her as; Gloriana, as celebrated by the poet Edmund Spenser, and the ageless Virgin Queen as portrayed in miniatures by the artist Nicholas Hilliard. Only her most intimate ladies-in-waiting were privy to Elizabeth's private self – the wrinkled, grey-haired old woman dependent on cosmetics, hair-pieces, gowns, and jewels to create her alter egos each day. On such a morning, 28 September 1599, the Queen's ritual of preparing herself for show was interrupted by a disturbance outside her Privy Chamber at the Palace of Nonsuch. Before her women could find out what all the noise was about, a dirty and dishevelled figure burst through the door. It was the Earl of Essex. Elizabeth was startled. Not only was she half dressed, being 'newly up, the hair about her face', but Essex was also supposed to be in Ireland. Utterly vulnerable and afraid, Elizabeth dared not provoke him. Instead, she greeted him with all smiles. Essex fell to his knees and gratefully kissed her hands. He was not expected back, he said excitedly, but he had great news. He had met with Tyrone in person, and the rebel leader had agreed to a ceasefire. He could not wait, he continued breathlessly, until he had told her in person.

Elizabeth played it cool. She expressed joy at his return, and the Earl, finding such 'a sweet calm at home', had no reason to doubt her sincerity. She was just as gracious when she met him again later in the day – in full dress and regalia, of course – and Essex debriefed her about his mission in Ireland. But after Elizabeth was assured he had no army with him – she was 'much changed'. At nightfall, Essex was ordered 'to keep [to] his chamber'.

The Earl's offences were great. He had disobeyed the Queen's orders to stay put at his post, and she was far from pleased at the truce he had made. He had been expected to crush Tyrone, not to make deals with him. Furthermore, Essex had again conferred knighthoods without permission, and he was 'overbold [in] going to Her Majesty's bedchamber'. Nevertheless, Elizabeth had to tread softly in her handling of Essex. Since Cádiz, he had become immensely popular with the people – another Philip Sidney it seemed – and it would be wise not to be too severe with him. Instead of laying formal charges against Essex, the Queen deemed it sufficient to have him reprimanded by the Council in June 1600, and to have him kept under house arrest.

Forbidden to come to court, Essex grew more and more agitated as the months went by. The Queen was no longer showing him favour. At New Year 1601, he sent Elizabeth a gift only to have it returned to him, and his letters, addressed from the 'saddest soul on earth', went unanswered. In August, Essex was granted his freedom at last. But what Elizabeth gave with one hand, she took with another. Since 1590, a large part of the perennially cash-strapped Earl's income had been dependent on a monopoly on revenues from imported sweet wines. The grant was a gift from the Queen in their happier days, and was good for ten years. If she did not renew it - and the lease was about to expire - Essex faced ruin. Frantic, he sent off another batch of letters filled with flowery praises. Upon receiving them, Elizabeth cynically remarked how they were 'but a preparative to a suit for the renewing of the farm of sweet wines'. In September, she announced that henceforth, the lease would be reverted to the Crown.

Bankrupt, Essex turned from begging to conspiring. He was convinced that his enemies at court – Robert Cecil, Raleigh, and others – were plotting his destruction, and his only remedy lay in rebellion. To remove them from the Queen, Essex turned to Scotland. He knew how impatient James VI was to sit on the English throne, and he convinced the Scottish King that Cecil was plotting to make the Infanta Isabella, the daughter of the late Philip of Spain (he had died in 1598), Elizabeth's heiress. There was no truth to Essex's claim, but it was enough to rile James. He began a secret correspondence with the Earl encouraging his revolt.

Backed by Scotland, and by friends such as his new stepfather, Sir Christopher Blount, Lord Monteagle, and the Earls of Southampton, Rutland, and Bedford, Essex was ready to strike. To stiffen his resolve, he sponsored and attended a performance of William Shakespeare's *Richard II* on 7 February 1601. That the play concerned the overthrow and murder of a monarch said much about his intentions. Emboldened, Essex and his followers took to the city streets the next morning. 'For the Queen! For the Queen! A plot is laid for my life!', the Earl shouted, but not one citizen heeded his call to join him. About 10 o'clock that night, a mere twelve hours after his uprising had begun, a shattered Essex, cornered at his house, surrendered to the authorities.

For years, Elizabeth had indulged his excesses and overlooked his faults, but she could not do so again, not when high treason was involved. 'I had put up with but too much disrespect to my person', Elizabeth was to say later, 'but I warned him that he should *not* touch my sceptre.' She made certain Essex had no opportunity again. After he had been condemned to death by his peers at his trial, she signed his death warrant with a steady hand on 20 February. When the terrible sentence was carried out five days later, Elizabeth shed no tears for Robert Devereux. She was practising on the virginals when the news arrived. She paused for a moment as if lost in thought, and then, without a word, resumed her playing.

As confident as Elizabeth still was of her abilities, her people were less so as the new century began. The execution of the popular Essex had been ill received, and other concerns – mainly economic - were threatening her popularity as well. People grumbled at the rising cost of inflation, at the burdensome taxes to fight Spain and to pacify Ireland, and at the fiscal corruption within the Queen's regime.

The machinery of government, many complained, seemed to be greased by the wholesale giving and accepting of bribes. There was also great resentment towards monopolies. These grants, such as Essex's on sweet wines, had long been a convenient means for the Queen to pay or reward her servants without having to dip into her own purse. Unfortunately, the burden was then assumed by her subjects who had to pay the holders of such leases whatever prices they fixed on the goods – starch, paper, playing cards, beer, pots, bottles, and so forth - they controlled. Sir Walter Raleigh, for example, made a handsome profit from his monopolies on tin and wine.

In the autumn of 1601, when Elizabeth was obliged to go cap in hand to Parliament to seek more money for her war chest, the Commons were adamant on voting her no new funds unless the granting of monopolies ceased. Anticipating a fight on her hands, the Queen was a bundle of nerves that October. Her godson, Sir John Harington, who visited Elizabeth, wrote how she ate little, how she was testy with her ladies, and how she paced nervously in her Privy Chamber, 'stamp[ing] with her feet at ill news'. When she was in an especially awful mood, his elderly godmother, Harington said, would 'thrust her rusty sword at times into the arras in great rage'.

The Commons were just as bad tempered, and there was a noticeable lack of respect paid to the Queen when she attended Parliament on 30 October. On her way through a crowded chamber packed by members of the Lower House, very few shouted the customary 'God bless your Majesty!' and many were slow to give Elizabeth passage. When her usher asked them to stand back, one individual shouted loudly, 'If you will hang us, we can make no more room!' Apparently, Elizabeth did not hear him, or she pretended not to, being surrounded by so many hostile faces.

During the sitting of Parliament in November, it was left to Robert Cecil to tame the Commons. But he found himself powerless against 'so great confusion'. He was unable to curb debate on the abuse of monopolies, or to stop the introduction of a bill limiting the Crown's power to grant them. When Walter Raleigh spoke against it - to protect his own interests of course - he was met by a disdainful silence. Others defending the Queen's prerogative were shouted down or heckled. An exasperated Cecil had to scold the Lower House for behaving more like unruly schoolboys than Parliamentarians, but his chiding went unheeded. If they failed to stem the abuses, the Commons reminded themselves, what would prevent the very bread they ate from being turned into a monopoly one day?

For years, Elizabeth had been aware of the unpopularity of the grants, but the extent of the resentment towards them caught her by surprise. The forcefulness with which the Commons fought was not expected, and they had made it clear that unless she ended the practice, her subsidy would be denied. In the past, Elizabeth had stood firm whenever Parliament demanded she marry and name her successor, but this time, it was different. By right, monopolies were hers to bestow as she pleased, but they were hurtful to her people. As 'she loved them no less than they her', as she had once told Monsieur de Maisse, Elizabeth gave in. She would grant no more such leases, and many of those already gifted were to be revoked.

The Commons were overjoyed. To render their thanks, they begged an audience of the Queen. But when she asked for only a selection of delegates to come before her, they would not have it so - the Queen must see them all. She graciously consented. On the afternoon of 30 November, Elizabeth sat enthroned before a packed Council chamber at Whitehall. Having surrendered her prerogative to please her people, she made her love for them the theme of her speech:

> 'I do assure you there is no Prince that loves his subjects better, or whose love can countervail our love. There is no jewel, be it of never so rich a price, which I set before this jewel - I mean your love. For I do esteem it more than any treasure or riches; for that we know how to prize, but love and thanks I count invaluable. And, though God hath raised me high, yet this I count the glory of my Crown, that I have reigned with your loves. This makes me that I do not so much rejoice that God hath made me to be a queen, as to be a queen over so thankful a people. Therefore, I have cause to wish nothing more than to content the subject and that is a duty which I owe. Neither do I desire to live longer days than I may see your prosperity and that is my only desire.'

Elizabeth then touched on the monopolies: Her 'kingly dignity' would not suffer them to be abused, and she was determined on reform. As for those 'varlets and lewd persons not worthy of the name of subjects' who had exploited the leases, they would be punished, she promised. Having said that, Elizabeth spoke again of her affection:

> 'There will never Queen sit in my seat with more zeal to my country, care to my subjects, and that will sooner with willingness venture her life for your good and safety than myself. For it is my desire to live nor reign no longer than my life and reign shall be for your good. And though you have had, and may have, many princes more mighty and wise sitting in this seat, yet you never had, nor shall have, any that will be more careful and loving.'

In an age when men wept unashamedly when deeply affected, an abundance of tears were shed at the Queen's oration. The day was made even more memorable for the Commons when Elizabeth then invited each and every member – all one hundred and forty people - to come forward and kiss her hand.

≡

In her 'Golden Speech', as it was later called, Elizabeth had promised not to outlive her usefulness. Her yielding on the issue of monopolies was a popular move, but still, after more than forty years of her reign, her subjects were yearning for change. The people were looking towards 'the sun rising, and neglected her as now ready to set', just as Elizabeth long ago knew they would.

Even Robert Cecil, the most powerful man in the kingdom after Elizabeth, was planning for the future. He was discretely writing to the King of Scots, preparing him for his inheritance. The Queen had never once named her successor, but James, by his royal state, closeness of blood, and her good will towards him, was obviously her preferred choice. It is probable that Elizabeth already knew that Cecil was in secret contact with James, but true to her motto - *video et taceo* - she said nothing. During her lifetime, she had never allowed anyone to champion a successor, but now, as her death was not far off, Elizabeth allowed Cecil to do what must be done.

By the beginning of 1603, the vigour Elizabeth had sustained into her old age was fading. She was often sapped of energy, unable to sleep or eat, and subject to fits of melancholy. It was thought that a change of scenery would do her good, and on 21 January, the court moved from Whitehall to Richmond. It was an inauspicious journey. The weather was extremely foul, being 'very windy and rainy', and along the way, the Queen might have recalled how her astrologer John Dee had once warned her against going to Richmond in her old age.

Settled in her 'warm box', as she called the palace built by her grandfather, Elizabeth's spirits were lifted by the good news from abroad. The Earl of Tyrone, who had earlier suffered a disastrous defeat at the hands of her Lord Deputy, Lord Mountjoy, was finally prepared to submit. Also, the Republic of Venice, which had never opened diplomatic ties with her government before, was finally sending a representative to the English court. In February, Elizabeth received the envoy in all her splendour. Wearing a dress of silver taffeta, a wig of a 'light colour never made by nature', and dripping with jewels, she impressed him with her 'most gracious words', and by her fluency in Italian. She had learnt it as a child, she told the ambassador proudly, and had never forgotten it.

But just a few short weeks after her meeting with the Venetian diplomat, it was evident that the Queen's invigoration could not last. Her beloved cousin, the Countess of Nottingham, had recently passed away, and Elizabeth was near inconsolable. The Countess' nephew, Robert Carey, visited the Queen to cheer her up - but to no avail. He found his royal kinswoman 'sitting low upon her cushions', and when he inquired how she was, she wrung his hand, and looking at him sadly replied, 'No, Robin, I am *not* well.' She had been ill for the past ten or twelve days, Elizabeth said, and she then 'fetched not so few as forty or fifty great sighs'. She had never been so sad, Carey observed, except at the Queen of Scots' execution. Elizabeth seemed to be better by nightfall, and she announced her intention to attend worship the next day. But when morning came, she was so weary that she had to hear divine service propped up on cushions by the chapel door. 'From that day forwards', Carey noted wistfully, 'she grew worse and worse'.

Elizabeth's depression was elevated by the loss of her coronation ring. She had worn it since the day she became Queen, and it had never left her finger. But in the forty-four years since, it had grown into her flesh and was presently causing her pain. When it had to be filed off, Elizabeth took it as a 'sad presage'. The ring represented her 'marriage to her kingdom', and now it was symbolically dissolved.

Lying on a heap of cushions still, Elizabeth refused any medicine her doctors brought her, and she waved away her ladies when they begged her to take nourishment. Weak and emaciated, the Queen would sit on the floor with her finger in her mouth staring into space. But if any of her courtiers thought the fire in her was extinguished, they were mistaken. When Cecil told his mistress she *must* go to bed, she looked him squarely in the eye, telling him the word 'must' 'was not to be used to princes'. To lie down was to take to her deathbed, and that she refused to do. Summoning her ladies to her, Elizabeth had them help her onto her feet. Once she was up, she waved them aside and stood. For what seemed an eternity, she remained standing - stock-still and silent like a waxwork - defying her Councillors and defying Death. But after fifteen hours, her Herculean struggle was lost. The Queen collapsed to the floor. This time, too feeble to resist, she was duly put to bed.

It was said that Thursday was an unlucky day for the Tudors. Henry VIII had died on that day, and, coincidentally, both Edward VI and Mary as well. Elizabeth, the last and greatest of her family, upheld the sad tradition. On the early morning of 24 March - another Thursday, and the Eve of the Annunciation of the Blessed Virgin – she slipped away, 'most quietly departing this life'.

=

A flurry of activity followed the passing of the Queen. Her death was announced by proclamation on the morning of her passing, and Robert Cecil made good on his promise to King James. Immediately after Elizabeth was pronounced dead, he dispatched Robert Carey to Scotland with the news James had been eagerly awaiting for years. Meanwhile, the remains of the old Queen were prepared for her funeral. It did not take place until 28 April. The city streets were crowded with thousands wanting to take a last look at their departed sovereign. The sight of the hearse with a lifelike effigy of Elizabeth lying in state on top with her 'whole body in her Parliament robes, with a crown on her head, and a sceptre in her hands' drew a heartfelt response from the crowd, with much 'sighing, groaning, and weeping as the like hath not been seen or known in the memory of man'. When the procession arrived at Westminster Abbey, Elizabeth was laid in the tomb of her grandparents – Henry VII, the founder of her dynasty, and Elizabeth of York after whom she had been named.

With the subsequent arrival of King James in London, and the preparations for his coronation, it was not until the end of May that Robert Cecil had time to reflect on the passing of the Queen. In a letter to her godson Harington, he paid tribute to his late mistress. She was, as Cecil wrote, 'more than a man, and in troth, sometimes less than a woman'.

Elizabeth, who had boasted of having the 'heart and stomach of a king', might have smiled at the compliment.

Figure 30   The new Stuart dynasty's descent from Elizabeth of
York and Henry VII is depicted in the centre
The National Gallery of Art, Washington D.C.

ENDNOTES

Chapter 1: Beginnings: The Cousins' War

Henry Tudor's promise to marry Elizabeth of York is in Vergil, *English History*, p. 203.

Henry VI's great piety is from James, *Henry the Sixth*, p. 27. Margaret of Anjou's fierce character is in *The Paston Letters*, III, no. 322. The King's insanity is in no. 270. The Duke of York as Protector: Hallam, *Chronicles*, p. 212 and p. 214 quoting the chronicler John Benet. Henry's recovery is in *The Paston Letters*, III, no. 270.

The Battle of St. Albans is described by the chronicler Jean de Waurin in Hallam, *Chronicles*, p. 216, and in Hall, *Chronicle*, pp. 232-233. Warwick as a man of 'stout stomach and invincible courage' is in Hall, *Chronicle*, p. 296. The day of reconciliation is on p. 238.

The Yorkists' setback at Ludford Bridge, and their later triumph, is in Hallam, *Chronicles*, p. 220 and p. 222, quoting Benet. The Duke of York's claim to the Crown, and its settlement upon him: Hall, *Chronicle*, pp. 245-249. For his death, see Stow, *Annales*, pp. 412-413, and Hall, *Chronicle*, pp. 250-251.

Edward IV as the new King: Hall, *Chronicle*, p. 254. Henry VI's deposition is commented upon by de Waurin in Hallam, *Chronicles*, p. 224. The French mockery of Edward is also from de Waurin, mentioned in Ross, *Edward IV*, p. 63, note 2. A description of Edward's good looks is in Vergil, *English History*, p. 172. He was 6 feet and 3 inches tall according to his remains uncovered in 1789: *The Journal of the British Archaeological Association*, vol. XXV, 1869, pp. 84-85. His character is in Mancini, *Richard the Third*, pp. 64/65-66/67.

That the King would wed the Lady Bona: Hall, *Chronicle*, p. 263. His marriage to Elizabeth Woodville instead, and Warwick's reaction to it is in Vergil, *English History*, pp. 116-118, and in Hall, *Chronicle*, pp. 264-265.

The birth of Elizabeth of York is in Fabyan, *The New Chronicles*, p. 655.

Chapter 2: The King's Daughter

Edward IV's falling out with Warwick: Hall, *Chronicle*, p. 275. His defeat and exile are in De Commines, *Memoirs*, pp. 191-192. Warwick's truce with Queen Margaret is in Vergil, *English History*, p. 131.

The Tower of London's accommodations are described in Thurley, 'Royal Lodgings', pp. 36-57, and in Lapper and Parnell, *The Tower of London*, p. 24. The fortification of the Tower and the royal family taking sanctuary are in Warkworth, *Chronicle*, p. 13. The people's denunciation of King Edward is on p. 12. Prince Edward's christening is in Fabyan, *The New Chronicles,* p. 659, and in Hall, *Chronicle,* p. 285.

Henry VI's prophecy about the future Henry VII is from Vergil, *English History,* p. 135, and from Hall, *Chronicle,* p. 287.

For Edward IV's return to England, refer to Warkworth, *Chronicle,* p. 14; Vergil, *English History,* p. 142; and *Chronicles of the White Rose of York,* p. 60. For the Battle of Barnet, see pp. 63-67; Vergil, *English History,* pp. 144-147; and Hall, *Chronicle,* pp. 295-296.

The Battle of Tewkesbury is in *Chronicles of the White Rose of York,* pp. 79-82, and Vergil, *English History,* pp. 151-152. Edward's triumphant entry into London is on pp. 92-93, and also in Kingsford, *Chronicles of London,* p. 184. The death of Henry VI is mentioned in *Chronicles of the White Rose,* p. 93, and in Vergil, *English History,* pp. 155-156.

Edward IV's magnificent court is in *Chronicles of the White Rose,* pp. 146-150. The young Prince's upbringing is on pp. 153-154.

Clarence's desire to marry Mary of Burgundy is in Hall, *Chronicle,* p. 326. His treasonous behaviour is in Mancini, *Richard the Third,* p. 62. Ankarette Twynyho's arrest and execution are in *Calendar of the Patent Rolls, 1476-1485,* pp. 72-73. 'To defend his cause with his own hand': *The Croyland Chronicle,* p. 480. The prophecy about the letter 'G': Vergil, *English History,* p. 167. Clarence's death remains a mystery. Rather than an expected death by decapitation, it was commonly believed that he was drowned in a butt of Malmsey wine instead.

The marriage of the young Duke of York and Duchess of Norfolk: Black, *Ancient State and Chivalry,* pp. 27-40. Prince Edward's appearance is from Mancini, *Richard the Third,* p. 92/93.

The jilting of Elizabeth by the French is in Hall, *Chronicle,* pp. 329-330. That the King had had grown fat in his later years is in More, *King Richard the Third,* p. 5.

'Cursed be the land where the Prince is a child': Hallam, *Chronicles,* p. 196, quoting de Waurin.

Chapter 3: The King's Sister

That Richard blamed the Woodvilles for Clarence's death is in Mancini, *Richard the Third,* pp. 62/63. Buckingham's disdain for his Woodville wife is on p. 74/75.

Edward V in the hands of his uncle: *The Croyland Chronicle,* p. 486; Kingsford, *Chronicles of London,* p. 190; and Mancini, *Richard the Third,* p. 74/75. The Queen in sanctuary again is mentioned in More, *King Richard the Third,* pp. 21-23, and in Mancini, *Richard the Third,* p. 78/79.

Hastings plotting with the Woodvilles is discussed in Cheetham, *Richard III,* pp. 111-112. Gloucester's summons to his northern supporters is in Davies, *York Records,* pp. 148-150.

For the besiegement of Westminster Abbey: More, *King Richard the Third*, p. 23, and Cunningham, *Richard III, pp. 41-42* (Simon Stallworth letter). The surrender of Prince Richard, and Gloucester's taking of the Crown is in *The Croyland Chronicle*, pp. 488-489, and in More, *King Richard the Third*, pp. 34-42. The announcement about Edward IV and Edward V's common illegitimacy is in Mancini, *Richard the Third*, pp. 94/95-96/97.

Chapter 4: The King's Niece

The Archbishop's reluctance to crown Richard King is in Mancini, *Richard the Third*, p. 100/101.

The alleged murder of the 'Princes in the Tower' is in Mancini, *Richard the Third*, p. 92/93; More, *King Richard the Third*, pp. 85-88; and Vergil, *English History*, pp. 188-189.

The plot to send the Princesses abroad is in *The Croyland Chronicle*, p. 491. Buckingham's failed rebellion is in Vergil, *English History*, pp. 193 – 201. For the proposed marriage between Henry Tudor and Elizabeth of York, see p. 196. That Edward IV had schemed to lure Henry Tudor back to England: pp. 164-167. Elizabeth Woodville's reaction to the deaths of her sons is on p. 189. That Margaret Beaufort was the 'head of that conspiracy' against Richard is on p. 204.

For *Titulus Regius*, refer to Halsted, *Richard III*, vol. 2, Appendix Y.

Richard and Anne's grief over the loss of their son is in *The Croyland Chronicle*, pp. 496-497.

The King's public vow to act as his nieces' guardian is in Ellis, *Original Letters*, 2nd series, vol. 1, pp. 149 –150. Richard III's apparent infatuation with Elizabeth of York is in *The Croyland Chronicle*, pp. 498-499. That he was dissuaded from marrying her is on pp. 499-500.

For *The Song of the Lady Bessy*, see Gairdner, *Richard III*, pp. 345-359. Elizabeth's alleged letter to the Duke of Norfolk is mentioned in Buck, *King Richard the Third*, pp. 190-191.

Henry Tudor's reaction to Richard's proposed marriage to Elizabeth is in Holinshed, *Chronicles*, pp. 433-434. Elizabeth Woodville's plea to her son to abandon Richmond is in Vergil, *English History*, p. 210. The anonymous letter to the Duke of Norfolk: Hall, *Chronicle*, p. 419. The Battle of Bosworth is described in *The Croyland Chronicle*, pp. 501-504. and in Vergil, *English History*, pp. 221-224.

Chapter 5: The King's Wife

For Margaret Beaufort's affection for her son: Wood, *Letters of Royal and Illustrious Ladies*, I, p. 118. Henry's appearance is in Vergil, *Anglica Historia*, pp. 144-145.

For Henry VII's right to the throne, see *Rotuli Parliamentorum*, VI, p. 268. That he would wed Elizabeth of York: p. 278. For Giovanni de Giglis' letter, see *CSP Ven.*, I, no. 506. That a descendent of Cadwallader would assume the English Crown: Hall, *Chronicle,* p. 423.

The ordinances for the Queen's confinement and the christening of her child are in Leland, *Collectanea,* IV, pp. 179-184, and p. 249.

For the conspiracy involving Lambert Simnel, see Hall, *Chronicle,* pp. 428-435.

The loss of Elizabeth Woodville's lands and possessions: Vergil, *Anglica Historia,* pp. 16/17-18/19, and Hall, *Chronicle,* p. 431. For an alternative explanation, refer to Okerlund, *Elizabeth Wydeville,* pp. 246-247.

That Henry VII was supposedly aloof towards his wife is from Bacon, *Henry the Seventh,* pp. 206-207. Inventories with items decorated with the royal couple's initials are in *L&P,* IV, no. 5114 and no. 6789. That the King paid Elizabeth's debts: Bentley, *Excerpta Historica,* p. 111. The couple's affectionate messages to each other are in Nicolas, *Privy Purse Expenses of Elizabeth of Yo*rk, p. xcvi.

Elizabeth's coronation is in Leland, *Collectanea,* IV, pp. 216-233.

Margaret of Burgundy's continuing grudge against Henry VII: Vergil, *Anglica Historia,* pp. 14/15-16/17, and Hall, *Chronicle,* p. 430. The Duchess' championing of Perkin Warbeck: *Anglica Historia,* p. 64/65; and Hall, *Chronicle,* p. 463. See also Arthurson, *Perkin Warbeck,* p. 56, and for his confession, refer to pp. xi-xii. Later, to justify the Earl of Warwick's execution, he was accused of plotting, along with Warbeck, to escape from the Tower of London. This was construed as treason, and both men were sentenced to death. See Hall, *Chronicle,* p. 491.

For Katherine of Aragon's French lessons, see *CSP Span.,* I, no. 203, and no. 294. Her letter from Prince Arthur is in Wood, *Letters of Royal and Illustrious Ladies,* I, p. 121. Katherine's coming to England and her marriage is described in The Receyt of the Ladie Kateryne. Also: Grose et al., *Antiquarian Repertory,* II, pp. 251-290; Vergil, *Anglica Historia,* p. 122/123; and Hall, *Chronicle,* pp. 493-494.

Henry VII's letter to Spain is in *CSP Span.,* I, no. 311. Prince Arthur as a happy newlywed is in no. 312.

The King and Queen's mutual grief is described in Leland, *Collectanea,* V, pp. 373-374.

The birth of a daughter and the death of the Queen is in Kingsford, *Chronicles of London,* p. 258. That Elizabeth would live to a ripe old age: Armstrong, 'Astrology at the Court of Henry VII', p. 452.

Chapter 6: The Greatest Trouble and Anguish in the World

Vives' assessment of Katherine is in Watson, *Luis Vives,* pp. 75–76.

Elizabeth of York as the 'most gracious and best loved', and Henry VII's mourning for her are taken from a contemporary description of her funeral, reprinted in Grose et al, *The Antiquarian Repertory,* IV, p. 655. The baby Katharine died not long after her mother: Strickland, *Lives of the Queens of England,* p. 60.

Her parents' desire to have Katherine back, and their resistance to her marriage to Henry VII are in *CSP Span.,* I, no. 360.

Henry VII presenting Katherine and her ladies with jewels is described in *The Receyt of the Ladie Kateryn,* pp. 77-78. His taking her hunting with him is in *CSP Span.,* I, no. 398.

Estrada's praise of Prince Henry is from *CSP Span.,* I, no. 398. His sheltering is described in *Correspondencia de Gutierre Gómez de Fuensalida,* p. 449, and in *CSP Span.,* I, no. 513. Henry dancing at Katherine's wedding is from *The Receyt of the Ladie Kateryn,* p. 58.

Henry VII's refusal to interfere with Katherine's dysfunctional household: *CSP Span.,* I, no. 400. His mistreatment of her is from *CSP Span.,* I, no. 311. Katherine's complaints against de Puebla and the loss of Doña Elvira: Wood, *Letters,* I, LII. See also: *CSP Span.,* I, no. 440, no. 441, and no. 539.

For Joanna and Philip's visit, refer to Wood, *Letters,* I, LIII, and also to *CSP Span.,* I, no. 451. For Henry VII's loan of money to Philip: Bentley, *Excerpta Historica,* pp. 132-133.

'All but naked': Wood, *Letters,* I, LIII (*CSP Span.,* I, no. 459).

Katherine's preference for making her confessions in Spanish is from *CSP Span.,* IV (ii), no. 1165 (*L&P,* VI, no. 1571).

For Katherine's letter to Joanna, refer to *CSP Span.,* I, no. 553. De Puebla's approval of a marriage between Joanna and Henry VII is mentioned in *CSP Span.,* I, no. 511. As late as 1518, Philip's embalmed corpse was still unburied and accompanying his distraught widow wherever she went. The bizarre situation 'cannot be avoided' as it was explained to her son Charles: *CSP Span.,* Supplement I and II, no. 36.

For the complaints against Fray Diego: *CSP Span.,* Supplement I and II, no. 2 and no. 4.

Katherine's wish to return to Spain is in *CSP Span.,* I, no. 603. Ferdinand's sympathy for her and his plans for her second marriage: *CSP Span.,* II, no. 1.

For Henry VII's decline: *CSP Span.,* I, no. 511, and *CSP Ven.,* I, no. 939.

Chapter 7: Well and Prosperous

Henry VII as an obstacle to Katherine's marriage to his son: *CSP Span.,* II, no. 10. Ferdinand's belated payment of the dowry and his friendship with his new son-in-law are from no. 13. His criticism of the late Henry VII can be found in no. 11.

The friary church outside Greenwich Palace is usually pointed out as the location of the marriage ceremony, but William Thomas, who served as a witness, said it took place in the Queen's Closet. See *L&P,* IV, no. 5774.

Henry and Katherine's coronation is in Hall, *Triumphant Reigne*, I, pp. 4-14. The King's magnificent physique is noted in *CSP Span.*, I, no. 552. For Margaret Beaufort's attendance at the festivities, see Hayward, *Dress at the Court of King Henry VIII*, p. 44.

Lord Mountjoy's letter to Erasmus is from Allen, *Opus Epistolarum*, I, no. 215. The arrest of Empson and Dudley: Hall, *Triumphant Reigne*, I, p. 1. For the royal couple's happiness, see *CSP Span.*, II, no. 21 and no. 22; *L&P*, I, no. 127; and Hall, *Triumphant Reigne*, I, pp. 10-11. For Henry VIII's good qualities: *CSP Span.*, I, no. 552.

Ferdinand's advice to his pregnant daughter: *CSP Span.*, II, no. 28. Katherine's letter to Spain is in *CSP Span.*, II, no. 43. Fray Diego's more truthful explanation to the King: *CSP Span.*, Supplement I and II, no. 7.

The birth and death of the Prince are in in Hall, *Triumphant Reigne*, I, pp. 22-27.

Henry VIII's pastimes are described in Hall, *Triumphant Reigne*, I, p. 19 and p. 28; *CSP Span.*, II, no. 19; and *CSP Ven.*, II, no. 1287.

For the King's rivalry with France, see *L&P*, I, no. 156. His alliance with Ferdinand: *CSP Span.*, II, no. 23. For the failed English expedition to Spain, refer to Hall, *Triumphant Reigne*, I, pp. 43-51.

The great esteem for Margaret of Austria: Sergeant, *Anne Boleyn*, Appendix, p. 276.

For Thérouanne: *CSP Ven.*, II, no. 333. The capture of the Duke of Longueville and the preparation to fight the Scots: *L&P*, I, no. 2226.

James IV's betrayal of England is in *CSP Milan*, I, no. 655. Katherine's speech to her troops is from *L&P*, I, no. 2299. For the English victory at Flodden: *CSP Milan*, I, no. 654 and no. 655; *L&P*, I, no. 2268; *CSP Ven.*, II, no. 329.

For Mary Tudor's marriage: *CSP Ven.*, II, no. 51; *Triumphant Reigne*, I, p. 123; *L&P*, I, no. 3146; *CSP Ven.*, II, no. 505; *L&P*, I, no. 3171; and *Letters of Royal and Illustrious Ladies*, I, LXII.

Katherine's miscarriage of November 1514 is in *CSP Ven.*, II, no. 555.

Her new 'Englishness': *CSP Span.*, II, no. 201.

That King Ferdinand's death was withheld from the Queen, and that Henry VIII's was still optimistic for male children, see Giustinian, *Four Years*, I, pp. 181-182. For Princess Mary's christening, see *L&P*, II, no. 1573.

The Spanish Princesses taught needlework: Vives, *De Institutione Feminae Christianae*, p. 22/23. Peter Martyr as tutor to the royal family is from Du Boys, *Catharine of Aragon*, I, p. 20. Katherine as Princess Mary's Latin teacher: Ellis, *Original Letters*, 1st series, II, CVII. Vives' dedication is in *De Institutione Feminae Christianae*, p. 10/11.

For Vives' views, see: *De Institutione Feminae Christianae*, p. 40/41 and p. 18/19. For Princess Mary's programme of study, see Dowling, *Humanism in the Age of Henry VIII*, pp. 223-229.

Chapter 8: To Submit and Have Patience

For the contrast between the royal couple, see *CSP Ven.,* II, no. 624 and no. 1287. Elizabeth Blount's attractions are from Hall, *Triumphant Reigne,* II, p. 49.

For the Queen's great piety: Clifford, *The Life of Jane Dormer,* pp. 73-74.

Wolsey's banishment of the 'minions' at court: Hall, *Triumphant Reigne,* I, p. 175 and pp. 177-178.

For the betrothal of Princess Mary: *L&P,* II, no. 4480 and no. 4481.

For the rivalry between Henry VIII and Francis I, see Giustinian, *Four Years,* I, pp. 90-91, and *State Papers, King Henry the Eighth,* VIII, DCCX.

The arrival of Emperor Charles to England: *CSP Ven.,* III, no. 50.

Descriptions of The Field of the Cloth of Gold are found in *CSP Ven.,* III, no. 50, no. 69, and no. 88.

Mary's betrothal to the Dauphin of France: *L&P,* II, no. 4504.

The Emperor's subsequent visit to England: Hall, *Triumphant Reigne,* I, p. 246.

Henry VIII's fear of the Duke of Buckingham: *CSP Ven.,* II, no. 1287.

Charles V's falling out with Henry and Katherine: *CSP Span.,* III (i), no. 106 and no. 621.

The elevation of Henry Fitzroy is in *CSP Ven.,* III, no. 1053.

Chapter 9: The King's Great Matter

The Shrovetide revels of 1522: Hall, *Triumphant Reigne,* I, pp. 237-240.

For the controversy surrounding Anne Boleyn's birth date, see: Paget, 'The Youth of Anne Boleyn' favouring 1501; and Warnicke, 'Anne Boleyn's Childhood and Adolescence' arguing for 1507.

Margaret of Austria's praise of Anne: Le Glay, *Correspondance,* II, p. 461, note 2. Her appearance: *CSP Ven.,* IV, no. 824, and De Carles, Épistre, p. 5.

Henry Percy's pursuit of Anne is described in Cavendish, *The Life of Cardinal Wolsey,* pp. 121-129.

Thomas Wyatt's poem referring to Anne Boleyn can be found in Wyatt, *Collected Poems,* p. 7.

Katherine reported to be 'full of apprehension': *CSP Span.,* III (ii), no. 69. She is finally confronted by the King in *CSP Span.,* III (ii), no. 113.

Felipez's escape to the Emperor: *State Papers, King Henry the Eighth,* I, CXVIII. Charles V's promise of assistance to his aunt can be found in *CSP Span.,* III (ii), no. 131.

For the sack of Rome, refer to *CSP Span.,* III (ii), no. 70.

Anne Boleyn's arrogance towards Wolsey: *CSP Span.,* III (ii), no. 224.

Katherine's tolerance of her: Cavendish, *The Life of Cardinal Wolsey*, p. 131. The episode of the two ladies at cards together is from the Appendix p. 428.

For Gardiner and Fox at Orvieto, see Pocock, *Records of the Reformation*, I, XLVI (*L&P*, IV, no. 4090).

That Princess Mary should reside 'near the King's person': *L&P*, IV, no. 4096.

For the plague of 1517: Hall, *Triumphant Reigne*, I, p. 165. The King's letters referring to Anne's illness: Ridley, *Love Letters*, p. 39 and p. 57.

Anne's new residence and her luxurious upkeep: Cavendish, *The Life of Cardinal Wolsey*, p. 131 and p. 240.

'The pride and ambition of the Cardinal': Hall, *Triumphant Reigne*, I, p. 168. Wolsey's gift of tunny to Lady Boleyn: Ellis, *Original Letters*, 3rd series, II, p. 133.

Anne's letter (with a postscript by the King) to Wolsey: Ridley, *Love Letters*, p. 69. For the Wilton affair: Ridley, *Love Letters*, p. 59

'More Lutheran than Luther himself': *CSP Span.*, IV (ii), no. 664. However, Anne's commitment to traditional religion is mentioned in William Kingston's letters. While in the Tower in May 1536, Anne asked for the Eucharist to be exposed in her oratory that she might pray before it, and she expressed certainty in going to Heaven as she had done many righteous deeds in her lifetime. This went against the Protestant view that good works in themselves were insufficient for salvation. Also, in February 1533, Anne expressed her intention to go on a pilgrimage if she was still not pregnant yet. See Friedmann, *Anne Boleyn*, I, p. 189.

Anne Boleyn's interest in religious discussion is in William Latymer, 'Cronickille of Anne Bulleyne', p. 62. Louis de Brun's tribute to Anne's piety is transcribed in Ives, *Anne Boleyn*, p. 269.

For Simon Fish: Foxe, *Acts and Monuments*, IV, pp. 659-664. His distribution of illegal English Bibles is in Strype, *Ecclesiastical Memorials*, I (ii), pp. 63-65. 'For me and all Kings to read': Strype, *Ecclesiastical Memorials*, I (i), pp. 171-172. Anne's protection of Thomas Forman: *L&P*, IV, Appendix, no. 197.

Campeggio's arrival in England is in *L&P*, IV, no. 4857. For his meeting with Henry, see *L&P*, IV, no. 4858. That Katherine would not be forced to take the veil: *L&P*, IV, no. 4897.

According to Campeggio, besides allowing Princess Mary to keep her place in the succession, the King even entertained the idea of marrying her to her stepbrother the Duke of Richmond: *L&P*, IV, no. 4881.

Katherine's meeting with Campeggio: *L&P*, IV, no. 4875.

For the Spanish Brief: *L&P*, IV, no. 4842, and *State Papers, King Henry the Eighth*, Vol. VIII, CCXXXVI.

Katherine's appeal at Blackfriars: Cavendish, *The Life of Cardinal Wolsey*, p. 211- 218; *L&P*, IV, no. 5702; and *CSP Ven.*, IV, no. 482. The depositions of the various witnesses are in *L&P*, IV, no. 5774.

For Wolsey's end: Cavendish, *The Life of Cardinal Wolsey*, pp. 387-388.

Katherine's continuing popularity: *L&P*, IV, no. 5702. For the insults directed at her rival: Ellis, *Original Letters*, 1ˢᵗ series, II, CXV; and *CSP Span.*, IV, no. 980.

Elizabeth Barton's reputation for saintliness: *L&P*, VI, no. 1419. Thomas More's regard for her is in *L&P*, VI, no. 1468. Despite giving ear to some of Elizabeth Barton's utterings, More had been careful not to implicate himself with her. For the Nun's predictions against the King: *L&P*, VI, no. 1466. His offer to make her an abbess is found in *L&P*, VI, no. 1468.

Anne's defiant motto: *CSP Span.*, IV (i), no. 547. For her complaint about her years wasted, see *CSP Span.*, IV (i), no. 224. Her ferocity: *CSP Span.*, IV (ii), no. 584.

For Henry VIII's first meeting with Cranmer: Foxe, *Acts and Monuments*, VIII, pp. 7-8. Cranmer as 'most bound' to Anne: Burnet, *History of the Reformation*, I, p. 323.

Chapuys as Katherine's 'especial friend': *CSP Span.*, V (i), no. 134.

For Anne eavesdropping on the King's meeting with Chapuys, see *CSP Span.*, IV (i), no. 492.

The Christmas festivities of 1530 are described in Hall, *Triumphant Reigne*, II, p. 183. Henry and Katherine's argument: Friedmann, *Anne Boleyn*, I, p. 130.

Thomas Cromwell's qualities: *CSP Span.*, V (i), no. 228 (*L&P*, IX, no. 862).

For Anne's rejoicing: *CSP Span.*, IV (ii), no. 635 (*L&P*, V, no. 105).

Katherine's refusal to leave her husband: *CSP Span.*, IV (ii), no. 720 (*L&P*, V, no. 238). For her abandonment at Windsor Castle, see *CSP Span.*, IV (ii), no. 765 (*L&P*, V, no. 340), and *CSP Span.*, IV (ii), no. 833.

Chapter 10: The Most Happy

The Queen's exile at The More is described in *CSP Ven.*, IV, no. 682.

Anne appointing courtiers to her service, and her expectation to be married soon are from *CSP Span.*, IV (ii); no. 1047 (*L&P*, VI, no. 142); and *CSP Span.*, IV (ii), no. 765. Her anger at Henry Guilford is from *CSP Span.*, IV (ii), no. 739 (*L&P*, V, no. 287).

Henry VIII called to Rome, and the Queen's defence of the Pope's authority are from *CSP Span.*, IV (ii), no. 739 (*L&P*, V, no. 287).

The Richard Hunne scandal is described in Hall, *Triumphant Reigne*, I, pp. 129-142.

For Henry's appeal to Parliament, see Hall, *Triumphant Reigne*, II, p. 210.

Anne's elevation to Marquis of Pembroke is in *L&P*, V, no. 1274; *CSP Span.*, IV (ii), no. 993 (*L&P*, V, no. 1292); and *CSP Ven.*, IV, no. 802. For her precedence over the other ladies at court, see *CSP Span.*, IV (i), no. 232. Anne's demand for the Queen's jewels is from *CSP Span.*, IV (ii), no. 1003 (*L&P*, V, no. 1377).

For the strange omens, refer to *CSP Ven.*, IV, no. 816. Anne's desire to be married in Westminster Abbey is in *CSP Span.*, IV (ii), no. 802. The Calais trip is described in Hall, *Triumphant Reigne*, II, p. 220.

25 January 1533 is generally accepted as the date of Henry and Anne's secret marriage. This was stated by Cranmer in Ellis, *Original Letters*, 1st series, II, CXIV, p. 39 (*L&P*, VI, no. 661), and is backed up by Chapuys in *CSP Span.*, IV (ii), no. 1072. However, a wedding date of 14 November 1532 is given in Hall, *Triumphant Reigne*, II, p. 222. Perhaps the earlier date was given out to imply that the Princess Elizabeth was properly conceived in wedlock.

For Anne as Queen at Easter of 1533, see *CSP Span.*, IV (ii), no. 1069 (*L&P*, VI, no. 351). Her craving for apples is from Friedmann, *Anne Boleyn*, I, pp. 189-190. That she actually said 'plums', see Bernard, *Anne Boleyn*, p. 67 and p. 208 (note 108). Her rich plate is from *CSP Span.*, IV (ii), no. 1055 (*L&P*, VI, no. 212).

Cranmer's request to try the divorce and Henry's assent to it is from *L&P*, VI, no. 327 and no. 332 respectively. The achievement of the divorce is in Hall, *Triumphant Reigne*, II, p. 224, and in Ellis, *Original Letters*, 1st series, II, CXIV, pp. 35-36 (*L&P*, VI, no. 661).

Anne's coronation is described in 'The Noble Triumphant Coronation of Queen Anne – Wife Unto the Most Noble King Henry VIII' in Pollard, *Tudor Tracts*, pp. 798-805; Ellis, *Original Letters*, 1st series, II, CXIV, pp. 36-39; *L&P*, VI, no. 563, no. 583, no. 584, no. 585, and no. 601; Wriothesley, *Chronicle*, I, pp. 18-22; Hall, *Triumphant Reigne*, II, pp. 228-242; Spelman, *Reports*, I, pp. 68-70; and Hume, *Chronicle*, pp. 12-14. Anne's seizure of Katherine's barge is from *CSP Span.*, IV (ii), no. 1077 (*L&P*, VI, no. 556).

The joyous atmosphere of the new Queen's court is mentioned in *L&P*, VI, no. 613. Anne's demand for the French bed, and her fight with Henry is told in *CSP Span.*, IV (ii), no. 1123 (*L&P*, VI, no. 1069). Her insistence on Katherine's christening cloth is in *CSP Span.*, IV (ii), no. 1107 (*L&P*, VI, no. 918).

Chapter 11: She is My Death, and I am Hers

For the birth announcement, see Doran, *Elizabeth*, p. 14, no. 9. 'They ought to thank God' is from *L&P*, VI, no. 1125.

The christening ceremony is described in Wriothesley, *Chronicle*, I, pp. 22-23, and in Hall, *Triumphant Reigne*, II, pp. 242-244. That the water in the font was 'not hot enough' is from *L&P*, VII, no. 939.

Mary's refusal to call Elizabeth other than 'sister' is in *CSP Span.*, IV (ii), no. 1164. (*L&P*, VI, no. 1558). Her message to her father calling herself 'Princess' is in *L&P*, VI, no. 1207. The new liveries for her servants are in *L&P*, VI, no. 1125.

The move of the two sisters to Hatfield is in *CSP Span.*, IV (ii), no. 1158 (*L&P*, VI, no. 1510). For the reduction of Mary's circumstances, see *CSP Span.*, V (i), no. 1 (*L&P*, VII, no. 14). Mary taking the better seat on the barge is in *CSP Span.*, V (i), no. 86 (*L&P*, VII, no. 1095), and her being manhandled into her litter is in *CSP Span.*, V (i), no. 32 (*L&P*, VII, no. 393).

Lady Hussey in trouble is mentioned in *L&P*, VII, no. 1036.

Chapuys' sighting of Mary in her barge is in *CSP Span.*, V (i), no. 102 (*L&P*, VII, no. 1297). The interrogation of the Princess's maid is in *CSP Span.*, V (i), no. 111.

Lady Shelton's empathy for Mary is in *CSP Span.*, V (i), no. 17 (*L&P*, VII, no. 214). Her later change of heart is in *CSP Span.*, V (i), no. 45 (*L&P*, VII, no. 530). For Anne's vow to harm Mary, see *CSP Span.*, V (i), no. 68 and no. 231.

The King's dispatch of his physician to Mary is in *CSP Span.*, V (i), no. 118 (*L&P*, VII, no. 1554). His glimpse of Mary at Hatfield is described in *CSP Span.*, V (i), no. 4 (*L&P*, VII, no. 83).

Elizabeth Barton's indictment is mentioned in *L&P*, VI, no. 1445. For the Marchioness of Exeter's repudiation of the Nun: *L&P*, VI, no. 1464 and 1465. More and Fisher's dealings with Elizabeth Barton are in *CSP Span.*, V (i), no. 22 (*L&P*, VII, no. 296). Her execution is described in Hall, *Triumphant Reigne*, II, p. 259, and in Wriothesley, *Chronicle*, I, p. 24.

Henry's undiminished love for Anne is from *CSP Span.*, IV (ii), no. 1144 (*L&P*, VI, no. 1392).

For Anne's abortive efforts to befriend Mary, refer to *CSP Span.*, V (i), no. 22 (*L&P*, VII, no. 296). Her letter to Lady Shelton: *CSP Span.*, V (ii), no. 13 (*L&P*, X, no. 199) and *L&P*, X, no. 307. Mary describing herself as without clothes: *CSP Span.*, V (i), no. 17 (*L&P*, VII, no. 214). The incident in the chapel is from Clifford, *Life of Jane Dormer*, pp. 81-82.

Mary's warning to her doctor about her safety is in *CSP Span.*, V (i), no. 45 (*L&P*, VII, no. 530). The government may have gotten wind of Mary's little ruse. Five months later, when the King's doctors visited Mary again, they were instructed to speak only in English to her, and in the presence of witnesses: *CSP Span.*, V (i), no. 90.

Chapuys' pleas on Mary's behalf are in *CSP Span.*, V (i), no. 19 (*L&P*, VII, no. 232). His advice to her to dissimulate is in *CSP Span.*, V (i), no. 102 (*L&P*, VII, no. 1297).

For the Act of Succession and the oath upholding the King's new marriage: Gee and Hardy, *Documents,* pp. 232-243 and pp. 245-246 respectively. The insults against Anne are from *L&P,* VIII, no. 196 and *L&P,* VI, no. 923.

Henry VIII's affair with a new lady and her affection for Mary, as well as Lady Rochford's banishment from court are described in *CSP Span.,* V (i), no. 97 (*L&P,* VII, no. 1257).

Chabot's visit to the English court is in *CSP Span.,* V (i), no. 112, no. 114 (*L&P,* VII, no. 1507), no. 118 (*L&P,* VII, no. 1554), and no. 127 (*L&P,* VIII, no. 48). For Anne's fears told to the French, see *L&P,* VIII, no. 174.

Chapter 12: Pride and Vainglory

Doubts about Henry VIII's virility are from *CSP Span.,* V (ii), no. 55 (*L&P,* X, no. 908).

For the supposed miraculous preservation of Fisher's head: *CSP Span.,* V (i), no. 231. Thomas More's regard for God before the King is from a letter (3 June 1535) to his daughter Margaret Roper. See De Silva, *Last Letters,* p. 119.

Chapuys' intrigues are in *CSP Span.,* V (i), no. 45 (*L&P,* VII, no. 530). Katherine of Aragon's refusal to be involved is in *CSP Span.,* V (i), no. 1 (*L&P,* VII, no. 14).

The layover at Wolf Hall is documented in *L&P,* IX, no. 729, items 6-8. The royal couple was 'very merry' according to *L&P,* IX, no. 525 and no. 571.

Lady Willoughby's arrival at Kimbolton is described in *L&P,* X, no. 28. Chapuys' visit to the dying Katherine is in *CSP Span.,* V (ii), no. 3 (*L&P,* X, no. 59) and *CSP Span.,* V (ii), no. 4 (*L&P,* X, no. 60). Her last letter to Henry VIII is in Vergil, *Anglica Historia,* pp. 334-337. Katherine having her meals prepared in her own chambers is mentioned in *CSP Span.,* V (i), no. 4. Her last hours and her autopsy: *CSP Span.,* V (ii), no. 9 (*L&P,* X, no. 141). For the continuing belief that Katherine was poisoned by Anne Boleyn, see: Clifford, *Life of Jane Dormer,* p. 77.

For Katherine's will and legacies, see *L&P,* X, no. 40. The court's reaction to her demise is in *CSP Span.,* V (ii), no. 9 (*L&P,* X, no. 141), and in Hall, *Triumphant Reigne,* II, p. 266.

For Mary's effort to discover the truth about her mother's death, Chapuys' belief that it was 'partly by poison', the circumstances and results of the autopsy, and Katherine's final bequests and burial, refer to *CSP Span.,* V (ii), no. 9 (*L&P,* X, no. 141).

Anne Boleyn's uneasiness after Katherine's death is told in *CSP Span.,* V (ii), no. 13 (*L&P,* X, no. 199). Chapuys' attempt to win over Lady Shelton is in *CSP Span.,* V (ii), no. 9 (*L&P,* X, no. 141) and in *CSP Span.,* V (ii), no. 13 (*L&P,* X, no. 199).

Mary's plans to escape from England are in *CSP Span.,* V (ii), no. 9 (*L&P,* X, no. 141); *CSP Span.,* V (ii), no. 13 (*L&P,* X, no. 199); and *CSP Span.,* V (ii), no. 21 (*L&P,* X, no. 307).

The King's jousting accident is in *L&P,* X, no. 200. Anne's miscarriage is described in *CSP Span.,* V (ii), no. 21 (*L&P,* X, no. 282). The foetus was about three to four months old according to Chapuys. That God did not wish to give Henry male children is in *CSP Span.,* V (ii), no. 29 *(L&P,* X, no. 351).

Jane Seymour engaged to work against the Queen, and her hint of marriage to the King are in *CSP Span.,* V (ii), no. 43 (*L&P,* X, no. 601). Chapuys' report that Jane and her party were emboldened to criticise the King's marriage - and to his face - is suspect. This was a treasonable offence, and despite whatever problems there were in the marriage, Henry VIII was still firmly committed to Anne as demonstrated in his negotiations with the Emperor later that April.

Anne's jealousy of her rival is from Clifford, *Life of Jane Dormer,* p. 79.

Anne's falling out with Cromwell is proposed by Ives, *Anne Boleyn,* pp. 307-312. Anne was also compared to Esther during the reign of Elizabeth by John Aylmer in his *An Harborowe for Faithfull and Trewe Subjects.* See Doran, *Elizabeth I and Her Circle,* p. 22. Anne's anger at Cromwell is taken from *CSP Span.,* V (ii), no. 43 (*L&P,* X, no. 601).

Chapuys' visit to court in Easter of 1536 is described in *CSP Span.,* V (ii), no. 43a (*L&P,* X, no. 699). That the Bishop of London declined to give his opinion on a divorce is in *CSP Span.,* V (ii), no. 47 (*L&P,* X, no. 752).

Anne Boleyn's quarrel with Norris is from *L&P,* X, no. 793. She came before the King with Elizabeth in her arms according to *CSP For.,* I, p. 527. Anne's encounter with Smeaton is in *L&P,* X, no. 798. The musician was probably tortured according to Constantine, 'Memorial', p. 64.

Chapter 13: Much Joy and Pleasure in Death

For the May Day joust, refer to Hall, *Triumphant Reigne,* II, p. 268. Henry VIII's offer of a pardon to Norris comes from Constantine, 'Memorial', p. 64.

For Anne's arrest and imprisonment: Wriothesley, *Chronicle,* I, p. 36; *CSP For.,* I, p. 527-528; and *L&P,* X, no. 793, no. 797, no. 798, no. 890, no. 902, and no. 910. Her insults at the Duke of Norfolk are in *CSP Span.,* V (i), no. 122 (*L&P,* VIII, no. 1). Anne's maintenance in the Tower is in *L&P,* XI, no. 381. Sir Thomas Wyatt and Sir Richard Page were also arrested in connection with the Queen, but the charges were later dropped.

Cranmer's letter to the King is in *L&P,* X, no. 792. For the King's behaviour after the Queen's arrest, refer to *CSP Span.,* V (ii), no. 54 (*L&P,* X, no. 909) and *CSP Span.,* V (ii), no. 55 (*L&P,* X, no. 908).

Hopes for Weston's release are in *L&P,* X, no. 865, and in *CSP Span.,* V (ii), no. 55 (*L&P,* X, no. 908). For the trial of the four commoners, see Wriothesley, *Chronicle,* I, p. 36; *CSP Span.,* V (ii), no. 55 (*L&P,* X, no. 908), and *L&P,* X, no. 876.

For the trials of Anne and her brother, see Wriothesley, *Chronicle,* I, pp. 37-38; Spelman, *Reports,* pp. 70-71; *CSP Span.,* V (ii), no. 55 (*L&P,* X, no. 908); Constantine, 'Memorial', p. 66; and *L&P,* X, no. 876. The charge of incest was not as incredible as it seemed to Anne and George Boleyn's contemporaries. Juan Vives wrote 'of the horrible crimes that even brother and sisters dared to commit when the opportunity of seclusion offered itself'. See: Vives, *De Institutione Feminae Christianae,* pp. 136/137- 138/139.

The people's murmuring against King: *CSP Span.,* V (ii), no. 55 (*L&P,* X, no. 908). Jane Seymour as the next Queen is from *CSP Span.,* V (ii), no. 55 (*L&P,* X, no. 908). The ballad against Henry and Jane: Ridley, *Love Letters,* p. 75.

Jane Parker's plea to Cromwell is in Ellis, *Original Letters,* 1st series, II, CXXIV.

The Earl of Northumberland was already observed to be ill – seized by 'vertigo and weakness' - at the Garter ceremony held on 23 April, three weeks before Anne's trial: *L&P,* X, no. 715.

For 17 May executions: *L&P,* X, no. 902 and no. 911; *CSP Span.,* V (ii), no. 55 (*L&P,* X, no. 908); Bentley, *Excerpta Historica,* pp. 262-264; Wriothesley, *Chronicle,* I, pp. 39-40; and Constantine, 'Memorial', p. 64-66.

The grounds for the nullification of the marriage are in *L&P,* X, no. 782; *CSP Span.,* V (ii), no. 54 (*L&P,* X, no. 909); and Wriothesley, *Chronicle,* I, pp. 40-41.

From Marchioness to Queen to martyr, see Montagu, *Works of Francis Bacon,* I, p. 396. Anne's affirmation of her innocence is taken from *L&P,* X, no. 910 and *CSP Span.,* V (ii), no. 55 (*L&P,* X, no. 908).

Aless's meeting with Cranmer is told in *CSP For.,* I, p. 528.

Anne's execution is described in *L&P,* X, no. 911, no. 918, no. 919, and no. 920; *The Lisle Letters,* 3, p. 698; Bentley, *Excerpta Historica,* pp. 264-265; Wriothesley, *Chronicle,* I, pp. 41-42; Hall, *Triumphant Reigne,* II, pp. 268-268; and *CSP Span.,* V (ii), no. 55 (*L&P,* X, no. 908).

Chapter 14: Bound to Obey and Serve

Cromwell's praise for the late Queen Anne is in *CSP Span.,* V (ii), no. 61 (*L&P,* X, no. 1069). The King 'hath come out of hell' according to *L&P,* X, no. 1047. Chapuys' initial opinions about Jane Seymour are in *L&P,* X, no. 901.

News of Anne Boleyn's condemnation in *CSP Span.,* V (ii), no. 55 (*L&P,* X, no. 908). The licence for Henry and Jane's marriage is in *L&P,* X, no. 915. Jane's formal recognition as Queen is described in Wriothesley, *Chronicle,* I, pp. 43-44. The postponement of her coronation is in *CSP Span.*, V (ii), no. 103 (*L&P*, XI, no. 528). For the river pageant and Henry VIII's going to Parliament, see Wriothesley, *Chronicle*, I, pp. 44-45.

Praise for the new Queen is from *L&P*, X, no. 1134 and no. 1047. Chapuys' meeting with Jane Seymour is in *CSP Span.*, V (ii), no. 61 (*L&P*, X, no. 1069).

Mary's removal to Hunsdon, and the return of her former servants is in *CSP Span.*, V (ii), no. 55 (*L&P*, X, no. 908). For Cromwell's sympathy for her, see *CSP Span.*, V (ii), no. 17. Mary's initial letter to Cromwell is in *L&P*, X, no. 968.

The King's scolding of Jane is in *CSP Span.*, V (ii), no. 55 (*L&P*, X, no. 908). Mary's plea for Cromwell's further intercession is in *L&P*, X, no. 1108. Her visit by the King's delegation is from *CSP Span.*, V (ii), no. 70 (*L&P*, XI, no. 7). The Earl of Essex, by his own admission, was the one who used 'injurious words' to the Princess.

Henry VIII's consultation with the judges, and his anger at Jane Seymour, are from *CSP Span.*, V (ii), no. 70 (*L&P*, XI, no. 7). Lady Hussey's arrest is mentioned in *CSP Span.*, V (ii), no. 70 (*L&P*, XI, no. 7) and in *L&P*, XI, no. 10.

Cromwell's angry letter to Mary is in Hearne, *Sylloge Epistolarum*, pp. 137-138. Her surrender is in *CSP Span.*, V (ii), no. 70 (*L&P*, XI, no. 7). Her formal submission is in Hearne, *Sylloge Epistolarum*, pp. 142-143. Her letter of thanks to Cromwell are on pp. 144-145.

Mary's naiveté is mentioned in Simpson, *The Spanish Marriage*, p. 99.

The visit of Henry and Jane to Hunsdon is in *CSP Span.*, V (ii), 71 (*L&P*, XI, no. 40. Cromwell's gift of a ring to Mary is in *L&P*, XI, no. 148.

The death of Henry Fitzroy, and the suspicion of poison by Anne Boleyn and Lord Rochford are in Wriothesley, *Chronicle*, I, p. 53-54.

The postponement of Jane's coronation is from Wriothesley, *Chronicle*, I, p. 55-56.

Anne Basset entering into royal service is in *The Lisle Letters*, 4, no. 887. The Queen's very English tastes are in no. 895 and no. 896. Her gifts to her ladies are described in *L&P*, XII (ii), no. 973.

Chapter 15: Most Precious Jewel

The Northerners' grievances against the Crown are in Hall, *Triumphant Reigne*, pp. 270-271; Wriothesley, *Chronicle*, I, pp. 56-58; *CSP Span.*, V (ii), no. 114; and *L&P*, XI, no. 944, no. 947, no. 955, no. 956, and no. 957.

For Mary and Elizabeth at court together, and for Jane's intercession for the abbeys, see *L&P*, XI, no. 860.

The move to Greenwich is in Wriothesley, *Chronicle*, I, pp. 59-60.

For Robert Aske at court, see *L&P,* XII (i), no. 43 and no. 44. Also, see Scarisbrick, *Henry VIII,* p. 345. The defeat and punishment of the rebels is in Wriothesley, *Chronicle,* I, pp. 60-65, and in *L&P,* XII (i), no. 1124.

Jane's craving for quails is in *The Lisle Letters,* 4, no. 887, and in Madden, *Privy Purse Expenses,* p. 30. The King's reluctance to venture far is in *L&P,* XII (ii), no. 77.

The birth and christening of Prince Edward is in Wriothesley, *Chronicle,* I, pp. 66-68. Thomas Boleyn's reduced circumstances are mentioned in *L&P,* XI, no. 17. After the disgrace of his two children, Boleyn was relieved of his office of Lord Privy Seal, and the honour was conferred on Thomas Cromwell instead. One of his last official duties before his death in March 1539 was as a mourner at Queen Jane's funeral (*L&P,* XII (ii), no. 1060). Boleyn's wife, Elizabeth Howard, predeceased him in April 1538. After the death of William Carey, Mary Boleyn married William Stafford in 1534. She died in 1543. Her children Henry Carey (later Baron Hunsdon) and Katherine Carey (later mother to Lettice Knollys) went on to serve their cousin Queen Elizabeth.

The regulations for the Prince's care are in Nichols, *Literary Remains,* I, pp. xxvii-xxx.

Jane fell ill days just after Prince Edward's birth according to *L&P,* XII (ii), no. 970. Cromwell's blaming of her servants is in no. 1004. For prayers for Jane's recovery, see Wriothesley, *Chronicle,* I, p. 69. Norfolk's letter to Cromwell is in *L&P,* XII (ii), no. 971.

For Jane's death and funeral, see *L&P,* XII (ii), no. 977; Wriothesley, *Chronicle,* I, pp. 71-72; and *L&P,* XII (ii), no. 1060. Her epitaph is in Foxe, *Acts and Monuments,* V, p. 148.

Chapter 16: Of Excellent Beauty?

Henry VIII's letter to King Francis is in *L&P,* XII (ii), no. 972. Mourning at court for Queen Jane is in Hall, *Triumphant Reigne,* II, p. 280.

Prince Edward's good health is in *L&P,* XII (ii), no. 1004 (*State Papers, Henry the Eighth,* VIII, CCCCLXVIII).

For the Emperor's plans for a marriage alliance with England, see *L&P,* X, no. 888.

Christina of Denmark's qualities are in *State Papers, Henry the Eighth,* VIII, CCCCLXXXI and CCCCLXXXVI. Also: *L&P,* XII, (ii), no. 1187.

The King's hesitation to consider a foreign bride is in *CSP Span.,* V (ii), no. 61 (*L&P,* X, no. 1069).

Henry's interest in Mary of Guise is in *L&P,* XII, (ii), no. 1285. For his suggestion of a beauty parade at Calais: Kaulek, *Correspondance Politique,* no. 99 (*L&P,* XIII (ii), no. 77).

Wriothesley's meeting with Christina is in *State Papers, Henry the Eighth,* VIII, DXXVII. Holbein's journey to Brussels to paint her is in

CCCCLXXXVIII. Her reference to Henry's previous wives is in *L&P,* XIV (ii), no. 400. Her alleged joke of having two heads is from Walpole, *Anecdotes,* I, pp. 113-114.

Cromwell's instructions to Christopher Mont are in: *L&P,* XIV (i), no. 103. His assessment of Anne, and his failure to obtain her portrait is in *L&P,* XIV (i), no. 552.

Wotton and Beard's mission to Germany is in *L&P,* XIV (i), no. 920. Wotton's description of Anne, and the 'liveliness' of Holbein's picture are in *L&P,* XIV (ii), no. 33.

Anne's pre-contract to Francis of Lorraine is in *L&P,* XIV (ii), no. 33.

That Anne will be crowned at Candlemas: Kaulek, *Correspondance Politique,* no. 170 (*L&P,* XIV (ii), no. 607).

The Germans' preference for an overland journey to England is in *L&P,* XIV (ii), no. 258. Henry VIII's scheme to smuggle Anne over by sea is discussed in Starkey, *Henry VIII - A European Court,* p. 149, and in *L&P,* XIV (ii), no. 389. The request for her safe conduct is in *L&P,* XIV (ii), no. 356, and also in *CSP Span.,* VI (i), no. 91.

Anne was 'never far' from her mother's side according to *L&P,* XIV (ii), no. 33. The composition of her suite, as well as the German wedding custom of gift giving are mentioned in *L&P,* XIV (ii), no. 634. For her itinerary, see *L&P,* XV, no. 14.

Lord Lisle's preparations to receive Anne are in *L&P,* XIV (ii), no. 347. Her arrival and stay in Calais are in Hall, *Triumphant Reigne,* pp. 294-295, and in *L&P,* XIV (ii), no. 677. Lady Lisle's opinion of Anne is in *L&P,* XIV (ii), no. 718. The learning of a card game is from *State Papers, Henry the Eighth,* VIII, DXLVIII.

Anne's arrival in England is in Wriothesley, *Chronicle,* I, p. 109, and in Hall, *Triumphant Reigne,* p. 295. The Duchess of Suffolk, Katherine Willoughby, was the daughter of Maria de Salinas (who had served Katherine of Aragon) and an English nobleman William Willoughby, the 11th Baron Willoughby de Eresby. She married Charles Brandon shortly after the death of Mary Tudor in 1533. For the late night journey to Dover Castle, and Anne's reception in Canterbury, refer to *L&P,* XIV (ii), no. 754.

The preparation of lodgings at Saint Augustine's in Canterbury is in Colvin, *King's Works,* IV, pp. 59-60. Her reception is in *L&P,* XIV (ii), no. 754, and in Hall, *Triumphant Reigne,* p. 295.

Anne's insistence on hurrying to her meeting with the King is in *L&P,* XIV (ii), no. 754. Her welcome at Rochester is Wriothesley, *Chronicle,* I, p. 109. The official versions of Henry's meeting with Anne in Rochester are in Wriothesley, *Chronicle,* I, pp. 109-110, and in Hall, *Triumphant Reigne,* pp. 295-296. Anthony Browne's differing account is given in Strype, *Ecclesiastical Memorials,* I (ii), pp. 456-458.

The King's complaints about Anne are in *L&P,* XV, no. 822, no. 823, and no. 824. Her 'queenly manner': *L&P,* XV, no. 822.

The reception at Blackheath is in Wriothesley, *Chronicle,* I, pp. 110-111; Hall, *Triumphant Reigne,* pp. 296-301; and *L&P,* XV, no. 18. De Marillac's description of Anne is from Kaulek, *Correspondance Politique,* no. 178 (*L&P,* XV, no. 22) and no. 179 (*L&P,* XV, no. 23).

Henry VIII's attempt to delay his marriage: *L&P,* XV, no. 822, no. 823, and no. 824. The two presiding at court is in Wriothesley, *Chronicle,* I, p. 111. Their wedding is in *L&P,* XV, no. 823, p. 391, and in Hall, *Triumphant Reigne,* p. 302.

Chapter 17: There Must Be More Than This

The couple's wedding night is in *L&P,* XV no. 823 and no. 824. Anne's fictionalized attempts to distract Henry VIII from having sex with her were depicted in film *The Private Life of Henry VIII* (1933), and in the television series *The Six Wives of Henry VIII* (1970).

The German envoys' description of the wedding day, and the King's gifts are in Bouterwek, 'Anna von Cleve', pp. 106-107. I am grateful to Dr. Martin Spies (Justus Liebig University Giessen, Germany) for translating this and other passages for me.

The celebratory jousts and the Germans' leave-taking are mentioned in Hall, *Triumphant Reigne,* p. 303. The popularity of the French hood is mentioned in *Chronicle of the Grey Friars,* p. 43.

The Lisles' attempt to place Katharine Basset at court is in *The Lisle Letters,* 6, no. 1650. After much persistence, she was able to secure a place later on.

The river pageant to Whitehall is from Wriothesley, *Chronicle,* I, p. 112.

The King's confiding in Denny is in Strype, *Ecclesiastical Memorials,* pp. 218-219. Anne's wilfulness towards the King is in *L&P,* XV, no. 823.

For Henry VIII's pursuit of Katheryn Howard, see Kaulek, *Correspondance Politique,* no. 235 (*L&P,* XVI, no. 848), and *L&P,* XVI, no. 578.

Cromwell was created Earl of Essex when Henry Bouchier, the previous holder of the title, died in a riding accident in March 1540. Cromwell's alleged treasons are in *History of the Reformation,* IV, pp. 417-423. His arrest is described in Kaulek, *Correspondance Politique,* no. 231. The Earl of Surrey's glee is from a document in The Public Record Office, SP 1/227, fo. 97. Cromwell's abject letter to the King is *L&P,* XV, no. 823.

Chapter 18: No More Spoken Of

The May Day jousts are mentioned in Wriothesley, *Chronicle,* I, pp. 116-117.

Anne's move to Richmond is in Kaulek, *Correspondance Politique,* no. 235 (*L&P,* XVI, no. 848).

Parliament's request to the King to investigate the legality of his marriage, and Anne's reaction to it, are in *State Papers, Henry the Eighth,* VIII, DCXII. The Councilors who met with her downplayed her reaction to the King. According to them, she agreed to Henry VIII's demands 'without alteration of countenance'. See: Original Letters, 2ⁿᵈ series, II, p. 159. But her non-cooperation, and her grief were reported by Harst in Bouterwek, 'Anna von Cleve', p. 171.

The investigation by Convocation into the marriage is in *State Papers, Henry the Eighth,* VIII, DCXVII. The doctors' statements and those of the Queen's ladies are in Strype, *Ecclesiastical Memorials,* pp. 220-222. An interpreter had to be employed to convey the King's wishes according to Ellis, *Original Letters,* 2ⁿᵈ series, II, CLXI.

The dissolving of the marriage is contained in *State Papers, Henry the Eighth,* I, CXXXIX, and in *State Papers, Henry the Eighth,* VIII, DCXVII. Her letter of submission is in *State Papers, Henry the Eighth,* I, CXL. See also CXLII.

Henry's divorce settlement is in *State Papers, Henry the Eighth,* VIII, DCXVII; *L&P,* XV, no. 925; and in Kaulek, *Correspondance Politique,* no. 238 (*L&P,* XV, no. 901).

The people's continuing affection for Anne is in Kaulek, *Correspondance Politique,* no. 238 (*L&P,* XV, no. 901).

The return of her wedding ring is in *L&P,* XV, no. 925. Anne's apparent cheerfulness after her divorce is described in Kaulek, *Correspondance Politique,* no. 244, no. 247, and no. 248 (*L&P,* XV, no. 976, *L&P,* XVI, no. 11, and no. 12 respectively).

She was 'no more spoken of' according to de Kaulek, *Correspondance Politique,* no. 268 (*L&P,* XVI, 223).

Chapter 19: Lambeth and Horsham

For Cromwell's demotion from his titles: Kaulek, *Correspondance Politiques,* no. 231 (*L&P,* XVI, no. 804). His execution is described in Wriothesley, *Chronicle,* I, p. 120, and in Hall, *Triumphant Reigne,* pp. 306-307.

Katheryn Howard was 'very small of stature' according to *L&P,* XVI, no. 578. 'Small and slender', said the French envoy: Kaulek, *Correspondance Politiques,* no. 248 (*L&P,* XVI, no. 12).

Katheryn's proposed birth date of circa 1521 is in Smith, *A Tudor Tragedy,* pp. 209-211. For Lord Edmund Howard's frustrated life and career, see pp. 37-45.

Katheryn's affair with Manox is in *L&P,* XVI, no. 1320 and no. 1321. Manox had a wife according to no. 1416.

Katheryn's affair with Francis Dereham at Lambeth is in *L&P,* XVI, no. 1416 and no. 1469. Also: Burnet, *History of the Reformation,* VI, pp. 249-252.

Chapter 20: Perfect Jewel of Womanhood

That the King fell in love with Katheryn at first sight is in *L&P,* XVI, no. 1409. Her appearance and her French clothes are in Kaulek, *Correspondance Politiques,* no. 248 (*L&P,* XVI, no 12). Rumours of their love affair were circulated 'before Saint John's Day' (24 June 1540), according to *L&P,* XVI, no. 578. 'Being solicited by his Council to marry again': *L&P,* XVI, no. 1334.

Katheryn's first public appearance as Queen is in Wriothesley, *Chronicle,* I, p. 122. As a 'perfect jewel of womanhood': *L&P,* XVI, no. 1334. Henry VIII's displays of affection for Katheryn, and her chosen motto are in Kaulek, *Correspondance Politiques,* no. 248 (*L&P,* XVI, no. 12). His gifts of jewelry are listed in *L&P,* XVI, no. 1389).

Katheryn's row with Princess Mary is in *CSP Span.,* VI (i), no. 143 (*L&P,* XVI, no. 314). Their reconciliation: *CSP Span.,* VI (i), no. 149 (*L&P,* XVI, no. 436); *CSP Span.,* VI (i), no. 161 (*L&P,* XVI, no. 835); and *L&P,* XVI, no. 1389.

According to Gregorio Leti's not always accurate life of Elizabeth I, Katheryn had her at court where she was much honoured. See: Leti, *La Vie d'Elizabeth,* p. 140. Gifts of jewellery to the Princess are in *L&P,* XVI, no. 1389. Elizabeth riding in the Queen's barge is in *L&P,* XVI, no. 804.

For the tensions within the Howard family, see *L&P,* XII (ii), no. 976, and *L&P,* XIV (i), no. 160.

The preferment of Katheryn's relatives at court is in *L&P,* XV, no. 21, and in Kaulek, *Correspondance Politiques,* no. 290 (*L&P,* XVI, no. 449). For Katheryn's household, see Strickland, *Lives of the Queens of England,* IV, p. 295. For Joan Bulmer's pleading letter, see p. 292 (*L&P,* XV, no. 875).

Francis Dereham's coming to court is in *L&P,* XVI, no. 1416. Lord William Howard was fond of Dereham too. He was a great 'maintainer of the young man since the Queen's marriage' (*L&P,* XVI, no. 1469). He even took Dereham's side in his quarrel with Henry Manox: *L&P,* XVI, no. 1416. Dereham's arrogance is in *L&P,* XVI, no. 1339.

Henry VIII's visit to Anne of Cleves is in Thomas, *The Pilgrim,* p. 153, and in Kaulek, *Correspondance Politiques,* no. 241. For her coming to court, see Kaulek, Correspondance Politiques, no. 290 (*L&P,* XVI, no. 449), and *CSP Span.,* VI (i), no. 149 (*L&P,* XVI, no. 436).

The King's new vigour is described in Kaulek, *Correspondance Politiques,* no. 275 (*L&P,* XVI, no. 311). His poor health: Kaulek, *Correspondance Politiques,* no. 306 and 307 (*L&P,* XVI, no. 589 and 590 respectively).

The river pageant from Westminster to Greenwich is in Wriothesley, *Chronicle*, I, p. 124. The Queen's intercession for Wyatt is described in *CSP Span.*, VI (i), no. 155 (*L&P*, XVI, no. 662). The often repeated story (for example in Strickland, *Lives of the Queens of England*, IV, pp. 298-299) that Katheryn also took pity on Margaret Pole, imprisoned in the Tower of London, is doubtful. The request to provide the old Countess with new clothes was actually initiated by a Tower official named Thomas Phillips to Cromwell. Though the items were later paid out of the King's household expenses (and hence 'bought and made' by the Queen's tailor John Scutte) there is no evidence that Katheryn herself ever intervened. Refer to *L&P*, XIII, no. 1176 and *L&P*, XVI, no. 1489.

The Queen was thought to be pregnant in April 1541 according to Kaulek, *Correspondance Politiques*, no. 326 (*L&P*, XVI, no. 712).

The disgruntlement of the Poles and their friends is discussed in Pierce, *Margaret Pole*, pp. 130-133. The dispatch of the Tower's prisoners is in Kaulek, *Correspondance Politiques*, no. 345 and no. 350 (*L&P*, XVI, no. 868 and no. 941 respectively). Margaret Pole's interrogation is in *L&P*, XIII (ii), no. 855. Her execution is in Wriothesley, *Chronicle*, I, p. 124; Kaulek, *Correspondance Politiques*, no. 345 (*L&P*, XVI, no. 868); and *CSP Span.*, VI (i), no. 166 (*L&P*, XVI, no. 897).

The Northern Progress is in Kaulek, *Correspondance Politiques*, no. 345, no. 350, no. 359, and no. 361 (*L&P*, XVI, no. 868, no. 941, no. 1130, and no. 1183 respectively), and in *L&P*, XVI, no. 1088.

For the King's thanksgiving for his life with Katheryn: *L&P*, XVI, no. 1334.

Chapter 21: No More to Dance

The investigation into Mary Hall's allegations are in *L&P*, XVI, no. 1320 and no. 1334, and in Kaulek, *Correspondance Politiques*, no. 376 (*L&P*, XVI, no. 1366). John Lascelles may have been the same who was executed alongside of Anne Askew in July 1546: Wriothesley, *Chronicle*, I, pp. 169-170.

Henry VIII's breakdown before his Councillors is in *L&P*, XVI, no. 1334. Katheryn's interrogation and confessions: *L&P*, XVI, no. 1325 and no. 1334; Burnet, *History of the Reformation*, VI, pp. 249-252; and *Cal. Marquis of Bath*, II, pp. 8-10.

Culpepper's arrest is in *Cal. Marquis of Bath*, II, p. 10. Katheryn's letter to him is from *L&P*, XVI, no. 1134 (transcribed in full in Smith, *A Tudor Tragedy*, pp. 168-169.

The ejection of Katheryn's sister in favour of Lady Rochford is in Kaulek, *Correspondance Politiques*, no. 376 (*L&P*, XVI, no. 1366). Her testimony, as well as Culpepper's, are in *L&P*, XVI, no. 1339. Katheryn's claim that Lady Rochford encouraged her to love Culpepper is in *Cal. Marquis of Bath*, II, p. 9. See also *L&P*, XVI, no. 1338.

Henry VIII's outburst about killing Katheryn himself is in Kaulek, *Correspondance Politiques*, no. 380 (*L&P,* XVI, no. 1426).

The Queen's removal to Syon House is in *State Papers, King Henry the Eighth,* I, CLXIII and CLXIV (*L&P,* XVI, no. 1331 and no. 1333 respectively). The King's merciful treatment of her is in *CSP Span.,* VI (i), no. 207 (*L&P,* XVI, no. 1359). Also: Kaulek, *Correspondance Politiques,* no. 376 (*L&P,* XVI, no. 1366).

Katheryn's jewels were confiscated according to *State Papers, King Henry the Eighth,* I, CLXIV. That some were 'taken by the King into his own hands' is in *L&P,* XVI, no. 1389. The government went so far as to even have Anne of Cleves surrender a ring Katheryn gave to her; perhaps the one presented to her at Hampton Court in January 1541. See: *CSP Span.,* VI (i), no. 232 (*L&P,* XVII, no. 124).

The pardoning of Mary Hall is in *State Papers, King Henry the Eighth,* I, CLXIX and CLXX. The testimonies of various witnesses about Katheryn's past are in *L&P,* XVI, no. 1337, no. 1338, no. 1339, no. 1416, no. 1469, and no. 1470.

The Howards' disassociation of themselves from the scandal is from Kaulek, *Correspondance Politiques,* no. 380 (*L&P,* XVI, no. 1426).

Dereham and Culpepper's condemnation is in *L&P,* XVI, no. 1395. Their executions are in Wriothesley, *Chronicle,* I, pp. 131-132.

The Dowager Duchess of Norfolk sending a spy to court is in *State Papers, King Henry the Eighth,* I, CLXV, and in *L&P,* XVI, no. 1415. The breaking of Dereham's coffers is in *L&P,* XVI, no. 1414, no. 1416, and no. 1423. The Duchess consulted the book of statutes according to *L&P,* XVI, no. 1414, no. 1416, no. 1425, and no. 1409.

The arrest and interrogation of the Howards are in *State Papers, King Henry the Eighth,* I, CLXX, CLXXII, CLXXIII, CLXXIV, and CLXXXI. The Duchess' claim of innocence is in *L&P,* XVI, no. 1415, no. 1416, and no. 1422. She attempted to warn William Howard according to *L&P,* XVI, no. 1414. Lord William and the Countess of Bridgewater's knowledge of the late night parties is in *L&P,* XVI, no. 1469. Ashby's testimony is in *L&P,* XVI, no. 1423.

The Duke of Norfolk's denunciation of his relatives is in *State Papers, King Henry the Eighth,* I, CLXXIX, and in *L&P,* XVI, no. 1359.

Katheryn's mood at Syon, and her desire for a private execution is in *CSP Span.,* VI (i), no. 228 (*L&P,* XVII, no. 63).

The legal proceedings against the Queen, and her submission are in *Journals of The House of Lords,* I, p. 171 and p. 176. Also: *CSP Span.,* VI (i), no. 232 (*L&P,* XVII, no. 124). Speculation that the old Duchess may be executed too is in Kaulek, *Correspondance Politiques,* no. 393 (*L&P,* XVII, no. 100).

Katheryn's confinement in the Tower and her execution are in Kaulek, *Correspondance Politiques,* no. 393 (*L&P,* XVII, no. 100); *CSP Span.,* VI (i), no. 232 (*L&P,* XVII, no. 124); Ellis, *Original Letters,* 1st series, II, CXLVII, (*L&P,* XVII, no. 106). Lady Rochford's madness is mentioned in *CSP Span.,* VI (i), no. 209 (*L&P,* XVI, no. 1401). The romanticised version of Katheryn's last words is in *Chronicle of King Henry VIII,* p. 86. Lady Rochford's supposed exoneration of her husband and his sister Queen Anne is in Leti, *La Vie D'Elizabeth,* p. 145.

'No more the time to dance': Kaulek, *Correspondance Politiques,* no. 371 (*L&P,* XVI, no. 1332).

The new law concerning future royal brides is *CSP Span.,* VI (i), no. 232 (*L&P,* XVII, no. 124).

Chapter 22: As Truly God is God

'The Gospels cause me no shame': Strype, *Ecclesiastical Memorials,* VI, p. 319 (*L&P,* XXI (i), no. 279).

Chapuys' comment is in *CSP Span.,* VI (i), no. 211 (*L&P,* XVI, no. 1403). Henry VIII's merrymaking after Katheryn Howard's fall is in *CSP Span.,* VI (i), no. 230, (*L&P,* XVII, no. 92).

Speculation about Anne of Cleves: *CSP Span.,* VI (i), no. 162 *(L&P,* XVI, no. 864), and *L&P,* XVI, no. 1407, no. 1410, and no. 1414. For the French pamphlet, see *L&P,* XVII, no. 126. The Emperor's fear of another Anglo-German alliance is from *CSP Span.,* VI (i), no. 238. The King's refusal to take back Anne is in *L&P,* XVI, no. 1457.

The Scotsmen's boast is in Loades, *Chronicles of the Tudor Kings,* p. 194.

For the King's wedding to Katharine Parr, refer to *L&P,* XVIII (i), no. 873.

Negotiations for the Parr and Scrope marriage: Strickland, *Lives of the Queens of England,* V, p. 14 (*L&P,* III, no. 3649), and p. 15. See also the letter on pp. 13-14; and *L&P,* IV, 162.

Margaret Neville's praise of Katharine is in Cokayne, *Complete Peerage,* Latimer, VII, p. 484, note a. For a full transcription see James, *Kateryn Parr,* Appendix III, pp. 417 – 418, and pg. 214, note 79 for the correct date of 1546 (not 1545) for Margaret's death.

Katharine's view of her wifely duties is from 'Lamentations of a Sinner': Mueller, *Katherine Parr,* pp. 481-482.

Lord Latimer's ornate chapel is mentioned in *L&P,* IV, no. 1596. The attack on his house is from *L&P,* XII (i), no. 173.

That Katharine served in Princess Mary's household is in James, *Kateryn Parr,* p. 90.

Her amiable nature is from Madden, 'Visit of the Duke of Najera', pp. 352-353.

'As truly God is God': Mueller, *Katherine Parr,* pp. 129-131. Anne Boleyn's fondness for religious discussion is in William Latymer, 'Cronickille of Anne Bulleyne', p. 62. Lord Borough's avid support of Anne had him seizing Katherine of Aragon's barge and hacking off her badges for the new Queen. See: *CSP Span.*, IV (ii), no. 1077 (*L&P* VI, no. 556).

Katharine's conversion of faith is thoroughly described in 'Lamentations of a Sinner', transcribed in Mueller, *Katherine Parr*, pp. 447-485.

Chapter 23: Most Illustrious Queen

Katharine's friendship with Mary and Elizabeth in June 1543 is in *L&P*, XVIII (i), no. 740. The King's regard for himself over Mary: *L&P*, XVII, no. 246. As the 'unhappiest lady in Christendom': Kaulek, *Correspondance Politiques*, no. 418 (*L&P* XVII, no. 371). Her gifts from the new Queen are in Madden, *Privy Purse Expenses of the Princess Mary*, p. 91 and p. 185.

Udall's tribute to Katharine and Mary is in Wood, Letters of Royal and Illustrious Ladies, III, p. 180.

Lady Bryan's praise of Elizabeth is in *L&P*, XI, no. 203. Wriothesley's admiration for her is in Hearne, *Sylloge Epistolarum*, pp. 150–151.

Mary of Hungary inquiring about the English royal family is from *L&P*, XVIII (ii), no. 501.

Elizabeth's letter to her stepmother about the translation is in Hearne, *Sylloge Epistolarum*, pp. 161-162. The following year (1545), Elizabeth did a translation, from English into Latin, French, and Italian, of Katharine's *Prayers and Meditations* for Henry VIII. Again, she embroidered the cover, adding Henry and Katharine's joined initials.

Prince Edward and his 'pretty toys': Wood, Letters of Royal and Illustrious Ladies, III, p. 112. His education: Nichols, *Literary Remains*, II, pp. 209-210.

How much Latin Katharine knew remains uncertain. For different views, see Dowling, *Humanism in the Age of Henry VIII*, p. 236, and James, *Kateryn Parr*, pp. 31-32. Elizabeth's Italian letter: Mueller, *Katherine Parr*, p. 82.

Edward's letter to the Queen praising her progress in Latin is in Nichols, *Literary Remains*, I, Letter XVII. For his other correspondence, see Letters X and XIV. Edward's admonishment of Mary is in Letter X.

Although Henry VIII included the Suffolk line of his sister Mary Tudor in his will, he bypassed her two daughters Frances and Eleanor Brandon. After Princess Elizabeth and any children she might have, Frances' daughter Jane Grey was next in line to the throne.

The Duke of Najera's visit with Katharine: 'Visit of the Duke of Najera', pp. 351-354. See also *CSP Span.*, VII, no. 39 (*L&P* XIX (i), no. 118).

For the war against the Scots: Hall, *Triumphant Reigne*, II, p. 347, and *L&P*, XIX (ii), no. 58. Also: Mueller, *Katherine Parr*, pp. 66-67. For Katharine as Regent: *L&P* XIX (ii), no. 201; *CSP Span.*, VII, no. 148; and Strype, *Ecclesiastical Memorials*, II (ii), pp. 331 – 332. Her prayer for victory is from Mueller, *Katherine Parr,* pp. 418-419. The King's return is in Hall, *Triumphant Reigne,* II, p. 350.

Katharine's meeting with Chapuys is described in *CSP Span.,* VIII, no. 51 (*L&P,* XX (i), no. 689.

For the Queen's religious circle, see Foxe, *Acts and Monuments,* V, p. 553. 'Every day a Sunday': *L&P,* XVIII (ii), no. 531.

The colleges and so forth to be 'committed to the King's order': Hall, *Triumphant Reigne,* II, p. 353. The Queen's letter to Cambridge is in Strype, *Ecclesiastical Memorials,* VI, pp. 318-20 (*L&P,* XXI (i), no. 279).

Chapter 24: The Lord Chancellor's Plot

For Henry VIII's piety, refer to *L&P,* XIV (i), no. 967, and also Sander, *Rise and Growth of the Anglican Schism,* pp. 161 – 162.

For *Lamentations of a Sinner* see: Mueller, *Katherine Parr,* pp. 443-485. For the executions in July 1540: Wriothesley, *Chronicle,* I, pp. 120-121.

The Duchess of Suffolk's dislike of Gardiner is described in Foxe, *Acts and Monuments,* VIII, p. 570.

Wriothesley's earlier praise of Katharine is from *State Papers, King Henry the Eighth,* V, CCCCXLVIII.

For Anne Askew, refer to Foxe, *Acts and Monuments,* V, pp. 546-548. The plot against the Queen: pp. 553-561.

The fall of the Earl of Surrey is in *L&P,* XXI (ii), no. 548 and no. 555.

'To die in the arms of so faithful a spouse' is from Thomas, *The Pilgrim,* p. 59. Henry VIII's deathbed is described in Foxe, *Acts and Monuments,* V, p. 689. For his funeral see Strype, *Ecclesiastical Memorials,* II (ii), pp. 289-311.

Chapter 25: The Merry Widow

For Henry VIII's Will, see *L&P,* XXI (ii), no. 634.

The Queen Dowager's letters to Thomas Seymour are in Mueller, *Katherine Parr,* pp. 129-131, and pp. 134-135. Edward VI's letter of condolence to his stepmother is in Strype, *Ecclesiastical Memorials,* II (ii), p. 512. His approval of the marriage is in Nichols, *Literary Remains,* I, Letter XLVI. For the Lord Protector's response, see Nichols, *Literary Remains,* II, p. 215.

The fight over Katharine's jewels is in *CSP Edward VI,* no. 185. The Duchess of Somerset's faults: Mueller, *Katherine Parr,* pp. 129-131. See also *CSP Span.,* IX, p. 429. On the other hand, Princess Mary was a great friend to the Duchess. See Mary's letter to her in Strickland, *Lives of the Queens of England,* V, pp. 163-164. Anne Stanhope's refusal to bear Katharine's train in Camden, *Elizabeth,* p. 401.

Katharine's anger at the Lord Protector: Mueller, *Katherine Parr,* pp. 140-141. Also: James, *Kateryn Parr,* p. 308.

Mary's refusal to interfere: Mueller, *Katherine Parr,* pp. 145-146. Gregorio Leti's biography of Elizabeth includes a letter written by her to Mary expressing her disapproval of Katharine Parr's new marriage. However, the letter like much of Leti's material cannot be authenticated. See, Leti, *La Vie d'Elizabeth,* pp. 169-170 (Wood, *Letters of Royal and Illustrious Letters,* III, pp. 193-194).

That service with the Lord Admiral was 'ever joyful' is in Harington, *Nugae Antiquae,* I, p. 65. His misbehaviour towards Elizabeth is in Haynes, *State Papers,* pp. 96-100.

Lady Jane Grey's disapproval of Mary is in Strype, *John Aylmer,* pp. 195-196.

Elizabeth's letters to Katharine are from Hearne, *Sylloge Epistolarum,* pp. 151-152, and pp.165-166.

Somerset's congratulations to his brother are in Strickland, *Lives of the Queens of England,* V, p. 82.

After the execution of Thomas Seymour, the orphaned Mary Seymour was put into the care of the Duchess of Suffolk. Afterwards, no more was heard of the little girl, and it has always been assumed that she died young. Agnes Strickland, however, had put forward the claim that Mary Seymour survived and even married, becoming matriarch to the Lawson family of Yorkshire and Westmoreland. See Strickland, *Lives of the Queens of England,* V, pp. 94-95.

Katharine's delirium is in Haynes, *State Papers,* pp. 103-104. Her final wishes are in Mueller, *Katherine Parr,* pp. 178-179.

Chapter 26: A Maiden Professing Godliness

The portrait of Jane Grey (engraved by Francesco Bartolozzi) reproduced in this book is based on a posthumous likeness circulated in the 16th century. Bartolozzi had mistakenly identified the sitter as Jane Shore, the mistress of King Edward IV.

Cecil's notation of Jane as the 'ex-Queen': *Chronicle of Queen Jane and Queen Mary,* Appendix, pp. 104-105.

Katharine Parr's funeral is transcribed in Strickland, *Lives of the Queens of England,* V, p. 85-86.

The sale of Jane's wardship is in Haynes, *State Papers,* p. 76. Thomas Seymour's jealousy of his brother is on p. 82. 'This day died a man…' is from Leti, *Vie d'Elizabeth,* p. 182.

The Duke of Suffolk's marriage to Katherine Willoughby: *CSP Span.,* IV (ii), no. 1123 (*L&P,* VI, no. 1069).

The portrait, by Hans Eworth, said to be of Frances Brandon and her second husband Adrian Stokes was re-identified as being of Lady Mary Neville and her son. See: Hearn, *Dynasties,* pp. 68-69. The only known authentic likeness of Frances is from her tomb effigy in Westminster Abbey.

Princess Mary as Frances' godmother: *L&P,* II, no. 3489. Actually, Mary (and her mother Queen Katherine, Frances' other godmother) was not present at the ceremony. Proxies ('Lady Boleyn', perhaps Elizabeth Howard, the wife of Sir Thomas Boleyn, and Lady Elizabeth Grey, the Marchioness of Exeter) were used. The Queen's absence may have been due to an illness she had that late summer lasting till August (*CSP Ven.,* II, no. 942), while Mary, barely eighteen months old, was hardly old enough to take part.

The cousins' gift giving is listed in Madden, *Privy Purse Expenses of the Princess Mary,* p. 96, p. 143, and p. 197.

Henry Grey's character is in Holinshed, *Chronicle,* p. 1101; Wingfield, 'Vita Mariae Reginae', p. 245; and *CSP Span.,* X, p. 6. Ulmis' praise of him is from Robinson, *Original Letters,* second portion, pp. 392-393 and pp. 406-407. Henry Grey's correspondence with Heinrich Bullinger is in *Original Letters,* first portion, pp. 3-4.

That Frances and Eleanor Brandon were in the Protestant circle of Anne Askew is mentioned by Parsons, *Treatise,* second part, p. 493.

Jane's correspondence with Bullinger: Robinson, *Original Letters,* first portion, pp. 4-7. The Dorsets' fondness for gambling is on pp. 282-283.

Jane's interest in languages is in Robinson, *Original Letters,* second portion, p. 432. According to Sir Thomas Chaloner, writing in the reign of Elizabeth I, Jane was learning 'Chaldean words' as well, and knew up to eight languages. See Ives, *Lady Jane Grey,* p. 66.

Jane's conversation with Ascham: Ascham, *English Works,* pp. 216-217.

Agnes Paston's directive to her son's tutor is in Gairdner, *Paston Letters,* III, no. 362. Grey's letter to Thomas Seymour is in Haynes, *State Papers,* pp. 78-79.

'What embellishment and adornment': Robinson, *Original Letters,* first portion, p. 278. Elizabeth's plainness is in note 1.

Mary of Guise's visit to the English court: Wriothesley, *Chronicle,* II, pp. 60-61. The dukedom of Suffolk passed to Henry Grey in October 1551 through his wife, Frances. Her brother, the Earl of Lincoln, who would have inherited the title, had died young in 1534. See Godwin, *Annales of England,* p. 244.

Jane's rejection of the dress is in Strype, *John Aylmer,* pp. 195-196.

Jane's disdain for the veneration of the Host is from Foxe, *Acts and Monuments,* VIII, p. 700.

Chapter 27: More Suffering Than Any Illness

Edward's letter of 1546 to Mary is in Nichols, *Literary Remains,* I, Letter IX.

Mary's scheme to leave the country is in *CSP Span.,* X, pp. 124-135.

Mary's defence of her Mass, and the arrest of her chaplains is from *CSP Span.*, X, pp. 410-411. Somerset on Mary's religion: *CSP Span.*, IX, p. 382. Mary's opinion of John Dudley is from *CSP Span.*, X, p. 6.

Edward's scolding of his sister is in *CSP Span.*, X, pp. 209-212. Her reply is on pp. 212-213.

Mary's refusal to go to court for Christmas is in *CSP Span.*, X, pp. 6-7. Her journey to Westminster in the following March is described in Machyn, *Diary*, pp. 4-5. For her meeting with the King: *CSP Span.*, X, pp. 258-260.

Charles V's threat of war, and the government's response are in Nichols, *Literary Remains*, II, p. 309. The attempt to force Mary into submission is in *Acts of the Privy Council*, III, p. 333, and pp. 347-352.

Somerset's execution: Wriothesley, *Chronicle*, II, p. 65.

Edward VI's enjoyment of sports is in *CSP Span.*, X, p. 293 and p. 300. For Cardano's visit to England and his horoscope of the King, see Nichols, *Literary Remains*, I, pp. ccxiv-ccxvii. Edward's declining health is in *CSP Span.*, XI, p. 70.

Jane's refusal to wed is from a Venetian account mentioned in Strickland, *Lives of the Tudor Princesses*, pp. 135-136. She and Guilford Dudley were nonetheless betrothed by 5 May 1553 as stated in *CSP Span.*, XI, p. 38. The nuptials are described on p. 40 and p. 47. See also Godwin, *Annales of England*, p. 255.

For various descriptions of Jane's appearance, see Ives, *Lady Jane Grey*, pp. 14-15. The often quoted Spinola letter (Davey, *The Nine Days' Queen*, p. 253) giving an eyewitness description of Jane as the new Queen, may be suspect: 'Faking Jane' by Leanda de Lisle, *The New Criterion*, Sept. 2009.

Edward VI's provisions for the weddings are in Strype, *Ecclesiastical Memorials*, II (ii), pp. 111-112.

The King's appearance at a window is in *CSP Span.*, XI, p. 70. His decline is mentioned on p. 40. The *Device for the* Succession is transcribed in Davey, *The Nine Days' Queen*, pp. 254-255. After the male heirs of Katherine or Mary Grey, the throne would go to the male descendants of their cousin Margaret Clifford (daughter of Frances Brandon's late sister Eleanor). In an earlier draft of the Will, before the nomination of Jane Grey as his successor, her mother Frances was to be 'Governor of the Realm' if there were absolutely no male heirs to be found. After Frances would be her daughters or Margaret Clifford as Governor until a Suffolk male was born. For a full discussion of the Device, refer to Ives, *Lady Jane Grey*, chapter 14.

Edward ordering the acceptance of Jane as Queen: Foxe, *Acts and Monuments*, VI, p. 384. Wingfield, 'Vita Mariae Angliae Reginae', p. 248, also has John Gosnard, the Solicitor General, refusing to accept Jane as well.

For the woman's attempt to cure the King, see *CSP Span.*, XI, p. 70. Edward's dying prayer is from Foxe, *Acts and Monuments*, VI, p. 352.

Chapter 28: The Reluctant Queen

That supposed non-consummation of Jane's marriage is from *CSP Span.*, XI, p. 47.

Jane's coming to the throne as told by her to Queen Mary is transcribed in Stone, *The History of Mary I*, pp. 496-499. See also: Pollini, *L'Historia Ecclesiastica*, pp. 358-359. Her reception at the Tower: Wriothesley, *Chronicle*, II, p. 85; *Chronicle of the Grey Friars*, pp. 78-79; Grose, *The Antiquarian Repertory*, I, p. 226; and *CSP Span.*, XI, p. 80.

The proclamation of Jane as Queen is in *The Harleian Miscellany*, I, pp. 318-321. Gilbert Potter's arrest is in Machyn, *Diary*, pp. 35-36, and in Wriothesley, *Chronicle*, II, p. 86.

Mary's battle for the Crown is fully documented in Wingfield, 'Vita Mariae Angliae Reginae', and in De Guaras, *The Accession of Queen Mary*. See also *CSP Span.*, XI, pp. 106-116. Her slim hopes are in *CSP Span.*, XI, pp. 72-75. Mary's letter to the Council is in Foxe, *Acts and Monuments*, VI, p. 385.

The letter to raise support for Jane is from *The Chronicle of Queen Jane and Queen Mary*, Appendix II, pp.103-105. Northumberland's preparations against Mary are in Machyn, *Diary*, p. 36. The Council's letter to her is in Foxe, *Acts and Monuments*, VI, pp. 385-386. The letters to Hoby are in Ellis, *Original Letters*, 3rd series, III, pp. 309-312.

For Winchester's giving of the crown to Jane, refer to Stone, *The History of Mary I*, pp. 498-499. For the valuables she was given access to, see Davey, *The Nine Days' Queen*, pp. 270-272. Guilford's regal airs are in *CSP Span.*, XI, p. 113, and in Stone, *The History of Mary I*, pp. 498-499. See the latter for Jane's fight with her mother-in-law, and for her fear of being poisoned.

John Dudley as commander of Jane's forces is in *The Chronicle of Queen Jane and Queen Mary*, pp. 5-8.

Chapter 29: Queen Jane or Queen Mary?

Ridley's preaching against the two Princesses is in Wriothesley, *Chronicle*, II, p. 88.

The letter to support Jane's regime is from Strype, *Thomas Cranmer*, II, Appendix, LXX.

The navy declaring for Mary, and the Council's defection are in *The Chronicle of Queen Jane and Queen Mary*, pp. 8-9. See also: De Guaras, *The Accession of Queen Mary*, pp. 93-95.

The joy over Mary's victory: *The Chronicle of Queen Jane and Queen Mary*, pp. 11-12; *CSP Span.*, XI, p. 108; and De Guaras, *The Accession of Queen Mary*, p. 96. Jane no longer Queen: *CSP Span.*, XI, pg. 113-114. The Council's submission to Mary is in Strype, *Thomas Cranmer*, II, Appendix, LXXI.

Northumberland's arrest is in *The Chronicle of Queen Jane and Queen Mary*, pp. 10-11; *Chronicle of the Grey Friars*, pp. 80-81; Wingfield, 'Vita Mariae Angliae Reginae', pp. 266-268, De Guaras, *The Accession of Queen Mary*, pp. 97-99; and *CSP Span.*, XI, p. 120.

Mary's triumphal entry in *The Chronicle of Queen Jane and Queen Mary*, p. 14; *CSP Span.*, XI, pp. 150-151, and p. 209; Wingfield, 'Vita Mariae Angliae Regina', pp. 271-272; *Chronicle of the Grey Friars*, pp. 81-82; and Machyn, *Diary*, p. 37. Mary compared to Moses: *CSP Span.*, XI, p. 106.

Chapter 30: Queen Regnant

The initial doubts surrounding Mary's victory are in *CSP Span.*, XI, pp. 88-89, and p. 108. The Emperor's advice to the new Queen is on pp. 110-111.

For the Duchess of Northumberland's failed attempt to see Mary, see *CSP Span.*, XI, p. 125.

Jane Grey's letter is in Stone, *The History of Mary I*, pp. 496-499. Also: Pollini, *L'Historia Ecclesiastica*, pp. 355-358. Mary's defence of Jane is from *CSP Span.*, XI, p. 168.

Northumberland's trial is described in *The Chronicle of Queen Jane and Queen Mary*, p. 41; *CSP Span.*, XI, pp. 184-185; Wriothesley, *Chronicle*, II, p. 99; and De Guaras, *The Accession of Queen Mary*, pp. 101-104. His conversion is described in *The Chronicle of Queen Jane and Queen Mary*, p. 18, and in Machyn, *Diary*, p. 42. The encounter with the vengeful woman is described in Godwin, *Annales of England*, p. 251. The Duke's final speech is in Strype, *Thomas Cranmer*, II, Appendix, LXXIII. His execution: *CSP Span.*, XI, p. 210.

Warwick and Northampton's conversions are in *The Chronicle of Queen Jane and Queen Mary*, pp. 19-20, and in Haynes, *State Papers*, p. 183. Later, even Jane's detention was relaxed. She was allowed to 'walk in the Queen's garden and on the hill' (*The Chronicle of Queen Jane and Queen Mary*, p. 33). The 'hill' was not Tower Hill outside the Tower of London as usually supposed, but the 'hill within the Tower' (mentioned in Wriothesley, *Chronicle*, II, p. 95). This meant the upslope open green surrounding the White Tower.

Jane's denunciation of Northumberland is in *The Chronicle of Queen Jane and Queen Mary*, pp. 25-26.

Mary's coronation is in Wingfield, 'Vita Mariae Angliae Reginae', pp. 276-277; De Guaras, *The Accession of Queen Mary*, pp. 117-123; Machyn, *Diary*, pp. 43-46; *The Chronicle of Queen Jane and Queen Mary*, pp. 27-32; and *CSP Span.*, XI, pp. 259 – 260. The hopes for the new reign were expressed in Nichols, 'Life of Fitzalan', p. 120. Mary humbling herself before the Council is in *CSP Span.*, XI, pp. 259 – 260.

The debasement of Henry VIII's coinage is in Buck, *Medieval English Groats*, p. 52 and p. 55. See also *CSP Span.*, XI, pp. 214-215. Mary's financial policies are in Hughes and Larkin, *Tudor Royal Proclamations,* II, no. 391 and no. 392; and in Wriothesley, *Chronicle,* II, p. 102. In the next reign, Elizabeth I went a step further by recalling all debased money out of circulation and replacing it with coins of full value.

She would not 'compel or constrain other men's consciences': Haynes, *State Papers,* p. 168. The restoration of the churches is in Machyn, *Diary,* p. 50. The reestablishment of Mary's legitimacy in Parliament is in The Statutes of the Realm, IV (i), pp. 200-201

Mary's dependence on a husband is described in *CSP Span.,* XI, p. 131. Her continual devotion to Charles V, and the question of her marriage are in *CSP Span.,* XI , p. 132, and pp. 205 –207.

The Queen at odds with her Council: *CSP Span.,* XI, p. 205. For her annoyance with Parliament, see *CSP Span.,* XI, p. 364.

Philip's portrait was sent to England according to *CSP Span.,* XI, p. 367. Mary had 'never felt that which is called love': *CSP Span.,* XI, p. 213. That she was divinely inspired to accept Philip is in *CSP Span.,* XI, p. 328.

Chapter 31: I Fear Them Nothing At All

For the trial at the Guildhall, see *The Chronicle of Queen Jane and Queen Mary,* p. 32; *Fourth Report of the Deputy* Keeper, pp. 237-238; and Wingfield, 'Vita Mariae Angliae Reginae', p. 274. The charges against Cranmer are in *Acts of the Privy Council,* IV, p. 347.

Jane Grey and her sisters were to be declared bastards according to *CSP Span.,* XI, p. 334 and p. 393. However, this issue was never seriously pursued. Even in the next reign, despite their threat to Elizabeth I as potential heiresses, the Queen never questioned Katherine and Mary Grey's legitimacy.

The reception of Charles V's ambassadors is described in *The Chronicle of Queen Jane and Queen Mary,* p. 34. That the citizens should behave with 'humbleness and rejoicing': Stow and Howes, *Annales,* p. 618.

For the Wyatt Rebellion, see Machyn, *Diary,* pp. 53-54; *CSP Span.,* XII, pp. 85-87; and *The Chronicle of Queen Jane and Queen Mary,* pp. 42-52. Courtney's involvement is mentioned in *CSP Span.,* XII, p. 130 and p. 139. Suffolk's participation is in *The Chronicle of Queen Jane and Queen Mary,* p. 37 and pp. 60-61. The proclamation against him and the rebels is in Hughes and Larkin, *Tudor Royal Proclamations,* II, no. 400. The Queen's rousing speech at the Guildhall is in Foxe, *Acts and Monuments,* VI, pp. 414-415. Mary's irritation at Suffolk is from *CSP Span.,* XI, p. 359. His supposed apostasy was reported in *CSP Span.,* XI, p. 366, but this is contradicted by a later report (*CSP Span.,* XII, p. 125) that Grey refused to be converted before his execution. His failed rebellion is in Wriothesley, *Chronicle,* II, p. 108 and p. 110. His attempted escape is in *The Chronicle of Queen Jane and Queen Mary,* Appendix, pp. 124 – 125, and in *CSP Mary I,* no. 781.

That Feckenham preached on the nature of the Sacrament is in Machyn, *Diary*, p. 48. His 'discourse' with Jane Grey is in Foxe, *Acts and Monuments*, VI, pp. 415-417.

Gardiner's speech is in *The Chronicle of Queen Jane and Queen Mary*, p. 54. The many scaffolds and gibbets throughout London were noted in Machyn, *Diary*, p. 55. Guilford and Jane's executions are in *The Chronicle of Queen Jane and Queen Mary*, pp. 54–59. See also Pollini, *L'Historia Ecclesiastica*, pp. 358-359; Godwin, *Annales of England*, pp. 296-297; and De Vertot, *Ambassades*, III, pp. 125-127.

Chapter 32: The Marriage With Spain

The religious services at court are mentioned in *CSP Span.*, XI, p. 188. The requiem for the late King: *CSP Span.*, XI, p. 131. Elizabeth's apparent conformity to the Catholic faith is in *CSP Span.*, XI, pp. 220-221. Her absence at Mass was noted in *CSP Span.*, XI, p. 240.

Mary's gifts to Elizabeth in September 1553 are in Madden, *Privy Purse Expenses of the Princess Mary*, p. 194 and p. 197. For Elizabeth's departure from court in December, see *CSP Span.*, XI, p. 440. For her supposed treachery, refer to Elizabeth's letter in Marcus et al, *Elizabeth I - Collected Works*, pp. 41-42. Her illness is mentioned in Tytler, *Reigns of Edward VI and Mary*, II, pp. 426-427. The journey to Whitehall is in *CSP Span.*, XII, p. 106 and p. 125.

Wyatt's interrogation is *The Chronicle of Queen Jane and Queen Mary*, pp. 69-70. For Elizabeth's arrest, refer to *CSP Span.*, XII, p. 167; *The Chronicle of Queen Jane and Queen Mary*, pp. 70-71; and Foxe, *Acts and Monuments*, VIII, pp. 608-610. Her letter of appeal to Mary is in Marcus et al, *Elizabeth I - Collected Works*, pp. 41-42. Her request for a death by a swordsman: De Castelnau, *Mémoires*, p. 289. Her interrogation is in Foxe, *Acts and Monuments*, VIII, pp. 610-611.

For the angel in the wall: Wingfield, 'Vita Mariae Angliae Reginae', p. 288.

Wyatt's exoneration of Elizabeth and Courtney is from *The Chronicle of Queen Jane and Queen Mary*, pp. 73-74.

The delay in Philip's arrival: *CSP Span.*, XII, pp. 308-309. Mary's longing for him is in *CSP Span.*, XII, p. 14. Her gifts of jewels are described in *CSP Span.*, XII, p. 309; Hume, *Philip II of Spain*, p. 34; and Hume, 'The Visit of Philip II', p. 261. Concerns over Philip's behaviour: *CSP Span.*, XII, p. 185.

Mary and Philip's meeting is in Tytler, *Reigns of Edward VI and Mary*, II, pp. 430-432, and in *CSP Span.*, XIII, p. 7- 10. That Mary understood Spanish but didn't speak it that well is in *CSP Span.*, XIII, p. 12. For Philip's languages, see *CSP Ven.*, VI (ii), no. 884. Mary's appearance is described in *CSP Span.*, XIII, p. 2, p. 26, and p. 31. Her wedding is in *CSP Span.*, XIII, p. 10.

The reconciliation with Rome is in Grafton, *Chronicle*, II, pp. 549-551.

Chapter 33: Bloody Mary

Elizabeth's return to court and her meeting with Mary are in Foxe, *Acts and Monuments,* VIII, pp. 620-621. According to Clifford, *The Life of Jane Dormer,* p. 88, it was Philip who had Elizabeth brought to court.

Letters announcing the birth of a 'prince' are found in *CSP Mary I,* nos. 183-187. The cradle is mentioned in Foxe, *Acts and Monuments,* VII, p. 126. Mary's brisk walking: *CSP Span.,* XIII, p. 175. Her depression is described in De Vertot, *Ambassades de Messieurs De Noailles,* IV, pp. 341-342.

Spanish opinions of England and its inhabitants are in *CSP Span.,* XIII, pp. 31-33, and pp. 60-62. The Spaniards' dislike of English ladies was not universal. Jane Dormer, an attendant of Queen Mary, attracted the attentions of the envoy Don Gomez Suarez de Figueroa, and of the Duke de Feria whom she married.

Philip's departure and Mary's grief are mentioned in *CSP Ven.,* VI, no. 200, no. 204, and no. 213. Philip's carousing in the Low Countries is mentioned in no. 336. Mary's supposed rage at her husband is in *CSP Mary I,* no. 339, and no. 367.

For the executions of the Protestant martyrs (Rogers, Ridley, Latimer, and Cranmer), refer to Foxe, *Acts and Monuments,* VI, pp. 611- 612; VII, pp. 550-551; and VIII, pp. 89-90. Mary's instructions regarding the burnings: Burnet, *History of the Reformation,* V, pp. 440-441. Jane Dormer's defence of Mary's policy is in Clifford, *The Life of Jane Dormer,* p. 92-93. John Knox's condemnation of her is in Knox, *First Blast,* p. 45. 'God grant she be the last of her religion': Holinshed, *Chronicles,* IV, p. 154.

The arrival of Christina of Denmark in England is in *CSP Span.,* XIII, p. 448. Mary's jealousy of her is in *CSP Ven.,* VI, no. 929.

For the Anglo-Spanish marriage contract, see *Tudor Royal Proclamations,* II, no. 398. Stafford's' proclamation against the Queen is in Strype, *Ecclesiastical Memorials,* III (ii), p. 513. That he had received 'armour, money, munition, and ships': *Tudor Royal Proclamations,* II, no. 434. See also *CSP Ven.,* VI, no. 883.

Archbishop Pole as Mary's confidante is in *CSP Ven.,* VI, no. 200, no. 204, and no. 884. Mary's uneasy relationship with Elizabeth is in no. 884 as well. Her praising of her baby sister is from Hearne, *Sylloge Epistolarum,* p. 131 (*L&P,* XI, no. 132).

Philip's interventions on Elizabeth's behalf are in *CSP Ven.,* VI, no. 884, and in Clifford, *The Life of Jane Dormer,* p. 88-90. Renard's advice to marry Elizabeth to the Duke of Savoy is in *CSP Span.,* XIII, no. 417. Mary's abject letter to Philip is in Strype, *Ecclesiastical Memorials,* III (ii), p. 418-419.

The Queen's supposed pregnancy: *CSP Span.,* XIII, no. 382. Her lament over the loss of Calais is in Foxe, *Acts and Monuments,* VIII, p. 625.

Mary's last Will, dated 30 March 1558, is transcribed in Madden, *Privy Purse Expenses of the Princess Mary,* Appendix IV, clxxxv-ccv. Her deathbed is in Clifford, *The Life of Jane Dormer,* p. 70.

Elizabeth as the new Queen is in Naunton, *Fragmenta Regalia,* p. 4.

Chapter 34: The Husband This Woman May Take

Edward VI's interest in astronomy/astrology (synonymous in the Tudor era) is described in his *Defence of Astronomy*: British Library, Additional MS 4724, fo. 104.

For Elizabeth's coronation, refer to *The Quenes Maiesties Passage*; Fabyan, *The New Chronicles,* pp. 719-722; *CSP Ven.,* VII, no. 10; and Hayward, *Annals,* pp. 15-18. Ironically, Mary Tudor as well had adopted the device *Truth is the Daughter of Time* for herself at her coronation. Even John Knox used the expression for an edition of his notorious *The First Blast of the Trumpet Against the Monstrous Regimen of Women.* The Elevation of the Host at Christmas is mentioned in *CSP Span. Eliz.,* 1558-1567, no. 6. Elizabeth's exhaustion afterwards: *CSP Ven.,* VII, no. 10.

The hope for England's continued obedience to Rome is in *CSP Ven.,* VII, no. 10. Count de Feria's opinion of the new Queen is in *CSP Span. Eliz.,* 1558-1567, no. 4.

Thomas Smith's assessment is from Strype, *The Life of the Learned Sir Thomas Smith,* pp. 249-250. The threat of France as noted by Armagil Waad is from Read, *Mr. Secretary Cecil and Queen Elizabeth,* p. 124. For the appointment of the new Council, see Camden, *Elizabeth,* pp. 12-13. Winchester as 'a pliable willow' is from Naunton, *Fragmenta Regalia,* p. 12. The Queen's special charge to Cecil is in Marcus et al, *Elizabeth I - Collected Works,* p. 51.

'There was one Jesus Christ': De Maisse, *Journal,* p. 58. 'Not liking to make windows into men's hearts': Bacon, *Works,* V, p. 429. Elizabeth's annoyance at the monks is from *CSP Ven.,* VII, no. 15, and *CSP Span. Eliz.,* 1558-1567, no. 13. Bacon's speech is from D'Ewes, *Journals,* p. 12. For Elizabeth's religious settlement, see Camden, *Elizabeth,* pp. 18-21 and pp. 27-31. Also Hayward, *Annals,* pp. 19-29.

De Feria on Elizabeth's marriage: *CSP Span. Eliz.,* 1558-1567, no. 1. The deputation to Whitehall is from Nichols, *Progresses and Public Processions,* I, pp. 63-65. In private, Archduke Ferdinand was actually already a husband in a morganatic marriage, but this did not prevent the Imperialists from proposing him as a husband to Elizabeth. That Philip might wed his former sister-in-law is in *CSP Span. Eliz.,* 1558-1567, no. 1 and no. 24.

Arundel's wooing of the Queen is in *CSP Span. Eliz.,* 1558-1567, no. 6, and in Von Klarwill, *Queen Elizabeth and Some Foreigners,* no. 26. For William Pickering, see *CSP Ven.,* VII, no. 18, and also *CSP Span. Eliz.,* 1558-1567, no. 31. Erik of Sweden's wooing of Elizabeth: *CSP For. Eliz.,* 1559-1560, no. 5, no. 6, and no. 766.

Elizabeth and Dudley's early friendship is mentioned in a document (Public Record Office, State Papers, 31/ 3/ 26 fol. 134). That the Tower prisoners were allowed outdoors, see *Acts of the Privy Council*, IV, p. 379. Dudley as 'the gypsy': Naunton, *Fragmenta Regalia*, p. 17. Kat Ashley's rebuke of the Queen is from Von Klarwill, *Queen Elizabeth and Some Foreigners*, no. 26. That Elizabeth and Dudley had children together, see Wright, *Queen Elizabeth*, I, p. 374. 'Never been forgetful of her honour': Von Klarwill, *Queen Elizabeth and Some Foreigners*, p. 113.

'Carnal marriages begin with happiness and end in strife': Cecil Papers at Hatfield House, 155, art. 29. Cecil's belief that Dudley would murder his wife is from *CSP Span. Eliz.*, 1558-1567, no. 119. The death of Amy Robsart is discussed in Aird, 'The Death of Amy Robsart'. Aird argues that Amy's fall was accidental, the result of a spontaneous fracture of her spine due to the softening of her bones brought on by breast cancer. In April 1559, she was reported to be suffering from a 'malady in one of her breasts'. For an alternative theory that Amy was indeed murdered, refer to Skidmore, Chris, *Death and the Virgin: Elizabeth, Dudley and the Mysterious Fate of Amy Robsart*, London: Weidenfeld & Nicolson, 2010.

The Act establishing Elizabeth's right to the throne is in *Statutes of the Realm*, IV, pp. 358-359. The Act making her inheritable to her mother and to her Boleyn relatives is on p. 397.

John Knox's denouncement of female rulers: Knox, *The First Blast*, p. 11.

The siege of Leith is described in Knox, *The History of the Reformation of Religion in Scotland*, p. 198. The comparison between Scotland and France is made in *Hayward, Annals, p. 75*.

Elizabeth's willingness to receive Mary at her court is in Camden, *Elizabeth, p. 5*. Mary's declaration to Throckmorton is from *CSP For. Eliz.*, 1561-1562, no. 336.

Chapter 35: Both King and Queen

That Elizabeth was supposedly a better dancer than the Queen of Scots: Melville, *Memoirs*, p. 51.

Her refusal to appoint a successor is in Marcus et al., *Elizabeth I - Collected Works*, p. 65, and in Montagu, *Works of Francis Bacon*, I, p. 398.

The Queen's bout of smallpox is recounted in *CSP Span. Eliz.*, 1558-1567, no. 187, no. 188, no. 189, and no. 190. See also Halliday, 'Queen Elizabeth I and Dr Burcot'.

Dudley's elevation to the peerage is in Nichols, *Progresses, pp. 190-191, and in Melville, Memoirs, p. 47*. Melville's interview with the Queen is in *Melville, Memoirs, pp. 48-51*. Lord Darnley's appearance is on *p. 56*. For Elizabeth and Leicester's quarrel: *CSP Span. Eliz.*, 1558-1567, no. 310, no. 316, and no. 317. Elizabeth's lament over her barrenness is from Melville, *Memoirs, pp. 69-70*.

That virginity *'was not meet for a prince'*: Marcus et al., *Elizabeth I - Collected Works*, p. 79. The Commons' criticism of the Queen is Camden, *Elizabeth, pp. 84-85*. Her row with her Council members is in *CSP Span. Eliz.*, 1558-1567, no. 388. Her reply to the deputation from Parliament is in Marcus et al., *Elizabeth I - Collected Works*, pp. 94-98. To 'declare the succession in such convenient time': Neale, *Elizabeth I and her Parliaments*, I, pp. 174-175.

Chapter 36: The Daughter of Debate

Mary Stuart's arrival in England: *CSP Scotland, II, no. 661, no. 662, and no. 664.*

'Happily brought to bed of her son James': Camden, *Elizabeth, p. 82.* Darnley's lack of manliness according to his contemporaries: Melville, *Memoirs, p. 48.* Mary Stuart's abandonment by her French in-laws is from *CSP Ven.*, VII, no. 393. Cecil's directives for Mary's confinement: Pryor, *Elizabeth I - Her Life in Letters*, p. 51. For Mary's letter to Elizabeth, see Ellis, *Original Letters,* 1st series, II, CXC. Elizabeth's willingness to receive her cousin: Teulet, *Relations Politiques, II, pp. 369-370; CSP Span. Eliz.*, *1568-1579, no. 26;* and *CSP Ven., VII, no. 426.* The cost of Mary's upkeep is in *CSP Scotland, II, no. 737.*

Debate over the Casket Letters continues. For the argument that the letters were genuinely pointing to Mary's guilt, see Wormald, *Mary, Queen of Scots, pp. 180-182. F*or an opposing view: Guy, *Queen of Scots, pp. 384-423.*

Sussex's negotiations with the Imperial court are in Camden, *Elizabeth, pp. 100-102.* 'She wanteth or meaneth never to proceed in the matter': Public Record Office, State Papers 70/94 fo. 175v.

Norfolk's former disavowal of Mary is in Murdin, *State Papers, p. 180.* Mary's affection for him is in Strickland, *Letters of Mary, Queen of Scots*, I, pp. 196-198. 'To the end of the world in her petticoat': Tytler, *History of Scotland, VII, pp. 87-88.* Norfolk's involvement with Mary is in *CSP Scotland, IV, no. 43,* and in Camden, *Elizabeth, pp. 129-130.*

Lady Westmorland's denunciation of her brother: *Williams, Thomas Howard, p. 165.* For the Northern Rebellion, see Camden, *Elizabeth*, pp. 133-137. Elizabeth's refusal of Norfolk's gift: Starkey, *Rivals in Power*, p. 188. Mary's letter to the imprisoned Norfolk is in Strickland, *Letters of Mary, Queen of Scots*, I, p. 198.

Elizabeth's excommunication is in *CSP Ven.,* VII, no. 475.

The Bishop of Ross's confession is in *The Harleian Miscellany,* I, pp. 405-408. Mary as the 'daughter of debate' is in Marcus et al, *Elizabeth I - Collected Works,* pp. 133-134. Norfolk's execution is in Camden, *Elizabeth,* pp. 177-178.

Chapter 37: The Frog Prince

Burghley's complaints about the Queen's policies are in *CSP Scotland, IV, no. 287*.

'There are but ten years between us': Fénélon, *Correspondance Diplomatique, III, p. 468*. Catherine de' Medici's overtures to Elizabeth are in *Pryor, Letters*, p. 66-67.

Preparations for receiving the Queen (in Sandwich) are in Nichols, *Progresses*, I, p. 337. Her 1572 summer progress is on pp. 307-321.

Walsingham's warning to the Queen is in Digges, *The Complete Ambassador*, p. 258. Elizabeth's reaction to the St. Bartholomew's Day Massacre is in Fénélon, *Correspondance Diplomatique*, CCLXXIV.

'Neither prejudice nor disgrace unto him': Camden, *Elizabeth, p. 194*. When Henry of Anjou succeeded to the French throne as Henry III, his dukedom was given to his younger brother Francis. However, he was still commonly called the Duke of Alençon. Interestingly, Alençon also shared part of his late older brother King Francis II's name. The Duke was christened 'Hercules Francis'.

Jean de Simier's talents are in Camden, *Elizabeth, p. 227*. Alençon's secret arrival is in *CSP Span. Eliz.*, 1568-1579, no. 593.

John Stubbs's punishment is in Camden, *Elizabeth, p. 270*, and in Harington, *Nugae Antiquae, I, pp. 154-157*.

Elizabeth's anger at her Councillors: Murdin, *State Papers, pp. 336-337*. Leicester's secret marriage was as practical as it was romantic. Before he married Lettice Knollys, Leicester had a relationship with a lady named Douglas Sheffield. The liaison produced a son, but young Robert Dudley (1574-1649) was illegitimately conceived, and his father needed a legal heir. Leicester did father another son (also named Robert) with his wife Lettice in 1581, but the boy died young three years later.

Elizabeth and Alençon's marriage contract is in Camden, *Elizabeth, pp. 255-256*. Her promise to marry him is in *CSP Span. Eliz.*, 1580-1586, no. 173. Her subsequent reluctance is in no. 186 and no. 189. Her final rejection of the Duke: Camden, *Elizabeth, p. 268*. 'She would give a million..'.: *CSP Span. Eliz.*, 1580-1586, no. 221. 'For reasons which she would not indulge': *CSP Span. Eliz.*, 1580-1586, no. 189.

That Alençon should refer to Elizabeth as 'my wife the Queen of England', see *CSP Span. Eliz., 1580-1586, no. 221*. Her reaction to his death is in Robinson, *'Queen Elizabeth and the Valois Princes'*, p. 77, and in Stump and Felch, *Elizabeth I and Her Age, pp. 273-274*.

To be given 'a town in each province' as collateral is from Motley, *History of the United Netherlands, I, p. 324*.

Leicester's campaign in the Netherlands is described in Camden, *Elizabeth, pp. 327-330*. See also Doran, *Elizabeth, pp. 224-225*. The Queen's letter of rebuke is from Bruce, *Correspondence of Robert Dudley, XXXIX*.

Leicester's affection for Philip Sidney: Wallace, *The Life of Sir Philip Sidney*, *p. 380*.

Chapter 38: That Wicked Murderess

Mary Stuart as a constant danger is from *CSP Scotland, II, no. 1164*. As 'the worst woman in the world': *CSP Span. Eliz.*, 1568-1579, no. 493. That 'wicked murderess': Strickland, *Letters of Mary, Queen of Scots*, III, p. 323. For Mary's refusal to acknowledge an English court, see Labanoff, *Marie Stuart*, VII, pp. 36-38. Her trial: Camden, *Elizabeth*, pp. 353-362. The executions of Babington and the other conspirators are on p. 344.

Elizabeth's speeches declaring her reluctance to proceed against Mary are in Marcus et al, *Elizabeth I - Collected Works*, pp. 196-204. According to Elizabeth herself, she might have pardoned Mary if she openly confessed to the Babington Plot. However, the Scottish Queen was contemptuous of any such offers. Earlier, following the execution of the Duke of Norfolk, Mary had told the French ambassador, 'I am determined, and will have none of her pardons. She may take away my life, but not the constancy which Heaven has produced and fortified within me. I will die Queen of Scotland. Posterity will judge on whom the blame will fall'. (Strickland, *Letters of Mary, Queen of Scots*, III, p. 293).

The comet (actually Halley's Comet) appearing to King Harold in 1066 is illustrated in the Bayeux Tapestry. The omens for Mary Stuart and Charles IX are in Teulet, *Relations Politiques*, IV, pp. 163-164, and in Camden, *Elizabeth*, p. 190. The signing of Mary's death warrant is in *CSP Scotland, IX, no. 284, and no. 285*. Paulet's refusal to murder Mary is in Morris, *Sir Amias Poulet, pp. 361-362*. For her execution, refer to Teulet, *Relations Politiques*, IV, pp. 156-163; Wyngfield, 'Circumstantial Account', pp. 255-262; and *CSP Ven.*, VIII, no. 484. For Elizabeth's reaction, see Camden, *Elizabeth*, p. 388; Carey, *Memoirs of the Life of Robert Cary*, p. 137; Teulet, *Relations Politiques*, IV, p. 197; *CSP Ven.*, VIII, no. 483; and *CSP Scotland, IX, no. 280*.

Chapter 39: The Enterprise of England

'The theatre of the whole world..'.: Camden, *Elizabeth*, p. 350.

De Mendoza's letter to King Philip is in *CSP Span. Eliz.*, 1587-1603, no. 28. For the King's reply, see no. 57. His claim to the English throne is in no. 17.

'A sieve that spends as it receives to little purpose': *CSP For. Eliz.*, XXI (ii), p. 195.

For prophecies about the year 1588, see: Camden, *Elizabeth*, p. 402, and Mattingly, *The Defeat of the Spanish Armada*, pp. 159-160.

Elizabeth's peace talks with Parma are in Camden, *Elizabeth*, pp. 407-408. The description of the Armada is on p. 411. William Allen's letter to

King Philip is in *CSP Span. Eliz.,* 1587-1603, no. 41. The battle against the
Armada: Camden, *Elizabeth,* pp. 411-418. The Queen's speech at Tilbury is
transcribed in Marcus et al, *Elizabeth I - Collected Works,* pp. 325-326.

Leicester's final letter to Elizabeth is in Pryor, *Letters,* pp. 100-101.

Chapter 40: Not So Old As They Think

Hatton is described in Naunton, *Fragmenta Regalia,* p. 30. For Raleigh,
see pp. 33-35.

Elizabeth's first encounter with Essex is in Devereux, *Lives and Letters,* I,
pp. 169-170 (a variant of the story, probably apocryphal, has the young Earl
reacting in terror at the Queen's kiss). Her fondness for him is on p. 186.
'One mistress, and no master': Naunton, *Fragmenta Regalia,* p. 5. Essex's
character is on p. 37. See also De Maisse, *Journal,* p. 7. The Queen's angry
letter to him is in Devereux, *Lives and Letters,* I, pp. 204-205.

Lord Burghley's decline is in De Maisse, *Journal,* p. 27. For Robert Cecil's
appearance, see Naunton, *Fragmenta Regalia,* p. 38.

Essex as a 'new man" is in Devereux, *Lives and Letters,* I, pp. 282-283.

The Lopez affair is mentioned in Camden, *Elizabeth,* pp. 484-485.

Essex's military glory: Camden, *Elizabeth,* pp. 518-523.

For De Maisse's various impressions of England and its Queen, see De
Maisse, *Journal.*

Nicander Nucius's observations are in Nucius, *Travels,* pp. 23-25.
William Thomas' opinion of the Irish is from Thomas, *The Pilgrim,* p. 66.

Elizabeth's mourning for Burghley is described in Harington, *Nugae
Antiquae, I, p. 314.*

Essex's rage at the Queen is in Camden, *Elizabeth, pp. 555-556.* His
sudden arrival at Nonsuch and his disgrace are in Devereux, *Lives and
Letters,* II, pp. 77-80. His pleas to the Queen are on p. 83. Her refusal to
renew his wines license: Bacon, *Works,* III, p. 229. For the Essex uprising,
see Camden, *Elizabeth,* pp. 609-611. Elizabeth's assessment of him to the
French ambassador is from Birch, *Queen Elizabeth,* II, p. 505. Her reaction
to his death: Strickland, *Queen Elizabeth,* p. 553.

The Queen's foul temper in the autumn of 1601 is in Harington, *Nugae
Antiquae, I, pp. 317-318.* Elizabeth's Parliament of 1601 and her 'Golden
Speech' are from Townshend, *Historical Collections, pp. 173-266. Elizabeth
as* 'the setting sun': Camden, *Elizabeth,* p. 659.

The reception of the Venetian envoy is in *CSP Ven., IX, no. 1135.* Robert
Carey's visit to court is in Carey, *Memoirs, pp. 136-138.*

The Queen's final days were recounted by her lady-in-waiting Elizabeth
Southwell. See: Stump and Felch, *Elizabeth I and Her Age,* pp. 524-526. That
Henry VIII and his children all died on a Thursday, see the commonplace
book (circa 1625) in Ziegler, *Elizabeth – Then and Now,* p. 120. The

peacefulness of Elizabeth's death is in Camden, *Elizabeth*, p. 661. Mourning for the Queen is in Stow and Howes, *Annales,* p. 815. In 1606, Elizabeth's remains were removed from Henry VII's tomb to its present location by King James.

'More than a man, and in troth…' is from Harington, *Nugae Antiquae, I, p. 345.*

BIBLIOGRAPHY

Acts of the Privy Council, New Series, 1542-1631, (edited by J.R. Dasent), London: H.M.S.O., 1890-1918. 32 Vols.

ADLARD, GEORGE, *Amye Robsart, The Earl of Leycester & Kenilworth*, London: John Russell Smith, 1870.

AIRD, IAN, 'The Death of Amy Robsart,' *English Historical Review (EHR)*, LXXI, Jan. 1956.

ALLEN, P.S., (edited by), *Opus Epistolarum Des. Erasmi Roterodami*, Oxford: Henry Frowde, 1906. 12 vols.

ARMSTRONG, C.A.J., 'Astrology at the Court of Henry VII,' *Italian Renaissance Studies*, (edited by E.F. Jacob), London: Faber and Faber, 1960.

ARTHURSON, IAN, *The Perkin Warbeck Conspiracy, 1491-1499*, Stroud, Gloucestershire: A. Sutton, 1994.

ASCHAM, ROGER, *The English Works of Roger Ascham, Preceptor to Queen Elizabeth*, London: printed for White, Cochrane, and Co., 1815.

BACON, FRANCIS, *The History of the Reign of King Henry the Seventh*, (annotated by Jerry Weinberger), Ithaca: Cornell University Press, 1996.

BACON, FRANCIS, *The Works of Francis Bacon, Lord Chancellor of England*, (edited by Basil Montagu), London: William Pickering, 1826. 16 vols.

BENTLEY, SAMUEL, *Excerpta Historica or Illustrations of English History*, London, 1831.

BERNARD, G.W., *Anne Boleyn: Fatal Attractions*, New Haven: Yale University Press, 2010.

BIRCH, THOMAS, *Memoirs of the Reign of Queen Elizabeth, From the Year 1581 till Her Death*, New York: The AMS Press Inc., 1970 (reprint of 1754 edition published in London). 2 vols.

BLACK, WILLIAM HENRY, *Illustrations of Ancient State and Chivalry From Manuscripts Preserved in the Ashmolean Museum*, London: William Nicol, Shakespeare Press, 1840.

BOUTERWEK, A. W., 'Anna von Cleve, Gemahlin Heinrich VIII, König von England,' *Zeitschrift des Bergischen Geschichtsvereins*, 6, 1869.

BRUCE, JOHN, *Correspondence of Robert Dudley, Earl of Leycester, During His Government of the Low Countries in the Years 1585 and 1586*, London: printed for The Camden Society, 1844.

BRUCE, MARIE LOUISE, *Anne Boleyn*, New York: Coward, McCann & Geoghegan, 1972.

BUCK, GEORGE, *The History of King Richard the Third*, (edited by Arthur Noel Kincaid), Gloucester: Alan Sutton, 1979.

BUCK, IVAN, *Medieval English Groats,* Witham: Greenlight Publishing, 2000.

BURNET, GILBERT, *The History of the Reformation of the Church of England,* (edited by Nicholas Pocock), Oxford: Clarendon Press, 1865. 7 vols.

Calendar of Letters and State Papers, Relating to English Affairs Preserved Principally in the Archives at Simancas (CSP Span. Eliz.), (edited by M.A.S. Hume), London: H.M.S.O., 1892-1899. 4 vols.

Calendar of Letters, Despatches, and State Papers Relating to the Negotiations between England and Spain Preserved in the Archives at Simancas and Elsewhere (CSP Span.), (edited by G.A. Bergenroth, Pascual de Gayangos, M.A.S. Hume, and R. Tyler), London: Longman, Green, Longman, and Roberts, 1862-1954. 13 vols.

Calendar of State Papers and Manuscripts Existing in the Archives and Collections of Milan (CSP Milan), (edited by Allen B. Hinds), London: H.M.S.O., 1912.

Calendar of State Papers and Manuscripts Relating to English Affairs Existing in the Archives and Collections of Venice (CSP Ven.), (edited by Rawdon Brown et al.), London: Longman, Green, Reader, and Dyer; also H.M.S.O., 1864-1947. 38 vols.

Calendar of State Papers, Domestic Series of the Reign of Edward VI, 1547-1553 *(CSP Edward VI),* (edited by C.S. Knighton), London: Public Record Office, 1992.

Calendar of State Papers, Domestic Series of the Reign of Mary I, 1553-1558 (CSP Mary I), (edited by C.S. Knighton), London: Public Record Office, 1998.

Calendar of State Papers, Foreign Series, of the Reign of Elizabeth (CSP For. Eliz.), (edited by A.J. Butler et al.), London: Longman, Green, Longman, Roberts, and Green; also H.M.S.O., 1863-1950. 23 vols.

Calendar of the Manuscripts of the Marquis of Bath Preserved at Longleat, Wiltshire (Cal. Marquis of Bath), Dublin: H.M.S.O., 1907. 3 vols.

Calendar of the Manuscripts of the Most Honourable The Marquis of Salisbury, KG, Preserved at Hatfield House, Hertfordshire (Cal. Marquis of Salisbury), London: H.M.S.O., 1883. 10 vols.

Calendar of the Patent Rolls Preserved in the Public Record Office – Edward IV, Edward V, Richard III, A.D. 1476-1485, London: H.M.S.O., 1901.

Calendar of the State Papers Relating to Scotland and Mary Queen of Scots, 1547-1603, Preserved in the Public Record Office, the British Museum, and Elsewhere in England (CSP Scotland), (edited by J. Bain et al.), Edinburgh: H.M. General Register House, 1898. 13 vols.

CAMDEN, WILLIAM, *The History of the Most Renowned and Victorious Princess Elizabeth, Late Queen of England,* New York: AMS Press Inc., 1970 (reprint of 4th edition of 1688 published in London).

CANNON, JOHN and RALPH GRIFFITHS, *The Oxford Illustrated History of the British Monarchy,* Oxford: Oxford University Press, 1988.

CAREY, ROBERT, *Memoirs of the Life of Robert Cary, Baron of Leppington, and Earl of Monmouth. Written By Himself,* London: J. Hughes (for R. and J. Dodsley), 1759.

CHAPMAN, HESTER W., *Anne Boleyn,* London: Jonathan Cape, 1974.

CHEETHAM, ANTHONY, *The Life and Times of Richard III,* New York: Welcome Rain, 1998.

CLIFFORD, HENRY, *The Life of Jane Dormer, Duchess of Feria,* (transcribed by Canon E.E. Estcourt and edited by Rev. Joseph Stevenson). London: Burns and Oates Limited, 1887.

Chronicle of King Henry VIII of England, (translated by M.A.S. Hume), London: George Bell and Sons, 1880.

The Chronicle of Queen Jane and of Two Years of Queen Mary, (edited by John Gough Nichols), London: printed for the Camden Society, 1850.

Chronicle of the Grey Friars of London, (edited by John Gough Nichols), London: printed for The Camden Society, 1852.

The Chronicles of the White Rose of York, A Series of Historical Fragments, Proclamations, Letters, and Other Contemporary Documents Relating to the Reign of King Edward the Fourth, London: James Bohn, 1845.

COKAYNE, GEORGE E., (edited by), *The Complete Peerage of England, Scotland, Ireland, Great Britain and the United Kingdom, Extant, Extinct, or Dormant,* London: St. Catherine Press: 1910-59. 13 vols.

A Collection of Ordinances and Regulations for the Government of the Royal Household. London: Society of Antiquaries, 1790.

COLVIN, H.M., *The History of the King's Works,* London: H.M.S.O., 1963-1982. 6 vols.

CONSTANTINE, GEORGE, 'A Memorial from George Constantine to Thomas Lord Cromwell', (edited by T. Amyot), *Archaeologia,* 23 (1831), London: Society of Antiquaries of London.

Correspondencia de Gutierre Gómez de Fuensalida, embajador en Alemania, Flandes é Inglaterra (1458-1509), Madrid, 1907.

CUNNINGHAM, SEAN, *Richard III – A Royal Enigma,* Kew: The National Archives, 2003.

DAVEY, RICHARD, *The Nine Days' Queen: Lady Jane Grey and Her Times,* (edited by Martin Hume), London: Methuen & Co., 1909.

DAVIES, ROBERT, *York Records, Extracts from the Municipal Records of the City of York,* London: J. B. Nichols and Son, 1843.

DE CASTELNAU, MICHEL, *Mémoires,* Paris, 1794.

DE CARLES, LANCELOT, *Épistre contenant le procès criminel faict à l'encontre de la royne Anne Boullant d'Angleterre,* Lyons, 1545.

DE COMMINES, PHILIP, *Memoirs,* (edited by Andrew R. Scoble), London: George Bell and Sons, 1877.

DE GUARAS, ANTONIO, *The Accession of Queen Mary,* (edited by Richard Garnett, London: Lawrence and Bullen, 1892.

DE SILVA, ALVARO, (edited by), *The Last Letters of Thomas More,* Grand Rapids: Wm. B. Eerdmans Publishing Co., 2000.

DE MAISSE, ANDRE HURAULT, *A Journal of All That Was Accomplished by Monsieur de Maisse Ambassador in England from Henry IV to Queen Elizabeth, Anno Domini 1597,* (translated and edited by G.B. Harrison and R.A. Jones), Bloomsbury: The Nonesuch Press, 1931.

DEVEREUX, WALTER BOUCHIER, *Lives and Letters of the Devereux Earls of Essex, in the Reigns of Elizabeth, James I, and Charles I,* London: John Murray, 1853. 2 vols.

DE VERTOT, RENÉ-AUBERT, *Ambassades de Messieurs De Noailles en Angleterre,* Leyden, 1763. 5 vols.

D'EWES, SIMONDS, *The Journals Of All The Parliaments During The Reign Of Queen Elizabeth,* Shannon: Irish University Press, 1973.

DEWHURST, JOHN, 'The Alleged Miscarriages of Catherine of Aragon and Anne Boleyn,' *Medical History,* 28, 1984.

DIGGES, DUDLEY, (compiled by), *The Complete Ambassador, Or Two Treaties Of The Intended Marriage of Queen Elizabeth of Glorious Memory,* London: Thomas Newcomb, 1655.

DORAN, SUSAN, (edited by), *Elizabeth – The Exhibition at the National Maritime Museum,* London: Chatto & Windus, 2003.

DORAN, SUSAN, (edited by), *Man & Monarchy – Henry VIII,* London: The British Library, 2009.

DOWLING, MARIA, 'A Woman's Place? Learning and the Wives of Henry VIII', *History Today,* 41, 1991.

DOWLING, MARIA, *Humanism in the Age of Henry VIII,* London: Croom Helm Ltd., 1986.

DU BOYS, ALBERT, *Catharine of Aragon and the Sources of the English Reformation,* (edited by Charlotte M. Yonge), London: Hurst and Blackett, 1881. 2 vols.

ELLIS, HENRY, *Original Letters Illustrative of English History,* London: printed for Harding, Triphook, and Lepard, 1824. 3 vols.

ERICKSON, CAROLLY, *Bloody Mary,* New York: Doubleday & Company, Inc. 1978.

ERICKSON, CAROLLY, *The First Elizabeth,* New York: Summit Books, 1983.

ERICKSON, CAROLLY, *Great Harry – The Extravagant Life of Henry VIII,* New York: Summit Books, 1980.

ERICKSON, CAROLLY, *Mistress Anne,* New York: Summit Books, 1984.

FABYAN, ROBERT, *The New Chronicles of England and France,* London: printed for F. C. & J. Rivington, 1811.

FANTAZZI, C. and MATHEEUSSEN, C., (edited and translated by) *De Institutione Feminae Christianae,* New York: E.J. Brill, 1996. 2 vols.

FÉNÉLON, BERTRAND DE SALIGNAC DE LA MOTHE, *Correspondance Diplomatique,* (edited by Charles Purton Cooper and Jean Baptiste Alexandre Theodore Teulet), Paris: Béthune et Plon, 1838-1840. 6 vols.

Fourth Report of the Deputy Keeper of the Public Records (February 28, 1843), London: H.M.S.O., 1843.

FOXE, JOHN, *Acts and Monuments,* (edited by Stephen Reed Cattley), London: R.B. Seeley and W. Burnside, 1837-1841. 8 vols.

FRASER, ANTONIA, *Mary Queen of Scots,* London: George Weidenfeld & Nicolson Limited, 1969.

FRASER, ANTONIA, *The Wives of Henry VIII,* New York: Viking, 1992.

FRIEDMANN, PAUL, *Anne Boleyn: A Chapter of English History, 1527-1536,* London: Macmillan, 1884. 2 vols.

GAIRDNER, JAMES, *History of the Life and Reign of Richard the Third,* Cambridge: University Press, 1898.

GEE, HENRY and WILLIAM JOHN HARDY, *Documents Illustrative of English Church History,* London: Macmillan and Co., 1914.

GIUSTINIAN, SEBASTIAN, *Four Years at the Court of Henry VIII,* (edited and translated by Rawdon Brown), London: Smith, Elder, & Co., 1854. 2 vols.

GODWIN, FRANCIS and MORGAN, *Annales of England, Containing the Reigns of Henry the Eighth, Edward the Sixth, Queen Mary,* London: A. Islip and W. Stansby, 1630.

GRAFTON, RICHARD, (compiled by), *Chronicle, or History of England,* London: printed for J. Johnson et al., 1809. 2 vols.

GRAHAM, WINSTON, *The Spanish Armadas,* New York: Doubleday & Company, Inc., 1972.

GROSE, FRANCIS et al. (compiled by), *The Antiquarian Repertory: A Miscellany Intended to Preserve and Illustrate Several Valuable Remains of Old Times,* London: Edward Jeffery, 1809. 4 vols.

GUY, JOHN, *Queen of Scots – The True Life of Mary Stuart,* Boston: Houghton Mifflin Company, 2004.

HALL, EDWARD, *Hall's Chronicle; Containing the History of England, During the Reign of Henry the Fourth and the Succeeding Monarchs,* London: printed for J. Johnson, 1809.

HALL, EDWARD, *The Triumphant Reigne of Kyng Henry the VIII,* London: T.C. & E.C. Jack, 1904. 2 vols.

HALLAM, ELIZABETH, (edited by), *The Chronicles of The Wars of the Roses,* Markham: Viking (Penguin Books Canada Ltd.), 1988.

HALLIDAY, F.E., 'Queen Elizabeth I and Dr Burcot,' *History Today,* vol. 5, no. 8, Aug. 1955.

HALSTED, CAROLINE A., *Richard III as Duke of Gloucester and King of England*, London: Longman, Brown, Greene, and Longmans, 1844. 2 vols.

HARINGTON, JOHN, *Nugae Antiquae*, (edited by Henry Harington), London: J. Wright, 1804. 2 vols.

The Harleian Miscellany, (edited by Samuel Johnson and William Oldys), London: printed for Robert Dutton, 1808-1811. 12 volumes.

HARRISON, G.B., (edited by), *The Letters of Queen Elizabeth I*, London: Cassell & Company Ltd., 1968.

HARVEY, JOHN, *The Plantagenets*, Glasgow: Fontana/Collins, 1979.

HAYNES, SAMUEL, (edited by), *A Collection of State Papers Relating to Affairs in the Reigns of King Henry VIII, King Edward VI, Queen Mary, and Queen Elizabeth From the Year 1542 to 1570... Left by William Cecil, Lord Burghley*, London: William Bowyer, 1740.

HAYWARD, JOHN, *Annals of the First Four Years of the Reign of Queen Elizabeth*, London: printed for The Camden Society, 1811.

HAYWARD, MARIA, (edited by), *Dress at the Court of King Henry VIII*, Leeds: Maney Publishing, 2007.

HEARN, KAREN, (edited by), *Dynasties – Painting in Tudor and Jacobean England, 1530-1630*, London: Tate Gallery, 1995.

HEARNE, THOMAS, *Sylloge Epistolarum*, Oxford, 1716.

HIBBERT, CHRISTOPHER, *The Virgin Queen – The Personal History of Elizabeth I*, New York: Viking, 1990.

HOLINSHED, RAPHAEL, *Chronicles: England, Scotland and Ireland*, New York: AMS Press Inc., 1976 (reprint of 1807/1808 edition published in London). 6 vols.

HUGHES, PAUL L. and JAMES F. LARKIN, *Tudor Royal Proclamations*, New Haven: Yale University Press, 1969. 3 vols.

HULSE, CLARK, *Elizabeth I - Ruler and Legend*, Chicago: University of Illinois Press (for The Newberry Library), 2003.

HUME, MARTIN A.S., *Philip II of Spain*, London: Macmillan and Co., 1906.

HUME, MARTIN A.S., 'The Visit of Philip II', *The English Historical Review*, VII (April 1892). London: Longman, 1892.

IMPREY, EDWARD and GEOFFREY PARNELL, *The Tower of London – The Official Illustrated History*, London: Merrell Publishers, 2000.

Ingulph's Chronicle of the Abbey of Croyland (The Croyland Chronicle), (translated by Henry T. Riley), London: Henry G. Bohn, 1854.

IVES, E.W., *Lady Jane Grey – A Tudor Mystery*, Chichester: Wiley-Blackwell, 2009.

IVES, E.W., *The Life and Death of Anne Boleyn*, Oxford: Blackwell Publishing, 2004.

JAMES, M.R., (translated by), *Henry the Sixth – A Reprint of John Blacman's Memoir,* Cambridge: Cambridge University Press, 1919.

JAMES, SUSAN E., *Kateryn Parr – The Making of a Queen,* Aldershot: Ashgate Publishing Ltd., 1999.

JENKINS, ELIZABETH, *Elizabeth the Great,* New York: Coward-McCann, Inc., 1959.

JOHNSON, PAUL, *Elizabeth I – A Study in Power and Intellect,* London: Futura Publications Limited, 1976.

The Journal of the British Archaeological Association, vol. XXV, 1869, London.

Journals of The House of Lords, London: Eyre and Spottiswoode, and H.M.S.O., 1817-1910. 12 vols.

KAULEK, JEAN, (edited by) *Correspondance Politique De MM. de Castillon et De Marillac, Ambassadeurs de France en Angleterre (1537-1542),* Paris: La Commission des Archives Diplomatiques, 1885.

KEAY, ANNA, *The Elizabethan Tower of London – The Haiward and Gascoyne Plan of 1597,* London: London Topographical Society, 2001.

KENDALL, PAUL MURRAY, *Richard the Third,* New York: W.W. Norton & Company Inc., 1955.

KINGSFORD, CHARLES LETHBRIDGE, (edited by), *Chronicles of London,* Oxford: Clarendon Press, 1905.

KNOX, JOHN, *The First Blast of the Trumpet Against the Monstrous Regiment of Women,* (edited by Edward Arber), London, 1878.

KNOX, JOHN, *The History of the Reformation of Religion in Scotland,* Glasgow: Blackie & Son, 1841

LABANOFF, PRINCE ALEXANDRE, *Lettres, Instructions et Mémoires de Marie Stuart, Reine D'Ecosse,* London: Charles Dolman, 1844. 7 vols.

LACEY, ROBERT, *The Life and Times of Henry VIII,* London: Weidenfeld and Nicolson, 1972.

LACEY, ROBERT, *Robert, Earl of Essex,* New York: Atheneum, 1971.

LAPPER, IVAN and GEOFFREY PARNELL, *The Tower of London – A 2000-Year History,* Oxford: Osprey Publishing, 2000.

LATYMER, WILLIAM, 'Cronickille of Anne Bulleyne,' (edited by Maria Dowling), *Camden Miscellany,* XXX, 4th series, 39, 1990.

LAYNESMITH, J.L., *The Last Medieval Queens,* Oxford: Oxford University Press, 2004.

LE GLAY, M., (edited by), *Correspondance de L'Empereur Maximilien Ier et de Marguerite D'Autriche Sa Fille, Gouvernante de Pays-Bas, de 1507 à 1519,* Paris: Jules Renouard et Cie, 1939. 2 vols.

LELAND, JOHN, *Antiquarii Rebus Britannicis Collectanea,* London, 1770. 6 vols.

LETI, GREGORIO, *La Vie d'Elizabeth Reine D'Angleterre,* Amsterdam: Henry Desbordes, 1714.

Letters and Papers, Foreign and Domestic, of the Reign of Henry VIII (L&P), (edited by J.S. Brewer), London: Longmans, H.M.S.O., 1862-1910.

LEVIN, CAROLE, *The Heart and Stomach of a King, Elizabeth I and the Politics of Sex and Power,* Philadelphia: University of Pennsylvania Press, 1994.

The Lisle Letters, (edited by Muriel St. Clare Byrne), Chicago: University of Chicago Press, 1981. 6 vols.

LOADES, DAVID, (edited by), *The Chronicles of the Tudor Kings,* New York: Viking, 1990.

LOADES, DAVID, (edited by), *Chronicles of the Tudor Queens,* Stroud: Sutton Publishing, 2002.

LOADES, DAVID, *Henry VIII and His Queens,* Stroud: Sutton Publishing, 1994.

LOADES, DAVID, *Mary Tudor- A Life,* Oxford: Blackwell Publishers Ltd., 1995.

MACCAFFREY, WALLACE, *Elizabeth I,* London: Edward Arnold, 1993.

MACCULLOCH, DIARMAID, *Thomas Cranmer – A Life,* New Haven: Yale University Press, 1996.

MACHYN, HENRY, *The Diary of Henry Machyn, Citizen and Merchant Tailor of London, from A.D. 1550 to A.D. 1563,* (edited by J.G. Nichols), London: printed for The Camden Society, 1848.

MADDEN, FREDERICK, 'Narrative of the Visit of the Duke of Najera to England, in the Year 1543-4', *Archaeologia,* 23 (1831), London: Society of Antiquaries of London.

MADDEN, FREDERICK, *Privy Purse Expenses of the Princess Mary, Daughter of King Henry the Eighth, Afterwards Queen Mary, With a Memoir of the Princess, and Notes,* London: William Pickering, 1831.

MANCINI, DOMINIC, *The Usurpation of Richard the Third,* (translated by C.A.J. Armstrong, Oxford: Clarendon Press, 1969.

MARCUS, LEAH S., JANEL MUELLER, MARY BETH ROSE, (edited by), *Elizabeth I – Collected Works,* Chicago: University of Chicago Press, 2000.

MATTINGLY, GARRETT, *Catherine of Aragon,* New York: Vintage Books, 1941.

MATTINGLY, GARRETT, *The Defeat of the Spanish Armada,* London: Jonathan Cape, 1959.

MARTIENSSEN, ANTHONY, *Queen Katherine Parr,* New York: McGraw-Hill Book Company, 1973.

MELVILLE, JAMES, Memoirs, London, 1683.

MONTAGU, BASIL, *The Works of Francis Bacon, Lord Chancellor of England,* Philadelphia: A. Hart, 1852. 3 vols.

MORE, THOMAS, *The History of King Richard the Third and Selections from the English and Latin Poems,* (edited by Richard S. Sylvester), New Haven: Yale University Press, 1976.

MORRIS, CHRISTOPHER, *The Tudors,* Glasgow: Fontana/Collins, 1979.

MORRIS, JOHN, (edited by), *The Letter-Books of Sir Amias Poulet, Keeper of Mary Queen of Scots,* London: Burns and Oates, 1874.

MOTLEY, JOHN LOTHROP, *History of the United Netherlands,* New York: Harper & Brothers, 1866. 4 vols.

MUELLER, JANEL, (edited by), *Katherine Parr, Complete Works and Correspondence,* Chicago: The University of Chicago Press, 2011.

MURDIN, WILLIAM, *A Collection of State Papers Relating To Affairs In The Reign Of Queen Elizabeth From The Year 1571 To 1596,* London: William Bowyer, 1759.

NAUNTON, ROBERT, *Fragmenta Regalia,* 1641.

NEALE, J. E., *Elizabeth I and Her Parliaments,* London: Cape, 1953 and 1957. 2 vols.

NICHOLS, JOHN GOUGH, 'Life of Fitzalan', *Gentlemen's Magazine,* 1st series, 103, ii (1833).

NICHOLS, JOHN GOUGH, *The Literary Remains of King Edward the Sixth,* New York: Burt Franklin, 1842. 2 vols.

NICHOLS, JOHN GOUGH, *The Progresses and Public Processions of Queen Elizabeth,* London: John Nichols and Son, 1823. 3 vols.

NICOLAS, NICHOLAS HARRIS, *Life of William Davison Secretary of State and Privy Counsellor to Queen Elizabeth,* London: John Nichols and Son, 1823.

NICOLAS, NICHOLAS HARRIS, *Privy Purse Expenses of Elizabeth of York: Wardrobe Accounts of Edward the Fourth. With a Memoir of Elizabeth of York, and Notes,* London: William Pickering, 1830.

NUCIUS, NICANDER, *The Second Book of the Travels of Nicander Nucius of Corcyra,* (edited and translated by J. A. Cramer), London: printed for The Camden Society, 1841.

OKERLUND, ARLENE, *Elizabeth of York,* New York: Palgrave Macmillan, 2009.

OKERLUND, ARLENE, *Elizabeth Wydeville – The Slandered Queen,* Stroud: Tempus, 2005.

PAGET, HUGH, 'The Youth of Anne Boleyn', *Bulletin of the Institute of Historical Research,* 55, 1981.

PARSONS, ROBERT, *A Treatise of Three Conversions of England from Paganisme to Christian Religion,* 1604. 3 parts.

The Paston Letters, A.D. 1422-1509, (edited by James Gairdner), London: Chatto & Windus, 1904. 6 vols.

PIERCE, HAZEL, *Margaret Pole, Countess of Salisbury, 1473-1541, Loyalty, Lineage and Leadership,* Cardiff: University of Wales Press, 2003.

PLOWDEN, ALISON, *Danger to Elizabeth – The Catholics Under Elizabeth I,* Stroud: Sutton Publishing, 1999.

PLOWDEN, ALISON, *Elizabeth Regina – The Age of Triumph, 1588-1603,* Stroud: Sutton Publishing, 2000.

PLOWDEN, ALISON, *Lady Jane Grey & the House of Suffolk,* London: Sidgwick & Jackson, 1985.

PLOWDEN, ALISON, *Marriage With My Kingdom - The Courtships of Queen Elizabeth I,* New York: Stein and Day, 1977.

PLOWDEN, ALISON, *The Young Elizabeth,* Trowbridge: Redwood Press Limited (for Readers Union Limited), 1972.

POLLARD, A. F., *Tudor Tracts 1532-1588,* Westminster: A. Constable and Co., 1903.

POLLINI, GIROLAMO, *L'Historia Ecclesiastica Della Rivoluzion D'Inghilterra,* Rome: Presso Guglielmo Facciotti, 1594.

PRYOR, FELIX, *Elizabeth I - Her Life in Letters,* Berkeley: University of California Press, 2003.

The Quenes Maiesties Passage through the Citie of London to Westminster the Day before her Coronation, (edited by James M. Osborn), New Haven: Yale University Press, 1960.

READ, CONYERS, *Mr. Secretary Cecil and Queen Elizabeth,* New York: Alfred A. Knopf, 1961.

The Receyt of the Ladie Kateryne, (edited by Gordon Kipling), Oxford: Oxford University Press, 1990.

The Reports of Sir John Spelman, (edited by J.H. Baker), London: Publications of the Selden Society, 1976 and 1978, 2 vols.

RIDLEY, JASPER, *The Love Letters of Henry VIII,* London: Cassell, 1988.

ROBINSON, A.M.F., 'Queen Elizabeth and the Valois Princes,' *English Historical Review, II, 1887.*

ROBINSON, HASTINGS, (edited by), *Original Letters Relative to the English Reformation, Written During the Reigns of King Henry VIII, King Edward VI, and Queen Mary, Chiefly From the Archives of Zurich,* Cambridge: Cambridge University Press (for The Parker Society), 1846. 2 vols.

ROSS, CHARLES, *Edward IV,* Berkeley: University of California Press, 1974.

Rotuli Parliamentorum; ut et Petitiones, et Placita in Parliamento (Rolls of Parliament, Comprising the Petitions, Pleas, and Proceedings of Parliament), London: Prepared and edited by order of a committee of The House of Lords, vol. 6, 1832.

SAALER, MARY, *Anne of Cleves – Fourth Wife of Henry VIII,* London: The Rubicon Press, 1995.

SANDER, NICOLAS, *Rise and Growth of the Anglican Schism,* (translated by David Lewis), London: Burns and Oates, 1877.

SCARISBRICK, J.J., *Henry VIII,* London: Eyre & Spottiswoode, 1968.

SERGEANT, PHILIP W. *Anne Boleyn*, London: Hutchinson & Co., Ltd., 1924.

SIMPSON, HELEN, *The Spanish Marriage*, Edinburgh: Peter Davies, 1933.

SKIDMORE, CHRIS, *Edward VI – The Lost King of England*, New York: St. Martin's Press, 2007.

SMITH, LACEY BALDWIN, *Henry VIII – The Mask of Royalty*, London: Jonathan Cape, 1971.

SMITH, LACEY BALDWIN, *A Tudor Tragedy – The Life and Times of Catherine Howard*, London: Jonathan Cape, 1961.

SOMERSET, ANNE, *Elizabeth I*, London: Fontana, 1992.

SPELMAN, JOHN, *The Reports of Sir John Spelman*, (edited by J. H. Baker), London: Selden Society, 1977-1978.

STARKEY, DAVID, *Elizabeth: Apprenticeship*, London: Chatto & Windus, 2000.

STARKEY, DAVID, (edited by), *Henry VIII – A European Court in England*, New York: Cross River Press, 1991.

STARKEY, DAVID, *The Reign of Henry VIII – Personalities and Politics*, London: George Philip, 1985.

STARKEY, DAVID, (edited by), *Rivals in Power – Lives and Letters of the Great Tudor Dynasties*, New York: Grove Weidenfeld, 1990.

STARKEY, DAVID, *Six Wives – The Queens of Henry VIII*, London: Chatto & Windus, 2003.

State Papers, King Henry the Eighth, London: published under the authority of His Majesty's Commission, 1831-1852, 11 vols.

The Statutes of the Realm. Printed by command of His Majesty King George the Third, in pursuance of an address of The House of Commons of Great Britain from original records and authentic manuscripts. London, 1810-1828. 11 vols.

STONE, J.M., *The History of Mary I Queen of England*, New York: E.P. Dutton and Co., 1901.

STOW, JOHN and HOWES, EDMUND, *Annales, Or A General Chronicle of England*, London: Richard Meighen, 1631.

STRICKLAND, AGNES, *Letters of Mary, Queen of Scots*, London: Henry Colburn, 1845. 2 vols.

STRICKLAND, AGNES, *Lives of the Queens of England*, Philadelphia: Blanchard and Lea, 1856. 12 vols.

STRICKLAND, AGNES, *Lives of the Tudor Princesses*, London: Longmans, Green, and Co., 1868.

STRICKLAND, AGNES, *Memoirs of Elizabeth, Second Queen Regnant of England and Ireland*, Philadelphia: Blanchard and Lea, 1853.

STRONG, ROY, *Tudor and Jacobean Portraits*, London: H.M.S.O., 1969. 2 vols.

STRYPE, JOHN, *Ecclesiastical Memorials,* Oxford: Clarendon Press, 1822. 7 vols.

STRYPE, JOHN, *Historical Collections of the Life and Acts of the Right Reverend Father in God, John Aylmer, Lord Bp. Of London in the Reign of Queen Elizabeth,* Oxford: Clarendon Press, 1821.

STRYPE, JOHN, *The Life of the Learned Sir Thomas Smith,* Oxford: Clarendon Press, 1820.

STRYPE, JOHN, *Memorials of the Most Reverend Father in God, Thomas Cramer, Sometime Lord Archbishop of Canterbury,* London: George Routledge & Co., 1853. 2 vols.

STUMP, DONALD and SUSAN M. FELCH, *Elizabeth I and Her Age,* New York: W.W. Norton & Company, 2009.

TEULET, ALEXANDRE, *Relations Politiques de la France et de L'Espagne Avec L'Ecosse au XVIe Siècle,* Paris: Librairie de la Société de L'Histoire de France, 1862. 5 vols.

THOMAS, WILLIAM, *The Pilgrim: A Dialogue of the Life and Actions of King Henry the Eighth,* (edited by J.A. Froude), London: Parker, Son, and Bourn, 1861.

THURLEY, SIMON, 'Royal Lodgings at the Tower of London, 1216-1327', *Architectural History,* vol. 38, 1995.

THURLEY, SIMON, *The Royal Palaces of Tudor England,* New Haven: Yale University Press (for The Paul Mellon Centre for Studies in British Art), 1993.

TOWNSHEND, HAYWARD, *Historical Collections: Or An Exact Account of the Proceedings of the Four Last Parliaments of Q. Elizabeth,* London: printed for T. Basset, W. Crooke, and W. Cademan, 1680.

Two London Chronicles From the Collections of John Stow, (edited by Charles Lethbridge Kingsford), London: Royal Historical Society, 1910.

TYTLER, PATRICK FRASER, *England Under the Reigns of Edward VI and Mary,* London: Richard Bentley, 1839. 2 vols.

TYTLER, PATRICK FRASER, *The History of Scotland From The Accession of Alexander III to The Union,* Edinburgh: William P. Nimmo, 1866. 10 vols.

VERGIL, POLYDORE, *The Anglica Historica of Polydore Vergil,* (edited and translated by Denys Hay), Camden Series, vol. LXXIV, London: Offices of the Royal Historical Society, 1950.

VERGIL, POLYDORE, *Three Books of Polydore Vergil's English History Comprising the Reigns of Henry VI, Edward IV, and Richard III,* (edited by Henry Ellis), London: printed for The Camden Society, 1844.

VIVES, JUAN, *De Institutione Feminae Christianae,* (edited by C. Fantazzi and C. Matheeussen; translated by C. Fantazzi), New York: E.J. Brill, 1996. 2 vols.

VON KLARWILL, VICTOR, (edited by), *Queen Elizabeth and Some Foreigners, Being A Series of Hitherto Unpublished Letters From the*

Archives of the Hapsburg Family, (translated by T.H. Nash), London: John Lane, 1928.

WALPOLE, HORACE, *Anecdotes of Painting in England; With Some Account of the Principal Artists; and Incidental Notes on Other Arts; Collected by the Late Mr. George Vertue,* London: printed for J. Dodsley, 1786. 4 vols.

WARKWORTH, JOHN, *Chronicle of the First Thirteen Years of the Reign of King Edward the Fourth,* (edited by James Orchard Halliwell), London: printed for the Camden Society, 1839.

WARNICKE, RETHA M., 'Anne Boleyn's Childhood and Adolescence', *The Historical Journal,* 28, 4, 1985.

WARNICKE, RETHA M., *The Rise and Fall of Anne Boleyn,* Cambridge: Cambridge University Press, 1989.

WATSON, FOSTER, *Luis Vives, El Gran Valenciano, (1492-1540),* Oxford: Oxford University Press, 1922.

WEIR, ALISON, *The Six Wives of Henry VIII,* London: The Bodley Head, 1991.

WILLIAMS, NEVILLE, *All the Queen's Men – Elizabeth I and Her Courtiers,* New York: The Macmillan Company, 1972.

WILLIAMS, NEVILLE, *Henry VIII and His Court,* New York: The Macmillan Company, 1971.

WILLIAMS, NEVILLE, *The Life and Times of Elizabeth I,* London: Weidenfeld and Nicolson, 1972.

WILLIAMS, NEVILLE, *Thomas Howard Fourth Duke of Norfolk,* New York: E.P. Dutton & Co., 1964.

WINGFIELD, ROBERT, 'Vita Mariae Angliae Reginae', (edited and translated by Diarmaid MacCulloch), *Camden Miscellany*, XXVIII, 4th series, 29, 1984.

WOOD, MARY ANNE EVERETT, (edited by), Letters of Royal and Illustrious Ladies of Great Britain, London: Henry Colburn, 1842. 3 vols.

The Works of Sir Francis Bacon, London: J. Crowder and E. Hemsted, 1803. 10 vols.

WORMALD, JENNY, *Mary, Queen of Scots: Politics, Passion and a Kingdom Lost,* London: Tauris Parke Paperbacks, 2001.

WRIGHT, THOMAS, (edited by), *Queen Elizabeth and Her Times,* London: Henry Colburn, 1838. 2 vols.

WRIOTHESLEY, CHARLES, *A Chronicle of England During the Reigns of the Tudors, From A.D. 1485 to 1559,* London: printed for The Camden Society, 1875-77. 2 vols.

WYATT, THOMAS, *Collected Poems,* (edited by Kenneth Muir), London: Routledge and Kegan Paul Ltd., 1949.

WYNGFIELD, ROBERT, 'A Circumstantial Account of the Execution of Mary, Queen of Scots', *The Clarendon Historical Society's Reprints,* series II, 1886.

ZIEGLER, GEORGIANNA, (edited by), *Elizabeth I – Then and Now,* Washington D.C.: The Folger Shakespeare Library, 2003.

ABOUT THE AUTHOR

Roland Hui received his degree in Art History from Concordia University in Canada. After completing his studies, he went on to work in Interpretive Media for California State Parks, The U.S. Forest Service, and The National Park Service.

Roland has written for *Renaissance Magazine* and for *Tudor Life Magazine*. He blogs about 16th century English art and personalities at *Tudor Faces* at: tudorfaces.blogspot.com.

Index

D

E

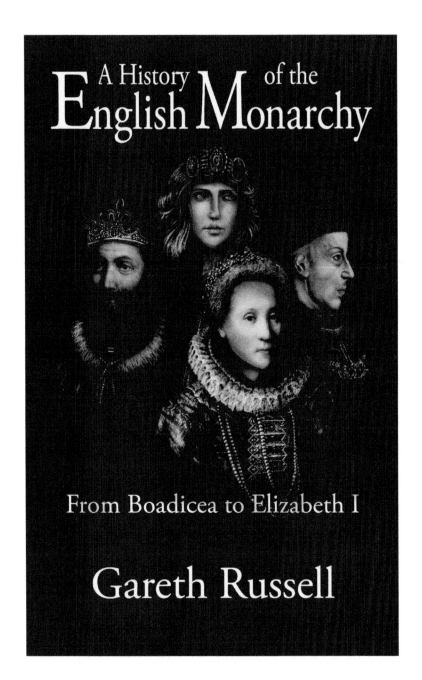

A History of the English Monarchy

From Boadicea to Elizabeth I

Gareth Russell

ISBN-13: 978-8494372124

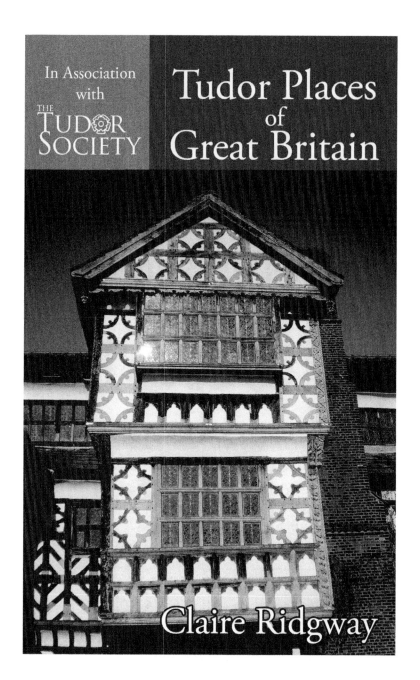

In Association
with
THE
TUD⊕R
SOCIETY

Tudor Places
of
Great Britain

Claire Ridgway

ISBN-13: 978-8494457463

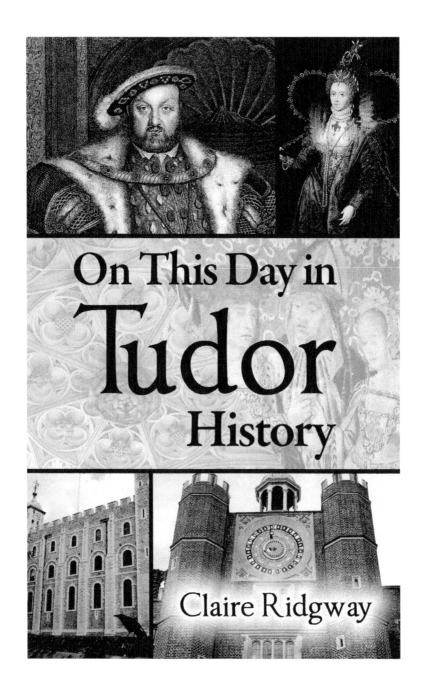

On This Day in
Tudor
History

Claire Ridgway

ISBN-13: 978-8494372193

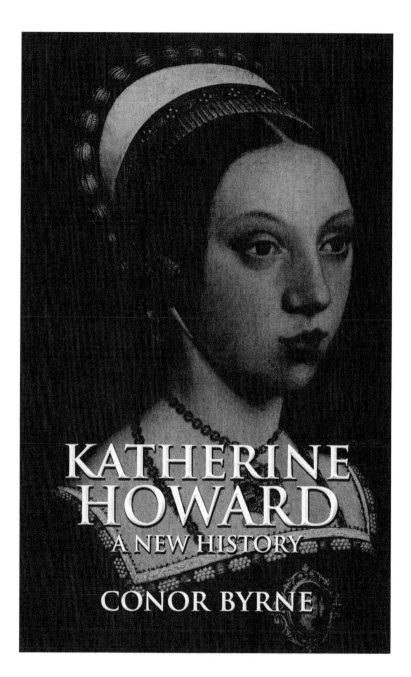

KATHERINE
HOWARD
A NEW HISTORY

CONOR BYRNE

ISBN-13: 978-8493746469

GEORGE
BOLEYN

TUDOR POET,
COURTIER & DIPLOMAT

CLARE CHERRY &
CLAIRE RIDGWAY

ISBN-13: 978-8493746452

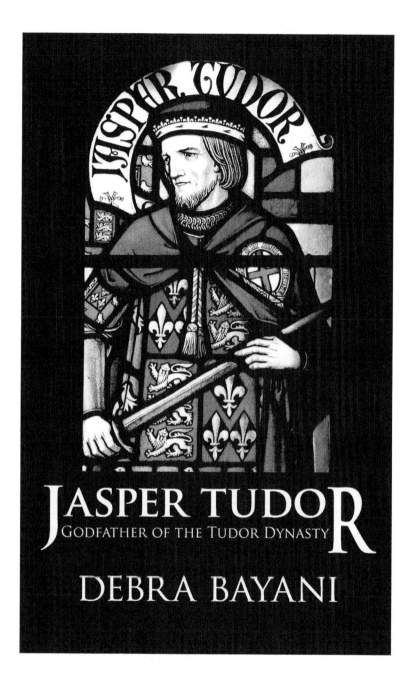

JASPER TUDOR
GODFATHER OF THE TUDOR DYNASTY

DEBRA BAYANI

ISBN-13: 978-8494372100

HISTORY IN A NUTSHELL SERIES

Sweating Sickness - **Claire Ridgway**
Mary Boleyn - **Sarah Bryson**
Thomas Cranmer - **Beth von Staats**
Henry VIII's Health - **Kyra Kramer**
Catherine Carey - **Adrienne Dillard**

The Pyramids - **Charlotte Booth**
The Mary Rose - **Philip Roberts**
Whitehall Palace - **Philip Roberts**
Cesare Borgia - **Samantha Morris**
Edward VI - **Kyra Kramer**

NON FICTION HISTORY

Anne Boleyn's Letter from the Tower - **Sandra Vasoli**
Jasper Tudor - **Debra Bayani**
Tudor Places of Great Britain - **Claire Ridgway**
Illustrated Kings and Queens of England - **Claire Ridgway**
A History of the English Monarchy - **Gareth Russell**
The Fall of Anne Boleyn - **Claire Ridgway**
George Boleyn: Tudor Poet, Courtier & Diplomat - **Ridgway & Cherry**
The Anne Boleyn Collection - **Claire Ridgway**
The Anne Boleyn Collection II - **Claire Ridgway**
Two Gentleman Poets at the Court of Henry VIII - **Edmond Bapst**
A Mountain Road - **Douglas Weddell Thompson**

HISTORICAL FICTION

The Devil's Chalice - **D.K.Wilson**
Falling Pomegranate Seeds - **Wendy J. Dunn**
Struck with the Dart of Love: Je Anne Boleyn 1 - **Sandra Vasoli**
Truth Endures: Je Anne Boleyn 2 - **Sandra Vasoli**
The Colour of Poison - **Toni Mount**
Between Two Kings: A Novel of Anne Boleyn - **Olivia Longueville**
Phoenix Rising - **Hunter S. Jones**
Cor Rotto - **Adrienne Dillard**
The Claimant - **Simon Anderson**
The Truth of the Line - **Melanie V. Taylor**

CHILDREN'S BOOKS

All about Richard III - **Amy Licence**
All about Henry VII - **Amy Licence**
All about Henry VIII - **Amy Licence**
Tudor Tales William at Hampton Court - **Alan Wybrow**

PLEASE LEAVE A REVIEW

If you enjoyed this book, *please* leave a review at the book
seller where you purchased it. There is no better way to thank
the author and it really does make a huge difference!
Thank you in advance.

Printed in Great Britain
by Amazon

12320486R00318